T0215414

COM and .NET Interoperability

ANDREW TROELSEN

Originally published by Apress in 2002

ISBN 978-1-59059-011-9 ISBN 978-1-4302-0824-2 (eBook)
DOI 10.1007/978-1-4302-0824-2

Technical Reviewers: Habib Heydarian, Eric Gunnerson
Editorial Directors: Dan Appleman, Peter Blackburn, Gary Cornell, Jason Gilmore, Karen Watterson, John Zukowski
Managing Editor: Grace Wong
Copy Editors: Anne Friedman, Ami Knox
Proofreaders: Nicole LeClerc, Sofia Marchant
Compositor: Diana Van Winkle, Van Winkle Design
Artist: Kurt Krames
Indexer: Valerie Robbins
Cover Designer: Tom Debolski
Marketing Manager: Stephanie Rodriguez

This book is dedicated to Mary and Wally Troelsen (aka Mom and Dad). Thanks for buying me my first computer (the classic Atari 400) so long ago and for staying awake during my last visit when I explained (in dreadful detail) how System.Object is so much better than IUnknown. I love you both.

Contents at a Glance

Contents at a Glance

Contents

Acknowledgments

As always, I must give a very real and heartfelt thanks to all of the fine people at Apress. First, thanks to Gary Cornell and Dan Appleman for building such a great place for writers to do their work. A mammoth thanks to Grace Wong for gently pushing me forward in order to get this book out on time and for putting up with me in general. And thanks to Stephanie Rodriguez and Hollie Fischer for their awesome work in spreading the word about Apress titles both at home and across the globe.

A huge thanks also goes to Ami Knox, Nicole LeClerc, Sofia Marchant, and Anne Friedman, all of whom did fantastic jobs smoothing over any grammatical glitches on my part. Thanks to Habib Heydarian and Eric Gunnerson for providing excellent technical assistance. Further thanks to Diana Van Winkle, Kurt Krames, and Tom Debolski for making the book look respectable and professional inside and out. Special thanks to Valerie Robbins for working on (yet another) tight deadline in order to index these chapters.

As for those individuals a bit closer to home, a heartfelt thanks to all my coworkers at Intertech, Inc. (`http://www.intertech-inc.com`), for making my "real job" a wonderful place to be. The previous praise does not apply to Tom Salonek, whom I still don't care much for at all (. . . well, maybe just a little). Further thanks are in order for my family and friends for remaining patient when I became "just a bit grumpy" during the last month of this project. Last but not least, I must thank my wife Amanda for supporting me through yet another stint of sleepless nights and for remaining positive and encouraging when I was anything but. Thanks all!

Introduction

The funny thing about writing a book on COM and .NET interoperability is that one author could craft a five- to ten-page article describing the basic details that you must understand to get up and running with interop-related endeavors. At the same time, another author could write volumes of material on the exact same subject. So, you may be asking, how could this massive discrepancy between authors possibly exist?

Well, stop and think for a moment about the number of COM-aware programming languages and COM application frameworks that exist. Raw C++/IDL, ATL, MFC, VB 6.0, and Object Pascal (Delphi) each have their own syntactic tokens that hide the underbelly of COM from view in various ways. Thus, the first dilemma you face as an interop author is choosing which language to use to build the COM sample applications.

Next, ponder the number of .NET-aware programming languages that are either currently supported or under development. C#, VB .NET, COBOL .NET, APL .NET, PASCAL .NET, and so on, each have their own unique ways of exposing features of the CTS to the software engineer. Therefore, the next dilemma is choosing which language to use to build the .NET applications.

Even when you solve the first two dilemmas and choose the languages to use during the course of the book, the final dilemma has to do with the assumptions made regarding the readers themselves. Do they have a solid understanding of IDL and the COM type system? Do they have a solid understanding of the .NET platform, managed languages, and metadata? If not, how much time should be spend pounding out such details?

Given the insane combinations of language preferences and reader backgrounds, I have chosen to take a solid stance in the *middle ground.* If I have done my job correctly, you will walk away from this text with the skills you need to tackle any interop-centric challenge you may encounter. Also, I am almost certain you will learn various tantalizing tidbits regarding the COM and .NET type systems.

My ultimate goal in writing this book is to provide you with a solid foundation of COM and .NET interoperability. To achieve this goal, I have chosen to provide material that defines the finer details of the COM and .NET architectures. For example, over the course of the first six chapters, you will learn how to *programmatically* generate and parse COM IDL, dynamically generate C# and VB .NET source code on the fly (via System.CodeDOM), and build .NET applications that can read COM type information. After all, when you need to build a software solution that makes use of two entirely unique programming paradigms, you had better have a solid understanding of each entity.

However, once this basic foundation has been laid, the bulk of this book describes the process of making COM and .NET binaries coexist in harmony. As an added bonus, I cover the process of building .NET code libraries that can leverage the services provided by the COM+ runtime layer (via System.EnterpriseServices).

Now that you have the big picture in your mind, here is a chapter-by-chapter breakdown of the material:

Chapter 1: Understanding Platform Invocation Services

I open this examination of COM/.NET interoperability by focusing on the role of a single .NET class type: DllImportAttribute. In this chapter, you learn how to access custom C-based (non-COM) DLLs as well as the Win32 API from a managed environment. Along the way, you investigate how to marshal C structures, interact with traditional callback functions, and extract exported C++ class types from within a managed environment. This chapter also examines the role of the Marshal class, which is used in various places throughout the book.

Chapter 2: The Anatomy of a COM Server

The point of this chapter is to document the internal composition of a classic COM server using raw C++ and COM IDL. Given that many COM frameworks (such as VB 6.0) hide the exact underpinnings of COM, this chapter also examines the use of the system registry, required DLL exports, the role of the class factory, late binding using IDispatch, and so on. As you might guess, the COM server you construct during this chapter is accessed by managed code later in the text.

Chapter 3: A Primer on COM Programming Frameworks

Given that you build a number of COM servers over the course of the book, this (brief) chapter provides an overview of two very popular COM frameworks: the Active Template Library (ATL) and Visual Basic 6.0. Knowledge mappings are made between the raw C++ server created in Chapter 2 and the binaries produced by the ATL/VB 6.0 COM frameworks. Along the way, you also explore the key COM development tool, oleview.exe.

Chapter 4: COM Type Information

This chapter examines the gory details of the COM type system, including a number of very useful (but not well-known) tasks such as constructing custom IDL attributes, applying various IDL keywords such as [appobject], [noncreatable], and so forth. More important, this chapter also illustrates how to read and write COM type information programmatically using ICreateTypeLibrary, ICreateTypeInfo, and related COM interfaces. This chapter wraps up by examining how to build a managed C# application that can read COM type information using interop primitives.

Chapter 5: The Anatomy of a .NET Server

The goals of this chapter are to examine the core aspect of a .NET code library, including various deployment-related issues (for example, XML configuration files, publisher policy, and the like). This chapter also provides a solid overview of a seemingly unrelated topic: dynamically generating and compiling code using System.CodeDOM. Using this namespace, developers are able to dynamically generate code in memory and save it to a file (*.cs or *.vb) on the fly. Once you have investigated the role of System.CodeDOM, you will have a deeper understanding of how various interop-centric tools (such as aximp.exe) are able to emit source code via command line flags.

Chapter 6: .NET Types

If you haven't heard by now, understand that the .NET type system is 100 percent different than that of classic COM. Here, you solidify your understanding of the .NET type system, including the use of custom .NET attributes. This chapter also examines the role of the System.Reflection namespace, which enables you to dynamically load an assembly and read the contained metadata at runtime. This chapter also illustrates late binding under .NET and the construction of custom managed attributes. I wrap up by showing you how to build a Windows Forms application that mimics the functionality provided by ILDasm.exe.

Chapter 7: .NET-to-COM Interoperability—The Basics

In this chapter, the focus is on learning how to build .NET applications that consume classic COM servers using a Runtime Callable Wrapper (RCW). You begin with the obvious (and most straightforward) approach of using the integrated wizards of Visual Studio .NET. Next, you learn about the tlbimp.exe tool (and the numerous command line options). Along the way, you are exposed to the core conversion topics, including COM/.NET data type conversions, property and method mappings, and other critical topics.

Chapter 8: .NET-to-COM Interoperability—Intermediate Topics

This chapter builds on the previous one by examining a number of intermediate topics. For example, you learn how .NET clients can make use of COM VARIANTs and SafeArrays, COM Error Objects, COM enums, COM connection points, and COM collections. Topics such as exposing COM interface hierarchies are also examined in detail.

Chapter 9: .NET-to-COM Interoperability—Advanced Topics

Here you learn to import ActiveX controls and augment the work performed by the aximp.exe command line utility to account for COM [helpstring] attributes that are lost during the conversion process. Furthermore, this chapter examines the process of manually editing the metadata contained in a given interop assembly. For example, you learn how to support [custom] IDL attributes in terms of .NET metadata and understand how to compile *.il files using ilasm.exe. This chapter also describes how a COM type can implement .NET interfaces to achieve "type compatibility" with other like-minded .NET types. You wrap up by learning how to build a custom type library importer application using C#.

Chapter 10: COM-to-.NET Interoperability—The Basics

This chapter focuses on how COM clients (written in VB 6.0, C++, and VBScript) can make use of .NET types using a COM Callable Wrapper (CCW). Here, I cover class interfaces, the tlbexp.exe/regasm.exe command line tools, and various registration and deployment issues. This chapter also examines how a COM client can interact with the types contained in the core .NET assembly, mscorlib.dll.

Chapter 11: COM-to-.NET Interoperability—Intermediate Topics

This chapter builds on the materials presented in Chapter 10 by examining how .NET enumerations, interface hierarchies, delegates, and collections are expressed in terms of classic COM. You also learn how to expose custom .NET exceptions as COM error objects, as well as about the process of exposing .NET interface hierarchies to classic COM.

Chapter 12: COM-to-.NET Interoperability—Advanced Topics

This advanced COM-to-.NET–centric chapter examines how a .NET programmer is able to build "binary-compatible" .NET types that integrate with classic COM. You see how a .NET type can implement COM interfaces, and you also get a chance to explore the details of manually defining COM types using managed code. This chapter also examines how to interact with the registration process of an interop assembly. The final topics of this chapter address the process of building a custom host for the .NET runtime (using classic COM) and the construction of a custom .NET-to-COM conversion utility.

Chapter 13: Building Serviced Components (COM+ Interop)

Despite the confusion, .NET programmers are able to build code libraries that can be installed under COM+. In this final chapter, I begin by examining the role of the COM+ runtime and reviewing how it fits into n-tier applications. The bulk of this chapter is spent understanding the System.EnterpriseServices namespace and numerous types of interest. You learn how to program for JITA, object pools, construction strings, and transactional support using managed code. I wrap up by constructing an n-tier application using managed code, serviced components, Windows Forms, and ASP .NET.

Now that you have a better understanding about the scope of this book and the mindset *I* have regarding the material that follows, understand that I have written this book based on the following assumptions about *you*:

- You are not satisfied with clicking a button of a given wizard and thinking "I guess it worked . . . somehow . . . I think." Rather, I assume you would love to know the inner details of what that wizard does on your behalf and *then* click the button.

- You are aware of the role of COM, have created a number of COM servers, and feel confident building COM solutions in the language mapping of your choice. As well, I am assuming that you still find the process of learning the finer details of COM a worthwhile endeavor. As you will see, most of the COM servers built during the course of this book make use of VB 6.0, unless a particular COM atom cannot be expressed using the vernacular of BASIC. In these cases, I make use of the ATL framework.

- You are aware of the role of .NET, have (at the very least) explored the syntax of your favorite managed language, and (at the very most) created a number of .NET applications during the process. While many of my managed examples make use of C#, I also make use of VB .NET when necessary.

Finally, be aware that the source code for each example can be obtained from the Apress Web site in the Downloads section at `http://www.apress.com`.

It is my sincere hope that as you read though the text you enjoy yourself and expand your understanding of COM, the .NET platform, and the techniques used to blend each architecture into a unified whole.

Andrew Troelsen
Minneapolis, Minnesota

CHAPTER 1

Understanding Platform Invocation Services

Platform Invocation Services (PInvoke) provides a way for managed code to call unmanaged functions that are implemented in traditional Win32 (non-COM) DLLs. PInvoke shields the .NET developer from the task of directly locating and invoking the exact function export. PInvoke also facilitates the marshalling of managed data (for example, intrinsic data types, arrays, structures) to and from their unmanaged counterparts.

In this chapter, you learn how to interact with unmanaged C DLLs using a small set of types found within the System.Runtime.InteropServices namespace. As you will see, PInvoke is basically composed of two key members. The DllImport attribute is a .NET class type that wraps low-level LoadLibrary() and GetProcAddress() calls on your behalf. System.Runtime.InteropServices.Marshal is the other key PInvoke-centric type, and it allows you to transform various primitives (including COM types) from managed to unmanaged equivalents and vice versa.

The Two Faces of Unmanaged Code

As I am sure you are aware, code built using a .NET-aware programming language (C#, VB .NET, and so on) is termed *managed code.* Conversely, code that was compiled without a .NET-aware compiler is termed *unmanaged code.* Unmanaged code really comes in two flavors:

- Traditional C-style Win32 DLLs/EXEs
- COM-based DLLs/EXEs

Obviously, the majority of this book is concerned with interoperating with COM-based binary images. However, the .NET platform does support the ability for managed code to call methods exported from a traditional (non-COM) C-style DLL. Formally, this facility is known as *Platform Invocation*, or simply PInvoke.

However, you will seldom be in a position where you absolutely need to directly call a Win32 API function, given the very simple fact that the .NET class libraries will typically provide the same functionality using a particular assembly. If you can find a .NET type that satisfies your needs, make use of it! Not only will it require less work on your part, but you can rest assured that as the .NET platform is ported to other operating systems, your code base will not be contingent upon a Windows-centric DLL.

Nevertheless, PInvoke is still a useful technology. First of all, many shops make use of a number of proprietary C-based DLLs in their current systems. Thus, if you have the best bubble sort algorithm known to humankind contained in a C-style DLL, your shiny new .NET applications will still be able to make use of it through PInvoke. Given that PInvoke can trigger the functionality contained in *any* Win32-based DLL (custom or otherwise), I spend the majority of this chapter examining how to invoke members exported from custom DLLs. However, you also get to see an example of using PInvoke to call prefabricated Win32 APIs (as you might guess, the process is identical).

Understanding the C-Style DLL

As you certainly know, Win32 EXEs define a WinMain() method that is called by the OS when the application is launched. In contrast, COM-based DLLs export a set of four functions that allow the COM runtime to extract class factories, register and unregister the COM server, and poll the DLL for its "unloadability." Unlike a Windows EXE or COM-based DLL, custom C-style DLLs are not required to support a set of well-known functions for consumption by the Windows OS.

However, although a custom DLL does not *need* to support a fixed member infrastructure, most do indeed support a special method named DllMain(), which will be called by the OS (if present) to allow you to initialize and terminate the module itself. DllMain() does have a fixed signature, which looks like the following:

```
// DllMain()'s prototype.
BOOL APIENTRY DllMain(HANDLE hModule,
    DWORD  ul_reason_for_call,
    LPVOID lpReserved);
```

The most relevant parameter for this discussion is the DWORD parameter, which contains a value (set by the OS) describing how the DLL is being accessed by the outside world. As you would hope, you are provided with a prefabricated set of programming constants to represent each possibility. In a nutshell, two of these constants are used to test if the DLL is being loaded or unloaded (for the first or last time), and two are used to capture instances when a new thread attaches to or detaches from the module. To account for each of these possibilities, you could implement DllMain() as follows:

```
// The optional, but quite helpful, DllMain().
BOOL APIENTRY DllMain( HANDLE hModule,
    DWORD  ul_reason_for_call,
    LPVOID lpReserved)
{
    switch (ul_reason_for_call)
    {
        case DLL_PROCESS_ATTACH: break;
        case DLL_THREAD_ATTACH: break;
        case DLL_THREAD_DETACH: break;
        case DLL_PROCESS_DETACH: break;
    }
    return TRUE;
}
```

Obviously, what you do within the scope of DllMain() is contingent on the module you are constructing. Possible tasks include assigning values to module-level data members, allocating (and deallocating) memory, and so forth. Of course, a DLL that only defines DllMain() is not very useful. You need custom content to make your DLL interesting to the outside world.

Exporting Custom Members

A traditional C-style DLL is not constructed using the building blocks of COM and does not have the same internal structure as a .NET binary. Rather, unmanaged DLLs contain some set of global functions, user-defined types (UDTs), and data points that are identified by a friendly string name and ordinal value. Typically, a *.def file is used to identify the available exports. For example, assume you have written a C-based DLL that exports four global functions. The corresponding *.def file might look something like the following:

```
; MyCBasedDll.def : Declares the module parameters.
LIBRARY "MyCBasedDll.dll"

EXPORTS
    MethodA   @1 PRIVATE
    MethodB   @2 PRIVATE
    MethodC   @3 PRIVATE
    MethodD   @4 PRIVATE
```

Note that the LIBRARY tag is used to mark the name of the *.dll that contains the member exports. The EXPORTS tag documents the set of members that are reachable from another binary client (DLL or EXE). Finally, note only the name of each member (not the parameters or return values) is identified using a simple numerical identifier (@1, @2, @3, and so on). As an interesting side note, understand that COM-based DLLs also make use of a standard *.def file to export the core functions accessed by the COM runtime (more details in Chapter 2):

```
; ATLServer.def : Declares the module parameters.
LIBRARY "ATLServer.DLL"

EXPORTS
    DllCanUnloadNow         @1 PRIVATE
    DllGetClassObject       @2 PRIVATE
    DllRegisterServer       @3 PRIVATE
    DllUnregisterServer     @4 PRIVATE
```

The Dllexport Declaration Specification

Although traditional *.def files have stood the test of time, the Visual C++ compiler also supports a specific *declaration specification* (declspec) that can be used to expose a member from a C-based DLL without the need to maintain and update a stand-alone *.def file. Following convention, the dllexport declspec will be used to build a simple macro that can be prefixed to a given function, data member, or class that needs to be visible from outside the binary boundary. The macro definition could be written as follows:

```
// A custom macro which will mark a DLL export.
#define MYCSTYLEDLL_API __declspec(dllexport)
```

You would then expose MethodA() from a given DLL as shown here (note that the prototype and member implementation both need to be qualified with the MYCSTYLEDLL macro):

```
// Function prototype (in some header file).
extern "C" MYCSTYLEDLL_API int MethodA(void);

// Function implementation (in some *.cpp file).
extern "C" MYCSTYLEDLL_API int MethodA(void)
{return 1234;}
```

This same shortcut can be used when you wish to export a single point of data (such as some fixed global constants) or an entire class module (not a COM class mind you, but a vanilla-flavored C++ class).

Building a Custom C-Based DLL

During the course of this chapter, you learn how to use the DllImport attribute to allow your managed .NET code to call members contained in a traditional C-style DLL (including Win32 DLLs). To be sure, DllImport is most commonly used to trigger Win32 API functions; however, this same .NET attribute can be used to interact with your custom proprietary modules. Given this, let's build a simple Win32 DLL named MyCustomDLL. If you wish to follow along, fire up Visual Studio 6.0 (or VS .NET if you prefer) and select a Win32 DLL project workspace (Figure 1-1).

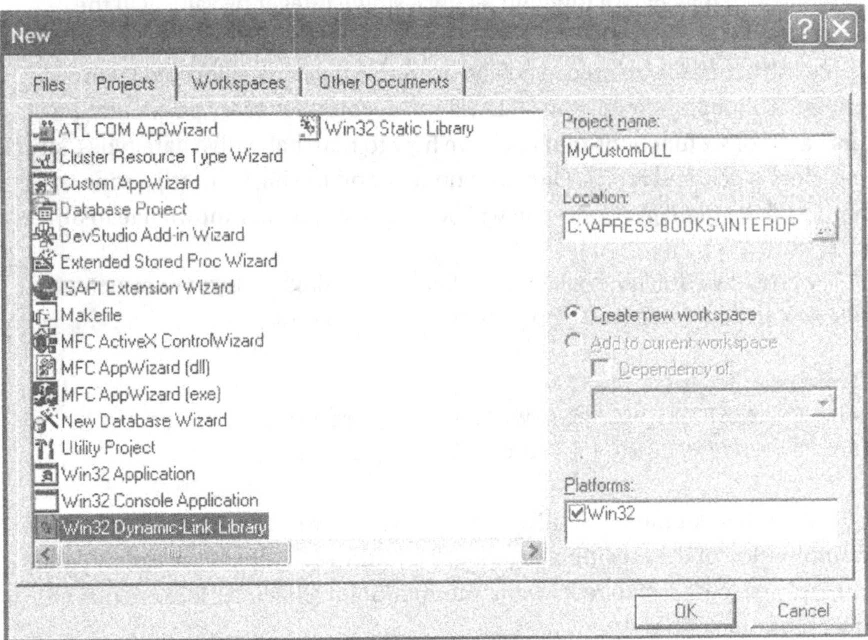

Figure 1-1. Creating your C-style DLL

From the resulting wizard, simply select "A simple DLL" project. The first order of business is to establish the custom declspec macros, which will be used under two circumstances. First, if the code base defines the MYCSTYLEDLL_EXPORTS symbol, the macro will expand to __declspec(dllexport). On the other hand, if an external code base #includes the files that define the custom members (and thus does not define the MYCSTYLEDLL_EXPORTS symbol), the macro will expand to __declspec(dllimport). For simplicity, simply add the following macro logic in the current MyCustomDLL.h file:

```
// The helper macro pair.
#ifdef MYCSTYLEDLL_EXPORTS
#define MYCSTYLEDLL_API __declspec(dllexport)
#else
#define MYCSTYLEDLL_API __declspec(dllimport)
#endif
```

Functions Using Basic Data Types and Arrays

A proprietary DLL could contain members of varying complexity. On the simple side of life, you may have a function taking a single integer by value. On the complex end of the spectrum, you may have a function that receives an array of complex structures by reference (which of course may be reallocated by the module). Although your custom DLL will not account for every possibility, it will export a set of six functions that illustrate how to marshal native data types, structures, class types, and arrays. Once you understand the basics of triggering these members from managed code, you will be able to apply this knowledge to other DLL exports.

Your first two functions allow the caller to pass single integer parameters as well as an array of integers. The prototypes are as follows:

```
// Prototypes for basic functions.
extern "C" MYCUSTOMDLL_API int AddNumbers(int x, int y);
extern "C" MYCUSTOMDLL_API int AddArray(int x[], int size);
```

The implementation of AddNumbers() is as you would expect (simply return the summation of the incoming arguments). AddArray() allows the caller to pass in an array of some size to receive the summation of all items. Here are the implementations:

```
// 1) A very simple DLL export.
extern "C" MYCUSTOMDLL_API int AddNumbers(int x, int y)
{ return x + y; }

// 2) A method taking an array.
extern "C" MYCUSTOMDLL_API int AddArray(int x[], int size)
```

```
{
    int ans = 0;
    for(int i = 0; i < size; i++)
    {
        ans = ans + x[i];
    }
    return ans;
}
```

Functions Receiving Structures (and Structures Containing Structures)

The next two function exports allow the user to pass in a complex structure for processing as well as return an array of structures to the caller. Before you see the methods themselves, here are definitions of the CAR and CAR2 UDTs:

```
// A basic structure.
typedef struct _CAR
{
    char* make;
    char* color;
} CAR;

// A structure containing another structure.
typedef struct _CAR2
{
    CAR theCar;
    char* petName;
} CAR2;
```

As you can see, the basic CAR structure defines two fields that document the color and make of a give automobile. CAR2 extends this basic information with a new field (petName), which allows the user to assign a friendly name to the car in question. The first structure-centric function, DisplayBetterCar(), takes a CAR2 type as an input parameter that is displayed using a Win32 MessageBox() call:

```
// Function prototype.
extern "C" MYCUSTOMDLL_API void DisplayBetterCar(CAR2* theCar);

// 3) A method taking a struct.
extern "C" MYCUSTOMDLL_API void DisplayBetterCar(CAR2* theCar)
```

```
{
    // Read values of car and put in message box.
    MessageBox(NULL, theCar->theCar.color, "Car Color", MB_OK);
    MessageBox(NULL, theCar->theCar.make, "Car Make", MB_OK);
    MessageBox(NULL, theCar->petName, "Car Pet Name", MB_OK);
}
```

The next DLL export, GiveMeThreeBasicCars(), returns a fixed array of CAR types to the caller as an output parameter. Given that you will be dynamically allocating structures on the fly, you make use of CoTaskMemAlloc(), which is defined in objbase.h (so be sure to #include this file in your project). Here is the code:

```
// Function prototype.
extern "C" MYCUSTOMDLL_API void GiveMeThreeBasicCars(CAR** theCars);

// 4) A Method returning an array of structs.
extern "C" MYCUSTOMDLL_API void GiveMeThreeBasicCars(CAR** theCars)
{
    int numbOfCars = 3;
    *theCars = (CAR*)CoTaskMemAlloc( numbOfCars * sizeof( CAR ));

    char* carMakes[3] = {"BMW", "Ford", "Viper"};
    char* carColors[3] = {"Green", "Pink", "Red"};

    CAR* pCurCar = *theCars;
    for( int i = 0; i < numbOfCars; i++, pCurCar++ )
    {
        pCurCar->color = carColors[i];
        pCurCar->make = carMakes[i];
    }
}
```

Functions Using Class Types

The final two function exports defined by your custom DLL allow the outside world to obtain and destroy a (non-COM) C++ class type named CMiniVan:

```
// A class to be exported.
class MYCUSTOMDLL_API CMiniVan
{
public:
    CMiniVan(){m_numbKids = 52;}
    int DisplayNumberOfKids()
    { return m_numbKids;}
private:
    int m_numbKids;
};
```

To interact with this class type, you provide the final two functions:

```
// Prototypes for class marshaling.
extern "C" MYCUSTOMDLL_API CMiniVan* CreateMiniVan();
extern "C" MYCUSTOMDLL_API void DeleteMiniVan(CMiniVan* obj);

// 5) Method to create a CMiniVan.
extern "C" MYCUSTOMDLL_API CMiniVan* CreateMiniVan()
{ return new CMiniVan(); }

// 6) Method to destroy a CMiniVan
extern "C" MYCUSTOMDLL_API void DeleteMiniVan(CMiniVan* obj)
{ delete obj; }
```

That's it! Go ahead and compile the project. Over the course of this chapter, you will trigger these members from managed and unmanaged code bases.

CODE *The MyCustomDLL project is included under the Chapter 1 directory.*

Viewing Your Imports and Exports Using dumpbin.exe

The dumpbin.exe utility is a command line tool that allows you to view a number of details for a given unmanaged DLL (or EXE). Like most command line tools, dumpbin.exe supports a set of command line flags you use to inform it exactly what you are interested in viewing. Table 1-1 illustrates some of the more common options.

Table 1-1. Common dumpbin.exe Flags

dumpbin.exe Flag	Meaning in Life
/all	This option displays all available information except code disassembly.
/disasm	This option displays disassembly of code sections, using symbols if present in the file.
/exports	This option displays all definitions exported from an executable file or DLL.

Table 1-1. Common dumpbin.exe Flags (continued)

dumpbin.exe Flag	**Meaning in Life**
/imports	This option displays all definitions imported to an executable file or DLL.
/summary	This option displays minimal information about sections, including total size. This option is the default if no other option is specified.

First, let's check out the set of *imported* modules used by MyCustomDLL.dll. As you recall, your code base made use of the MessageBox() API (defined in user32.dll), the CoTaskMemAlloc() API (ole32.dll), and the mandatory kernel32.dll. Given this, if you were to open a command window, navigate to the location of MyCustomDLL.dll, and apply the /imports command to dumpbin.exe as follows:

```
C:\ >dumpbin /imports mycustomdll.dll
```

you would find the listing shown in Figure 1-2.

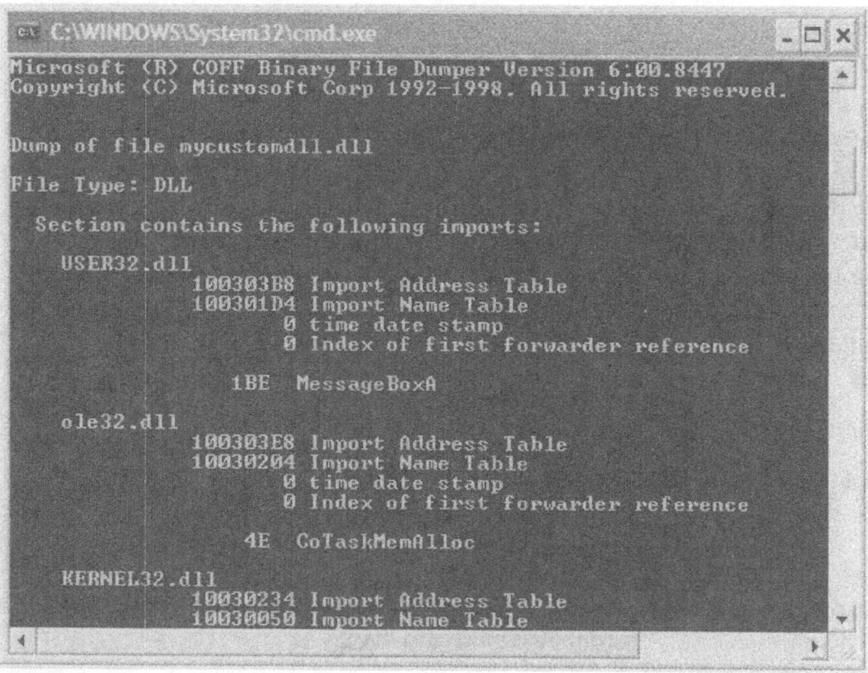

Figure 1-2. Dumping the imports of MyCustomDLL.dll

As you may be aware, .NET assemblies catalog the same sort of imported information using the assembly manifest (via the [.assembly extern] tag). Of greater interest to you at the current time is the list of *exports*:

```
C:\ >dumpbin /exports mycustomdll.dll
```

As you can see from Figure 1-3, the __declspec(dllexport) specification has assigned unique ordinal numbers to each exported member.

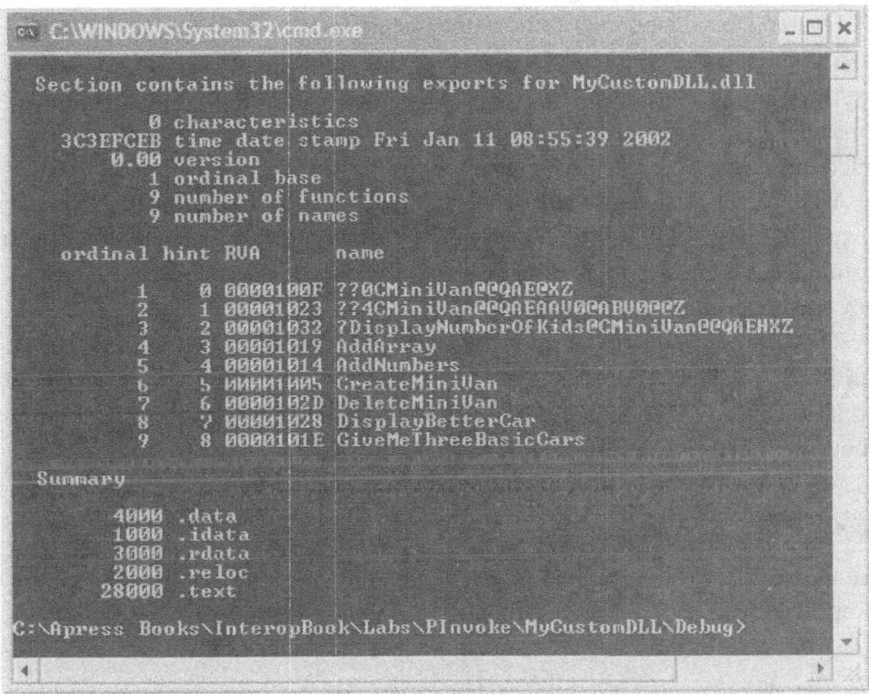

Figure 1-3. The exports of MyCustomDLL.dll

Notice that the CMiniVan class is internally represented using a common C++ complier technique termed *named mangling*. Basically, name mangling is a way to assign a unique internal name to a given class member. Typically, C++ developers do not need to be concerned with the internal mangled representation of a given class member. However, do be aware that when you wish to trigger a class method from managed code, you *will* need to obtain this internal name. For example, later in this chapter when you invoke CMiniVan::DisplayNumberOfKids(), you need to refer to this member as

```
?DisplayNumberOfKids@CMiniVan@@QAEHXZ
```

Deploying Traditional DLLs

Now that you have created a custom DLL, you are ready to begin building a number of client applications (both managed and unmanaged) that can access the exported member set. Before you get to that point, you need to address a rather obvious question: How will the runtime locate the custom C-based module?

As you may know (and will see in detail in Chapter 2), COM-based DLLs can be placed anywhere within the host computer's directory structure, given that COM servers are explicitly registered in the system registry. On the other hand, .NET-based DLLs are not registered in the system registry at all, but are typically deployed in the same directory as the launching client (that is, as a private assembly). As an alternative, .NET DLLs can be shared by multiple client applications on a given machine by placing the assembly within a well-known location called the *Global Assembly Cache* (GAC).

Traditional C-style DLLs are deployed much like a .NET DLL, given that they are not registered within the system registry. The simplest approach to deploy your custom DLLs is to place them directly in the directory of the calling client (typically called the *application directory*).

This brings about a rather interesting side note, however. As you know, the Windows OS defines a number of system-level DLLs that supply a number of core services such as GDI, file IO, and so forth. For sake of reference, Table 1-2 documents some of the critical system DLLs to be aware of.

Table 1-2. Core System-Level DLLs

Core Windows DLL	Meaning in Life
advapi32.dll	Advanced API services library supporting numerous APIs, including many security and registry calls
comdlg32.dll	Common dialog API library
gdi32.dll	Graphics Device Interface API library
kernel32.dll	Core Windows 32-bit base API support
mpr.dll	No, not Minnesota Public Radio, but rather Multiple Provider Router library
netapi32.dll	32-bit Network API library
shell32.dll	32-bit Shell API library
user32.dll	Library for user interface routines
version.dll	Version library
winmm.dll	Windows multimedia library

Obviously, when you are building a custom Win32 application, you are not required to create private copies of these core DLLs in the client's application directory. How then are these DLLs located by the runtime? The Windows OS maintains a well-known location for its system-level DLLs, specifically %windir%\System32 (Figure 1-4).

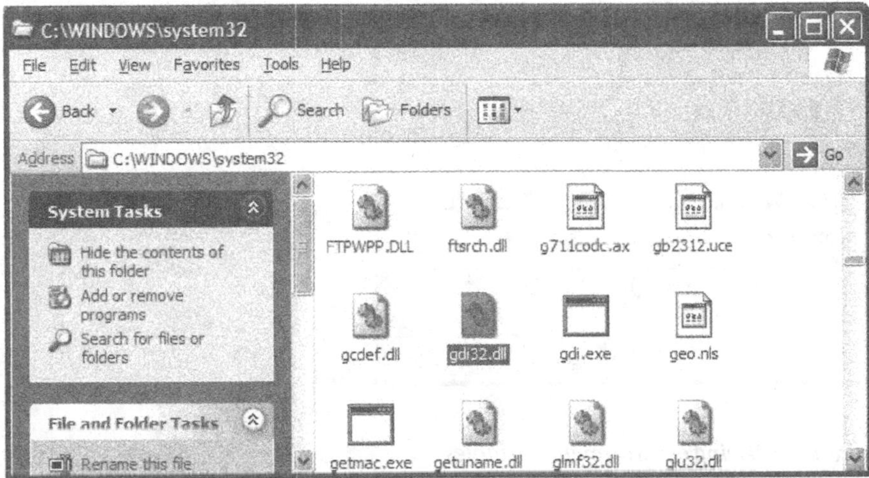

Figure 1-4. The %windir%\System32 subdirectory is the location of core Win32 DLLs.

This location is documented using a system path variable that can be found by taking the following steps on a Windows XP machine (some steps may vary for other OSs):

- Right-click the My Computer icon.
- Click the Environment Variables button on the Advanced Tab.
- View the Path value under the System Variables list box (Figure 1-5).

Figure 1-5. Viewing environment variables

Using this path value, the Windows OS understands where to look when it is attempting to locate a distinct Win32 (non-COM/non-.NET) DLL. Given that the "Path" variable defines numerous values (separated by semicolons), you are free to place your custom DLLs in within any documented paths. For the remainder of this chapter, I will assume that you have placed a copy of MyCustomDLL.dll in your %windir%\System32 subdirectory (Figure 1-6).

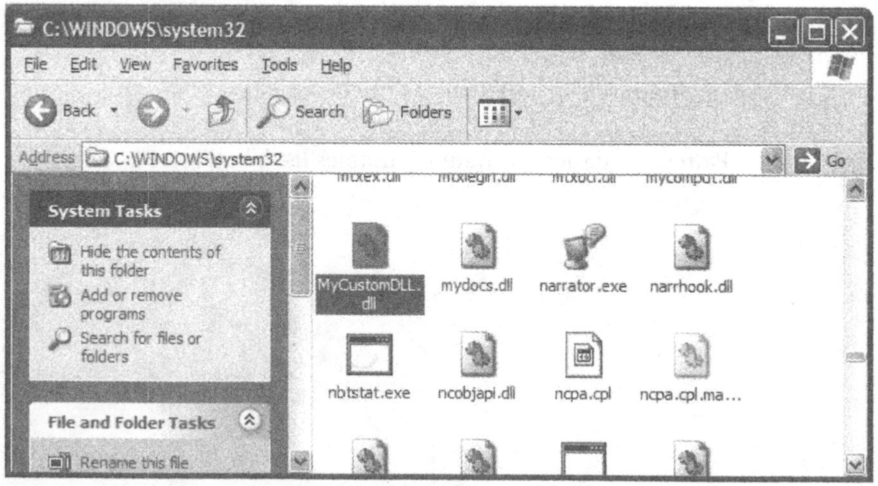

Figure 1-6. Your custom DLL is now within the %windir%\System32 path.

A Dynamic C++ DLL Client

Before you learn how to trigger function exports using managed languages, let's take a brief look at a traditional C-based client application. Now, if you wanted to take the simple (that is, uninteresting) approach, you would build a C++ client that directly links to the MyCustomDLL.dll binary. However, let's take a more interesting approach and load (and invoke) members of the *.dll on the fly at runtime. As you will see, the managed DllImport attribute mimics the same pattern found with the LoadLibrary()/GetProcAddress() APIs.

To begin, assume you have a new Win32 console application named MyCustomDLLCppClient (a "simple project" will be fine). First, place a copy of the MyCustomDll.h file directly in the project directory (you do this because the file has the C definitions of your custom UDTs). When you need to load a C-based DLL and invoke its members dynamically, you must make use of three key Win32 API calls, which are explained in Table 1-3.

Table 1-3. Library-Centric Win32 API Functions

Library-Centric API Function	Meaning in Life
FreeLibrary()	This API decreases the *.dll's internal use counter by one and removes the binary from memory when the counter is at zero.
GetProcAddress()	This API function is used to invoke a given export within the loaded module.
LoadLibrary()	This API function loads a specific *.dll module using the search heuristics explained previously.

Dynamically Loading an External Library

Calling LoadLibrary() is quite painless, given that the only parameter is the string name of the DLL you wish to load into the current process. The return value is of type HINSTANCE, which represents a handle to the currently loaded binary (as you will see, GetProcAddress() requires this value as a parameter). To begin, update Main() as shown here:

```
#include "stdafx.h"
#include <windows.h>
#include <iostream>
#include "MyCustomDLL.h"
using namespace std;
int main(int argc, char* argv[])
```

```
{
    // A handle to the loaded library.
    HINSTANCE dllHandle = NULL;

    // Load the DLL and keep the handle to it.
    // Assume this DLL is in the same folder as the
    // client EXE or under \System32.
    dllHandle = LoadLibrary("MyCustomDll.dll");

    // If the handle is valid, try to call members.
    if (NULL != dllHandle)
    {
        ...
        // Free the library when finished.
        FreeLibrary(dllHandle);
    }
    return 0;
}
```

Invoking Members

Given that the example has not directly linked the DLL to its compilation cycle, you are not currently able to directly resolve the names of the exported functions. What you need is a generic way to represent the address of a given function. Lucky for you, GetProcAddress() will return a pointer to a specific function upon successful completion. So, how do you represent a generic function pointer? The standard approach is to build a C-style type definition that represents a pointer to the method as well as its set of arguments and return value. For example, if you craft such a pointer for the AddNumbers() method, you can build the following typedef:

```
// A typedef to hold the address of the AddNumbers() method.
typedef int (*PFNADDNUMBERS) (int, int);

// Create a variable of this type.
PFNADDNUMBERS pfnAddMethod;
```

A similar typedef could be created for any of your exported members. Here is another example for the DisplayBetterCar() method, which as you recall takes a CAR2 structure type as its sole parameter:

```
// A typedef to hold the address of the DisplayBetterCar() method.
typedef int (*PFNDISPLAYBETTERCAR) (CAR2*);
PFNDISPLAYBETTERCAR pfnDisplayBetterCar;
```

Once you have a generic pointer to a given function, you can now call GetProcAddress() to obtain a valid pointer to said method. Here is an update to the Main() loop that will call AddNumbers() and DisplayBetterCar() dynamically at runtime (without statically linking to the MyCustomDLL.dll):

```
if (NULL != dllHandle)
{
    // Get pointer to AddNumbers() using GetProcAddress.
    pfnAddMethod = (PFNADDNUMBERS)
        GetProcAddress(dllHandle, "AddNumbers");

    // If the function address is valid, call AddNumbers().
    if (NULL != pfnAddMethod)
    {
        int retVal = pfnAddMethod(100, 100);
        cout << "100 + 100 is: " << retVal << endl;
    }

    // Make a better car.
    CAR2 myCar;
    myCar.petName = "JoJo";
    myCar.theCar.make = "Viper";
    myCar.theCar.color = "Red";

    pfnDisplayBetterCar = (PFNDISPLAYBETTERCAR)
        GetProcAddress(dllHandle, "DisplayBetterCar");

    // If the function address is valid, call DisplayBetterCar().
    if (NULL != pfnDisplayBetterCar)
    {
        pfnDisplayBetterCar(&myCar);
    }

    // Free the library.
    FreeLibrary(dllHandle);
}
```

As you can see, GetProcAddress() requires you to specify the module to examine (represented by the HINSTANCE returned from LoadLibrary()) and the name of the member you wish to invoke. The result is a pointer to the correct function, which can be invoked as if you had a direct function definition! When you run this application, you should see the result of adding 100 and 100, followed by a series of message boxes describing your new red Viper named JoJo.

CODE *The MyCustomDLLCppClient application is found under the Chapter 1 directory.*

The Atoms of PInvoke

Now that you have created a custom DLL (and checked out the process of dynamically invoking members using the Win32 API), you will spend the rest of this chapter examining the process of calling C-based function exports from managed code. In order to do so, you need to be comfortable with a small set of .NET types and a basic set of data conversion rules.

The two .NET types in question (the Marshal class and DllImport attribute) are both defined within the System.Runtime.InteropServices namespace, which as you will see throughout this book is the key namespace that makes COM/.NET interoperability possible. This namespace is defined within the core .NET assembly, mscorlib.dll, which is part of every managed application. Therefore, all you need to do to access these types is simply make reference to the namespace itself using the syntax of your favorite managed language. For example:

```
// C#.
using System.Runtime.InteropServices;

' VB .NET.
Imports System.Runtime.InteropServices
```

Data Type Conversions

As C++ programmers are painfully aware, the Windows API has billions (or thereabout) of type definitions that represent primitive data types. Although these typedefs can take a bit of getting used to at first, they do save you a few keystrokes. For example, if you wish to define a constant string of Unicode characters, you could write the following C-style declaration:

```
/* A constant Unicode string of characters in C */
const wchar_t* myUnicodeString;
```

or make use of the following Windows typedef:

```
/* Same string, fewer keystrokes…*/
LPCWSTR myOtherUnicodeString;
```

These predefined type definitions are based on a naming convention called *Hungarian notation*, which is used to make a data type a bit more self-describing. For example, LPCWSTR can be read as a "pointer to a constant wide string." When you are making use of PInvoke, you don't make use of these Win32-centric type definitions directly, but rather a managed equivalent. Table 1-4 documents the mapping between Win32 typedefs (and their C representation) and the correct .NET data type.

Table 1-4. Data Type Representation

Unmanaged Type in wtypes.h	Unmanaged C Language Type	Managed Type Representation	Meaning in Life
BOOL	long	System.Int32	32 bits
BYTE	unsigned char	System.Byte	8 bits
CHAR	char	System.Char	ANSI string
DOUBLE	double	System.Double	64 bits
DWORD	unsigned long	System.UInt32	32 bits
FLOAT	float	System.Single	32 bits
HANDLE	void*	System.IntPtr	32 bits
INT	int	System.Int32	32 bits
LONG	long	System.Int32	32 bits
LPCSTR	const char*	System.String or System.StringBuilder	ANSI string
LPCWSTR	const wchar_t*	System.String or System.StringBuilder	Unicode string
LPSTR	char*	System.String or System.StringBuilder	ANSI string
LPWSTR	wchar_t*	System.String or System.StringBuilder	Unicode string
SHORT	short	System.Int16	16 bits
UINT	unsigned int	System.UInt32	32 bits
ULONG	unsigned long	System.UInt32	32 bits
WORD	unsigned short	System.UInt16	16 bits

The Marshal Class

System.Runtime.InteropServices.Marshal is a key type that is used with all facets of .NET interoperability. This sealed class defines a healthy dose of static (Shared in terms of VB .NET) members that provides a bridge between managed and unmanaged constructs. When you are working with PInvoke proper (meaning you are not interested in communicating with COM-based DLLs), you really only need to access a very small subset of its overall functionality. In fact, a majority of the members provided by the Marshal type are most useful when dealing with COM/.NET interop issues.

Nevertheless, in this section, I outline the full functionality of Marshal, by grouping members by related functionality. You will see additional aspects of Marshal during the remainder of this text, so don't panic due to the sheer volume of members. Table 1-5 documents a number of members that allow you to interact with low-level COM primitives such as IUnknown, VARIANT transformations, and moniker bindings (among other things).

Table 1-5. COM-Centric Members of the Marshal Type

General COM-Centric Member of the Marshal Type	Meaning in Life
AddRef()	Increments the reference count on the specified interface
BindToMoniker()	Gets an interface pointer identified by the specified moniker
GenerateGuidForType()	Returns the GUID for the specified type, or generates a GUID using the algorithm employed by the Type Library Exporter (TlbExp.exe)
GenerateProgIdForType()	Returns a ProgID for the specified type
GetActiveObject()	Obtains a running instance of the specified object from the Running Object Table (ROT)
GetComInterfaceForObject()	Returns an IUnknown pointer representing the specified interface for an object
GetIDispatchForObject()	Returns an IDispatch interface from a managed object
GetIUnknownForObject()	Returns an IUnknown interface from a managed object

Table 1-5. COM-Centric Members of the Marshal Type (continued)

General COM-Centric Member of the Marshal Type	Meaning in Life
GetObjectForNativeVariant()	Converts a COM VARIANT to an object
GetObjectsForNativeVariants()	Converts an array of COM VARIANTs to an array of objects
GetNativeVariantForObject()	Converts an object to a COM VARIANT
IsComObject()	Indicates whether a specified object represents an unmanaged COM object
IsTypeVisibleFromCom()	Indicates whether a type is visible to COM clients
QueryInterface()	Requests a pointer to a specified interface from an existing interface
Release()	Decrements the reference count on the specified interface
ReleaseComObject()	Decrements the reference count of the supplied Runtime Callable Wrapper (RCW)

Closely related to the members in Table 1-5 are the following set of COM type library–specific members of the Marshal type (Table 1-6).

Table 1-6. Type Library–Centric Members of the Marshal Class

COM Type Library-Centric Member of the Marshal Type	Meaning in Life
GetITypeInfoForType()	Returns an ITypeInfo interface from a managed type
GetTypeForITypeInfo()	Converts an ITypeInfo into a managed System.Type object
GetTypeInfoName()	Retrieves the name of the type represented by an ITypeInfo
GetTypeLibGuid()	Retrieves the GUID of a type library
GetTypeLibGuidForAssembly()	Retrieves the GUID that is assigned to a type library when it was exported from the specified assembly
GetTypeLibLcid()	Retrieves the LCID of a type library
GetTypeLibName()	Retrieves the name of a type library

Of course, there are a number of members of the Marshal type that allow you to convert between the managed System.String type and all 20,000 (or so) textual variations found in the raw Win32 APIs (Table 1-7).

Table 1-7. String Conversion Members of the Marshal Type

String Conversion Member of the Marshal Type	Meaning in Life
FreeBSTR()	Frees a BSTR using SysFreeString
PtrToStringAnsi()	Copies all or part of an ANSI string to a managed System.String object
PtrToStringAuto()	Copies an unmanaged string to a managed System.String object
PtrToStringBSTR()	Copies a Unicode string stored in native heap to a managed System.String object
PtrToStringUni()	Copies an unmanaged Unicode string to a managed System.String object
StringToBSTR()	Allocates a BSTR and copies the string contents into it
StringToCoTaskMemAnsi()	Copies the contents of a string to a block of memory allocated from the unmanaged COM task allocator
StringToCoTaskMemAuto()	Copies the contents of a string to a block of memory allocated from the unmanaged COM task allocator
StringToCoTaskMemUni()	Copies the contents of a string to a block of memory allocated from the unmanaged COM task allocator
StringToHGlobalAnsi()	Copies the contents of a managed System.String object into native heap, converting into ANSI format as it copies
StringToHGlobalAuto()	Copies the contents of a managed System.String object into native heap, converting into ANSI format if required
StringToHGlobalUni()	Copies the contents of a managed System.String object into native heap

Perhaps the most directly useful members of the Marshal type (especially when working with PInvoke) are the following set of structure and/or memory manipulation members of the Marshal type (Table 1-8).

Table 1-8. Memory/Structure-Centric Members of the Marshal Type

Memory/Structure-Centric Member of the Marshal Type	**Meaning in Life**
AllocCoTaskMem()	Allocates a block of memory of specified size from the COM task memory allocator using CoTaskMemAlloc
AllocHGlobal()	Allocates a block of memory using GlobalAlloc
DestroyStructure()	Frees all substructures pointed to by the specified native memory block
FreeCoTaskMem()	Frees a block of memory allocated by the unmanaged COM task memory allocator with AllocCoTaskMem
FreeHGlobal()	Frees memory previously allocated from the unmanaged native heap of the process with AllocHGlobal
PtrToStructure()	Marshals data from an unmanaged block of memory to a managed object
ReAllocCoTaskMem()	Resizes a block of memory previously allocated with AllocCoTaskMem
ReAllocHGlobal()	Resizes a block of memory previously allocated with AllocHGlobal
SizeOf()	Returns the unmanaged size of a class used via Marshal in bytes
StructureToPtr()	Marshals data from a managed object to an unmanaged block of memory

The error-centric members listed in Table 1-9 compose the next major aspect of the Marshal type.

Table 1-9. Error-Centric Members of the Marshal Type

Error-Centric Member of the Marshal Type	Meaning in Life
GetExceptionCode()	Retrieves a code that identifies the type of the exception that occurred
GetExceptionPointers()	Retrieves a machine-independent description of an exception and information about the machine state that existed for the thread when the exception occurred
GetHRForException()	Converts the specified exception to an HRESULT
GetHRForLastWin32Error()	Returns the HRESULT corresponding to the last error incurred by Win32 code executed using Marshal
GetLastWin32Error()	Returns the error code returned by the last unmanaged function called using Platform Invoke that has the SetLastError() flag set
ThrowExceptionForHR()	Throws an exception with a specific HRESULT value

Finally, be aware that the Marshal type defines a number of members that allow you to read and write data to and from unmanaged memory (Table 1-10).

Table 1-10. Bit Reading/Writing–Centric Members of the Marshal Type

Data Reading/Writing Members of the Marshal Type	Meaning in Life
ReadByte() WriteByte()	Reads or writes a single byte from an unmanaged pointer
ReadInt16() WriteInt16()	Reads or writes a 16-bit integer from native heap
ReadInt32() WriteInt32()	Reads or writes a 32-bit integer from native heap
ReadInt64() WriteInt64()	Reads or writes a 64-bit integer from native heap
ReadIntPtr() WriteIntPtr()	Reads or writes a processor native-sized integer from native heap

Again, you are *not* required to make use of all of these members when working with COM/.NET interop or PInvoke. Many of the static members seen in the previous tables are more low level than you will need for your day-to-day programming tasks. However, you will see useful examples when necessary throughout the remainder of this text.

The DllImportAttribute Type

The final piece of the PInvoke puzzle is the DllImportAttribute type. In many ways, this single .NET type combines the functionality of the Win32 LoadLibrary() and GetProcAddress() APIs into a well-encapsulated class. On a related note, also understand that DllImport is a direct .NET equivalent to the VB 6.0–style declare statement. In fact, under VB .NET, the legacy Declare statement, although still supported, has been retrofitted to make use of the services of PInvoke. Given this, I will avoid examining the use of VB .NET's Declare keyword and stick to the DllImport attribute.

Like most .NET attributes, DllAttribute defines a number of public fields that allow you to control its behavior. Also, like most .NET attributes, these fields are typically set as named constructor arguments. First, ponder the formal type definition:

```
// The essence of PInvoke.
public sealed class DllImportAttribute : Attribute
{
    // Fields (first two listings are not typos!)
    // These fields are used to control exactly
    // how the attribute should be applied to the
    // unmanaged function export.
    public CallingConvention CallingConvention;
    public CharSet CharSet;
    public string EntryPoint;
    public bool ExactSpelling;
    public bool PreserveSig;
    public bool SetLastError;

    // Constructor (string param used to set fields
    // as name / value pairs).
    public DllImportAttribute(string dllName);

    // Properties.
    public object TypeId { virtual get; }
    public string Value { get; }
```

```
    // Methods (basic .NET infrastructure stuff).
    public virtual bool Equals(object obj);
    public virtual int GetHashCode();
    public Type GetType();
    public virtual bool IsDefaultAttribute();
    public virtual bool Match(object obj);
    public virtual string ToString();
}
```

As you can see, DllImportAttribute defines two fields (CallingConvention and CharSet), which may be assigned a value from enumerations of the same name:

```
// Specifies the calling convention required
// to call methods implemented in unmanaged code.
public enum CallingConvention
{
    Cdecl,
    FastCall,    // Not supported under .NET version 1.0.*.
    StdCall,
    ThisCall,
    Winapi
}

// Dictates which character set should be used to marshal strings.
public enum CharSet
{
    Ansi,
    Auto,
    None,
    Unicode
}
```

You will see exactly how these three types are used during the remainder of this chapter. Before tackling the topic of accessing your custom DLL, let's take PInvoke out for a simple test drive and get to know the various fields of DllImportAttribute at the same time.

A Trivial PInvoke Example

The most typical use of PInvoke is to allow .NET components to interact with the Win32 API in the raw. As you already know, the .NET base class library exists for the very purpose of hiding the low-level API from view. Thus, although you might not ever need to drop down to the raw Win32, PInvoke provides the ability to do so. To illustrate the use of PInvoke, let's build a C# console application (SimpleAPIInvoke) that makes a call to the Win32 MessageBox() function. First, the code:

```
namespace SimpleAPIInvoke
{
    using System;
    // Must reference to gain access to the PInvoke types.
    using System.Runtime.InteropServices;

    public class PInvokeClient
    {
        // The Win32 MessageBox() function lives in user32.dll.
        [DllImport("user32.dll")]
        public static extern int MessageBox(int hWnd, String  pText,
            String  pCaption, int uType);

        public static int Main(string[] args)
        {
            // Send in some managed data.
            String pText = "Hello World!";
            String pCaption = "PInvoke Test";
            MessageBox(0, pText, pCaption, 0);
            return 0;
        }
    }
}
```

The process of calling a C-style DLL begins by declaring the function you wish to call using the static and extern C# keywords (this step is not optional). Notice that when you declare the C function prototype, you must list the return type, function name, and arguments in terms of *managed data types*. So you do not send in char* or wchar_t* arrays, but the managed System.String type. Once you have prototyped the method you intend to call, your next step is to adorn this member with the DllImport attribute. At absolute minimum, you need to specify the name of the raw DLL that contains the function you are attempting to call as shown here:

```
[DllImport("user32.dll")]
public static extern int MessageBox(…);
```

As you can see, the DllImportAttribute type defines a set of public fields that may be specified to further configure the process of binding to the function export. Table 1-11 gives a rundown of these fields.

Table 1-11. Fields of the DllImportAttribute Type

DllImportAttribute Field	**Meaning in Life**
CallingConvention	Used to establish the calling convention used in passing method arguments. The default is CallingConvention.WinAPI, which corresponds to __stdcall.
CharSet	Indicates how string arguments to the method should be marshaled (CharSet.Ansi is the default).
EntryPoint	Indicates the string name or ordinal number of the function to be called.
ExactSpelling	PInvoke attempts to match the name of the function you specify with the "real" name as prototyped. If this field is set to true, you are indicating that the name of the entry point in the unmanaged .dll must exactly match the name you are passing in.
PreserveSig	When set to true (the default setting), an unmanaged method signature will *not* be transformed into a managed signature that returns an HRESULT and has an additional [out, retval] argument for the return value.
SetLastError	When set to true, indicates that the caller may call Marshal.GetLastWin32Error() to determine if an error occurred while executing the method; the default is false in C# but true in VB .NET.

If you wish to set these values for your current DllImportAttribute object instance, simply specify each as a name/value pair to the class constructor. If you check out the definition of the DllImportAttribute constructor, you can see it takes a single parameter of type System.String:

```
class DllImportAttribute
{
    // Constructor takes a string that holds all field values.
    public DllImportAttribute( string val );
...
}
```

Given this bit of information, it should be clear that the order in which you specify these values does not matter. The DllImport class will simply parse the string internally and use the values to set its internal state data.

Specifying the ExactSpelling Field

The first field of interest is ExactSpelling, which is used to control whether the name of the managed function is identical to that of the name of the unmanaged function. For example, as you may know, there is no such function named MessageBox in the Win32 API. Rather, you have an ANSI version (MessageBoxA) and a Unicode version (MessageBoxW). Given the fact that you specified a method named MessageBox, you can correctly assume that the default value of ExactSpelling is false. However, if you were to set this value to true as follows:

```
[DllImport("user32.dll", ExactSpelling = true)]
public static extern int MessageBox(…);              // Uh-oh!
```

you would now receive an EntryPointNotFoundException exception, because there is no function named MessageBox in user32.dll! As you can see, the ExactSpelling field basically allows you to be "lazy" and ignore the W or A suffixes. However, PInvoke clearly needs to ultimately resolve the exact name of the function you wish to call. When you leave ExactSpelling at its default value ("false"), the letter *A* is appended to the method name under ANSI environments and the letter *W* under Unicode environments.

Specifying the Character Set

If you wish to explicitly specify the character set used to marshal data between managed code and the raw DLL export, you may set the value of the CharSet field using a member from the related CharSet enumeration (Table 1-12).

Table 1-12. CharSet Values

CharSet Member Name	Meaning in Life
Ansi	Specifies that strings should be marshaled as ANSI 1-byte chars
Auto	Informs PInvoke to marshal a string correctly as required by the target platform (Unicode on WinNT/Win2000 and ANSI on Win 9*x*)
None	Signifies that you didn't specify how to marshal strings (default) and you wish the runtime to figure things out automatically
Unicode	Specifies that strings should be marshaled as Unicode 2-byte chars

By way of example, if you wish to enforce that all strings be marshaled as Unicode (and thus risk your code not working correctly on Win95, Win98, or WinME platforms), you would write the following:

```
// Demand the exact name, and specify the Unicode character set.
[DllImport("user32.dll", ExactSpelling = true, CharSet=CharSet.Unicode)]
public static extern int MessageBoxW(…);
```

Generally speaking, it is safer to set the CharSet value to CharSet.Auto (or simply accept the default). In this way, textual parameters will be marshaled correctly regardless of the target platform, leaving your code base far more portable.

Specifying Calling Conventions

The next field of interest is CallingConvention. As you know, Win32 API functions can be adorned with a number of typedefs that specify how parameters should be passed into the function (C declaration, fast call, standard call, and so forth). The CallingConvention field may be set using any value from the CallingConvention enumeration. As you might suspect, this enum specifies values such as Cdecl, Winapi, StdCall, and so forth. The default of this field is StdCall, so you can typically ignore explicitly setting this field (given that this is the most common Win32 calling convention). Nevertheless, Table 1-13 documents the possible values of the CallingConvention enumeration. (Do note the CallingConvention.ThisCall value, which will be used later in this chapter to trigger methods of exported C++ class types.)

Table 1-13. CallingConvention Values

CallingConvention Enumeration Value	**Meaning in Life**
Cdecl	The caller cleans the stack. This enables calling functions with varargs.
FastCall	This calling convention is not currently supported (but is reserved for future use).
StdCall	The callee cleans the stack. This is the default convention for calling unmanaged functions from managed code.
ThisCall	The first parameter is the "this" pointer and is stored in register ECX. Other parameters are pushed on the stack. This calling convention is used to call methods on classes exported from an unmanaged DLL.
Winapi	Uses the default platform calling convention. For example, Windows uses StdCall and Windows CE uses Cdecl.

Specifying Function Entry Points

Next up is the EntryPoint field. By default, this field will be the same as the name of the function you are prototyping. Therefore, in the following declaration, EntryPoint is implicitly set to MessageBoxW.

```
// EntryPoint automatically set to 'MessageBoxW'.
[DllImport("user32.dll", ExactSpelling = true, CharSet=CharSet.Unicode)]
public static extern int MessageBoxW(...);
```

If you wish to establish an alias for the exported function, you may specify the "real name" of the exported function using the EntryPoint field, effectively renaming the function for use in your managed code. Obviously, this is a helpful way to avoid possible name clashes. To illustrate, here is the final iteration of the PInvoke example that maps the MessageBoxW() function to a friendly alias (DisplayMessage):

```
public class PInvokeClient
{
    // Map the MessageBoxW() function to 'DisplayMessage'.
    [DllImport("user32.dll", ExactSpelling = true,
    CharSet=CharSet.Unicode, EntryPoint = "MessageBoxW")]
    public static extern int DisplayMessage(int hWnd, String  pText,
        String  pCaption, int uType);

    public static int Main(string[] args)
    {
        String pText = "Hello World!";
        String pCaption = "PInvoke Test";

        // This really calls MessageBoxW()...
        DisplayMessage(0, pText, pCaption, 0);
        return 0;
    }
}
```

Also, be aware that if you wish to refer to an unmanaged method by ordinal position (rather than the friendly string name), make use of a pound prefix followed by the numerical value:

```
// The ordinal value of MessageBoxW() is 484 (ala dumpbin.exe).
[DllImport("user32.dll", ExactSpelling = true,
CharSet=CharSet.Unicode, EntryPoint = "#484")]
public static extern int DisplayMessage(int hWnd, String  pText,
    String  pCaption, int uType);
```

SetLastError and Marshal.GetLastWin32Error()

The final field of DllImportAttribute is SetLastError, which is false by default under C#. When you set this field to true, you are informing PInvoke that you wish to receive any Win32 error that was returned from the exported function. For example, as you most likely know, the first parameter to MessageBox{A|W}() is the HWND, which identifies the parent window of the message box. Assume you assigned a bogus value to this parameter:

```
// There is no window with the handle 99999!
DisplayMessage(99999, pText, pCaption, 0);
```

Given that the value 99999 is well within the bounds of a System.Int32, the program compiles without fail. However, when you run the application, the message fails to display. If you wish to obtain the error number thrown from MessageBoxW(), simply make use of the Marshal type:

```
// Get the error!
DisplayMessage(999, pText, pCaption, 0);
Console.WriteLine("Last Win32 Error: {0}",
    Marshal.GetLastWin32Error());
```

If you run the application, you now find the output shown in Figure 1-7.

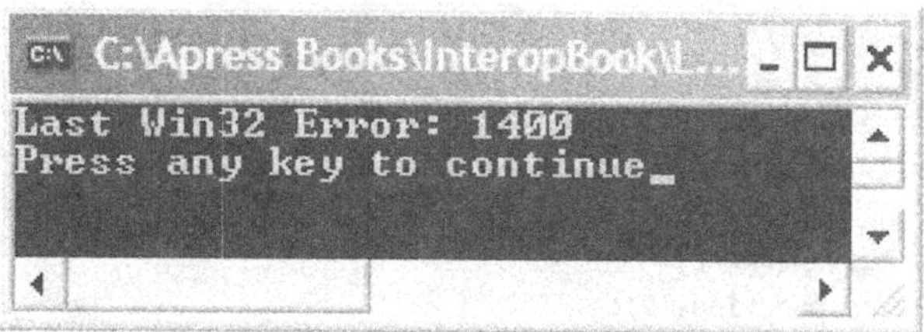

Figure 1-7. Obtaining the last Win32 error

Well, what good is it to know that the numerical value of the error is 1400? The truth of the matter is that each predefined Win32 error code is assigned a friendly text string that describes the error in question. These descriptions are located in the winerror.h header file; however, it is much simpler to discover the error description at design time using the Error Lookup utility located under the Tools | Error Lookup menu selection of the VS. NET IDE. If you paste in the value 1400, you will find the helpful hint shown in Figure 1-8.

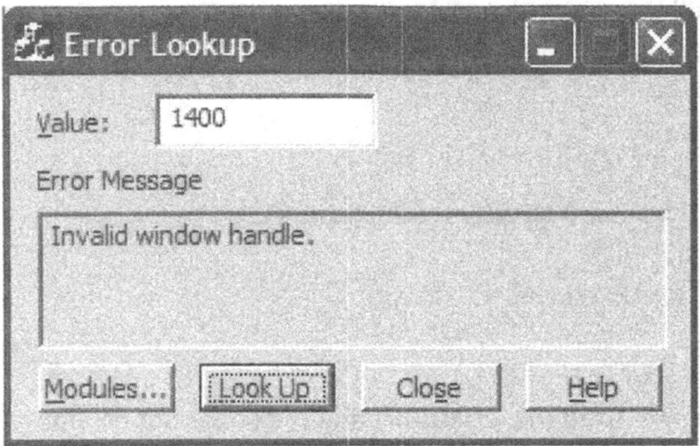

Figure 1-8. The meaning of the mysterious 1400

Now, what if you wish to obtain this string message programmatically? The FormatMessage() API function (defined in kernel32.dll) will return the correct string value based on the numerical error. Given that FormatMessage() is contained within a traditional C-based DLL, you would need to create a separate DllImport statement mapping to FormatMessage(); however, I'll leave that as a task for the interested reader.

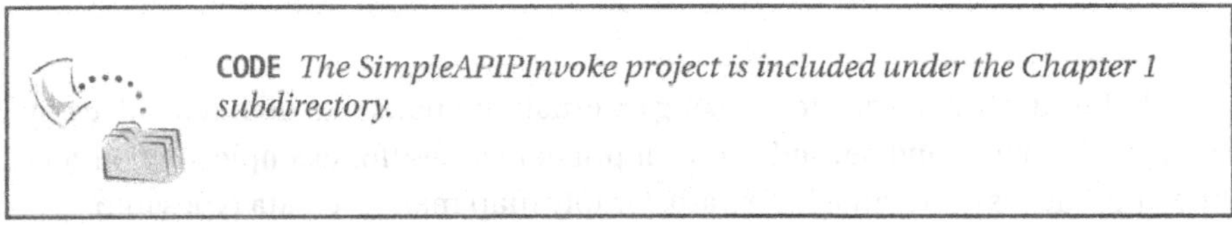

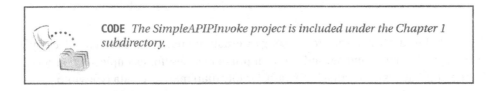

CODE *The SimpleAPIPInvoke project is included under the Chapter 1 subdirectory.*

Interacting with MyCustomDLL.dll

Now that you have seen how to customize the behavior of DllImport to access an API function taking simple data types, let's build a new C# console application (PInvokeCustomDLL) that triggers each member of the custom DLL you created earlier in this chapter. To do so, make use of a common PInvoke strategy, which is to build a custom class type that wraps the collection of DllImport statements on behalf of the caller using various static members. Given this, assume you have defined the following class within the new namespace:

```
// The Custom DLL wrapper class.
public class MyCustomDLLWrapper
{
   // ...all the DllExports...
}
```

The first member you will interact with is AddNumbers(), which is a very clear mapping between managed and unmanaged types:

```
public class MyCustomDLLWrapper
{
    // extern "C" MYCUSTOMDLL_API int AddNumbers(int x, int y);
    [DllImport("MyCustomDll.dll")]
    public static extern int AddNumbers(int x, int y);
}
```

Calling this external function from the C# Main() method could not be any simpler:

```
class CustomDLLInvoker
{
    [STAThread]
    static void Main(string[] args)
    {
        // Add some numbers.
        Console.WriteLine("Invoking AddNumbers()...");
        Console.WriteLine("10 + 10 is {0}",
            MyCustomDLLWrapper.AddNumbers(10, 10));
 }
```

To be sure, when you are invoking external functions that do not involve any parameters above and beyond simple input data types (for example, no pointers), the approach is quite straightforward. Simply map managed data types into unmanaged types using the information presented earlier in Table 1-4.

Marshaling Arrays

Passing arrays of intrinsic data types is also quite simple. Recall that the AddArray() member of the custom DLL requires the caller to pass in an array of ints (and the size of the incoming array) to obtain the summation of each item. Here is the DllImport:

```
public class MyCustomDLLWrapper
{
...
    // extern "C" MYCUSTOMDLL_API int AddArray(int x[], int size);
    [DllImport("MyCustomDll.dll")]
    public static extern int AddArray(int[] x, int y);
}
```

The managed C# code is again quite straightforward:

```
// Add array of numbers.
Console.WriteLine("\nInvoking AddArray()...");
int[] theVals = {10, 23, 83, 9, 12};
Console.WriteLine("Sum of array is {0}",
    MyCustomDLLWrapper.AddArray(theVals, theVals.Length));
```

Passing Structures

When you need to call an exported DLL function that requires a structure, you have a bit of additional work to do. As you may assume, the .NET class libraries do not contain a managed definition for every Win32 structure (and obviously has no way to know the layout of custom structures such as CAR or CAR2). To interact with this sort of function export, you need to build a managed equivalent of the raw Win32 structure using the syntax of your favorite programming language. One odd point to be aware of is that you are able to define the managed version of the raw structure via a custom structure *or* class definition.

In either case, when you are building a managed version of an unmanaged structure, you need to adorn the type with the StructLayout attribute in order to instruct PInvoke how to represent each member in the UDT. StructLayout can be assigned any value of the LayoutKind enumeration:

```
// How should the class / struct definition be
// marshaled to the unmanaged layer?
public enum LayoutKind
{
    Auto,
    Explicit,
    Sequential
}
```

In reality, you will almost always want to make use of LayoutKind.Sequential, which informs PInvoke to preserve the order of the fields when mapping the type between managed and unmanaged environments. LayoutKind.Auto is simply evil, because it gives permission to the runtime to *reorder* the fields at its leisure for reasons of efficiency. Never employ this option when marshaling structures using PInvoke.

The final option, LayoutKind.Explicit, allows you to be in charge of calculating the physical position of fields of the class or structure when marshaling the type into an unmanaged binary. Types marked as StructLayout(LayoutKind.Explicit) require you to make use of another attribute (FieldOffset) to mark the locations of each field. You have no need to make use of this option for the CAR and CAR2 types, given that many of your fields can have varying lengths (the strings). However, by way of a simple example, assume the following managed POINT representation:

```
[StructLayout(LayoutKind.Explicit)]
public struct POINT
{
    [FieldOffset(0)] int x;
    [FieldOffset(4)] int y;
}
```

Representing CAR and CAR2 As Class Types

Assume you wish to build a managed representation of the CAR and CAR2 types using the C# class keyword. CAR is simple enough (recall that unmanaged char* maps into a managed System.String):

```
[StructLayout(LayoutKind.Sequential)]
public class CAR
{
    public string make;
    public string color;
}
```

However, what about the CAR2 type, which makes use of an embedded CAR type? Because CAR is defined as a C# class type, you can simply allocate an instance within the CAR2 class definition as follows:

```
// A structure containing another structure.
[StructLayout(LayoutKind.Sequential)]
public class CAR2
{
    public CAR theCar = new CAR();
    public string petName;
}
```

This approach will also simplify the DllImport definition and client-side invocation. First update the wrapper to invoke DisplayBetterCar():

```
public class MyCustomDLLWrapper
{
...
    // extern "C" MYCUSTOMDLL_API void DisplayBetterCar(CAR2* theCar);
    [DllImport("MyCustomDll.dll", CharSet=CharSet.Ansi)]
    public static extern int DisplayBetterCar( CAR2 c);
}
```

The client-side code begins by creating a new CAR2 structure, filling in the field data, and passing it along to the unmanaged export:

```
// Display a better car.
Console.WriteLine("\nInvoking DisplayBetterCar()...");
Console.WriteLine("...message boxes are displaying...");
CAR2 myCar = new CAR2();
myCar.petName = "Frank";
myCar.theCar.color = "Rust";
myCar.theCar.make = "Colt";
MyCustomDLLWrapper.DisplayBetterCar(myCar);
```

Receiving Allocated Structures

Now, if you wish to invoke GiveMeThreeBasicCars(), you would need to build the DllImport statement using the C# out keyword, given that this method will allocate three CAR types on your behalf.

```
public class MyCustomDLLWrapper
{
...
    // extern "C" MYCUSTOMDLL_API
    // void GiveMeThreeBasicCars(CAR** theCars);
    [DllImport("MyCustomDll.dll", CharSet=CharSet.Ansi)]
    public static extern void GiveMeThreeBasicCars(out IntPtr theCars);
}
```

Notice that you have not sent in an output parameter of type CAR[], but a System.IntPtr that will point to the memory allocated by the unmanaged export. When you wish to filter the memory for a given structure, you need to make use of four key members of the Marshal type: PtrToStructure(), SizeOf(), DestroyStructure(), and FreeCoTaskMem(). First, the calling code:

```
// Get three basic cars.
Console.WriteLine("\nInvoking GiveMeThreeBasicCars()...");
int size = 3;

// Pass in an IntPtr as an output parameter.
IntPtr outArray;
MyCustomDLLWrapper.GiveMeThreeBasicCars(out outArray);

// Allocate an array big enough to hold the
// memory returned to use.
CAR[] carArray = new CAR[size];
IntPtr current = outArray;

// Print out each structure.
for( int i = 0; i < size; i++ )
{
    // Get next CAR using Marshal.PtrToStructure()
    carArray[ i ] = new CAR();
    Marshal.PtrToStructure( current, carArray[ i ]);
    Console.WriteLine( "Structure {0}: {1} {2}", i,
        carArray[ i ].make, carArray[ i ].color);

    // Destroy memory held by current structure.
    Marshal.DestroyStructure( current, typeof(CAR) );

    // Calculate location of next structure using Marshal.SizeOf().
    current = (IntPtr)((int)current + Marshal.SizeOf(carArray[ i ] ));
}

// Free memory for the allocated array.
Marshal.FreeCoTaskMem( outArray );

// Just to make sure that we fail
// immediately if we try to use this again.
outArray = IntPtr.Zero;
```

It really isn't as bad as it looks. The process begins by calling the unmanaged export to receive a block of memory contained within a System.IntPtr. Because the managed CAR class type has been defined using LayoutKind.Sequential, you can rest assured that the memory contained within the IntPtr type can be mapped exactly to an array of CAR types. Given this assumption, the bulk of the work simply iterates over IntPtr three times to pull out the current CAR using Marshal.PtrToStructure().

Once you free up the memory contained within the current CAR using Marshal.DestroyStrucutre(), you figure out the position of the next CAR in the IntPtr using the old C programmers' sizeof hack (a la Marshal.SizeOf()). Finally, once you have sucked out and displayed each CAR, you free the memory of the allocated array using Marshal.FreeCoTaskMem().

Interacting with Exported Class Types

The final exports of MyCustomDLL.dll allow the outside world to interact with the internal CMiniVan type. Recall that the unmanaged CreateMiniVan() and DestroyMiniVan() functions made use of a strongly typed CMiniVan. In terms of managed code, you will represent this type using System.IntPtr.

Also recall during my discussion of the dumpbin.exe utility that the members of exported class types are referenced using a mangled name generated by the C++ compiler. When you wish to call an exported class member from managed code, you need to generate a *separate* DllImport statement that makes explicit use of the EntryPoint field. Given that DisplayNumberOfKids() method will be called on the class level, you need to specify the CallingConvention as CallingConvention. ThisCall (this, as in the "this" pointer). This being said, here are the final three static methods of the MyCustomDLLWrapper type:

```
public class MyCustomDLLWrapper
{
...
    // extern "C" MYCUSTOMDLL_API CMiniVan* CreateMiniVan();
    [DllImport("MyCustomDll.dll")]
    public static extern IntPtr CreateMiniVan();

    // extern "C" MYCUSTOMDLL_API void DeleteMiniVan(CMiniVan* obj);
    [DllImport("MyCustomDll.dll")]
    public static extern void DeleteMiniVan(IntPtr obj);

    // CMiniVan::DisplayNumberOfKids
    [DllImport( "MyCustomDll.dll", EntryPoint =
    "?DisplayNumberOfKids@CMiniVan@@QAEHXZ",
    CallingConvention=CallingConvention.ThisCall )]
    public static extern int GetTheKids(IntPtr thisPointer);
}
```

The C++ CMiniVan can be manipulated from your C# console application as follows:

```
// Manipulate a CMiniVan type.
Console.WriteLine("\nInvoking CMiniVan.DisplayNumberOfKids()...");
IntPtr instancePtr = MyCustomDLLWrapper.CreateMiniVan();
int kidCount = MyCustomDLLWrapper.GetTheKids(instancePtr);
Console.WriteLine("Number of kids in Mini Van is: {0} \n", kidCount);
MyCustomDLLWrapper.DeleteMiniVan(instancePtr);
```

If you run the application, you will see the output shown in Figure 1-9.

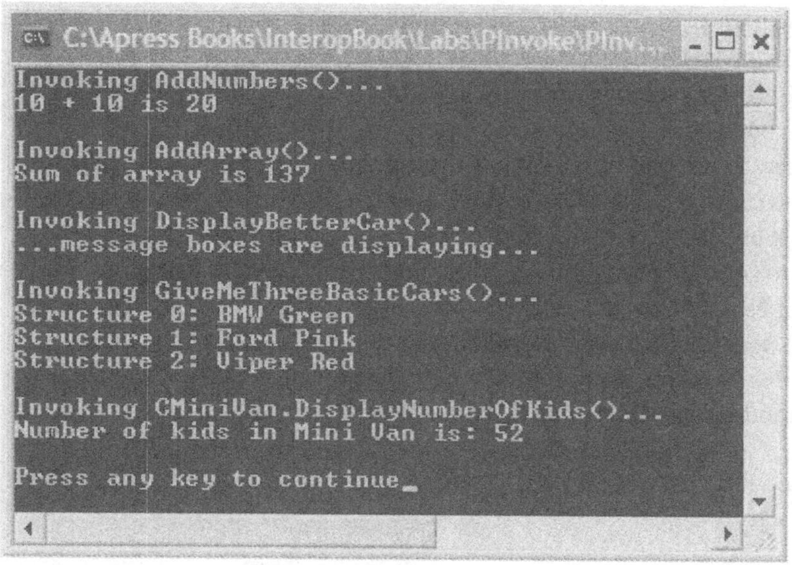

Figure 1-9. A C# client interacting with MyCustomDLL.dll

CODE *The PInvokeCustomDLL project is included under the Chapter 1 directory.*

Examining the Underlying IL

There is one final point of interest regarding the current C# client application. You may be wondering exactly how a given DllImport attribute is represented under the hood in terms of the underlying IL. Assume you have loaded the PInvokeCustomDLL.exe assembly into ILDasm.exe. If you examine the IL (intermediate language) for any DllImport statement defined by the wrapper class, you will find that the [pinvokeimpl] tag is used to inform mscoree.dll that this method will invoke a member in an external unmanaged DLL. For example, consider the IL for the AddNumbers() method:

```
.method public hidebysig static pinvokeimpl("MyCustomDll.dll" winapi)
        int32  AddNumbers(int32 x, int32 y) cil managed preservesig
{
}
```

Because you did not specify an EntryPoint value, you have a one-to-one mapping between the managed and unmanaged method names. However, if you check out the IL for the managed GetTheKids() method, you will find that the [pinvokeimpl] tag is qualified with an "as" statement that points to the correct mangled name of the export:

```
.method public hidebysig static pinvokeimpl("MyCustomDll.dll" as
"\?DisplayNumberOfKids@CMiniVan@@QAEHXZ" thiscall)
        int32  GetTheKids(native int thisPointer) cil managed preservesig
{
}
```

When the engine encounters the [pinvokeimpl] tag, the following tasks ensue:

- The runtime locates the DLL containing the function.
- The runtime loads the DLL into memory.
- The runtime locates the address of the function in memory and marshals parameters as required.
- Control is transferred to the unmanaged function.

Once the unmanaged function receives control, the runtime waits for the method call to return and hands back any function return values in terms of managed code. Figure 1-10 illustrates the basic process.

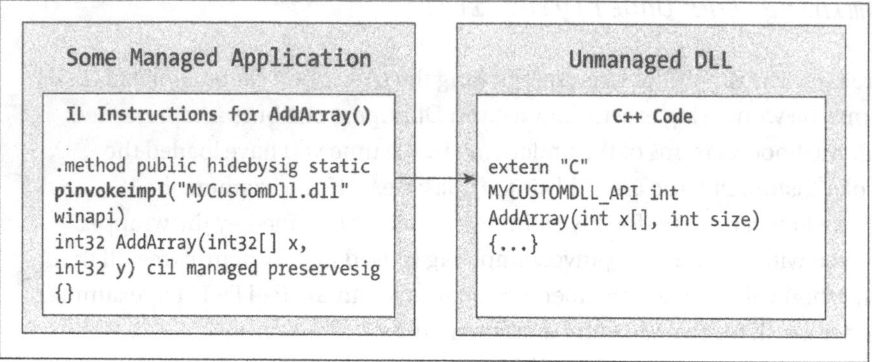

Figure 1-10. Behold, the guts of PInvoke.

Working with Unmanaged Callbacks

To wrap up this chapter, let's check out how PInvoke allows managed code to interact with traditional Win32 *callback functions*. First question: What exactly is a callback function? Simply put, a callback function is a function defined by a DLL, but implemented by the caller, that can be called by the DLL. Typically, callback functions are used when the unmanaged DLL needs to report back to the invoker. This may be to simply signal that a given task is completed or indicate that the unmanaged DLL needs additional information from the caller. Figure 1-11 documents the basic callback pattern.

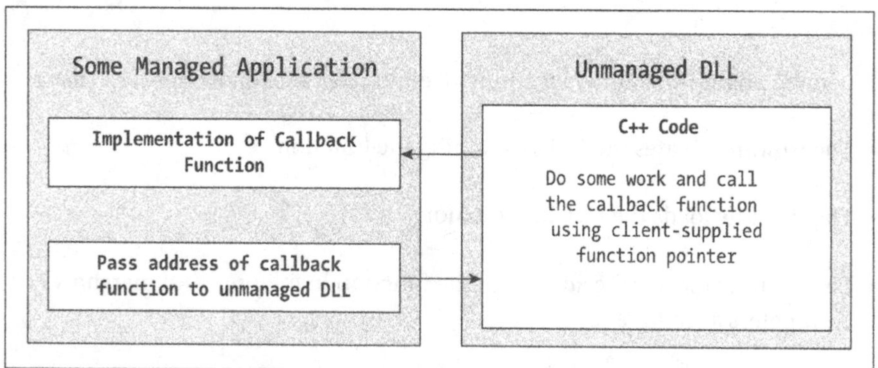

Figure 1-11. The basic callback pattern

This basic pattern of passing one part of a system a pointer to a function located at another part of the system is a common theme in Windows development. As you may know, the COM connection point architecture takes the same basic approach using interface references. Likewise, Win32-style callbacks are the forerunner of the modern day .NET delegation protocol.

A Simple Callback Example

To illustrate the process of interacting with Win32 callbacks from managed code, assume you have created a new Win32 DLL project workspace named MyCustomCallbackDLL. The first order of business is to define a prototype of the method that will be implemented *by the caller*. Think this one through just a bit. If the unmanaged DLL is going to be passed a pointer to a function implemented elsewhere, it must be able to understand the calling conventions of said function (such as the parameters and return type). To keep things simple, your first callback prototype will take no parameters and return a boolean (to signal if the client has successfully completed its share of the workload):

```
// Simple Callback prototype.
typedef bool (CALLBACK *SIMPLECALLBACKFUNCTION)();
```

The lack of arguments is syntactically signified by the empty parentheses. The CALLBACK tag is defined within windef.h as follows:

```
#define CALLBACK     __stdcall
```

To keep your wits about you, I'll take the opportunity here to remind you that this function will be *implemented* by the caller but *prototyped* by the unmanaged DLL.

The next step is to define a function export that can take a pointer to this function and trigger the client-side implementation at a later time. Again to keep things simple, your export will verify the current invocation and immediately trigger the callback using the supplied function pointer:

```
extern "C" MYCUSTOMCALLBACKDLL_API void
VerifyAndReportBack(SIMPLECALLBACKFUNCTION pf)
{
    MessageBox(NULL, "You called me...about to call you!",
        "Unmanaged DLL", MB_OK);
```

```
    // Call the managed function using incoming pointer.
    bool res = (*pf)();

    // Get result from callback.
    if( res )
        MessageBox(NULL, "Callback says TRUE",
            "Unmanaged DLL", MB_OK);
    else
        MessageBox(NULL, "Callback says FALSE",
        "Unmanaged DLL", MB_OK);
}
```

Notice that when the VerifyAndReportBack() export wishes to call the client-side callback, it simply makes use of the supplied function pointer:

```
// This line basically says "I am calling a
// function which matches the calling
// conventions established by the
// SIMPLECALLBACKFUNCTION callback
// definition."
bool res = (*pf)();
```

A More Interesting Callback Function

Let's add one additional callback to your new DLL that allows the caller to pass in not only a pointer to some function on their end, but also a single argument of type THEPOINT. The client will allocate a THEPOINT structure that will be manipulated by the export and passed to the client's callback. Here are the complete details:

```
// A basic structure.
typedef struct _THEPOINT
{
    int x;
    int y;
} THEPOINT;

// THEPOINT Callback prototype.
typedef bool (CALLBACK *POINTCALLBACKFUNCTION)( THEPOINT* i );

extern "C" MYCUSTOMCALLBACKDLL_API void
ChangePOINTAndReportBack(POINTCALLBACKFUNCTION pf,
THEPOINT* thePoint)
```

```
{
    MessageBox(NULL, "Received THEPOINT and am about to change it...",
        "Unmanaged DLL", MB_OK);

    // Take the incoming THEPOINT and change it.
    thePoint->x = 10000;
    thePoint->y = 20000;

    // Call the managed function.
    bool res = (*pf)(thePoint);

    // Get result from callback.
    if( res )
    MessageBox(NULL, "Callback says TRUE",
        "Unmanaged DLL", MB_OK);
    else
    MessageBox(NULL, "Callback says FALSE",
        "Unmanaged DLL", MB_OK);
}
```

In this case, the client will pass in a function pointer that matches the calling conventions defined by the POINTCALLBACKFUNCTION callback definition. Thus, the following unmanaged code:

```
// Call the managed function.
bool res = (*pf)(thePoint);
```

says in effect: I will call a function on the client which takes a THEPOINT parameter and returns a Boolean.

CODE *The MyCustomCallbackDLL project is located under the Chapter 1 subdirectory.*

Building a C# Callback Client

Now that you have a custom DLL that defines two callback prototypes, you are in the position to build a C# application to provide an implementation. When you wish to interact with a traditional Win32 callback from managed code, you follow a very fixed set of steps:

1. Define a .NET delegate that represents the unmanaged callback.
2. Build a DllImport statement for the unmanaged export, using the .NET delegate as the function pointer parameter.
3. Assign a managed function to the delegate.
4. Trigger the unmanaged export.

Confused? Don't be. To see each piece fit together, ponder the following C# code, which interacts with the SIMPLECALLBACKFUNCTION prototype:

```
namespace CustomCallbackClient
{
    class ManagedCallBackApp
    {
        // typedef bool (CALLBACK *SIMPLECALLBACKFUNCTION)();
        // 1) Define a delegate representing the unmanaged callback
        // prototype.
        public delegate bool ReportBackHere();

        // 2) Build the DllImport (note the parameter is our delegate).
        [DllImport("MyCustomCallbackDLL.dll")]
        public static extern void VerifyAndReportBack(ReportBackHere callback);

        [STAThread]
        public static void Main()
        {
            // 3) Assign a function for the delegate to call.
            ReportBackHere simpleCallback =
                new ReportBackHere(ManagedCallBackApp.Report);

            // 4) Call the unmanaged export.
            VerifyAndReportBack(simpleCallback);
        }
```

```
        // This will be called by the unmanaged DLL.
        public static bool Report()
        {
            Console.WriteLine("I was called by the DLL!");
            return false;
        }
    }
}
```

Notice that the managed delegate maps identically to the unmanaged callback prototype, in that both return a Boolean and neither takes any arguments.

```
// The C++ callback prototype.
typedef bool (CALLBACK *SIMPLECALLBACKFUNCTION)();

// The C# managed delegate.
public delegate bool ReportBackHere();
```

When you build the DllImport statement, you make use of this delegate in place of the unmanaged SIMPLECALLBACKFUNCTION. Again, ponder the relationship:

```
// The C++ export takes a pointer to a function that matches.
// SIMPLECALLBACKFUNCTION.
extern "C" MYCUSTOMCALLBACKDLL_API
void VerifyAndReportBack(SIMPLECALLBACKFUNCTION pf)
{…}

// The C# DllImport statement uses the delegate.
[DllImport("MyCustomCallbackDLL.dll")]
public static extern void VerifyAndReportBack(ReportBackHere callback);
```

The remainder of the logic simply defines and implements the method called by the delegate. Now, what of the POINTCALLBACKFUNCTION prototype? The only difference is to build a managed equivalent of the THEPOINT structure. Other than that, simply repeat the process:

```
namespace CustomCallbackClient
{
    [StructLayout(LayoutKind.Sequential)]
    public class THEPOINT
    {
```

```
        public int x;
        public int y;
    }

    class ManagedCallBackApp
    {
        public delegate bool SendTHEPOINTHere(THEPOINT pt);

        [DllImport("MyCustomCallbackDLL.dll")]
        public static extern viod ChangePOINTAndReportBack
            (SendTHEPOINTHere callback, THEPOINT pt);

        [STAThread]
        public static void Main()
        {
            SendTHEPOINTHere theCallBack = new
                SendTHEPOINTHere(ManagedCallBackApp.GiveMeThePoint);

            THEPOINT pt = new THEPOINT();
            pt.x = 10;
            pt.y = 10;
            Console.WriteLine("Point is:");
            Console.WriteLine("X = {0}\nY = {1}", pt.x, pt.y);
            ChangePOINTAndReportBack(theCallBack, pt);
        }

        public static bool GiveMeThePoint(THEPOINT pt)
        {
            Console.WriteLine("New Point is:");
            Console.WriteLine("X = {0}\nY = {1}", pt.x, pt.y);
            return true;
        }
    }
}
```

CODE *The CustomCallbackClient project is included under the Chapter 1 subdirectory.*

At this point, you have examined the process of building managed .NET applications that are able to communicate with traditional C-style DLLs. While not as sexy as the act of COM/.NET communication, PInvoke is helpful when you need to access legacy (non-COM) binary modules. Although this chapter focused on the process of interacting with custom *.dll files, all of the information presented here applies directly to the process of triggering a Win32 API function.

Summary

PInvoke is the aspect of the .NET Framework that is specifically geared toward the task of invoking functions defined in non-COM DLLs. As you have seen, the backbone of PInvoke is the DllImport attribute, which allows you to map a managed method to an unmanaged equivalent. This class type contains a number of fields that allow you to specify calling conventions, string representations, and error information.

In addition to the DllImportAttribute type, activities involving PInvoke typically make use of the Marshal class, which defines a number of static members that allow you to transform raw memory (System.IntPtr) into strongly typed UDTs (for example, Marshal.PtrToStructure() and friends). Finally, this chapter illustrated how .NET delegate types can represent traditional Win32 callback prototypes. Once you have defined an appropriate delegate, this can be passed into the unmanaged function export as if it were indeed an unmanaged function pointer.

Now that you have seen how to interact with traditional C-based DLLs, the next chapter drills into the specifics of the internal composition of COM-based DLLs.

CHAPTER 2

The Anatomy of a COM Server

In terms of software longevity, Microsoft's Component Object Model (COM) has enjoyed a lengthy and successful life. Formally solidified circa 1993, COM formalized a specific process for building reusable, binary software components. When developers abide by the rules of COM, they are presented with a number of desirable byproducts. One of the great byproducts of COM components is their language-independent nature. This trait allows software developers to build COM servers in one language (such as VB 6.0) and reuse them in any number of other COM-aware languages (such as C++). However, depending on your programming tool of choice, the internal composition of a COM server may be a bit of a mystery.

Given that the only way to truly comprehend COM/.NET interoperability is to understand the nuances of both architectures, this chapter is intended to provide a concise overview of the COM paradigm. During the process, you build a complete COM binary (using raw C++ and IDL [Interface Definition Language]) that will be accessed by various .NET-aware languages later in this text. Along the way, you will be reminded of the role of the system registry, the COM library, and related entities such as the IUnknown, IClassFactory, and IDispatch interfaces. However, before you dive into the guts of a COM DLL, let's begin by formalizing the role of interface-based programming.

Of Classes and Interfaces

One of the central architectural foundations in COM programming is the separation of implementation (class) from protocol (interface). Simply put, an *interface* is a collection of semantically related methods that may be implemented by a given COM class (often called a *coclass*). Once a coclass has been instantiated by a particular client, the in-memory representation is termed a *COM object*.

The odd thing about programmatic interfaces (as opposed to GUI interfaces) is the fact that the interfaces never define member variables, implementation logic, or other coding items that would mark them as a useful entity. Rather, the sole purpose of a programmatic interface is to specify the calling conventions a client must abide by to communicate with the implementing coclass.

Once an interface has been defined (using the syntax of your favorite programming language), any number of COM classes may choose to support the specified interface. Given that an interface is a grouping of semantically related methods, it is common (and helpful) to regard an interface as a specific *behavior* that the class in question supports. A key point to understand is that it is completely possible (and very common) for multiple COM classes to support the identical interface in unique ways. As you may already be aware, this is yet another form of programmatic polymorphism (more on this tidbit in just a moment). It is also quite possible (and very common) for a single coclass to support multiple interfaces.

Interfaces from a Non-COM Perspective

Although using interfaces is inescapable in COM development, it is possible to make use of this programming discipline from non-COM environments. To illustrate the basic mechanics of interfaced-based programming, I'll open this chapter with a simple C++ example named Interfaces. If you wish to follow along, launch Visual Studio 6.0 and create a new Win32 Console Application (Figure 2-1).

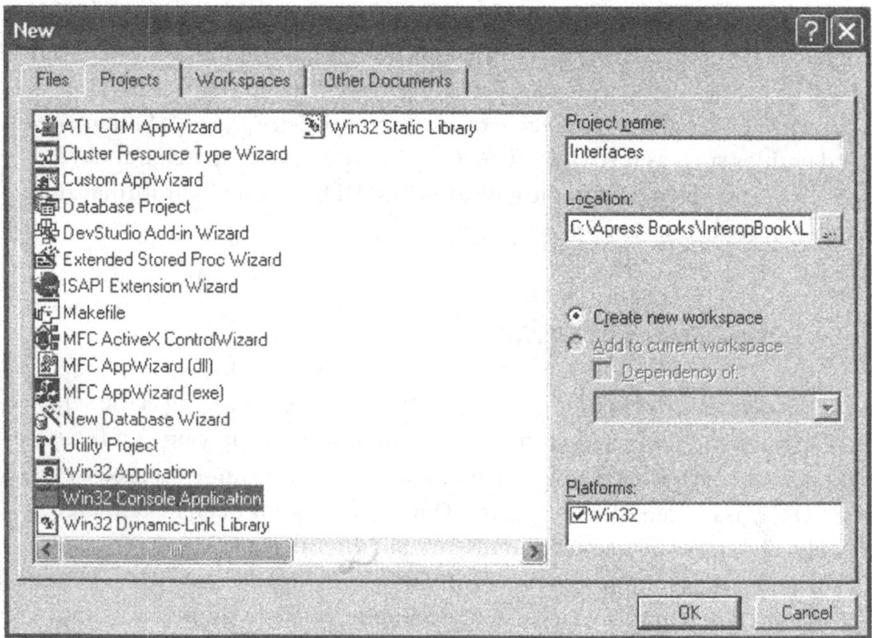

Figure 2-1. Creating a new Win32 Console Application project

Once you click the OK button, select A simple application from the resulting dialog box (Figure 2-2).

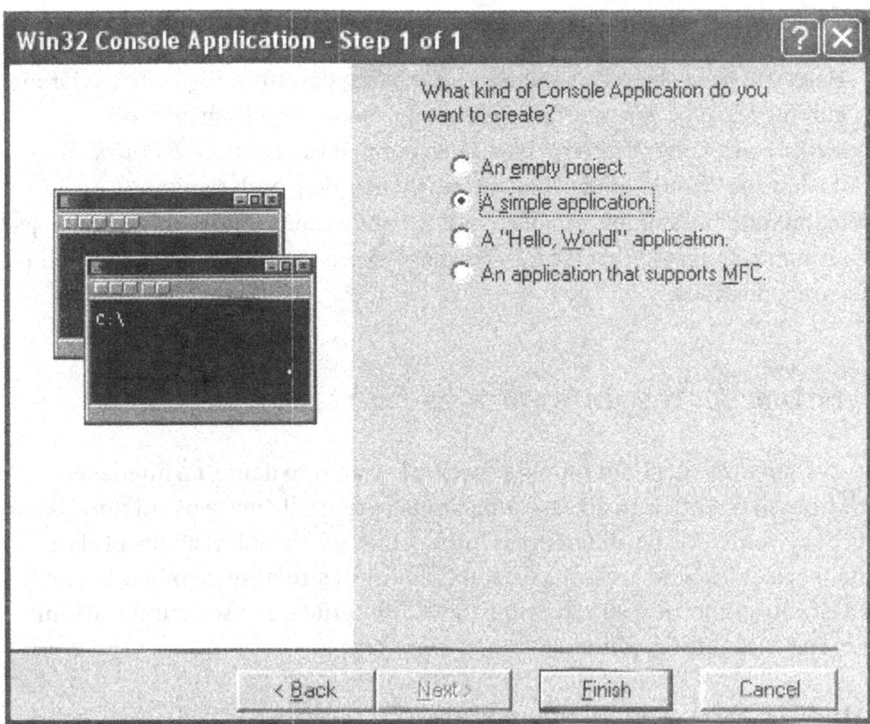

Figure 2-2. A "simple application" fits the bill.

This option generates a *.cpp file that defines an empty main() function. As you are most likely aware, each and every C++ executable application requires a main() function (or in the case of a Windows application, WinMain()) that marks the entry point to the program. To begin coding your interface example, define the following interface using generic C++ in the same file that defines the main() function:

```
// We contend with IUnknown, GUIDs, and IDL soon enough...
class ICar
{
public:
    virtual void SpeedUp(long delta) = 0;
    virtual void CurrentSpeed(long *currSp) = 0;
};
```

```
int main(int argc, char* argv[])
{
    return 0;
}
```

Here, you have defined an interface (ICar) that describes a basic behavior for any automobile type you may be constructing. Notice that both methods (SpeedUp() and CurrentSpeed()) have been defined as *pure virtual functions* (marked by the "virtual" prefix and "=0" suffix adorning each signature). Again, given that interfaces simply establish calling conventions for the object and object user, it stands to reason that the C++ language expresses interfaces as a named set of abstract methods.

Cleaning Up the Interface Definition

The C++ language does not supply a specific keyword to define an interface (COM-based or not). Instead, C++ programmers typically make use of the class or struct keywords. The big difference is the fact that the default visibility of class members is *private,* whereas the default visibility of structure members is *public.* Thus, if you so choose, you can define the ICar interface as a structure and omit the public visibility keyword:

```
// Structure members are public by default.
struct ICar
{
    virtual void SpeedUp(long delta) = 0;
    virtual void CurrentSpeed(long *currSp) = 0;
};
```

If you really want to make your interface definitions stand out, you can also make use of the "interface" symbol defined in objbase.h as follows:

```
// Must include objbase.h (or simply windows.h) to
// use the 'interface' symbol.
#define interface struct
```

Given that "interface" is just an alias to the struct keyword, you wind up with the final iteration of the C++ ICar interface definition:

```
// The final ICar interface.
interface ICar
```

```
{
    virtual void SpeedUp(long delta) = 0;
    virtual void CurrentSpeed(long *currSp) = 0;
};
```

Building the Class Types

Because interfaces define a set of pure virtual function, any class that wishes to implement an interface is obligated to flesh out the details of each member. The simplest way to implement an interface in C++ is to make use of classic inheritance. Assume that you have two concrete classes (Car and HotRod) implementing the ICar interface in their unique manners (again, feel free to implement these class in the initial *.cpp file):

```
// The basic Car.
class Car : public ICar
{
private:
    long m_currSpeed;
public:
    Car() { m_currSpeed = 0; }
    virtual ~Car(){}

    // ICar implementation.
    void SpeedUp(long delta)
    {
        cout << "I am a basic car" << endl;
        m_currSpeed += delta;
    }

    void CurrentSpeed(long *currSp)
    { *currSp = m_currSpeed;}
};

// The wicked cool car.
class HotRod: public ICar
{
private:
    long m_currSpeed;
public:
    HotRod() { m_currSpeed = 0; }
    virtual ~HotRod(){}
```

```
    // ICar implementation (massive turbo booster!)
    void SpeedUp(long delta)
    {
        cout << "I am a hot rod!" << endl;
        m_currSpeed += (delta * 20);
    }

    void CurrentSpeed(long *currSp)
    { *currSp = m_currSpeed;}
};
```

As you can see, when you ask a simple Car to speed up by some amount, the internal speed is adjusted verbatim. However, if you ask a HotRod to speed up using the same interface, you find the automobile advances at breakneck speed (20 times delta!). Because each class supports the same interface, the user of each object can treat them identically (that's the point of polymorphism). To see your cars in action, assume you have updated the application's main() loop as follows (the output can be seen in Figure 2-3):

```
// Don't forget to include iostream.h to access cout.
int main(int argc, char* argv[])
{
    // Create an array of two ICar interfaces.
    ICar* theCars[2];
    theCars[0] = new Car();
    theCars[1] = new HotRod();

    // Speed up each car 5 times, using the ICar interface.
    for (int j = 0; j < 5; j++)
    {
        for(int i = 0; i < 2; i++)
        {
            theCars[i]->SpeedUp(10);
            long currSp =  0;
            theCars[i]->CurrentSpeed(&currSp);
            cout << "  ->Speed: " << currSp << endl;
        }
    }
    // Clean up memory.
    delete[] *theCars;
    return 0;
}
```

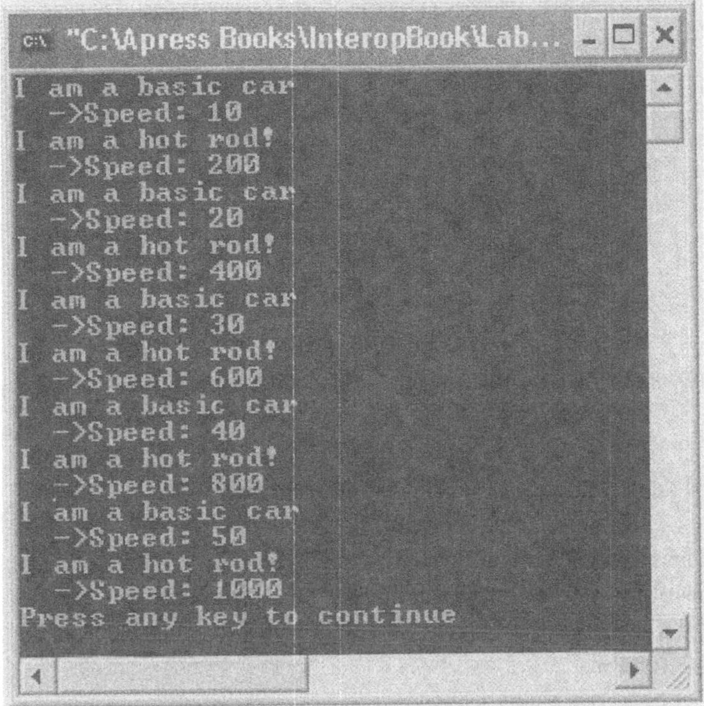

Figure 2-3. Driving your cars using interface references

Here, the main() function creates an array of ICar pointers, each member of which is set to a unique automotive type. Given that both Car and HotRod implement the behavior defined by ICar, you are able to interact with each type using a simple ICar reference. However, because each class responds uniquely to the same request ("Speed up by delta") we have injected polymorphic behavior into the application. Consider Figure 2-4, which illustrates this concept using the popular COM lollipop notation.

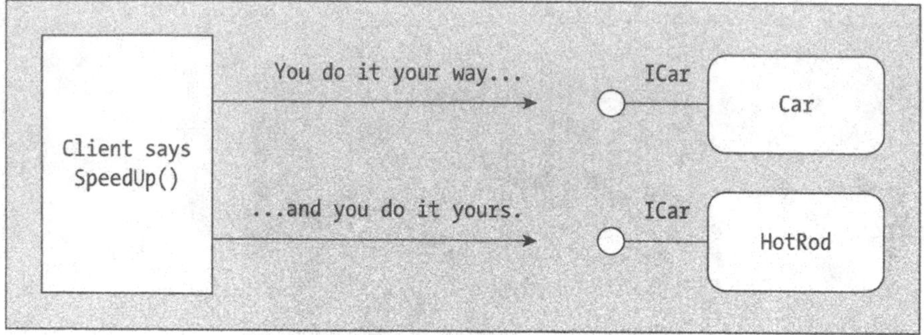

Figure 2-4. Polymorphic behavior a la interface-based programming

Interfaces Are Strongly Typed Variables

In addition to the fact that you can manipulate classes using interface references, you are able to use interfaces as method parameters (and return types). For example, if you had a global method named RevEngine() which takes an ICar* as its sole argument as follows:

```
// Rev the engine of a given automobile.
void RevEngine(ICar* pCar)
{
    long currSp = 0;
    for(int i = 0; i < 5; i++)
    {
        pCar->SpeedUp(10);
        pCar->CurrentSpeed(&currSp);
        cout << "Speed: " << currSp << endl;
    }
    for(i = 5; i > 0; i--)
    {
        pCar->SpeedUp(-10);
        pCar->CurrentSpeed(&currSp);
        cout << "Speed: " << currSp << endl;
    }
}
```

you can safely pass in any type that supports the ICar interface, as shown here:

```
// Make some cars and rev the engines.
ICar* pAnotherCar = new Car();
ICar* pAnotherHotRod = new HotRod();
RevEngine(pAnotherCar);
RevEngine(pAnotherHotRod);
delete pAnotherCar;
delete pAnotherHotRod;
```

If you attempt to pass in an incompatible type (such as a CellPhone object):

```
// The CellPhone class does not implement ICar!
CellPhone cp;
RevEngine(cp);  // Error!
```

you will (thankfully) be issued a compile time conversion error:

```
error C2664: 'RevEngine' : cannot convert parameter 1 from 'class CellPhone'
to 'struct ICar *'
```

Classes Can Support Multiple Interfaces

The next concept you must understand about interface-based programming is that it is possible for a single class type (COM-based or otherwise) to implement multiple interfaces. Assume you define another interface named IConvertible:

```
// Another possible behavior a class may support.
interface IConvertible
{
    virtual void LetTheSunIn(bool isOpening) = 0;
};
```

Certainly not all cars are convertibles. However, you can equip some automobiles to support IConvertible (the hot rod, of course) while other cars (say, minivans) do not. Pictorially, you can view the behaviors as shown in Figure 2-5.

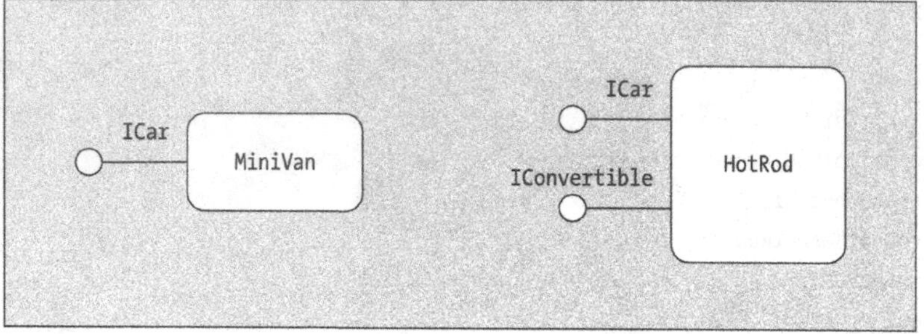

Figure 2-5. A single class may support multiple behaviors.

When C++ programmers build classes that support numerous interfaces, the simplest approach is to use standard multiple inheritance. Thus, you could update the HotRod definition as follows:

```
// The HotRod now supports two behaviors.
class HotRod: public ICar, IConvertible
{
    … same as before…

    // IConvertible impl.
    void LetTheSunIn(bool isOpening)
    {
        if(isOpening)
            cout << "Opening sun roof" << endl;
        else
            cout << "Closing sun roof" << endl;
    }
};
```

Of course, for the object user to make use of this new behavior, there must be a manner by which to query the type for a discrete interface (ICar or IConvertible). Ideally, the object itself would be able to return interface references to the user on request, rather than forcing the object user to perform awkward pointer casting directly. As you may already know, this is one of the core duties of the standard COM interface: IUnknown. You will see this interface in action later in this chapter, so let's hold off on discussing the details of client-side usage of classes supporting multiple interfaces.

Interfaces Provide a Versioning Scheme

The final aspect of interfaced-based programming that I cover here is the fact that interfaces may be *versioned*. By way of a simple example, assume that you wish to update the original behavior defined by the ICar interface to support the following new member:

```
// ICar was initially defined March 24th 2001.
interface ICar
{
    virtual void SpeedUp(long delta) = 0;
    virtual void CurrentSpeed(long *currSp) = 0;

    // Added this method April 1st 2001.
    virtual void TurnOnRadio(bool state) = 0;
};
```

While this might seem like a rather harmless approach, check out the code comments. Here you can see that the initial ICar interface was created 3/24/01. The new member was added some time after the fact (4/1/01). Now, what if you had a code base that defined two automobile types, each supporting different iterations of the ICar interface? This would be a horrible thing.

A central rule of interface-based programming is that interfaces (once in production) should never change. If you make a change, you have just broken polymorphism! Consider the following (problematic) code:

```
// The MiniVan supports the ICar defined on 3/24/01.
ICar* pMV = new MiniVan();
pMV->TurnOnRadio(true);      // Bomb!

// The HotRod supports the ICar defined on 4/1/01.
ICar* pHR = new HotRod();
pHR->TurnOnRadio(true);      // OK.
```

As you can see, although both class types claim to support the ICar interface, the truth of the matter is they each support a *version* of the same interface. If you attempt to turn on the radio for your current MiniVan type, you bomb at runtime, given that the TurnOnRadio() member is not defined as of 3/24/01, and therefore is not supported by the MiniVan class.

When you wish to version an existing interface, the standard approach is to derive a new interface from an existing base interface. Keeping with convention, each derived interface is suffixed with a numerical version identifier (following n+1 increments). That said, ponder the following (safe) extension of the ICar interface:

```
// ICar.
interface ICar
{
    virtual void SpeedUp(long delta) = 0;
    virtual void CurrentSpeed(long *currSp) = 0;
};

// ICar2 (derives from ICar).
interface ICar2 : public ICar
{
    // Added this method April 1st 2001.
    virtual void TurnOnRadio(bool state) = 0;
};
```

Notice that the new ICar2 interface derives from ICar, and therefore inherits the abstract members defined by its base type. If the HotRod was now derived from ICar2, the type has brought in support for the simpler ICar interface as well:

```
// HotRod now supports three interfaces (ICar, ICar2, and IConvertible).
class HotRod: public ICar2, IConvertible
{
    ...
    // ICar impl.

    // ICar2 impl.

    // IConvertible impl.
};
```

Using this versioning scheme, the object user can determine if a type in question supports the newer ICar2 behavior. If not, you can fall back on the initial ICar functionality. Again, as you may already know, the IUnknown COM interface equips a COM type to return "yes" or "no" to the question "Do you support this interface?" You see the exact details of this functionality a bit later in the chapter. That wraps up your initial look at interfaces from a simple C++ (non-COM) perspective. With this introduction aside, you can now focus your attention on COM proper.

CODE *The Interfaces application can be found under the Chapter 2 subdirectory.*

The Composition of a COM DLL

So much for our brief overview of the key benefits of interface-based programming. For the remainder of this chapter, you focus your attention on the process of building a COM DLL server (and various clients) using C++ and IDL. Before you pound out the code, Figure 2-6 illustrates the core atoms of the initial binary image you will be constructing.

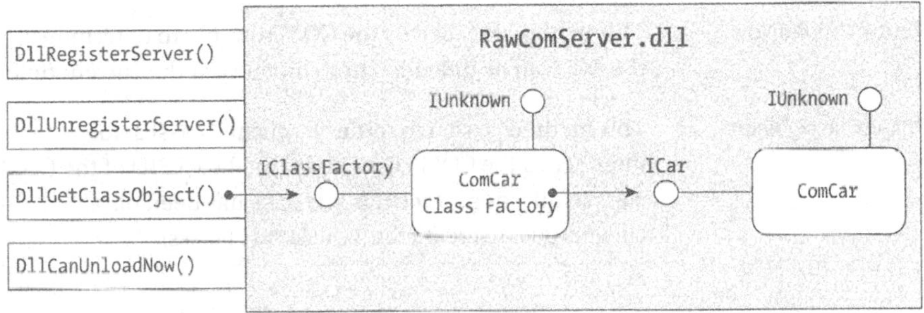

Figure 2-6. The composition of a COM DLL server

All COM DLLs have the same internal composition regardless of which COM-aware language you build them in. First, a COM server contains some number of coclasses (which as you recall is a type supporting at minimum the mandatory IUnknown interface). Because IUnknown is so critical in COM programming, this interface is represented as a lollipop mounted on the top of a given coclass. To the left of the coclass is the set of auxiliary interfaces. Assume that the RawComServer.dll contains a single coclass named ComCar. This COM type supports two interfaces, ICar and IUnknown.

COM servers also support a special sort of COM type termed a *class factory* (also termed a *class object*). COM class factories also support the mandatory IUnknown, as well as another standard interface named IClassFactory. This interface allows the COM client to create a given coclass in a language- and location-neutral manner. As you may be aware, it is possible for a COM class factory to support the IClassFactory2 interface (which derives from IClassFactory).

The role of IClassFactory2 is to define additional methods to check for a valid license file before activating the object.

In addition to the set of coclasses and class factories, COM DLLs must support a small set of function exports. These function exports allow the COM runtime to interact with the internal types, as well as perform registration and unregistration of the COM binary itself. Table 2-1 provides a breakdown of each DLL export.

Table 2-1. COM DLL Function Exports

COM DLL Function Export	Meaning in Life
DllRegisterServer()	This method, which is technically optional, is used to install the necessary entries into the system registry.
DllUnregisterServer()	This method (also technically optional) removes any and all entries inserted by DllRegisterServer().
DllCanUnloadNow()	This method is called by the COM runtime to determine if the DLL can be unloaded from memory at the current time.
DllGetClassObject()	This method is used to retrieve a given IClassFactory interface to the COM client based on the CLSID of the COM class in question. Once this interface has been obtained, the client is able to create the associated coclass.

The final points of interest are the global variables (realized in Figure 2-6 as g_ObjectCount and g_lockCount). COM DLLs need to monitor the number of active coclasses it contains (seen here as g_ObjectCount). As you will see, every time a COM class (including class factories) is created, the server-wide object counter is incremented by 1. When a given object is destroyed, this same counter is decremented by 1.

The lock counter (g_lockCount), on the other hand, represents the number of active locks on the DLL at any given time. Using a valid IClassFactory(2) interface reference, a COM client can lock (and unlock) the server in memory. In this way, a COM client can say in effect "although I don't plan on creating coclasses right now, stay in memory for the time being."

These two global counters are ultimately consulted by the DllCanUnloadNow() function export. If the number of active objects and active locks are both zero, the DLL may be safely unloaded from memory.

The Role of Type Libraries

Given the language-neutral aspect of COM, it makes little sense to define an interface using the syntax of a particular and specific programming language. For example, consider the previous C++ definition of ICar. If you wish to build a COM client using VB 6.0, you are out of luck. Simply put, how can the VB 6.0 compiler understand an interface defined in C++? It cannot. On a related note, what if you defined ICar using VB 6.0? Certainly Delphi, C++, C, and Java (J++) clients have little understanding of the syntax of VB 6.0. What is needed is a way to define a COM type in a language-neutral format.

The IDL is the metalanguage used to describe COM items in language-independent terms. Once you have created an *.idl file describing the COM types in a given COM server, the resulting *.idl file is sent into the Microsoft IDL compiler: midl.exe. The midl.exe compiler emits a binary equivalent termed a *type library*. This library contains the same information as the raw IDL, tokenized into a language-neutral format. By convention, type libraries end with the *.tlb file extension. This file, however, may be bundled into the COM server itself to keep the binary image more modular.

As an example, assume that you have created such an IDL file and produced an equivalent type library using the MIDL compiler. If you were to build a VB 6.0 client, you could reference this information using the IDE's Project | References menu option. The resulting dialog (Figure 2-7) lists all type libraries that are registered on the development machine.

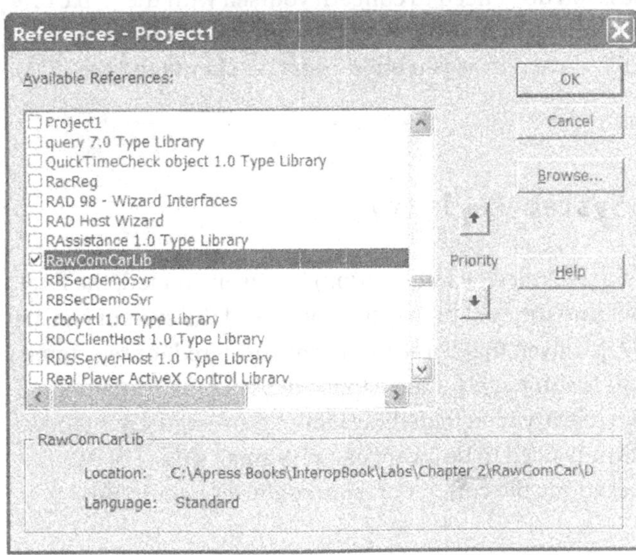

Figure 2-7. Type information is binary IDL (and is thus language-independent).

The Full MIDL Output

In addition to the *.tlb file, the MIDL compiler also generates a number of files that are intended to be used during the development of the COM server and C++ COM clients. Figure 2-8 illustrates the complete MIDL output.

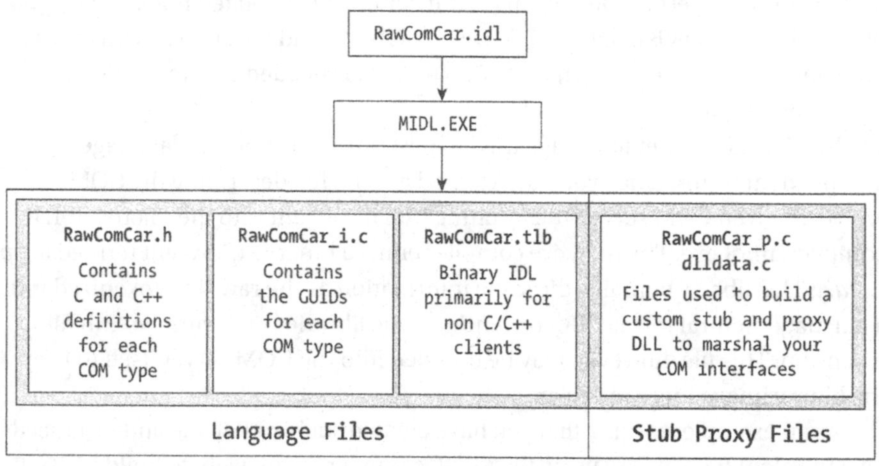

Figure 2-8. Output of the Midl.exe compiler

As you can see, the name of each output file is based on the name of the initial IDL file. For your purposes, you don't need to concern yourself with the *._p.c or dlldata.c files, as you will not need to marshal your interfaces out of process. You will see the *._i.c and *.h files in action as you build your C++ client (and the COM server itself).

The Role of the System Registry

Once a COM server (and the related type information) has been created, the final step is to catalog the server into the system registry. The role of the system registry cannot be overstated in COM, given that if a server is not registered (or registered incorrectly) the COM client is completely unable to make use of the contained types. Although the system registry is an incredibly complex beast, the good news is that COM programmers only need to be aware of a very small subset of its overall functionality. You examine the core set of registry entries later in this chapter.

Creating the COM DLL Project Workspace

Now that you have seen the high-level layout of the COM server you will be constructing, we can get down to the business of building the DLL itself. To begin, create a new Win32 Dynamic-Link Library project workspace named RawComCar (Figure 2-9). From the resulting dialog, select "A simple DLL project" (Figure 2-10).

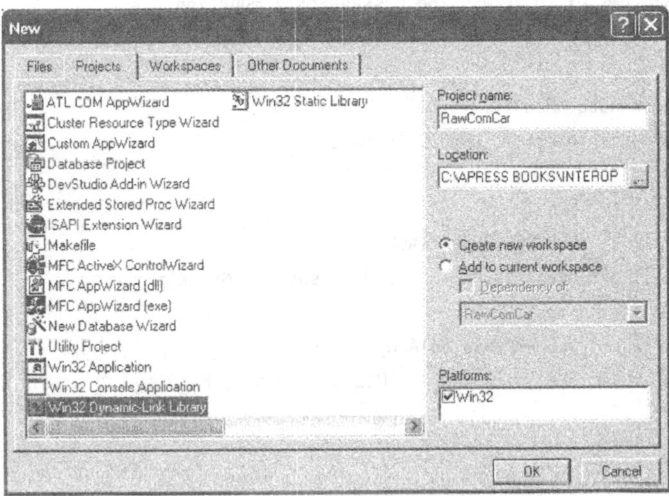

Figure 2-9. Creating the DLL project workspace

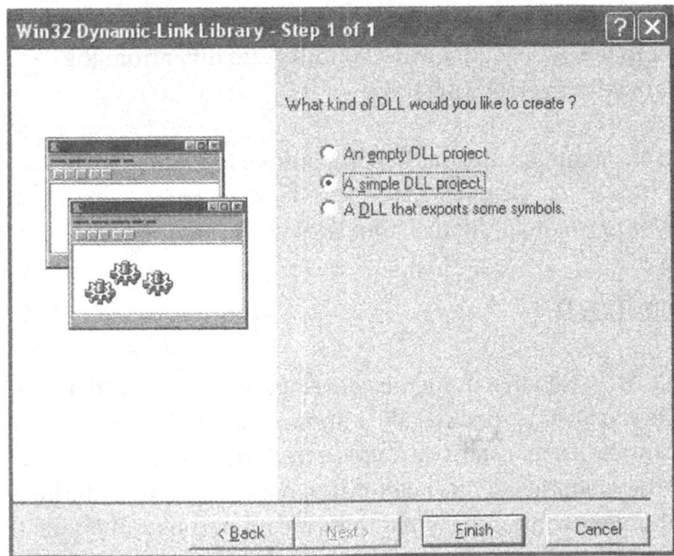

Figure 2-10. Selecting the DLL project type

As you can see, your project workspace contains a single *.cpp file that contains a definition for DllMain(). Technically speaking, COM DLLs do not need to support DllMain(), however, if the DLL does indeed support this method, it is called automatically when the binary is loaded and unloaded from memory (see Chapter 1). For illustrative purposes, update the dummy implementation to display a Win32 message box based on the reason for the invocation.

```
// Need to include <windows.h> to access the MessageBox() function.
#include <windows.h>

BOOL APIENTRY DllMain( HANDLE hModule,
            DWORD ul_reason_for_call, LPVOID lpReserved)
{
  // Just for fun...
  if (ul_reason_for_call = = DLL_PROCESS_ATTACH)
    MessageBox(NULL, "I have been loaded!", "DllMain says:", MB_OK);

  if (ul_reason_for_call = = DLL_PROCESS_DETACH)
    MessageBox(NULL, "I have been Unloaded!", "DllMain says:", MB_OK);
  return TRUE;
}
```

Understanding COM Interfaces

Like the previous ICar interface, COM interfaces are a collection of semantically related functions. When you wish to define a true COM interface, you typically make use of IDL rather than C++. In addition, COM interfaces differ from the previous C++ ICar interface in the following ways:

- COM interfaces are identified using a Globally Unique Identifier (GUID).
- COM interfaces *must* eventually derive from IUnknown.

The Role of the GUID

First, let's qualify the GUID. Given that numerous developers may decide that the string token "I-C-a-r" is a great alias for a specific interface, name clashes are almost certain. For example, if you install five COM servers on your development machine and three of these binaries define an interface named ICar, imagine how confused the COM runtime becomes, given that there are numerous entities identified by the same string token.

To solve these potential name clashes, COM demands that each and every interface be uniquely specified using a GUID. A GUID is a 128-bit number that is statically unique. Physically, a GUID is a four-field structure defined as follows:

```
// GUIDs define numerous COM entities.
typedef struct _GUID
{
  DWORD Data1;
  WORD  Data2;
  WORD  Data3;
  BYTE Data4[8];
} GUID;
```

When you want to generate a new GUID, you can do so programmatically by using the COM library function CoCreateGuid():

```
// Get a GUID on the fly.
GUID myInterfaceID;
CoCreateGuid(&myInterfaceID);
```

When you need a GUID at design time, it is far simpler to make use of the guidgen.exe utility supplied with Microsoft Visual Studio. You will find guidgen.exe installed under your "<drive>:\Program Files\Microsoft Visual Studio\Common\Tools" directory (provided you used the default install paths). Guidgen.exe defines four possible formats. However, when you create IDL files, the only option you care about is the Registry Format selection (Figure 2-11).

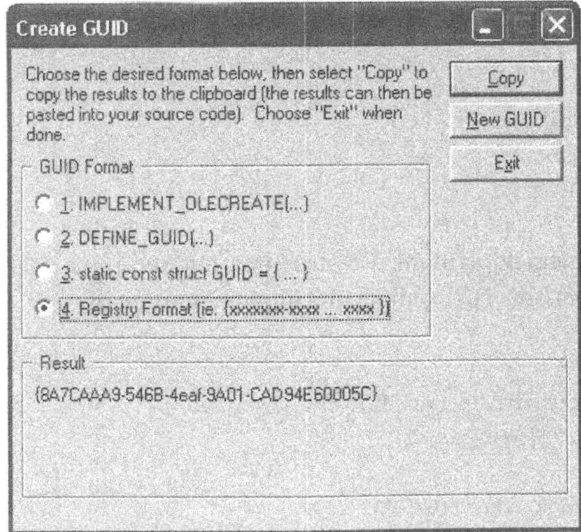

Figure 2-11. Obtaining a GUID at design time

A GUID by Any Other Name…

One aspect of COM development that can be a source of confusion is the fact that the same GUID structure is used to describe any sort of COM-ism. For example, when a GUID is used to define a COM interface, this is termed an IID (interface ID). If the GUID is used to specify the coclass itself, the GUID is called a CLSID (class ID). Similar terms exist to define a COM type library (LIBID), COM category (CATID), and the COM server application itself (AppID). Always remember that regardless of what the GUID is referring to, it is the same GUID structure defined in winnt.h.

Common GUID Helpers

The COM library provides a set of useful functions and types for working with GUIDs programmatically. Many COM library functions take GUIDs as parameters, and given that a 128-bit number might be a bit hefty to pass by value, a number of system defines (found in wtypes.h) are provided to pass these structures around by reference:

```
// wtypes.h lists a number of defines to work with GUIDs in code.
#define REFGUID    const GUID * const
#define REFIID    const IID * const
#define REFCLSID    const CLSID * const
```

You are also given a set of COM library functions to do comparisons of two existing GUIDs:

```
// Defined in objbase.h
BOOL IsEqualGUID(REFGUID g1, REFGUID g2);
BOOL IsEqualIID(REFIID i1, REFIID i2);
BOOL IsEqualCLSID(CLSID c1, CLSID c2);
```

Each function performs a memcmp() of the two structures and returns a BOOL as the result of the comparison. For example, the implementation of IsEqualGUID() follows:

```
// IsEqualGUID can be used to determine if two GUIDs are identical.
BOOL IsEqualGUID(REFGUID rguid1, REFGUID rguid2)
{
   return !memcmp(&rguid1, &rguid2, sizeof(GUID));
}
```

In addition to IsEqualGUID(), the COM library has overloaded the C++ equality operator (= =) and the not equal operator (!=), allowing you to compare two GUIDs as follows:

```
// We may also use = = and != with two existing GUIDs, as
// we have overloaded operators at our disposal.
if(g1 = = g2) {…}   // GUIDs are the same!
if(g1 != g2) {…}    // GUIDs are different!
```

The implementation of the operator = = function calls IsEqualGUID(), while the operator != implementation simply leverages operator = =:

```
// The overloaded operators simply call IsEqualGUID()
BOOL operator == (const GUID& guidOne, const GUID& guidOther)
{
    return IsEqualGUID(guidOne,guidOther);
}

BOOL operator != (const GUID& guidOne, const GUID& guidOther)
{
    return !(guidOne == guidOther);
}
```

The Role of IUnknown

Next, you must reflect on the role of the kingpin of COM: IUnknown. This standard COM interface is like any other COM interface in that it defines a set of semantically related functions. The official (slightly simplified) definition found in unknwn.idl is as follows (note the predefined GUID that identifies this interface):

```
 [object, uuid(00000000-0000-0000-C000-000000000046)]
interface IUnknown
{
  HRESULT QueryInterface([in] REFIID riid,
                   [out, iid_is(riid)] void **ppvObject);
  ULONG AddRef();
  ULONG Release();
};
```

As you see in far greater detail in Chapter 4, IDL supports the notion of attributes. In IDL, an attribute is simply a set of keywords (or a single keyword) that is used to disambiguate a given type definition. These keywords are always placed within square brackets ([,]) and apply to the item directly below or to the immediate right. Here, you see that the IUnknown interface is qualified using the [object] and [uuid] attributes. The two parameters to the QueryInterface() method take additional attributes: [in] and [out, iid_is()]. Again, I comment on numerous IDL attributes throughout this text. For the time being, simply understand that IDL attributes are used to remove any hint of ambiguity as to the function of a given COM entity.

IUnknown defines three methods, which provide two discrete behaviors to every coclass:

- Lifetime management of the COM object
- The ability to obtain interfaces from the COM object

First, IUnknown is used to manage the lifetime of a given COM object. One marked difference from traditional C++ memory management is the fact that the COM client is completely decoupled from the direct creation and destruction of a given COM class. Under the COM paradigm, a client never directly creates a coclass but does so indirectly using COM library calls. On a similar note, a COM client never directly deletes a given COM type from memory. So how is a coclass deallocated?

COM memory management is a joint venture between the client and object. Every COM object maintains a private internal reference counter that reflects the number of outstanding references on the object (represented by an unsigned long, or ULONG, data type). When a client receives a given COM interface reference, the client is obligated to call IUnknown::Release() when it is finished using the interface pointer. As you may have guessed, this action decrements the internal reference counter by one. When the reference count is exactly zero, the object deallocates itself from memory.

On the other side of the coin, you have the COM object. Recall that COM objects typically support a great number of interfaces, each representing a specific behavior the COM type is capable of providing. When a COM client asks for an interface that is supported by the COM type, the COM object itself calls IUnknown::AddRef() to increment its reference by one. In effect, an object's reference counter reflects the current number of active users at any given time.

The second role of IUnknown is to provide a manner in which an external client can discover the interfaces supported on a particular COM object. Recall that by definition, a COM class (coclass) must support at least IUnknown, but will need to support at least one additional interface to be deemed useful. More often than not, a given COM class supports numerous interfaces to fully qualify its behavior (consider an ActiveX control, which supports anywhere between 10 and 15 COM interfaces). The QueryInterface() method allows a COM client to ask the object if it supports a particular interface (specified using an IID) at runtime. If the object in question supports the requested interface, the object returns an interface reference for use by the client (and increments its internal reference counter).

Defining the ICar Interface in IDL

Now that you have a better feel for the role of IUnknown, you are able to define the ICar interface. Using the File | New menu selection, inset a new *.txt file into your current project workspace and save it under the name "rawcomcar.idl". Using IDL syntax, populate your file as follows:

```
// Bring in the core COM data types.
import "oaidl.idl";

// The ICar interface.
[uuid(710D2F54-9289-4f66-9F64-201D56FB66C7), object]
interface ICar : IUnknown
{
  HRESULT SpeedUp([in] long delta);
  HRESULT CurrentSpeed([out, retval] long* currSp);
};
```

As you can see, this iteration of the ICar interface is quite different than the previous C++ version. First and foremost, this custom interface has been adorned with the mandatory [uuid] and [object] attributes. As you may assume, the GUID used to identify this COM type was generated using the guidgen.exe utility. The [object] attribute is used to mark this interface as a COM-style interface, rather than an older RPC interface (which has nothing to do with COM itself).

Of course, the ICar interface derives from the IUnknown interface (also note that unlike C++, inheritance is not specified using the public keyword). Recall that the formal IDL definition of IUnknown is contained within unknwn.idl. However, given that most IDL files need additional COM type definitions, it is commonplace to import oaidl.idl, which will import unknwn.idl on your behalf. Oaild.idl defines a number of core COM types such as IDispatch, BSTR, VARIANT, and other important data types that are typical for most COM applications.

The Role of the HRESULT

Our ICar interface supports two methods. As you can see, each returns the standard function return type: HRESULT. The COM HRESULT is a 32-bit number that contains statistics concerning the success or failure of the method invocation.

As you may have seen during your career as a COM developer, there are numerous predefined HRESULTs that can be used to report information to the COM client. The most common HRESULTs are simply S_OK (the function completed without error) and E_FAIL (something went wrong).

As you will see, C++ COM clients often make use of the SUCCEEDED and FAILED macros to test for a successful method invocation. Visual Basic programmers typically do not directly see the returned HRESULT value, however, it is possible to obtain the return code using the intrinsic VB Err object. Other COM-aware language mappings contend with the HRESULT in their own ways. As you see later in this text, .NET COM clients map HRESULTs (and COM error objects) into the paradigm of structured exception handling (SEH).

IDL Parameter Attributes

COM interface method parameters also take IDL attributes that are used to disambiguate how a given argument is to be marshaled across a given process boundary. You examine the exact details of IDL parameter attributes in greater detail in Chapter 4. For the time being, Table 2-2 hits the highlights.

Table 2-2. IDL Parameter Attributes

IDL Parameter Attribute	Meaning in Life
[in]	The parameter is passed by value (which is to say, a copy of the data is supplied to the called function).
[out]	[out] parameters are sent into the method as unassigned values. The called method fills the outbound parameter to a set value.
[in, out]	Value is assigned by caller, but may be reallocated by the called function. The classic "pass by reference" scenario.
[out, retval]	This parameter configuration is used by higher level languages such as VB 6.0. The role of an [out, retval] parameter is to map a logical return value to a physical return value.

Defining the Coclass (ComCar) in IDL

Given that COM interfaces are rather useless on their own, most IDL files also define the set of coclasses that reside within the binary COM server. When you want to define a COM class, your goal is to define a unique CLSID value as well as document each custom interface supported by the COM type. Assume that you wish to define a COM-aware automobile (ComCar) in IDL syntax (again, use guidgen.exe to obtain new GUIDs).

```
// Bring in the core IDL COM data types.
import "oaidl.idl";

// The ICar interface.
[uuid(710D2F54-9289-4f66-9F64-201D56FB66C7), object]
interface ICar : IUnknown
{
  HRESULT SpeedUp([in] long delta);
  HRESULT CurrentSpeed([out, retval] long* currSp);
};

// The Raw Car Library.
[uuid(D679F136-19C9-4868-B229-F338AE163656), version(1.0)]
library RawComCarLib
{
  // Bring in the COM type definitions with our own library.
  importlib("stdole32.tlb");

  // Define the COM class.
  [uuid(096AC71D-3EB6-4974-A071-A3B1C0B7FC8D)]
  coclass ComCar
  {
     [default] interface ICar;
  };
};
```

As you can see, coclass definitions are placed within a special section of an IDL file termed the *library statement* (marked by the IDL library keyword). Libraries are typically attributed with a [version] attribute to mark the current version of the COM server. COM libraries must also be marked with a [uuid] attribute, which as you recall is termed a library identifier (LIBID).

Each coclass in the server is marked using the *coclass* keyword and the mandatory CLSID. Following the coclass definition is a list of each and every nth-most interface supported by the COM class. By "nth-most" I am referring to the fact that you do not list the base IUnknown directly in your coclass definition, given that ICar "is-a" IUnknown.

Defining the [default] Interface

On a related coclass-centric topic, note the use of the [default] IDL attribute. Recall that COM demands the use of interfaces. Also recall that some higher level COM-aware programming languages attempt to hide that simple fact from view to make the process of working with COM a bit more intuitive. The [default] attribute is used to mark the interface that is automatically returned to the COM client once instantiated. Again, using VB 6.0 as an example:

```
Dim myCar as ComCar
Set myCar = New ComCar  ' [default] ICar returned automatically!
myCar.SpeedUp 10
```

On the other hand, C++ itself does not honor the [default] attribute. Rather, the user of the ComCar is required to ask directly for the ICar interface via QueryInterface(). I formalize client-side COM code at later in this chapter.

Defining and Supporting Multiple Interfaces

To make our ComCar coclass a bit more interesting, assume you have defined an additional COM interface named IRadio.

```
// The IRadio interface
[uuid(3B6C6126-92A8-47ef-86DA-A12BFFD9BC42), object]
 interface IRadio : IUnknown
{
  HRESULT CrankTunes();
};
```

If you want the ComCar to support the ability to blare music and annoy passersby, you can update the coclass definition as follows:

```
// Our COM class.
[uuid(096AC71D-3EB6-4974-A071-A3B1C0B7FC8D)]
coclass ComCar
{
  [default] interface ICar;
  interface IRadio;
};
```

Compiling the IDL File with the MIDL Compiler

Now that you have created the IDL file that describes the COM types contained in the RawComCar.dll, you can compile it with the MIDL compiler. While you are free to run midl.exe from the command line, your task will be much simpler if you make use of Visual Studio when compiling your *.idl files. First, right-click anywhere on the open file window and select "Insert File into Project" from the context menu.

The MIDL compiler itself can be configured using the MIDL tab of the project settings dialog box (found under the Project | Settings menu). By default, MIDL is set to the MkTypLib-compatible option, which means all IDL code is expected to conform under the older ODL syntax rather than modern day IDL. Be sure to turn this feature *off* in your raw C++ COM projects (see Figure 2-12).

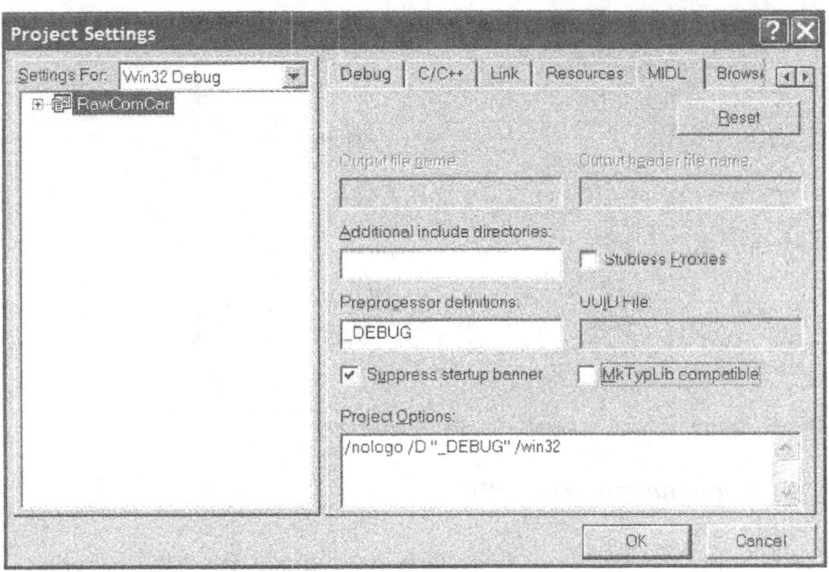

Figure 2-12. Configuring the MIDL compiler

Once you insert a *.idl file into the project workspace, you can simply right-click the file from FileView and select Compile. This activates the MIDL compiler and automatically sends the output files into your project directory. The MIDL compiler also runs automatically when you build your projects, if you have inserted one or more *.idl files.

Examining the MIDL-Generated Files

Assuming your IDL file has compiled without error, you will find the MIDL-generated files have been dumped into your project folder. First, locate and open the generated type library file (RawComCar.tlb). As shown in Figure 2-13, the type library is little more than a binary, tokenized version of the original IDL.

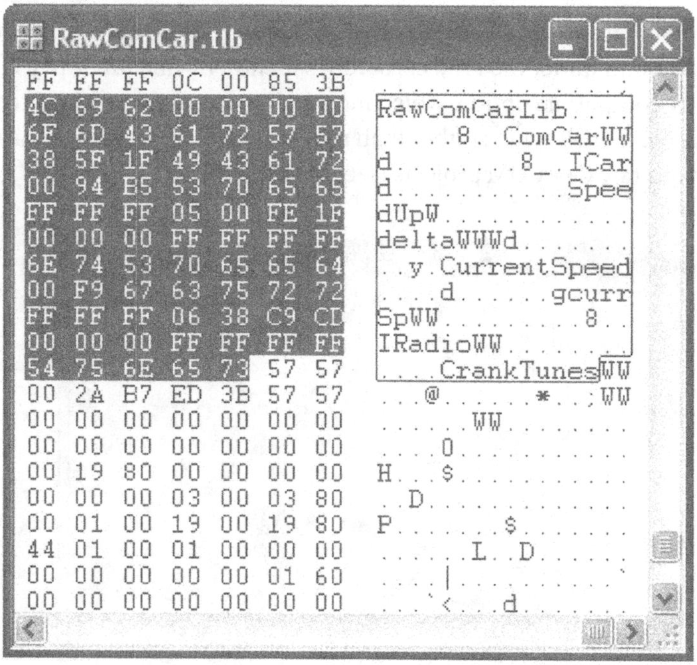

Figure 2-13. Type libraries are binary IDL.

The contents of the RawComCar_i.c file is quite simple. The MIDL compiler creates this file to define C/C++ constants for every GUID contained in the IDL. As you can guess, whenever the MIDL compiler encounters a [uuid] attribute, a new constant is generated. Note that the name of each constant is prefixed with CLSID_, IID_, or LIBID_ (depending on what the [uuid] attribute was describing).

```
const IID IID_ICar =
{0x710D2F54,0x9289,0x4f66,{0x9F,0x64,0x20,0x1D,0x56,0xFB,0x66,0xC7}};

const IID IID_IRadio =
{0x3B6C6126,0x92A8,0x47ef,{0x86,0xDA,0xA1,0x2B,0xFF,0xD9,0xBC,0x42}};
```

```
const IID LIBID_RawComCarLib =
{0xD679F136,0x19C9,0x4868,{0xB2,0x29,0xF3,0x38,0xAE,0x16,0x36,0x56}};

const CLSID CLSID_ComCar =
{0x096AC71D,0x3EB6,0x4974,{0xA0,0x71,0xA3,0xB1,0xC0,0xB7,0xFC,0x8D}};
```

Finally, you have the generated header file, RawComCar.h. This file contains C/C++ language definitions for each custom interface (as well as COM enumerations and COM structures) found in the IDL file. For example, here is the C++ ICar interface definition (IRadio is also defined in this file):

```
ICar : public IUnknown
{
  public:
    virtual HRESULT STDMETHODCALLTYPE SpeedUp(
      /* [in] */ long delta) = 0;

    virtual HRESULT STDMETHODCALLTYPE CurrentSpeed(
      /* [retval][out] */ long __RPC_FAR *currSp) = 0;
};
```

A Brief Word on COM-Centric Macros

While the MIDL-generated code contains a number of COM-centric macros (STDMETHODCALLTYPE) to define the interface, the essence of the ICar interface should look familiar. C++ COM developers typically make use of these COM macros to provide some degree of platform neutrality. For example, the STDMETHOD and STDMETHOD_ macros are used in C++ coclass header files to ensure that the method prototypes expand correctly on various target platforms. STDMETHODIMP and STDMETHODIMP_ are used in the corresponding C++ implementation files for the same reason. Table 2-3 defines the use of each of these core COM macros (all of which are defined in objbase.h, so take a peek if you are interested).

Table 2-3. C++ COM-Centric Macros

COM-Centric Macro	Meaning in Life
STDMETHOD	Used to define a method prototype that returns the HRESULT data type.
STDMETHOD_	Used to define a method prototype that does not return an HRESULT. The first parameter to this macro is the data type to return.
STDMETHODIMP	Used to implement (IMP) a method that returns an HRESULT.
STDMETHODIMP_	Used to implement a method that does not return an HRESULT.

Implementing the ComCar

Since the MIDL compiler was kind enough to generate the *_i.c and *.h files that express the IDL definitions in C++, you can now implement the ComCar type. Begin by inserting a new C++ class definition using the Insert | New Class menu selection (Figure 2-14). Name your class ComCar, and if you desire, change the names of the header and implementation files to suit your fancy. Finally, specify ICar as the base class for your new type (ignore the warning generated when you dismiss the dialog).

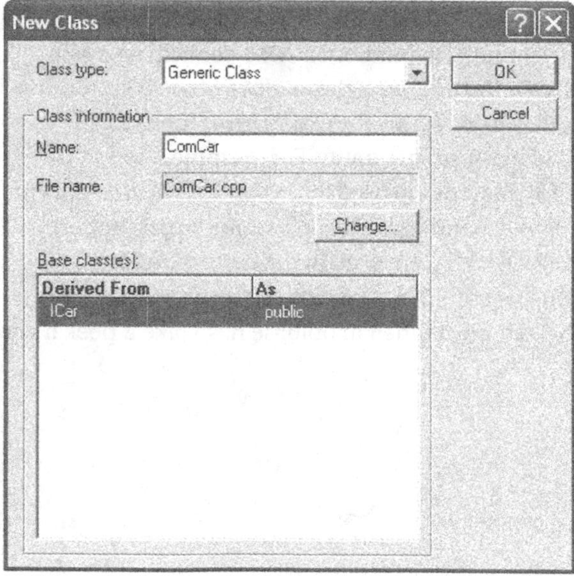

Figure 2-14. Inserting the ComCar class

When implementing a coclass in C++, the standard approach is to simply inherit from each interface you wish the coclass to support. Given that our type information states that ComCar supports the ICar and IRadio interfaces (which in turn derive from IUnknown), the ComCar must now implement a total of six interface methods. Here is the class definition (making use of the correct COM macros):

```
#include <windows.h>
// MIDL generated file!
#include "rawcomcar.h"

// ComCar implements IUnknown, ICar, and IRadio.
class ComCar : public ICar, IRadio  // Add IRadio to the list.
{
public:
    ComCar();
    virtual ~ComCar();

    // IUnknown methods.
    STDMETHOD_(ULONG,AddRef)();
    STDMETHOD_(ULONG,Release)();
    STDMETHOD (QueryInterface)(REFIID riid, void**);

    // ICar methods.
    STDMETHOD (SpeedUp)(long delta);
    STDMETHOD (CurrentSpeed)(long* currSp);

    // IRadio impl.
    STDMETHOD (CrankTunes)();

    // Ref counter for this COM object.
    ULONG m_refCount;

    // Current speed!
    long m_currSpeed;
};
```

Implementing IUnknown

As you recall, the AddRef() and Release() methods of IUnknown are used to control the lifetime of a COM object. Simply put, AddRef() increments the class' reference counter by one. Release decrements this counter by one and checks for the final release (meaning the Release() invocation that sets the reference counter to zero). At that time, the COM type removes itself from memory. Add the following implementation code into your ComCar.cpp implementation file.

```
// Don't forget to set your member variables to a default value!
ComCar::ComCar() : m_refCount(0), m_currSpeed(0) {}
ComCar::~ComCar() {}

STDMETHODIMP_(ULONG) ComCar::AddRef()
{ return ++m_refCount; }

STDMETHODIMP_(ULONG) ComCar::Release()
{
  if(--m_refCount = = 0)
    delete this;
  return m_refCount;
}
```

Notice that both AddRef() and Release() return the current number of outstanding interface pointers to the client. Never use this value for any purpose other than general debugging. The COM specification does not state that this returned reference count is a perfect reflection of the object's number of clients. Although a client can examine this return value to get a general feel of the object in use, it should never use this value in production code.

Implementing QueryInterface() is also fairly simple. Recall that this method allows the client to ask the object "Do you support an interface named X?" The interface in question is identified (of course) by the associated IID. If the COM type does indeed implement the requested interface, the client receives a reference that forces the COM object to AddRefs itself. As for the physical HRESULT return value, convention dictates that E_NOINTERFACE is used when the client asks you for an interface you do not support. If you do, simply return S_OK. Given that ComCar supports three interfaces, you must test for three possible IIDs.

```
// Note! All standard COM interfaces (such as IUnknown) have a predefined GUID
// constant that can be obtained by simply including windows.h.
STDMETHODIMP ComCar::QueryInterface(REFIID riid, void** ppInterface)
{
  // Remember! Always AddRef() when handing out an interface.
  if(riid = = IID_IUnknown)
  {
    *ppInterface = (IUnknown*)(ICar*)this;
    ((IUnknown*)(*ppInterface ))->AddRef();
    return S_OK;
  }
```

```
    else if(riid = = IID_ICar)
    {
      *ppInterface = (ICar*)this;
      ((IUnknown*)(*ppInterface ))->AddRef();
      return S_OK;
    }
    else if(riid = = IID_IRadio)
    {
      *ppInterface = (IRadio*)this;
      ((IUnknown*)(*ppInterface ))->AddRef();
      return S_OK;
    }
    else
    {
      *ppInterface = NULL;
      return E_NOINTERFACE;
    }
}
```

Implementing ICar and IRadio

The final step in building your coclass is to implement the interface methods themselves. To keep focused on the COM architecture, I offer the following trivial implementation:

```
// Increase the speed of the Car.
STDMETHODIMP ComCar::SpeedUp(long delta)
{
    m_currSpeed += delta;
    return S_OK;
}

// Return the current speed as an output parameter.
STDMETHODIMP ComCar::CurrentSpeed(long* currSp)
{
    *currSp = m_currSpeed;
    return S_OK;
}

// Jam.
STDMETHODIMP ComCar::CrankTunes()
{
  MessageBox(NULL, "Cranking music!", "ComCar", MB_OK);
  return S_OK;
}
```

Understanding IClassFactory

Because COM is a language-independent architecture, a client cannot create a COM object using a *language-specific* keyword. For example, the C++ "new" operator has no built-in ability to create a new instance of a binary object. Also, a COM client can create a server that may be located at any location in the Enterprise. Given these two issues (locality- and language-independence), you need a language- and location-neutral way in which a client can create a COM object. This is accomplished through another standard COM interface named IClassFactory. IClassFactory (also defined in unknwn.idl) defines two methods:

```
// The IClassFactory interface.
[object,
uuid(00000001-0000-0000-C000-000000000046)]
interface IClassFactory : IUnknown
{
    HRESULT CreateInstance(
        [in, unique] IUnknown * pUnkOuter,
    [in] REFIID riid,
    [out, iid_is(riid)] void **ppvObject);

    HRESULT LockServer( [in] BOOL fLock);
};
```

The most critical (and most often called) method is CreateInstance(), which creates an instance of the associated coclass on behalf of the calling client. LockServer() is used less often and is used to hold the binary server itself in memory per client request (recall the global lock counter?).

Class objects exist only to create another type of COM object. This is how COM provides a language- and location-neutral means by which a client can create a coclass located in a binary server. If every COM-enabled language has some way to access the IClassFactory interface, every client is able to create the object it desires in a language-independent manner. Furthermore, as the actual implementation of the IClassFactory methods is hidden at the binary level, you (as the object creator) can use whatever language keywords you have at your disposal (such as the C++ new operator) to create the associated coclass. If you like, consider the COM class factory to be a language- and location-independent new operator.

Building Your Class Factory

Your class factory, which I will call ComCarCF, is responsible for creating ComCar objects for a client and returning some interface pointer from ComCar. The definition of ComCarCF should appear straightforward:

```
#include <windows.h>

// Class factories NEVER implement the interfaces
// of the COM class they create!
class ComCarCF : public IClassFactory
{
public:
  ComCarCF();
      virtual ~ComCarCF();
  // IUnknown methods.
  STDMETHOD_(ULONG,AddRef)();
  STDMETHOD_(ULONG,Release)();
  STDMETHOD (QueryInterface)(REFIID riid, void** pInterface);

  // IClassFactory methods.
  STDMETHOD (CreateInstance)(LPUNKNOWN pUnkOuter,
                          REFIID iid, void** pInterface);
  STDMETHOD (LockServer)(BOOL lock);

  // Ref counter (set to zero in constructor).
  ULONG m_refCount;
};
```

As with any COM object, the implementation of AddRef() and Release() for a class factory simply increments or decrements the internal reference counter, and checks for the final release to remove itself from memory:

```
// Class objects, being COM objects, maintain a reference count.
STDMETHODIMP_(ULONG) ComCarCF::AddRef()
{ return ++m_refCount; }

STDMETHODIMP_(ULONG) ComCarCF::Release()
{
  if(--m_refCount = = 0)
  {
    delete this;
    return 0;
  }
  return m_refCount;
}
```

QueryInterface() simply hands out pointers to the standard IUnknown or IClassFactory interfaces (if the class factory is checking for a valid license file, you could also implement and test for IClassFactory2):

```
// Note that class factories never supported the
// interfaces of the related coclass (ComCar)!
STDMETHODIMP ComCarCF::QueryInterface(REFIID riid, void** pIFace)
{
  if(riid = = IID_IUnknown)
    *pIFace = (IUnknown*)this;
  else if(riid = = IID_IClassFactory)
    *pIFace = (IClassFactory*)this;

  if(*pIFace){
    ((IUnknown*)(*pIFace))->AddRef();
    return S_OK;
  }
  *pIFace = NULL;
  return E_NOINTERFACE;
}
```

Implementing IClassFactory::CreateInstance()

As mentioned, CreateInstance() is responsible for creating a new instance of the associated COM object, asking the object for the client-specified interface, and returning it back to the client.

The first parameter of CreateInstance() is used in conjunction with COM aggregation. I do not examine the details of aggregation here. Assume this parameter is always NULL (which specifies no aggregation support is being requested). The second parameter is the IID of the interface the client is interested in obtaining from the coclass once it has been created. The final parameter (of course) is a pointer to the fetched interface. Without further ado, here is the implementation of CreateInstance():

```
// Create the related coclass.
STDMETHODIMP ComCarCF::CreateInstance(LPUNKNOWN pUnkOuter,
                                      REFIID riid, void** ppInterface)
{
  // We do not support aggregation in this class object.
  if(pUnkOuter != NULL)
    return CLASS_E_NOAGGREGATION;
```

```
    ComCar* pCarObj = NULL;
    HRESULT hr;

    // Create the car.
    pCarObj = new ComCar;

    // Ask car for an interface.
    hr = pCarObj -> QueryInterface(riid, ppInterface);

    // Problem? We must delete the memory we allocated.
    if (FAILED(hr))
        delete pCarObj;
    return hr;
}
```

Implementing IClassFactory::LockServer()

Finally, you need to address the LockServer() method of IClassFactory to finish up your ComCar class factory. LockServer() provides a way for a client to lock the COM binary in memory, even if there are currently no active objects in the server. The reason to do so is client optimization. Once a client obtains an IClassFactory pointer, it may call LockServer(TRUE), which will bump up a global level lock counter maintained by the server. When the COM runtime attempts to unload a server from memory, this lock count is consulted first. If the value of the global lock counter is not zero (which signifies that there are locks), COM will stop by later and ask again.

Any client that calls LockServer(TRUE) must call LockServer(FALSE) before terminating, to decrement the server's global lock counter. With that said, create a global ULONG named g_lockCount in your rawcomcar.cpp file. The LockServer() method may then be implemented as follows:

```
// Assume that the lock counter has been defined in the rawcomcar.cpp file.
extern ULONG g_lockCount;

// LockServer() simply increments or decrements
// the server level global lock counter.
STDMETHODIMP ComCarCF::LockServer(BOOL lock)
{
  if(lock)
    g_lockCount++;
  else
    g_lockCount--;
  return S_OK;
}
```

Implementing DLL Component Housing

The next major hurdle facing you before ComCar is ready for client access is creating a binary home for itself and its class object to dwell. As you recall, every COM-based DLL exports (through a standard *.def file) four well-known functions.

The implementation of DllGetClassObject() creates a new class factory and returns the correct IClassFactory interface to the client. If your server contains a collection of coclasses, you should examine the incoming CLSID parameter of DllGetClassObject() to determine which class factory to create. This method has the following signature:

```
// Creates a given class factory for
// the client based on the CLSID of the coclass.
STDAPI DllGetClassObject(REFCLSID rclsid, REFIID riid, void** ppv);
```

Here then is an implementation of the first server export, DllGetClassObject():

```
// DllGetClassObject() is in charge of creating a class factory, and returning the
// IClassFactory interface to the COM client.
STDAPI DllGetClassObject(REFCLSID rclsid, REFIID riid, LPVOID* ppv)
{
  // We only know how to make cars!
  if(rclsid = = CLSID_ComCar)
  {
    // Make a ComCarCF and return requested interface.
    ComCarCF* pCarCF = new ComCarCF();
    return pCarCF->QueryInterface(riid, ppv);
  }
  else
  {
    return CLASS_E_CLASSNOTAVAILABLE;
  }
}
```

Managing Server Lifetime: DllCanUnloadNow()

In addition to the global lock counter, COM DLLs maintain a global object counter that identifies the number of active objects in the server at any given time. Whenever a coclass (ComCar) or class object (ComCarCF) is created, the constructors of these types should bump up this global object counter variable by one. Whenever a coclass (ComCar) or class object (ComCarCF) is terminated, the destructors should decrement this global object counter by one. Here is the revised ComCar class, which properly adjusts the serverwide object counter (ComCarCF would also need to be retrofitted in the same way):

```
// Assume that the object counter has been defined in the rawcomcar.cpp file
extern ULONG g_ObjectCount;

ComCar::ComCar()
{
    g_objCount++;    // Also increment in class factory.
}

// Server lost an object.
ComCar ::~ComCar
{
    g_objCount--;   // Also decrement in class factory.
}
```

A COM DLL can be unloaded safely by the COM runtime only if there are no server locks and no active objects within the server. DllCanUnloadNow() can check the two global variables maintaining this information, and return S_OK or S_FALSE accordingly:

```
// The DllCanUnloadNow() server export informs the COM runtime when it is
// safe to unload the DLL from memory.
ULONG g_lockCount = 0; // Modified by ICF::LockServer.
ULONG g_objCount = 0;  // Modified by ctor & dtor of any coclass in the server.

STDAPI DllCanUnloadNow(void)
{
  if(g_lockCount = = 0 && g_objCount = = 0)
    return S_OK;  // Unload me.
  else
    return S_FALSE; // Keep me alive.
}
```

Contending with DllRegisterServer() and DllUnregisterServer()

If you were to implement these two remaining DLL exports, you would have a good deal of code to contend with. Not only would you need to build numerous structures to represent every registry entry, but you would also need to be comfortable programming the registry using numerous API calls. Given that this would take you a bit off task, we will simply define the following stub code and enter your registry information using a (much simpler) *.reg file.

```
// Typically these methods are called by an installation program or using
// the regsvr32.exe command line tool.
STDAPI DllRegisterServer(void)
{
  MessageBox(NULL, "If I had code, I would register these types...",
    "DllRegisterServer", MB_OK);
  return S_OK;
}

STDAPI DllUnregisterServer(void)
{
  MessageBox(NULL, "If I had code, I would UN-register these types...",
    "DllUnregisterServer", MB_OK);
  return S_OK;
}
```

Exporting the Exports

Now that you have implemented the necessary exports, you need to expose them to the outside world. To export these DLL functions, you need to assemble a standard Win32 *.def file, which must be included into your current project. The name of the library is the exact same name as your project workspace:

```
; RawComCar.def : Declares the module parameters.
LIBRARY "RawComCar.dll"
EXPORTS
DllCanUnloadNow       @1 PRIVATE
DllGetClassObject     @2 PRIVATE
DllRegisterServer     @3 PRIVATE
DllUnregisterServer   @4 PRIVATE
```

At this point, you have created the necessary infrastructure for a C++-based COM DLL server! (As you can tell, building COM binaries in raw C++ is a labor of love.) However, before a client could create and use the object, you must enter the correct information in the system registry.

Registering the COM Server

The registry is a local system database, which specifies (among other things) all the COM-centric information for a given computer. You may access the Registry Editor by running regedit.exe from the Run command. The registry is broken into a series of topmost nodes called *hives*. The most important hive for COM developers is HKEY_CLASSES_ROOT (abbreviate to HKCR). Figure 2-15 illustrates the hives found on a Windows XP Professional installation.

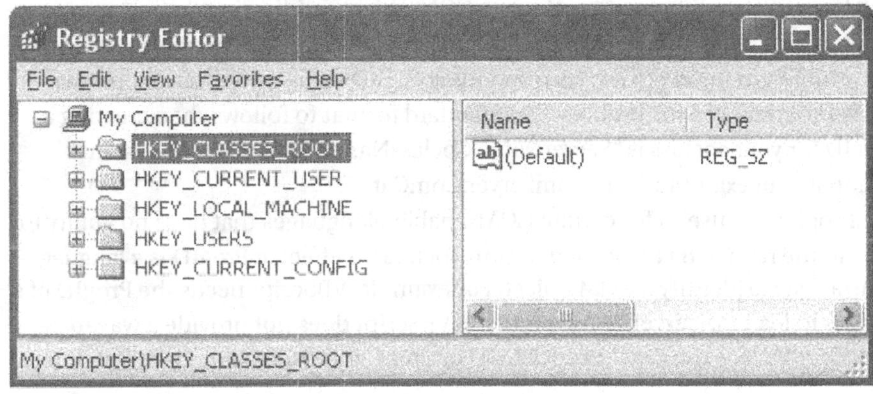

Figure 2-15. The core COM hive (HKCR)

Entries under a hive are called *keys*, which may contain *subkeys*. A given key or subkey may contain string or numerical values. Entire books have been written about the layout and programming of the Windows registry; luckily COM developers only need to understand a small subset of its overall functionality, beginning with the ProgID.

Programmatic Identifiers (ProgIDs)

The first thing listed under HKCR is a long list of file extensions, which we have no interest in at all. Scroll past this list until you find the first real text entry located after the final file extension. When you find that item, expand it as shown in Figure 2-16.

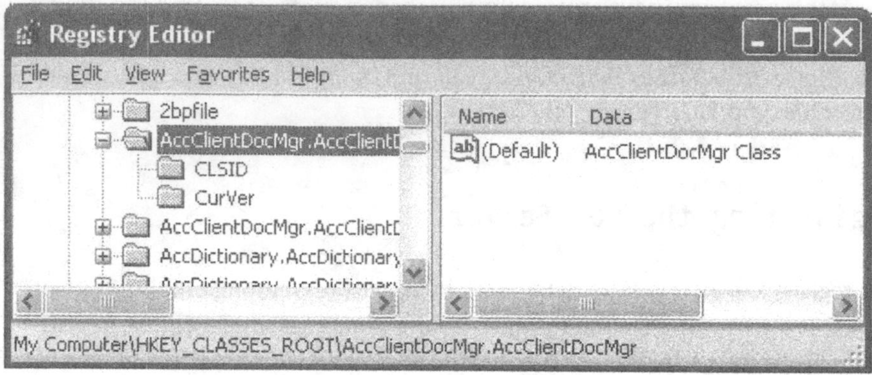

Figure 2-16. ProgIDs are listed off HKCR.

These strings are termed *Programmatic Identifiers* (ProgIDs). ProgIDs are a text-based alternative used to refer to a COM object residing in some server. ProgIDs are simply text mappings for CLSIDs. As you can see, every ProgID listing has a subkey mapping to the corresponding CLSID value as well as an optional CurVer (current version) subkey. The standard format to follow when creating a ProgID for your coclass is "ServerName.CoclassName.Version" (the version is optional). For example: "RawComServer.ComCar.1".

ProgIDs are useful for certain COM-enabled languages that have no ability to refer to the raw GUID associated to your coclass. In effect, a ProgID is a language-neutral way to identify a COM object. For example, VBScript needs the ProgID of a coclass to load the server into memory as VBScript does not provide a way to directly reference the raw 128-bit CLSID of ComCar (as seen later in this chapter).

A Critical Key: HKEY_CLASSES_ROOT \ CLSID

The next point of interest is the CLSID key. The CLSID key is where SCM ultimately ends up when it looks for the physical path to your COM server. Each subkey of HKCR\CLSID begins with the GUID for the entry. Figure 2-17 reveals the CLSID of Microsoft's Data Access Object's (DAO) DBEngine coclass.

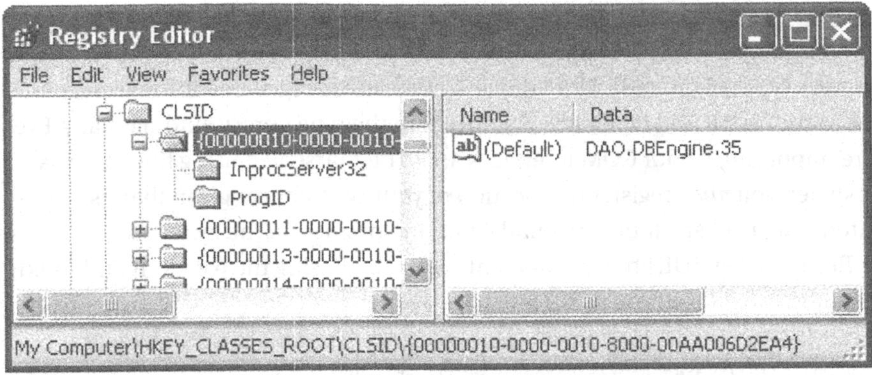

Figure 2-17. CLSIDs are used to resolve the location of a COM type.

Under a given CLSID entry, you may find any of the following core subkeys listed in Table 2-4.

Table 2-4. Core Entries Under HKCR\CLSID

HKCR\CLSID Subdirectory	Meaning in Life
ProgID	This key maps to the ProgID associated with the coclass. When you call ProgIDFromCLSID(), the COM runtime returns the ProgID subkey for a given CLSID listing.
VersionIndependentProgID	Same value as the ProgID key, without the version suffix. Recall that ProgIDs do not have to be versioned.
InprocServer32	For in-process COM servers, this is the most important of all CLSID subkeys. This value is the physical path to the DLL server (for example, "C:\MyServers\Cars\Debug\RawComCar.dll").
LocalServer32	If you have COM objects that live in an EXE, rather than a DLL, the value of LocalServer32 is the path to the COM executable (for example, "C:\MyServers\Cars\Debug\Cars.exe").

Another Critical Key: HKEY_CLASSES_ROOT\TypeLib

A server's type information file (*.tlb) also needs to be registered if you expect tools such as the VB 6.0 Add Reference dialog to find the type library automatically. Even more important, if your COM interfaces are to be marshaled using the universal marshaler, you *must* register the location of your type library, given that its contents are read at runtime to build stubs and proxies on the fly.

Recall that an IDL library statement is qualified using the [version] and [uuid] attributes:

```
[uuid(D679F136-19C9-4868-B229-F338AE163656), version(1.0)]
library RawComCarLib
{ … }
```

This very same information is listed under HKCR\TypeLib. The location of the *.tlb file is placed under the \0\Win32 subdirectory ("0" marks the default locale of the type library, which I will assume to be US English). Be aware that many COM frameworks such as VB 6.0 and ATL embed the *.tlb file as a resource of the binary DLL or EXE COM server. Thus, the value contained under the \Win32 subdirectory could be the path to an *.tlb, *.dll, or *.exe file. For example, Figure 2-18 shows the entry for your current RawComServer (which you have yet to formally register).

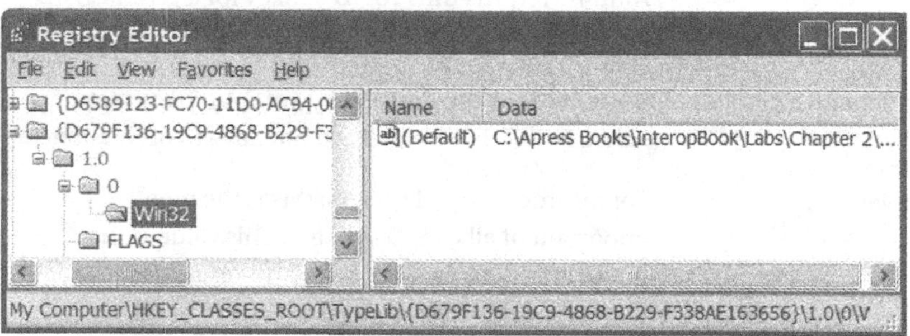

Figure 2-18. Type information is located under HKCR\TypeLib.

Other COM Registration Possibilities

In addition to ProgIDs, CLSIDs, and LIBIDs, there are two other valid registration entries of note. First, HKCR\Interface is the place to log your custom COM interfaces. Understand that you are not required to register your COM interfaces *unless* they are intended to be marshaled out of process. Given that our

RawComServer.dll is always accessed in process (by a client with the same threading model), you do not have to register the IRadio or ICar interfaces.

The final subfolder of interest is HKCR\Component Categories. It is possible to generate a GUID termed a CATID, which is used to refer to a COM category. These GUIDs are used to group like objects together under a unique ID, even if the members of the category are located in independent COM servers. Using CATIDs, the COM client may make a request (using the COM library) for a list of all coclasses that belong to a given Component Category. The result is a set of CLSIDs, which can then be used to activate each member.

Registering Your COM Servers

So much for your tour of the Windows registry. As mentioned, you will write your own registry scripts (*.reg files) that can be used to merge your server information into the registry automatically, bypassing the need to code DllRegisterServer() by hand. Thus, insert a new *.txt file and save it under the name RawComServer.reg.

Here is the complete registration syntax for the RawComCar.dll. To save yourself the pain of typing in each line by hand, feel free to simply copy and adjust the *.reg file supplied with the downloaded code. Be aware that the GUIDs used in the *.reg file must match the values found in your IDL code (your paths may differ from mine, so update accordingly)!

```
REGEDIT

; This is the ProgID!
HKEY_CLASSES_ROOT\RawComCar.CoCar\
CLSID = {096AC71D-3EB6-4974-A071-A3B1C0B7FC8D}

; A CLSID entry typically has these lines (at minimum).
HKEY_CLASSES_ROOT\CLSID\
{096AC71D-3EB6-4974-A071-A3B1C0B7FC8D} = RawComCar.CoCar

HKEY_CLASSES_ROOT\CLSID\{096AC71D-3EB6-4974-A071-A3B1C0B7FC8D}
\InprocServer32 = C:\Apress Books\InteropBook\Labs
\Chapter 2\RawComCar\Debug\RawComCar.dll

HKEY_CLASSES_ROOT\CLSID\
{096AC71D-3EB6-4974-A071-A3B1C0B7FC8D}\
TypeLib = {D679F136-19C9-4868-B229-F338AE163656}
```

```
; TypeLib Settings
HKEY_CLASSES_ROOT\TypeLib\
{D679F136-19C9-4868-B229-F338AE163656} = Car Server Type Lib

HKEY_CLASSES_ROOT\TypeLib\{D679F136-19C9-4868-B229-F338AE163656}
\1.0\0\Win32 = C:\Apress Books\InteropBook\
Labs\Chapter 2\RawComCar\Debug\RawComCar.tlb
```

Once you save this file, simply double-click it from within Windows Explorer. Using regedit.exe, you will now be able to find your ProgID (Figure 2-19), CLSID (Figure 2-20), and LIBID (seen previously in Figure 2-18).

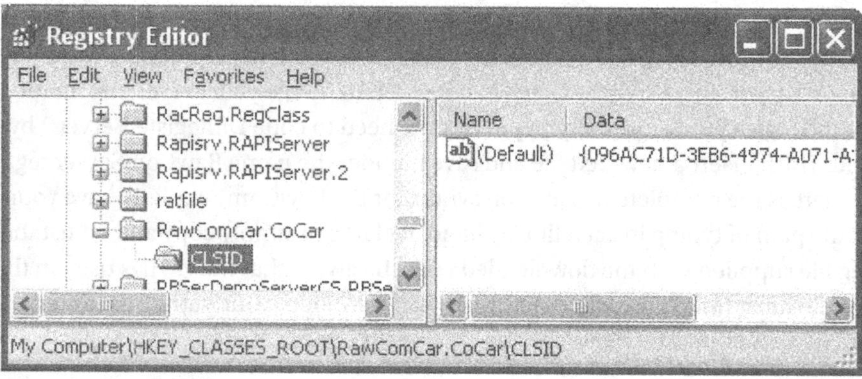

Figure 2-19. The ProgID

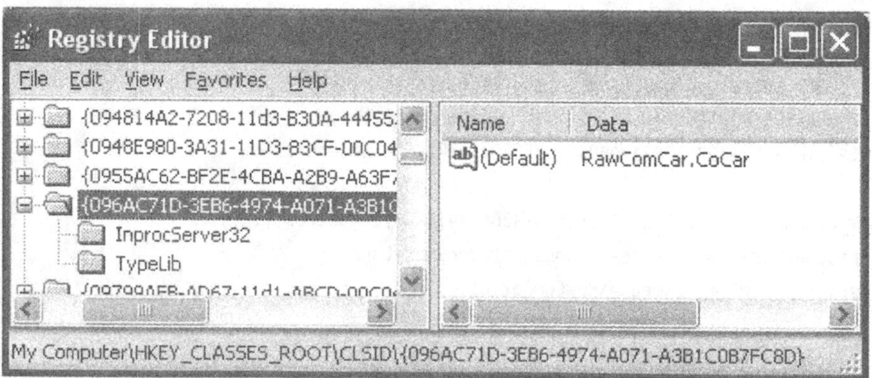

Figure 2-20. The CLSID

Excellent! If you followed along with this example, you have successfully created a COM DLL from the ground up. As you have seen, building a COM server using raw C++ can be quite an undertaking. In the next chapter, you briefly examine two popular COM frameworks (ATL and Visual Basic 6.0) that help lessen the burden of creating COM binaries.

CODE *The RawComCar application is included under the Chapter 2 subdirectory.*

Developing a C++ COM Client

Now that you have implemented your first COM-based in-process server, you need to investigate the necessary COM library calls to access it. Regardless of the client's language, under the hood the same basic sequence of COM library calls are used. Some COM language mappings (such as VB) hide this process so well that the developer has little exposure to what is happening under the hood.

When COM developers make requests to runtime, they do so by calling COM library functions, which (for the most part) are contained in the granddaddy of all COM system DLLs, ole32.dll. This core system file is the gateway between your client code and the COM runtime. The very first thing COM clients must be sure to do is initialize the COM subsystem. Each and every thread using the COM libraries must make a call to CoInitialize() before making any further requests from the COM runtime. When that thread is finished with the COM subsystem, a complementing call to CoUninitialize() must be made to clean things up.

Activating COM Objects

Once the COM runtime is ready to receive your requests, clients typically make calls to one of two COM activation functions, CoGetClassObject() or CoCreateInstance(), to load a server and create a new COM object. You examine the use of CoGetClassObject() first, as CoCreateInstance() is simply a helper function, wrapping the call to CoGetClassObject() on your behalf. CoGetClassObject() tells COM runtime to locate, load, and retrieve the IClassFactory pointer for a given coclass.

From this pointer, you can create an instance of the associated coclass, (via CreateInstance()) and go to town. Here is the signature of CoGetClassObject():

```
// This activation function is used to return the
// IClassFactory pointer for a given
// class factory. Using this interface, the client
// can then create the corresponding class object.
HRESULT CoGetClassObject(REFCLSID rclsid, DWORD dwClsContext,
      COSERVERINFO * pServerInfo,
      REFIID riid, LPVOID * ppv);
```

The first parameter is the CLSID of the coclass you wish to create, for example CLSID_ComCar. As you entered this information into the system registry, the COM SCM knows where to find the path to the binary and load the server. The second parameter is a member from the CLSCTX enumeration, which specifies the class context of the server. You know that COM offers you location transparency, and this parameter allows you to specify if you wish an in-proc, local, or remote version of the server. The core values of the CLSCTX are as follows:

```
// The class context allows a COM client to specify
// which 'local' they are interested in.
enum tagCLSCTX
{
    CLSCTX_INPROC_SERVER = 0x1,  // In-proc server.
    CLSCTX_LOCAL_SERVER = 0x4,   // Local server.
    CLSCTX_REMOTE_SERVER = 0x10  // Remote server
}CLSCTX;
```

You specify CLSCTX_INPROC_SERVER if you desire in-proc servers, CLSCTX_LOCAL_SERVER for local servers, or CLSCTX_REMOTE_SERVER for a remote server. You may also combine any of the CLSCTX flags, and SCM finds the server closest to the client. If you specify the predefined CLSCTX_SERVER (which is an OR-ing together of INPROC, LOCAL, and REMOTE) you can effectively say to SCM "Just give me the one closet to me." If SCM finds an in-proc version, you get this version. Next is local, followed by remote (resolved using the AppID).

The third parameter, COSERVERINFO, is a structure that specifies useful information about a remote server machine. Of course, if you are not accessing a remote COM server, you can simply send in NULL. The fourth and fifth parameters identify the IID of the interface you want from the coclass and a place to store it (void**).

Let's write some client code that loads up the RawComCar.dll server and returns the IClassFactory pointer for the ComCarCF coclass. Before you do so, you must copy over the MIDL-generated RawComCar_i.c and RawComCar.h files from your server project into the new this Win32 Console application (given that the client must be able to understand the IRadio, ICar, and GUID definitions). Once you have done so, you can take your car out for a test drive as follows.

```
// Client side C++ COM code.
#include "RawComCar_i.c" // Defines GUIDs.
#include "RawComCar.h"  // Defines interface definitions.

int main(int argc, char* argv[])
{
  CoInitialize(NULL);
  ICar* pCar = NULL;
  HRESULT hr = E_FAIL;
  IClassFactory* pCF = NULL;

  // Use CoGetClassObject().
  hr = CoGetClassObject(CLSID_ComCar, CLSCTX_INPROC_SERVER,
                  NULL, IID_IClassFactory, (void**)&pCF);
  hr = pCF->CreateInstance(NULL, IID_ICar, (void**)&pCar);

  // Speed up car.
  if(SUCCEEDED(hr))
  {
    for(int i = 0; i < 5; i++)
    {
      long currSp = 0;
      pCar->SpeedUp(10);
      pCar->CurrentSpeed(&currSp);
      cout << "Car Speed: " << currSp << endl;
    }
  }

  // Turn on radio.
  IRadio* pRadio = NULL;
  pCar->QueryInterface(IID_IRadio, (void**)&pRadio);
  pRadio->CrankTunes();

  // Clean up.
  if(pCar != NULL) pCar->Release();
  if(pCF!= NULL) pCF->Release();
```

```
  if(pUnk!= NULL) pUnk->Release();
  if(pRadio!= NULL) pRadio->Release();
  CoUninitialize();
  return 0;
}
```

When using CoGetClassObject(), the client is required to directly create the COM class using the returned IClassFactory interface. Once you have exercised your ComCar type, you must call Release() on each acquired interface when you are finished in order for the server's object counter to eventually reach zero (and thus be unloaded).

Accessing a Coclass Using CoCreateInstance()

Having seen CoGetClassObject() in action, you can now look at CoCreateInstance(). This function is useful if you only require a single instance of the coclass. CoCreateInstance() finds the class object and calls CreateInstance()from the IClassFactory pointer automatically. All you do is pass in the CLSID and IID you are looking for:

```
// CoCreateInstance() creates the class factory for you automatically.
HRESULT CoCreateInstance( REFCLSID rclsid, LPUNKNOWN pUnkOuter,
  DWORD dwClsContext, REFIID riid,
  LPVOID * ppv);
```

The only difference from CoGetClassObject() is the second parameter, pUnkOuter. This parameter is used only in COM aggregation. Do not worry about this now; simply pass in NULL. Because CoCreateInstance() does not provide direct access to IClassFactory, you can alter the client code using CoCreateInstance(), thus bypassing any reference to the class object. For illustrative purposes, let's ask for the IUnknown interface right off the bat. Here is the relevant update:

```
int main(int argc, char* argv[])
{
  CoInitialize(NULL);
  IUnknown* pUnk = NULL;
  ICar* pCar = NULL;
  HRESULT hr = E_FAIL;

  // Specify CLSID, context and IID (and a place to store the pointer).
  hr = CoCreateInstance(CLSID_ComCar, NULL, CLSCTX_INPROC,
                        IID_IUnknown, (void**)&pUnk);
```

```
   // Now ask for ICar.
   if(SUCCEEDED(hr))
     hr = pUnk->QueryInterface(IID_ICar, (void**)&pCar);
...
}
```

Regardless of which COM library function you use, the result is seen in Figure 2-21 followed by a message box informing you the radio has been turned on.

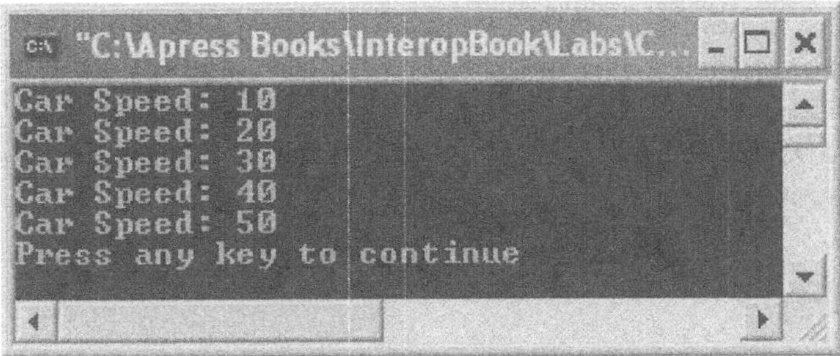

Figure 2-21. The C++ COM client

So, using this function looks a lot easier than CoGetClassObject(). Why would you not use CoCreateInstance() every time? Realize that when you use CoCreateInstance(), the class object is created and destroyed each and every time. Thus, if you are interested in creating, say, ten ComCar objects, CoCreateInstance() creates and destroys the class factory ten times. CoGetClassObject() is far more efficient when you wish to create a batch of objects, as you are directly holding the IClassFactory pointer.

Furthermore, as CoCreateInstance() does not give you back an IClassFactory pointer directly, your client could never lock the server. Whenever you wish to lock a server into memory, you must do so using an IClassFactory pointer, and thus must use CoGetClassObject().

CODE *The CppRawComClient application is included under the Chapter 2 subdirectory.*

Building a C++ Client Using the #import Directive

When developers make use of the COM library "in the raw," tradition dictates making manual calls to the methods of IUnknown, CoCreateInstance(), CoInitialize(), and other COM primitives. While this allows developers to get rather close to the action, direct manipulation to the COM API can be a bit verbose. To help lessen the burden, many C++ programmers choose to make use of the Visual C++ #import directive.

Essentially, the #import directive reads the type information of a given COM server and generates entities named *smart pointers*. These generated types wrap up the raw COM types into more convenient object instances. While I do not want to dive into a full discourse of this C++ directive, here is some sample usage (do understand that MSDN online help contains complete details of this aspect of C++ COM client programming).

```
// CppImportClient.cpp
#include "stdafx.h"
#include <iostream.h>

// Import the type info for the rawcomcar.dll (adjust your path accordingly).
#import "C:\ RawComCar\Debug\RawComCar.tlb" \
    no_namespace named_guids

int main(int argc, char* argv[])
{
  CoInitialize(NULL);

  // Create the ComCar and get ICar..
  ICarPtr spCar(__uuidof(ComCar));
  spCar->SpeedUp(10);
  cout << "Speed is: " << spCar->CurrentSpeed() << endl;

  // Now turn on the radio.
  IRadioPtr spRadio = spCar;  // Calls QueryInterface().
  spRadio->CrankTunes();

  // Clean up.
  spCar = NULL;
  spRadio = NULL;
  CoUninitialize();
  return 0;
}
```

As you may be able to tell, the generated smart pointers make C++ client-side programming look a bit more like VB 6.0 programming and a bit less like raw COM API development (depending on your view, this may be either a good thing or a bad thing). Speaking of Visual Basic 6.0...

CODE *The CppImportClient application is included under the Chapter 2 subdirectory.*

A Visual Basic 6.0 COM Client

Given that you have described the types within your C++ RawComServer.dll, you are able to build client applications using any number of languages. To illustrate, assume you have launched Visual Basic 6.0 (not VB .NET!) and created a brand-new Standard EXE application. Using the VB 6.0 ToolBox, assemble a simple GUI that allows the user to speed up the ComCar (and view the current speed) as well as turn on the radio. Figure 2-22 shows a possible UI .

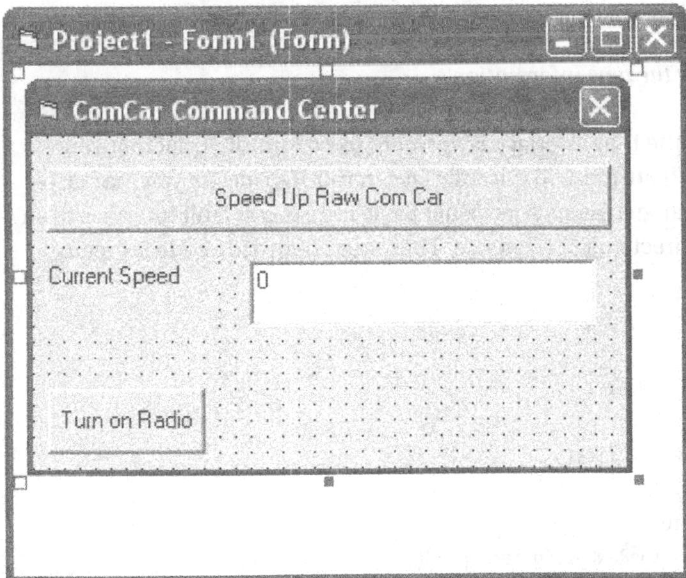

Figure 2-22. The VB 6.0 client UI

Now, before you are able to build the code base, you must set a reference to the COM server's type information using the Project | References menu option. Given that you registered the type library, you see the RawComCar library is listed alphabetically. Once you have set a reference to this type information, open the VB 6.0 Object Browser utility (F2 is the hotkey). Check out Figure 2-23.

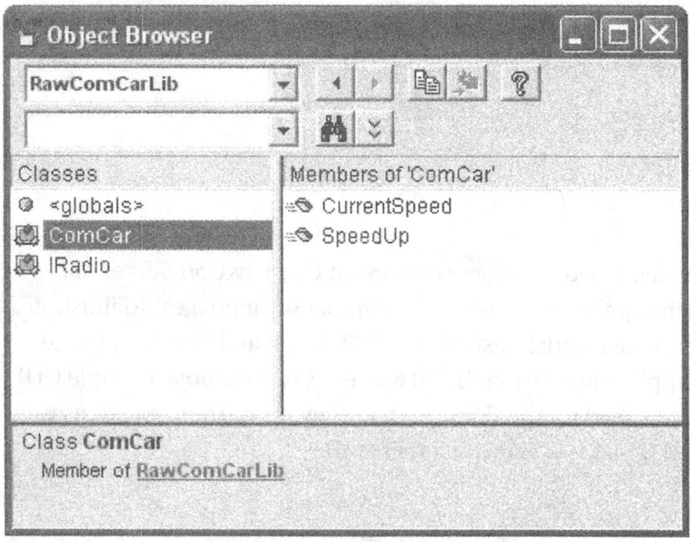

Figure 2-23. Viewing the type information

As you can see, the ICar interface is nowhere to be found! Recall that you assigned the [default] attribute to this interface in our IDL file. As you may also recall, higher-level languages such as Visual Basic hide the default interface from view to simulate a direct object reference. Thus, our client-side code is greatly simplified.

```
' The car.
Private theRawCar As ComCar

Private Sub btnUseRawCar_Click()
  ' Speed up raw car.
  theRawCar.SpeedUp 10
  txtCurrSpeed.Text = theRawCar.CurrentSpeed()
End Sub

Private Sub Form_Load()
  Set theRawCar = New ComCar
End Sub
```

```
Private Sub Form_Unload(Cancel As Integer)
  ' Explicitly decrement ref count.
  Set theRawCar = Nothing
End Sub
```

Notice that VB 6.0 client-side code hides the low-level COM library calls from view. Remember, when you create a new instance of a COM class as follows:

```
Dim o as ComCar
Set o = New ComCar  ' Really holds a reference to ICar!
```

Visual Basic automatically calls CoCreateInstance(), obtains the default interface, and stores it into the declared variable. VB 6.0 automatically calls Release() on all interfaces when they fall out of scope. However, if you wish to explicitly force a call from Release() using VB, simply set the variable to Nothing.

Finally, when you wish to trigger QueryInterface() using VB syntax, declare a variable of the type of interface you desire and set it to an active interface reference. Thus, to trigger the CrankTunes() method of IRadio from VB 6.0, you can write

```
Private Sub btnTurnOnRadio_Click()
  ' Declare an IRadio variable.
  Dim itfRadio As IRadio
  Set itfRadio = theRawCar ' Calls QueryInterface() for IID_IRadio
  itfRadio.CrankTunes
  Set itfRadio = Nothing
End Sub
```

CODE *The Vb6RawCarClient application is included under the Chapter 2 subdirectory.*

Understanding COM Properties

Until this point you have created interfaces supporting a collection of semantically-related *methods*. Beyond this, COM supports the use of *properties* in an interface definition. In a nutshell, properties are a shorthand notation for traditional accessor and mutator methods (for example, GetPetName() and SetPetName()). In Visual Basic 6.0, a class property (such as PetName) is internally represented by a pair of Property Let (or Property Set if the property wraps an object type) and

Property Get methods. The VB object user indirectly triggers the correct variation based on the calling syntax. If you, as a VB class builder, write the following code in a CLS file (named CVBCar), you can define a property (PetName) for a single private String called mName:

```
Private mName as String

' A read/write COM property.
Public Property Get PetName() as String
  PetName = mName
End Property

Public Property Let PetName(n as String)
  mName = n
End Property
```

IDL Syntax for Interface Properties

As you would expect, COM properties have a particular IDL notation. Given the previous VB 6.0 example, you can see that your single PetName property has been mapped to two separate function definitions. In IDL, the [propget] attribute marks a method as an accessor function, whereas [propput] marks a mutator. Here is the IDL generated by VB for the PetName property (you address IDispatch and the [id] attribute later in the chapter):

```
// Properties do not have to be part of an IDispatch derived
// interface!
// They can be supported by any IUnknown derived interface.
interface _CVBCar : IDispatch
{
  [id(0x68030000), propget]
  HRESULT PetName([out, retval] BSTR* );
  [id(0x68030000), propput]
  HRESULT PetName([in, out] BSTR* );
};
```

Keep in mind that COM properties are always represented internally as methods. Interfaces can *only* contain methods, and the fact that some languages support properties is not much more than "syntactic sugar" provided by COM languages.

If you write an IDL property definition by hand and examine the MIDL-generated header file, you would see two functions named put_PetName() and get_PetName():

```
// IDL property syntax.
interface ICarStats: IUnknown
{
  [propget] HRESULT PetName([out, retval] BSTR* );
  [propput] HRESULT PetName([in, out] BSTR* );
};

// A single property resolves to 'get' and 'put' functions.
STDMETHOD(get_PetName)(/*[out, retval]*/ BSTR *pVal);
STDMETHOD(put_PetName)(/*[in]*/ BSTR newVal);
```

Properties: The Client's Point of View

Clients using straight C++ access the PetName property as any other interface method (more on BSTRs in Chapter 4):

```
// Create a new car named Fred.
BSTR carName;
carName = SysAllocString(L"Fred");
pMyCar -> put_PetName(carName);
SysFreeString(carName);

// Print out name of my car.
char buff[80];
pMyCar -> get_PetName(&carName);
WideCharToMultiByte(CP_ACP, NULL, carName, -1, buff, 80, NULL, NULL);
cout << "Your car is called" << buff << endl;
SysFreeString(carName);
```

Visual Basic developers can get at the PetName property as follows:

```
' A little VB code illustrating property manipulation.
Dim myCar as New ComCar
myCar.PetName = "Fred"                          ' [propput]
MsgBox myCar.PetName, , "My car is named…"      ' [propget]
```

Building Scriptable Objects (Using IDispatch)

The final topic of this chapter is to refresh the role of IDispatch. As you have just seen, C++ and Visual Basic 6.0 are able to exercise early binding when making use of COM types. *Early binding* describes the process of understanding the calling conventions for a given interface method at compile time rather than at runtime. Using this (preferred) technique, a COM client is able to make sure that the method name and parameter format is abiding by the contract laid out in the server's type library. This is quite helpful given that any syntactic errors are found at compile time.

Other COM clients are not so fortunate in having a detailed understanding of an interface's methods at compile time for the simple reason that they are not compiled! Consider for example Web-scripting languages such as VBScript. When a Web developer wishes to make use of a COM object from an HTML or classic ASP page, the only way to do so is by using an intrinsic method named CreateObject(), which returns a loosely typed Object variable (stored in a COM VARIANT). As the late-bound client interprets the scripting code, it is at runtime that the caller is able to determine if a given method exists, and if so, whether the parameters are of the correct type and order. Obviously, this is far less robust a programming model than early binding. However, for scripting clients, this is the only option given that the external GUIDs and type information have not been compiled into the code base of the scripting engine!

When a coclass wishes to allow late-bound clients to access its functionality, it must support a standard COM interface named IDispatch. This standard COM interface allows a late-bound client to call any method or property on the object's IDispatch implementation (termed a *dispinterface*) using two well-known methods: GetIDsOfNames() and Invoke(). In addition to these core members, IDispatch defines two members of lesser importance (as far as the client is concerned) named GetTypeInfo() and GetTypeInfoCount(). The latter members are of great importance when you wish to read type information at runtime (as you will do in Chapter 4). Here is the IDL definition of IDispatch (defined in oaidl.idl):

```
[ object, uuid(00020400-0000-0000-C000-000000000046)]
interface IDispatch : IUnknown
{
  // Allows a client to see if the object can provide a type library.
  HRESULT GetTypeInfoCount( [out] UINT * pctinfo );

  // Get type information for the supporting type.
  HRESULT GetTypeInfo( [in] UINT iTInfo, [in] LCID lcid,
  [out] ITypeInfo ** ppTInfo );
```

```
  // Find the numerical ID of some method or property in the object.
  HRESULT GetIDsOfNames( [in] REFIID riid,
  [in, size_is(cNames)] LPOLESTR * rgszNames,
  [in] UINT cNames, [in] LCID lcid,
  [out, size_is(cNames)] DISPID * rgDispId );

  // Call a method or property.
  HRESULT Invoke( [in] DISPID dispIdMember,
  [in] REFIID riid, [in] LCID lcid, [in] WORD wFlags,
  [in, out] DISPPARAMS * pDispParams,
  [out] VARIANT * pVarResult,
  [out] EXCEPINFO * pExcepInfo,
  [out] UINT * puArgErr );
};
```

Table 2-5 gives a breakdown of the role of each method.

Table 2-5. The Methods of IDispatch

Method of IDispatch	Meaning in Life
GetTypeInfoCount()	This method is used by clients wishing to know if the object's functionality is described in an associated type library. This coclass fills the [out] parameter to zero (0) if the object does not support type information.
GetTypeInfo()	Allows a client to obtain type information for a given COM type.
GetIDsOfNames()	A client calls this method to retrieve a numerical cookie (termed a DISPID) that identifies the number of the method or property it is attempting to call.
Invoke()	This is the method that invokes the property or method on behalf of the client, based on the numerical cookie (DISPID) obtained from GetIDsOfNames().

Understanding Dispinterfaces and DISPIDs

A *dispinterface* is the term for a specific implementation of IDispatch by a given coclass. As a scriptable coclass exposes its functionality using a single interface, it must identify each property and method with a numerical cookie called a DISPID (dispatch identifier), which is defined in oaidl.idl as a simple LONG:

```
typedef LONG DISPID; // DISPIDs are not GUIDs.
```

If you build a COM class that can only be accessed using IDispatch (which is not typical in this day and age), you could define your dispinterface using the following IDL (note that the dispinterface keyword must be contained in a library statement):

```
 [uuid(D679F136-19C9-4868-B229-F338AE163656), version(1.0)]
library RawComCarLib
{
  [uuid(0899D87E-80FE-4e9e-A831-6FCF0A149A9B)]
  dispinterface _CarDispinterface
  {
    properties:
    methods:
    [id(1)] HRESULT PopTheTrunk(VARIANT_BOOL popIt);
  };

  [uuid(1A57D988-6A5F-4ef6-B991-7D64C51003A0)]
  coclass LateBoundOnlyCar
  {
    [default] dispinterface _CarDispinterface;
  };
};
```

Notice that when you build an IDispatch-only based COM class, you simply add all your properties and methods to the [default] dispinterface. The reason is simple: Late-bound clients can *only* access members defined by the [default]. Thus, although you could write the following IDL coclass statement:

```
[uuid(1A57D988-6A5F-4ef6-B991-7D64C51003A0)]
coclass LateBoundOnlyCar
{
  [default] dispinterface _CarDispinterface;
  interface ICantBeUsed;
  interface ICantBeUsedEither;
};
```

a late-bound client can only make use of the members defined by the IDispatch-based _CarDispinterface (by the way, the under-bar prefix is not required. It is simply a naming convention that informs various object browsers to hide this interface from view).

Obtaining DISPIDs

Because late-bound clients do not have compile-time access to a server's type information, the first step to triggering the object's functionality is to see if the type in question supports a given method. To obtain the associated DISPID for some property or method, the late-bound client sends in the textual name of the method or property it hopes the object supports by calling GetIDsOfNames(). Using this method, a late-bound client is able to obtain the numerical value of a given property or method in the dispinterface. GetIDsOfNames() takes a total of five parameters:

```
// Breaking down GetIDsOfNames().
HRESULT GetIDsOfNames(
  [in] REFIID riid,    // Reserved, and will always be IID_NULL.
  [in] LPOLESTR * rgszNames,    // Text name of method/property.
  [in] UINT cNames,    // Number of names.
  [in] LCID lcid,  // The language ID.
  [out] DISPID * rgDispId );  // Place to hold the DISPIDs.
```

The first parameter is reserved for (possible) future use, and is always IID_NULL. The second and third parameters represent the string name and the number of names requested, respectively. The fourth parameter is the "locale" requested (for example, US English). The final parameter is a place to store the numerical value of the method or property (aka, the DISPID).

Invoking the Member

Once the client knows the DISPID that identifies the property or method, a call to Invoke() may be made to actually trigger the item in the dispinterface. As you can guess, one of the parameters to Invoke() is the DISPID. Here is a breakdown of each parameter of the Invoke() method:

```
// Breaking down the Invoke() method.
HRESULT Invoke(
  [in] DISPID dispIdMember,  // DISPID of method or property.
  [in] REFIID riid, // Reserved (also IID_NULL)
  [in] LCID lcid, // Locale ID (again).
  [in] WORD wFlags, // Flag used to specify a property or method.
  [in, out] DISPPARAMS * pDispParams, // An array of parameters for the method.
  [out] VARIANT * pVarResult, // A place to store the logical return value.
  [out] EXCEPINFO * pExcepInfo, // Error information (if any).
  [out] UINT * puArgErr ); // Error information index (if any).
```

Because of the fact that a dispinterface can contain properties and/or methods, the value of the WORD parameter (wFlags) specifies if the client wants to invoke a method (DISPATCH_METHOD), a "put" version of a property (DISPATCH_PROPERTYPUT), or a "get" version of the property (DISPATCH_PROPERTYGET). Recall that an interface property is identified by two methods in the object and marked in IDL with the [propput] or [propget] attributes. Using this flag, Invoke() can call the correct get_ or put_ method in the coclass.

The DISPPARAMS structure is an array of VARIANT-compatible data types, which contains the parameters for the invoked method (you see the details of this structure in a moment). Finally, beyond the final two parameters (which are used for automation error-handling), you have a [out] parameter of type VARIANT*. This is used to hold the logical return value of the method (if any).

The VARIANT Data Type

As you can see, the DISPPARAMS structure and the VARIANT data type are interrelated. COM programmers have long been aware of a special data type termed the VARIANT. The VARIANT itself is realized in C++ as a union of all possible [oleautomation] compatible data types. Beyond specifying the union of all possible data types, the VARIANT structure also specifies a VARTYPE field. You use this field to specify what sort of thing the VARIANT represents (a BSTR, long, short, IUnknown pointer, and so forth). The definition of the VARIANT is expressed in IDL (oaidl.idl) as the following:

```
// The VARIANT structure may take on the value of any possible automation
// data type.
struct tagVARIANT {
  union {
  VARTYPE vt; // What is my current type?
    union {
    LONG     lVal;              /* VT_I4 */
    BYTE      bVal;             /* VT_UI1 */
    SHORT  iVal;                /* VT_I2 */
    FLOAT   fltVal;             /* VT_R4 */
    DOUBLE  dblVal;             /* VT_R8 */
    VARIANT_BOOL  boolVal;      /* VT_BOOL */
    _VARIANT_BOOL  bool;        /* (obsolete) */
    SCODE  scode;               /* VT_ERROR */
    CY    cyVal;                /* VT_CY */
    DATE   date;                /* VT_DATE */
```

```
        BSTR   bstrVal;              /* VT_BSTR */
        IUnknown *   punkVal;        /* VT_UNKNOWN */
        IDispatch *  pdispVal;       /* VT_DISPATCH */
        SAFEARRAY *  parray;         /* VT_ARRAY */
        BYTE *    pbVal;             /* VT_BYREF|VT_UI1 */
        SHORT *    piVal;            /* VT_BYREF|VT_I2 */
        LONG *    plVal;             /* VT_BYREF|VT_I4 */
        FLOAT *    pfltVal;          /* VT_BYREF|VT_R4 */
        DOUBLE *   pdblVal;          /* VT_BYREF|VT_R8 */
        VARIANT_BOOL *  pboolVal;    /* VT_BYREF|VT_BOOL */
        _VARIANT_BOOL * pbool;       /* (obsolete) */
        SCODE *    pscode;           /* VT_BYREF|VT_ERROR */
        CY *     pcyVal;             /* VT_BYREF|VT_CY */
        DATE *    pdate;             /* VT_BYREF|VT_DATE */
        BSTR *    pbstrVal;          /* VT_BYREF|VT_BSTR */
        IUnknown **  ppunkVal;       /* VT_BYREF|VT_UNKNOWN */
        IDispatch ** ppdispVal;      /* VT_BYREF|VT_DISPATCH */
        SAFEARRAY ** pparray;        /* VT_BYREF|VT_ARRAY */
        VARIANT *   pvarVal;         /* VT_BYREF|VT_VARIANT */
        PVOID   byref;               /* Generic ByRef */
        CHAR     cVal;               /* VT_I1 */
        USHORT    uiVal;             /* VT_UI2 */
        ULONG     ulVal;             /* VT_UI4 */
        INT      intVal;             /* VT_INT */
        UINT     uintVal;            /* VT_UINT */
        DECIMAL *   pdecVal;         /* VT_BYREF|VT_DECIMAL */
        CHAR *    pcVal;             /* VT_BYREF|VT_I1 */
        USHORT *    puiVal;          /* VT_BYREF|VT_UI2 */
        ULONG *    pulVal;           /* VT_BYREF|VT_UI4 */
        INT *     pintVal;           /* VT_BYREF|VT_INT */
        UINT *    puintVal;          /* VT_BYREF|VT_UINT */
        };
...
   };
};
```

The comments that appear in the definition of the VARIANT type are the flags used to set the underlying type of VARIANT you are working with. In essence, the VARIANT structure allows you to express any [oleautomation]-compatible data types that can be understood by all COM-aware languages. The whole of these data types is expressed as a C style union. To specify the sort of VARIANT you are defining, set the VARTYPE field of the structure using the correct VT_ flag.

Working with VARIANTs (in C++)

When you want to create a VARIANT data type in the C++ programming language, you make use of a handful of COM library functions, which shield you from the need to manage the memory associated with a given VARIANT. To create a brand-new VARIANT, you begin by defining a VARIANT variable and initialize it using the VariantInit() COM library function:

```
// Create and initialize a VARIANT in C++
VARIANT myVar;
VariantInit(&myVar);
```

At this point, you have an empty (but safe) VARIANT structure. To establish what sort of data the variant is holding (BSTR, long, short, pointer to a BSTR, and so on) you set the VARTYPE field, by specifying the correct VT_ flag. Let's say you want to create a VARIANT that starts out life as a short, which is to say VT_I2:

```
VARIANT myVar;
VariantInit(&myVar);
myVar.vt = VT_I2;
```

Next, you need to establish the value of this short, by setting the correct member in the union with an appropriate value. As you can see from the definition of the VARIANT structure, a short is identified as the iVal member of the union. Thus, to create a short with the value of 20 using the VARIANT data type:

```
VARIANT myVar;
VariantInit(&myVar);
myVar.vt = VT_I2;
myVar.iVal = 20;
```

As another example, here is a VARIANT of type long, with the value of 5000:

```
VARIANT myOtherVar;
VariantInit(&myOtherVar);
myVar.vt = VT_I4;
myVar.lVal = 5000;
```

In addition to VariantInit(), the COM library defines a set of additional functions that operate on the VARIANT data type. Some of the most common are shown in Table 2-6.

Table 2-6. VARIANT COM Library Functions

VARIANT-Centric COM Library Function	Meaning in Life
VariantInit()	Initializes a VARIANT structure.
VariantClear()	Frees up any memory consumed by the current VARIANT. This method automatically frees BSTRs, release interface pointers, and so forth.
VariantCopy()	Copies the content of one VARIANT to another VARIANT. This method also frees any memory of the destination before performing the copy.
VariantChangeType()	Sets the underlying type of the VARIANT to another type.

Working with VARIANTs (in VB 6.0)

As you would expect, all this nastiness is hidden from view when using the Visual Basic Variant data type:

```
Dim v as Variant
v = "Hello there"          ' vt = VT_BSTR
v = 100                    ' vt = VT_I4
Set v = txtCarPetName      ' vt = VT_BYREF | VT_DISPATCH
```

The DISPPARAMS Structure

Once you can create a single VARIANT, you can build the DISPPARAMS structure. Using IDispatch from a C++ client can be difficult. The trouble comes from needing to package any necessary parameters to the method in the form of an array of VARIANTS, which is represented by the DISPPARAMS structure. DISPPARAMS is defined in <oaidl.idl> as the following (do note that the VARIANTARG type is a simple typedef to the VARIANT structure):

```
// The DISPARAMS structure allows you to send over all required parameters to
// a method using one data structure.
typedef struct tagDISPPARAMS {
  [size_is(cArgs)] VARIANTARG * rgvarg;                 // Array of arguments.
  [size_is(cNamedArgs)] DISPID * rgdispidNamedArgs;     // Array of named arguments.
  UINT cArgs;          // # of items in array.
  UINT cNamedArgs;     // # of named arguments.
} DISPPARAMS;
```

More often than not, you only need to concern yourself with the first and third fields of the DISPPARAMS structure. As for the other fields, automation objects can support the idea of named arguments. The Visual Basic language allows developers to call a method and send in any required parameters in an order *different* from the one in which the method was declared. To keep things simple, I will not support any named arguments, so the values of these fields will be NULL.

The other fields of the DISPARAMS structure specify the upper bound of the array of VARIANT parameters and the array itself. If a C++ client is calling a member of a dispinterface that takes no parameters, the DISPPARAMS structure can be assembled quite easily:

```
// When you are calling a member of a dispinterface that does not require
// any arguments at all (named or otherwise) set up your DISPPARAMS as follows:
DISPPARAMS params = {0, 0, 0, 0};
```

A C++ IDispatch Example

Most members of a dispinterface do, of course, take parameters, and thus you are required to create some VARIANTS. For example, the _CarDispinterface defines the PopTheTrunk() method which takes a single VARIANT Boolean. If you call this method using C++, you would build the following DISPPARAMS structure:

```
// C++ late binding code.
void main()
{
  CoInitialize(NULL);
  IDispatch* pDisp = NULL;
  CLSID clsid;
  DISPID dispid;

  // Go look up the CLSID from the ProgID.
  CLSIDFromProgID(OLESTR("RawComCar.LateBoundOnlyCar"),&clsid);
  LPOLESTR str = OLESTR("PopTheTrunk");

  // Create object and get IDispatch...
  CoCreateInstance(clsid, NULL, CLSCTX_SERVER, IID_IDispatch,
                   (void**)&pDisp);

  // Get DISPID from object...
  pDisp->GetIDsOfNames(IID_NULL, &str, 1,
                 LOCALE_SYSTEM_DEFAULT, &dispid);
```

```
    // Build dispatch parameters.
    VARIANT myVars[1];
    VariantInit(&myVars [0]);
    myVars [0].vt = VT_ BOOL;
    myVars [0].lVal = VARIANT_TRUE;
    DISPPARAMS myParams = { myVars, 0, 1, 0};

    // Call PopTheTrunk() using Invoke().
    pDisp->Invoke(dispid, IID_NULL, LOCALE_SYSTEM_DEFAULT,
      DISPATCH_METHOD, &myParams, NULL, NULL, NULL);

    // Clean up...
    pDisp->Release();
    CoUninitialize();
}
```

Assuming that you have indeed implemented the LateBoundOnlyCar COM type (including the methods of IDispatch) and registered the server with the system, you would be able to activate and manipulate this coclass using nothing but the well-known IDispatch interface. In the previous code, notice that there are no #includes for MIDL-generated files or #imported type information. Everything is happening on the fly at runtime. For example, notice that you obtain the CLSID of the LateBoundOnlyCar dynamically using the type's ProgID (and the CLSIDFromProgID() COM library function).

A Visual Basic IDispatch Client

Although you may never need to build a C++ client that makes use of pure late binding, you hopefully have a better idea (and appreciation) what Visual Basic is doing on your behalf. For example, here is a late-bound Visual Basic 6.0 client:

```
' obj is pointing to IDispatch!
Dim obj as Object
Set obj = CreateObject("RawComCar.LateBoundOnlyCar")
obj.PopTheTrunk True
```

Understanding the Dual Interface

As mentioned, most COM classes do not support pure dispinterfaces, given that this would force all clients to interact with the type using IDispatch (which can be a pain). Objects that support *dual interfaces* provide both an IDispatch implementation as well as the set of custom COM interfaces supported by the object. In this way, early-bound clients can simply access your custom interfaces (ICar, IRadio) as expected (and by pass any dynamic lookup of DISPIDs) while the late-bound clients are still able to make use of your coclass using IDispatch.

Building a dual interface object is quite simple if you make use of the COM library. For the most part, you write the IDL to describe the dual interface and use the associated COM library calls to fill in the details of GetTypeInfoCount(), GetTypeInfo(), GetIDsOfNames(), and Invoke(). This leaves your only task to implement your interface methods as usual.

However, dual interfaces do have one very important restriction. If you build a dual interface object, every single parameter of every single method must be variant compliant (meaning, it must be able to be represented in a VARIANT structure). Just like a raw dispinterface, it is important to understand that late-bound clients are only able to access the [default] dual interface (even though it is technically possible to build a COM class with multiple [dual] interfaces).

Defining a Scriptable Object

To illustrate the use of [dual] interfaces and see a complete implementation of IDispatch, let's add a new coclass to the current RawComCar project. As with most things in COM, writing a dual interface begins with the IDL code. Defining a dual interface in IDL looks like the following (note you are defining a COM property):

```
// The IScriptableCar interface
[uuid(DBAA0495-2F6A-458a-A74A-129F2C45B642), dual, object]
interface IScriptableCar : IDispatch
{
  [id(1), propput] HRESULT Speed([in] long currSp);
  [id(1), propget] HRESULT Speed([out, retval] long* currSp);
  [id(2)] HRESULT CrankTunes();
};
```

Like any COM interface, dual interfaces are marked with the [uuid] and [object] attributes. However, you must also specify the [dual] attribute and derive your custom interface directly from IDispatch. Furthermore, each member in the dispinterface must be marked with a unique DISPID using the [id] attribute.

As you can see, [dual] interfaces are a hybrid of traditional COM interfaces and the pure dispinterface.

Now assume that you have updated your library statement to support the following coclass (notice that we are making use of the interface keyword rather than the dispinterface keyword when specifying a [dual] interface):

```
[uuid(D679F136-19C9-4868-B229-F338AE163656), version(1.0)]
library RawComCarLib
{
  importlib("stdole32.tlb");

  // The first ComCar as before…

  // Our other COM class.
  [uuid(7AD9AFC9-771C-495c-A330-006D54A23650)]
  coclass ScriptableCar
  {
    [default] interface IScriptableCar;
  };
};
```

Implementing IScriptableCar

If you insert a new C++ class named ScriptableCar, you would suddenly be in the position of implementing a total of ten methods on the type. Here is the header file:

```
class ScriptableCar : public IScriptableCar
{
public:
  ScriptableCar();
  virtual ~ScriptableCar();

  // IUnknown.
  STDMETHOD_(DWORD, AddRef)();
  STDMETHOD_(DWORD, Release)();
  STDMETHOD (QueryInterface)(REFIID riid, void** ppv);

  // IDispatch.
  STDMETHOD (GetTypeInfoCount)( UINT *pctinfo);
  STDMETHOD (GetTypeInfo)( UINT iTInfo, LCID lcid, ITypeInfo **ppTInfo);
  STDMETHOD (GetIDsOfNames)( REFIID riid, LPOLESTR *rgszNames,
                  UINT cNames, LCID lcid, DISPID *rgDispId);
```

```
  STDMETHOD (Invoke)( DISPID dispIdMember, REFIID riid, LCID lcid,
                WORD wFlags, DISPPARAMS *pDispParams,
                VARIANT *pVarResult, EXCEPINFO *pExcepInfo,
                UINT *puArgErr);

  // Members of IScriptableCar.
  STDMETHOD (put_Speed)(long delta);
  STDMETHOD (get_Speed)(long* currSp);
  STDMETHOD (CrankTunes)();

  long m_currSpeed;
  ULONG m_refCount;
  // To hold onto our type information (see below).
  ITypeInfo* m_ptypeInfo;
};
```

Like any COM class, ScriptableCar needs to implement the three methods of IUnknown. I won't bother listing this here, but check your companion code for full details (it should be no surprise that QueryInterface() is returning three possible interfaces!).

When it comes down to the process of implementing the methods of IDispatch, you have a number of possible techniques ranging from building a custom lookup table to leveraging your own type information. The simplest possible way to support IDispatch is to make use of your own type information and a small set of COM library functions as shown in Table 2-7.

Table 2-7. IDispatch Helper Functions

IDispatch-Centric COM Library Function	**Meaning in Life**
LoadRegTypeLib()	This COM library function loads a type library into memory. The returned ITypeLib interface represents this in-memory hook, and from it you are able to obtain a valid ITypeInfo interface that describes the current COM type.
DispGetIDsOfNames()	This method of the COM library maps a string name to the correct DISPID by reading your type information.
DispInvoke()	This COM library function calls a method on our C++ class based on the current DISPID.

Using these members of the COM library, you are able to equip your COM class to read its *own* type information to obtain the correct DISPID for the caller, as well as route the invocation request to a member on your C++ class type.

Notice how the ScriptableCar type maintains a private ITypeInfo interface member variable. This standard COM interface represents a pointer to a specific COM type in a loaded type library. You learn much more about this interface later in the text. Just understand for the time being that this standard COM interface allows you to read type information about a COM item at runtime.

Given the fact that ITypeInfo represents the type information for the ScriptableCar, the first step is to load the type information into memory (represented by the ITypeLib interface), and hold onto your type information using the ITypeInfo member variable. When the COM class self-destructs, you need to release the interface reference. Here is the initial update:

```
// Load our type information on start up.
ScriptableCar::ScriptableCar() : m_currSpeed(0), m_ptypeInfo(NULL),
                                 m_refCount(0)
{
  ++g_ObjectCount;

  // When our object is constructed, we are going to
  // load up the *tlb file and store it in our ITypeInfo pointer.
  ITypeLib* pTypeLibrary = NULL;
  HRESULT hr;
  hr = LoadRegTypeLib(LIBID_RawComCarLib, 1, 0,
                 LANG_NEUTRAL, &pTypeLibrary);
  if(SUCCEEDED(hr))
  {
    pTypeLibrary->GetTypeInfoOfGuid(IID_IScriptableCar, &m_ptypeInfo);
    pTypeLibrary->Release();
  }
}

// Release our type information on shut down.
ScriptableCar::~ScriptableCar()
{
  --g_ObjectCount;
  m_ptypeInfo->Release();
}
```

Now that you have a handle to your type information, the implementation of IDispatch is rather straightforward. Here is the code (with analysis to follow):

```
STDMETHODIMP ScriptableCar::GetTypeInfoCount( UINT *pctinfo)
{
  // Return type info count.
  *pctinfo = 1;
  return S_OK;
```

```
}

STDMETHODIMP ScriptableCar::GetTypeInfo( UINT iTInfo,
  LCID lcid, ITypeInfo **ppTInfo)
{
  // Return reference to our ITypeInfo interface.
  *ppTInfo = m_ptypeInfo;
  m_ptypeInfo->AddRef();
  return S_OK;
}

STDMETHODIMP ScriptableCar::GetIDsOfNames( REFIID riid,
  LPOLESTR *rgszNames, UINT cNames, LCID lcid, DISPID *rgDispId)
{
  // Now we just delegate the work of the look-up to our type library.
  return DispGetIDsOfNames(m_ptypeInfo, rgszNames, cNames, rgDispId);
}

STDMETHODIMP ScriptableCar::Invoke( DISPID dispIdMember, REFIID riid,
     LCID lcid, WORD wFlags, DISPPARAMS *pDispParams,
     VARIANT *pVarResult, EXCEPINFO *pExcepInfo, UINT *puArgErr)
{
  // Again, delegate work to the type library.
  return DispInvoke(this, m_ptypeInfo, dispIdMember, wFlags, pDispParams,
                pVarResult, pExcepInfo, puArgErr);
}
```

The implementation of GetTypeInfoCount() fills the incoming UINT to 1, which is the standard way of informing the caller that this COM object has access to its own type information (1 being the number of ITypeInfo interfaces the type is maintaining). If the client wishes to obtain access to our type information, GetTypeInfo() returns a reference to the caller.

The real point of interest is GetIDsOfNames(), which delegates the work to the COM library function DispGetIDsOfNames(). Using our type information, this function obtains the correct DISPID for the client based on the incoming string value. Invoke() is also rather simple, given that DispInvoke() will do the work of calling the correct method on the ScriptableCar based on the incoming DISPID (note that the first parameter to this COM library function is a pointer to the implementing object!).

Building the Class Factory

Given that the ScriptableCar is a creatable COM class, it must have a unique class factory to activate it. The truth of the matter is that all COM class factories have a very similar look and feel and are quite boilerplate in nature. In fact, if you copy and paste the ComCar's class factory definition (changing the name of the class of course), the only update of note is in the implementation of CreateInstance(). This time you construct a ScriptableCar type:

```
STDMETHODIMP ScriptableCarCF::CreateInstance(LPUNKNOWN pUnkOuter,
                 REFIID riid, void** ppInterface)
{
  if(pUnkOuter != NULL)
    return CLASS_E_NOAGGREGATION;

  ScriptableCar* pCarObj = NULL;
  HRESULT hr;

  // Create the scriptable car.
  pCarObj = new ScriptableCar;
  hr = pCarObj -> QueryInterface(riid, ppInterface);

  if (FAILED(hr))
    delete pCarObj;
  return hr;
}
```

The remainder of the ScriptableCarCF class is identical to ComCarCF.

Updating DllGetClassObject

Recall that the role of DllGetClassObject() is to return the correct IClassFactory interface based on the CLSID of the coclass provided by the client. Given that our COM server now contains two coclasses, you must update your previous DllGetClassObject() implementation to test against two MIDL-generated constants:

```
// Don't forget to #include "scriptablecarcf.h"
STDAPI DllGetClassObject(REFCLSID rclsid, REFIID riid, LPVOID* ppv)
{
  // Which Car do you want?
  if(rclsid == CLSID_ComCar)
    {
```

```
    ComCarCF* pCarCF = new ComCarCF();
    return pCarCF->QueryInterface(riid, ppv);
  }
  else if(rclsid == CLSID_ScriptableCar)
  {
    ScriptableCarCF* pCarCF = new ScriptableCarCF();
    return pCarCF->QueryInterface(riid, ppv);
  }
  else
    return CLASS_E_CLASSNOTAVAILABLE;
}
```

Updating the Server's Registration File

Finally, like all COM objects, you must ensure that the type is registered in the system registry. Here are the new entries to your current *.reg file (be sure to reregister this information by double-clicking the file!).

```
; Scriptable car entries.
HKEY_CLASSES_ROOT\RawComCar.ScriptableCar\CLSID
= {7AD9AFC9-771C-495c-A330-006D54A23650}

HKEY_CLASSES_ROOT\CLSID\{7AD9AFC9-771C-495c-A330-006D54A23650}
= ScriptableCar.CoCar

HKEY_CLASSES_ROOT\CLSID\{7AD9AFC9-771C-495c-A330-006D54A23650}
\InprocServer32 = C:\Apress Books\InteropBook\Labs\Chapter 2
\RawComCar\Debug\RawComCar.dll

HKEY_CLASSES_ROOT\CLSID\{7AD9AFC9-771C-495c-A330-006D54A23650}
\TypeLib = {D679F136-19C9-4868-B229-F338AE163656}
```

Building a VBScript Late-Bound Client

The point of IDispatch really hits home when you look at the process of using a COM object from an existing piece of software. Consider, for example, Microsoft Internet Explorer. Obviously, you do not have the source code for this desktop application, and therefore cannot simply #include the MIDL-generated files into the code base. Nevertheless, IE still needs to make use of the same GUIDs, member names, and type information as would an application that you constructed yourself. Using your HTML editor of choice, activate the COM type using the VBScript CreateObject() method and trigger some functionality:

```
<HTML>
  <HEAD>
    <TITLE>Document Title</TITLE>
  </HEAD>
  <BODY>
    <H1>Behold, the need for <i>IDispatch</i>.</H1>
    <SCRIPT language="VBScript">
      Dim o
      Set o = CreateObject("RawComCar.ScriptableCar")
      o.CrankTunes
      o.Speed = 100
      MsgBox o.Speed
    </SCRIPT>
  </BODY>
</HTML>
```

If you now load this file (simply by double-clicking) you find something like what you see in Figure 2-24.

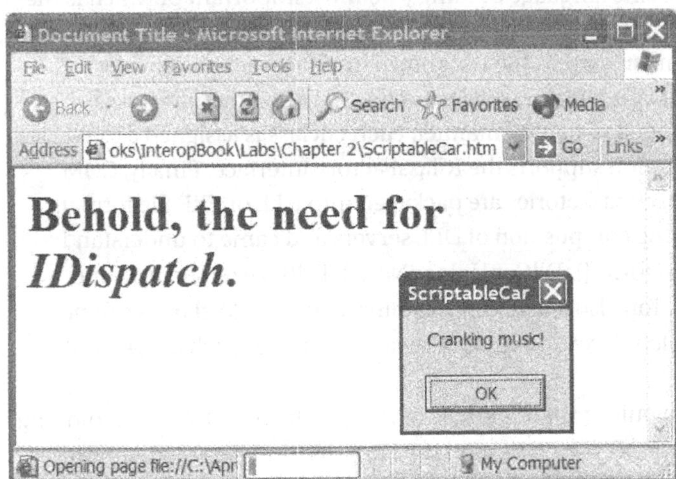

Figure 2-24. IDispatch in action

So, with this you reach the conclusion of Chapter 2. Based on your current exposure to the guts of COM, this chapter may have been quite illuminating, or a rather obvious reiteration of facts you have committed to memory long ago. In either case, I hope this chapter has clarified the core aspects of COM development. The next chapter offers a quick-and-dirty compare and contrast between two popular COM frameworks: ATL 3.0 and Visual Basic 6.0.

CODE *The ScriptableCar.htm file as well as a C++ late-bound client (CppLateBoundClient) are included under the Chapter 2 subdirectory.*

Summary

The stated goal of this chapter was to examine the internal composition of a COM DLL server. To reach this objective, you spent a good deal of time digging into the inner goo that constitutes the COM infrastructure. As you have learned, all COM types (interfaces, coclasses, enumerations, and structures) are defined in IDL. IDL, as a language-neutral way to define COM types, is sent into the MIDL compiler to produce language-specific language binding (the most important of which is the type library file).

All COM classes must support the IUnknown interface, which provides memory management and interface navigation for the implementing coclass. To be activated in a language-neutral manner, each coclass is assigned a COM class factory, which by definition supports the IClassFactory interface. Finally, COM classes and the related class factories are packaged into DLL or EXE file formats. Here, you focused on the composition of DLL servers and came to understand the role of DllGetClassObject(), DllCanUnloadNow(), DllRegisterServer(), and DllUnregisterServer(). You also spent time examining how COM classes can be activated and manipulated by various COM-aware languages such as C++ and Visual Basic 6.0.

Finally, you took a quick tour of the role of IDispatch and related late-binding atoms such as the VARIANT data type, and the ITypeLib and ITypeInfo interfaces. Using IDispatch, a late-bound client is able to invoke members on a COM type without needing to reengineer its code base to reference external dependencies (GUIDs, interface constants, and whatnot).

Now on to a (very) short course on ATL 3.0 and VB 6.0.

CHAPTER 3

A Primer on COM Programming Frameworks

The previous chapter introduced you to the process of building COM DLLs using raw C++ and IDL. Although it is illuminating to see exactly what takes place under the hood to build a COM server from the ground up, I am sure you agree that the process is tedious and error prone. In this chapter, I draw your attention to the creation of COM servers using two popular frameworks, namely the Active Template Library 3.0 (ATL 3.0) and Microsoft Visual Basic 6.0. This chapter also illustrates how to make use of a core development tool: the OLE/COM Object Viewer (oleview.exe), which will be used throughout this text.

Obviously, entire books have been written about COM development using ATL 3.0 and VB 6.0. To be sure, a single chapter cannot do justice to each COM framework. However, given that this book is all about getting the COM and .NET architecture to coexist in harmony, I feel compelled to cover the basics of each of these COM toolkits. Even if you are a seasoned veteran of ATL 3.0 and VB 6.0, I invite you to read along and build the sample applications, given that you make use of these COM servers later in the text. So without further introductory fluff, let's formalize the role of ATL.

The Role of the Active Template Library

ATL is a very popular C++ COM development framework that consists of a number of templates, magic macros, and base class types. The overall goal of ATL is to provide default boilerplate implementations for the necessary COM infrastructure (IUnknown, class factories, IDispatch, and so on), giving you more time to concentrate on the business problem you are trying to solve. Consider for example the C++ ComCar you created in Chapter 2. Although all you really wanted to do was allow the outside world to access this functionality:

```
// The essence of the ComCar.
STDMETHODIMP ComCar::SpeedUp(long delta)
{
    m_currSpeed += delta;
    return S_OK;
}
STDMETHODIMP ComCar::CurrentSpeed(long* currSp)
{
    *currSp = m_currSpeed;
    return S_OK;
}
STDMETHODIMP ComCar::CrankTunes()
{
    MessageBox(NULL, "Cranking music!", "ComCar", MB_OK);
    return S_OK;
}
```

you were required to implement the methods of IUnknown, build IDL type definitions, and construct a class factory, as well as contend with several DLL exports (not to mention register the critical server information in the system registry). If you choose to build your COM servers using C++, ATL will be a welcome addition to your programmer's bag of tricks.

Understand that even though ATL does provide stock implementations of numerous COM atoms, you are always able to extend and override this default behavior if you so choose. In any case, ATL does not exonerate you from the need to understand IDL or the constructs of COM. To illustrate the basics, you will construct an ATL DLL that mimics the functionality of the previous RawComCar.dll.

Generating the Component Housing

Every ATL project begins by making use of the ATL COM AppWizard utility, which can be activated from the File | New menu of the Visual Studio 6.0 IDE (Figure 3-1). If you wish to follow along, name your project AtlCarServer and click the OK button.

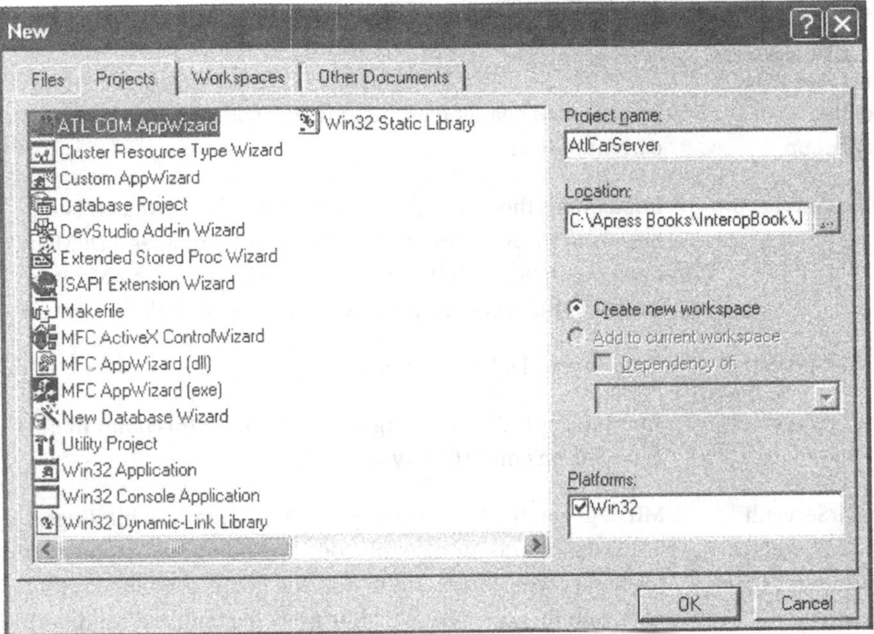

Figure 3-1. ATL projects begin here.

The ATL COM AppWizard allows you to choose among a small set of options. Most important, you are able to specify if you wish to build an in-process server (DLL) or a COM-based EXE server (used for local or remote access). For the current example, leave all the default settings to receive a new DLL. The only purpose of this tool is to generate the necessary files for a COM server. Thus, at this point you do not have any interface or coclass IDL definitions or C++ coclass implementations.

The ATL Project Files

When you create a new ATL DLL project workspace, you are provided with a number of files that represent the component housing. Table 3-1 documents the role of each file.

Table 3-1. Generated ATL Project Workspace Files

ATL COM AppWizard Generated File	Meaning in Life
stdafx.h stdafx.cpp	Precompiled header files. Includes the core ATL files into your current project.
AtlCarServer.cpp	Implements the DLL export functions for this server, enlisting help from the ATL class, CComModule. Also defines a DllMain() implementation to initialize and terminate the CComModule instance and declares the server's OBJECT_MAP data structure.
AtlCarServer.def	Exports your DLL functions.
AtlCarServer.idl	Your project's IDL file, doing nothing more at this point than declaring an empty library statement.
AtlCarServer.h AtlCarServer_i.c AtlCarServer_p.c dlldata.c. AtlCarServer.tlb	MIDL-generated files to hold your C/C++ interface bindings, GUID definitions, proxy/stub code (including DLL exports), and the binary type library. These files will not be generated until after your first compile (which triggers the midl.exe compiler).
AtlCarServer.mk AtlCarServer.def	ATL-generated makefile and DEF file used to build a custom stub/proxy DLL using the nmake.exe utility.
resource.h AtlCarServer.rc	Minimal resource files for this project.

At this point, if you view the list of global members using ClassView, you will be pleased to find that each of the required DLL exports have been implemented on your behalf (Figure 3-2).

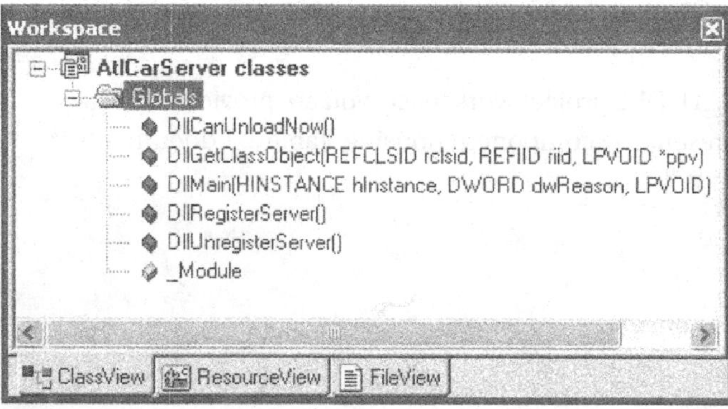

Figure 3-2. ATL autogenerates the necessary DLL exports.

Now compile this project (to run the MIDL compiler) and switch to FileView. You should now be able to see the full set of files that constitute the empty COM DLL (Figure 3-3).

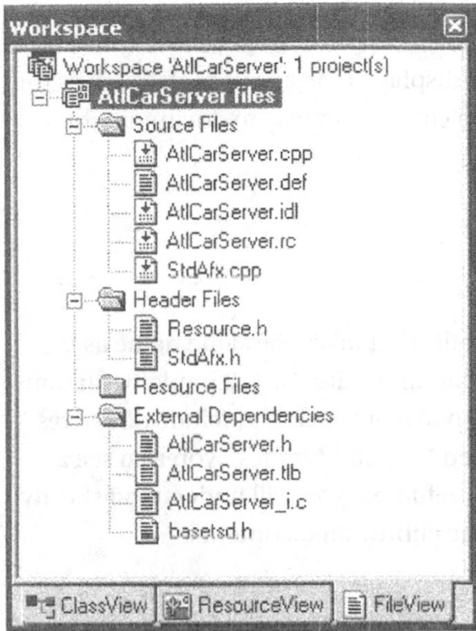

Figure 3-3. Initial project files

Although you do not need to examine the contents of each and every file, take the time to check out three important files. (I'll assume you'll investigate the remaining files in whatever level of detail you so choose.)

The Initial IDL File

If you open the generated IDL file, you will see an empty library definition, complete with a generated LIBID, version, and a new IDL attribute termed a [helpstring]:

```
import "oaidl.idl";
import "ocidl.idl";
[
  uuid(B6D55CDA-D4AA-42E5-A5E3-D3034DE6A575),
  version(1.0), helpstring("AtlCarServer 1.0 Type Library")
]
library ATLCARSERVERLib
```

```
{
  importlib("stdole32.tlb");
  importlib("stdole2.tlb");
};
```

The [helpstring] attribute may be applied to the libraries, coclasses, interfaces, and methods. These simple text strings are displayed in various tools (such as the VB 6.0 Object Browser utility) and provide a convenient way to document the functionality of your COM binary.

The AtlCarServer.cpp File

Every ATL project contains a primary *.cpp file that takes the same name as the current project. Within this C++ implementation file are the full implementations of the four required DLL exports. In addition to a number of #include directives (including references to the MIDL-generated *_i.c and *.h files), you also see a global object of type CComObject (whose usefulness you will understand shortly) and a server-wide "object map." Here are the abbreviated contents:

```
// All ATL projects have a single global CComModule…
CComModule _Module;
// …and a server-wide object map.
BEGIN_OBJECT_MAP(ObjectMap)
END_OBJECT_MAP()
extern "C"
BOOL WINAPI DllMain(HINSTANCE hInstance, DWORD dwReason,
                    LPVOID /*lpReserved*/)
{
  if (dwReason == DLL_PROCESS_ATTACH)
  {
    _Module.Init(ObjectMap, hInstance, &LIBID_ATLCARSERVERLib);
    DisableThreadLibraryCalls(hInstance);
  }
  else if (dwReason == DLL_PROCESS_DETACH)
    _Module.Term();
  return TRUE;  // ok
}
STDAPI DllCanUnloadNow(void)
{ return (_Module.GetLockCount()==0) ? S_OK : S_FALSE; }
STDAPI DllGetClassObject(REFCLSID rclsid, REFIID riid, LPVOID* ppv)
{ return _Module.GetClassObject(rclsid, riid, ppv); }
STDAPI DllRegisterServer(void)
```

```
{ return _Module.RegisterServer(TRUE); }
STDAPI DllUnregisterServer(void)
{ return _Module.UnregisterServer(TRUE); }
```

The Project's *.def File

Finally, you are provided with a properly configured *.def file that is used to expose your DLL exports.

```
; AtlCarServer.def : Declares the module parameters.
LIBRARY    "AtlCarServer.DLL"
EXPORTS
  DllCanUnloadNow       @1 PRIVATE
  DllGetClassObject     @2 PRIVATE
  DllRegisterServer     @3 PRIVATE
  DllUnregisterServer   @4 PRIVATE
```

Inserting COM Objects Using the ATL Object Wizard

Once you have established the component housing using the ATL COM AppWizard, you make use of another integrated tool, the ATL Object Wizard, when you wish to insert COM objects into the binary DLL. You can use numerous methods to activate this wizard, the simplest of which is the Insert | New ATL Object menu selection. When you make this selection, you are greeted by the dialog box in Figure 3-4.

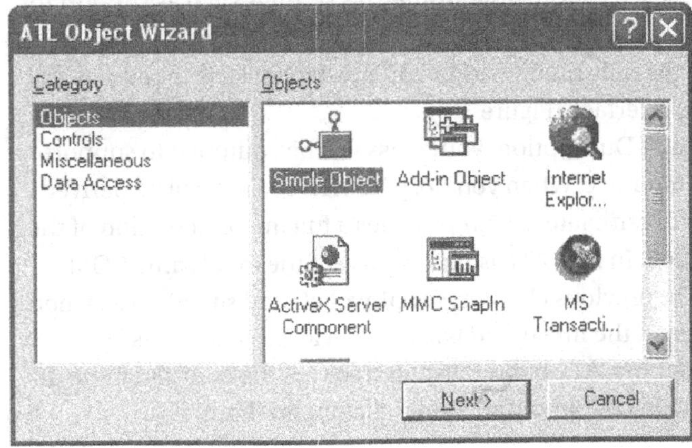

Figure 3-4. The ATL Object Wizard

As you can tell, the ATL Object Wizard defines a number of COM object types ranging from a simple coclass (Simple Object) to complete ActiveX controls (found under the Controls category). For the purposes of this example, you only need to concern yourself with Simple Object types. These COM object types are initially configured using two tabs: Names and Attributes.

The Names tab is simple enough. Here, you are able to specify the names of each generated C++ file as well as various COM atoms (such as the ProgID and name of the default interface). Insert a new type named ComCar (Figure 3-5). Notice the ProgID is based on the name of your COM server and the object you are about to insert.

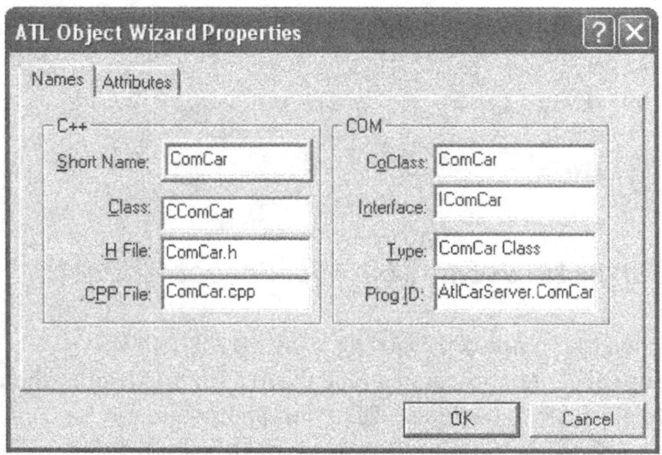

Figure 3-5. Establishing the names of your new coclass

The Attributes tab is used to configure numerous settings such as support for COM error handling, COM connection points (the COM event model), and various threading details. Here, the only modification you need to make is to select a custom rather than dual interface (Figure 3-6).

If you select the default Dual option, your class will be equipped to support the standard IDispatch interface. When you do, your ATL coclass will be derived from the IDispatchImpl<> template, which provides a full implementation of the four members of IDispatch. In fact, ATL is making use of the exact same COM library calls you did in the previous chapter (DispInvoke() and so on). Also, when you choose a dual interface, the integrated wizards will automatically assign DISPIDs to each new member. ATL hides IDispatch so well that you can more or less forget about the details and simply add your custom methods.

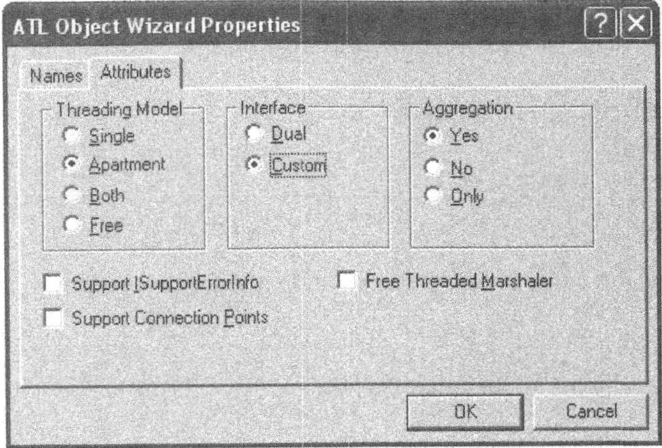

Figure 3-6. Configuring various coclass attributes

Code Updates

Once you have inserted your new Simple Object, the coclass and [default] interface will be reflected in your original IDL. Although the Object Wizard is kind enough to make this initial IDL update, don't be lulled into believing that you can forget about manually editing your *.idl files. When you wish to add support for additional COM interfaces, you will need to do so manually. Here are the relevant changes:

```
[object, uuid(16C19100-5881-40E0-8844-8C0B8436B603),
helpstring("IComCar Interface"), pointer_default(unique) ]
interface IComCar : IUnknown
{};
[uuid(B6D55CDA-D4AA-42E5-A5E3-D3034DE6A575),
version(1.0),helpstring("AtlCarServer 1.0 Type Library")]
library ATLCARSERVERLib
{
  importlib("stdole32.tlb");
  importlib("stdole2.tlb");

  [ uuid(8225387E-8453-484C-96D4-CBB4FF3A5329),
  helpstring("ComCar Class")]
  coclass ComCar
  {
    [default] interface IComCar;
  };
};
```

In addition to updating your type information, the Object Wizard also alters your server-wide "object map" with a new OBJECT_ENTRY macro.

```
// Each object in your ATL server will be listed here.
BEGIN_OBJECT_MAP(ObjectMap)
  OBJECT_ENTRY(CLSID_ComCar, CComCar)
END_OBJECT_MAP()
```

The major code updates come by way of the addition of three new source code files:

- ComCar.h: The header file for your new coclass
- ComCar.cpp: The implementation file for your new coclass
- ComCar.rgs: The registration script file for your new coclass

Let's examine each file in turn, focusing on the provided functionality.

ATL's Implementation of Your Coclass

Once of the best things about the ATL framework is that you never need to manually implement the methods of IUnknown for your COM types. The framework provides a default implementation using two core base-class templates: CComObjectRootEx<> and its immediate parent, CComObjectRoot<>. These templates work in conjunction with another entity termed the *COM map*. This may be one of the most misnamed entities in the ATL class libraries, given that the COM map is used to catalog the set of *interfaces* supported by the current COM class. Although the internal construction of the ATL COM map (and related templates) is a bit outside the scope of this text, do understand that helper functions of these templates will make calls to the COM map whenever an external QueryInterface() request is made on the object. Thus, keeping your COM map up-to-date is just as critical to the health of your COM object as manually updating the QueryInterface() of a coclass written in raw C++.

In addition to providing a default implementation of IUnknown, ATL provides a free default implementation of the IClassFactory interface. Each creatable ATL class has CComCoClass<> as a member of its inheritance chain. Nested deep within this template definition is a macro named DECLARE_CLASSFACTORY. When expanded, this macro defines a C++ class that implements IClassFactory::LockServer() and IClassFactory::CreateInstance() on your behalf. Here then is the initial header file definition of ComCar:

```
// Recall! These base class templates provide an automatic
// implementation of IUnknown and IClassFactory.
class ATL_NO_VTABLE CComCar :
  // Core IUnknown support here.
  public CComObjectRootEx<CComSingleThreadModel>,
  // Class factory defined here!
  public CComCoClass<CComCar, &CLSID_ComCar>,
  // Custom interface(s) here!
  public IComCar
{
public:
  CComCar(){}
DECLARE_REGISTRY_RESOURCEID(IDR_COMCAR)
DECLARE_PROTECT_FINAL_CONSTRUCT()
// Table driven QueryInterface().
BEGIN_COM_MAP(CComCar)
  COM_INTERFACE_ENTRY(IComCar)
END_COM_MAP()
};
```

ATL's Registration Support

Recall from Chapter 2 that a given COM server requires a good deal of system registration. If you were to build a C++ implementation of DllRegisterServer() and DllUnregisterServer(), you would have a good deal of code on your hands. Using *.reg files is a less code-intensive alternative; however, the syntax of a *.reg file is hardly friendly. One extra bit of white space (or not enough in the correct places) can cause a number of corrupt entries to be encoded under HKEY_CLASSES_ROOT. The ATL framework takes a middle-of-the-road approach using *.rgs files.

When an ATL COM server is told to register itself with the system (via regsvr32.exe or some installation software package), the implementation of DllRegisterServer() simply makes a call on the global CComModule helper class:

```
STDAPI DllRegisterServer(void)
{
  return _Module.RegisterServer(TRUE);
}
```

CComModule::RegisterServer() in turn consults the server-wide object map and walks the list of entries (that is, each OBJECT_ENTRY listing), calling each member's UpdateRegistry() method. For this example, you have a single listing in your object map for the ComCar type. Notice how the second parameter to the OBJECT_ENTRY macro is the name of the C++ class that has the implementation code for the given CLSID.

```
// The CComModule type walks the list of
// entries and tells each C++ class to register
// itself by calling the UpdateRegistry() method.
BEGIN_OBJECT_MAP(ObjectMap)
  OBJECT_ENTRY(CLSID_ComCar, CComCar)
END_OBJECT_MAP()
```

Sadly, if you look in the CComCar header file, you will not see a method named UpdateRegistry(). You should, however, notice the following macro:

```
class ATL_NO_VTABLE CComCar :
  public CComObjectRootEx<CComSingleThreadModel>,
...
{
...
  DECLARE_REGISTRY_RESOURCEID(IDR_COMCAR)
};
```

If you examine the expansion of this macro, you will see a method named UpdateRegistry(). Notice how the macro parameter (IDR_COMCAR) is passed as an argument to the CComModule::UpdateRegistryFromResource() helper function:

```
// This ATL macro expands to define UpdateRegistry()
// for your class.
#define DECLARE_REGISTRY_RESOURCEID(x)\
  static HRESULT WINAPI UpdateRegistry(BOOL bRegister)\
  {\
    return _Module.UpdateRegistryFromResource(x, bRegister);\
  }
```

So, if you are following the bouncing ball, you will see that ATL's default implementation of DllRegisterServer() calls CComModule::RegisterServer(). This method calls the UpdateRegistry() method (supplied via the DECLARE_REGISTRY_RESOURCEID macro) for each C++ class listed in the object map. The final question is, what is this magical parameter IDR_COMCAR that is passed into CComModule.UpdateRegistryFromResource()? If you examine your ResourceView tab, you will see a new custom resource folder named "REGISTRY" (Figure 3-7).

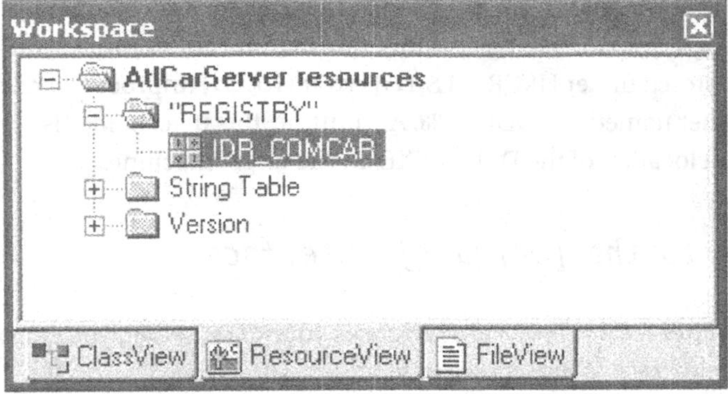

Figure 3-7. IDR_xxx is a custom resource.

These "IDR_" resources are a binary equivalent of the autogenerated *.rgs file. This file is compiled into a "REGISTRY" resource, which is then embedded in your COM DLL (or EXE). Thus, each ATL COM server has all the necessary information to register and unregister itself on demand. Here is the *.rgs file that describes ComCar:

```
HKCR
{
  AtlCarServer.ComCar.1 = s 'ComCar Class'
  {
    CLSID = s '{8225387E-8453-484C-96D4-CBB4FF3A5329}'
  }
  AtlCarServer.ComCar = s 'ComCar Class'
  {
    CLSID = s '{8225387E-8453-484C-96D4-CBB4FF3A5329}'
    CurVer = s 'AtlCarServer.ComCar.1'
  }
  NoRemove CLSID
  {
    ForceRemove {8225387E-8453-484C-96D4-CBB4FF3A5329} = s 'ComCar Class'
    {
      ProgID = s 'AtlCarServer.ComCar.1'
      VersionIndependentProgID = s 'AtlCarServer.ComCar'
      InprocServer32 = s '%MODULE%'
      {
        val ThreadingModel = s 'Apartment'
      }
      'TypeLib' = s '{B6D55CDA-D4AA-42E5-A5E3-D3034DE6A575}'
    }
  }
}
```

Even if you have never seen ATL's Registry Scripting Language, you should be able to pull out the ProgID and CLSID registration information. For example, you can see that the value stored under HKCR\CLSID\{<your GUID>}\InprocServer32 is based on a placeholder named %MODULE%. At runtime, this placeholder is replaced by the current location of the DLL or EXE on the target machine.

Adding Members to the [Default] Interface

Now that you have a better feel for how ATL composes your COM server, you can begin to add your custom logic. When you wish to add methods to a given COM interface, you certainly could make the necessary code adjustments by hand. However, ATL projects support yet another wizard to facilitate this process. Simply right-click an interface icon from ClassView and select Add Method (or if you wish, Add Property) from the context menu (Figure 3-8).

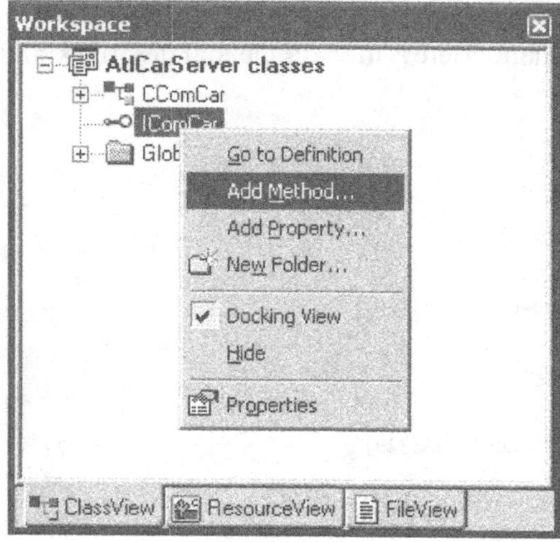

Figure 3-8. Adding methods a la ATL

The resulting dialog box prompts you for the name, return type, and parameter list of the new interface method. Be aware that all parameters are entered as IDL (so don't forget about the [in], [out], [in, out], and [out, retval] attributes). If you add the SpeedUp() method shown in Figure 3-9, you will find that your *.idl, ComCar.h, and ComCar.cpp files have been updated as follows:

```
// IDL file update.
interface IComCar : IUnknown
{
   [helpstring("method SpeedUp")] HRESULT SpeedUp([in] long delta);
```

```
};
// Header file update.
class ATL_NO_VTABLE CComCar :
    public CComObjectRootEx<CComSingleThreadModel>,
    public CComCoClass<CComCar, &CLSID_ComCar>,
    public IComCar
{
...
public:
    STDMETHOD(SpeedUp)(/*[in]*/ long delta);
};
// Implementation file update.
STDMETHODIMP CComCar::SpeedUp(long delta)
{
  // TODO: Add your implementation code here
  return S_OK;
}
```

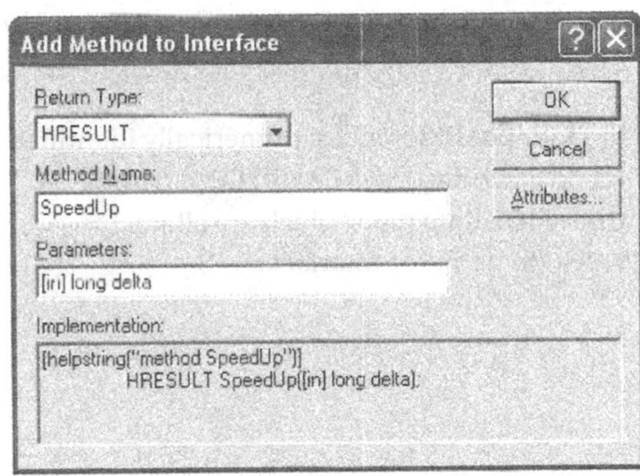

Figure 3-9. Adding interface methods

As you can see, ATL is making use of the same COM-centric macros shown in Chapter 2. Now assume you have added a private data member (m_currSpeed) to your ATL ComCar to hold the current speed. The implementation of SpeedUp() is trivial:

```
STDMETHODIMP CComCar::SpeedUp(long delta)
{
  // Speed up.
  m_currSpeed = m_currSpeed + delta;
  MessageBox(NULL,"Speeding Up", "ATL ComCar", MB_OK);
  return S_OK;
}
```

Adding a More Interesting Method

SpeedUp() is a step in the right direction for this iteration of ComCar. However, to make things a bit more enticing (and preview some additional COM types), add one more method to the IComCar interface. The TurnOnRadio() method takes a single inbound argument that just happens to be a COM enumeration. Like C(++) enumerations, the IDL enum keyword is used to define a custom user-defined type with a fixed set of name/value pairs. When defining enums in IDL, you are not required to add any IDL attributes to the enum type itself, but you are required to make use of the C typedef syntax. To illustrate, assume your IDL file now has the following COM type:

```
// IDL COM enum definition.
typedef enum RADIOTYPE
{
  EIGHT_TRACK,
  CD,
  AM_RADIO,
  FM_RADIO
} RADIOTYPE;
```

The RADIOTYPE enumeration has four possible values, numerically identified as {0, 1, 2, 3}. The TurnOnRadio() method can now take a RADIOTYPE parameter in the exact same manner as any intrinsic IDL data type (which are all fully defined in the next chapter). Here is the updated ICar interface:

```
interface IComCar : IUnknown
{
  [helpstring("method SpeedUp")]
  HRESULT SpeedUp([in] long delta);
  [helpstring("method TurnOnRadio")]
  HRESULT TurnOnRadio([in] RADIOTYPE make);
};
```

When this IDL file is processed by the MIDL compiler, the IDL enumeration is embedded in the type library and is therefore usable by any COM-aware language. C++ clients (as well as the COM server) can also opt to make use of the definition placed in the MIDL-generated header file:

```
// MIDL-generated C++ enum definition.
typedef enum RADIOTYPE
{  EIGHT_TRACK = 0,
   CD = EIGHT_TRACK + 1,
   AM_RADIO = CD + 1,
   FM_RADIO = AM_RADIO + 1
}RADIOTYPE;
```

To flesh out the details of the TurnOnRadio() method, you can take the easy route and display a message based on the value of the client-supplied RADIOTYPE:

```
// Play some tunes.
STDMETHODIMP CComCar::TurnOnRadio(RADIOTYPE make)
{
  switch(make)
  {
  case EIGHT_TRACK:
    MessageBox(NULL, "Upgrade your system!", "ATL ComCar", MB_OK);
  break;
  case CD:
    MessageBox(NULL, "Good choice...", "ATL ComCar", MB_OK);
  break;
  case AM_RADIO:
    MessageBox(NULL, "Sports talk radio on!", "ATL ComCar", MB_OK);
  break;
  case FM_RADIO:
    MessageBox(NULL, "Top 40 crap on...", "ATL ComCar", MB_OK);
  break;
  }
  return S_OK;
}
```

You'll see your COM enum in action a bit later in this chapter.

Supporting Additional COM Interfaces

The final ATL topic I address here is how to add additional COM interfaces to an ATL-based coclass. The process begins by writing an empty interface definition in your IDL file. Once the interface has been defined, you must add it to the list of supported interfaces for each implementing coclass. For example:

```
[object,
uuid(E98B898C-5C0A-4318-AFCB-541695E4945D),
helpstring("This interface floors it")]
interface ITurbo: IUnknown
{
};
[uuid(2EE867E1-C237-48FC-B6C7-D2804FB52C68),
version(1.0), helpstring("AtlCarServer 1.0 Type Library")]
library ATLCARSERVERLib
```

```
{
...
  coclass ComCar
  {
    [default] interface IComCar;
    interface ITurbo;
  };
};
```

You now need to compile your IDL file once again to correctly activate the Implement Interface Wizard utility. To do so, right-click the CComCar icon in ClassView (Figure 3-10).

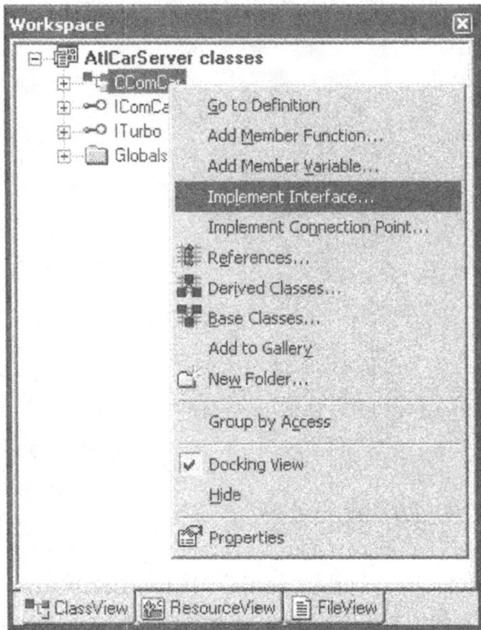

Figure 3-10. Activating the Implement Interface Wizard

The resulting dialog box lists each IDL interface that is currently *not* supported by the C++ ATL coclass. Once you check off support for ITurbo (Figure 3-11), you see the following source code modifications:

- The new interface has been added to the class' inheritance chain.
- The class' COM map has been updated with a new COM_INTERFACE_ENTRY listing.

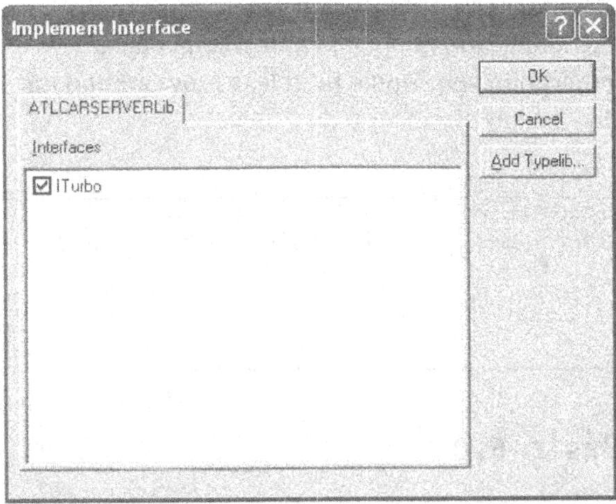

Figure 3-11. Supporting a new COM interface using ATL

Here are the relevant code updates:

```
// After running the wizard, your ATL coclass is
// equipped to return the new interface.
class ATL_NO_VTABLE CComCar :
  public CComObjectRootEx<CComSingleThreadModel>,
  public CComCoClass<CComCar, &CLSID_ComCar>,
  public IComCar,
  public ITurbo
...
BEGIN_COM_MAP(CComCar)
  COM_INTERFACE_ENTRY(IComCar)
  COM_INTERFACE_ENTRY(ITurbo)
END_COM_MAP()
```

At this point, you can make use of the Add Method tool as before:

```
STDMETHODIMP CComCar::TurboBlast()
{
  MessageBox(NULL, "Turbo blast!!", "ATL ComCar", MB_OK);
  return S_OK;
}
```

So, that wraps up this rapid-fire tour of developing basic COM servers with ATL. As I am sure you would agree, ATL greatly simplifies the creation of C++-based COM servers. Obviously, there is a great deal more to ATL than what I have covered here. You will see additional aspects of ATL when you examine COM connection points, COM error handling, and the COM enumeration object (IEnumXXXX). Nevertheless, at this point you should be able to move around the ATL framework a bit more fluidly.

CODE *The AtlCarServer application is included under the Chapter 3 subdirectory.*

The Role of Visual Basic 6.0

ATL is a vast improvement to the raw C++/IDL development cycle, yet it poses one minor problem (depending on your point of view): ATL still uses C++. To be frank, C++ will never win an award for the most elegant programming language (or most user friendly, or most intuitive, or . . .). C++ is a powerful language, and when you need to build a very complex COM server that makes use of numerous advanced techniques such as tear-off interfaces, COM categories, custom marshaling, and so forth, C++ is an absolute necessity. However, when it comes to raw productivity, nothing comes close to Visual Basic 6.0.

When developers build COM servers using VB 6.0, they are making a conscious choice to focus on nothing but the business logic of the current problem domain. As alluded to in the previous paragraph, VB COM servers are unable to take advantage of advanced COM programming patterns. Likewise, VB 6.0 does not allow you to directly establish GUID values, edit (or alter) the generated IDL code, or participate in exotic COM threading models. Nevertheless, VB 6.0 is the most popular COM development paradigm in use, given that many applications don't *need* to use these advanced features in the first place. To see just how simple building a COM server can be, let's re-create the essence of ComCar from the cozy confines of VB 6.0.

Building COM Servers Using Visual Basic 6.0

Visual Basic supports two core project workspace types used to build in-proc or local (and remote) COM servers: ActiveX DLLs and ActiveX EXEs (see Figure 3-12).

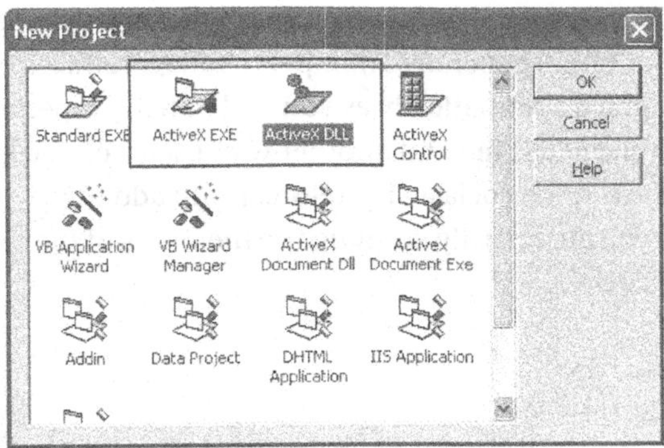

Figure 3-12. Core VB 6.0 COM project types

Having chosen an ActiveX DLL project workspace, you will be presented with a single *.cls file. Unlike most programming languages, VB 6.0 does not support specific language keywords that are used to build class and interface definitions. Rather, each COM type is placed in a *.cls file (as you may be aware, VB .NET does support specific keywords). To begin, change the name of this initial class type to CoCar using the (Name) property in the Properties window (Figure 3-13).

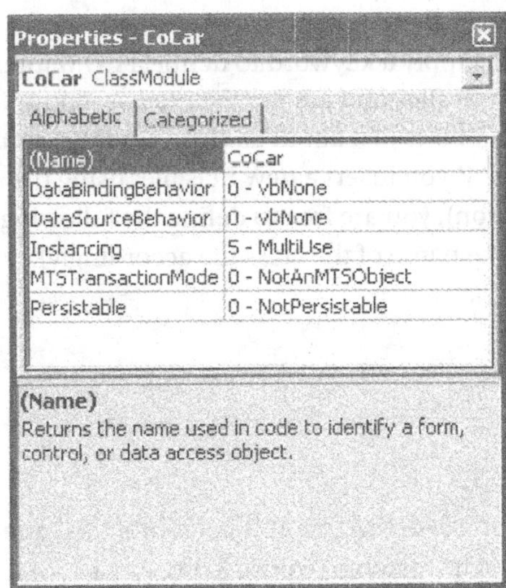

Figure 3-13. Naming your coclass

As you learned in the previous chapter, COM development demands the use of interfaces. However, given that VB 6.0 generally attempts to hide interfaces from view, you receive a [default] interface automatically as you add Public properties, functions, and subroutines to a given *.cls file. Put another way, each *.cls file is expressed as the [default] interface of the coclass. Therefore, if you add the following VB code to CoCar.cls, you are actually defining the members of the [default] interface of the CoCar coclass.

```
Option Explicit
' Define class level variables in the
' [General][Declaration] section.
Private mCurrSpeed As Long
Public Property Get Speed() As Long
  Speed = mCurrSpeed
End Property
Public Property Let Speed(delta As Long)
  mCurrSpeed = mCurrSpeed + delta
End Property
```

Defining Auxiliary Interfaces

As mentioned, Visual Basic 6.0 does not supply a keyword to define a COM interface. Rather, interfaces are placed into *.cls files and are represented as empty method (or property) implementations. This is just about as close as VB 6.0 comes to the concept of a pure virtual function. If you insert a new *.cls file (using the Project | Add Class Module menu selection), you are free to define the following IVBTurbo interface (be sure to change the name of the class file accordingly):

```
' A VB 6.0 interface definition
Option Explicit
Public Sub TurboBlast()
End Sub
```

When you are building a VB 6.0 interface definition, it is good practice to set the type's Instancing property to PublicNotCreatable (Figure 3-14).

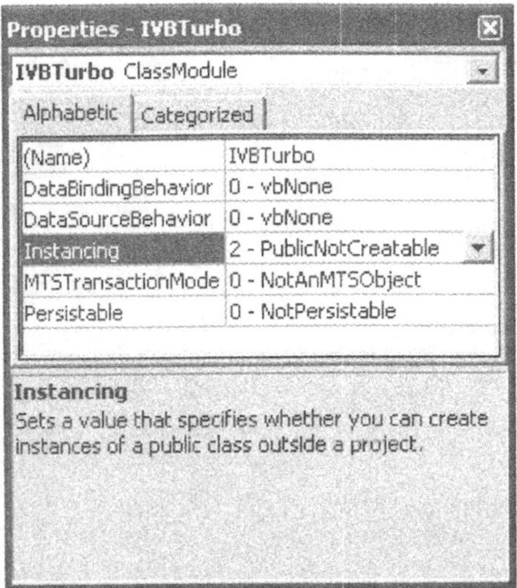

Figure 3-14. Interfaces should not be directly creatable.

This is considered good practice because it will prevent the COM client from directly "New-ing" the interface. Any attempt to do so will result in a compiler error:

```
' PublicNotCreatable types cannot be directly created!
Dim itfIVBTurbo as New IVBTurbo   ' Nope!
```

Implementing Interfaces in VB 6.0

When you wish to implement additional interfaces on an existing COM type, make use of the Implements keyword. Note that Implements definitions must appear in the [General] [Declarations] section of a given *.cls file. Once you have specified which behaviors your coclass supports, you may make use of the VB 6.0 IDE to generate stub code for each member of a particular interface. Simply select the interface (by name) from the left-hand drop-down list and each interface member from the right-hand drop-down list. The finished product is shown in Figure 3-15.

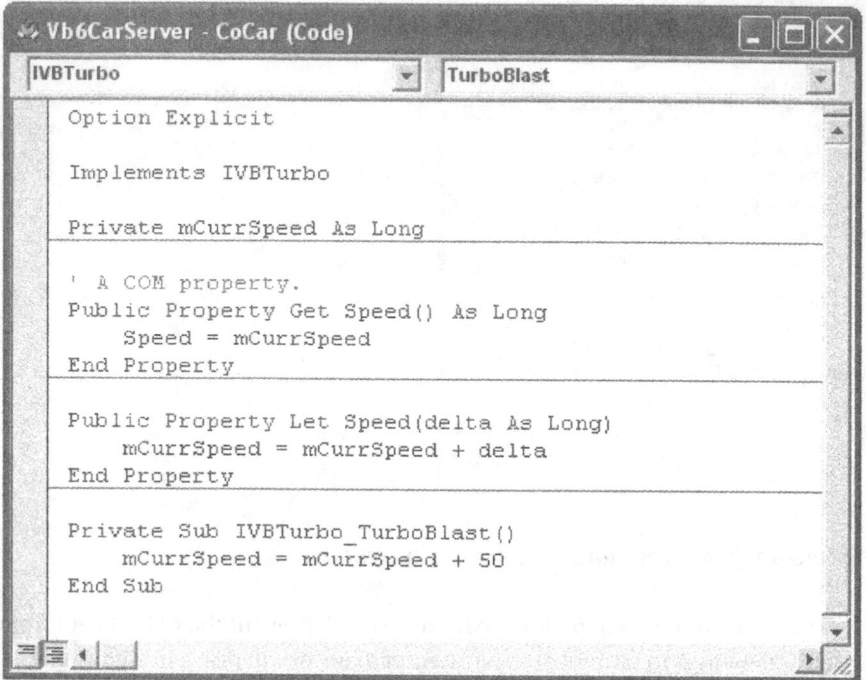

Figure 3-15. The completed VB 6.0 CoCar

When you make use of the VB 6.0 IDE to generate default stub code, notice that the members are declared as Private rather than Public:

```
' This seems strange…
Private Sub IVBTurbo_TurboBlast()
  mCurrSpeed = mCurrSpeed + 50
End Sub
```

The reason for this is simple. If you declare this type as Public, you will suddenly have a member named IVBTurbo_TurboBlast() as a member of the [default] public interface! In such a case, the object user would need to make use of the following oddball syntax:

```
' Yuck.
Dim c3 as CoCar
Set c3 = New CoCar
c3.IVBTurbo_TurboBlast
```

By defining the TurboBlast() method of the IVBTurbo interface as Private, you force the user to obtain the IVBTurbo interface explicitly:

```
' Better.
Dim c4 as CoCar
Set c4 = New CoCar
Dim iftIVBTurbo as IVBTurbo
Set iftIVBTurbo = c4
IftIVBTurbo.TubroBlast
```

At this point, you are free to compile your VB 6.0 COM server using the File | Make menu selection. Notice that you don't need to manually create any IDL definitions. Also notice that each DLL export and the required class factory have been supplied on your behalf.

As a final positive note, VB 6.0 will automatically register this COM server on your development machine as part of the compilation cycle (thus you can hunt down the registration entries using regedit.exe).

Setting Binary Compatibility

I have one final point to make regarding VB 6.0 COM development. Because VB is attempting to simplify the creation of COM servers, GUIDs are assigned automatically behind the scenes. In fact, each time you compile your project, VB 6.0 will generate *new GUIDs* for your COM types! This is obviously a huge annoyance, given that any existing clients using this COM server are effectively broken.

To prevent this GUID generation madness from occurring, get in the habit of enabling binary compatibility as soon as you have performed your first compile. When you do so, VB will stop generating new GUIDs and freeze the current identifiers. If you attempt to alter the definition of any interface, you will be warned through a series of dialog boxes. To specify this type of version compatibility, choose the Binary Compatibility option in the Project Properties dialog box (Figure 3-16).

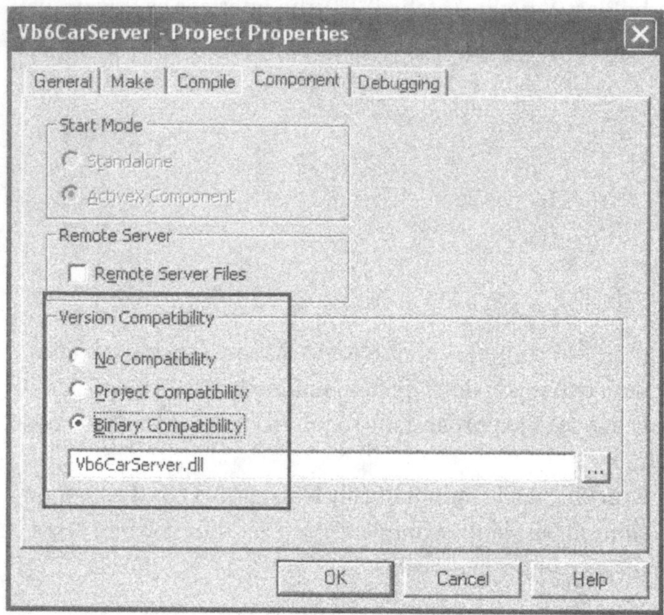

Figure 3-16. Freezing the current GUID values

Viewing the Generated IDL Using Oleview.exe

To prove that the VB 6.0 IDE is maintaining the same binary standard as a COM server created using C++ or ATL, you need to be introduced to the oleview.exe utility. This tool, which ships with Visual Studio, allows you to investigate the set of registered COM servers on your development machine. Using oleview.exe, you are able to view the set of interfaces supported on a given object (provided the interface has been registered under HKCR\Interface), the underlying IDL, and the numerous registration entries for the COM binary. Figure 3-17 shows the set of expandable nodes.

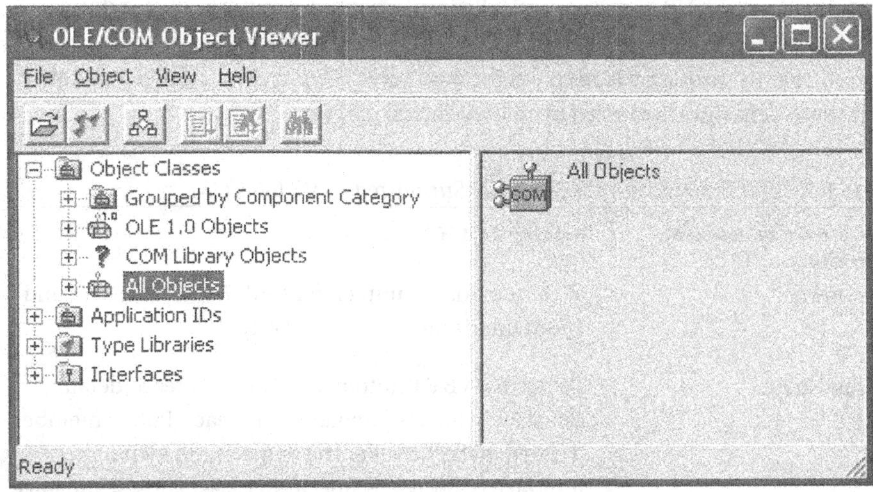

Figure 3-17. The oleview.exe utility

The most important node in this instance is the All Objects category. Once you expand this node, you will be able to find the CoCar and IVBTurbo types listed alphabetically by ProgID (Figure 3-18).

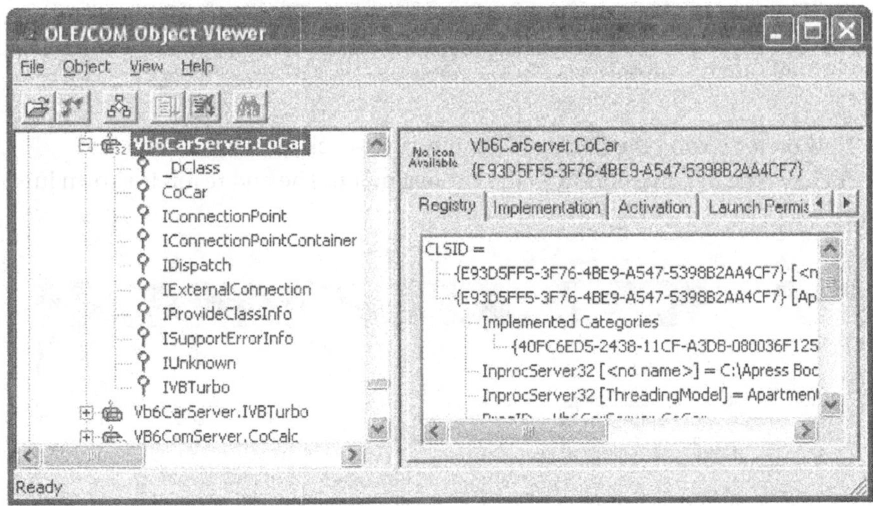

Figure 3-18. Locating your VB 6.0 COM types

As you can see, VB has automatically implemented a number of standard COM interfaces on the CoCar type. You will get to know the role of these interfaces as you progress through the text, but for now Table 3-2 provides a quick rundown of the core behaviors (grouped by related functionality).

Table 3-2. COM Interfaces Automatically Supported by VB 6.0 COM

VB 6.0 Autoimplemented Interface	Meaning in Life
IUnknown	VB automatically implements AddRef(), Release(), and QueryInterface() for each COM type.
<_ClassName>	Recall that VB 6.0 automatically generates a [default] interface, which is populated with each Public member defined in the *.cls file. The name of the [default] interface is always _NameOfTheClass. Thus, if you have a class named CoCar, the default interface is _CoCar.
IConnectionPointContainer IConnectionPoint	These two interfaces allow a COM class to send events to a connected client.
IDispatch IProvideClassInfo	Provide late-binding capabilities. Required for late-bound scripting languages such as VBScript.
ISupportErrorInfo	Allows a COM class to send COM "error" objects to report a processing error.

Now on to viewing the IDL itself. Simply right-click the coclass icon and select View Type Information from the context menu. The end result is shown in Figure 3-19.

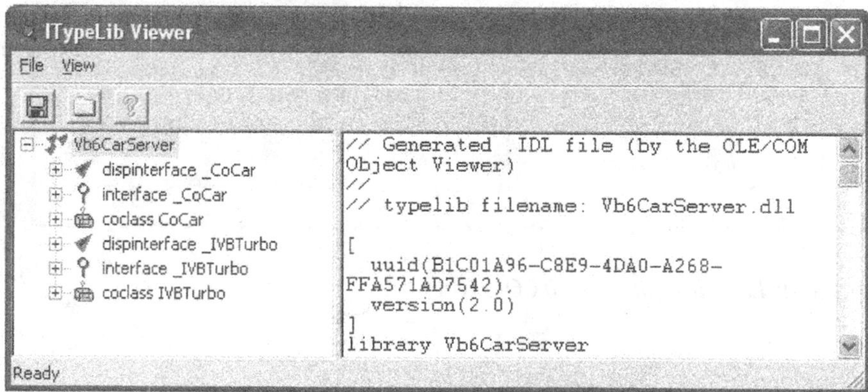

Figure 3-19. Viewing the IDL

If you select the CoCar type, you will see an IDL definition that should look quite familiar at this point.

```
// The VB CoCar type definition.
[ uuid(E93D5FF5-3F76-4BE9-A547-5398B2AA4CF7),
version(1.0)]
coclass CoCar {
  [default] interface _CoCar;
  interface _IVBTurbo;
};
```

Here, you can see that the [default] interface is indeed _CoCar. This interface defines a single COM property. As you may remember, COM properties are defined using the [propget] and [propput] IDL keywords.

```
// The [default] interface.
[ odl, uuid(BFC753BA-4CEB-4682-BD63-8973D3CB2186),
 version(1.0), hidden, dual,
 nonextensible, oleautomation ]
interface _CoCar : IDispatch {
  [id(0x68030000), propget]
  HRESULT Speed([out, retval] long* );
  [id(0x68030000), propput]
  HRESULT Speed([in, out] long* );
};
```

You can see from the _CoCar IDL definition that VB 6.0 always creates dual interfaces, which by definition support the [dual] interface and are derived directly from IDispatch rather than IUnknown. As mentioned in Chapter 2, this core COM interface provides a way for late-bound clients (such as scripting clients) to determine the functionality of a COM class at runtime.

The auxiliary IVBTurbo interface is not directly listed in the coclass statement, however. Rather, an intermediate interface, _VBTurbo, is listed, and it has the following IDL definition:

```
[ odl, uuid(0FE9EC86-7959-42CA-97B3-61B14214718D),
 version(1.0), hidden, dual, nonextensible,
 oleautomation]
interface _IVBTurbo : IDispatch {
  [id(0x60030000)] HRESULT TurboBlast();
};
```

While examining the remaining IDL definitions, also notice that VB has assembled a COM library statement listing each type, as well as a raw dispinterface definition for each COM interface. In the next chapter, I drill much deeper into the world of COM type information. For the time being, simply understand that VB 6.0 manually generates the correct COM metadata.

CODE *The Vb6CarServer project is included under the Chapter 3 subdirectory.*

Making Use of Your COM Servers

To test the functionality of your ATL and VB 6.0 COM servers, you wrap up by creating a new standard EXE VB application. As always, before you can use the COM types created in a separate binary file, you must set references to the COM type information (Figure 3-20).

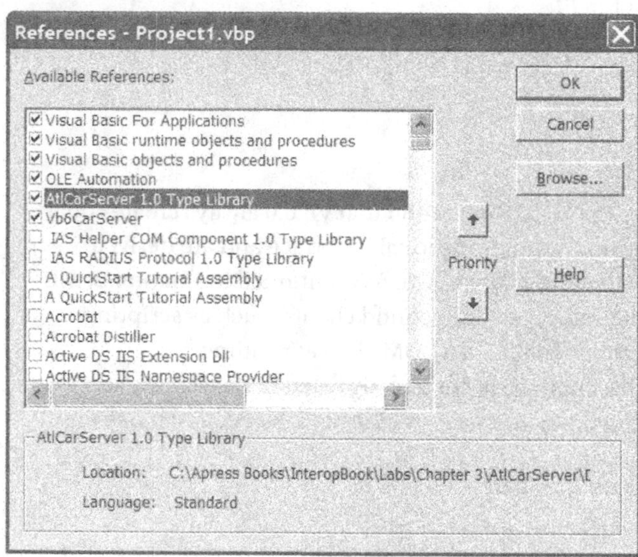

Figure 3-20. Setting references to the COM type libraries

If you examine the Object Browser (Figure 3-21), you will see that the COM enumeration you defined in your ATL server project has mapped correctly to the Visual Basic language (observe as well that the various [helpstrings] are displayed in the lower pane of the tool).

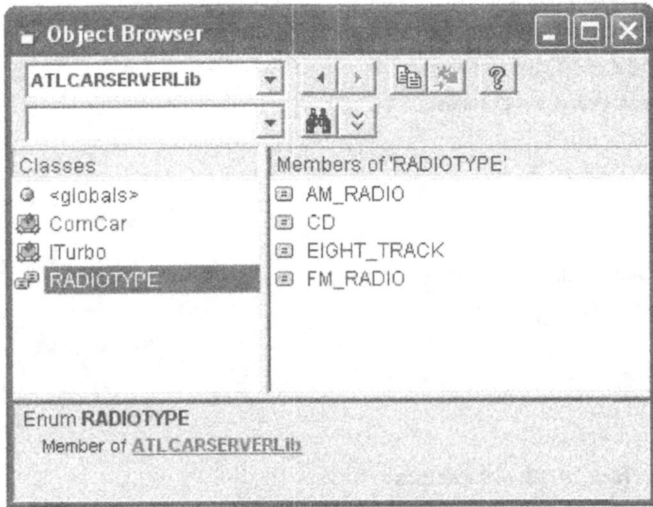

Figure 3-21. Viewing IDL COM types

The user interface of your VB client is short and sweet. As shown in Figure 3-22, you are simply providing a way for the client to activate the ATL ComCar and VB 6.0 CoCar.

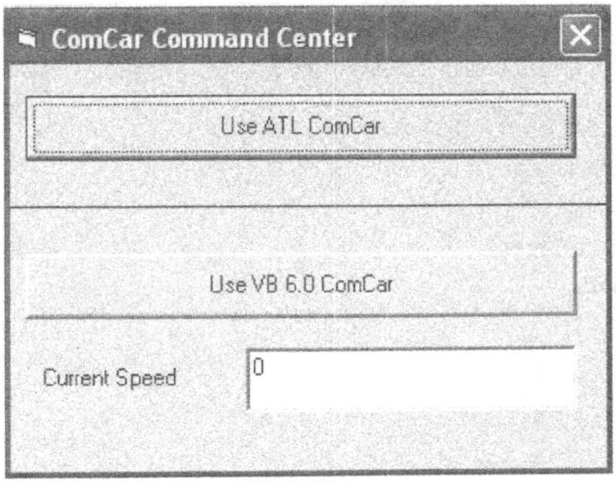

Figure 3-22. Another COM client

As for the code, things look much like they did when you accessed your RawComCar types in Chapter 2. Here is the complete code behind the VB form:

```
Option Explicit
' The cars.
Private vbCar As Vb6CarServer.CoCar
Private atlCar As ATLCARSERVERLib.ComCar
Private Sub btnATLCoCar_Click()
  ' Speed up ATL car and crank some tunes.
  atlCar.SpeedUp 10
  atlCar.TurnOnRadio AM_RADIO

  ' Get ITurbo.
  Dim itfTurbo As ATLCARSERVERLib.ITurbo
  Set itfTurbo = atlCar
  itfTurbo.TurboBlast
  Set itfTurbo = Nothing
End Sub
Private Sub btnUseVb6Car_Click()
  ' Use [default] interface of VB 6.0 coclass.
  vbCar.Speed = vbCar.Speed + 10

  ' Get IVBTurbo
  MsgBox "Turbo boosting", , "Message from Car Command..."
  Dim itfVbTurbo As IVBTurbo
  Set itfVbTurbo = vbCar
  itfVbTurbo.TurboBlast
  txtCurrVbSpeed.Text = vbCar.Speed
  Set itfVbTurbo = Nothing
End Sub
Private Sub Form_Load()
  Set vbCar = New Vb6CarServer.CoCar
  Set atlCar = New ATLCARSERVERLib.ComCar
End Sub
Private Sub Form_Unload(Cancel As Integer)
  ' Explicitly decrement ref counts.
  Set vbCar = Nothing
  Set atlCar = Nothing
End Sub
```

CODE *The Vb6CarsClient application is included under the Chapter 3 subdirectory.*

Excellent! At this point, you have learned the basic process of building COM servers using raw C++, the Active Template Library, and Visual Basic 6.0. Better yet, you now have a total of three COM servers that you make use of through various .NET-aware languages later in this text.

Summary

This chapter and the preceding one have guided you through the process of building three COM servers, beginning with the most complex (but most powerful) technique of using raw C++/IDL. The Active Template Library (ATL) attempts to lessen the burden of C++ COM server development by defining a number of base-class templates (and integrated wizards). Visual Basic 6.0 is far and away the least painful approach to COM server development, given that VB hides the low-level COM grunge from view. Now that you have seen the process of building various COM servers, the next (and final) COM-centric chapter drills into the type system of classic COM.

CHAPTER 4

COM Type Information

The previous two chapters were more concerned with the internal composition of COM in-process servers than the finer details of IDL (or COM type information in general). Understanding COM type information is critical when exploring the issues behind COM and .NET interoperability for one simple reason: When a .NET type attempts to access a legacy COM type, an intermediate object (termed a Runtime Callable Wrapper, or simply RCW) is responsible for translating between COM types and .NET types. For example, COM SAFEARRAY types map into the .NET System.Array class, COM BSTR types map into System.String, and so on. A similar operation occurs when a .NET type makes use of a legacy COM type (using an intervening COM Callable Wrapper, or simply CCW). Because IDL types are mapped into managed equivalents (and vice versa), this chapter pounds out the finer details of COM IDL.

In this chapter, you not only solidify the set of core COM types and intrinsic data types, but you also learn how to generate COM type information *at runtime*. The COM library contains a small set of interfaces, functions, and data structures that allow developers to generate COM type information on the fly, and save out the resulting *.tlb file to storage. It is also possible to build applications that are capable of reading type information at runtime (think the VB 6.0 Object Brower utility).

Just in case you are thinking that the topics of dynamically reading and writing COM type information are obsolete with the advent of .NET, understand that the System.Runtime.InteropServices namespace defines a good number of members that expose identical functionality using managed types. Therefore (hang onto your hat) it is completely possible to build a .NET application that emits and reads COM type libraries (!). In fact, you explore this very topic during the second half of this chapter.

As a friendly heads-up, understand that the only unmanaged language that is directly capable of dynamically writing and reading COM IDL is (alas) C++. For my fellow Visual Basic friends not familiar with C++, and who may not be thrilled with another chapter of pointer arithmetic, just grin and bear it for the time being.

The Format of a COM IDL File

To open this chapter, I want to ensure that you are comfortable with the overall structure of an IDL file. In general, an IDL file can be stratified into two regions: the library statement and everything else outside the library statement. To be specific, if a given COM type is only defined outside the IDL library statement, you have created an item that is only usable from the C(++) COM language mapping. Be aware that it is the case that some IDL constructs (such as cpp_quote and const) are only valid outside an IDL library statement in the first place and (therefore) are only applicable to C(++) COM projects. On the other hand, any type that is referenced (or explicitly defined) within a library statement is visible from any COM-aware language mapping (provided that the language in question honors the IDL). Here then, is the general layout of an IDL file:

```
/***** MyIDL.idl *****/
// Bring in core IDL definitions.
#import "oaidl.idl";

// Items outside of the library statement
// will be placed in the MyIDL_i.c and
// MyIDL.h C(++) files. If these items are
// not referenced within the library statement,
// they will not be part of the type library!

// The library statement.
[uuid(<some GUID>), version(<major.minor>)]
library MyIDL_Library
{
  // Bring in any standard COM
  // definitions using importlib().
  importlib("stdole32.tlb");

  // Any item referenced or defined within
  // the library will be placed
  // within the *.tlb file,
  // and (typically) usable from all
  // COM language mappings.
};
```

Recall from Chapter 2 that type information defined outside an IDL library statement is placed in the MIDL-generated *_i.c and *.h files. The *_i.c file contains C(++)-friendly GUID constants that are created based on the [uuid] value of each item. The *.h file contains C(++)-friendly interface definitions. Clearly, these two files will be used during the construction of a C(++) COM server as well as a C(++) COM client.

Although a library statement is not a mandatory requirement of a well-formed IDL file, as far as the language-independent nature of COM is concerned, a given COM type is only usable if (and only if) it is accounted for within the library statement. Even if you define dozens of elaborate COM interfaces, enums, and structures outside a library statement (and fail to reference the item within the library statement), they will be unreachable from any language other than C(++).

The IDL library statement itself must be qualified with the [uuid] attribute (which functions as the LIBID for the type information) at minimum. In addition, most type libraries support a [version] attribute that is of the form <Major.Minor> (if you do not specify a [version] attribute, the default version is <0.0>). As you are aware, whenever you update a type library that is in production, the numerical version should be updated and reregistered on each target machine.

Defining COM Types

As you have seen over the course of the previous two chapters, COM is all about coclasses and their supported interfaces. In COM IDL, the coclass and interface keywords are used to define these core types. However, COM also defines additional data types that may (or may not) be recognized in a given COM-aware programming language. When I speak of COM types I am not referring to COM data types. Simply put, COM types are the set of custom user defined types (UDTs) that you can express using IDL syntax. COM data types, on the other hand, represent a set of intrinsic data members (int, long, BSTR and so forth) that you can send between COM binaries as method parameters or as building blocks for other COM types (such as enums and structures).

To make things a bit more intriguing, understand that you can also create COM interface methods that take other COM types as method parameters (as seen in the previous chapter when you examined COM enumerations). Table 4-1 defines the core set of COM types.

Table 4-1. COM Types

COM Type	IDL Keyword	Meaning in Life
Interface	interface	By now you should understand that the COM universe demands that clients and server objects communicate using interface references (the same is not true for .NET). An interface is little more than a named set of semantically related methods that ultimately derive from IUnknown.
Coclass	coclass	A coclass is simply a concrete implementation of some number of interfaces.
Enumerations	enum	Enumerations are a way to programmatically express a range of name/value pairs. Using enums, you are able to avoid cluttering your global namespace with magic numbers.
Structures and Unions	struct union	Structures can best be understood as a lightweight class type. Specifically, structures are a collection of disparate data types bound under a shared name. C(++) style unions are also supported in IDL: however, the only language that can make use of them is C(++). Given this, I do not address this COM type in this chapter (after all, interoperating with the same language is not all that interesting . . .).

Primitive COM Data Types

In addition to the set of COM types, IDL also supports a set of COM data types. Now be clear on the distinction here. COM types represent the set of possible UDTs you can create to represent the programming entities in your programs. COM data types represent the intrinsic data types of COM IDL (pardon the redundancy). Given that COM IDL does not allow you to define global-level data types, understand that COM data types must be used within the context of a method parameter or structure field.

> **NOTE** *COM IDL does allow you to make use of the const keyword. Like C++, the IDL const keyword can be used to define shared programming constants. Understand, however, that IDL constants are translated into C(++) #define statements and are not understood by other COM-aware languages (such as VB 6.0).*

As you may already be aware, Microsoft IDL is based on an older IDL format that was specifically geared to the task of describing C-style data types for RPC (remote procedure calls). Given COM IDL's legacy in a very C-centric description language, MIDL supports the following core base types (Table 4-2). Do note that most of these core data types may support the signed and unsigned IDL keywords and each may be declared as a pointer variable.

Table 4-2. The Core IDL Data Types

Base MIDL Data Type	**Meaning in Life**	**Default Sign**
boolean	8 bits. This Boolean data type is *not* usable from any language other than C(++).	Unsigned
byte	8 bits.	(not applicable)
char	8 bits.	Unsigned
double	64-bit floating-point number.	(not applicable)
float	32-bit floating-point number.	(not applicable)
hyper	64-bit integer.	Signed
int	32-bit integer. On 16-bit platforms, cannot appear in remote functions without a size qualifier such as short, small, long, or hyper.	Signed
__int32	32-bit integer. Equivalent to long.	
__int3264	An integer that is 32-bit on 32-bit platforms, and is 64-bit on 64-bit platforms.	Signed
__int64	64-bit integer. Equivalent to hyper.	
long	32-bit integer.	Signed
short	16-bt integer.	Signed

Table 4-2. The Core IDL Data Types (continued)

Base MIDL Data Type	Meaning in Life	Default Sign
small	8-bit integer.	Signed
void	Indicates that the procedure does not return a value.	(not applicable)
wchar_t	16-bit predefined type for wide characters.	Unsigned

If you build COM interface definitions (or structures) using these core IDL base types, the chances are very good that you have built a COM entity that can only be accessed by C and C++ clients. For example, the IDL boolean data type does not translate into a VB 6.0 Boolean. C(++)-style string representation (null terminated character arrays) does *not* translate correctly into other COM-aware languages. Because one of the driving forces behind COM is language independence, most programmers make use of an alternate set of COM IDL data types termed the *oleautomation-compatible* data types (also known as the *variant-compliant* types).

The Oleautomation (aka Variant) Data Types

The term *oleautomation* is used to describe a COM interface that is accessible through late binding (that is, using IDispatch). Any oleautomation interface (which is to say a dispinterface) must make use of the set of oleautomation data types, given that the universal marshaler can *only* build stubs and proxies for interfaces making use of this well-known set. Formally speaking, this well-known set is any data type that can be represented as a VARIANT data type (see Chapter 2). The core oleautomation data types (and constructs) are showcased in Table 4-3.

Table 4-3. The Core [oleautomation]-Compatible Data Types

Oleautomation-Compatible Data Type/Construct	Description
VARIANT_BOOL	The VARIANT-compliant Boolean data type.
double	64-bit IEEE floating-point number.
float	32-bit IEEE floating-point number.
int	Integer whose size is system dependent. On 32-bit platforms, MIDL treats int as a 32-bit signed integer.

Table 4-3. The Core [oleautomation]-Compatible Data Types (continued)

Oleautomation-Compatible Data Type/Construct	Description
long	32-bit signed integer.
short	16-bit signed integer.
BSTR	The de facto COM string type.
CY	8-byte fixed-point number (formerly represented as the CURRENCY data type).
DATE	64-bit floating-point fractional number of days since December 30, 1899.
enum	Signed integer, whose size is system dependent. In remote operations, enum objects are treated as 16-bit unsigned entities. Applying the [v1_enum] attribute to an enum type definition allows enum objects to be transmitted as 32-bit entities.
struct	C(++) and Visual Basic 6.0 clients are able to map IDL structures. This IDL construct is not supported by all COM language mappings.
IDispatch *	Pointer to IDispatch interface (VT_DISPATCH).
IUnknown *	Pointer to interface that is not derived from IDispatch. (Any COM interface can be represented by its IUnknown interface.)
VARIANT	Parameters can be expressed as a VARIANT, which allows you to pass any variant-compliant type as a single argument.
SAFEARRAY	When you wish to send arrays of data between the caller and COM class, use the SAFEARRAY structure. In essence, a SAFEARRAY is a self-describing array of VARIANTs.

IDL Method Parameter Attributes

As you recall from Chapter 2, parameters can take the [in], [out], [in, out], and [out, retval] attributes. Using these attributes, you are able to configure how a parameter should be passed to and from an interface method. You can also directly influence how a given parameter is represented in various COM language mappings. In Table 4-4, you see a bit more detail of these attributes than seen earlier in this text.

Table 4-4. IDL Parameter Attributes

IDL Parameter Attribute	**Meaning in Life**
[in]	Indicates that this parameter is allocated by the caller and passed into the method. Be aware that if an IDL parameter attribute is not used, [in] is assumed. This IDL attribute maps to the VB 6.0 ByVal parameter modifier.
[out]	Indicates that this parameter is a pointer supplied by the caller and filled by the method. Be aware that while VB COM clients are able to call methods taking [out] parameters, VB COM objects *cannot* implement interfaces with methods containing [out] parameters.
[in, out]	When a parameter has both [in] and [out] IDL attributes on a single parameter, this represents passing a data item by reference. Thus, the caller supplies an initial value that may be changed within the method implementation. Be aware that [in, out] parameters must be defined as pointers (realized in VB 6.0 as the ByRef parameter modifier).
[out, retval]	This combination of parameter attributes is a cue to higher level languages (such as VB 6.0) that this parameter should be mapped as a physical return value. The literal HRESULT return value will be mapped to some other language-specific entity (such as the intrinsic VB Err object).

To illustrate, assume you have the following IDL interface:

```
interface IParams : IUnknown
{
  [helpstring("This method only takes [in] params")]
  HRESULT InParamsOnly([in] long x, [in] long y);
  [helpstring("This method only takes [out] params")]
  HRESULT OutParamsOnly([out] long* x, [out] long* y);
  [helpstring("Takes two [in, out] params.")]
  HRESULT InAndOutParams([in, out] long* x, [in, out] long* y);
  [helpstring("method SumByRetVal")]
  HRESULT SumByRetVal([in] long x, [in] long y,
                      [out, retval] long* answer);
};
```

Also assume you have an ATL Simple Object (see Chapter 3) that implements these methods as follows:

```
STDMETHODIMP CParams::InParamsOnly(long x, long y)
{
  // Just use the incoming data…
  return S_OK;
}
STDMETHODIMP CParams::OutParamsOnly(long *x, long *y)
{
  // Allocate data for the caller.
  *x = 100;
  *y = 200;
  return S_OK;
}

STDMETHODIMP CParams::InAndOutParams(long *x, long *y)
{
  // Client sends us some initial data, but we can
  // reallocate.
  *x = *x + 100; // Add 100 to x.
  *y = *y + 100; // Add 100 to y.
  return S_OK;
}
STDMETHODIMP CParams::SumByRetVal(long x, long y, long *answer)
{
    // Return sum.
    *answer = x + y;
    return S_OK;
}
```

A Visual Basic client could call each of the methods of interest as follows:

```
Private Sub btnUseMethods_Click()
  Dim o As Params
  Set o = New Params
  Dim x As Long, y As Long, z As Long

  ' Use [out] params.
  o.OutParamsOnly x, y
  MsgBox "x = " & x & vbLf & "y = " & y, , "After [out] call"

  ' Use [in, out] params.
```

```
    o.InAndOutParams x, y
    MsgBox "x = " & x & vbLf & "y = " & y, , "After [in, out] call"

    ' Use [out, retval]
    z = o.SumByRetVal(x, y)
    MsgBox "x = " & x & vbLf & "y = " & y & vbLf & "z = " & z _
        , , "After [out, retval] call"
End Sub
```

The output of this application is seen in three message boxes, as shown in Figures 4-1 to 4-3.

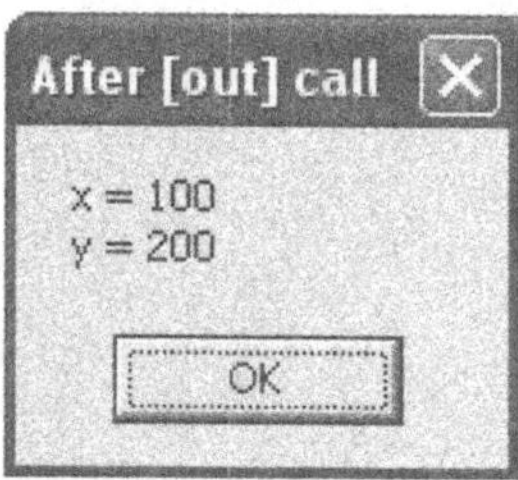

Figure 4-1. Using [out] parameters

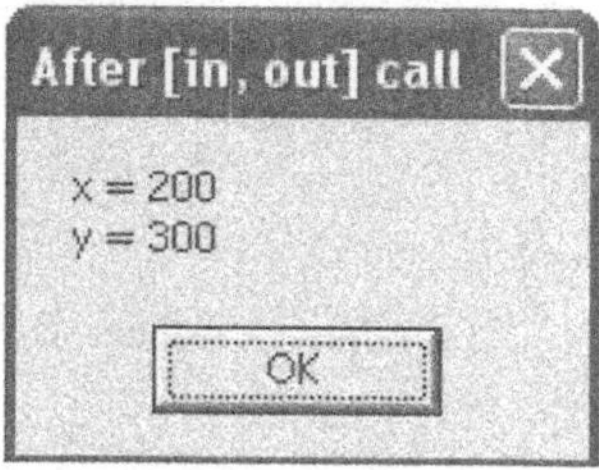

Figure 4-2. Using [in, out] parameters

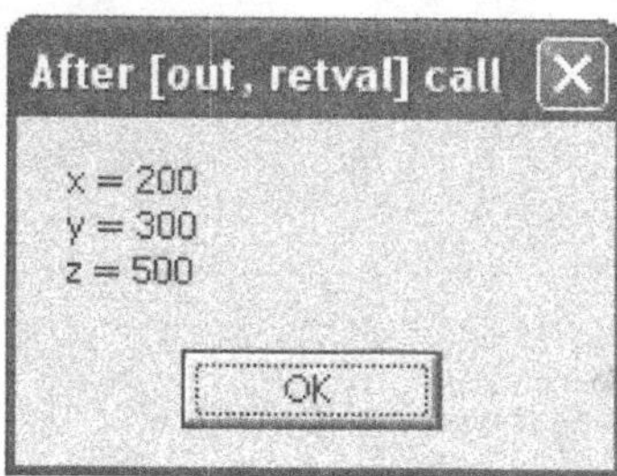

Figure 4-3. Using [out, retval] parameters

[in], [out], and [in, out] parameters in C++ are self-explanatory (raw C++ COM clients ignore [out, retval] parameters).

```
// Assume we have already created the coclass
// and obtained an IParams interface.
long x = 0; long y = 0; long z = 0;
pIParams->OutParamsOnly(&x, &y);
pIParams->InAndOutParams (&x, &y);
pIParams->SumByRetVal(&x, &y, &z);.
```

Now that you have seen the set of COM types and IDL data types, you are ready to formalize the IDL syntax used to express each COM type. Understand that each COM type can be qualified using various IDL keywords. Although this chapter does not provide an exhaustive description of each and every IDL keyword, I will point out items of interest. If you require additional information, check out the MIDL Language Reference document using online Help.

Defining COM Interface Types in IDL

You have already seen how to build interface types in the previous two chapters. However, now that you have seen IDL data types in a more formal light, let's walk through the IDL syntax used to define the COM interface type, while at the same time making further mention of oleautomation compliance.

Defining Raw Dispinterfaces

The first form of a COM interface is termed a *dispinterface,* which is always defined within the scope of an IDL library statement. Each member of the dispinterface is assigned a corresponding DISPID using the IDL [id] keyword (by necessity, DISPIDs are numbered beginning at 1 and must be unique within the definition. Microsoft has reserved all negative DISPID values). Recall from Chapter 2 that dispinterfaces are a set of properties and methods that can only be invoked using late binding (via IDispatch). When you build raw dispinterfaces, every member is automatically oleautomation compliant. Here is the syntax behind a raw dispinterface:

```
// Raw dispinterfaces must be within a type library!
[uuid(E5909DB1-F271-433C-BB02-4D0BFA95D387),
version(1.0), helpstring("My Type Library 1.0")]
library MyTypeLibrary
```

```
{
  importlib("stdole32.tlb");
  importlib("stdole2.tlb");
  // A pure IDispatch based interface (dispinterface).
  [uuid(A8B2AA3A-1138-4C43-8596-D99CBD2BDAA3),
  helpstring("IDispOnlyInterface")]
  dispinterface _IDispOnly
  {
    properties:
    methods:
    [id(1), helpstring("method LateBoundMethod")]
    HRESULT LateBoundMethod([in] BSTR msg );
  };
};
```

In this day and age, raw dispinterfaces are most commonly used when you wish to build an outbound interface with the COM connection point model (more details on this later in this text). When you are building an inbound interface designed to be supported by a given COM object, dispinterfaces are not all that helpful, given that the only way to access the object's members is through late binding.

Defining Dual Interfaces

Recall that COM also supports dual interfaces. This form of COM interface is very helpful when you wish to build an interface that can be accessed using both early and late binding. When you build a dual interface, you make use of the [dual] attribute to force the MIDL compiler to ensure oleautomation conformance (recall that Visual Basic 6.0 COM classes are always configured to support [dual] interfaces automatically). The core IDL is as follows:

```
// A dual interface.
[object,
uuid(62401BC6-7892-46A0-939E-5D19D3B764D2),
dual, helpstring("Dual Interface")]
interface IDualInterface : IDispatch
{
  [id(1), helpstring("method MethodA")]
  HRESULT MethodA();
};
```

Dual interfaces are indeed a hybrid of a raw dispinterface as well as a standard IUnknown-derived interface. Note that dual interface members still must have an associated DISPID (for the late-bound clients) and derive from IDispatch (to ensure the implementing object contends with the four methods of IDispatch). However, the interface itself (IDualInterface) may also be directly accessed by type-safe, early-bound clients such as VB 6.0 and C(++). When a client makes use of the custom IDualInterface reference, the members of IDispatch are generally ignored.

Building IUnknown-Derived Interfaces

Finally, you should be aware that it is completely possible to build standard IUnknown-derived interfaces that are also oleautomation compliant, by explicitly making use of the [oleautomation] attribute (note the lack of the [id] attribute):

```
[object,
uuid(60FBF1E1-3F08-4893-94BB-4A2C4B341342),
oleautomation, helpstring("IDispOnly Interface")]
interface IUseUniversalMarshaling : IUnknown
{
  [helpstring("method MethodA")]
  HRESULT MethodA();
};
```

[oleautomation]-compatible custom interfaces can be helpful for two reasons. First, if you intend your COM interfaces to be used by any COM-aware language, the presence of the [oleautomation] attribute again forces the MIDL compiler to perform sanity checks. Furthermore, if you wish to leverage the universal marshaler (and therefore avoid the need to build your own stub and proxy DLL), the ATL compilation cycle registers each interface to use the universal marshaler (oleaut32.dll).

Common IDL Interface Modifiers

COM interfaces (excluding dispinterfaces) are required to take the [object] and [uuid] attributes at minimum. In addition to the [dual] and [oleautomation] attributes seen in the previous sections, IDL does allow COM interfaces to be defined with other attributes to further qualify their usage. Table 4-5 lists some of the more interesting attributes.

Table 4-5. Additional IDL Interface Attributes

IDL Interface Attribute	Meaning in Life
hidden	When a COM type (including a type library) is marked with the [hidden] attribute, it will not be displayed within the Visual Basic 6.0 Object Browser utility. Other browser types may or may not honor this IDL keyword.
pointer_default	This IDL attribute is used to describe how parameters expressed as C(++) pointers should be marshaled between boundaries. When set to "ref," pointers are handled in the same manner as a C++ reference (and is typically what you require).
local	If an interface is marked with the [local] attribute, it cannot be marshaled across boundaries and is only usable from another in-process COM object. Local interfaces are permitted to return values other than the mandatory HRESULT.

Defining COM Classes in IDL

Coclasses are defined in IDL using the coclass keyword and must be configured with the [uuid] attribute. Within the scope of the coclass definition is a list of each interface supported by the COM class. For example, here is a library containing two coclasses, each of which supports two distinct COM interfaces (recall that the [default] attribute is used to identify which interface is returned automatically when used by a higher level language such as VB 6.0).

```
// This type library contains two coclasses.
[uuid(E5909DB1-F271-433C-BB02-4D0BFA95D387),
version(1.0), helpstring("My Type Library 1.0")]
library MyTypeLibrary
{
  importlib("stdole32.tlb");
  importlib("stdole2.tlb");
  [uuid(5C3D4955-17C1-4ACC-BB1C-72F6B63D22F2),
  helpstring("First COM Class")]
  coclass CoClassOne
  {
    [default] interface IA;
    interface IB;
  };
```

```
  [uuid(5C3D4955-17C1-4ACC-BB1C-72F6B63D22F3),
  helpstring("Another COM Class")]
  coclass AnotherCoClass
  {
    [default] interface IOne;
    interface ITwo;
  };
};
```

In addition to the mandatory [uuid] IDL attribute (and optional help-centric modifiers), coclasses can be assigned additional IDL keywords, to help further qualify their usage. Table 4-6 documents two of the more common coclass modifiers (both of which are ignored by C(++) COM clients).

Table 4-6. Additional IDL Coclass Attributes

IDL Coclass Attribute	Meaning in Life
appobject	When a coclass is marked with the [appobject] attribute, Visual Basic will automatically create an instance of the object for use at the global level (therefore, the client code does not need to make use of the VB New keyword).
noncreatable	At times, you might want to have a coclass only directly creatable by another coclass. In this situation, the object user must obtain the noncreatable object from a method of the creatable object. By using the IDL [noncreatable] attribute, you force higher-level languages such as VB 6.0 to generate compiler errors if the client attempts to "New" the object.

For example, if your library contained the following coclass definitions:

```
[uuid(E817E78F-E13E-4954-AC63-FF1B36A46C05),
helpstring("GlobalObject Class"), appobject]
coclass GlobalObject
{
  [default] interface IGlobalObject;
};
[uuid(E1B45767-3909-4838-B035-D04F9B459D98),
noncreatable, helpstring("CantCreateDirectly Class")]
coclass CantCreateDirectly
{
  [default] interface ICantCreateDirectly;
};
```

Visual Basic 6.0 could make use of the application object as follows (note the lack of the New keyword):

```
' VB 6.0 Client calling [appobject] aware COM type.
GlobalObject.SomeMethod
```

On the other hand, VB would not be able to directly 'New' a [noncreatable] object:

```
Dim wontWork as CantCreateDirectly
Set wontWork = New CantCreateDirectly  ' Error!
```

Defining IDL Enumerations

As you have seen, COM also supports enumerations. These name/value pairs are defined by the IDL enum keyword. Like C(++), the first member of an enumeration is automatically assigned the value of zero, following an n+1 incrementation. COM enums may be assigned a [uuid] value, and may be defined as [hidden] should the need arise. The only enum attribute that deserves special mention is [v1_enum]. By default, enumerations are transmitted between boundaries as 16-bit entities. When you qualify your custom enumerations to support [v1_enum], variables of this type are transmitted as 32-bit entities:

```
[v1_enum, uuid(2358F2E6-3887-405e-BD25-4F73EDF32400)]
enum MyEnum
{ FIRST, SECOND, THIRD };
```

As you have already seen in Chapter 3, COM IDL enums translate directly into C(++) enumerations and VB 6.0 Enum constants.

Defining IDL Structures

The final COM type you examine is the structure. Structures have long been used in C to represent a user-defined data type. Like classes, structures allow you to group related data under a common name. Unlike classes, you have no true support for polymorphic behavior or type extension. Nevertheless, structures can be helpful when you want to build lightweight types. Consider the classic MYPOINT example:

```
// IDL structures may take the [uuid] attribute,
// especially if the structure is to be stuffed
// into a VARIANT or SAFEARRAY.
[uuid(FB58A440-ABD8-43a3-969D-0B7D8700664A)]
```

```
typedef struct
{
  long xPos;
  long yPos;
}MYPOINT;
```

Be aware that if you intend your IDL structures to function correctly in Visual Basic 6.0, you must pass all structures by reference! Therefore, the following IDL interface definition translates correctly in both C(++) and VB 6.0:

```
// Structures must be passed by reference ([in, out])
// not by value ([in]) to work correctly in VB 6.0.
[object, uuid(C3CBCB15-901F-44d6-885C-16836DD267F5)]
interface IDraw
{
  HRESULT DrawALine([in, out] MYPOINT* p1,
                    [in, out] MYPOINT* p2);
};
```

If you had an implementing class named Drawer that supported IDraw as the [default] interface, you would make use of DrawALine() from VB 6.0 as follows:

```
' Assume Drawer specified IDraw as the
' default interface.
Dim o As Drawer
Set o = New Drawer
' COM structs map to VB 6.0 Types.
Dim p1 As MYPOINT, p2 As MYPOINT
p1.xPos = 100
p1.yPos = 100
p2.xPos = 300
p2.yPos = 100
o.DrawALine p1, p2
```

COM String Representation

COM strings should always be exposed as BSTR data types, period. The reason is that different COM languages internally represent string data in different ways. For example, C(++) programmers view strings as a null-terminated array of char data types (char*). However, you should understand that (a) COM strings demand to be expressed as Unicode and (b) Visual Basic can't understand strings represented as char*. While you might be tempted to represent your strings as wchar_t* (a null-terminated array of Unicode characters) you have resolved issue (a) but are still left to contend with issue (b).

Visual Basic does not internally represent string data as an array of null-terminated characters (char* or wchar_t) but rather a *byte-length prefixed* null-terminated array of Unicode characters. This string format is termed a BSTR (BASIC String). Visual Basic programmers generate BSTR data types whenever they declare a variable of type String:

```
' A VB 6.0 BSTR data type.
Dim s as String
```

C(++) programmers, on the other hand, make use of a set of COM library functions specifically geared toward the creation, manipulation, and destruction of BSTRs. Whenever you work with the raw BSTR data type, be sure to make use of the core library functions defined in Table 4-7, as they will properly configure the byte-length prefix of the BSTR.

Table 4-7. BSTR COM Library Functions

BSTR COM Library Function	Meaning in Life
SysAllocString()	Creates a BSTR based on an array of Unicode characters. Typically this array of Unicode characters is represented programmatically as an array of OLECHAR data types (OLECHAR*).
SysReAllocString()	Reallocates an existing BSTR to a new value (with new byte-length-prefix) given a new OLECHAR*.
SysFreeString()	Used to free the memory attached to a BSTR created by SysAllocString(). When C(++) COM clients obtain a BSTR from a method invocation, be sure to call SysFreeString()! If you create a BSTR locally in some scope (and don't pass it back to the client) be sure to call SysFreeString()!
SysStringLen()	Returns the character length of an existing BSTR.

While it is completely possible to make use of these raw COM API functions, it is a bit of a hassle. It is far more common to make use of (or create) a C++ class that hides these raw calls from view. For example, ATL programmers typically make use of the CComBSTR class to manipulate raw BSTRs. CComBSTR also defines a set of helper functions (and overloaded operators) to simplify COM string types. For example:

```
// ATL CComBSTR at work.
STDMETHODIMP CCoClass::UseABstr()
{
  USES_CONVERSION;
  // SysAllocString() called automatically.
  CComBSTR message("Hello There!");
  message.ToLower();
  MessageBox(NULL, W2A(message), "Lower case BSTR", MB_OK);
  message.ToUpper();
  MessageBox(NULL, W2A(message), "Upper case BSTR", MB_OK);
  // SysFreeString() called when object drops out of scope.
  return S_OK;
}
```

A Brief Comment on ATL Conversion Macros

The previous code block made use of two ATL string conversion macros: USES_CONVERSION and W2A. These macros (defined in atlconv.h) allow the programmer to translate between Unicode and ANSI string encoding with minimal fuss and bother. Although a great many of these macros exist, the pair to be aware of is W2A (Unicode to ANSI) and A2W (ANSI to Unicode), both of which require that the USES_CONVERSION macro be placed in the method performing the conversion.

In the previous code example, you converted the Unicode BSTR into an ANSI char* to place the value into the MessageBoxA() method. No, that is not a typo. Recall from Chapter 1 that under Win32, there is actually no function called MessageBox(). Rather, an ANSI version and Unicode (or *wide*) version both exist. Based on your project settings, all API calls taking textual parameters expand to the wide (that is, Unicode) or ANSI equivalent. Unless you are willing to create a Unicode-only build of your project (and work incorrectly on various versions of Windows), you need to do such manual conversions. In this case, W2A and A2W are your greatest allies.

COM (Safe)Array Representation

Arrays are also supported in COM IDL, and as you would expect, different COM language mappings express arrays in unique manners. When you wish to use arrays that can be used from all COM-aware language mappings, you should stick to the SAFEARRAY data type as opposed to variable or fixed-length C-style arrays. The COM SAFEARRAY (which has multidimensional capabilities) may contain any [oleautomation]-compliant data type, which is to say, is able to hold any data type that can be expressed as a VARIANT. The SAFEARRAY itself is a structure defined in oaidl.idl as follows:

```
// The COM SAFEARRAY structure.
typedef struct tagSAFEARRAY {
  USHORT cDims;        // Number of dimensions.
  USHORT fFeatures;    // Flags which describe the data.
  ULONG cbElements;    // Holds size of an element in the array.
  ULONG cLocks;        // Holds number of locks on this array.
  PVOID pvData;        // Pointer to the actual data.
  SAFEARRAYBOUND rgsabound[];
} SAFEARRAY;
```

Notice that the last field of the SAFEARRAY structure is an array of yet another structure of type SAFEARRAYBOUND. This entity is used to catalog the upper and lower bound for each dimension in the array:

```
typedef struct tagSAFEARRAYBOUND {
  ULONG cElements;
  LONG lLbound;
} SAFEARRAYBOUND, * LPSAFEARRAYBOUND;
```

As you might be suspecting, Visual Basic always represents array types as SAFEARRAYs. Thus, if you build an interface definition as follows:

```
' [default] interface of the VB 6.0 CoSafeArray class.
Option Explicit
' This parameter is a COM SAFEARRAY.
Public Sub UseArrayOfStrings(theStrings() As String)
  Dim i As Integer
  For i = 0 To UBound(theStrings)
    MsgBox theStrings(i), , "BSTR says:"
  Next i
End Sub
```

you would find the resulting IDL:

```
// Recall! VB 6.0 always builds [dual] interfaces.
interface _CoSafeArray : IDispatch
{
  [id(0x60030000)]
  HRESULT UseArrayOfStrings([in, out] SAFEARRAY(BSTR)* theStrings);
};
```

The manipulation of the SAFEARRAY type is far more robust (which is to say far more complex and painful) than when using Visual Basic. Much like the BSTR data type, C++ programmers make use of the COM library to allocate, fill, access, and destroy items in this complex data type. Table 4-8 lists some (but by no means all) of the core library functions.

Table 4-8. SAFEARRAY COM Library Functions

SAFEARRAY COM Library Function	Meaning in Life
SafeArrayCreate() SafeArrayCreateVector()	Allocates a SAFEARRAY based on the underlying type, dimensions, and bounds. The vector variation allocates a fixed-size SAFEARRAY.
SafeArrayDestroy()	Cleans up all memory stuffed in the SAFEARRAY. By reading the fFeatures flag, this function is able to call Release() on interface references, SysFreeString() on BSTR references, and so forth.
SafeArrayGetUBound() SafeArrayGetLBound()	Gets the upper/lower bounds for a given dimension of the safe array.
SafeArrayAccessData() SafeArrayUnaccessData()	These methods lock/unlock the SAFEARRAY (by adjusting the cLocks field) and provide access to the underlying data. Unaccessing the data results in NULLing the pointer to the data.

Making use of these C++ COM library APIs in not impossible, but it is very (very) verbose. To illustrate, assume you have an interface that allows the user to send in a SAFEARRAY of BSTRs for display by the COM object, as well as another method that returns an array of BSTRs for use by the COM client. Here is the IDL:

```
// One of many ways to define safe array parameters.
interface ISafeArray : IUnknown
{
  [helpstring("Pass in a SafeArray of Strings.")]
  HRESULT UseThisSafeArray([in] SAFEARRAY(BSTR)* ppStrings);
  [helpstring("Return a SafeArray of Strings.")]
  HRESULT GiveMeSomeStrings([out, retval] SAFEARRAY(BSTR)* ppStrings);
};
```

If you had an ATL coclass that supports this COM interface, you could make use of the SAFEARRAY COM library functions to build the following implementation:

```
// Show each item in the array.
STDMETHODIMP CCoWidget::UseThisSafeArray(SAFEARRAY** ppStrings)
{
  USES_CONVERSION;
  SAFEARRAY* pSA = *ppStrings;
  // Be sure we don't have a multidimensional array.
  UINT numbOfDims = SafeArrayGetDim(pSA);
  if(numbOfDims != 1)
    return E_INVALIDARG;
  // Be sure we have strings in the array.
  VARTYPE vt = 0;
  SafeArrayGetVartype(pSA, &vt);
  if(vt != VT_BSTR)
    return E_INVALIDARG;
  // Get upper bound of array.
  long ubound = 0;
  SafeArrayGetUBound(pSA, 1, &ubound);
  // Now show each string.
  BSTR* temp = NULL;
  SafeArrayAccessData(pSA, (void**)&temp);
  for(int i = 0; i <= ubound; i++)
  {
    MessageBox(NULL, W2A(temp[i]), "BSTR says...", MB_OK);
  }
  SafeArrayUnaccessData(pSA);
  return S_OK;
}
// Build an array and return to the caller.
STDMETHODIMP CCoWidget::GiveMeSomeStrings(SAFEARRAY** ppStrings)
{
  // Send back some strings to the client.
  SAFEARRAY *pSA;
  SAFEARRAYBOUND bounds = {4, 0};

  // Create the array
  pSA = SafeArrayCreate(VT_BSTR, 1, &bounds);
  // Fill the array with data.
  BSTR *theStrings;
  SafeArrayAccessData(pSA, (void**)&theStrings);
```

```
  theStrings[0] = SysAllocString(L"Hello");
  theStrings[1] = SysAllocString(L"from");
  theStrings[2] = SysAllocString(L"the");
  theStrings[3] = SysAllocString(L"coclass!");
  SafeArrayUnaccessData(pSA);
  // Set return value.
  *ppStrings = pSA;
  return S_OK;
}
```

For ease of use, assume a simple VB 6.0 COM client that triggers each function as follows (VB destroys the SAFEARRAY structure automatically):

```
Private Sub btnSafeArray_Click()
  Dim w As CoWidget
  Set w = New CoWidget
  Dim itfSA As ISafeArray
  Set itfSA = w

  ' Send strings to object.
  Dim theStrings(2) As String
  theStrings(0) = "Hello"
  theStrings(1) = "from"
  theStrings(2) = "Visual Basic!"
  itfSA.UseThisSafeArray theStrings

  ' Get strings from object.
  Dim moreStrings() As String
  moreStrings = itfSA.GiveMeSomeStrings()
  Dim i As Integer
  For i = 0 To UBound(moreStrings)
    MsgBox moreStrings(i), , "Strings from COM object"
  Next i
End Sub
```

As you would expect, when you run the application you see a total of six message boxes pop up as the array of BSTRs is sent across boundaries. Understand that the SAFEARRAY structure is capable of containing more complex types (such as custom structures, interface pointers, and so forth). You see additional examples of COM array manipulation later in this text.

ATL 4.0 SAFEARRAY Helper Templates

Until the advent of ATL 4.0, C++ developers were forced to pound out dozens of lines of code all for the sake of creating a simple array of types (Visual Basic programmers are free to emit a hearty belly laugh at this point). However, ATL 4.0 now supplies the CComSafeArray and CComSafeArrayBounds helper templates. I'll assume you will check out online Help for further details.

CODE *The ATL WidgetServer server and VB 6.0 client application (WidgetClient) are included under the Chapter 4 subdirectory.*

COM Interface Types As Method Parameters

As mentioned at the start of this chapter, COM interface methods may take other COM types (including interfaces) as parameters. During the course of this chapter, you have already seen how to pass structures and enumerations between caller and callee, however, you have not yet examined how to pass interface types between COM entities. Notice that I did not say "how to pass coclass types." It is always important to remember that COM clients can never access an object's functionality except using an interface pointer. Therefore, it is not possible to pass a COM object reference to another part of your system.

Passing interface references is quite common when building a COM collection object that exposes a set of inner objects. For example, you might have a coclass named Garage that maintains a set of internal Car types. In IDL, you might concoct the following IGarage interface:

```
interface IGarage : IUnknown
{
  HRESULT GetCar([in] long carID, [out, retval] ICar** pTheCar);
  HRESULT InsertNewCar([in] ICar* pTheCar);
};
```

Assuming you do indeed have an implementation of the IGarage and ICar interfaces, we would be able to make use of these types in VB 6.0 as follows:

```
' Make a Garage and insert new Car.
Dim g as Garage
Set g = New Garage
```

```
Dim c as Car
Set c = New Car
g.InsertNewCar c
' Get back car number with ID 123
Dim c123 as Car
c123 = g.GetCar (123)
```

You examine the code behind this sort of collection (and other related patterns) later in this text. At this point in the chapter you should now have a better understanding (or received a painless refresher) of the core COM types, intrinsic data types, and various IDL constructs. Understand that you will see additional IDL keywords (and COM concepts) where necessary during the remainder of this text. The remainder of this chapter examines the process of programmatically generating and reading COM type information at runtime using both unmanaged (C++) and managed (C#) code.

The ITypeInfo Interface

As you know, once you have defined your COM types in IDL syntax, you compile the IDL into a binary equivalent termed a *type library* (that may or may not be embedded into the COM binary). Programmatically speaking, when you wish to read information from a type library, you make use of the methods of the standard ITypeInfo COM interface. This single interface is able to return a wealth of information about any COM type (interface, coclass, enum, struct) at runtime. Sadly, there is not a unique one-to-one mapping of COM interface to COM type (thus you will not find a specific standard COM interface that *only* reads interface information, another that reads *only* coclass information, and so forth). ITypeInfo is your one-stop shop, and it is defined in IDL (within oaidl.idl) as follows:

```
// This interface allows you to examine COM types at runtime.
[object,
uuid(00020401-0000-0000-C000-000000000046)]
interface ITypeInfo : IUnknown
{
  HRESULT GetTypeAttr( [out] TYPEATTR ** ppTypeAttr);
  HRESULT GetTypeComp( [out] ITypeComp ** ppTComp);
  HRESULT GetFuncDesc([in] UINT index,
                      [out] FUNCDESC ** ppFuncDesc);
  HRESULT GetVarDesc( [in] UINT index,
                      [out] VARDESC ** ppVarDesc);
```

```
    HRESULT GetNames( [in] MEMBERID memid,
      [out,size_is(cMaxNames),length_is(*pcNames)] BSTR * rgBstrNames,
      [in] UINT cMaxNames, [out] UINT * pcNames);
    HRESULT GetRefTypeOfImplType( [in] UINT index,
      [out] HREFTYPE * pRefType);
    HRESULT GetImplTypeFlags( [in] UINT index,
      [out] INT * pImplTypeFlags);
    HRESULT GetIDsOfNames(
      [in, size_is(cNames)] LPOLESTR * rgszNames,
      [in] UINT cNames,
      [out, size_is(cNames)] MEMBERID * pMemId);
    HRESULT Invoke( [in] PVOID pvInstance,
      [in] MEMBERID memid,
      [in] WORD wFlags,
      [in, out] DISPPARAMS * pDispParams,
      [out] VARIANT * pVarResult,
      [out] EXCEPINFO * pExcepInfo,
      [out] UINT * puArgErr);
    HRESULT GetDocumentation( [in] MEMBERID memid,
      [out] BSTR * pBstrName,
      [out] BSTR * pBstrDocString,
      [out] DWORD * pdwHelpContext,
      [out] BSTR * pBstrHelpFile);
    HRESULT GetDllEntry( [in] MEMBERID memid,
      [in] INVOKEKIND invKind,
      [out] BSTR * pBstrDllName,
      [out] BSTR * pBstrName,
      [out] WORD * pwOrdinal);
    HRESULT GetRefTypeInfo( [in] HREFTYPE hRefType,
      [out] ITypeInfo ** ppTInfo);
    HRESULT AddressOfMember(
      [in] MEMBERID memid,
      [in] INVOKEKIND invKind,
      [out] PVOID * ppv);
    HRESULT CreateInstance( [in] IUnknown * pUnkOuter,
      [in] REFIID riid, [out, iid_is(riid)] PVOID * ppvObj);
    HRESULT GetMops( [in] MEMBERID memid,
      [out] BSTR * pBstrMops);
    HRESULT GetContainingTypeLib(
      [out] ITypeLib ** ppTLib,
      [out] UINT * pIndex);
    void ReleaseTypeAttr( [in] TYPEATTR * pTypeAttr);
    void ReleaseFuncDesc( [in] FUNCDESC * pFuncDesc);
    void ReleaseVarDesc( [in] VARDESC * pVarDesc);
};
```

Even though ITypeInfo defines a good number of members, the truth of the matter is that only a subset of these items are necessary when attempting to programmatically investigate a COM type library. Table 4-9 shows the highlights.

Table 4-9. Core Members of ITypeInfo

Relevant ITypeInfo Method	Meaning in Life
CreateInstance()	If the current ITypeInfo interface is pointing to a COM class (coclass), this method allows you to activate the object (assuming the coclass is implemented in a registered COM server).
GetContainingTypeLib()	This method allows you to gain an ITypeLib reference of the type library containing the COM type.
GetDocumentation()	Fetches the [helpstring] value for the type, as well as any help file information for the type.
GetFuncDesc()	Retrieves information about an interface method held in a FUNCDESC structure.
GetIDsOfNames() Invoke()	Much like the IDispatch equivalents, these methods allow you to obtain a DISPID given a string token and trigger a member of the dispinterface using late binding.
GetImplTypeFlags()	Returns a set of flags that describe the IDL attributes of a coclass' supported interface (e.g., [default], [hidden]).
GetNames()	Returns an array of BSTRs that describe a given member.
GetRefTypeInfo()	If the current type description references other type descriptions, this method returns the associated ITypeInfo for the referenced type.
GetRefTypeOfImplType()	If a type description describes a COM class, it retrieves the type description of the implemented interface types.
GetTypeAttr()	Returns a TYPEATTR structure that describes the current type.
GetVarDesc()	Returns a VARDESC structure that defines a variable in the type library.
ReleaseFuncDesc() ReleaseTypeDesc() ReleaseVarDesc()	These methods free the structure allocated for you when calling GetFuncDesc(), GetTypeDesc(), and GetVarDesc().

A Brief Word on ITypeInfo2

In addition to ITypeInfo, COM also defines a derived interface named (of course) ITypeInfo2. This interface extends the functionality of ITypeInfo by adding members that allow you to retrieve custom IDL attributes (identified with the [custom] attribute). You'll see the ITypeInfo2 interface in action a bit later in this chapter.

Related ITypeInfo Data Types

If you were reading over the previous table carefully, you should have noticed that many of the ITypeInfo accessor methods return various related structures. These structures are your key to ciphering among the numerous members that lurk within a COM type library. Table 4-10 documents some (but not all) of the items of interest.

Table 4-10. ITypeInfo-Related Structures (and Enums)

Related ITypeInfo Structure Type	Meaning in Life
ARRAYDESC	Array description referenced by TYPEDESC, containing the element type, dimension count, and a variable-length array.
ELEMDESC	Includes the type description and process-transfer information for a variable, a function, or a function parameter.
FUNCDESC	Describes a function.
FUNCFLAGS	Enumeration containing constants that are used to define properties of a function.
FUNCKIND	Enumeration for defining whether a function is accessed as a virtual, pure virtual, nonvirtual, static, or through IDispatch.
HREFTYPE	A handle identifying a type description.
PARAMDESC	Describes the type of the parameter.
IMPLTYPEFLAGS	Represents various flags that may adorn COM implementation types (interfaces and coclasses).
MEMBERID	Identifies the member in a type description. For IDispatch interfaces, this is the same as a DISPID.

Table 4-10. ITypeInfo-Related Structures (and Enums) (continued)

Related ITypeInfo Structure Type	Meaning in Life
TYPEATTR	Contains attributes of the current type.
TYPEDESC	Describes the type of a variable, the return type of a function, or the type of a function parameter.
TYPEFLAGS	Defines the properties and attributes of a type description.
TYPEKIND	Defines properties of a type.
VARDESC	Describes a variable, constant, or data member.
VARFLAGS	Used to set attributes of a variable.
VARKIND	Defines the kind of variable.

Generating COM Type Information Programmatically

Unless you happen to be a tool builder by trade, chances are that you will build your COM type information using the Keyboard Wizard and the MIDL compiler. However, it is worth pointing out that the COM library defines a small set of standard interfaces (used in conjunction with a small set of COM library functions) that allow you to *programmatically* generate type information at runtime. Of course, this in-memory type information may be then committed to file for later use. In a nutshell, creating type information requires the use of three core COM interfaces and a single COM library function. Table 4-11 hits the highlights.

Table 4-11. Type Library Creation Elements

COM Type Information Creation Element	Meaning in Life
ICreateTypeLib	This interface is used to establish the characteristics of the type ibrary itself (i.e., the library statement and its attributes).
ICreateTypeInfo	This interface is used to insert COM types into a type library.
CreateTypeLib()	This COM library function creates a coclass that supports the ICreateTypeLib interface.
ITypeInfo	As seen, while not really an interface that directly *creates* a COM type, this interface *represents* a COM type description in memory.

A Brief Word on ICreateTypeLib2 and ICreateTypeInfo2

In addition to this small set of COM type creators, you may wish to know that both the ICreateTypeLib and ICreateTypeInfo interfaces function as a base interface to two versioned equivalents (ICreateTypeLib2 and ICreateTypeInfo2). These interfaces support the ability to remove a given element from an existing library statement or COM type. If you wish to interact with these interfaces, you need to first call the CreateTypeLib2() COM library function (rather than CreateTypeLib() proper) to obtain the ICreateTypeLib2 interface. However, to keep things simple, I avoid using these interfaces (but check out online Help for a full description of the defined interface members).

The Target IDL

To illustrate the basic functionality of building type information at runtime, you make use of the items defined in Table 4-11 to build the following type information programmatically:

```
 [uuid(<some guid>), version(1.0),
 helpstring("The Hello Library")]
library HelloLibrary
{
  importlib("stdole32.tlb");
  [odl, uuid(<some guid>),
  helpstring("Hello Interface"), hidden]
  interface IHello : IUnknown
  {
    [helpstring("This method says hello...")]
    HRESULT _stdcall SayHello();
  };
  [uuid(<some guid>), helpstring("Hello Class")]
  coclass Hello
  {
    [default] interface IHello;
  };
};
```

As you can see, your COM class (Hello) supports a single [default] interface (IHello). The IHello interface contains a single method named (of course) SayHello(). To keep things simple, the SayHello() method does not take any parameters and returns the standard HRESULT. Do note, however, that you are making use of the [helpstring] attribute at various levels to help document the functionality of the type information. Finally, notice that the values assigned to the [uuid] attributes are generated on the fly using CoCreateGuid().

If you wish to follow along and build your own COM type generator (and I'm sure you do), begin by creating a brand-new Win32 Console Application named CppComTypeWriter using Visual Studio 6.0 (a simple application will be fine). All of your programming logic will be contained within the initial C++ file.

Building the Type Library (ICreateTypeLib)

The first step in your endeavor is to create a helper function that will create a new *.tlb file and return a valid ICreateTypeLib interface. Using this interface reference, you will be able to insert the individual types into the library definition. Here is the prototype:

```
// This global method will be called by main() in order
// to create the *.tlb file and obtain an ICreateTypeLib interface.
ICreateTypeLib* CreateTypeLibrary();
```

The ICreateTypeLib interface defines a number of methods that allow you to establish numerous library attributes ([version], [uuid], [helpstring], and so forth). The official IDL definition can be found in oaidl.idl and looks like the following (see Table 4-12 for an explanation of each method):

```
[object,
uuid(00020406-0000-0000-C000-000000000046),
pointer_default(unique), local]
interface ICreateTypeLib : IUnknown
{
  HRESULT CreateTypeInfo( [in] LPOLESTR szName,
        [in] TYPEKIND tkind,
        [out] ICreateTypeInfo ** ppCTInfo);
  HRESULT SetName( [in] LPOLESTR szName);
  HRESULT SetVersion(
        [in] WORD wMajorVerNum,
        [in] WORD wMinorVerNum);
  HRESULT SetGuid( [in] REFGUID guid);
  HRESULT SetDocString( [in] LPOLESTR szDoc);
  HRESULT SetHelpFileName(
        [in] LPOLESTR szHelpFileName);
```

```
  HRESULT SetHelpContext(
       [in] DWORD dwHelpContext);
  HRESULT SetLcid( [in] LCID lcid);
  HRESULT SetLibFlags( [in] UINT uLibFlags);
  HRESULT SaveAllChanges();
};
```

Table 4-12. Members of ICreateTypeLib

ICreateTypeLib Method	**Meaning in Life**
CreateTypeInfo()	Creates a new type description instance (interface, coclass, and so forth) within the type library.
SaveAllChanges()	Saves the type library to file.
SetDocString()	Sets the [helpstring] attribute for the type library.
SetGuid()	Sets the [uuid] attribute (LIBID) for the type library.
SetHelpContext() SetHelpFileName()	Sets the Help context ID and help file name for the type library.
SetLcid()	Sets the locale identifier (LCID) code indicating the national language associated with the library.
SetLibFlags()	Sets any library flags for the type library. Valid values are taken from the LIBFLAGS enumeration.
SetName()	Sets the name of the type library.
SetVersion()	Sets major and minor version numbers for the type library (the [version] attribute).

Now that you have a better idea of the behavior offered by the ICreateTypeLib interface, you can build the implementation of your custom CreateTypeLibrary() method:

```
// Create a type library and gain an ICreateTypeLib
// interface to reference it.
ICreateTypeLib* CreateTypeLibrary()
{
  cout << "Creating COM type library!" << endl;
  ICreateTypeLib *pCTL = NULL;
  GUID theGUID;
  CoCreateGuid(&theGUID);
  // Make the type lib file and get the ICreateTypeLib interface.
```

```
    CreateTypeLib(SYS_WIN32, L"MyTypeLib.tlb", &pCTL);
    // Set version, name and LIBID and return ICreateTypeLib.
    pCTL->SetVersion(1, 0);
    pCTL->SetName(L"HelloLibrary");
    pCTL->SetGuid(theGUID);
    pCTL->SetDocString(L"The Hello Library");
    return pCTL;      // Caller will Release().
}
```

This process begins filling our GUID (which will become the LIBID) using CoCreateGuid(). After this point, make use of the CreateTypeLib() COM library function to (a) define the target platform for this type information, (b) the name of the *.tlb file, and (c) specify storage for the returned ICreateTypeLib interface. The first parameter used to establish the target OS is a value from the SYSKIND enumeration:

```
// Yes, the Macintosh does support
// COM type information…
typedef [v1_enum] enum tagSYSKIND {
    SYS_WIN16 = 0,
    SYS_WIN32,  // This is all we care about…
    SYS_MAC
} SYSKIND;
```

Once you obtain a reference to the returned ICreateTypeLib interface, you make a number of calls to establish the form of the type library statement. In effect, you have just built the following IDL in memory:

```
// The story thus far.
[uuid(<some guid>), version(1.0),
helpstring("The Hello Library")]
library HelloLibrary
{
}
```

Creating the IHello Interface

Now that you have a valid ICreateTypeLib interface, you are able to insert the individual COM types. Now, let me warn you that you are about to view some terse C code (remember, knowledge is power). Assume you have defined the following new function prototype:

```
// Creates the IHello interface and returns an associated
// ITypeInfo pointer.
ITypeInfo* CreateInterface(ICreateTypeLib *pctlib);
```

The purpose of this helper function is to create the characteristics of the IHello interface ([uuid], base interface, and the single SayHello() method) and then insert it into the previously created type library. Notice that you need to pass in the ICreateTypeLib interface you obtained from the previous call to the CreateTypeLibrary() helper function. As you may expect, the returned ITypeInfo reference represents the in-memory representation of the IHello interface. Here is the complete method implementation (with analysis to follow):

```
// Add an interface to the incoming type library.
ITypeInfo* CreateInterface(ICreateTypeLib* pctlib)
{
  cout << "Creating IHello interface!" << endl;
  ICreateTypeInfo *pctinfo = NULL;
  HREFTYPE hreftype;
  ITypeInfo *ptinfoIUnknown = NULL;
  ITypeLib *ptlibStdOle = NULL;
  ITypeInfo* ptinfoIHello = NULL;
  GUID theGUID;
  FUNCDESC funcdesc;      // Used to define IHello::SayHello().
  CoCreateGuid(&theGUID);
  // Get type info for IUnknown (as it is the base interface
  // of IHello).
  LoadTypeLib(OLESTR("stdole32.tlb"), &ptlibStdOle);
  ptlibStdOle->GetTypeInfoOfGuid(IID_IUnknown, &ptinfoIUnknown);
  ptlibStdOle->Release();

  // Make the IHello interface.
  pctlib->CreateTypeInfo(OLESTR("IHello"), TKIND_INTERFACE, &pctinfo);
  pctinfo->SetGuid(theGUID);
  pctinfo->SetDocString(OLESTR("Hello Interface"));
  pctinfo->SetTypeFlags(TYPEFLAG_FHIDDEN);

  // Save typeinfo of IHello for others who may refer to it.
  pctinfo->QueryInterface(IID_ITypeInfo, (void**)&ptinfoIHello);
```

```
    // Output base interface of IHello (IUnknown)
    pctinfo->AddRefTypeInfo(ptinfoIUnknown, &hreftype);
    pctinfo->AddImplType(0, hreftype);

    // Make SayHello() method (using FUNCDESC structure).
    cout << "Creating IHello.SayHello() method!" << endl;
    OLECHAR * rgszFuncArgNamesSH[1] = {OLESTR("SayHello")};
    funcdesc.memid = 1;
    funcdesc.lprgscode = NULL;
    funcdesc.lprgelemdescParam = NULL;
    funcdesc.funckind = FUNC_PUREVIRTUAL;
    funcdesc.invkind = INVOKE_FUNC;
    funcdesc.callconv = CC_STDCALL;
    funcdesc.cParams = 0;
    funcdesc.cParamsOpt = 0;
    funcdesc.oVft = 0;
    funcdesc.cScodes = 0;
    funcdesc.elemdescFunc.tdesc.vt = VT_HRESULT;
    funcdesc.elemdescFunc.idldesc.dwReserved = NULL;
    funcdesc.elemdescFunc.idldesc.wIDLFlags = IDLFLAG_NONE;
    funcdesc.wFuncFlags = 0;
    pctinfo->AddFuncDesc(0, &funcdesc);
    pctinfo->SetFuncAndParamNames(0, rgszFuncArgNamesSH, 1);
    pctinfo->SetFuncDocString(0, OLESTR("This method says hello..."));
    pctinfo->LayOut();
    pctinfo->Release();
    // Return ITypeInfo for IHello.
    return ptinfoIHello;
}
```

Breaking Down the CreateInterface() Helper Method

Hmmm. This looks a bit more complex than the process of creating the type library itself. Well, that's why you get paid the big bucks. In reality it isn't all that bad if you break things down bit by bit. The function begins by loading the standard OLE type library (stdole32.tlb) to obtain a reference to the type information for IUnknown. This reference is held in an ITypeInfo interface (described in detail earlier in this chapter). Why do you need to do this? Well, as you recall, all COM interfaces must ultimately derive from this base interface, and therefore you best have access to its type information! Like all things in COM, once you have made use of a given interface, you call Release():

```
// Get type info for IUnknown (as it is the base interface
// of IHello).
ITypeInfo *ptinfoIUnknown = NULL;
ITypeLib *ptlibStdOle = NULL;
...
LoadTypeLib(OLESTR("stdole32.tlb"), &ptlibStdOle);
ptlibStdOle->GetTypeInfoOfGuid(IID_IUnknown, &ptinfoIUnknown);
ptlibStdOle->Release();
```

Once you have a reference to the base interface of IHello, you perform a series of steps to establish IHello. Here is the relevant code under dissection:

```
// Make the IHello interface.
HREFTYPE hreftype;
ICreateTypeInfo *pctinfo = NULL;
ITypeInfo* ptinfoIHello = NULL;
...
pctlib->CreateTypeInfo(OLESTR("IHello"), TKIND_INTERFACE, &pctinfo);
pctinfo->SetGuid(theGUID);
pctinfo->SetDocString(OLESTR("Hello Interface"));
pctinfo->SetTypeFlags(TYPEFLAG_FHIDDEN);
// Save typeinfo of IHello for others who may refer to it.
pctinfo->QueryInterface(IID_ITypeInfo, (void**)&ptinfoIHello);
// Output base interface of IHello (IUnknown)
pctinfo->AddRefTypeInfo(ptinfoIUnknown, &hreftype);
pctinfo->AddImplType(0, hreftype);
```

The key point to this code block is the call to ICreateTypeLib::CreateTypeInfo(). As you can see, you are specifying a name for your type (IHello as a Unicode string), storage for the returned ICreateTypeInfo interface, and the TKIND_INTERFACE member of the TYPEKIND enumeration (due to the fact that we are creating a COM interface type). Here is the IDL description of TYPEKIND:

```
// This IDL enum defined in oaidl.idl
typedef [v1_enum] enum tagTYPEKIND {
  TKIND_ENUM = 0,
  TKIND_RECORD,
  TKIND_MODULE,
  TKIND_INTERFACE,
  TKIND_DISPATCH,
```

```
  TKIND_COCLASS,
  TKIND_ALIAS,
  TKIND_UNION,
  TKIND_MAX          // End of enum marker
} TYPEKIND;
```

Once the [uuid] and [helpstring] values have been set (a la the ICreateTypeInfo::SetGuid() and ICreateTypeInfo::SetDocString() methods), you make a call to ITypeInfo::SetTypeFlags(). As suggested by the name of the method, SetTypeFlags() is used to further qualify the COM type with various IDL attributes. Given that a COM type may be any number of entities (interfaces, coclasses, and so forth), the parameters sent into SetTypeFlags()depend on the type you are attempting to generate. All in all, you may specify any of the following values of the TYPEFLAGS enumeration:

```
typedef enum tagTYPEFLAGS {
  TYPEFLAG_FAPPOBJECT = 0x01,
  TYPEFLAG_FCANCREATE = 0x02,
  TYPEFLAG_FLICENSED = 0x04,
  TYPEFLAG_FPREDECLID = 0x08,
  TYPEFLAG_FHIDDEN = 0x10,
  TYPEFLAG_FCONTROL = 0x20,
  TYPEFLAG_FDUAL = 0x40,
  TYPEFLAG_FNONEXTENSIBLE = 0x80,
  TYPEFLAG_FOLEAUTOMATION = 0x100,
  TYPEFLAG_FRESTRICTED = 0x200,
  TYPEFLAG_FAGGREGATABLE = 0x400,
  TYPEFLAG_FREPLACEABLE = 0x800,
  TYPEFLAG_FDISPATCHABLE = 0x1000,
  TYPEFLAG_FREVERSEBIND = 0x2000
} TYPEFLAGS;
```

Hopefully, Table 4-13 provides some degree of insight as to what the core TYPEFLAGS values mean in terms of COM IDL.

Table 4-13. Various TYPEFLAGS Values

TYPEFLAGS (Values You Might Actually Care About)	Meaning in Life
TYPEFLAG_FAPPOBJECT	Defines an application object. These types are automatically created on the loading of the COM server (think VB 6.0's Instancing =GlobalSingleUse).
TYPEFLAG_FCANCREATE	Instances of the type can be created by ITypeInfo::CreateInstance().
TYPEFLAG_FLICENSED	The type is licensed.
TYPEFLAG_FHIDDEN	The type should not be displayed to browsers.
TYPEFLAG_FDUAL	The interface supplies both late and early binding.
TYPEFLAG_FOLEAUTOMATION	The types used in the interface are fully compatible with Automation, including early binding support. Basically, this flag sets the [oleautomation] attribute.
TYPEFLAG_FRESTRICTED	Should not be accessible from macro languages. This flag is intended for system-level types or types that type browsers should not display.
TYPEFLAG_FAGGREGATABLE	The class supports aggregation.
TYPEFLAG_FDISPATCHABLE	Indicates that the interface derives from IDispatch, either directly or indirectly. This flag is computed.

Building the SayHello() Method

The final block of code within the CreateInterface() helper method (and the largest block of said code) is the establishment of the SayHello() method. Members of a COM interface are ultimately described using a FUNCDESC structure:

```
// Defined in oaidl.idl
typedef struct tagFUNCDESC
{
  MEMBERID memid;
  SCODE __RPC_FAR *lprgscode;
  ELEMDESC __RPC_FAR *lprgelemdescParam;
  FUNCKIND funckind;
  INVOKEKIND invkind;
  CALLCONV callconv;
```

```
  SHORT cParams;
  SHORT cParamsOpt;
  SHORT oVft;
  SHORT cScodes;
  ELEMDESC elemdescFunc;
  WORD wFuncFlags;
} FUNCDESC;
```

As you may be able to tell, many of the fields of the FUNCDESC are in fact enumeration values. Rather than detailing each and every possible value of each and every FUNCDESC-centric structure, let's just focus of the behavior established for the SayHello() method:

```
// Establish the SayHello() function.
FUNCDESC funcdesc;
...
OLECHAR* rgszFuncArgNamesSH[1] = {OLESTR("SayHello")};
funcdesc.memid = 1;
funcdesc.lprgscode = NULL;
funcdesc.lprgelemdescParam = NULL;
funcdesc.funckind = FUNC_PUREVIRTUAL;
funcdesc.invkind = INVOKE_FUNC;
funcdesc.callconv = CC_STDCALL;
funcdesc.cParams = 0;
funcdesc.cParamsOpt = 0;
funcdesc.oVft = 0;
funcdesc.cScodes = 0;
funcdesc.elemdescFunc.tdesc.vt = VT_HRESULT;
funcdesc.elemdescFunc.idldesc.dwReserved = NULL;
funcdesc.elemdescFunc.idldesc.wIDLFlags = IDLFLAG_NONE;
funcdesc.wFuncFlags = 0;

// Remember! pctinfo is a handle to IHello!
pctinfo->AddFuncDesc(0, &funcdesc);
pctinfo->SetFuncAndParamNames(0, rgszFuncArgNamesSH, 1);
pctinfo->SetFuncDocString(0, OLESTR("This method says hello..."));
pctinfo->LayOut();
pctinfo->Release();
```

In essence what we are saying is "Build a method named SayHello() that takes no parameters and returns an HRESULT" via various fields of the FUNCDESC structure (I'll assume you will check out each possible value at your leisure). Do note that it is *critical* to call ICreateTypeInfo::LayOut() once you have established a COM type to commit the changes (if you will). At this point, you have effectively created the following IDL in memory:

```
[uuid(<some guid.>),
helpstring("Hello Interface"), odl, hidden]
interface IHello : IUnknown
{
  [helpstring("This method says hello...")]
  HRESULT SayHello(void);
};
```

In case you are wondering why you attributed the [hidden] attribute to the IHello interface, understand that you are using type library creation interfaces to insert COM type definitions within a library statement (rather than outside the scope of the type library). Recall that if an interface is referenced within the scope of a library statement, it will be visible to higher-level languages such as VB 6.0. Given that the Hello coclass supports IHello as its [default] interface, it would be redundant (and a bit confusing) to have this same interface visible from the VB Object Browser.

Building the Hello Coclass

The final step of this exercise is to create type information for the Hello coclass itself. Given that coclasses support interfaces and are defined in a type library, it makes sense that your final function prototype takes the following parameters:

```
// Create a coclass using this type library (ICreateTypeLib)
// and list the IHello interface (ITypeInfo).
void CreateCoClass(ICreateTypeLib* pctlib, ITypeInfo* pCurrType);
```

The implementation is far less formidable than the creation of the interface itself:

```
void CreateCoClass(ICreateTypeLib* pctlib, ITypeInfo* ptinfoIHello)
{
  cout << "Creating Hello CoClass!" << endl;
  GUID theGUID;
  CoCreateGuid(&theGUID);
  ICreateTypeInfo *pctinfo = NULL;
  HREFTYPE hreftype;
```

```
  // Create the coclass.
  pctlib->CreateTypeInfo(OLESTR("Hello"), TKIND_COCLASS, &pctinfo);
  pctinfo->SetGuid(theGUID);
  pctinfo->SetTypeFlags(TYPEFLAG_FCANCREATE);
  pctinfo->SetDocString(OLESTR("Hello Class"));

  // List IHello in the coclass.
  pctinfo->AddRefTypeInfo(ptinfoIHello, &hreftype);
  pctinfo->AddImplType(0, hreftype);
  pctinfo->SetImplTypeFlags(0, IMPLTYPEFLAG_FDEFAULT);
  pctinfo->LayOut();
  pctinfo->Release();
}
```

Again, take the incoming ICreateTypeLib interface and make use of the call CreateTypeInfo(), this time specifying a TYPEKIND value of TKIND_COCLASS. Using the resulting ICreateTypeInfo reference, you are able to set the GUID, type flags, and [helpstring]. To specify IHello as the default interface requires little less than adding the correct ITypeInfo reference while specifying the IMPLTYPEFLAG_FDEFAULT flag. Once ICreateTypeInfo::LayOut() has been called, you have the following in-memory type IDL information:

```
[uuid(<some guid>),
helpstring("Hello Class")]
coclass Hello
{
   [default] interface IHello;
}
```

Testing the Application

With each of your three helper functions established, you can now configure main() as follows (without excessive error checking):

```
// Make that type information!
int main(int argc, char* argv[])
{
  CoInitialize(NULL);
  ICreateTypeLib *pCTL = NULL;
  ITypeInfo *pCurrType = NULL;
  // Create the type library.
  pCTL = CreateTypeLibrary();
```

```
    // Create IHello interface.
    pCurrType = CreateInterface(pCTL);

    // Now create the coclass.
    CreateCoClass(pCTL, pCurrType);
    // Save the type lib!
    pCTL->SaveAllChanges();

    // COM clean up.
    if(pCTL != NULL ) pCTL->Release();
    if(pCurrType != NULL ) pCurrType->Release();
    CoUninitialize();
    return 0;
}
```

Once you execute this application, you will find the MyTypeLib.tlb file is present and accounted for (Figure 4-4).

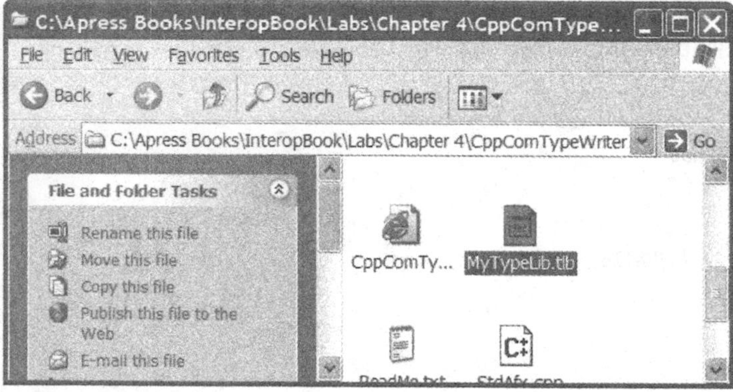

Figure 4-4. Proof that the exotic world of runtime COM type generation is possible

If you open this *.tlb file using the VB 6.0 Project | References menu option (and manually navigate to location of your new file using the Browse button), you will be able to view the types using the Object Browser tool (F2) as seen in Figure 4-5 (note the [helpstring] for the SayHello() method).

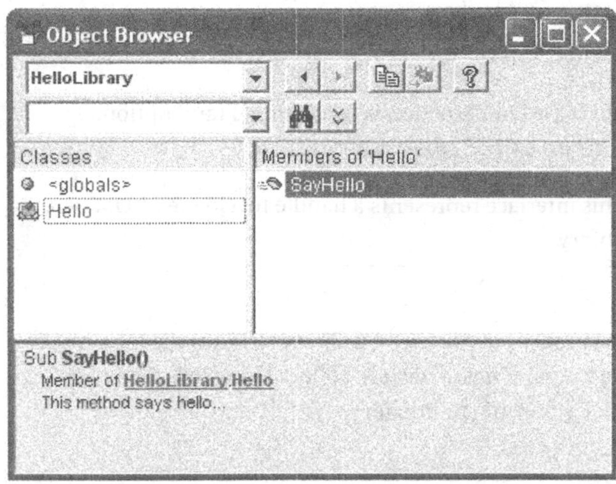

Figure 4-5. Recall! IHello is the [default] interface of Hello.

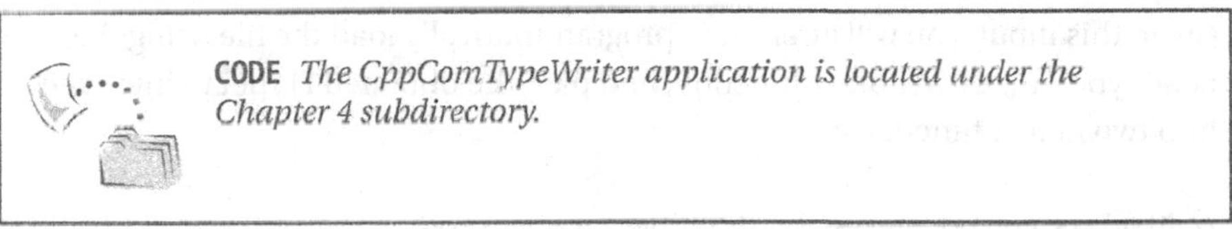

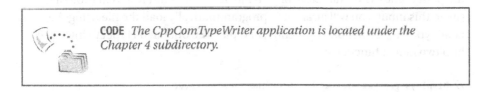

CODE *The CppComTypeWriter application is located under the Chapter 4 subdirectory.*

Programmatically Reading COM Type Information

So at this point you have received a lesson in the process of building COM type information on the fly using a small subset of the COM library. As you would expect, there are equivalent types that allow you to *read* COM type information at runtime. For example, consider the VB 6.0 Object Browser. Essentially all this tool does is load a *.tlb file from disk, read the contents, and display the binary IDL within a functional user interface.

Your next goal is to build your type library browser application. Of course, it will not look as sharp as the GUI-based tool (as you opt for a simple console window UI) but it should get the point across that it is completely possible to programmatically read type libraries at runtime. Formally speaking, this process is termed *reflection*. The key players involved in COM reflection services are listed in Table 4-14.

Table 4-14. Type Library-Centric COM Library Items

COM Type Information Reader Atom	Meaning in Life
LoadTypeLib()	This COM API function is used to load (and optionally register) a COM type library.
ITypeLib	This interface represents a handle to a loaded COM type library.

As you may suspect, the process of reading a COM type library is far simpler than creating one in memory. Again, if you wish to follow along, create a new Win32 Console Application (CppComTypeReader).

The Program Skeleton

Basically, your console application will prompt the user for input that specifies the path to the COM *.dll, *.exe, or *.tlb file he or she is interested in browsing. Given this input, you will attempt to programmatically load the file using the LoadTypeLib() COM library function, and pass the obtained ITypeLib interface into two helper functions:

```
// Displays general statistics about the type library.
void DumpLibraryStats(ITypeLib* pTypeLib);
// Iterates over each COM type and dumps
// selective information for each.
void DumpComTypes(ITypeLib* pTypeLib);
```

You will also construct a do/while loop to keep prompting for path names until the user tells you to stop this madness by typing **n** (No). Before you see the implementation of each function, here is the general form of the main() function (and some important preprocessor include directives to leverage ATL string conversion macros):

```
// Include these ATL files to get the string stuff...
#include <atlbase.h>
#include <atlconv.h>
#include <iostream.h>
...
int main(int argc, char* argv[])
```

```
{
  USES_CONVERSION;
  char oneMoreTime; // ('n' or 'y')
  char pathToComServer[100] = {0};
  do
  {
    // Get path to COM server.
    cout << "Please enter path to COM server (or *tlb file)";
    ITypeLib* pTypeLib = NULL;
    cin.ignore(0, '\n');
    cin.get(pathToComServer, 100);

    // Load type information for a COM server.
    if(SUCCEEDED(LoadTypeLibEx(A2W(pathToComServer),
                 REGKIND_DEFAULT, &pTypeLib)))
    {
      // Read info about the type lib.
      DumpLibraryStats(pTypeLib);
      // Read info about COM types.
      DumpComTypes(pTypeLib);
      // COM clean up.
      pTypeLib->Release();
    }
    // Want another?
    cout << "Do you want to enter another? (y or n)";
    cin >> oneMoreTime;
    }while (oneMoreTime != 'n');
  return 0;
}
```

Displaying COM Library Information

The implementation of DumpLibraryStats() takes the incoming ITypeLib interface and calls a series of methods to print out general traits. Table 4-15 showcases the core members of ITypeLib.

Table 4-15. Core Members of ITypeLib

ITypeLib Interface Member	Meaning in Life
FindName()	Finds occurrences of a type description in a type library.
GetDocumentation()	Retrieves the library's documentation string, name of the complete Help file name and path, and the context identifier for the library Help topic.
GetLibAttr()	Retrieves the structure (TLIBATTR) containing the library's attributes. The returned TLIBATTR must be released by calling ReleaseTLibAttr() to free the allocated memory.
GetTypeInfo()	Retrieves an ITypeInfo interface for a given COM type in the library.
GetTypeInfoCount()	Retrieves the number of types in the type library.
GetTypeInfoOfGuid()	Retrieves the type description corresponding to the specified globally unique identifier (GUID).
GetTypeInfoType()	Retrieves the type of a type description.
ReleaseTLibAttr()	Releases the TLIBATTR structure, originally obtained from ITypeLib::GetLibAttr().

With this, here is the implementation of DumpLibraryStats():

```
void DumpLibraryStats(ITypeLib* pTypeLib)
{
    pTypeLib->AddRef();
    cout << "****** Stats about the Library ******" << endl;
    USES_CONVERSION;
    TLIBATTR* libAttr;
    pTypeLib->GetLibAttr(&libAttr);
    CComBSTR bstrGuid(libAttr->guid);
    cout << "Major: " << libAttr->wMajorVerNum << endl;
    cout << "Minor: " << libAttr->wMinorVerNum << endl;
    cout << "LibID: " << W2A(bstrGuid.Copy()) << endl;
    cout << "Locale ID: " << libAttr->lcid << endl;
    pTypeLib->ReleaseTLibAttr(libAttr);
    pTypeLib->Release();
}
```

If you take a test run of the logic thus far (assuming you do not yet call the DumpComTypes() function), you will be able to read the MyTypeLib.tlb file generated by the CppComTypeWriter application (see Figure 4-6 for output).

Figure 4-6. Reading type library attributes at runtime

Dumping COM Type Information

Recall that every COM type can be represented by an ITypeInfo interface reference. Also recall that the TYPEKIND structure allows you to specify a given type programmatically. Given these two factoids, the DumpComTypes() helper function begins by asking the incoming ITypeLib interface to return the number of type definitions via GetTypeInfoCount(). Once you know exactly how many COM types are in the library, you are able to enter a loop to test for each member of the TYPEKIND enumeration. Here is the skeleton code (you fill in the case statements in just a bit):

```
void DumpComTypes(ITypeLib* pTypeLib)
{
  // Get number of COM types in this library.
  USES_CONVERSION;
  pTypeLib->AddRef();
  ULONG typeCount = pTypeLib->GetTypeInfoCount();
  cout << "\n****** The COM Types ******" << endl;
  cout << "There are " << typeCount << " in this type lib" << endl << endl;
  // Now list out each COM type.
  for(ULONG typeIndex = 0; typeIndex < typeCount; typeIndex++)
  {
    ITypeInfo* pInfo = NULL;
    TYPEATTR* typeAtt;
    CComBSTR temp;
```

```
        ULONG index = 0;
        ULONG numbMembers = 0;
        pTypeLib->GetTypeInfo(typeIndex, &pInfo);
        pInfo->GetTypeAttr(&typeAtt);
        switch(typeAtt->typekind)
        {
          case  TKIND_COCLASS:    // type is a coclass.
          break;
          case TKIND_DISPATCH:    // type is a IDispatch derived interface.
          break;
          case TKIND_INTERFACE:  // Type is an IUnknown derived interface.
          break;
          case TKIND_ENUM:        // Type is an COM enumeration.
          break;

          default:
            cout << "Some other type I don't care about..." << endl;
        }
        cout << endl;
        pInfo->ReleaseTypeAttr(typeAtt);
        pInfo->Release();
      }
      pTypeLib->Release();
    }
```

Listing CoClass Statistics

The case statement for TKIND_COCLASS prints out the number of interfaces on the object, its CLSID, its friendly name, and any supplied [helpstring]. To do so requires some COM string conversion mumbo-jumbo (simplified using the ATL CComBSTR helper class). Beyond this fact, the code is not too painful to observe:

```
case TKIND_COCLASS: // type is a coclass.
  cout << "(" << typeIndex << ")" << " Coclass with "
       << typeAtt->cImplTypes << " interface(s). ******" << endl;
  temp = typeAtt->guid;
  cout << "->CLSID: " << W2A(temp.Copy()) << endl;
  pInfo->GetDocumentation(-1, &temp, NULL, NULL, NULL);
  cout << "->Name: " << W2A(temp.Copy()) << endl;
break;
```

Listing IDispatch-Based Interface Statistics

TKIND_DISPATCH-based COM types will be asked to return the number of methods they define, each of which is represented by FUNCDESC. Using FUNCDESC, you will obtain the number of parameters for each method:

```
case TKIND_DISPATCH: // type is a IDispatch derived interface.
  cout << "(" << typeIndex << ")" << " IDispatch based interface with "
      << typeAtt->cFuncs << " method(s). ******" << endl;
  temp = typeAtt->guid;
  cout << "->IID: " << W2A(temp.Copy()) << endl;
  pInfo->GetDocumentation(-1, &temp, NULL, NULL, NULL);
  cout << "->Name: " << W2A(temp.Copy()) << endl;

  numbMembers = typeAtt->cFuncs;
  for(index = 0; index < numbMembers; index++)
  {
    FUNCDESC* fx;
    pInfo->GetFuncDesc(index, &fx);
    pInfo->GetDocumentation(fx->memid, &temp, NULL, NULL, NULL);
    cout << " ->" << W2A(temp.Copy()) << " has "
      << fx->cParams << " params" << endl;
    pInfo->ReleaseFuncDesc(fx);
  }
break;
```

Listing IUnknown-Based Interface Statistics

The story here is short and sweet. Basically, TKIND_INTERFACE is implemented identically as the case for TKIND_DISPATCH. In fact this is so much the case, I'll just assume you copy and paste the implementation between implementations (and tweak the cout statements).

Listing COM Enumeration Statistics

TKIND_ENUM is along the same lines as the other cases. This time, however, you are interested in printing out the number of members (identified by the VARDESC structure) for the enum and any specified [helpstring].

```
    case TKIND_ENUM: // Type is an enum.
    cout << "(" << typeIndex << ")" << " Enum with "
        << typeAtt->cVars << " member(s). ******" << endl;
    pInfo->GetDocumentation(-1, &temp, NULL, NULL, NULL);
    cout << "->Name: " << W2A(temp.Copy()) << endl;

    numbMembers = typeAtt->cVars;
    for(index = 0; index < numbMembers; index++)
    {
      VARDESC* var;
      pInfo->GetVarDesc(index, &var);
      pInfo->GetDocumentation(var->memid, &temp, NULL, NULL, NULL);
      cout << " ->" << W2A(temp.Copy()) << endl;
      pInfo->ReleaseVarDesc(var);
}
```

Reading the MyTypeLib.tlb file

So! If your fingers are not worn to the bone from the typing of these last two applications, you are now in the position to take the current application out for a test drive. For example, Figure 4-7 shows the output for specifying MyTypeLib.tlb as the input (which I have moved to my C:\ drive to save *myself* some typing).

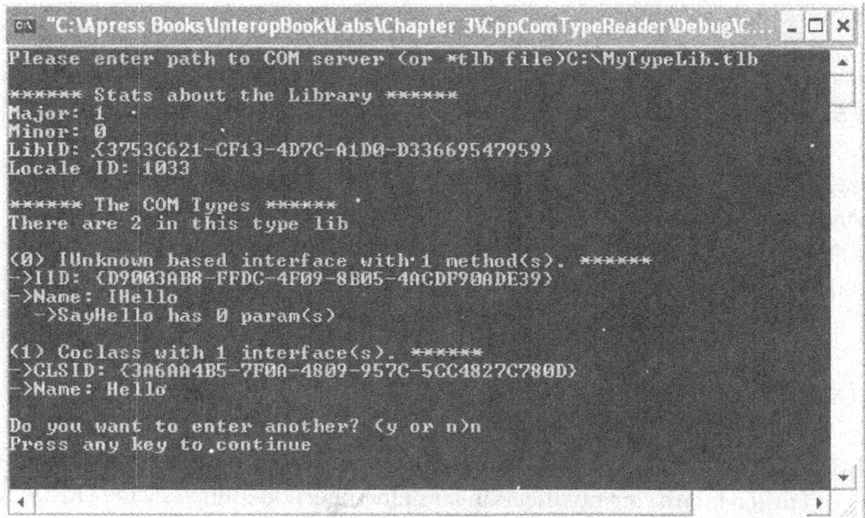

Figure 4-7. Reading the MyTypeLib.tlb file

Now, let's try something more exotic. If you enter in the path to msado15.dll (the COM server describing the Active Data Objects, or ADO), you see 96 different COM types whirl down the console application (you may want to update your code to print out 10 or so at a time to see them all). Figure 4-8 shows item 85 (remember, numbering starts at zero), which happens to be the Connection type.

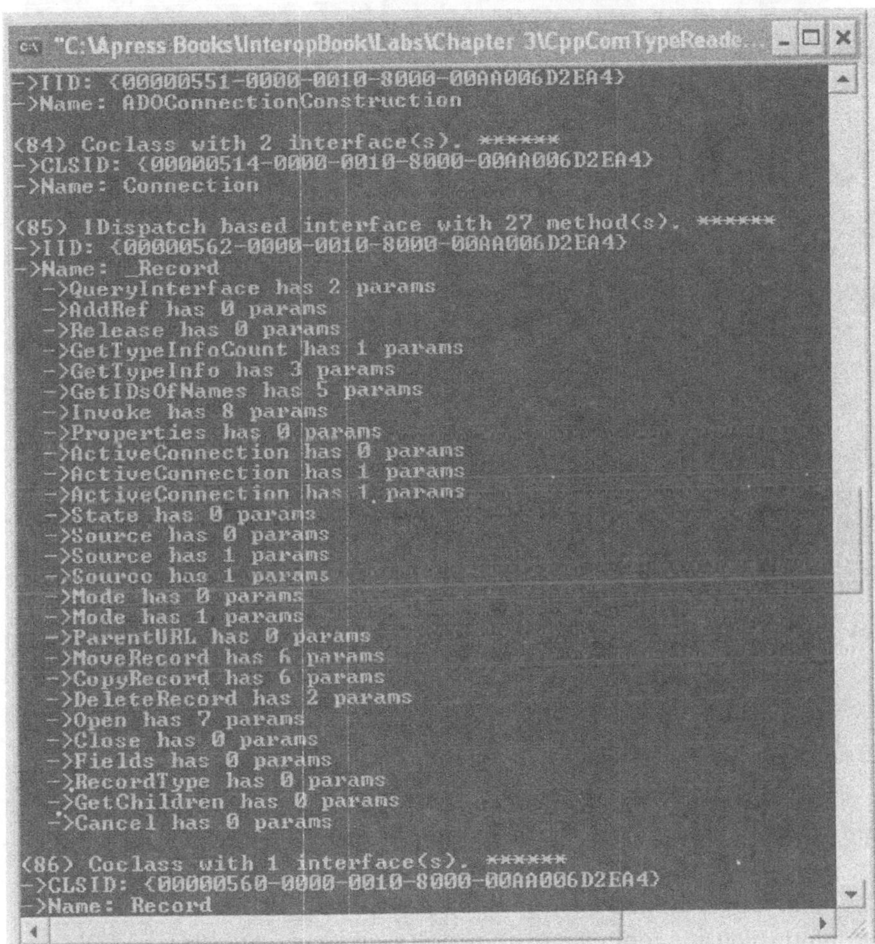

Figure 4-8. Reading the ADO type library

Of course you could reflect on the COM servers you created back in the previous chapters as well. For example, here is the Vb6CarSever.dll dump (Figure 4-9).

```
"C:\Apress Books\InteropBook\Labs\Chapter 3\CppComTypeReader\Debug...
Please enter path to COM server (or *tlb file)C:\Vb6CarServer.dll

****** Stats about the Library ******
Major: 2
Minor: 0
LibID: {B1C01A96-C8E9-4DA0-A268-FFA571AD7542}
Locale ID: 0

****** The COM Types ******
There are 4 in this type lib

(0) IDispatch based interface with 9 method(s). ******
->IID: {BFC753BA-4CEB-4682-BD63-8973D3CB2186}
->Name: _CoCar
  ->QueryInterface has 2 params
  ->AddRef has 0 params
  ->Release has 0 params
  ->GetTypeInfoCount has 1 params
  ->GetTypeInfo has 3 params
  ->GetIDsOfNames has 5 params
  ->Invoke has 8 params
  ->Speed has 0 params
  ->Speed has 1 params

(1) Coclass with 2 interface(s). ******
->CLSID: {E93D5FF5-3F76-4BE9-A547-5398B2AA4CF7}
->Name: CoCar

(2) IDispatch based interface with 8 method(s). ******
->IID: {0FE9EC86-7959-42CA-97B3-61B14214718D}
->Name: _IVBTurbo
  ->QueryInterface has 2 params
  ->AddRef has 0 params
  ->Release has 0 params
  ->GetTypeInfoCount has 1 params
  ->GetTypeInfo has 3 params
  ->GetIDsOfNames has 5 params
  ->Invoke has 8 params
  ->TurboBlast has 0 params

(3) Coclass with 1 interface(s). ******
->CLSID: {39780FBA-95C9-465E-8A34-59A6AA23DF8C}
->Name: IVBTurbo

Do you want to enter another? (y or n)
```

Figure 4-9. Reading your VB 6.0 COM server

I think you get the general idea. Using the COM library, you are able to build type information and commit it to file as well as programmatically read COM type information at runtime.

Defining Custom IDL Attributes

The IDL language is, to some extent, extendable. Using the [custom] IDL attribute, you are able to add your annotations to a COM type library. In effect, when you make use of the [custom] attribute, you are building new IDL attributes that can be programmatically obtained at runtime using the ITypeLib2 and ITypeInfo2 interfaces.

The key point to understand about defining custom IDL attributes is the fact that the semantics of these data points is meaningless unless some other piece of software is "aware" of their presence. If you do not specifically poll a type library for a chunk of custom data, it is completely ignored by COM-centric tools. However, as you will see later in this text, the [custom] attribute is quite helpful when working with COM/.NET interoperability issues.

Custom IDL attributes are realized as simple name/value pairs. The name of a custom attribute is (of course) a GUID. The value of the attribute can be any [oleautomation]-compliant data type (that is, the data type must be able to be represented as a VARIANT). To illustrate, assume you have the following *.idl file that establishes three custom attributes (each GUID has been generated using guidgen.exe):

```
[object,
uuid(267943B0-50E4-400C-8F79-4B68D4A839FA),
custom(1403B3A5-38FE-4ba9-94E2-54577F712E7A,
      "ToDo: Implement methods..."),
helpstring("IFoo Interface"),
pointer_default(unique)]
interface IFoo : IUnknown
{
  [helpstring("method MethodA")] HRESULT MethodA();
};
[uuid(365739ED-EE97-4F7C-A050-BC157F04663A),
version(1.0),
helpstring("CustomIDLServer 1.0 Type Library"),
custom(FF69F249-3FC0-4062-9CB6-7901E4DD3B7A,
      "Updated: 3/24/01")]
library CUSTOMIDLSERVERLib
{
  importlib("stdole32.tlb");
  importlib("stdole2.tlb");
  [uuid(EA0AF1B1-5EA7-4352-AF6D-E78606614CCA),
  helpstring("Foo Class"),
  custom(97240DA1-C8DD-4548-95B7-DFBEF217C026,
        "ProgID: CustomIDLServer.Foo")]
  coclass Foo
  {
    [default] interface IFoo;
  };
};
```

As you can see, each [custom] attribute makes use of a BSTR data type to represent its value. Again, these annotations are only of use to a software entity that is on the lookout for these GUIDs. What the application in question does with this information is a matter of choice. Here, your first two [custom] attributes are little more than internal notes for our development team (or simply ourselves). The third attribute however does have some value. Using the custom attribute named 97240DA1-C8DD-4548-95B7-DFBEF217C026, a client is able to automatically obtain the ProgID of the COM type (can anyone say late binding?).

Understand that the [custom] IDL attribute may be assigned to numerous aspects of a COM IDL file. Specifically, you are free to assign custom annotations to library statements, coclasses, interfaces (including dispinterfaces), methods, and even individual method parameters.

Reading Custom Attributes

Now that you have established a set of [custom] attributes, you need to learn how to extract these name/value pairs at runtime. Before you see the code, Figure 4-10 shows the output you are shooting for.

```
"C:\Apress Books\InteropBook\Labs\Chapter 3\CustomIDLDataReader\...
Custom data name is: {FF69F249-3FC0-4062-9CB6-7901E4DD3B7A}
Custom data value is: Updated: 3/24/01

Custom data name is: {97240DA1-C8DD-4548-95B7-DFBEF217C026}
Custom data value is: ProgID: CustomIDLServer.Foo

Custom data name is: {1403B3A5-38FE-4BA9-94E2-54577F712E7A}
Custom data value is: ToDo:  Implement methods...

Press any key to continue
```

Figure 4-10. Reading [custom] IDL attributes

When you wish to read [custom] IDL attributes, you must make use of the ITypeLib2 and ITypeInfo2 interfaces (in addition to the LoadTypeLibEx() COM library function). First, get to know ITypeLib2. This interface derives from ITypeLib and adds a number of methods specifically designed to read [custom] metadata from a COM type library. Table 4-16 lists the methods of interest.

Table 4-16. Core Members of ITypeLib2

ITypeLib2 Method	Meaning in Life
GetCustData()	Returns a VARIANT containing the value of a given [custom] attribute, based on the GUID of said [custom] attribute.
GetAllCustData()	Returns a CUSTDATA structure that contains the name/value pairs for all [custom] data in the library statement.

While ITypeLib2 allows you to read any [custom] attributes applied at the library level, when you wish to read [custom] information for a given COM type, you need to work with ITypeInfo2 (which of course derives from ITypeInfo). This interface actually defines a number of helpful methods that are not necessarily related to reading [custom] IDL metadata. I'll allow you to check out the full set of members from online Help and focus on the members listed in Table 4-17.

Table 4-17. Core Members of ITypeInfo2

ITypeInfo2 Method	Meaning in Life
GetCustData() GetAllCustData()	Returns a VARIANT or CUSTDATA structure for all custom attributes for the current COM type
GetFuntCustData() GetAllFuntCustData()	Returns a VARIANT or CUSTDATA structure for all custom attributes for all functions of the COM type
GetParamCustData() GetAllParamCustData()	Returns a VARIANT or CUSTDATA structure for all custom attributes for all parameters of a method supported by the COM interface
GetVarCustData() GetAllVarCustData()	Returns a VARIANT or CUSTDATA structure for all custom attributes for variables in the type library
GetImplTypeCustData() GetAllImplTypeCustData()	Returns a VARIANT or CUSTDATA structure for all custom attributes for all COM types

Both the ITypeLib2 and ITypeInfo2 interfaces define a number of methods that return a single VARIANT. If you know the exact GUID of the custom attribute you are looking for, you are able to crack of the value of the VARIANT and act accordingly. If you would rather obtain all custom attributes for a given COM type (or type library) you will call one of the "all" methods (that is, GetAllCustData() and friends) and obtain a CUSTDATA structure:

```
typedef struct tagCUSTDATA
{
  DWORD cCustData;  // Number of CUSTDATAITEMs.
  LPCUSTDATAITEM prgCustData;  // Array of CUSTDATAITEMs.
}CUSTDATA;
```

The cCustData field of the CUSTDATA structure represents the number of items in the CUSTDATAITEM array (LPCUSTDATAITEM). The CUSTDATAITEM structure contains (as you may guess) a GUID and VARIANT field:

```
typedef struct tagCUSTDATAITEM
{
  GUID guid;  // Name of custom attribute.
  VARIANTARG varValue;  // Value of custom attribute.
}CUSTDATAITEM;
```

Now that you understand the various types used to read [custom] IDL attributes, you can take a look at the code behind the CustomIDLDataReader console application. Here is the code used to read the [custom] attribute found in the library statement:

```
// …various #include statements…
int main(int argc, char* argv[])
{
  USES_CONVERSION;
  CoInitialize(NULL);
  ITypeLib2* pTLib2 = NULL;
  ITypeInfo2* pTInfo2 = NULL;

  // Load the type library and get ITypeLib2 interface.
  LoadTypeLibEx(L"customIDLServer.tlb",
     REGKIND_NONE, (ITypeLib**)&pTLib2);
  // Read out the custom data from the library.
  CUSTDATA theCustomData;
  pTLib2->GetAllCustData(&theCustomData);
  for(ULONG i = 0; i < theCustomData.cCustData; i++)
  {
    VARIANT customValue;
    VariantInit(&customValue);
    VariantCopy(&customValue, &theCustomData.prgCustData[i].varValue);
    if(customValue.vt == VT_BSTR)
    {
```

```
    // Display custom data.
    CComBSTR customGUID(theCustomData.prgCustData[i].guid);
    cout << "Custom data name is: " << W2A(customGUID) << endl;
    cout << "Custom data value is: " << W2A(customValue.bstrVal) << endl;
    VariantClear(&customValue);
   }
  }
}
```

Begin by obtaining an ITypeLib2 interface via LoadTypeLibEx(). Notice how you are able to obtain the number of [custom] attributes found on the library statement using the cCustData field of the CUSTDATA structure. As you look over each bit of metadata, you obtain the embedded GUID and VARIANT of the CUSTDATAITEM and (if the VARIANT is a BSTR) dump out the values to the console. You also make use of various ATL helper types (CComBSTR and various conversion macros) to ease the pain of BSTR manipulation.

Reading custom attributes for each type is more or less the same operation. Using the current ITypeLib2 interface, obtain each ITypeInfo2 interface (that is, get each COM type in the library) and act accordingly:

```
// For each COM type in the library...
for(UINT j = 0; j < pTLib2->GetTypeInfoCount(); j++)
{
  pTLib2->GetTypeInfo(j, (ITypeInfo**)&pTInfo2);
  pTInfo2->GetAllCustData(&theCustomData);
  // ...get the custom data...
  for(ULONG k = 0; k < theCustomData.cCustData; k++)
  {
   VARIANT customValue;
   VariantInit(&customValue);
   VariantCopy(&customValue, &theCustomData.prgCustData[k].varValue);
   if(customValue.vt == VT_BSTR)
   {
    // ...and display it.
    CComBSTR customGUID(theCustomData.prgCustData[k].guid);
    cout << "Custom data name is: " << W2A(customGUID) << endl;
    cout << "Custom data value is: " << W2A(customValue.bstrVal) << endl;
    VariantClear(&customValue);
   }
  }
  pTInfo2->Release();  // Release current type.
  cout << endl;
}
```

So! This concludes our examination of the core pieces of the COM architecture.

At this point you may be wondering why is it important to understand how to read and write COM type information. Now, think this one through just a bit. If a piece of software is able to read a description of all the COM types contained within a given server, it would be quite possible to build a translator, would it not? For example, you could say "Every time I find a COM BSTR, translate that type into a .NET System.String data type." You could also do more exotic things such as saying "Every time I find a coclass supporting a hierarchy of versioned interfaces (for example, ICar2 deriving from ICar), build a .NET class that is a union of all methods."

These exact rules (as well as many others) are the foundation of .NET to COM interoperability. As you'll see in later chapters, whenever a .NET type wishes to make use of a COM type, a translator termed the RCW (Runtime Callable Wrapper) reads COM type information and builds corresponding .NET equivalents. All that is required is a set of rules that make that translation possible (for example, BSTR/System.String). As mentioned, the bulk of this book is concerned with explaining these rules.

CODE *The CustomIDLServer and CustomIDLDataReader projects are included under the Chapter 4 subdirectory.*

Introducing the System.Runtime.InteropServices Namespace

To close the chapter, let's take a first look at the key .NET namespace that makes COM/.NET interoperability possible: System.Runtime.InteropServices. Using the types within this namespace, you are able to dynamically create, load, manipulate, and generate COM type information. Of course, this namespace also defines a number of .NET types that allows you to marshal information between the COM and .NET architectures, define how a .NET type should appear to COM, and various other interoperability-related tasks. You will see the full glory of this namespace throughout this text, but for the time being, Table 4-18 lists the .NET items specifically used to interact with COM type information.

Table 4-18. A Tiny Sampling of the System.Runtime.InteropServices Namespace

InteropServices COM Type Library-Centric Member	Meaning in Life
UCOMITypeComp	Managed definition of the ITypeComp interface
UCOMITypeInfo	Managed definition of the ITypeInfo interface
UCOMITypeLib	Managed definition of the ITypeLib interface
ELEMDESC	Contains the type description and process transfer information for a variable, function, or function parameter
FUNCDESC	Defines a function description
PARAMDESC	Contains information about how to transfer a structure element, parameter, or function return value between processes
TYPEATTR	Contains attributes of a UCOMITypeInfo
TYPEDESC	Describes the type of a variable, return type of a function, or the type of a function parameter
TYPELIBATTR	Identifies a particular type library and provides localization support for member names
VARDESC	Describes a variable, constant, or data member
CALLCONV	Identifies the calling convention used by a method described in a METHODDATA structure
DESCKIND	Identifies the type description being bound to
FUNCFLAGS	Identifies the constants that define the properties of a function
FUNCKIND	Defines how to access a function
IMPLTYPEFLAGS	Defines the attributes of an implemented or inherited interface of a type
LIBFLAGS	Defines flags that apply to type libraries
PARAMFLAG	Describes how to transfer a structure element, parameter, or function return value between processes
SYSKIND	Identifies the target operating system platform
TYPEFLAGS	Defines the properties and attributes of a type description
TYPEKIND	Specifies various types of data and functions
VARFLAGS	Identifies the constants that define the properties of a variable

The first item of note is the fact that many interfaces defined within the System.Runtime.InteropServices namespace have a UCOM prefix, which stands for "unmanaged COM." As you can see, you have managed equivalents for ITypeInfo, ITypeLib, and ITypeComp (which I have not addressed in this chapter). Next, notice that you have managed equivalents for a number of different COM structures (FUNCDESC, TYPEDESC, and so forth). Last but not least, you can see that numerous COM enumerations that are used during type library development also have a managed equivalent (VARFLAGS, SYSKIND, and so on).

It is important to note that System.Runtime.InteropServices does *not* define a managed equivalent for each and every possible COM interface or each and every COM type. Quite the contrary. The major purpose of this .NET namespace is to provide types that hide the raw COM infrastructure from view. Nevertheless, numerous managed COM types are present. If a required COM type is not represented in this namespace, you are free to build your managed equivalent (as you will soon see).

Building a C# COM Type Information Viewer

To take the System.Runtime.InteropServices namespace out for a spin, the remainder of this chapter illustrates how to build a C# .NET application that is able to load and display COM type library information. This Windows Forms–based application has a simple menu system that defines a File | Open and File | Exit option.

Your Form-derived type defines a number of ListBox member variables that will hold the coclasses, interfaces (IDispatch and IUnknown based), and COM enums found in the *.dll, *.exe, or *.tlb file. Finally, you have a simple Label object that will display some basic information about the type library itself. Figure 4-11 shows a test run after loading the MyTypeLib.tlb file that was generated by the CppComTypeWriter application you created earlier in this chapter.

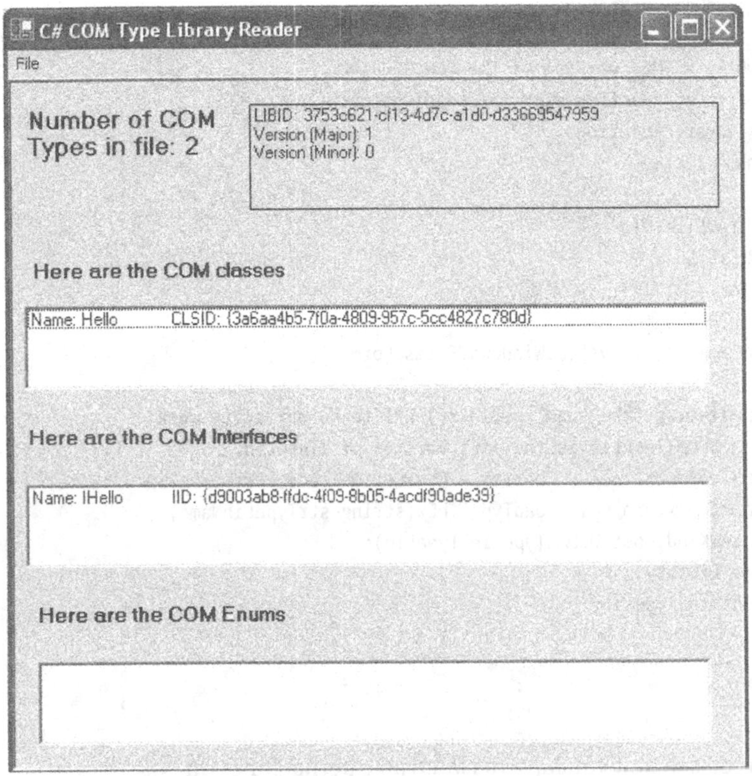

Figure 4-11. A C# application reading a COM type library

Loading the COM Type Library

If you checked out the COM type library-centric .NET types defined in System.Runtime.InteropServices, you may have noticed that this namespace does not define managed equivalents of COM library functions. Thus, you will not find a .NET version of LoadTypeLib(), CoCreateInstance(), CoGetClassObject(), or what have you. When you need to make a call to the Win32 API (COM library or otherwise) you need to make use of PInvoke. Recall that the core .NET type that constitutes the services of PInvoke is the DllImport attribute (see Chapter 1). Given this, ponder the following update to our initial Form type:

```
namespace ManagedComTypeReader
{
  // This enum is a .NET version of the COM REGKIND
  // enum used in conjunction with the LoadTypeLibEx()
  // API COM library function.
  internal enum REGKIND
  {
    REGKIND_DEFAULT = 0,
    REGKIND_REGISTER = 1,
    REGKIND_NONE = 2
  }
  public class mainForm: System.Windows.Forms.Form
  {
    // Need to leverage the LoadTypeLibEx() API to do our dirty work.
    // Param 3: UCOMITypeLib is the .NET version of ITypeLib.
    [DllImport("oleaut32.dll", CharSet = CharSet.Unicode, PreserveSig = false)]
    private static extern void LoadTypeLibEx(string strTypeLibName,
      REGKIND regKind, out UCOMITypeLib TypeLib);
    // The Type Library.
    UCOMITypeLib theTypeLib;
...
  }
}
```

Here you can see that you have declared an external function (LoadTypeLibEx()) which is mapped to the COM library function of the same name using DllImport. Thus, any time our Form wishes to load a type library, it is able to make a call to LoadTypeLibEx() and trigger the raw COM API. Also notice that you have rolled your managed version of the REGKIND enumeration. The reason is simple. Given that there is not a managed REGKIND equivalent, you need to establish the same entity for use by the LoadTypeLibEx() COM library call. The process of manually defining COM types using managed code is formally examined in Chapter 12 during your examination of advanced .NET to COM interop topics. Finally, notice that your Form defines a private member variable of type UCOMITypeLib to represent the loaded COM type information (recall that this is the managed version of ITypeLib).

Loading the COM Type Library

To allow the user to pick a file to open, you make use of the Windows Forms OpenFileDialog type. After prepping the object to our desired look and feel, you extract the file name (if you click on the OK button) and call the DLLImported LoadTypeLibEx() method. Also note that you pass in the name of the file to a helper function (LoadTypeLibrary()) to save the handle to the loaded COM library in your UCOMITypeLib member variable and print out various traits about the type library. Finally, you pass the UCOMITypeLib variable into a private helper function named FillListBoxes(), which I define in just a moment. Here is the code behind the File | Open menu Click handler:

```
private void mnuOpen_Click(object sender, System.EventArgs e)
{
  string typeLibFile = "";
  // Configure look and feel of open dlg.
  OpenFileDialog myOpenFileDialog = new OpenFileDialog();
  myOpenFileDialog.InitialDirectory = ".";
  myOpenFileDialog.Filter = "Type library files (*.tlb)|*.tlb|In-proc COM server"
  + "(*.dll)|*.dll|Local COM server (*.exe)|*.exe|All files (*.*)|*.*" ;
  myOpenFileDialog.FilterIndex = 1 ;
  myOpenFileDialog.RestoreDirectory = true ;
  // Do we have a file?
  // If so, open the type library.
  if(myOpenFileDialog.ShowDialog() == DialogResult.OK)
  {
    typeLibFile = myOpenFileDialog.FileName;
    LoadTypeLibrary(typeLibFile);
    // Fill ListBoxes.
    FillListBoxes(theTypeLib);
  }
}
```

The LoadTypeLibrary() helper function needs to do a bit of grunt work to handle the translation of COM structures into .NET equivalents. Recall that the ITypeLib COM interface defines a method named GetLibAttr(), which returns a TYPELIBATTR structure. The managed UCOMITypeLib interface also defines the GetLibAttr() method, however (alas), this method does not simply return a managed TYPELIBATTR type. Rather, UCOMITypeLib.GetLibAttr() takes a System.IntPtr type as an out parameter. The task, then, is to map a System.IntPtr type into a new managed TYPELIBATTR equivalent.

This involves the use of the System.Runtime.InteropServices.Marshal type. To keep focused on the reading of COM type information, I'll hold off on the details of the Marshal class, System.IntPtr types, and mapping pointers to structures until later in this book. Again, just ponder the following implementation of the LoadTypeLibrary() helper function:

```
private void LoadTypeLibrary(string typeLibFile)
{
```

```
    // Load type library via DllImported COM f(x).
    LoadTypeLibEx(typeLibFile, REGKIND.REGKIND_DEFAULT, out theTypeLib);
    string typLibStats;
    // Translate unmanaged TYPELIBATTR structure
    // into a managed TYPELIBATTR type.
    TYPELIBATTR libAtts = new TYPELIBATTR();
    Type TYPELIBATTRType = libAtts.GetType();
    int structSize = Marshal.SizeOf(TYPELIBATTRType);
    IntPtr ptr = IntPtr.Zero;
    ptr = Marshal.AllocHGlobal(structSize);
    theTypeLib.GetLibAttr(out ptr);
    libAtts = (TYPELIBATTR) Marshal.PtrToStructure(ptr, TYPELIBATTRType);
    // Print out stats and release memory.
    typLibStats = "LIBID: " + libAtts.guid.ToString()
      + "\nVersion (Major): " + libAtts.wMajorVerNum.ToString()
      + "\nVersion (Minor): " + libAtts.wMinorVerNum.ToString();
    lblTypeLibStats.Text = typLibStats;
    theTypeLib.ReleaseTLibAttr(ptr);
}
```

In a nutshell, this helper function creates a managed TYPELIBATTR structure and extracts its .NET type information (represented by System.Type). Using the static Marshal.SizeOf() method, you calculate the size of this structure, allocate the memory, and obtain a pointer to the memory (stored in a System.IntPtr type). Finally, you translate this pointer into the managed TYPELIBATTR structure. From here, you are able to read out various bits of information (version and LIBID).

Displaying the COM Types

The FillListBoxes() helper function will dump minimal but complete statistics about each COM type in the type library. I assume that you will extend the code to dump method names, parameters, or whatever suits your fancy. As you look over the following code, notice that it is basically the same look and feel as the CppComTypeReader program you created in C++ (in fact, I simply copied and pasted the C++ source code and performed the required cleanup). Also note that you are making use of numerous managed types defined within the System.Runtime.InteropServices namespace:

```
private void FillListBoxes(UCOMITypeLib itfTypeLib)
{
```

```
// Clear out current contents.
lstBoxCoclasses.Items.Clear();
lstBoxInterfaces.Items.Clear();
lstBoxEnums.Items.Clear();
// Get # of COM types in the library.
int typeCount = itfTypeLib.GetTypeInfoCount();
lblNumbOfTypes.Text = "Number of COM Types in file: "
                    + typeCount.ToString();

// Switch between COM type.
for(int typeIndex = 0; typeIndex < typeCount; typeIndex++)
{
  string typeInfoString;
  UCOMITypeInfo pInfo;
  // Get TYPEATTR structure set up.
  TYPEATTR typeAtt = new TYPEATTR();
  Type TYPEATTRType = typeAtt.GetType();
  int structSize = Marshal.SizeOf(TYPEATTRType);
  IntPtr ptr = IntPtr.Zero;
  ptr = Marshal.AllocHGlobal(structSize);

  // Get next type info.
  itfTypeLib.GetTypeInfo(typeIndex, out pInfo);
  pInfo.GetTypeAttr(out ptr);
  typeAtt = (TYPEATTR) Marshal.PtrToStructure(ptr, TYPEATTRType);
  // Based on the kind of COM type, print out some information.
  string typeName, helpFile, docString;
  int helpID;
  switch(typeAtt.typekind)
  {
     case TYPEKIND.TKIND_COCLASS: // type is a coclass.
      pInfo.GetDocumentation(-1, out typeName, out docString,
      out helpID, out helpFile);
      typeInfoString = "Name: " + typeName + "\tCLSID: {"
                     + typeAtt.guid.ToString() + "}";
      lstBoxCoclasses.Items.Add(typeInfoString);
    break;
    case TYPEKIND.TKIND_INTERFACE: // type is an interface.
    case TYPEKIND.TKIND_DISPATCH:
      pInfo.GetDocumentation(-1, out typeName, out docString,
      out helpID, out helpFile);
      typeInfoString = "Name: " + typeName + "\tIID: {"
                     + typeAtt.guid.ToString() + "}";
```

```
          lstBoxInterfaces.Items.Add(typeInfoString);
        break;
        case TYPEKIND.TKIND_ENUM: // type is an enum.
          pInfo.GetDocumentation(-1, out typeName, out docString,
                              out helpID, out helpFile);
          typeInfoString = "Name: " + typeName;
          lstBoxEnums.Items.Add(typeInfoString);
          break;
      }
    Marshal.DestroyStructure(ptr, typeAtt.GetType());
    }
}
```

As you can see, you again need to deal with translating structures to System.IntPtr types. The bulk of this method looks much like the previous C++ COM type reader application. Using the managed TYPEKIND type, you iterate over the number of types in the loaded type library and check for coclasses, interfaces (both IUnknown based and IDispatch based), and COM enums. The only major change is the need to make use of the C# out keyword when you wish to pass a parameter defined as an IDL [out] attribute. As another example, Figure 4-12 shows the dump of the ATL server created in Chapter 3.

Not too shabby, huh? By virtue of the System.Runtime.InteropServices namespace (and a bit of elbow grease) it is completely possible to create .NET applications that can read unmanaged COM type information. Although this key namespace does not support managed equivalents for COM type library creation entities (ICreateTypeLibrary and friends), you could build managed equivalents and make your own C# COM type library generator. You will look at building your own managed ICreateTypeLibrary interface later in this text when you examine the .NET to COM conversion process. However, as for the task of building a managed COM type library generator, I'll leave that to you.

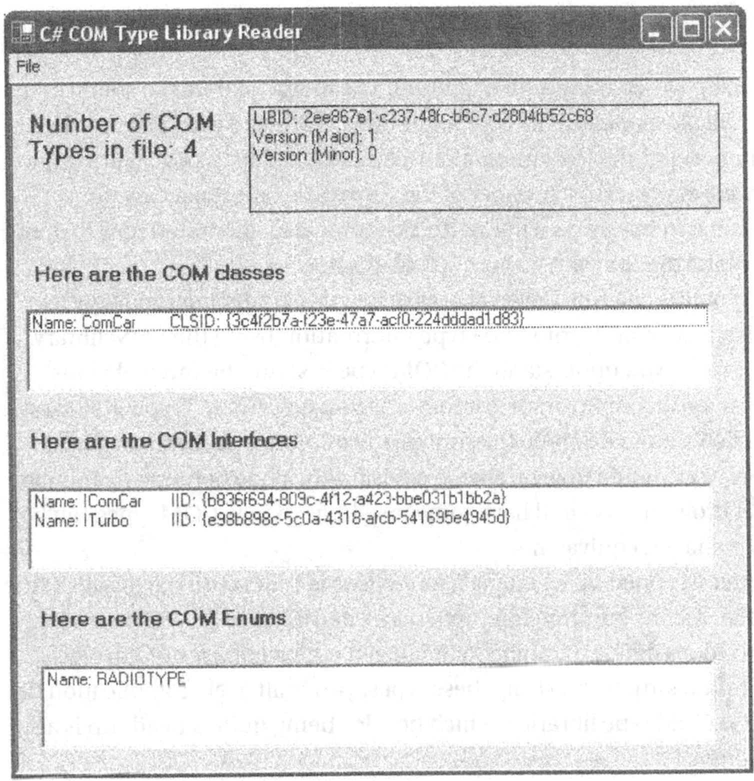

Figure 4-12. Reading your ATL COM server

CODE *The ManagedComTypeReader application is included under the Chapter 4 subdirectory.*

Summary

This chapter has covered quite a bit of ground. The initial goal was to solidify the format of an *.idl file as well as the core set of COM types and intrinsic IDL data types (most important, the [oleautomation]-compatible data types). During the process you were exposed to a number of IDL keywords (appobject, custom, hidden) that come in handy. As a bonus, this chapter also illustrated how to annotate your type information with custom IDL attributes.

A majority of this chapter, however, was devoted to understanding how to programmatically read and write COM type information using the COM library. To be sure, the more you understand the COM type system, the more obvious COM ⇔ .NET interoperability issues become. As you have seen, ITypeLib(2) and ITypeInfo(2) allow you to examine the contents of a *.tlb file at runtime. Given your work here, you should now be able to envision the code behind any number of COM object browser tools and have some insight as to how COM types can be mapped into managed equivalents.

This chapter wrapped up by taking a tour of some (but by no means all) of the members of the System.Runtime.InteropServices namespace. As you have seen, this namespace does define a number of managed equivalents for COM-type-library-centric data structures. Using these types, you built a .NET application that was able to read COM type libraries (which besides being quite a head trip is also very illuminating).

Now that you have pondered the intricacies of COM type metadata, the next two chapters pound out the details of .NET types. Then you will have all the information you need to dive into COM and .NET interoperability.

CHAPTER 5
The Anatomy of a .NET Server

Now that you have learned the core aspects of COM, it stands to reason that you should tackle the core building blocks of the .NET platform. Over the course of this chapter, you are given a grand tour of the composition of .NET code libraries as well as the opportunity to solidify your understanding of intermediate language (IL), type metadata, and assembly manifests. During the process, you build a private C# assembly (and a shared VB .NET assembly) that will be consumed by unmanaged COM clients later in this text. This chapter also pounds out the core details of the .NET runtime, such as the use of application configuration files (*.config) and the construction of shared assemblies.

I conclude this chapter by examining a very interesting .NET namespace that you may have not yet been introduced to formally: System.CodeDOM. Using this well-organized set of .NET types, you are able to represent managed code in memory using language-independent terms. Once you have defined the coding atoms, you are then able to save these tokens into language-specific source files (*.cs or *.vb) as well as compile the files at runtime into .NET assemblies. As you will see, the ability to represent (and possibly compile) code in memory is one aspect of COM/.NET interoperability and should be of special interest to the tool builders of the world.

Before you get started, do understand that the point of this chapter is *not* to discuss the syntax or semantics of the C# or VB .NET programming languages. My assumption is that you already have a handle of one (if not both) of these languages, and are already comfortable with the famed pillars of OOP (encapsulation, inheritance, and polymorphism) as well as interfaced-based programming. If you require additional information regarding the specifics of either language, I'll assume that you will consult your favorite language reference for further details.

The Philosophy of .NET

Traditionally, building applications for the Windows OS required an intimate understanding of the Win32 API, a set of C++ API wrapper classes such as MFC, or a more elaborate wrapper such as Visual Basic 6.0. The problem with these approaches is that they each rely on a specific programming language (C, C++, or VB 6.0, respectively) that makes the sharing of implementation logic extremely difficult; each language has its own type system, each language has its own set of supported syntactical constructs, and each language contends with the pillars of OOP in its own particular manner. To contend with this great lack of symmetry, developers tend to take one of two paths to make their lives simpler: the path of COM or the path of Java.

The path offered by classic COM is a standard binary format. As you have seen during the previous three chapters, each COM-aware language generates files that are up to snuff with the COM architecture. If COM programmers are disciplined enough to only expose [oleautomation] compatible types, COM servers (written in different programming languages) can communicate with each other rather well. The bottom-line vision of COM states "If you stick to the rules of COM, you can choose among different programming languages . . . as long as you only expect to run on the Windows OS."

The path of Java (and the numerous Java APIs) is to establish a way for a single code base to be compiled on the fly to different platforms using a just-in-time compiler. Although the capability to have a single code base run on numerous operating systems is a great boon, one obvious downfall with the Java solution is the fact that many solutions do not lend themselves to a single programming language for every need. The bottom-line vision of Java states "If you only make use of Java, your code can be run on any OS supporting the Java runtime."

.NET takes the philosophy of COM and the philosophy of Java and blends them into a brand-new architecture. For example, like Java, .NET binaries contain platform-neutral instructions (IL code) that can be compiled on the fly to .NET-aware operating systems using a just-in-time compiler. Like COM, .NET binaries written in different programming languages can communicate with each other in harmony. In effect, the bottom-line vision of .NET is "Build a code base using your choice of programming language (or combination thereof) and you can run on any operating system targeting .NET."

The ultimate endgame of .NET is to make the concept of programming language and operating system a matter of personal choice. At the time of this writing, literally dozens of languages are being retrofitted to take advantage of the .NET architecture (APL, COBOL, PL1, and so forth). As well, the .NET platform is already being ported to non–Microsoft-specific operating systems. When you combine the language- and platform-agnostic nature of .NET with the framework's liberal use of XML, SOAP, and other industry standards, developers can build extremely neutral and accessible software.

The Building Blocks of .NET

The fabric of the .NET philosophy can be summed up by three new acronyms: CLR, CTS, and CLS. First, let's check out the Common Type System (CTS). The CTS defines in gory detail the full set of valid programming constructs supported by the .NET architecture. For example, the CTS establishes the intrinsic data set supported by a .NET-aware programming language and defines all the possible ways in which classes, enumerations, structures, interfaces, and delegates may be represented. Obviously, if your job is to build a new .NET programming language (and the related compiler), the rules of the CTS are extremely important to understand.

However, the full set of programming idioms defined by the CTS may or may not be supported by every .NET programming language. For example, C# and Managed C++ both support the definition and use of overloaded operators (unlike VB .NET). As well, some languages (such as C#) support the use of unsigned types (for example, unsigned long), whereas others (VB .NET) do not. To offer programmers a well-defined set of agreed-on programming atoms, we are provided with the Common Language Specification (CLS). The CLS can be viewed as the modern day equivalent of the IDL [oleautomation] attribute. Recall that the [oleautomation] attribute defines a subset of known COM data types. The CLS builds upon this concept by not only defining a subset of possible data types, but programming constructs as well. In a nutshell, the CLS is a specific subset of the CTS, which is guaranteed to be supported by each and every .NET language mapping.

The rule of thumb is quite simple: If you wish to build a .NET code library that can be consumed by any .NET-aware programming language, be sure to expose only CLS-compliant types from your custom .NET assemblies. By default, VB .NET will always emit CLS-compliant assemblies. However, if you make use of a managed language (such as C#) that does allow you to use non–CLS-compliant idioms, you can apply the following assembly-level attribute to force the C# compiler to check your code for CLS compliance (you can examine the topic of attributes in full detail in Chapter 6):

```
// C# applications can force CLS compliance as so.
[assembly: System.CLSCompliant(true)]
```

The final building block of .NET is the common language runtime (CLR). The CLR can be viewed as two complementary pieces: a new runtime engine (mscoree.dll) and a plethora of existing code that can be leveraged (and extended) in your own custom solutions. The runtime engine is responsible for launching your application, locating the types within the binary using the contained metadata, managing allocated memory on your behalf, and performing numerous security checks.

The prefabricated code base (often called the *.NET base class libraries*) has been semantically divided into numerous "assemblies" (defined shortly) that can be referenced by your current application. As you are most likely aware, the base class libraries define types that can be used for file IO, object serialization, GUI-based development, XML manipulation, and the construction of Web applications/Web services (among many other common programming tasks).

Working with Managed Languages

When a programming language has a .NET-aware compiler, the source code itself is referred to as *managed code*. Code that does not target .NET (including classic COM languages) is thus termed *unmanaged code*. Visual Studio .NET ships with four managed languages out of the box. First you have C#, which is a brand-new programming language specifically geared for the construction of managed code. Like other members of the C++ family, C# is full of curly brackets, semicolons, and a streamlined (or, depending on your view, terse) set of language tokens. If you already have a background in other C++-based languages (Java, C[++], or Objective C), you will find the syntax of C# very natural.

Visual Basic .NET (VB .NET) is another key managed language, which is (of course) a member of the BASIC family of languages. VB .NET is *not* a simple upgrade from Visual Basic 6.0, however. Rather, VB .NET is best viewed as a brand-new language that just happens to look a little like VB 6.0. If that seems a bit alarmist in nature, understand that for the first time in BASIC's history, VB .NET offers developers full OOP support (inheritance, polymorphism, and encapsulation), parameterized constructors, method overloading, and so forth. Although VB .NET is a far cry from VB 6.0, VB .NET is likely to be the preferred choice for those with a VB 6.0 background.

Finally, VS .NET also provides JScript .NET (a compiled OO language) as well as a new set of keywords to the C++ programming language that enables programmers to build C++ applications that target the .NET platform. Formally speaking, this dialect of C++ is termed *C++ with managed extensions*, also known as *Managed C++*, and referred to by myself as the acronym *MC++*. To be honest, I really can't comment on the usefulness of JScript .NET. In fact, I will not make any real mention of this language outside of this paragraph.

As for MC++, the language can best be viewed as a great tool for migrating existing C++ code into the .NET platform. Even if you are a proficient C++ programmer, you will most likely find yourself more drawn to C# than MC++, given that (a) MC++ requires more typing and (b) numerous aspects of the C++ language are not supported under .NET (such as templates and multiple inheritance).

During the course of this book, I make use of C# for a majority of my managed code examples. This is really for no other reason than the fact that C# code is more compact on the printed page than the corresponding VB .NET code. In the spirit of fairness, however, this text will make use of VB .NET (as well as VB 6.0) where appropriate.

The Composition of a .NET Binary

Regardless of which managed language you choose, all .NET-aware compilers emit binaries that share the same internal composition. Although .NET binaries share the same file extension as a classic COM server (*.dll and *.exe), they are completely different under the hood. First and foremost, .NET binaries do not contain platform-specific instructions, but rather platform-agnostic IL code that is compiled to platform-specific instructions using a just-in-time compiler. In addition to the IL instruction set, .NET binaries contain full and complete metadata that describes each and every .NET type referenced within the binary. Finally, a .NET compiler emits binaries containing a *manifest* that describes the binary shell itself.

In addition to a unique internal fabric, .NET binaries have been given a new name, *assembly*. Assemblies are the unit of deployment and unit of versioning under the .NET platform. Specifically speaking, an assembly can be a single-file assembly or multifile assembly. Single-file assemblies (which are far and away the most common) are a single *.dll or *.exe file that contains all .NET types in a single unit. Multifile assemblies, on the other hand, are a collection of related files. When developers build multifile assemblies (using the command line compilers supplied with the .NET SDK), the end result is a collection of files that are versioned as a single unit. More interesting, the individual modules of a multifile assembly (which by convention take the file extension *.netmodule) are loaded on demand by the .NET runtime. This can be especially useful if a remote client needs to download an assembly to the local machine, given that the runtime will only need to download a subset of the entire file set (which can save time).

.NET assemblies differ from classic COM servers in other ways as well. Perhaps the most marked difference is that .NET assemblies are *not* registered in the system registry. To whet your appetite, Table 5-1 enumerates some key differences between COM binaries and .NET binaries (I drill into more specifies where necessary).

Table 5-1. COM Binaries and .NET Binaries Side by Side

Trait of the Binary Unit	COM Approach	.NET Approach
What is the code contained within the binary?	Platform-specific OS instructions	Platform-agnostic IL code
How are types described?	Using Interface Definition Language (IDL) code, which is compiled into a binary type library	Using .NET metadata
How is the binary itself described?	Using the IDL [library] attribute and numerous locations in the system registry, specifically: HKEY_CLASSES_ROOT\\<ProgID> HKEY_CLASSES_ROOT\CLSID HKEY_CLASSES_ROOT\AppID HKEY_CLASSES_ROOT\Interface HKEY_CLASSES_ROOT\Component Category	Using assembly metadata (aka the manifest)
How are external dependencies documented?	N/A (COM IDL has no way to document externally required binaries.)	Using assembly metadata (aka the manifest)
How can I generate custom metadata?	Using the [custom] IDL attribute	By creating a new type derived from System.Attribute
How is the binary located by the runtime?	By consulting the system registry	By looking in the application directory, the GAC, or elsewhere using an application configuration file

As you can see, a central theme in .NET is to place the required metadata and IL code base into the same location (the assembly). Given that a single assembly contains all the information it needs to be used by the runtime and by an interested client, assemblies are typically regarded as "self-describing" entities.

Building a C# Code Library

Now that I have wrapped up my brief but necessary .NET architecture preamble, I can turn your attention to the construction of your first C# .NET code library. Understand that you will reuse this assembly during the course of the text to be reachable by various COM clients. If you wish to follow along, open up VS .NET and build a new Class Library solution named CSharpCarLibrary (Figure 5-1).

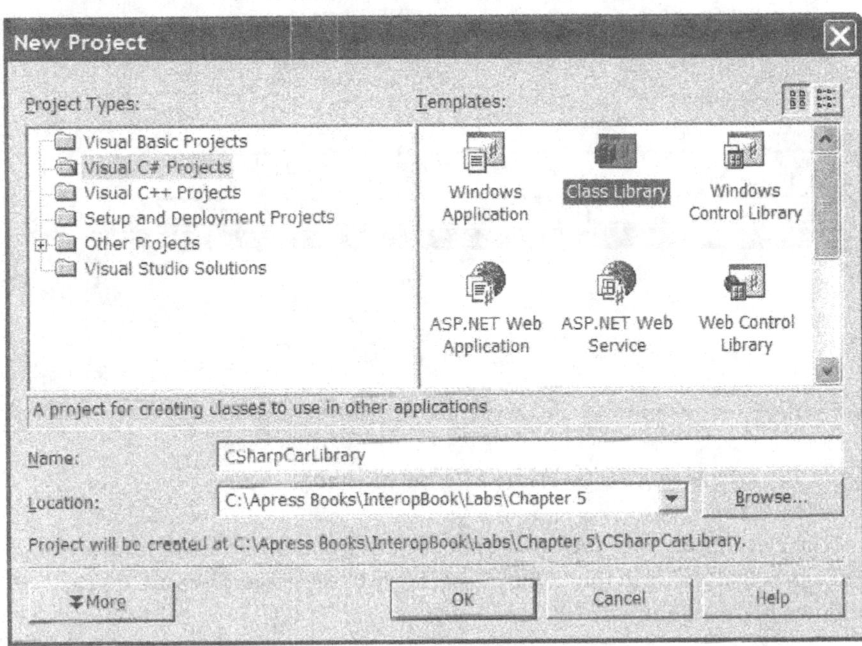

Figure 5-1. The C# Class Library

Given that your application will make use of the MessageBox class defined within the System.Windows.Forms.dll assembly, be sure to add a project reference (Figure 5-2).

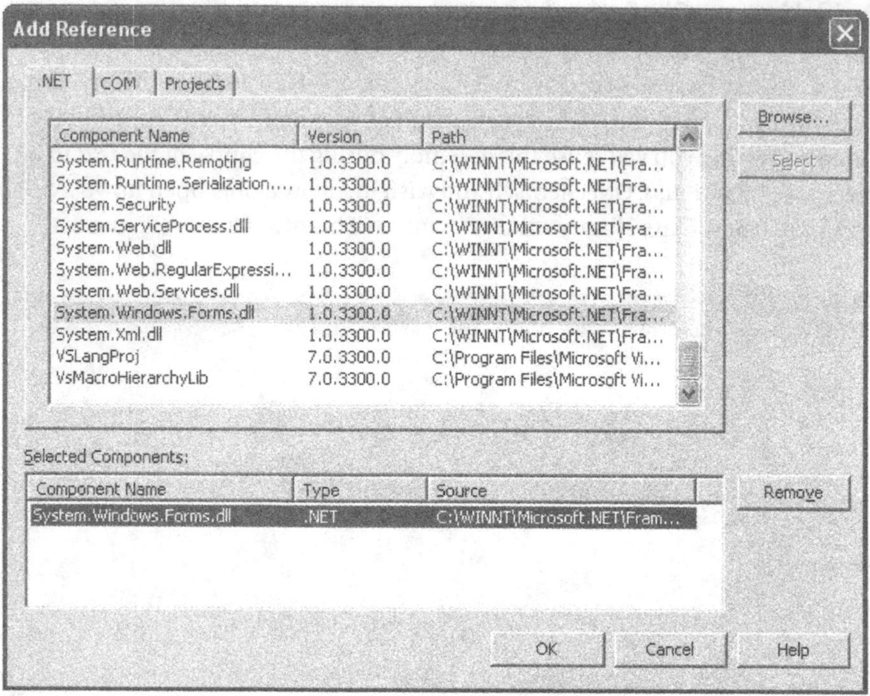

Figure 5-2. Referencing the necessary external assembly

The class library that you will be constructing contains a small number of .NET types that reside in the CSharpCarLibrary namespace. Here is a quick rundown of each item:

- An abstract base class named Car
- Three derived types named HotRod, MiniVan, and Roadster
- An enumeration (CarColor) used to specify the color of the automobile
- The IConvertible interface, which will be implemented by a subset of the automobiles

Figure 5-3 shows a logical view of the assembly you are constructing.

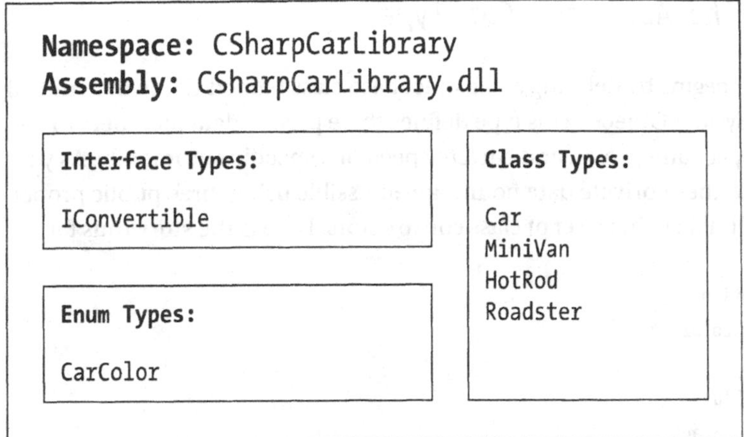

Figure 5-3. The logical view of your C# car assembly

Physically speaking, CSharpCarLibrary.dll will be constructed as a single-file assembly (as opposed to a number of discrete *.netmodule files). In terms of the class library itself, Figure 5-4 shows the relationships of the core types (using the familiar COM lollipop notation to represent supported interfaces).

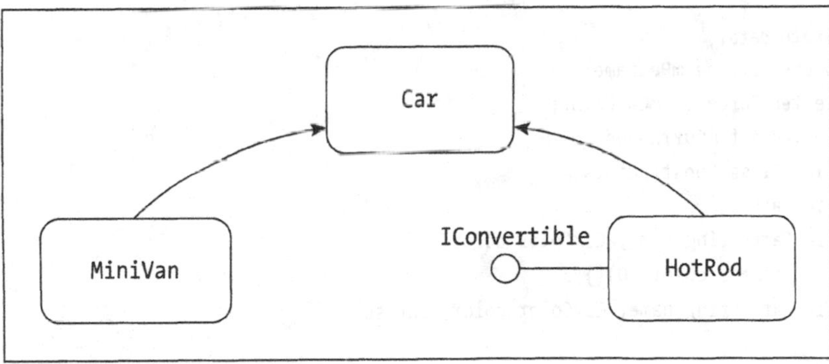

Figure 5-4. The automobile hierarchy

Building the Abstract Car Type

Your endeavor begins by defining an abstract base class named Car (which directly derives from System.Object). This type defines three private data members to represent the pet name, color, and current speed of a specific automobile. As you would imagine, these private data points are accessible using three public properties and initializable using a set of class constructors. Here is the story thus far:

```
// The enumeration.
public enum CarColor
{
  Red, Green, Blue,
  Pink, Yellow, Black
}

// The interface.
public interface IConvertible
{void OpenSunRoof(bool openIt);}

// The base class.
public abstract class Car
{
    // State data.
    protected string mPetName;
    protected CarColor mCarColor;
    protected int mCurrSpeed;
    #region Class Constructors
    public Car(){}
    public Car(string name, CarColor color)
      : this(name, color, 0){}
    public Car(string name, CarColor color, int sp)
    {
      mPetName = name;
      mCarColor = color;
      mCurrSpeed = sp;
    }
    #endregion
    #region Properties
    public string PetName
    {
      get{ return mPetName;}
      set{ mPetName = value;}
    }
```

```
    public CarColor Color
    {
      get{ return mCarColor;}
      set{ mCarColor = value;}
    }
    public int Speed // Read only!
    {get{ return mCurrSpeed;}}
    #endregion
}
```

Like all well-behaved base classes, the Car type defines a polymorphic interface for each derived type. First, you have an abstract method named SpeedUp(), which allows each type to adjust its internal speed in a specific manner. The virtual DisplayBumperStickerText() method provides a default text string, which may be overridden by child types:

```
public abstract class Car
{
  // Polymorphic interface.
  public abstract void SpeedUp();
  public virtual void DisplayBumperStickerText()
  {
    MessageBox.Show("If you can read this you're too close.",
                "C# Car Library");
  }
...
}
```

Finally, the Car base class overrides System.Object.ToString() to dump out its state data to interested invokers (using the StringBuilder type, which is defined within the System.Text namespace):

```
// Change ToString() for Cars.
public override string ToString()
{
  StringBuilder sb = new StringBuilder();
  sb.AppendFormat("[C#] PetName: {0} Color: {1} CurrentSpeed: {2}",
               mPetName, mCarColor, mCurrSpeed);
  return sb.ToString();
}
```

Building the Derived MiniVan Type

The MiniVan class, which extends Car, does not define any additional state data; however, it contends with the polymorphic interface as follows:

```
public class MiniVan : Car
{
  #region Constructors
  public MiniVan(){}
  public MiniVan(string name, CarColor color)
    : base(name, color){}
  public MiniVan(string name, CarColor color, int sp)
    : base(name, color, sp){}
  #endregion
  // Implement abstract SpeedUp(), but leverage the
  // default implementation of DisplayBumperStickerText().
  public override void SpeedUp()
  { mCurrSpeed += 10; }
}
```

Implementing the Convertibles

The HotRod and Roadster types each implement the IConvertible interface, speed up appropriately, and sport a custom bumper sticker. Notice that you are making use of explicit interface implementation to force the caller to obtain the IConvertible before letting the sunshine in. First, the HotRod:

```
public class HotRod : Car, IConvertible
{
  // IConvertible impl.
  void IConvertible.OpenSunRoof(bool openIt)
  {
    if(openIt)
      MessageBox.Show("Sun roof is open!", "C# Car Library");
    else
      MessageBox.Show("Closing sun roof...", "C# Car Library");
  }

  #region Overrides
  public override void SpeedUp()
  {mCurrSpeed += 20;}
```

```
  public override void DisplayBumperStickerText()
  {
    MessageBox.Show("Taking names and kickin' butt...",
                    "C# Car Library");
  }
  #endregion
  #region Constructors
  public HotRod() {}
  public HotRod(string name, CarColor color)
    : base(name, color){}
  public HotRod(string name, CarColor color, int sp)
    : base(name, color, sp){}
  #endregion
}
```

The Roadster type does define a new property (TrunkSpace) that allows the world to manipulate a private data member representing just how much luggage you can fit into the cramped confines of your super car (the overridden ToString() has also been updated to account for this new member):

```
public class Roadster : HotRod, IConvertible
{
  #region Constructors
  public Roadster(){}
  public Roadster(string name, CarColor color)
    : base(name, color){}
  public Roadster(string name, CarColor color, int sp)
    : base(name, color, sp){}
  public Roadster(string name, CarColor color, int sp, short trunkSpace)
    : base(name, color, sp)
    { mTrunkSpace = trunkSpace;}
  #endregion
  #region Overrides
  public override void SpeedUp()
  {mCurrSpeed += 20;}
  public override void DisplayBumperStickerText()
  {
    MessageBox.Show("Faster is better...", "C# Car Library");
  }
  public override string ToString()
  {
    StringBuilder sb = new StringBuilder();
    sb.Append(base.ToString());
```

```
      sb.AppendFormat(" Trunk space: {0}", mTrunkSpace);
      return sb.ToString();
    }
    #endregion
    // IConvertible impl.
    void IConvertible.OpenSunRoof(bool openIt)
    {
      if(openIt)
        MessageBox.Show("Sun roof is open!", "C# Car Library");
      else
        MessageBox.Show("Looking through small plastic window...",
                        "C# Car Library");
    }
    // Custom state data.
    private short mTrunkSpace;
    public short TrunkSpace
    {
      get{return mTrunkSpace;}
      set{mTrunkSpace = value;}
    }
  }
```

Establishing the Assembly Manifest

Before you compile, let's update your assemblyinfo.cs file to establish the current version of this .NET binary (1.0.0.0), enforce CLS compliance, and add any other bits of information you feel the need to express:

```
[assembly: System.CLSCompliant(true)]
[assembly: AssemblyTitle("The CSharp Car Library")]
[assembly: AssemblyDescription("Another book, more Car types")]
[assembly: AssemblyCompany("Intertech, Inc")]
[assembly: AssemblyVersion("1.0.0.0")]
```

With this, you are able to compile your single-file assembly. You will build a managed client in just a moment; however, for now let's check out your binary using ILDasm.exe.

Introducing ILDasm.exe

The ILDasm.exe tool allows you to view the internal types, underlying IL, type metadata, and assembly manifest for a given managed binary. As you will see in the next chapter, you are also able to build custom applications that can bind to a given assembly and reflect on the contained types at runtime using the System.Reflection namespace. For now, simply open up your new CSharpCarLibrary.dll using ILDasm.exe (Figure 5-5).

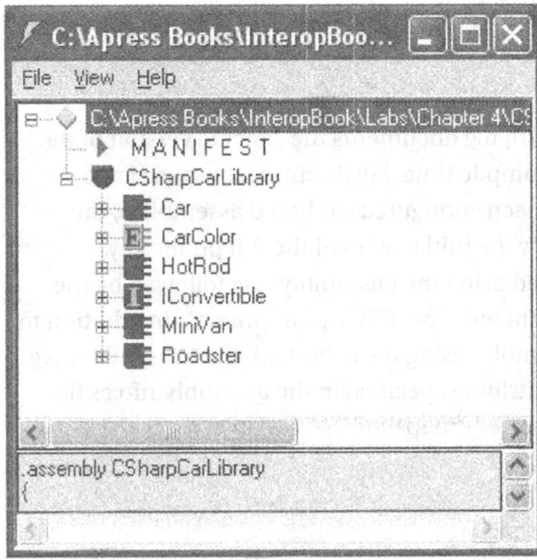

Figure 5-5. Viewing the types within your custom assembly

Viewing the Assembly Manifest

As you recall, every .NET binary contains assembly-level metadata, which is termed the *manifest*. The manifest is used to describe the version of the binary, the required external references and other assembly-level attributes. Later in this chapter, you will find that if (and only if) your assembly has been constructed to function as a shared assembly, the manifest also documents the public key for this binary. In its simplest form, the format of an assembly's manifest begins by listing each external assembly referenced by the current assembly using the [.assembly extern] directive:

```
.assembly extern mscorlib
{
 .publickeytoken = (B7 7A 5C 56 19 34 E0 89 )
 .ver 1:0:3300:0
}
.assembly extern System.Windows.Forms
{
 .publickeytoken = (B7 7A 5C 56 19 34 E0 89 )
 .ver 1:0:3300:0
}
```

Note how the [.assembly extern] tag documents the specific version of the external assembly referenced at compile time. Furthermore, because each of the referenced assemblies has been configured as shared assemblies, the [.publickeytoken] is used to specify the initial bytes of the full public key.

The assembly itself is identified using the [.assembly] tag followed by the friendly name of the .NET binary (in our case, CSharpCarLibrary). In addition to specifying the version of this assembly (using the [.ver] tag), the [.assembly] tag documents each assembly-level attribute specified in the assemblyinfo.cs file. Here is a partial (and slightly formatted) snapshot:

```
.assembly CSharpCarLibrary
{
 .custom instance void
[mscorlib]System.Reflection.AssemblyCompanyAttribute::.ctor(string)
= ( 01 00 0E 49 6E 74 65 72 74 65 63 68 2C 20 49 6E
// ...Intertech, Inc.
 .custom instance void [mscorlib]
System.Reflection.AssemblyDescriptionAttribute::.ctor(string)
= ( 01 00 1C 41 6E 6F 74 68 65 72 20 62 6F 6F 6B 2C
// ...Another book, more Car types.
 .custom instance void [mscorlib]
System.Reflection.AssemblyTitleAttribute::.ctor(string)
= ( 01 00 16 54 68 65 20 43 53 68 61 72 70 20 43 61
// ...The CSharp Car Library.
 .custom instance void
[mscorlib]System.CLSCompliantAttribute::.ctor(bool)
= ( 01 00 01 00 00 )
// true.
 .hash algorithm 0x00008004
 .ver 1:0:0:0
}
```

The last item of note regarding the CSharpCarLibrary.dll assembly is the [.module] tag, which is located at the end of the [.assembly] tag block and documents the name of the physical binary. Given that you have created a single-file assembly, the value assigned to the [.module] tag is simply the following:

```
.module CSharpCarLibrary.dll
```

As you can see, the assembly manifest is a great improvement to the IDL [library] keyword. Unlike classic COM, .NET manifests are able to document the necessary external binaries, which are required for this assembly to function correctly. This of course is a good thing, given that .NET assemblies "understand" the additional binaries that they have been compiled against (in this case, mscorlib.dll and System.Windows.Forms.dll).

Viewing the Type Metadata

In COM, IDL is used to describe the internal COM types found within a given COM server. In the same spirit of self-describing binaries, .NET code libraries support type metadata. Of course, the .NET type metadata does not have the same syntax as COM IDL! Rather, type metadata is listed as a more "tabular" format. Using ILDasm.exe, you are able to view the metadata that describes all types in the assembly, using the Ctrl-m keyboard option. The end result of applying this keystroke is seen in Figure 5-6.

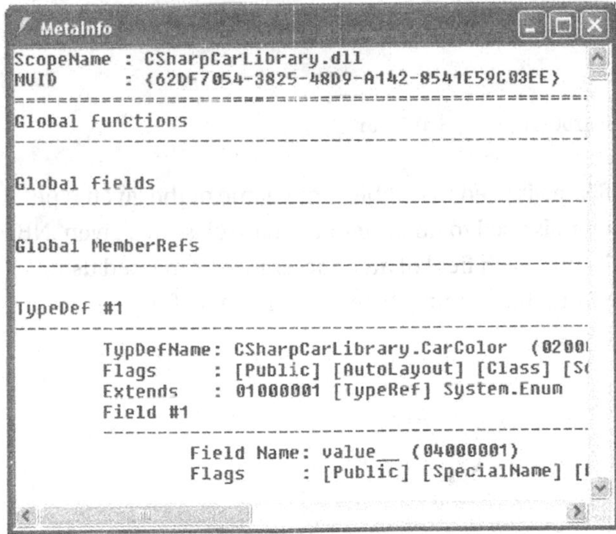

Figure 5-6. Viewing an assembly's metadata

.NET type metadata is very verbose when compared to COM IDL (for good reason). Using this embedded metadata, the .NET runtime is able to locate and load a given type for a calling client as well as obtain a complete description of each item. If I were to list the entire set of metadata generated for your CSharpCarLibrary.dll assembly, it would span several pages. Given that this would be a woeful waste of your time (and paper), let's just take a quick look at some of the key items.

Viewing (Partial) Metadata for the CarColor Enumeration

First, understand that each type contained within an assembly is documented using a "TypeDef *#n*" token. Given that the CarColor enumeration is the first type encountered by the C# compiler, you will find the following metadata description:

```
TypeDef #1
-------------------------------------------------------
  TypDefName: CSharpCarLibrary.CarColor (02000002)
  Flags    : [Public] [AutoLayout] [Class] [Sealed] [AnsiClass] (00000101)
  Extends   : 01000001 [TypeRef] System.Enum
...
  Field #3
  -------------------------------------------------------
  Field Name: Green (04000003)
  Flags    : [Public] [Static] [Literal] [HasDefault] (00008056)
  DefltValue: (I4) 1
  CallCnvntn: [FIELD]
  Field type: ValueClass CSharpCarLibrary.CarColor
```

As you can see, TypDefName is used to establish the name of the given type. The Extends metadata keyword is used to document the base class of a given .NET type (in this case, System.Enum). Each field of an enumeration is marked using the "Field *#n*" value. For brevity, I have simply listed the metadata for CarColor.Green (field 3).

Viewing (Partial) Metadata for the IConvertible Interface

The second metadata type definition (IConvertible) marks this entity as an interface and promptly documents the calling conventions of each member (notice how each member is automatically marked as abstract):

```
TypeDef #2
-------------------------------------------------------
  TypDefName: CSharpCarLibrary.IConvertible (02000003)
  Flags    : [Public] [AutoLayout] [Interface] [Abstract] [AnsiClass] (000000a1)
  Extends  : 01000000 [TypeRef]
  Method #1
  -------------------------------------------------------
  MethodName: OpenSunRoof (06000001)
  Flags    : [Public] [Virtual] [HideBySig] [NewSlot] [Abstract] (000005c6)
  RVA      : 0x00000000
  ImplFlags : [IL] [Managed] (00000000)
  CallCnvntn: [DEFAULT]
  hasThis
    ReturnType: Void
    1 Arguments
      Argument #1: Boolean
    1 Parameters
      (1) ParamToken : (08000001) Name : openIt flags: [none] (00000000)
```

Viewing (Partial) Metadata for a Derived Type

Each of the class types is also completely documented using the .NET metadata format. As you may expect, the complete metadata dump for a given type would again be pages worth of data. To hit the highlights, here is a partial dump of the Roadster type that illustrates (a) how a single type property is mapped to two discrete member functions and (b) how an interface is bound to an implementing type using the InterfaceImpl keyword:

```
TypeDef #6
-------------------------------------------------------
  TypDefName: CSharpCarLibrary.Roadster (02000007)
  Flags    : [Public] [AutoLayout] [Class] [AnsiClass] (00100001)
  Extends  : 02000005 [TypeDef] CSharpCarLibrary.HotRod
...
```

```
Method #9
-------------------------------------------------------
  MethodName: get_TrunkSpace (0600001F)
  Flags    : [Public] [HideBySig] [ReuseSlot] [SpecialName] (00000886)
     hasThis
     ReturnType: I2
     No arguments.
Method #10
-------------------------------------------------------
  MethodName: set_TrunkSpace (06000020)
  Flags    : [Public] [HideBySig] [ReuseSlot] [SpecialName] (00000886)
     hasThis
      ReturnType: Void
        1 Arguments
        Argument #1: I2
        1 Parameters
       (1) ParamToken : (0800001e) Name : value flags: [none] (00000000)
Property #1
-------------------------------------------------------
  Prop.Name : TrunkSpace (17000004)
  ...
    DefltValue:
    Setter  : (06000020) set_TrunkSpace
    Getter  : (0600001f) get_TrunkSpace
...
InterfaceImpl #1 (09000002)
-------------------------------------------------------
  Class    : CSharpCarLibrary.Roadster
  Token    : 02000003 [TypeDef] CSharpCarLibrary.IConvertible
```

Remaining Bits of Interesting Metadata

.NET metadata does far more than document the custom types you have defined using your managed language of choice. In addition, you will find metadata descriptions for every base class library item you referenced in your coding effort. For example, TypeRef tokens exist for each attribute type found in your assemblyinfo.cs file, the System.Windows.Forms.MessageBox type (because you displayed a number of message boxes), and the layout of the System.Text.StringBuilder class (because you made use of this type during the overriding of System.Object.ToString()).

Finally, at the very end of the metadata dump, you will find an "AssemblyRef #*n*" listing for each external assembly and a list of all string literals contained within the binary, as shown in this example:

```
AssemblyRef #2
-------------------------------------------------------
Token: 0x23000002
Public Key or Token: b7 7a 5c 56 19 34 e0 89
Name: System.Windows.Forms
Major Version: 0x00000001
Minor Version: 0x00000000
Build Number: 0x00000ce4
Revision Number: 0x00000000
Locale: <null>
HashValue Blob:
Flags: [none] (00000000)
User Strings
-------------------------------------------------------
70000001 : (38) L"If you can read this you're too close."
7000004f : (14) L"C# Car Library"
7000006d : (46) L"[C#] PetName: {0} Color: {1} CurrentSpeed: {2}"
700000cb : (17) L"Sun roof is open!"
700000ef : (19) L"Closing sun roof..."
70000117 : (32) L"Taking names and kickin' butt..."
70000159 : (19) L"Faster is better..."
70000181 : (17) L" Trunk space: {0}"
700001a5 : (39) L"Looking through small plastic window..."
```

Now, at this point you should not be too concerned with the exact syntax of each piece of .NET metadata. The bigger issue to be aware of is that .NET metadata is very descriptive and lists each custom (and referenced) type found in the code base. Thinking again along the terms of COM/.NET interoperability, you can most likely imagine a tool that could read .NET metadata and produce an equivalent COM type library. You will see this topic in action a bit later.

(Not) Viewing the Underlying IL Code

Although the ILDasm.exe utility also allows you to view the underlying IL code for a given item (simply by double-clicking an expanded node), you really don't need to check out the instructions that have been generated. To be honest, the crux of COM/.NET interoperability has to do with translating COM *metadata* into .NET *metadata* (not IL into OS-specific instructions). In most cases, any IL that is lurking under the hood is not as important (especially given that the interop-centric tools will generate it automatically). However, you certainly get a chance to take a look at relevant IL where necessary during the remainder of this text.

CODE *The CSharpCarLibrary and VbNetCarLibrary code libraries are located under the Chapter 5 subdirectory.*

Building a Managed Client

Before examining other interesting aspects of the .NET Framework, assume you have created a brand-new Windows Forms application that is making use of the CSharpCarLibrary type. The GUI of this Form-derived type simply maintains a single Button type, which has the following implementation in the Click event handler:

```
private void btnCSharpCars_Click(object sender, System.EventArgs e)
{
  // Make array of C# Cars.
  Car[] myCars =
  {
    new HotRod("Viper", CarColor.Red),
    new MiniVan("Clunky", CarColor.Green),
    new Roadster("Zippy", CarColor.Green, 50, 5)
  };
  // Loop over each array element using IEnumerator.
  foreach(Car c in myCars)
  {
    // Call each car's ToString()
    MessageBox.Show(c.ToString(), c.GetType().Name);
    // Display each car's bumper sticker.
    c.DisplayBumperStickerText();
      // Do we have a convertible?
      if(c is IConvertible)
      {
        IConvertible itfConvert;
        itfConvert = (IConvertible)c;
        // Enjoy the day!
        itfConvert.OpenSunRoof(true);
      }
  }
}
```

The code is quite straightforward. Using an array of base class Car types, you create a set of derived types. As you loop over the array, you call each member of the polymorphic interface defined by the abstract Car type, and check to see if the current automobile is IConvertible compatible. If so, open the sunroof and enjoy the ride!

CODE *The CarClientApplication is included under the Chapter 5 subdirectory.*

Configuring Private Assemblies

When you set a reference to an external assembly using VS .NET, the IDE responds by placing a copy of the assembly directly within the folder containing the client that is making use of the contained types. Formally speaking, the directory that contains the client application is known as the *application directory* (Figure 5-7).

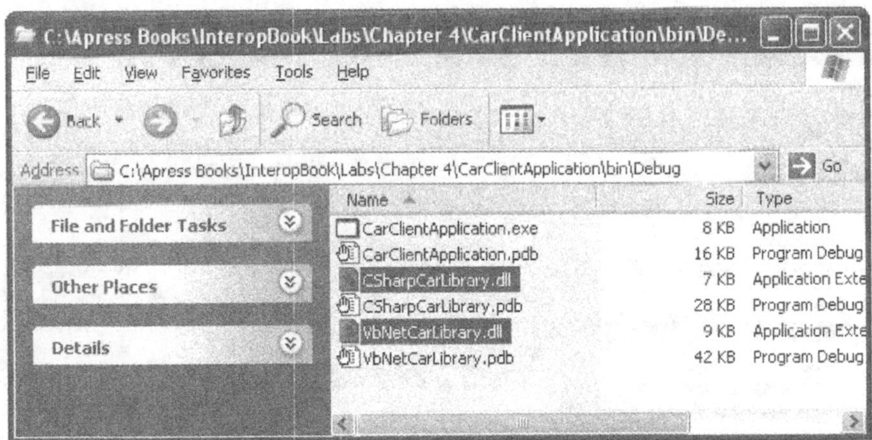

Figure 5-7. Viewing the application directory

Assemblies that reside in the same folder as the launching client are called *private assemblies.* By its very nature, a private assembly is not intended to be used by any other application on the machine other than the client it was compiled against. Obviously, this approach makes the deployment of the application a breeze: Simply copy the client and any referenced private assembly to a given location on a given hard drive and run the program (no registration required).

Although the process of placing all the required binaries into a single application directory greatly simplifies the deployment of a .NET solution, this has the unappealing byproduct of a rather unorganized file structure. What if you would rather have a subdirectory off the application directory called MyAsms, which contains the CSharpCarLibrary.dll assembly? The truth is that if you relocate the referenced assemblies and attempt to run the client once again, you will crash at runtime, as the location of the assemblies listed in the client manifest cannot be resolved.

When you wish to instruct the runtime to probe for referenced assemblies located within a given subfolder of the application directory, you must author an *application configuration file*. These XML-based files contain any number of "privatePath" attributes that will be read by the runtime as it attempts to resolve the location of a private assembly. You must be aware, however, that the runtime expects the name of the configuration file to be <NameOfTheClient>.exe.config. For example, the configuration file for your CarClientApplciation.exe client would be CarClientApplication.exe.config. Furthermore, the *.config file must be in the client's application directory.

Assume you have created a *.config file for your current client and moved the CSharpCarLibrary assembly into a subdirectory named MyAsms (Figure 5-8).

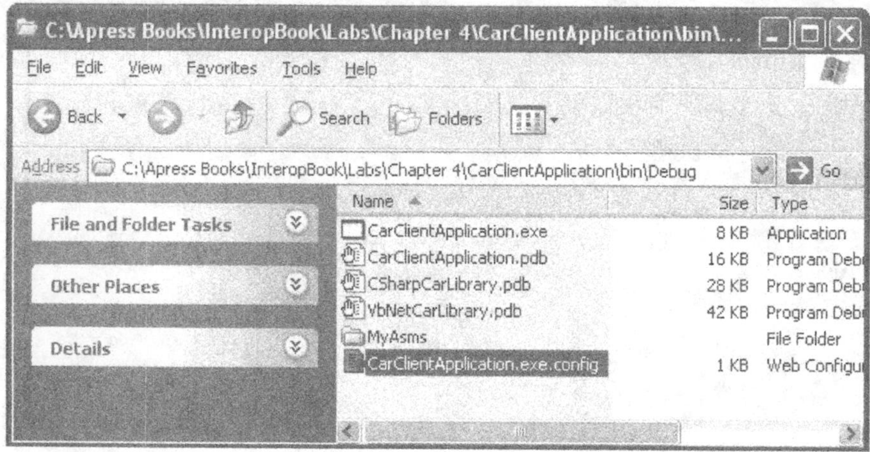

Figure 5-8. The private assemblies have been relocated under the MyAsms subdirectory.

To instruct the runtime to probe under \MyAsms, you would author the following XML:

```
<configuration>
  <runtime>
   <assemblyBinding xmlns="urn:schemas-microsoft-com:asm.v1">
     <probing privatePath="MyAsms" />
   </assemblyBinding>
  </runtime>
</configuration>
```

Configuration files must begin with the root element <configuration>. Before you specify the <probing privatePath> attribute, you must first specify the <runtime> and <assemblyBinding> elements. Also understand that you may specify multiple subfolders to be included in the probing process using a semi-colon delimited list:

```
<probing privatePath="MyCSharpAsms;MyVbNetAsms" />
```

If you were to now launch the CarClientApplication.exe client program, the execution engine would be able to locate the referenced assemblies using the corresponding *.config file.

Specifying Arbitrary Assembly Locations

As you may already be aware, you can create *.config files containing additional XML elements that instruct the runtime to load a specific localized assembly, as well as consult other subdirectories (for example, C:\AllMyAssemblies) during the probing process. Using the <codeBase> element, you are able to instruct the runtime engine to probe under any folder on your machine, a remote networked machine, or a given URL. For example, if you move C# car assembly under C:\MyCoolAsms, you will need to update the CarClientApplication.exe.config file as follows (the publicKeyToken value will be defined shortly):

```
<configuration>
  <runtime>
   <assemblyBinding xmlns="urn:schemas-microsoft-com:asm.v1">
    <dependentAssembly>
      <assemblyIdentity name="CSharpCarLibrary"
                        publicKeyToken="xxxxxxxxxxxxxxxx"
                        culture="neutral" />
```

```
        <codeBase
            href="file://c:/MyCoolAsms\CSharpCarLibrary.dll"/>
      </dependentAssembly>
    </assemblyBinding>
  </runtime>
</configuration>
```

Now that you understand the basic configuration of a private assembly, let me wrap up with a few final thoughts. First, although it is good protocol to document a specific assembly version (1.0.0.0, 2.0.0.0, and so on) for each assembly you may author, the runtime will *ignore* the version number when attempting to locate a private assembly. The reason is simple. Given that private assemblies are intended to be used by a single client, versioning is a bit of a nonissue. Second, private assemblies will more likely than not end up being exactly what you desire for a vast majority of your .NET development efforts. In fact, Visual Studio .NET is only able to compile code libraries that are intended to be deployed as private binaries. If you wish to build a shared assembly, you will need to make use of the command line compiler csc.exe (C#) or vbc.exe (VB .NET).

Understanding the Shared Assembly

Although it is true that private assemblies will most likely be your configuration option of choice, at times you will wish to share an assembly among multiple clients on a single machine. Consider the System.Windows.Forms.dll assembly (which, as you know, contains the types for building GUI desktop applications). If this binary were created as a private assembly, this would mean that every .NET application that has to show a simple message box would need to have a copy of the same *.dll. This would be insane, of course, given that such a situation would require hundreds of copies of the same binary to be installed on a given machine.

Rest assured that the .NET platform does provide a way for you to share a single copy of a given assembly among multiple clients. When you wish to build a shared assembly, you will ultimately place the binary into a very specific folder named the Global Assembly Cache (GAC), which is located under %windir%\Assembly (Figure 5-9).

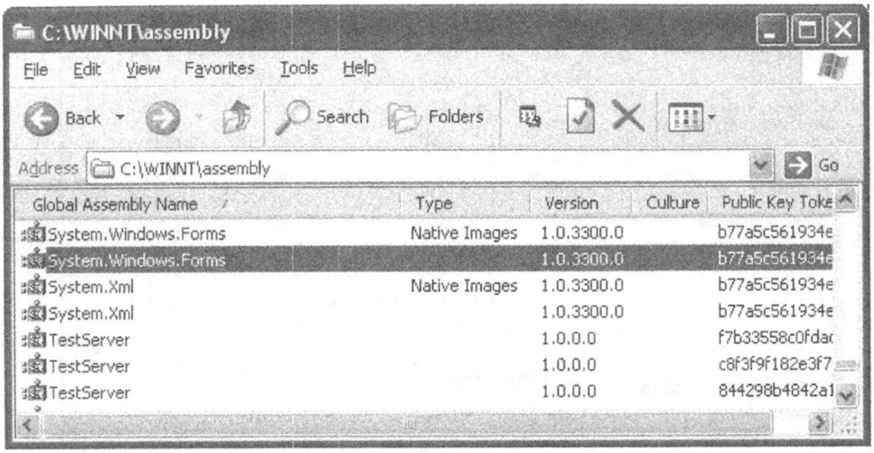

Figure 5-9. Shared assemblies are placed into the GAC.

However, you cannot simply take a private assembly, install it in the GAC, and expect to end up with a shared assembly. Rather, you must retrofit an assembly to support a *strong name* (also known as a *shared name*). A strong name is a combination of the simple name (for example, CSharpCarLibrary), culture information (for example, English, Urdu), a version number (for example, 1.0.0.0), a public key, and a digital signature. This strict level of identification provided by the strong name is far superior to the COM AppID given that (a) multiple versions of the same assembly can be installed in the GAC and (b) your company can create a unique identity used to identify each assembly that has been shipped.

Generating a Strongly Named Assembly

So, as mentioned, shared assemblies must have a strong name. A strong name consists of a friendly name, numerical version, culture ID, a public key, and a digital signature. Gathering all the pieces of a string name is much simpler than you may be thinking. To illustrate, let's create a brand-new code library (this time using VB .NET) named SharedVbNetAirVehicles (Figure 5-10).

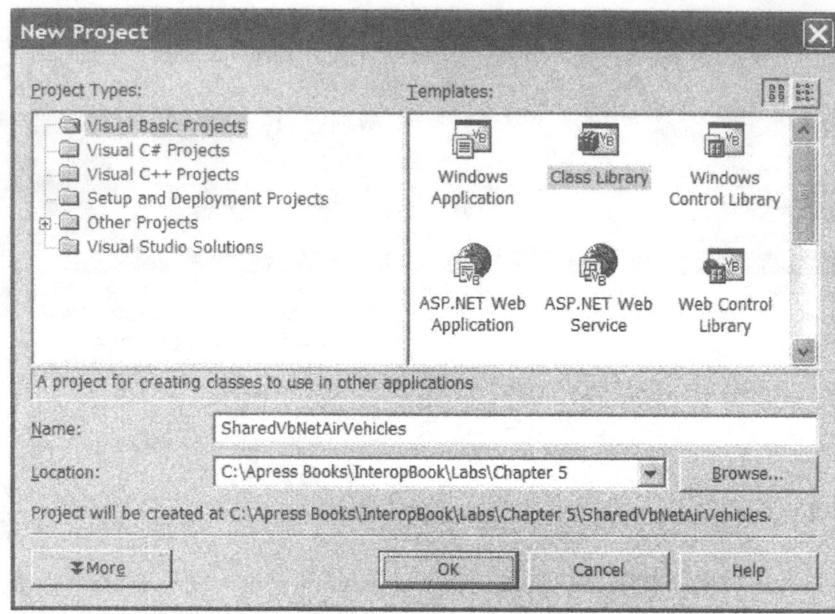

Figure 5-10. The VB .NET project workspace

To keep focused on the process of configuring a shared assembly, the VB .NET code library will be minimal but complete (as shown in Figure 5-11).

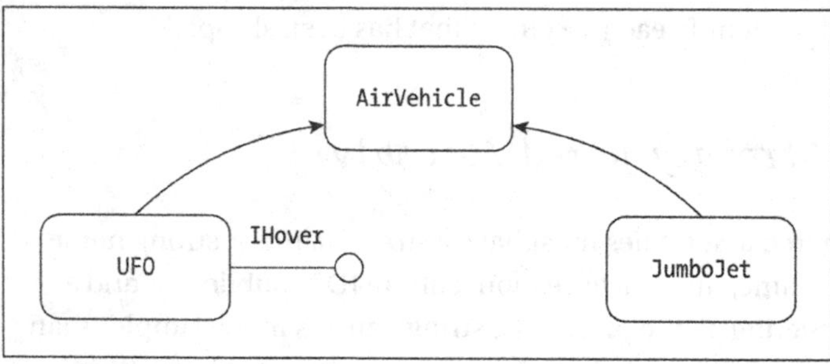

Figure 5-11. The AirVehicles hierarchy

Prepping the Project Workspace

Like the C# automobile assembly, your VB .NET AirVehicles library will make use of types contained within the System.Windows.Forms.dll assembly (go ahead and set a reference to this binary now). Recall that in C#, you make use of the using keyword whenever a source code file needs to reference external types. Although you could make use of the VB .NET Imports keyword for the same purpose, VB .NET also allows you to establish project-wide imports using the Project Property window (Figure 5-12).

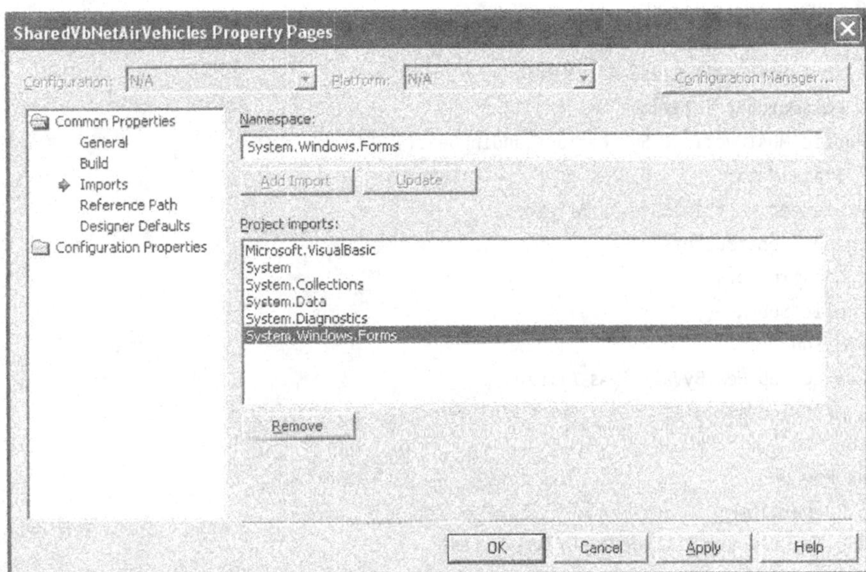

Figure 5-12. Setting up project-wide imports

As you would expect, this VB .NET shortcut allows each *.vb file in the project to make direct reference to types contained in external assemblies (without the need to explicitly use the Imports keyword).

Also be aware that every VB .NET project maintains an entity known as the *root namespace* (located under the General node of the Project Property window). The root namespace is another nicety provided by VB .NET, given that you can avoid the need to wrap each type definition within a namespace specification. Do note, however, that VB .NET does support the Namespace keyword when you wish to explicitly define a namespace definition.

Building the Air Vehicles

Your base type, AirVehicle, defines a single abstract method and a property of type AirLine (which happens to be a custom enumeration).

```
Public Enum AirLine
  SunnyCountry
  SouthEastAirlines
  Unknown
  ChucksInternationalAir
End Enum

Public MustInherit Class AirVehicle
  ' Polymorphic interface
  Public MustOverride Sub RetractLandingGear()
  ' State data
  Protected mAirLineName As AirLine
#Region "Constructors"
  ' Constructors.
  Public Sub New()
  End Sub
  Public Sub New(ByVal al As AirLine)
    mAirLineName = al
  End Sub
#End Region
  ' Properties
  Public Property AirLineName() As AirLine
    Get
      Return mAirLineName
    End Get
    Set(ByVal Value As AirLine)
      mAirLineName = Value
    End Set
  End Property
End Class
```

The JumboJet type derives from AirVehicle and implements RetractLandingGear() by issuing a friendly salutation:

```
Public Class JumboJet
  Inherits AirVehicle
  Public Overrides Sub RetractLandingGear()
    Dim s As String
    s = "Thanks for flying with " & Me.AirLineName.ToString()
```

```
    MessageBox.Show(s)
  End Sub
  Public Sub New(ByVal al As AirLine)
    Me.AirLineName = al
  End Sub
End Class
```

The UFO contends with the abstract RetractLandingGear() method by issuing a more ominous message. The IHover interface is also implemented as follows:

```
Public Class UFO
  Inherits AirVehicle
  Implements IHover
  Private canHover As Boolean
  ' Overrides
  Public Overrides Sub RetractLandingGear()
    Dim s As String
    s = "UFO's don't have landing gear" _
      & vbLf & "Activating molecule stimulator..."
    MessageBox.Show(s)
  End Sub
#Region "IHover Impl"
  Public Function CanHoverWithoutDetection() As Boolean _
        Implements IHover.CanHoverWithoutDetection
    Return canHover
  End Function
  Public Sub Hover() _
        Implements IHover.Hover
    If (CanHoverWithoutDetection()) Then
      MessageBox.Show("waiting and watching...")
    Else
      MessageBox.Show("Located by Earthling...Applying InvisoShield")
    End If
  End Sub
#End Region
  Public Sub AbductHuman()
    MessageBox.Show("Welcome aboard human...")
  End Sub
  Public Sub New()
    AirLineName = AirLine.Unknown
    canHover = True
  End Sub
End Class
```

Generating the Strong Name

Now that you have your hierarchy in place, you can establish the necessary strong name. Recall that this requires a number of individual pieces:

- The friendly name (for example, SharedVbNetAirVehicles)
- Culture information (for example, English, Urdu)
- A version number (for example, 1.0.0.0)
- A public key
- A digital signature

The friendly name is simply the name of the code library (not including the exact file extension). Also recall that your project's assemblyinfo.vb file allows you to establish the version of your assembly using the AssemblyVersion attribute. Given that the runtime takes the version of a shared assembly quite seriously, be sure you set the AssemblyVersion attribute accordingly:

```
<Assembly: AssemblyVersion("1.0.0.0")>
```

As far as the culture identity of an assembly goes, you will make use of the default "neutral" culture. Culture applies only if you are building an assembly that contains resources, such as strings and bitmaps, which need to be customized for various human languages. This type of assembly is called a *satellite assembly*, which by definition does not contain any IL code. Therefore, given that your SharedVbNetAirVehicles assembly does indeed contain implementation code, you will not be applying a specific culture.

Your final task is to create a public key (and thus your digital signature). To do so, you must make use of a command line tool named sn.exe to generate the *.snk file that represents a public/private key pair (which is accomplished by specifying the –k command line flag). Check out Figure 5-13.

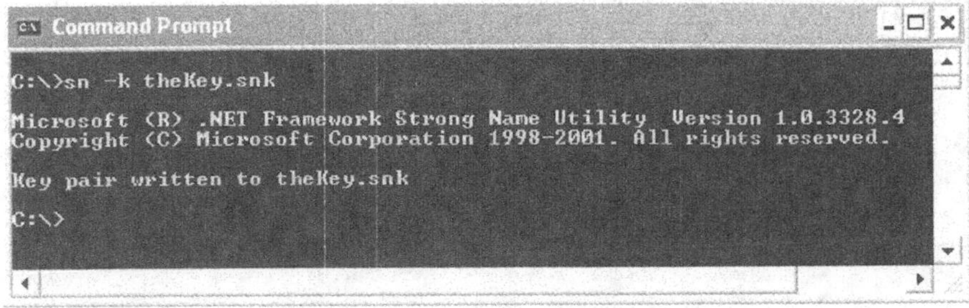

*Figure 5-13. Generating the *.snk file*

To bind the *.snk file into your current assembly, you make use of the assembly-level attribute AssemblyKeyFile:

```
<Assembly: AssemblyKeyFile("C:\theKey.snk")>
```

At this point, when you compile your project, the key pair will be used to sign the assembly.

Recall that assemblies containing strong names will have their public keys recorded within the assembly manifest. If you examine your completed SharedVbNetAirVehicles.dll using ILDasm.exe, you will find the [.publickey] value shown in Figure 5-14.

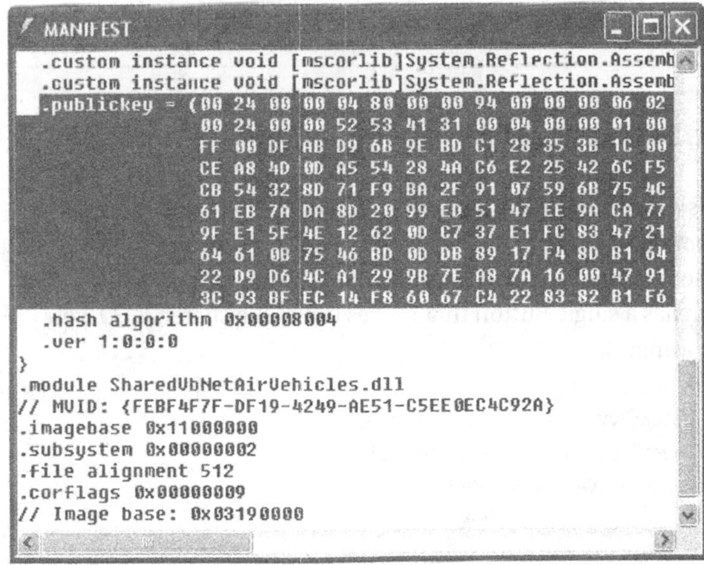

Figure 5-14. The mark of a shared assembly

Now that your assembly has been assigned a strong name, you are able to drag and drop your .NET binary into the GAC. Figure 5-15 shows the end result.

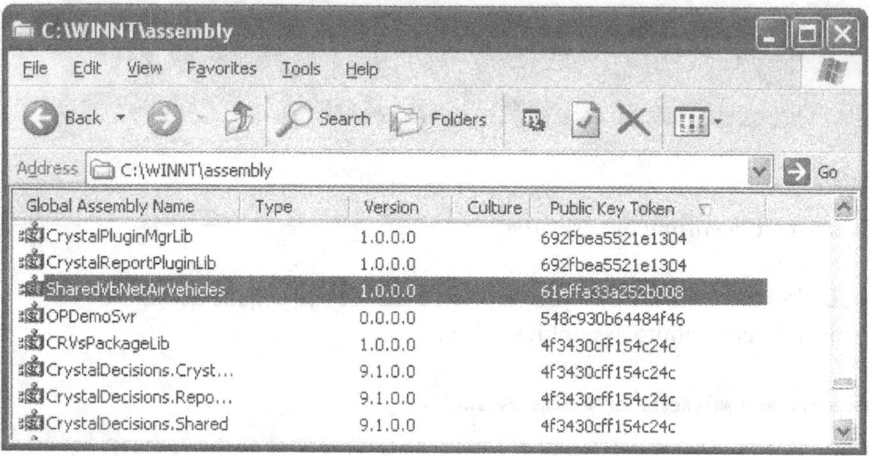

Figure 5-15. The VB .NET binary installed in the GAC

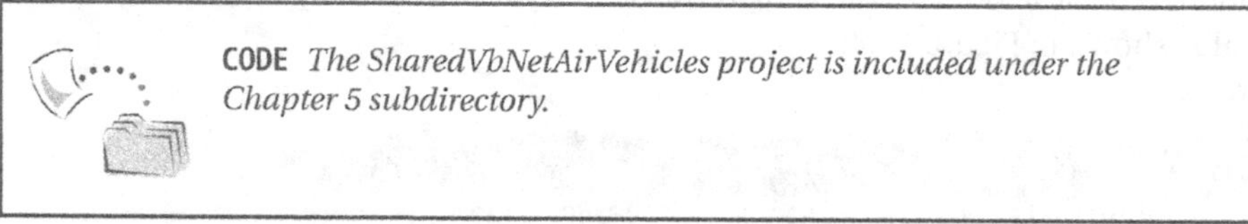

CODE *The SharedVbNetAirVehicles project is included under the Chapter 5 subdirectory.*

Using the Shared Assembly

As far as the client is concerned, using a shared assembly is identical to the act of using a private assembly. If you have a new VB .NET Windows Forms application at your disposal, you set a reference to the assembly (as always), and code away. For example, if the Form has a single Button that makes use of the shared UFO, you might write the following:

```
Private Sub Button1_Click(ByVal sender As System.Object, _
  ByVal e As System.EventArgs) Handles Button1.Click
  Dim u As New SharedVbNetAirVehicles.UFO()
  u.Hover()
  u.AbductHuman()
End Sub
```

The only additional point of interest is that when the IDE encounters a reference to a shared assembly (meaning the IDE is able to detect a [.publickey] value), it will *not* make a local copy of the binary (as noted in Figure 5-16).

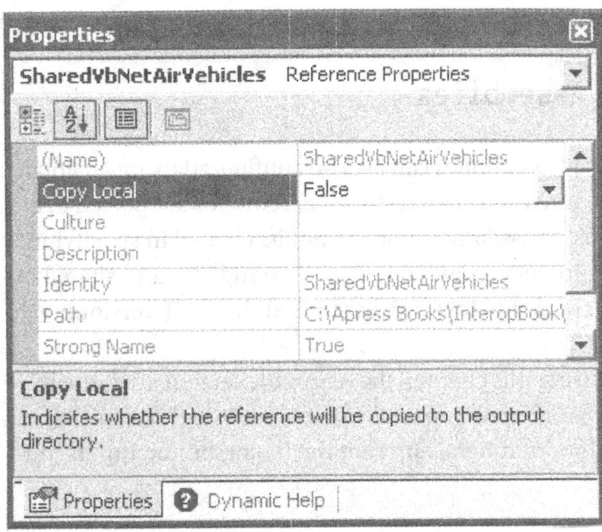

Figure 5-16. By default, strongly named assemblies are not copied into the application directory.

Also, recall that when a .NET client makes reference to a strongly named assembly, the manifest will record a token of the public key (marked with the [.publickeytoken] tag). This can be verified using ILDasm.exe (Figure 5-17).

```
MANIFEST
{
  .publickeytoken = (B7 7A 5C 56 19 34 E0 89 )
  .ver 1:0:3300:0
}
.assembly extern System.Xml
{
  .publickeytoken = (B7 7A 5C 56 19 34 E0 89 )
  .ver 1:0:3300:0
}
.assembly extern SharedVbNetAirVehicles
{
  .publickeytoken = (61 EF FA 33 A2 52 B0 08 )
  .ver 1:0:0:0
}
.assembly SharedAsmClient
{
  // --- The following custom attribute is added a
```

Figure 5-17. Recording a shared assembly

CODE *The SharedAsmClient project can be found under the Chapter 5 subdirectory.*

Versioning Shared Assemblies

Like a private assembly, shared assemblies can also be configured using an application configuration file. Of course, given that shared assemblies are placed in a well-known location (%windir%\Assembly), you are not interested in specifying privatePath attribute values. To understand the role of *.config files and shared assemblies, you need to step back and take a closer look at the .NET versioning scheme.

As you have observed during this chapter, the AssemblyVersion attribute is used to control the four-part numerical version of an assembly (private or shared). Specifically speaking, these four numbers represent the major, minor, build, and revision numbers:

```
' Format: <Major version>.<Minor version>.<Build number>.<Revision>
<Assembly: AssemblyVersion("1.0.0.0")>
```

When an assembly's version is recorded into the manifest, clients are able to record the assembly's version as well. For example, the SharedVbNetAirVehicles assembly was set to version 1.0.0.0. The SharedAsmClient application in turn records this value in its own assembly using the [.assembly extern] tag:

```
.assembly extern SharedVbNetAirVehicles
{
 .publickeytoken = (61 EF FA 33 A2 52 B0 08 )
 .ver 1:0:0:0
}
```

Now, by default, the .NET runtime will only launch the client without error if indeed there is a shared assembly named SharedVbNetAirVehicles, version 1.0.0.0 with a public key token of the value 61 EF FA 33 A2 52 B0 08 in the GAC. If any of these elements is not correct, the runtime will throw a LoadTypeException exception. Again, remember that version checking only applies to shared assemblies. Even though private assemblies can support a four-number version, this will be ignored by the runtime.

Application configuration files can be used in conjunction with shared assemblies whenever you wish to instruct the runtime to bind to a *different* version of a given assembly. For example, imagine that you have shipped version 1.0.0.0 of a given assembly and suddenly realized, to your horror, a major bug (or to be more politically correct, a runtime anomaly) has reared its ugly head. Your first option for corrective action would be to rebuild the client application to reference the correct version of the bug-free assembly (say, 1.0.0.1) and redistribute the new binaries to every client machine. Obviously, this would not be a very elegant solution.

Your other option is to ship the new code library and a simple *.config file that automatically instructs the runtime to bind to the new (bug-free) version. As long as the new version has been installed in the GAC, the client runs without recompilation or redistribution (or your fear of having to update your resume).

Another example: You have shipped the first version of a bug-free assembly (1.0.0.0) and after a year or two, you have added a number of new types to the current project to yield version 2.0.0.0. Obviously, previous clients that were compiled against version 1.0.0.0 have no clue about these new types (given that their code base makes no reference to them). New client applications, however, may need to make reference to the new functionality found in version 2.0.0.0.

Under the COM model, programmers were forced to deal with the simple-in-concept-but-hard-in-practice notion of interface versioning. A healthy dose of code versioning is also very important under .NET; however, it is equally possible to simply install both versions of the shared assembly into the GAC and allow a client to bind to whichever version has been recorded in the manifest.

Versioning the Shared VB .NET AirVehicles Assembly

To illustrate versioning shared assemblies, assume that you have frozen version 1.0.0.0 of the SharedVbNetAirVehicles assembly and added the following new class type:

```
Public Class MotherShip
  Inherits UFO
  Public Sub AbductOtherUFOs()
    MessageBox.Show("You have failed your mission...beam aboard.")
  End Sub
End Class
```

Assume as well that you have updated the version as follows:

```
<Assembly: AssemblyVersion("2.0.0.0")>
```

Once compiled, you are then able to place the new version into the GAC. Lo and behold, you have installed two versions of the *same* assembly on the *same* machine (a technique not possible under classic COM). Check out Figure 5-18.

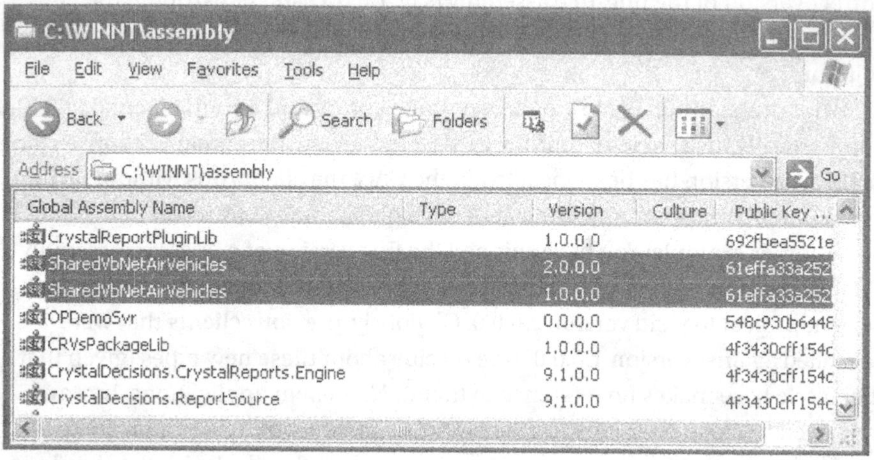
C:\WINNT\assembly
File Edit View Favorites Tools Help
Back Search Folders
Address C:\WINNT\assembly
Go
Global Assembly Name
Type
Version
Culture
Public Key ...
CrystalReportPluginLib 1.0.0.0 692fbea5521e
SharedVbNetAirVehicles 2.0.0.0 61effa33a252
SharedVbNetAirVehicles 1.0.0.0 61effa33a252
OPDemoSvr 0.0.0.0 548c930b6448
CRVsPackageLib 1.0.0.0 4f3430cff154c
CrystalDecisions.CrystalReports.Engine 9.1.0.0 4f3430cff154c
CrystalDecisions.ReportSource 9.1.0.0 4f3430cff154c

Figure 5-18. Side-by-side execution

Now, if you wish to redirect your existing SharedAsmClient to make use of version 2.0.0.0, for example, you could author the following *.config file:

```
<configuration>
  <runtime>
   <assemblyBinding xmlns="urn:schemas-microsoft-com:asm.v1">
     <dependentAssembly>
      <assemblyIdentity name="SharedVbNetAirVehicles"
               publicKeyToken="61effa33a252b008" />
      <bindingRedirect oldVersion="1.0.0.0"
                       newVersion="2.0.0.0" />
     </dependentAssembly>
   </assemblyBinding>
  </runtime>
</configuration>
```

Here, the bindingRedirect element specifies two attributes: oldVersion (the version documented in the client manifest) and newVersion (the, well, new version you wish to bind to). As long as the configuration file SharedAsmClient.exe.config is placed in the same directory as the client application, the runtime will automatically bind to the newer version, and thereby override the version listed in the client's manifest.

Of course, in this example you really have no need to redirect to version 2.0.0.0, given that the client code base is unable to make use of the MotherShip type without recompiling in the first place. To understand the big picture, assume that version 2.0.0.0 also fixed a bug (or two) found with the JumboJet type. In this case, the use of a *.config file is much more clear. Nevertheless, even if version 2.0.0.0 of the SharedVbNetAirVehicles assembly did not contain any additional bug fixes, there are still great benefits to having multiple copies of the same *.dll safely installed on a single machine.

Working with Publisher Policy Assemblies

I wish to comment on one additional aspect of *.config files termed *publisher policy*. As you have already seen, *.config files can be used by private assemblies to instruct the runtime to probe under various subdirectories when resolving the location of a given assembly. Shared assemblies can also make use of *.config files to dynamically bind to an assembly other than the version recorded in the client manifest. Do note that both of these approaches require that somebody (such as a system administrator) create and edit the *.config file on each client machine.

Publisher policy allows the *publisher* of a given assembly to ship a special binary version of a *.config file that is installed in the GAC along with the assembly it is responsible for influencing. When these unique *.config files are placed into the GAC, the client's application directory does *not* need to support a specific *.config file. Given this, the redirecting of shared assemblies is less of a burden on the individual responsible for configuring individual .NET clients. All he or she needs to do is install the new binary *.config file shipped by the publisher in the GAC and walk away.

To be honest, the *.config file itself is not literally installed in the GAC, due to the fact that the GAC will only accept files with a *.dll file extension. Rather, the publisher of the bug-ridden assembly is responsible for creating is a *.xml file that will be used to build a *.dll that contains the binary equivalent of the underlying XML using a tool named al.exe (assembly linker). Understand that VS. NET does not support the construction of publisher policy binaries, so you will be forced to drop down to the command prompt.

The good news is that the syntax of a XML publisher policy configuration file is identical to that of an application-specific *.config file. If you wish to retrofit the previous SharedAsmClient.exe.config file into the publisher policy format, you can run the following command at the command line:

```
al /link:SharedAsmClient.xml/out:policy.1.0.SharedVbNetAirVehicles.dll
/keyf:C:\theKey.snk /v:1.0.0.0
```

As you can see, you do need to specify the input *.xml file, the name of the output file (which must be in the format "policy.<major>.<minor>.assemblyToConfigure"), and the name of the file containing the public/private key pair.

Once the al.exe tool has executed, the end result is a new assembly that can be placed into the GAC (Figure 5-19) to force all clients to bind to version 2.0.0.0 of the SharedVbNetAirVehicles.dll file.

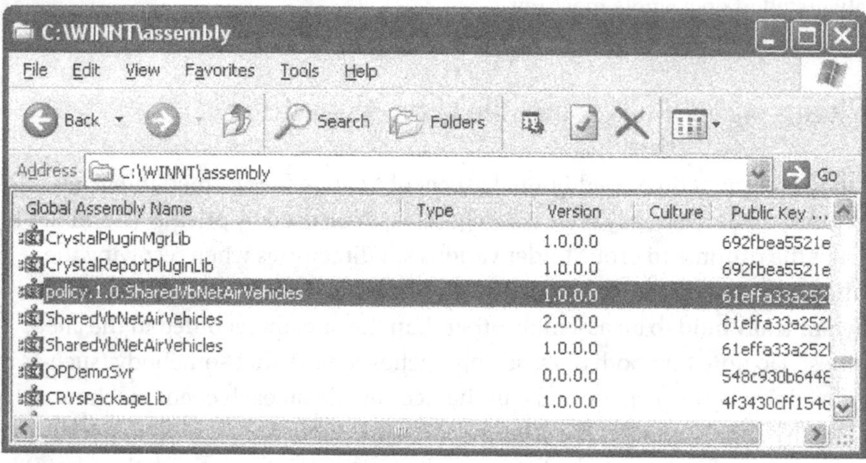

Figure 5-19. The policy assembly

If you are curious about exactly what is contained within the new .NET assembly, you can use ILDasm.exe to see that this binary contains little more than a bit of assembly metadata (Figure 5-20).

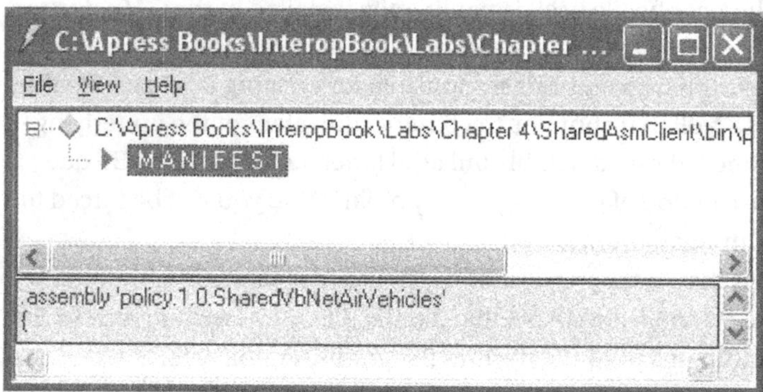

Figure 5-20. Inside the policy assembly

The manifest itself is rather bland. Simply put, the manifest lists the name of the XML file that was used to generate the assembly, which is embedded as an internal resource (Figure 5-21).

```
MANIFEST
  .hash algorithm 0x00008004
  .ver 1:0:0:0
}
.file nometadata SharedAsmClient.xml
    .hash = (31 A4 3D 9E D6 23 49 2C 7B F1 95 AA 2
             C8 B7 C0 72 )
.mresource public SharedAsmClient.xml
{
  .file SharedAsmClient.xml at 0x00000000
}
.module 'policy.1.0.SharedVbNetAirVehicles.dll'
// MVID: {55EB7E38-B7DB-4EB2-B7DE-95FFF545C59B}
.imagebase 0x00400000
.subsystem 0x00000003
.file alignment 512
```

Figure 5-21. The XML-based configuration file is embedded as an internal resource.

When the .NET runtime attempts to bind to the SharedVbNetAirVehicles assembly for a client specifying version 1.0.0.0, the policy assembly automatically redirects to version 2.0.0.0.

The Binding Process in a Nutshell

At this point, you have been exposed to each of the major facets of resolving the location of an external assembly. To summarize the process that is followed by the .NET runtime, here is a concise synopsis:

1. The runtime reads the client manifest for each [.assembly extern] tag and determines the friendly name of the referenced assembly (for example, CSharpCarLibrary).

2. The runtime then examines the [.assembly extern] tag to determine if a [.publickeytoken] is listed. If so, the GAC is consulted for (a) a publisher policy assembly and then (b) the shared assembly itself.

3. If the referenced assembly does not contain a [.publickeytoken], the runtime attempts to locate a *.config file. If a *.config file is present and accounted for, the underlying XML is parsed to locate the assembly in question. If a *.config file is not found, the application directory is probed.

4. If any of the preceding steps fail, a LoadTypeException exception is raised.

To be sure, other aspects of the .NET binding process exist that I do not need to comment on at this time (such as the machine-wide *.config file). Nevertheless, at this point you should have a much better idea how .NET has divorced itself from the COM-centric approach of server registration.

And Now for Something Completely Different: System.CodeDOM

To wrap up this chapter, I wish to introduce a namespace with which you may not be readily familiar: System.CodeDOM. Now I will be perfectly honest from the onset and admit that the types contained within this namespace do not directly relate to COM/.NET interoperability *per se*. In other words, when you are attempting to make COM types and .NET types coexist, you will not need to directly make use of the *Code Document Object Model* (CodeDOM), unless perhaps you happen to be a tool builder who needs to dynamically generate source code on the fly. However, to understand my rationale for discussing a seemingly unrelated namespace, let's begin by checking out a practical use of the System.CodeDOM namespace.

If you have worked with the ASP.NET Web Services, you are likely familiar with a utility named wsdl.exe (WSDL, being short for Web Service Description Language). When you build a Web Service, the exposed [WebMethods] are described using the WSDL metalanguage. Like other metalanguages (such as IDL and .NET metadata), WSDL lives to document the entities it is describing in a neutral format. For example, assume you have defined the following proverbial HelloWorld Web Service in C#:

```
// A very simple Web Service.
public class HelloWorldWS : System.Web.Services.WebService
{
...
  // This attribute qualifies this method as being "invokible" using HTTP
  // requests.
  [WebMethod]
  public string HelloWorld()
  { return "Hello World"; }
}
```

Once compiled, the generated WSDL describes how to access the HelloWorld() [WebMethod] using the HTTP GET, HTTP POST, and SOAP protocols. As you may know, WSDL documentation is expressed using XML syntax. You may also know that when a Web Service client wishes to activate a given [WebMethod], it is completely possible to build a client-side code base that is able to read the XML elements one-by-one in order to interact with the remote Web Service. Doing so, however, would be a very tedious and lengthy task, as suggested by Figure 5-22.

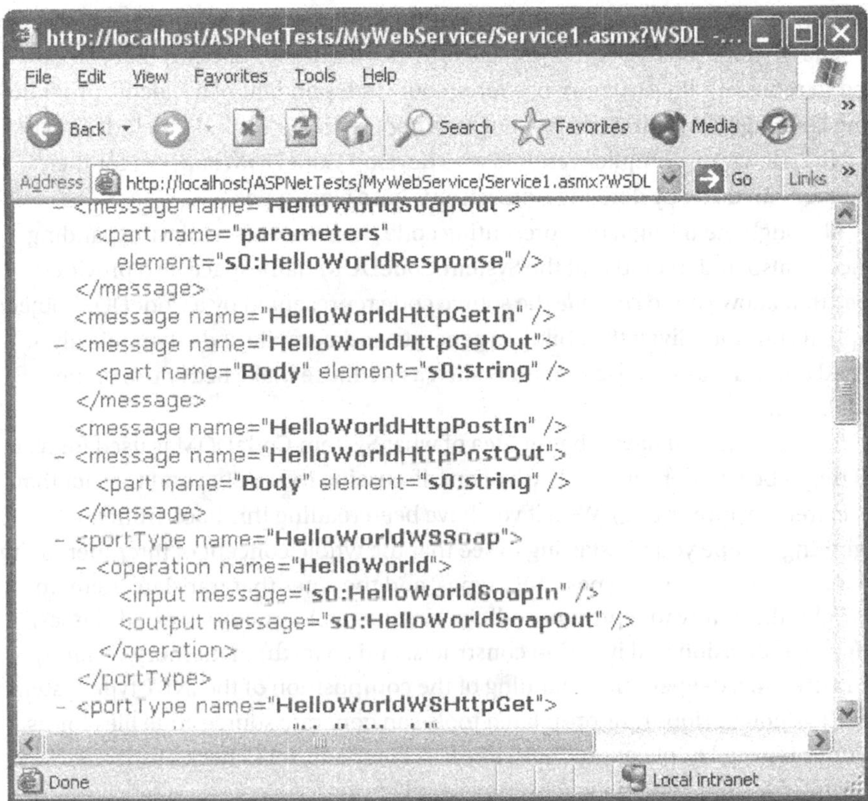

Figure 5-22. The raw WSDL

Given the verbose nature of WSDL syntax, few programmers are willing to manually parse the individual XML nodes. Lucky for you, using the wsdl.exe tool, you don't have to. This tool will read WSDL descriptions and dynamically generate a corresponding proxy class, which behaves like any other .NET type.

Under the hood, however, the proxy class itself contains methods that map to each exposed [WebMethod] at the given URL. In addition to specifying the wire protocol you wish to leverage to interact with the remote Web Service (GET, POST, or SOAP), the wsdl.exe tool also supports the "/language" flag, which allows you to instruct the wsdl.exe utility to generate the proxy using C#, VB .NET, or JScript .NET syntax. Enter System.CodeDOM.

System.CodeDOM: Its Meaning in Life

Tools such as wsdl.exe require the ability to generate and output source code in multiple languages at *runtime*. Using the CodeDOM you are able to build custom applications that can also output source code in multiple programming languages at runtime, using a single, unified .NET object model that represents the code to render.

The System.CodeDOM namespace provides a number of types that can be used to represent the structure of source code, independent of a specific programming language. Currently, the languages supported by CodeDOM include C# and VB .NET. However, compiler vendors who develop CodeDOM support for their language can do so by deriving from various base class types.

Although the thought of representing code in memory is a mind-expanding concept, also understand that the System.CodeDOM namespace also provides types that allow you to *compile* the source code represented by a CodeDOM object graph at runtime. Given the ability to generate and compile code dynamically, it should come as no surprise that tools such as wsdl.exe make heavy use of the CodeDOM.

So, now that you have a better idea of what System.CodeDOM is used for, you still might be wondering exactly why I am discussing its use (beyond the fact that it is extremely interesting). Well, if you have been reading this book from the beginning, I hope you are starting to see that the whole concept of interoperability is a matter of type: COM types, .NET types, and the rules that translate them. In this light, the ability to represent coding elements (constructors, nested classes, properties, decision and iteration constructs, and so forth) in memory certainly lends itself to a deeper understanding of the composition of the .NET type system as well as how various interop-related tools can generate source code files for use in your managed applications. So, without further ado, let's check out System.CodeDom and build an example application.

Introducing the System.CodeDOM Namespace

Given that CodeDOM is in charge of representing any possible .NET type (class, interface, structure, enumeration, or delegate), its members (properties, methods, and events), and their implementation (foreach loops, if/else statements, object manipulation), you are correct to assume that System.CodeDOM contains numerous types of interest. Although I will not bother to pound out the details of each and every type located in the System.CodeDOM namespace (to be sure, a small book in and of itself), let's just focus on the highlights. Before you drill into a number of tables, consider the generalized format of a .NET source code file, presented in dazzling pseudo-code:

```
// A namespace contains types.
NAMESPACE myNameSpace
[
  // Interfaces types.
  INTERFACE : <Other Interfaces>
  [
    {PROPERTY, METHOD, EVENT}
  ]
  // Class types.
  CLASS : <BaseClass>
  [
    {PROPERTY, METHOD, EVENT}
    [NESTED TYPES] * n where n >= 0
  ]
  // Enum types.
  ENUM : System.Enum : STORAGE
  [
    NAME = VAULE
  ]
  // Structure types.
  STRUCTURE : System.ValueType
  [
    {PROPERTY, METHOD, EVENT}
  ]
  // Delegates.
  DELEGATE : System.MulticastDelegate
  [
    {METHOD}
  ]
]

Where:
PROPERTY[OPTIONAL PARAMS]
[
  GET
  SET
]
METHOD[OPTIONAL PARAMS][RETURN VALUE]
EVENT[DELEGATE]
And:
{PROPERTY, METHOD, EVENT}
[
  [PARAMETER] * n where n >= 0
]
```

Obviously the previous skeleton is not using the syntax of a "real" managed language. Rather, notice how the pseudo-code is simply representing the layout of the possible types that can populate a .NET namespace. Once the form is understood, you can represent this layout in memory using a number of types of the CodeDOM. Next question: How exactly does System.CodeDOM represent these programming atoms?

The Types of System.CodeDOM

First, System.CodeDOM defines a number of types that allow you to programmatically represent a .NET namespace. In essence, you have two core types; however, Table 5-2 documents each namespace-centric type.

Table 5-2. Namespace-Building Types of CodeDOM

Namespace-Building CodeDOM Type	Meaning in Life
CodeNamespace CodeNamespaceCollection	Represents a single namespace declaration, or a collection of namespaces
CodeNamespaceImport CodeNamespaceImportCollection	Represents a single namespace import or a collection of namespace imports

As you know, .NET namespaces contain any number of types (classes, structures, enumerations, interfaces, and delegates). Each of these constructs can be represented by the CodeTypeDeclaration/CodeTypeDelegate types (or, if you rather, by a collection of related types). Check out Table 5-3.

Table 5-3. Type-Building Types of CodeDOM

Type-Building CodeDOM Type	Meaning in Life
CodeTypeDeclaration	A type declaration for a class, structure, enumeration, or interface (as well as a nested type contained within another type). The underlying type is established using the IsClass, IsInterface, IsStruct, and IsEnum properties.
CodeTypeDeclarationCollection	A type declaration collection.
CodeTypeDelegate	A delegate declaration.

Just as namespaces contain types, types contain any number of members (properties, methods, and events). As you would expect, System.CodeDOM also defines a number of members that allow you to represent the members of an in-memory type. Table 5-4 hits the core items of interest.

Table 5-4. Member-Building Types of CodeDOM

Member-Building CodeDOM Type	Meaning in Life
CodeTypeMember	An abstract base class that represents a member of a type
CodeTypeMemberCollection	A collection of members of a type
CodeMemberMethod	A class method declaration
CodeMemberField	A class field declaration
CodeMemberProperty	A class property declaration
CodeConstructor	A constructor for a type
CodeTypeConstructor	A static constructor for a type
CodeEntryPoint	A member that is the entry point of a program (for example, Main())
MemberAttributes	Attributes with identifiers that are used by CodeTypeMember
CodeMemberEvent	A class event declaration
CodeParameterDeclarationExpression	A parameter declaration

System.CodeDOM also defines a number of types that allow you to represent various looping and decision constructs, code comments, structured exception handling logic (try, catch, throw), and even the infamous Goto keyword. Again, the point of this final task of the chapter is not to provide an exhaustive description of System.CodeDOM types, but rather to facilitate the importance of type. In this light, let's see a concrete CodeDOM example and get to know various members of this namespace.

Building a CodeDOM Example

The application you will now construct is a console application (written in C#) named SimpleCodeDOM. The program is responsible for performing a series of steps in addition to generating a set of CodeDOM nodes. Here are the specifics:

- The user will be prompted to specify C# or VB .NET as the target of the source code.
- Once the code target has been obtained, you will build a namespace containing a single class using System.CodeDOM. As you will see, this class supports a property that manipulates a private string data type and a method to display the value.
- Once the *.vb or *.cs file has been saved to file, you will dynamically compile the source code into a .NET assembly (way cool).
- Finally, you prompt the user for a string value and make use of late binding to interact with the generated assembly and its internal types.

Basically, this exercise allows you to build a (painfully) simplified custom compiler that emits C# or VB .NET source code! Of course, the major limitation of this example program is that it only knows how to compile the following class (shown here in C#):

```
// This is the wicked cool Hello class.
namespace SimpleCodeDOMHelloClass {
  using System;
  using System.Windows.Forms;

  public class HelloClass : object {

    // The state data...
    private string mMsg;

    public HelloClass(string msg) {mMsg = msg;}
    public HelloClass() {}

    // The Message property.
    public string Message {
      get {return this.mMsg;}
      set {mMsg = value;}
    }
```

```
    // Show 'em what we got!
    public void Display() {
      MessageBox.Show(mMsg);
    }
  }
}
```

I will assume that you will take this example and add additional user interactivity to fix this limitation as you see fit.

Building the Main() Function

The CodeDOM program is driven by a Main() function that is in charge of triggering each aspect of your design specification. You do need to import a number of namespaces to interact with the C# and VB .NET code providers (Microsoft.CSharp and Microsoft.VisualBasic, respectively) as well as the types necessary to facilitate late binding (System.Reflection). I drill into the details of System.Reflection in the next chapter. Until then, here is your initial crack at the SimpleCodeDom application:

```
using System;
using System.CodeDom;
using System.CodeDom.Compiler;
using Microsoft.CSharp;
using Microsoft.VisualBasic;
using System.IO;
using System.Reflection;

namespace SimpleCodeDOM
{
  class HelloCodeGen
  {
    // Access to the code generator.
    private static ICodeGenerator itfCG;
    // Access to the code compiler.
    private static ICodeCompiler itfCC;
    // cs or vb?
    private static string syntaxTarget;
    private static string assemblyName;

    [STAThread]
    static void Main(string[] args)
```

```
{
  // Prompt for target language.
  Console.Write("Do you want to generate C# or VB .NET code? ");
  syntaxTarget = Console.ReadLine();

  // Get interface references from code provider type.
  switch(syntaxTarget.ToUpper())
  {
  case "C#":
  case "CSharp":
  case "CS":
    syntaxTarget = "cs";
    CSharpCodeProvider cdp = new CSharpCodeProvider();
    itfCG = cdp.CreateGenerator();
    itfCC = cdp.CreateCompiler();
  break;
  case "VB .NET":
  case "VB.NET":
  case "VB":
    syntaxTarget = "vb";
    VBCodeProvider vbdp = new VBCodeProvider();
    itfCG = vbdp.CreateGenerator();
    itfCC = vbdp.CreateCompiler();
  break;
  default:
  Console.WriteLine("Sorry...can't do it...");
  syntaxTarget = null;
  break;
  }
  // Only proceed if they picked a valid language
  // supported by System.CodeDOM.
  if(syntaxTarget != null)
  {
    // Now create the file and generate the code!
    TextWriter txtWriter = CreateFile(syntaxTarget);
    PopulateNamespace(itfCG, txtWriter);
    txtWriter.Close();
    Console.WriteLine("Done!");

    // Now compile the code into a .NET DLL.
    Console.WriteLine("Compiling code...");
    CompileCode(itfCC, syntaxTarget);
```

```
        // Now launch the application!
        Console.Write("Enter your message: ");
        string msg = Console.ReadLine();
        LoadAndRunAsm(msg);
        Console.WriteLine("Thanks for playing...");
      }
    }
  }
}
```

The crux of the Main() method is to build a "code provider" based on the user's choice of managed language. The Microsoft.CSharp and Microsoft.VisualBasic namespaces each define a code provider type (CSharpCodeProvider and VBCodeProvider, respectively) that support two interfaces, ICodeGenerator and ICodeCompiler (note that you have declared a member variable of each type in your HelloCodeGen class). Once you have figured out which language the user wishes to use, you extract interface references from the correct code provider type (also note that these interfaces are defined within the System.CodeDOM.Compiler namespace).

ICodeGenerator provides a number of methods that enable CodeDOM to create code in memory, given various aspects of the System.CodeDOM object model (that is, a namespace, a type, a code statement, and so forth). Here is the formal C# definition:

```
// This interface is used to generate source code using CodeDOM.
public interface System.CodeDom.Compiler.ICodeGenerator
{
  string CreateEscapedIdentifier(string value);
  string CreateValidIdentifier(string value);
  void GenerateCodeFromCompileUnit(CodeCompileUnit e,
      TextWriter w, CodeGeneratorOptions o);
  void GenerateCodeFromExpression(CodeExpression e,
      TextWriter w, CodeGeneratorOptions o);
  void GenerateCodeFromNamespace(CodeNamespace e,
      TextWriter w, CodeGeneratorOptions o);
  void GenerateCodeFromStatement(CodeStatement e,
      TextWriter w, CodeGeneratorOptions o);
  void GenerateCodeFromType(CodeTypeDeclaration e,
      TextWriter w, CodeGeneratorOptions o);
  string GetTypeOutput(CodeTypeReference type);
  bool IsValidIdentifier(string value);
  bool Supports(GeneratorSupport supports);
  void ValidateIdentifier(string value);
}
```

The ICodeCompiler, as you would guess, is used to compile a source code file (or set of source code files) into a .NET assembly:

```
// Used to compile code into a .NET assembly.
public interface System.CodeDom.Compiler.ICodeCompiler
{
  CompilerResults CompileAssemblyFromDom(CompilerParameters options,
     CodeCompileUnit compilationUnit);
  CompilerResults CompileAssemblyFromDomBatch(CompilerParameters options,
     CodeCompileUnit[] compilationUnits);
  CompilerResults CompileAssemblyFromFile(CompilerParameters options,
     string fileName);
  CompilerResults CompileAssemblyFromFileBatch(CompilerParameters options,
     string[] fileNames);
  CompilerResults CompileAssemblyFromSource(CompilerParameters options,
     string source);
  CompilerResults CompileAssemblyFromSourceBatch(CompilerParameters options,
     string[] sources);
}
```

Finally, once a reference to each interface has been obtained, the Main() loop calls a set of static helper functions to do the dirty work. Let's see each helper member in turn.

Building the File via CreateFile()

The first helper function, CreateFile(), simply generates a new *.vb or *.cs file and saves it in the current application directory. To make things a bit simpler, the name of this file will always be Hello.vb or Hello.cs:

```
// Build the physical file to hold the source code.
private static TextWriter CreateFile(string syntaxTarget)
{
  string fileName = String.Format("Hello.{0}", syntaxTarget);
  Console.WriteLine ("Creating source file {0}.", fileName);
  TextWriter t = new StreamWriter (new FileStream (fileName, FileMode.Create));
  return t;
}
```

Building the HelloClass (and Containing Namespace)

The PopulateNamespace() helper method is where most of the action happens. Although this is a rather lengthy code block, fear not. It is actually quite readable:

```
private static void PopulateNamespace(ICodeGenerator itfCG, TextWriter w)
{
  // Add a code comment.
  CodeCommentStatement c =
    new CodeCommentStatement("This is the wicked cool Hello class");
  itfCG.GenerateCodeFromStatement(c, w, null);

  // Build root namespace.
  CodeNamespace cnamespace =
    new CodeNamespace("SimpleCodeDOMHelloClass");

  // Reference other namespaces.
  cnamespace.Imports.Add(new CodeNamespaceImport ("System") );
  cnamespace.Imports.Add(new CodeNamespaceImport ("System.Windows.Forms") );

  // Insert the HelloClass.
  CodeTypeDeclaration co = new CodeTypeDeclaration ("HelloClass");
  co.IsClass = true;
  co.BaseTypes.Add (typeof (System.Object) );
  co.TypeAttributes = TypeAttributes.Public;
  cnamespace.Types.Add(co);

  // Make a custom constructor.
  CodeConstructor ctor = new CodeConstructor();
  ctor.Attributes = MemberAttributes.Public;
  ctor.Parameters.Add(new CodeParameterDeclarationExpression
     (new CodeTypeReference(typeof(string)), "msg"));
  ctor.Statements.Add((new CodeAssignStatement(new
    CodeArgumentReferenceExpression("mMsg"),
    new CodeArgumentReferenceExpression("msg"))));
    co.Members.Add(ctor);

  // Add the default constructor.
  ctor = new CodeConstructor();
  ctor.Attributes = MemberAttributes.Public;
  co.Members.Add(ctor);
```

```
    // Insert a String field (mMsg).
    CodeMemberField cf = new CodeMemberField("System.String", "mMsg");
    cf.Comments.Add(new CodeCommentStatement("The state data..."));
    cf.Attributes = MemberAttributes.Private;
    co.Members.Add(cf);

    // Add the Message property.
    CodeMemberProperty cp = new CodeMemberProperty();
    cp.Name = "Message";
    cp.Attributes = MemberAttributes.Public | MemberAttributes.Final ;
    cp.Type = new CodeTypeReference("System.String");
    cp.Comments.Add(new CodeCommentStatement("The Message property"));

    // Getter.
    cp.GetStatements.Add(new CodeMethodReturnStatement
    (new CodeFieldReferenceExpression(new
    CodeThisReferenceExpression(), "mMsg")));

    // Setter.
    cp.SetStatements.Add(new CodeAssignStatement(
      new CodeArgumentReferenceExpression("mMsg"),
      new CodeArgumentReferenceExpression("value")));
    co.Members.Add (cp);

    // Add the Display() method.
    CodeMemberMethod cm = new CodeMemberMethod();
    cm.Name = "Display";
    cm.Attributes = MemberAttributes.Public | MemberAttributes.Final ;
    cm.Comments.Add(new CodeCommentStatement("Show 'em what we got!"));
    cm.Statements.Add (new CodeMethodInvokeExpression
      (new CodeTypeReferenceExpression("MessageBox"), "Show",
       new CodeExpression [] {new CodeArgumentReferenceExpression ("mMsg")}));
    co.Members.Add(cm);

    // Generate the code!
    itfCG.GenerateCodeFromNamespace (cnamespace, w, null);
}
```

As you can see, you begin by defining the name of the namespace (SimpleCodeDOMHelloClass) and establish the set of additional namespaces that will be referenced.

```
// Build namespace.
CodeCommentStatement c =
  new CodeCommentStatement("This is the wicked cool Hello class");
itfCG.GenerateCodeFromStatement(c, w, null);
CodeNamespace cnamespace =
  new CodeNamespace("SimpleCodeDOMHelloClass");
cnamespace.Imports.Add(new CodeNamespaceImport ("System") );
cnamespace.Imports.Add(new CodeNamespaceImport ("System.Windows.Forms") );
```

Next, you create the HelloClass type, establish the characteristics of your class type, and add it to the namespace itself:

```
// Insert the HelloClass.
CodeTypeDeclaration co = new CodeTypeDeclaration ("HelloClass");
co.IsClass = true;
co.BaseTypes.Add (typeof (System.Object) );
co.TypeAttributes = TypeAttributes.Public;
cnamespace.Types.Add(co);
```

The HelloClass itself defines two constructors (one taking a System.String and the other being the default constructor), a private field (or type System.String), a property named Message, and a method called Display(), which shows the value of the private string using the Windows Forms MessageBox class. Most of the code is quite readable; however, when you wish to represent a method invocation in memory using System.CodeDOM, you will need to build a new CodeMethodInvokeExpression type.

The CodeMethodInvokeExpression type takes as constructor arguments a new CodeTypeReferenceExpression type that represents the name of the type you wish to invoke (MessageBox), the name of the member to invoke (Show), and a list of parameters to send into the method (represented as an array of CodeExpression types). For example, the following CodeDOM logic:

```
// Add the Display() message.
CodeMemberMethod cm = new CodeMemberMethod();
cm.Name = "Display";
cm.Attributes = MemberAttributes.Public | MemberAttributes.Final ;
cm.Comments.Add(new CodeCommentStatement("Show 'em what we got!"));
cm.Statements.Add (new CodeMethodInvokeExpression
  (new CodeTypeReferenceExpression("MessageBox"), "Show",
   new CodeExpression [] {new CodeArgumentReferenceExpression ("mMsg")}));
co.Members.Add(cm);
```

represents the following C# method implementation:

```
// Show 'em what we got!
public void Display()
{
  MessageBox.Show(mMsg);
}
```

Finally, before exiting your helper function, you save the object graph to your source code file using the namespace you have just created and the incoming TextWriter:

```
private static void PopulateNamespace(ICodeGenerator itfCG, TextWriter w)
{
  // … all the CodeDOM stuff…
  // Generate the code!
  itfCG.GenerateCodeFromNamespace (cnamespace, w, null);
}
```

Compiling the Assembly

Now that you have a source code file saved to disk, the CompileCode() method will make use of the obtained ICodeCompiler interface and build a .NET DLL assembly (always named HelloCSAsm.dll or HelloVBAsm.dll). If you have worked with the raw C# or VB .NET compilers at the command line before, this should look very familiar:

```
private static void CompileCode(ICodeCompiler itfCC, string syntaxTarget)
{
  // Set assembly name.
  assemblyName = String.Format("Hello{0}Asm", syntaxTarget.ToUpper());
  // Compile the code.
  CompilerParameters parms = new CompilerParameters();
  parms.OutputAssembly = assemblyName + ".dll";
  parms.CompilerOptions = "/t:library /r:System.Windows.Forms.dll";
  itfCC.CompileAssemblyFromFile(parms,
    String.Format("Hello.{0}", syntaxTarget));
}
```

Running the Assembly (Using Late Binding)

The final helper function of the application LoadAndRunAsm() loads the assembly into a new AppDomain and exercises the HelloClass using late binding. I comment on reflection and late binding in the next chapter. Until then, ponder the following code:

```
private static void LoadAndRunAsm(string msg)
{
  // Load the assembly into a new AppDomain.
  AppDomain ad = AppDomain.CreateDomain("HelloAppDomain");
  Assembly a = ad.Load(assemblyName);

  // Get the HelloClass type.
  Type helloClass = a.GetType("SimpleCodeDOMHelloClass.HelloClass");
  object obj = Activator.CreateInstance(helloClass);

  // Set message property.
  PropertyInfo pi = helloClass.GetProperty("Message");
  MethodInfo mi = pi.GetSetMethod(true);
  mi.Invoke(obj, new object[]{msg});

  // Display message!
  mi = helloClass.GetMethod("Display");
  mi.Invoke(obj, null);
}
```

Running Your Application

Now then, take your application out for a test drive. Assume you have run the application once for each target language. If you were to look at the application directory for your project, you would find four dynamically generated files (two source code files and two .NET assemblies). Check out Figure 5-23.

Figure 5-23. Your generated files, thanks to System.CodeDOM

The resulting console output (and message box display) would look something like what you see in Figure 5-24.

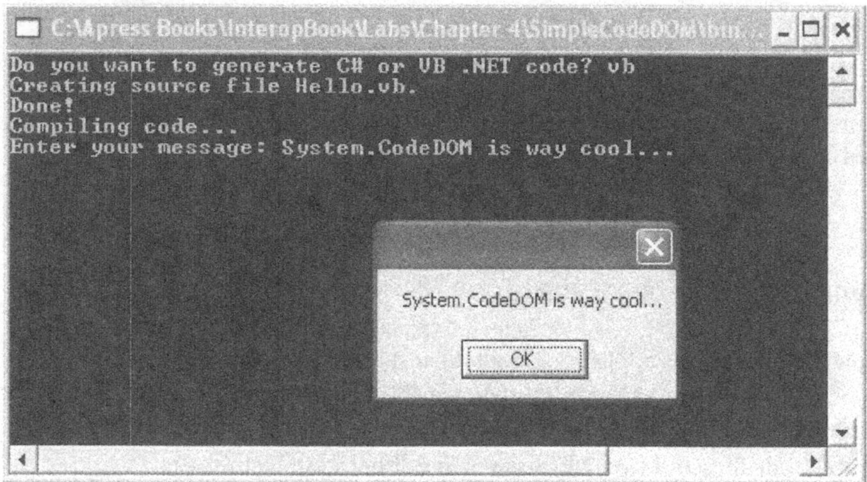

Figure 5-24. The completed application

Given that you have already seen the resulting C# code, here is the generated VB .NET code:

```
'This is the wicked cool Hello class
Imports System
Imports System.Windows.Forms
Namespace SimpleCodeDOMHelloClass

  Public Class HelloClass
    Inherits Object

    'The state data...
    Private mMsg As String

    Public Sub New(ByVal msg As String)
      MyBase.New
      mMsg = msg
    End Sub

    Public Sub New()
      MyBase.New
    End Sub

    'The Message property
    Public Property Message As String
      Get
        Return Me.mMsg
      End Get
      Set
        mMsg = value
      End Set
    End Property

    'Show 'em what we got!
    Public Sub Display()
      MessageBox.Show(mMsg)
    End Sub
  End Class
End Namespace
```

As you can see, System.CodeDOM is a critical .NET namespace for the tool builders of the world. Given that numerous interop-centric tools make use of System.CodeDOM under the hood, I hope you found the previous section enlightening.

CODE *The SimpleCodeDOM project is included under the Chapter 5 subdirectory.*

Summary

The .NET platform is a 100% new architecture that has no relationship to COM whatsoever. However, like COM, .NET supports the ideals of binary reuse, language independence, and interface-based programming. As you have seen, .NET assemblies contain platform-agnostic IL code, type metadata, and an assembly manifest. Collectively, these entities make .NET assemblies completely self-describing. Given this, assemblies are not registered within the system registry, but are located by the runtime by probing the application directory or the GAC. Recall that the binding process can be modified using application configuration files.

Within a given assembly, there will be some number of .NET types (classes, interfaces, enumerations, structures, and delegates). Of course, most of the time, you will simply fire up Visual Studio .NET and author your source code using the IDE. However, the System.CodeDOM namespace contains a number of items that allow you to represent .NET types and their implementations in memory and commit this object graph to a physical file using a specific managed language. Clearly, this is a very important aspect of building custom tools that can create source code for use by other applications (such as wsdl.exe).

In the next (and final) chapter before you begin to formally examine specific COM/.NET interoperability issues, you will get to understand the process of reading .NET type information at runtime using the System.Reflection namespace. As you will see, .NET makes the process of reading type information much simpler than the classic COM ITypeLib(2) and ITypeInfo(2) interfaces.

CHAPTER 6

.NET Types

In Chapter 5, you examined the core traits of .NET assemblies. During this discussion, I did not make much mention of the specific type system of the .NET platform. Therefore, the first task of this chapter is to document the set of CLS-compliant data types, their relationships, and how these core types map into C# and VB .NET–specific keywords. After that I formalize each of the possible user-defined types supported by the .NET Framework (classes, structures, interfaces, and enumerations).

The bulk of this chapter, however, examines how to build applications that are capable of reading the set of types contained within a given assembly using the System.Reflection namespace. Along the way, you are exposed to a number of related topics such as .NET attributes and late binding. Once you complete this chapter, you will have a solid handle on the .NET type system, as well as that of classic COM. In effect, you will be in a perfect position to truly understand the inner details of COM/.NET interoperability.

The Role of System.Object

No examination of the .NET type system would be complete without discussing the role of System.Object. This class type is the ultimate root of each and every class entity in the .NET universe. System.Object is defined within mscorlib.dll as follows:

```
// The chief base class.
public class Object
{
    public Object();
    // Instance methods.
    public virtual bool Equals(object obj);
    public virtual int GetHashCode();
    public Type GetType();
    public virtual string ToString();
    // Static (that's Shared in VB .NET) methods.
   public static bool ReferenceEquals(object objA, object objB);
   public static bool Equals(object objA, object objB);
}
```

As you can see, Equals(), GetHashCode(), and ToString() have each been declared virtual and can thus be overridden by a derived type. Also note that two members of System.Object (ReferenceEquals() and an alternative version of the Equals() method) have been declared static and can thus be called at the class level without first needing to create an object reference. Table 6-1 documents the functionality of each member.

Table 6-1. The Methods of System.Object

Method of System.Object	Meaning in Life
Equals()	This instance-level method is used to test if two object references point to the same object in memory. This method may be overridden to test for value-based semantics.
Equals()	The static version of Equals() compares two objects using value-based or reference-based semantics (depending on how the object being tested has been configured).
GetHashCode()	This method is used to return a numerical value that can identify an object held within a HashTable data structure.
GetType()	As far as this chapter is concerned, this is the most important member of System.Object. Using GetType() callers are able to obtain a Type object that fully describes the characteristics of a given object.
ReferenceEquals()	This static method compares two objects using reference-based semantics.
ToString()	By default, this method returns the fully qualified name of a given type (for example, Namespace.Type). This method is typically overridden to return a string that contains name/value pairs representing the state of the current object reference.

Overriding ToString()

To illustrate how a derived class can override the virtual members of System.Object, here is a simple Car type that has overridden ToString() to return its current state data as a set of formatted name/value pairs. Notice that I am making use of the StringBuilder type (defined in the System.Text namespace) for reasons of efficiency. Simply making use of a System.String and the overloaded + operator also fits the bill.

```
// Overriding ToString().
public class SimpleCar // : object implied.
{
   private string mPetName;
   private string mColor;
   private int mCurrSpeed;

   public SimpleCar(string petname, string color, int sp)
   {
      mPetName = petname;
      mColor = color;
      mCurrSpeed = sp;
   }
   public SimpleCar(){}
   public override string ToString()
   {
      StringBuilder sb = new StringBuilder();
      sb.AppendFormat("[Pet Name: {0}, ", mPetName);
      sb.AppendFormat("Color: {0}, ", mColor);
      sb.AppendFormat("Current Speed: {0}]", mCurrSpeed);
      return sb.ToString();
   }
}
```

If you take your class type out for a spin, you might build a Main() loop as follows:

```
class CarTester
{
   [STAThread]
   static void Main(string[] args)
   {
      SimpleCar car = new SimpleCar("Mel", "Yellow", 40);
      Console.WriteLine(car);    // ToString() called automatically.
    }
}
```

The output (of course) prints "[Pet Name: Mel, Color: Yellow, Current Speed: 40]" to the console window. If you did not override ToString(), you would simply see the fully qualified name of the SimpleCar type.

The Two Faces of Equality

System.Object defines several ways to allow you to test if two objects have the same internal state values (that is, value-based semantics) as well as if two object references are pointing to the same entity on the managed heap (that is, reference-based semantics). To illustrate the distinction, consider the following update to the Main() method:

```
class CarTester
{
   [STAThread]
   static void Main(string[] args)
   {
      SimpleCar car = new SimpleCar("Mel", "Yellow", 40);
      Console.WriteLine(car);

      // Test object refs.
      SimpleCar carRef = car;
      Console.WriteLine("Are Car and carRef pointing to same car? : {0}",
                                object.ReferenceEquals(car, carRef));

      // Compare new refs.
      SimpleCar car2 = new SimpleCar("Hank", "Pink", 90);
      Console.WriteLine("Are car and car2 pointing to same car? : {0}",
                                object.ReferenceEquals(car, car2));
   }
}
```

Here, you are first testing to see if the car and carRef variables are pointing to the same object allocated on the managed heap (which they are). Next, you call the static ReferenceEquals()on two distinct objects. In this case, you are told the object variables are not the same (which is correct). Figure 6-1 shows the output thus far.

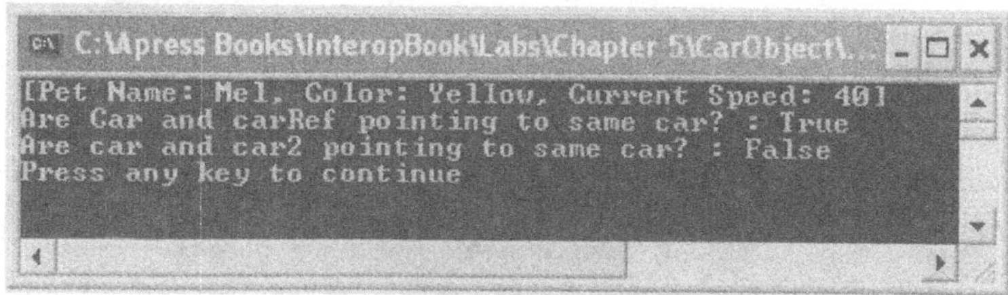

Figure 6-1. Testing object references

Now, let's assume you updated Main() once again as follows:

```
static void Main(string[] args)
{
...
   SimpleCar car2 = new SimpleCar("Hank", "Pink", 90);
   // Compare state?
   SimpleCar car3 = new SimpleCar("Hank", "Pink", 90);
   Console.WriteLine("Do car2 and car3 contain same state ? : {0}",
                           object.Equals(car2, car3));
   Console.WriteLine("Do car2 and car3 contain same state ? : {0}",
                           car2.Equals(car3));
}
```

Here, you begin by using the static System.Object.Equals() method as well as the default inherited implementation of Equals() currently used by the SimpleCar type. Notice that although car2 and car3 have been created with identical constructor arguments, the test for identical state data fails!

The reason is simple. Both the static and instance-level System.Object.Equals() methods, by default, only test *object references* and not the *state* data of an object. When you wish to retrofit your custom class types to perform value-based semantics, you need to explicitly override the Equals() method for your class. In addition, understand that classes that override Equals() should also override GetHashCode() to ensure that the object in question behaves property if placed in a hash container. Thus, you could update the SimpleCar class as follows:

```
// Overriding Equals() and GetHashCode().
public class SimpleCar : object
{
   ....
   public override bool Equals(object obj)
   {
      // Test values (not references).
      if((((SimpleCar)obj).mColor == this.mColor) &&
         (((SimpleCar)obj).mCurrSpeed == this.mCurrSpeed) &&
         (((SimpleCar)obj).mPetName == this.mPetName))
         return true;
      else
         return false;
   }
   // The System.String class implements a nice hash algorithm,
   // so we just leverage it using the pet name member variable.
   public override int GetHashCode()
   { return mPetName.GetHashCode(); }
}
```

If you now test the state values of car2 and car3 using the static or instance-level Equals() method, you find that they do indeed contain the same state data and will thus pump out the following to the console:

```
Do car2 and car3 contain same state? : True
```

The remaining member of System.Object, GetType(), is examined in gory detail a bit later in this chapter. Until then, let's get to know the set of intrinsic data members supported by the .NET runtime.

CODE *The CarObject project is located under the Chapter 6 subdirectory.*

Examining the .NET Data Type System

As you recall from the previous chapter, the Common Type System (CTS) is a set of rules that define the full set of programming constructs and data types that may be present in a given .NET-aware programming language. Figure 6-2 documents the intrinsic types supported by the CTS. Notice how all reference types ultimately derive from the mighty System.Object.

As you can see, the System.ValueType type is the base class for any and all intrinsic data types supported by a given programming language (for example, int, string, long, and so forth). The role of System.ValueType is to ensure that the derived type *automatically* obeys the rules of value-based semantics. Thus, when you compare two C# int types (which is an alias for the System.Int32 type) you are returned the result of the comparison of their underlying values, not their location in memory. In fact, ValueTypes are not placed on the managed heap at all! ValueTypes are always allocated on the stack (and thus are destroyed when they fall out of the defining scope). For example:

```
// Remember, the C# 'int' is just an alias for System.Int32,
// and therefore we can call inherited members directly!
int x = 99;
int y = 9;
Console.WriteLine("Equal? : {0}", x.Equals(y));      // False!
```

In contrast, types that do not derive from ValueType are allocated on the managed heap and typically make use of the default implementation of System.Object.Equals() (meaning equality tests are made using reference-based semantics).

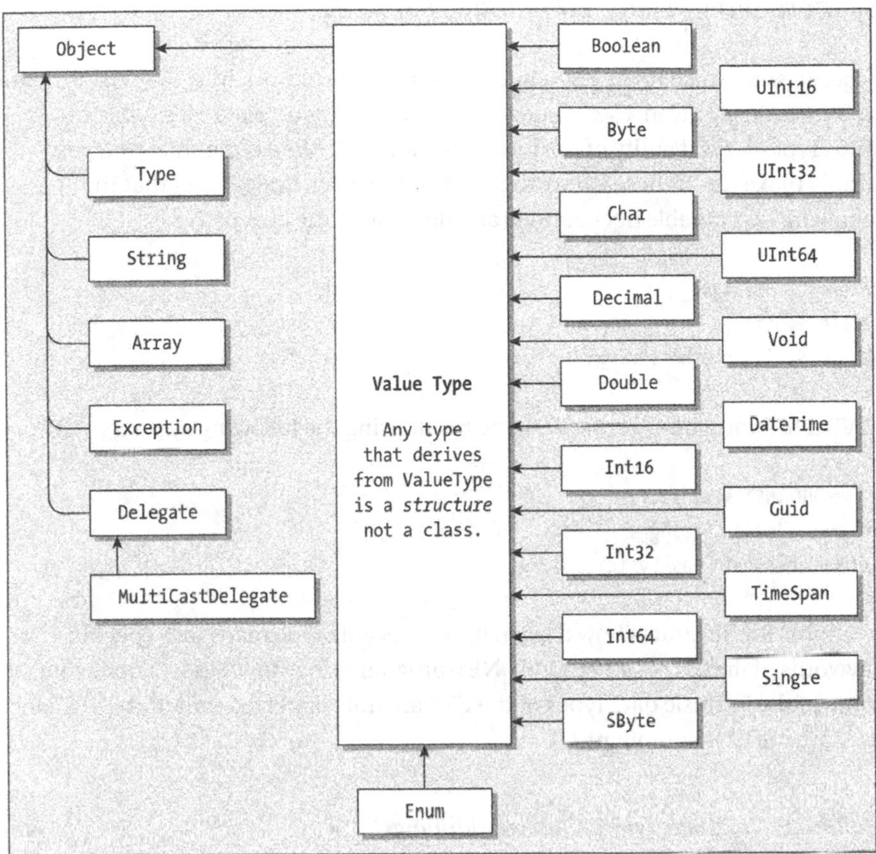

Figure 6-2. The hierarchy of core types

Do note, however, that even though System.String is not a ValueType (and is thus allocated on the heap) the designers of this class type have overridden Object.Equals() to use value-based semantics (just like you did for the SimpleCar type). Thus:

```
// System.String.Equals() works with values, not references.
string s1 = "Hello";
string s2 = "Hello";
Console.WriteLine("Equal? : {0}", s1.Equals(s2));     // True!
string s3 = "Oh the humanity...";
Console.WriteLine("Equal? : {0}", s1.Equals(s3));     // False!
```

System Data Type Language Mappings

Regardless of which managed language you choose to work with (C#, VB .NET, and so forth) you are given a set of language-specific keywords that alias the correct ValueType-derived entity of the base class libraries. More often than not, you simply make use of these keywords directly. However, understand that the following two variable declarations are identical in the eyes of .NET:

```
// Two C# strings.
string myString;
System.String myOtherString;
```

In VB .NET you would get to the same result using the following syntax:

```
' Two VB .NET strings.
Dim myString as String
Dim myOtherString as System.String
```

Table 6-2 illustrates how a given base class data type maps into specific keywords of the C#, MC++, and VB .NET programming languages. (Notice that some of the intrinsic data types of the CTS are not supported under VB .NET since they are not CLS-compliant.)

Table 6-2. .NET Data Type Language Mappings

.NET Base Class	Visual Basic. NET Representation	C# Representation	C++ with Managed Extensions Representation
System.Byte	Byte	byte	char
System.SByte	Not supported	Sbyte	signed char
System.Int16	Short	short	short
System.Int32	Integer	int	int or long
System.Int64	Long	long	__int64
System.UInt16	Not supported	ushort	unsigned short
System.UInt32	Not supported	uint	unsigned int or unsigned long
System.UInt64	Not supported	ulong	unsigned __int64

Table 6-2. .NET Data Type Language Mappings (continued)

.NET Base Class	Visual Basic. NET Representation	C# Representation	C++ with Managed Extensions Representation
System.Single	Single	float	float
System.Double	Double	double	double
System.Object	Object	object	Object*
System.Char	Char	char	__wchar_t
System.String	String	string	String*
System.Decimal	Decimal	decimal	Decimal
System.Boolean	Boolean	bool	bool

Obviously, these intrinsic data types are used to function as method parameters, member variables, and local variables in some method scope. Understand that given the fact that these language-specific keywords alias a specific type in the .NET base class library, and given the fact that all types ultimately derive from System.Object, you are able to write code such as the following:

```
// 12 is a C# int, which is really System.Int32, which derives from
// System.ValueType, which derives from System.Object.
Console.WriteLine(12.ToString());
Console.WriteLine(12.GetHashCode());
Console.WriteLine(12.Equals(12));
```

The Set of Custom .NET Types

In addition to the set of internal data types, you will certainly need to build custom data types for use in a given application. In the world of .NET, you have five possible type constructs that can be used. Table 6-3 documents each possibility.

Table 6-3. .NET Types

.NET Type	Meaning in Life
Class	When you build custom classes (or hierarchies of classes) you are building heap-allocated types that are managed by the .NET garbage collector. Class types benefit from each pillar of OOP, can work as base classes to other classes, and can define any number of members.
Structure	In essence, structures can be regarded as "lightweight class types" that are used to group logically related data items. Unlike classes, structures cannot be subclasses. They always derive directly from System.ValueType. As already mentioned, structures are allocated on the stack (rather than the heap) and are therefore a bit more efficient than a corresponding class definition.
Interface	Interfaces are a named set of abstract methods that may (or may not) be supported by a given class or structure. Given that interfaces are strongly typed data types, you can obtain an interface reference from a type and access a subset of its overall functionality, as well as use interface variables as function parameters and return values.
Enumeration	Enums are a set of name/value pairs that always derive from System.Enum. By default, the storage used for a given enumeration is System.Int32, but you are able to specify a different storage type if you are concerned with saving every byte of memory.

In addition to these four categories of .NET types, delegates are often considered a fifth possibility. As you may know, delegates are indeed classes that derive from the System.MulticastDelegate base class. More often than not, however, when you are building a custom delegate, you make use of a language-specific keyword (such as the C# delegate keyword). Whichever way you go, delegates are used to represent a type-safe (and object-oriented) function pointer, which provides the foundation for the .NET event model. I hold off on discussing delegate types until you formally examine COM/.NET event interoperability. Until then, let's check out the core four.

.NET Class Types

Every .NET-aware language supports the notion of a *class type*, which is the cornerstone of object-oriented programming. A *class* is composed of any number of properties, methods, and events that typically manipulate some set of state data. As you would expect, the CTS allows a given class to support abstract members that provide a polymorphic interface for any derived classes. CTS-compliant classes may only derive from a single base class (multiple inheritance is not allowed for a .NET class type). To help keep your wits about you, Table 6-4 documents a number of characteristics of interest to class types.

Table 6-4. .NET Class Characteristics

Class Characteristic	Meaning in Life
Is the class "sealed"or not?	Sealed classes are types that cannot function as a base class to other classes.
Does the class implement any interfaces?	An interface is a collection of abstract members that provides contract between the object and object user. The CTS allows a class to implement any number of interfaces.
Is the class abstract or concrete?	Abstract classes cannot be directly created, but they are intended to define common behaviors for derived types. Concrete classes are directly creatable.
What is the "visibility" of this class?	Each class must be configured with a visibility attribute. Basically, this trait defines if the class can be used by external assemblies or used only from within the containing assembly (for example, a private helper class).

Like other OO-based programming languages, managed languages support the use of "nested" classes. This programming construct allows an outer (or nesting class) to define and manipulate an inner (or nested) type. This technique is yet another way to force tight encapsulation of related types and is especially useful when you want to create an object factory using the nested type. For example:

```
// This type makes cars.
public class CarFactory
{
   ....
   // Return a Car type to the caller.
   public Car GetNewCar()
   { return new Car();}
   // Nested car type: CarFactory.Car.
   public class Car{ /* some members */}
}
```

.NET Structure Types

The concept of a structure is also formalized by the CTS. If you have a C background, you should be pleased to know that these user-defined types (UDTs) have survived in the world of .NET (although they behave a bit differently under the hood). In general, a structure is a lightweight class type, with a number of notable exceptions. For example, structures may define any number of *parameterized* constructors (the no-argument constructor is reserved). In this way, you are able to establish the value of each field during the time of construction. For example:

```
// Create a C# structure.
struct POINT
{
   // Structures can contain fields.
   public int mX, mY;
   public POINT(int x, int y)
   { mX = x; mY =y; }
}
```

All CTS-compliant structures automatically derive from a common base class: System.ValueType. As you have seen, this base class configures a structure to function as a value-based (stack) data type rather than a reference-based (heap) entity. Be aware that the CTS permits structures to implement any number of .NET interfaces. Structures, however, may not derive from other types and are therefore always "sealed."

.NET Interface Types

Unlike classic COM, .NET interfaces do *not* derive from a common base interface such as IUnknown. In fact, topmost interfaces have no parent class (not even System.Object!). Interfaces are nothing more than a collection of abstract methods, properties, and event definitions. On their own, interfaces are of little use. However, when a class or structure implements a given interface in its unique way, you are able to request access to the supplied functionality using an interface reference. When you build custom interfaces using a .NET-aware programming language, the CTS permits a given interface to derive from *multiple* base interfaces (something not possible in classic COM). In this way, you are able to build elaborate interface hierarchies. For example:

```
// A James Bond car is a submergible sports car.
public interface ISportsCar{}
public interface IUnderwaterVehicle{}
public interface IJamesBondCar : ISportsCar, IUnderwaterVehicle{}
```

.NET Enumeration Types

Finally, there are enumerations. These types are a handy programming construct that allows you to group name/value pairs under a specific name. For example, assume you are creating a video game application that allows the end user to select one of three player types (Wizard, Fighter, or Thief). Rather than keeping track of raw numerical values to represent each possibility, you could build a custom enumeration:

```
// A C# enumeration.
enum PlayerType
{ Wizard = 100, Fighter = 200, Thief = 300 };
```

The CTS demands that enumerated types derive from a common base class, System.Enum, which defines a number of members that allow you to interact with the name/value pairs (such as testing if a given name exists within a given enum). Also be aware that (by default) .NET enumerations make use of a System.Int32 for the underlying storage. If you so choose, you may change this underlying storage using the following syntax:

```
// Change storage type.
enum PlayerType : long
{ Wizard = 100, Fighter = 200, Thief = 300 };
```

Building a Complex Code Library

Now that you have had a chance to examine the essence of the .NET type system, let's build a complex C# code library that you can use during the remaining examples of this chapter. The assembly that you will construct (ComplexTypeLibrary.dll) will define the following types (in two distinct but interrelated namespaces) as shown by the following ILDasm.exe screen shot (Figure 6-3).

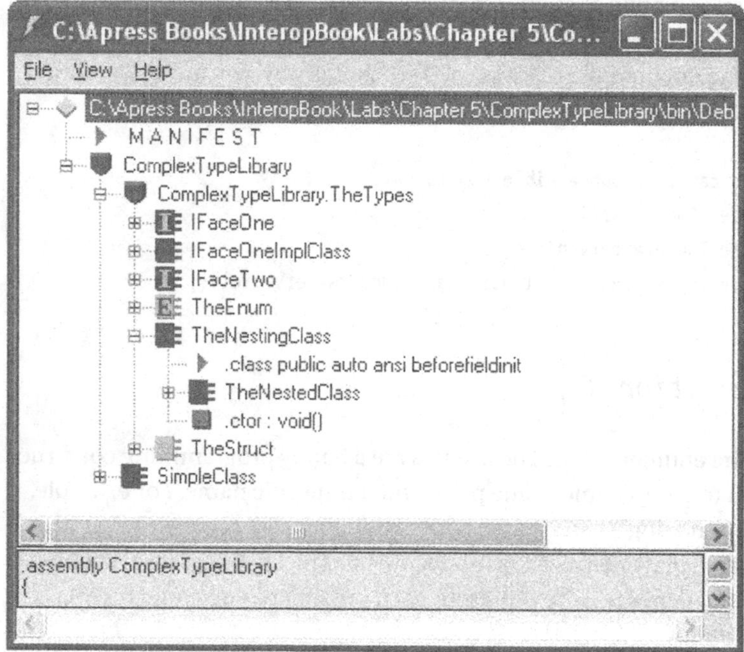

Figure 6-3. The ComplexTypeLibrary assembly

Because this chapter is more concerned with types than implementations of types, the code is short and sweet. Here is the complete listing (note the nested namespaces, nested classes, and interface definitions):

```
// Our 'complex' .NET code library.
namespace ComplexTypeLibrary
{
   // A class.
   public class SimpleClass{}
   namespace TheTypes // Nested namespace.
   {
```

```
      // An enum.
      public enum TheEnum
      {FieldA, FieldB}
      // Interfaces.
      public interface IFaceOne
      {
         string ReadOnlyProp{get;}
         string WriteOnlyProp{set;}
         TheEnum ReadWriteProp{get; set;}
      }
      public interface IFaceTwo
      {int SimpleMethod();}
      // A struct implementing an interface.
      public struct TheStruct : IFaceTwo
      {public int SimpleMethod(){return 0;}}
      // The nesting class
      public class TheNestingClass
      {
         // A nested class, with one property.
         public class TheNestedClass
         {
            private string someStrVal = "I'm nested!";
            public string GetInternalString()
            {return someStrVal;}
         }
      }
      // A class implementing an interface.
      public class IFaceOneImplClass : IFaceOne
      {
         public IFaceOneImplClass()
         {e = TheEnum.FieldB;}
         private TheEnum e;
         public string ReadOnlyProp
         {get{return "Hey!";}}
         public string WriteOnlyProp
         {set {string x = value;}}
         public TheEnum ReadWriteProp
         {get{return e;} set{e = value;}}
      }
   }
}
```

The ComplexTypeLibrary.dll is very generic (by design). Nevertheless, this gives us an interesting test bed to examine during the next topic under scrutiny: .NET reflection services.

Understanding Reflection

As you already know, ILDasm.exe is the tool of choice to examine the types within a given .NET assembly at design time (that is, after compilation). However, how exactly is ILDasm.exe able to read the assembly metadata? To be sure, ILDasm.exe is not making use of COM-centric type interfaces such as ITypeLib(2) or ITypeInfo(2).

The core problem with reading COM type information at runtime is the fact that you are forced to make use of a very non–OO-based architecture. As you recall from Chapter 4, the process of runtime type discovery under COM requires us to interact with the COM library and a small set of interfaces (and about 8 billion related structures).

Under .NET, however, developers are able to leverage the System.Type class and the related System.Reflection namespace. Like any other .NET namespace, System.Reflection makes use of the same well-designed, OOP-based protocol that is the .NET architecture. To begin, let's check out the role of the Type class itself.

Working with System.Type

The System.Type class represents the runtime representation of the metadata, which describes a given .NET type (class, interface, structure, enumeration, delegate). As you saw in Chapter 5, the .NET metadata format is quite verbose. The good news is that the type information contained within a Type reference is manipulated using a small set of members that shield you from the raw metadata information. Table 6-5 lists some (but not all) of the members of System.Type, grouped by related functionality.

Table 6-5. The Members of System.Type

System.Type Member	Meaning in Life
IsAbstract IsArray IsClass IsCOMObject IsEnum IsInterface IsPrimitive IsNestedPublic IsNestedPrivate IsSealed IsValueType	These properties (among others) allow you to discover a number of basic traits about the Type you are referring to (for example, if it is an abstract method, an array, a nested class, and so forth).
GetConstructors() GetEvents() GetFields() GetInterfaces() GetMethods() GetMembers() GetNestedTypes() GetProperties()	These methods (among others) allow you to obtain an array representing the items (interface, method, property, and so on) you are interested in. Each method returns a related array (for example, GetFields() returns a FieldInfo array, GetMethods() returns a MethodInfo array, and so forth). Be aware that each of these methods has a singular form (for example, GetMethod(), GetProperty()) that allows you to retrieve a specific item by name, rather than an array of all related items.
FindMembers()	Returns an array of MemberInfo types, based on search criteria.
GetType()	This method returns a Type instance given a string name.
InvokeMember()	This method allows late binding to a given item.

Do be aware that many of the more elaborate methods of Type (that is, GetProperties() and so forth) require that you explicitly make use of the types contained within the System.Reflection namespace. However, before you examine this namespace, let's check out how to read basic metadata information using some core members of the Type class.

Obtaining a Type Reference Using System.Object.GetType()

There are many ways to obtain a reference of System.Type. As you already are aware, System.Object defines a method named GetType() that returns (of course) the underlying Type describing the item. For example:

```
// Get a Type reference using Object.GetType().
Type t = 12.GetType();
Console.WriteLine("->Containing assembly: {0}", t.Assembly);
Console.WriteLine("->Base class: {0}", t.BaseType);
Console.WriteLine("->Full Name: {0}", t.FullName);
Console.WriteLine("->Is this an array? : {0}", t.IsArray);
Console.WriteLine("->Is this a COM object? :{0}", t.IsCOMObject);
```

Understand that when you wish to obtain metadata information for a given type using the inherited System.Object.GetType() method, you are required to have an active object reference. What if you do not wish (or need) to create an object reference but still require valid metadata?

Obtaining a Type Reference Using the C# typeof Operator

Another (perfectly valid) approach to obtaining a Type reference is to make use of the C# typeof operator. The nice thing about using typeof is the fact that you are not required to create an object of the entity you wish to examine. The only requirements are that you have

- Set a reference to the assembly containing the type you wish to examine
- Made use of the using or Imports statement (or whatever syntax is required by your managed language of choice) to scope the type (or make use of the fully qualified name)

Assume you have set a reference to the core ADO.NET assembly, System.Data.dll. Once you have done so, you can obtain type information for the DataSet class as follows:

```
// Now use typeof operator.
Console.WriteLine("Using typeof operator!");
Type t3 = typeof(DataSet);
```

```
Console.WriteLine("->Containing assembly: {0}", t3.Assembly);
Console.WriteLine("->Base class: {0}", t3.BaseType);
Console.WriteLine("->Full Name: {0}", t3.FullName);
Console.WriteLine("->Is this an array? : {0}", t3.IsArray);
Console.WriteLine("->Is this a COM object? :{0}", t3.IsCOMObject);
```

Again, notice that although you are reading the same bits of metadata for the DataSet type, using the typeof operator, you are not required to create an instance of this class type.

Obtaining a Type Reference Using the Type Class

The final, and most flexible, way of obtaining a Type reference is to make use of the static (or in terms of VB .NET, Shared) method Type.GetType(). The nice thing about this avenue of type acquisition is that you are able to specify the name of the assembly that contains the type you wish to examine. Like the C# typeof operator, you are still required to set a reference to the assembly containing the type you wish to examine and do not need to make an active object. Unlike the typeof operator, you are not required to make use of the "using"/"Imports" (or whatever) keyword in the file using Type.GetType() because the string sent into this method includes the name of the containing assembly. Assume you have set a reference to the ComplexTypeLibrary assembly you created earlier in this chapter. You could obtain type information for the SimpleClass type as follows:

```
// Now get a type in a different assembly using
// the static Type.GetType() method.
Console.WriteLine("Using static Type.GetType()!");
Type t2 =
   Type.GetType("ComplexTypeLibrary.SimpleClass, ComplexTypeLibrary");
Console.WriteLine("->Containing assembly: {0}", t2.Assembly);
Console.WriteLine("->Base class: {0}", t2.BaseType);
Console.WriteLine("->Full Name: {0}", t2.FullName);
Console.WriteLine("->Is this an array? : {0}", t2.IsArray);
Console.WriteLine("->Is this a COM object? :{0}", t2.IsCOMObject);
```

As you can see, the basic form of the string sent into Type.GetType() takes the following format:

```
// String format: "<namespace>.<typeName>, assemblyIdentity"
Type t2 =
   Type.GetType("ComplexTypeLibrary.SimpleClass, ComplexTypeLibrary");
```

Basically, a dot is used to separate namespaces and types, while a comma is used to mark the segment of the string that holds the name of the referenced assembly (minus the file extension). Type.GetType() also honors using additional string tokens, as seen in Table 6-6, which documents the core set of delimiters.

Table 6-6. Core Tokens Parsed by Type.GetType()

Type.GetType() Argument Token	**Meaning in Life**
Comma (,)	Precedes the Assembly name
Plus sign (+)	Precedes a nested class
Period (.)	Denotes namespace identifiers

Now then, assume you have a simple console application that makes use of each of the three techniques illustrated in this section (where all the logic is contained in the application's Main() method). Figure 6-4 shows the output.

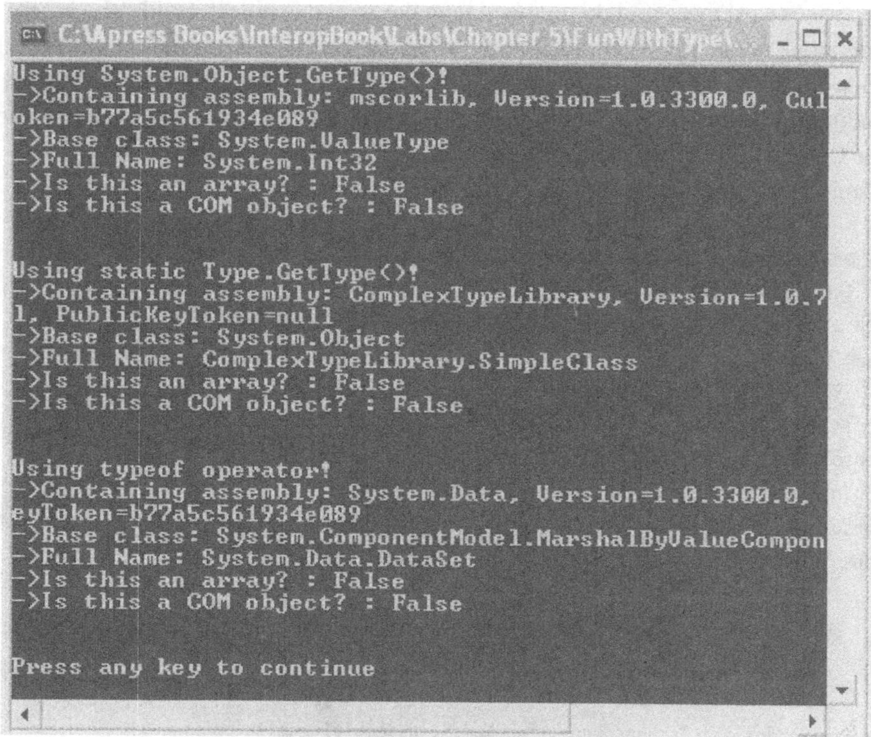

Figure 6-4. Fun with System.Type

CODE *The FunWithType project is located under the Chapter 6 subdirectory.*

The System.Reflection Namespace

Although the Type class allows you to obtain basic type information for a given item, most more elaborate methods of System.Type require additional types of the System.Reflection namespace. Using these members, you are able to drill into a reference type and obtain additional details such as the list of supported constructors, properties, methods, and events. Table 6-7 contains a (very) partial list of the members of the System.Reflection namespace.

Table 6-7. Select Members of the System.Reflection Namespace

Member of the System.Reflection Namespace	Meaning in Life
Assembly	This class (in addition to numerous related types) contains a number of methods that allow you to load, investigate, and manipulate an assembly.
AssemblyName	This class allows you to discover numerous details behind an assembly's identity (version information, culture information, and so forth).
EventInfo	Holds information for a given event.
FieldInfo	Holds information for a given field.
MemberInfo	This is the abstract base class that defines common behaviors for the EventInfo, FieldInfo, MethodInfo, and PropertyInfo types.
MethodInfo	Contains information for a given method.
Module	Allows you to access a given module within a multifile assembly.
ParameterInfo	Holds information for a given parameter.
PropertyInfo	Holds information for a given property.

Dynamically Loading an Assembly

The real workhorse of System.Reflection is the Assembly class. Using this type, you are able to dynamically load an assembly, invoke class members at runtime (late binding), as well as discover numerous properties about the assembly itself. Assume you have set a reference to the ComplexTypeLibrary assembly created previously in this chapter. The static Assembly.Load() method can be called by passing in the friendly string name:

```
// Investigate the ComplexTypeLibrary assembly.
using System;
using System.Reflection;
using System.IO; // Defines FileNotFoundException type.
...
public class MyReflector
{
public static int Main(string[] args)
{
   // Use Assembly class to load the ComplexTypeLibrary.
   Assembly a = null;
   try
   {
      a = Assembly.Load("ComplexTypeLibrary");
   }
   catch(FileNotFoundException e)
   {Console.WriteLine(e.Message);}
   return 0;
   }
}
```

Notice that the static Assembly.Load() method has been passed in the friendly name of the assembly you are interested in loading into memory. As you may suspect, this method has been overloaded a number of times to provide a number of ways in which you can bind to an assembly. One variation to be aware of is that the textual information sent into Assembly.Load() may contain additional string segments beyond the friendly name. Specifically, you may choose to specify a version number, public key token value, or locale (to load a shared assembly). You see this approach later in this chapter when you examine late binding under the .NET Framework.

Of equal interest is the static LoadFrom() method of the Assembly type. Using this method, you are able to load an assembly using an arbitrary path:

```
// Load an assembly given a specific path.
Assembly otherAsm = Assembly.LoadFrom(@"C:\MyAsms\foo.dll");
```

Enumerating Types in a Referenced Assembly

Once you have a reference to a loaded assembly, you may discover the characteristics of each .NET type it contains using Assembly.GetTypes(). This method returns an array of Type objects, from which you can call any of the members of the Type class. For example:

```
// List all members within the assembly.
// Assume 'a' is a currently loaded assembly.
Console.WriteLine("Listing all types in {0}", a.FullName);
Type[] types = a.GetTypes();
foreach(Type t in types)
   Console.WriteLine("Type: {0}", t);
```

Enumerating Class Members

Now assume you are interested in discovering the full set of members supported by one of the .NET types located within a given assembly. To do so, you can make use of the GetMembers() method defined by the Type class. As you recall, the Type class also defined a number of related methods (GetInterfaces(), GetProperties(), GetMethods(), and so forth) that allow you to specify a kind of member. GetMembers() itself returns an array of MemberInfo types. Again, by way of example:

```
// List all members of a given type.
Type t = a.GetType("ComplexTypeLibrary.SimpleClass");
MemberInfo[] mi = t.GetMembers();
foreach(MemberInfo m in mi)
   Console.WriteLine("Member Type {0}: {1} ",
                     m.MemberType.ToString(), m);
```

Enumerating Method Parameters

Not only can you use reflection to gather information for the members of a type, you can also obtain information about the parameters of a given member. To do so requires the use of MethodInfo.GetParameters(). This method returns a ParameterInfo array. Each item in this array contains numerous properties for a given parameter. Assume that you have added a Foo() method to the SimpleClass type and wish to read the metadata that describes its parameter set:

```
// Get information of the Foo() method..
Type t = a.GetType("ComplexTypeLibrary.SimpleClass");
MethodInfo mi = t.GetMethod("Foo");
// Show number of params.
Console.WriteLine("Here are the params for {0}", mi.Name);
ParameterInfo[] myParams = mi.GetParameters();
Console.WriteLine("Method has " + myParams.Length + " params");
// Show some info for param.
foreach(ParameterInfo pi in myParams)
{
   Console.WriteLine("Param name: {0}", pi.Name);
   Console.WriteLine("Position in method: {0}", pi.Position);
   Console.WriteLine("Param type: {0}", pi.ParameterType);
}
```

Building a Custom .NET Type Viewer

In the previous few pages, you have seen bits and pieces of reflection-centric code. To pull the related topics together into a cohesive unit, you now spend some time building your own custom .NET type viewer application. As you will see, you will basically build your own version of ILDams.exe. Specifically, this Windows Forms application allows the end user to do the following:

- Select a given assembly to examine using a standard File Open dialog.
- View select characteristics of the loaded assembly.
- View a list of all types contained within the loaded assembly.
- View member details for a given type.
- View the set of parameters for a given member of a given type.

If you want to follow along, create a new Windows Forms application named DotNetTypeReader. As you would expect, you have a topmost File menu that supports Open and Exit submenus (File | Exit simply calls the static Application.Exit() method). Once you open a valid .NET *.dll or *.exe, the type names are extracted and placed into one of four list boxes. For example, here is the dump of the ComplexTypeLibrary.dll assembly created earlier in this chapter (Figure 6-5).

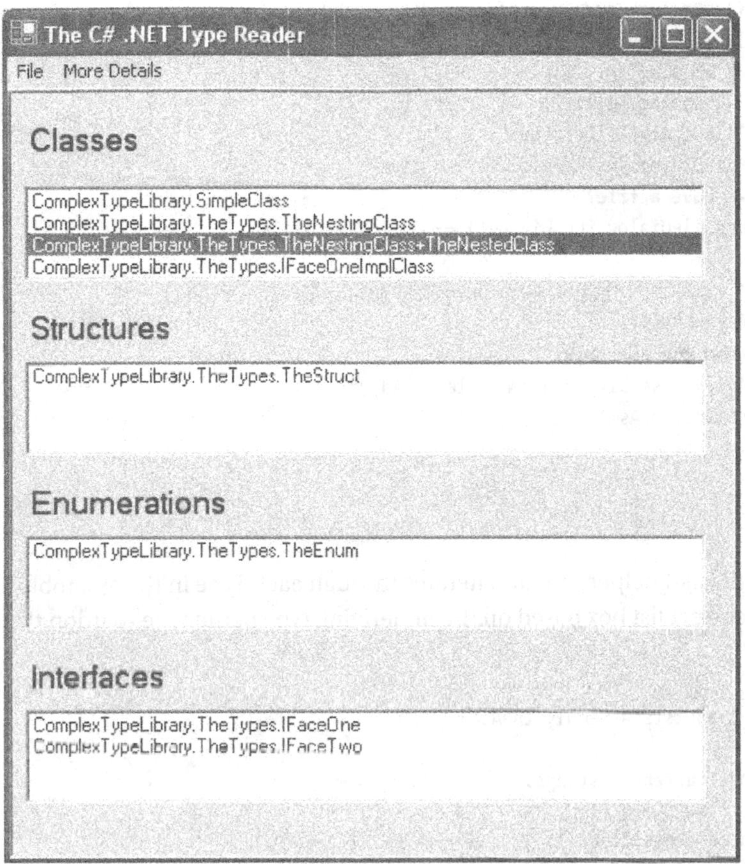

Figure 6-5. Viewing type names in a given assembly

In addition to the various GUI widgets, the Form maintains an Assembly data member that will be filled within the scope of the Click event handler for the Open menu. Once the assembly has been loaded using the OpenFileDialog class, you call a helper function named LoadLists(). Here is the code thus far:

```
public class MainForm : System.Windows.Forms.Form
{
   // Reference to the loaded assembly.
   private Assembly theAsm = null;
...
   private void mnuFileOpen_Click(object sender, System.EventArgs e)
   {
      // Show the FileOpen dialog and get file name.
      string fileToLoad = "";
```

```
            // Configure look and feel of open dlg.
            OpenFileDialog myOpenFileDialog = new OpenFileDialog();
            myOpenFileDialog.InitialDirectory = ".";
            myOpenFileDialog.Filter = "All files (*.*)|*.*" ;
            myOpenFileDialog.FilterIndex = 1 ;
            myOpenFileDialog.RestoreDirectory = true ;
            // Do we have a file?
            if(myOpenFileDialog.ShowDialog() == DialogResult.OK)
            {
               fileToLoad = myOpenFileDialog.FileName;
               theAsm = null;
               // Load the assembly.
               theAsm = Assembly.LoadFrom(fileToLoad);
               LoadLists(theAsm);
            }
      }
}
```

The LoadLists() helper function iterates through each Type in the assembly and fills the correct list box based on the underlying type of the type (pardon the redundancy!).

```
private void LoadLists(Assembly theAsm)
{
   // Clear out current listings.
   lstClasses.Items.Clear();
   lstInterfaces.Items.Clear();
   lstEnums.Items.Clear();
   lstStructs.Items.Clear();
   // Get all types in the assembly.
   Type[] theTypes = theAsm.GetTypes();

   // Fill each list box.
   foreach(Type t in theTypes)
   {
      if(t.IsClass)
         lstClasses.Items.Add(t.FullName);
      if(t.IsInterface)
         lstInterfaces.Items.Add(t.FullName);
      if(t.IsEnum)
         lstEnums.Items.Add(t.FullName);
      if(t.IsValueType && !t.IsEnum)          // enums are also value types!
         lstStructs.Items.Add(t.FullName);
   }
}
```

Showing Selected Type Details

At this point, you should be able to load a given assembly and view its contained types. The next aspect of your application is to intercept DoubleClick events for each list box. If the user double-clicks a given entry, you extract metadata for the selected item and display various details. The code behind each DoubleClick event handler is about identical. Simply obtain the current selection from the correct ListBox and call another helper method named ShowTypeStats(). For example:

```
// Do the same thing for the struct, enum, and interface list boxes,
// just be sure you refer to the correct ListBox variable.
private void lstClasses_DoubleClick(object sender, System.EventArgs e)
{
   // Get the current selection.
   string currItem = lstClasses.Text;
   Type t = theAsm.GetType(currItem);
   ShowTypeStats(t);
}
```

ShowTypeStat() takes an incoming Type and dumps out the following:

```
private void ShowTypeStats(Type t)
{
   // Build the stats.
   StringBuilder sb = new StringBuilder();
   sb.AppendFormat("Abstract? : {0}\n", t.IsAbstract);
   sb.AppendFormat("Sealed? : {0}\n", t.IsSealed);
   sb.AppendFormat("Base class? : {0}\n", t.BaseType);
   sb.AppendFormat("Nested Private? : {0}\n", t.IsNestedPrivate);
   sb.AppendFormat("Nested Public? : {0}\n", t.IsNestedPublic);
   sb.AppendFormat("Public Class? : {0}\n", t.IsPublic);
   MessageBox.Show(sb.ToString(),
                "Type Details for: " + t.FullName);
}
```

If you select your custom enumeration (TheEnum) contained within the ComplexTypeLibrary.dll, you find what appears in Figure 6-6.

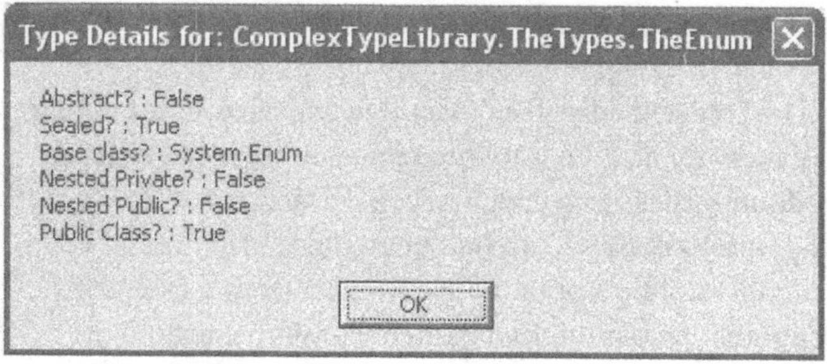

Figure 6-6. Viewing selected type information

Building the More Details Menu

The other topmost menu of the main Form provides additional options to view information about the assembly itself as well as the *members* of a given type (for example, the methods of an interface, the fields of an enumeration, and whatnot). Table 6-8 documents the name and purpose of each submenu.

Table 6-8. Listing the Submenus of the Topmost More Details Menu

More Details Submenu	Meaning in Life
Get Assembly Details	Launches a message box containing details of the currently loaded assembly.
Get Members of Selected Class	Launches a custom dialog box that lists each member for the currently selected class.
Get Members of Selected Structure	Launches a custom dialog box that lists each member for the currently selected structure.
Get Members of Selected Enum	Launches a custom dialog box that lists each member for the currently selected enumeration.
Get Members of Selected Interface	Launches a custom dialog box that lists each member for the currently selected interface.

Once you have constructed the menu system with the design-time menu editor, your next goal is to build an appropriate Click event handler for each submenu.

Viewing Assembly Details

The implementation of More Details | Get Assembly Details simply displays core bits of information using the Form's Assembly member variable:

```
private void mnuGetAsmDetails_Click(object sender, System.EventArgs e)
{
   if(theAsm != null)
   {
      StringBuilder sb = new StringBuilder();
      sb.AppendFormat("FullName? : {0}\n", theAsm.FullName);
      sb.AppendFormat("Loaded from GAC? : {0}\n", theAsm.GlobalAssemblyCache);
      sb.AppendFormat("Location? : {0}\n", theAsm.Location);
      MessageBox.Show(sb.ToString(), "Assembly Details");
   }
}
```

For example, the assembly details for the ComplexTypeLibrary.dll assembly would look something like Figure 6-7.

Figure 6-7. Viewing assembly details

Viewing Class, Enum, Interface, and Structure Details

The remaining Click event handlers each make use of a custom Windows Forms dialog box (which I have called MemberInfoDialog). The dialog box contains a ListBox type (to hold the method names), one Button that will function as the OK button, and a final Button that allows the user to view the set of parameters for a selected method (which you contend with in the next step). Once you have constructed the GUI (Figure 6-8), be sure to set the DialogResult property of your OK Button type to DialogResult.OK to ensure you can detect when the user has dismissed the Form.

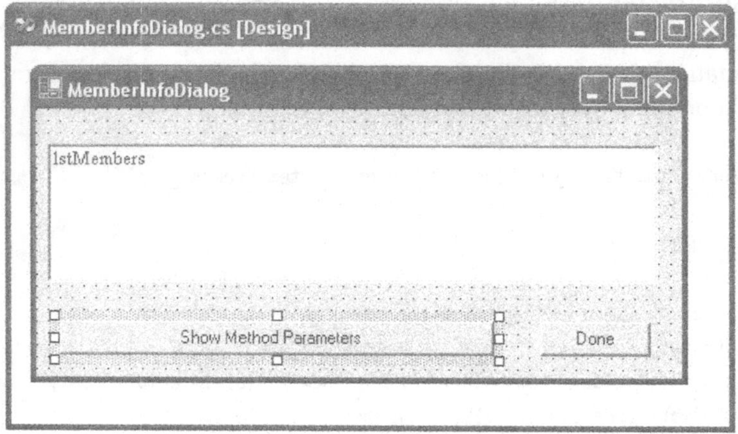

Figure 6-8. The initial GUI of your custom dialog

Given that this dialog box is required to display member information for the item that has been selected on the parent Form, you need to add a few methods to the MemberInfoDialog class. First, create a method named AddMember() to be called by the parent Form to populate the ListBox. Next, add a method named SetType() to set the value of a class-level Type reference. As you can guess, you use this object to examine the set of parameters for a given item (which you do in just a bit). Here are the relevant code updates:

```
// Extend your Form as so…
public class MemberInfoDialog : System.Windows.Forms.Form
{
   private Type theType = null;
…
   public void AddMember(string m)
   {lstMembers.Items.Add(m);}
   public void SetType(Type t)
   {theType = t;}
}
```

Now that you have a dialog box to hold the given member information, you can get back to the business of implementing the remaining menu Click events on the main Form. Much like the implementation of the ListBox DoubleClick event handlers, each submenu Click handler has a very similar code block: Simply identify the currently selected item in a given ListBox, ask the Assembly for its type information, and call a helper function named ShowMemberStats(). For example, here is the code behind mnuGetClassMethods_Click():

```
// The other submenu Click handlers are implemented
// in the same way (just change which ListBox to poll).
private void mnuGetClassMethods_Click(object sender, System.EventArgs e)
{
   if(theAsm != null && lstClasses.Text != "")
   {
      // Get the current selection.
      string currItem = lstClasses.Text;
      Type t = theAsm.GetType(currItem);
      ShowMemberStats(t);
   }
}
```

ShowMemberStats() displays and populates your custom dialog Form and sets the dialog's internal Type member variable using the SetType() helper method:

```
private void ShowMemberStats(Type t)
{
   // Create the dialog & set Type.
   MemberInfoDialog d = new MemberInfoDialog();
   d.SetType(t);
   // Get the members for the selected item.
   StringBuilder sb = new StringBuilder();
   MemberInfo[] allTheMembers = t.GetMembers();
   // Fill the dialog's ListBox with member info.
   foreach(MemberInfo mi in allTheMembers)
   {
      d.AddMember(mi.Name);
   }
   d.ShowDialog();
}
```

Now, to test your new functionality, again assume you have loaded the ComplexTypeLibrary.dll assembly, selected the SimpleClass item from the class ListBox, and activated the Get Class Members menu item. The results are seen in Figure 6-9 (note that I set this dialog's ListBox.Sorted property to True).

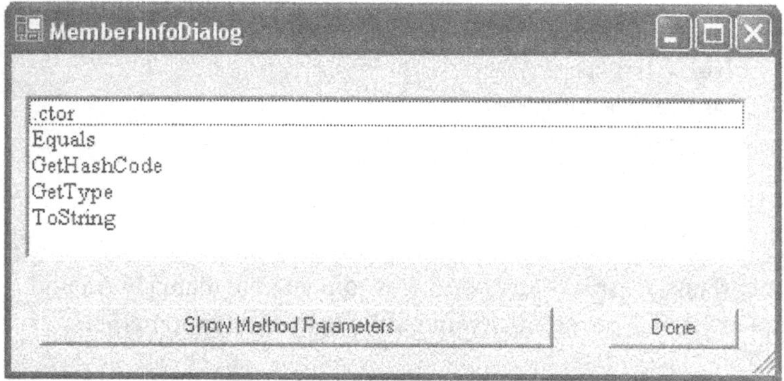

Figure 6-9. Showing class member information

Likewise, if you select the custom enumeration (TheEnum) from the main Form's enumeration ListBox and select Get Enum Members, you find something like what you see in Figure 6-10.

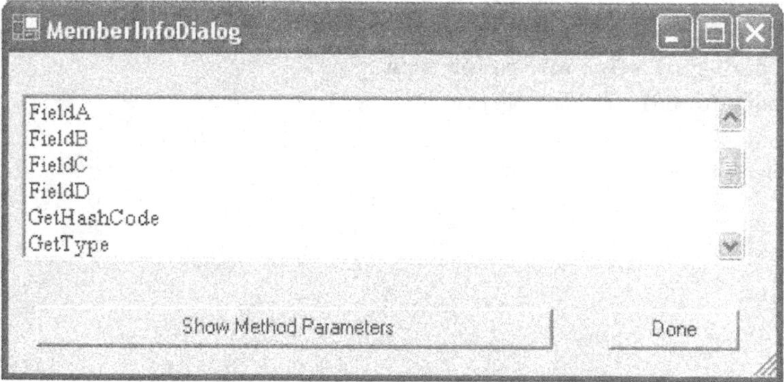

Figure 6-10. Viewing fields of a given enumeration

Viewing Member Parameters

The final step of your custom type viewer is to implement the code behind the dialog's Show Method Parameters Button. As you might expect, when the user selects a given item in the member ListBox (and clicks the Button), he or she sees a list of each parameter for the selected item. For simplicity's sake, the parameter information is displayed in a Windows Forms message box. Here is the implementation of the Click event handler:

```
// Show the params (if any)!
private void btnShowParams_Click(object sender, System.EventArgs e)
{
   if(theType != null)
   {
      try
      {
         string memberToExamine = lstMembers.Text;
         StringBuilder sb = new StringBuilder();
         ParameterInfo[] paramInfo =
            theType.GetMethod(memberToExamine).GetParameters();
         foreach(ParameterInfo pi in paramInfo)
         {
            sb.AppendFormat("Name: {0}, Type: {1}, Position: {2}\n",
                pi.Name, pi.ParameterType.ToString(),
                pi.Position);
         }

         MessageBox.Show(sb.ToString(), "Params for: " + lstMembers.Text);
      }
      catch(Exception ex)
      {
         MessageBox.Show(ex.Message, "Error building params!");
      }
   }
}
```

Given that some types do not have parameterized members (such as the fields of a .NET enumeration), I have wrapped the parameter-building logic within a generic try/catch statement. If you want to enhance this application, you may want to disable the parameter-centric Button if the type is an enumeration. Nevertheless, here is the parameter information for the inherited Equals() method of the ComplexTypeLibrary.SimpleClass type (Figure 6-11).

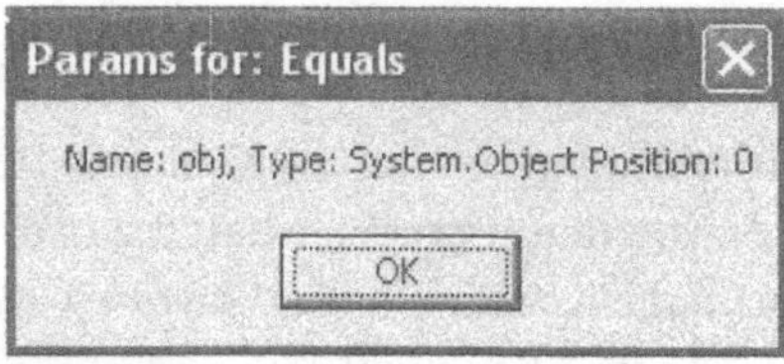

Figure 6-11. Parameter information

Your custom ILDasm-like application is now complete! To highlight the use of your application, Figure 6-12 shows the set of types contained within the System.Data.dll assembly (which, as you are aware, is the home of ADO.NET types).

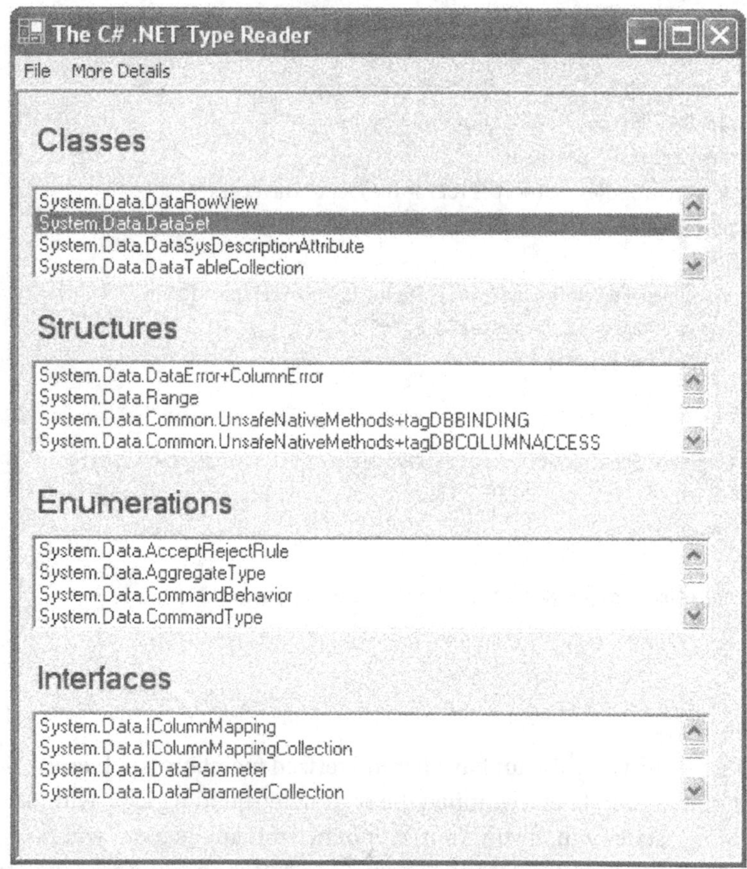

Figure 6-12. Viewing the types of ADO.NET using your custom type viewer

CODE *The DotNetTypeReader application is located under the Chapter 6 subdirectory.*

A Brief Word Regarding System.Reflection.Emit

Before moving to the next topic of the chapter, it is worth pointing out that the System.Reflection namespace defines a nested namespace called System.Reflection.Emit. Using these types, you can construct assemblies and the contained IL instructions at runtime, on the fly. As you have already seen in Chapter 5, the System.CodeDOM namespace defines a number of types that allow you to dynamically generate language-specific source code files using a language-independent object graph. The distinction between System.Reflection.Emit and CodeDOM is that System.Reflection.Emit allows you to bypass obtaining an ICodeCompiler interface to transform a given set of files into an assembly. Rather, the types found in the System.Reflection.Emit namespace allow you to directly build the entire assembly and IL code in one fell swoop. If you require additional information, may I (modestly) suggest my first two Apress texts: *C# and the .NET Platform* and *VB .NET and the .NET Platform: An Advanced Guide.*

Understanding .NET Attributes

At this point in the chapter, you have examined the details behind the .NET type system and spent time coming to understand the process of runtime type discovery using the System.Reflection namespace. Next, you need to examine exactly how the .NET platform honors the use of attribute-based programming.

As you recall, COM IDL attributes are basically keywords placed within square brackets (for example, [in, out]). As you recall from Chapter 4, the [custom] IDL attribute can be used to create a custom name/value pair that allows you to extend your type library with custom metadata. The major problem with custom IDL COM attributes is the fact that they are simple keywords that only exist to bind a GUID to a particular value.

Under .NET, attributes are objects. Specifically, .NET attributes are class types that extend the System.Attribute base class type. Table 6-9 documents the core members of the Attribute class.

Table 6-9. Core Members of System.Attribute

Member of System.Attribute	Meaning in Life
TypeId	This property is used to return a unique identifier for this Attribute (the default implementation returns the Type that describes this attribute). Using this unique tag, you are able to refer to this item at runtime.
GetCustomAttribute() GetCustomAttributes()	These static methods retrieve a custom attribute (or set of attributes) of a specified type.
IsDefaultAttribute()	When overridden in a derived class, returns an indication of whether the value of this instance is the default value for the derived class.
IsDefined	This static property determines whether any custom attributes of a specified type are applied to a specified type or the assembly itself.

In addition to building your own custom attributes, you should also understand that just about every .NET namespace defines a number of preexisting attributes. As you begin to see in Chapter 7 (as well as for the remainder of this book) COM/.NET interoperability makes heavy use of these existing attributes. In fact, a majority of the members of the System.Runtime.InteropServices namespace are System.Attribute-derived class types!

When you apply attributes to a given coding item, you are able to add custom bits of metadata to your .NET assemblies. Understand that attributes in and of themselves are useless. To be sure, attributes mean nothing unless some piece of software is able to account for their presence. This piece of software could be a custom application, a particular design-time tool, or a managed compiler.

For example, the System.ObsoleteAttribute attribute may be applied to a given piece of code to identify items that are considered out of fashion. As you recall, the ComplexTypeLibrary.dll assembly defined a rather uninteresting class (SimpleClass). If you update the class definition as follows:

```
[ObsoleteAttribute("This class is useless. Use anything else")]
public class SimpleClass{}
```

you inform a managed compiler to generate a compile time warning whenever the type is used (Figure 6-13).

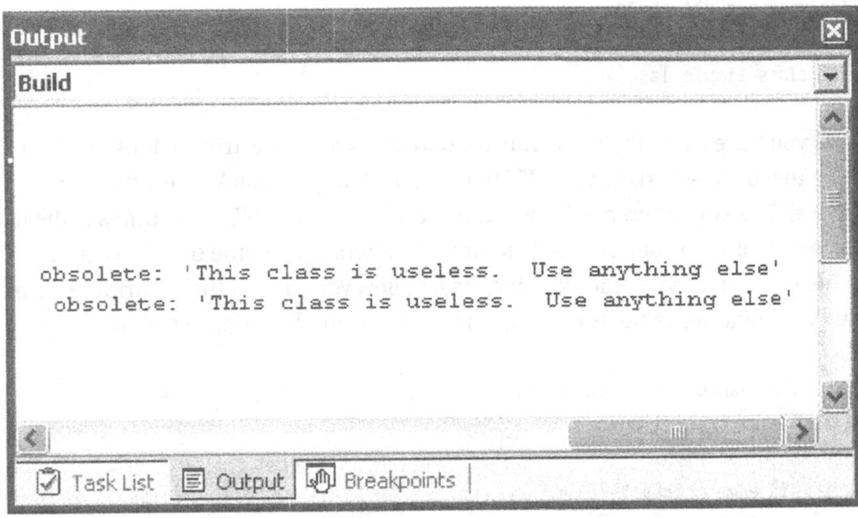

Figure 6-13. The Obsolete attribute in action

Creating and Applying Custom Attributes

To illustrate the process of building custom .NET attributes, let's add the following class definition to your existing ComplexTypeLibrary.dll assembly, which mimics the custom IDL attribute created in Chapter 4:

```
// The custom attribute.
public class ToDoAttribute : System.Attribute
{
   private string toDoComment;
   public ToDoAttribute(string comment)
   { toDoComment = comment;}

   public string Comment
   {get {return toDoComment;}}
}
```

Like any other class type, ToDoAttribute maintains a set of data members and may support any number of constructors, properties, or methods. Here, your custom attribute maintains a string that represents an annotation that may be applied to a given code block. For example, you could update the SimpleClass to make use of your custom attribute rather than the predefined ObsoleteAttribute:

```
// Applying our attribute.
[ToDoAttribute("Make this class do something!")]
public class SimpleClass{}
```

As you have seen, the C# syntax used to apply a .NET attribute looks quite a bit like that of classic IDL (VB .NET makes use of angled brackets for the same purpose). The key difference between IDL attributes and .NET attributes is the fact that you are able to specify constructor parameters at the time of application.

Also be aware that some .NET languages allow you to omit the "-Attribute" suffix. Thus, you could write the following (slightly shortened) attribute syntax:

```
// Some .NET languages allow you to
// make use of the following
// shorthand notation.
[ToDo("This enum stinks!")]
public enum TheEnum
{FieldA, FieldB}
```

Viewing the Applied Metadata

If you open the updated ComplexTypeLibrary.dll assembly using ILDasm.exe and examine the TheEnum type, you are able to view your custom metadata (Figure 6-14).

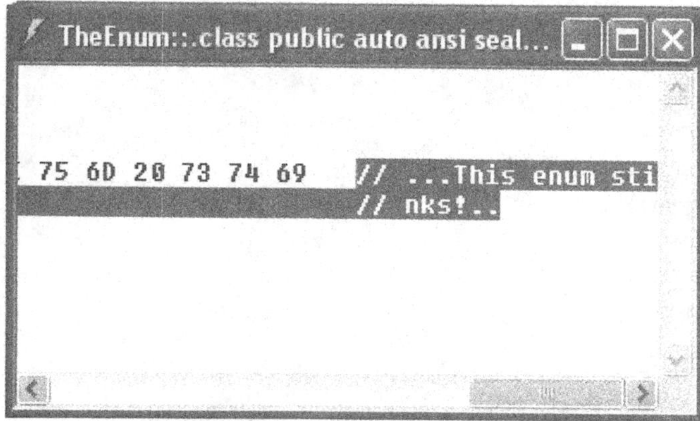

Figure 6-14. Viewing your custom metadata

Restricting Attribute Usage

Attributes can take attributes themselves. One of the more interesting attributes you can apply to your custom System.Attribute-derived types is the AttributesUsage type. Using this attribute, you are able to control exactly where your custom attribute is applied. By default, custom .NET attributes can be applied to any item (types, methods, parameters, or what have you). Obviously, some attributes only make sense in a given context. Consider the COM IDL [retval] attribute. Imagine how bizarre IDL definitions would become if [retval] was used in the context of a library statement, [in]-bound parameters, or coclass definition! To prevent this chaos, the AttributeUsage attribute may be assigned any values from the AttributeTarget enumeration:

```
// This enumeration is used to control
// how a custom attribute can be applied.
public enum AttributeTargets
{
   All,
   Assembly,
   Class,
   Constructor,
   Delegate,
   Enum,
   Event,
   Field,
   Interface,
   Method,
   Module,
   Parameter,
   Property,
   ReturnValue,
   Struct
}
```

For the sake of argument, if you wish to ensure that the ToDoAttribute can only be applied to classes, interfaces, structures, or enumerations, you could update the definition as follows:

```
// The restricted attribute.
[AttributeUsage(AttributeTargets.Class |
 AttributeTargets.Interface |
 AttributeTargets.Enum |
```

```
 AttributeTargets.Struct)]
public class ToDoAttribute : System.Attribute
{
   private string toDoComment;
   public ToDoAttribute(string comment)
   { toDoComment = comment;}

   public string Comment
   {get {return toDoComment;}}
}
```

If you now attempt to apply the ToDoAttribute attribute to a method as follows:

```
// Ugh! Not allowed.
public interface IFaceTwo
{
   [ToDo("Document this method...")]
   int SimpleMethod();
}
```

you are issued a compile-time error.

Assembly- (and Module-) Level Attributes

It is also possible to apply attributes on all types within a given assembly using the [assembly:] prefix. Recall the CLS-compliant attribute described in Chapter 5:

```
// Enforce CLS compliance!
[assembly:System.CLSCompliantAttribute(true)]
```

Visual Studio .NET projects define a file called AssemblyInfo.*. This file is a handy place to place all global-level attributes that are to be applied at the assembly level. Table 6-10 is run-through of some assembly-level attributes you should be aware of.

Table 6-10. Select Assembly-Level Attributes

Assembly-Level Attribute	Meaning in Life
AssemblyCompanyAttribute	Holds basic company information.
AssemblyConfigurationAttribute	Build information, such as "retail" or "debug."
AssemblyCopyrightAttribute	Holds any copyright information for the product or assembly.
AssemblyDescriptionAttribute	A friendly description of the product or modules that make up the assembly.
AssemblyInformationalVersionAttribute	Additional or supporting version information, such as a commercial product version number.
AssemblyProductAttribute	Product information.
AssemblyTrademarkAttribute	Trademark information.
AssemblyCultureAttribute	Information on what cultures or languages the assembly supports.
AssemblyKeyFileAttribute	Specifies the name of the file containing the key pair used to sign the assembly (that is, establish a shared name).
AssemblyKeyNameAttribute	Specifies the name of the key container. Instead of placing a key pair in a file, you can store it in a key container in the CSP. If you choose this option, this attribute contains the name of the key container.
AssemblyOperatingSystemAttribute	Information on which operating system the assembly was built to support.
AssemblyProcessorAttribute	Information on which processors the assembly was built to support.
AssemblyVersionAttribute	Specifies the assembly's version information, in the format major.minor.build.rev.

Reading Attributes at Runtime

To wrap up your examination of .NET attribute programming, let's examine how to read attributes at runtime. There are a number of ways to obtain attribute metadata from a loaded assembly. First, the Assembly class defines the GetCustomAttribute() and GetCustomAttributes() methods. The System.Type class defines members of the same name. To illustrate, assume you wish to obtain the ToDo comment for the TheEnum type. The following Main() method does the trick:

```
using System;
using System.Reflection;
using ComplexTypeLibrary;
using ComplexTypeLibrary.TheTypes;
...
static void Main(string[] args)
{
   // Get the Type of TheEnum.
   Type t = typeof(TheEnum);

   // Get all attributes on this type.
   object[] customAtts = t.GetCustomAttributes(false);

   // List TODO comment.
   foreach(ToDoAttribute a in customAtts)
      Console.WriteLine("ToDo: {0}", a.Comment);
}
```

The output can be seen in Figure 6-15.

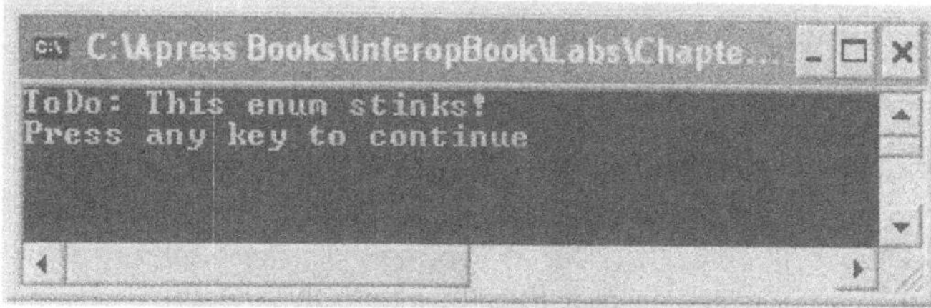

Figure 6-15. Reading TheEnum's ToDo comment

CODE *The AttributeReader application is included under the Chapter 6 subdirectory.*

Late Binding Under the .NET Platform

To wrap up the chapter, let's examine how the .NET platform contends with the notion of late binding. Recall that late binding is a technique in which you are able to resolve the existence of (and name of) a given type and its members at runtime (rather than compile time). Once the presence of a type has been determined, you are then able to dynamically invoke methods, access properties, and manipulate the fields of a given entity.

To be sure, when you build your custom .NET types, you never need to implement IDispatch to facilitate late binding. The truth of the matter is that you will not need to do anything at all to allow clients to dynamically invoke your members. When you build late-bound clients, however, you make use of the System.Reflection namespace.

Like any late-binding scenario, the client code base does not refer to the assembly containing the types it wishes to activate. In terms of managed code, this means you will *not* set a reference to the assembly (and therefore you will not have an [.assembly extern] tag in the client manifest) and you will *not* need make use of the C# using (Imports under VB .NET) keyword.

Do understand, however, that the .NET runtime makes use of the same search heuristics used with early binding (see Chapter 5). Thus, if the assembly you want to interact with is a private assembly, you need to manually copy the assembly into the current application directory (or author a *.config file). On the other hand, if you attempt to bind late to a shared assembly stored in the GAC, you need to refer to the assembly using the corresponding strong name. You will see each approach, but first you need to check out the Activator class.

The Activator Class

The System.Activator class is the key to late binding. Beyond the methods inherited from Object, Activator only defines a small set of members, all of which are static (Table 6-11).

Table 6-11. Members of the Activator Class

Static Method of the Activator Class	Meaning in Life
CreateComInstanceFrom()	Creates an instance of the COM object whose name is specified using the named assembly file and the constructor that best matches the specified parameters.
CreateInstance()	Overloaded. Creates an instance of the specified type using the constructor that best matches the specified parameters.
CreateInstanceFrom()	Overloaded. Creates an instance of the type whose name is specified, using the named assembly file and the constructor that best matches the specified parameters.
GetObject()	Overloaded. Creates a proxy for a currently running remote object, server-activated well-known object, or XML Web service.

Activator.CreateInstance() is perhaps the core method, which creates an instance of a type at runtime. This method has been overloaded numerous times, to provide a good deal of flexibility. One variation of the CreateInstance() member takes a valid Type object (representing the entity you wish to create) and returns a System.Object reference, which represents a handle to the newly created type.

Late Binding to a Private Assembly

By way of example, assume that you have manually copied the ComplexTypeLibrary.dll assembly into the application directory of a new console application named LateBinder.exe. To create an instance of the nested TheNestedClass type (found in the ComplexTypeLibrary.TheTypes namespace), you would write the following:

```
// Bind late to a private assembly.
Assembly asm = Assembly.Load("ComplexTypeLibrary");
// Get type in the assembly.
string typeIWant =
   "ComplexTypeLibrary.TheTypes.TheNestingClass+TheNestedClass";
Type t = asm.GetType(typeIWant);

// Create TheNestedClass on the fly.
object obj = Activator.CreateInstance(t);
```

Once you have a reference to the type you wish to manipulate, you are then able to make use of the members of System.Reflection to interact with the type's fields, methods, properties, and so forth. For example, to invoke the GetInternalString() method of the TheNestedClass type, you would make use of MethodInfo.Invoke():

```
// Get info for GetInternalString.
MethodInfo mi = t.GetMethod("GetInternalString");
// Invoke method ('null' for no parameters).
// The return value of Invoke() holds the methods
// physical return value.
object retval = mi.Invoke(obj, null);
Console.WriteLine(((string)retval).ToString());
```

If you run the application, you will be pleased to find what you see in Figure 6-16.

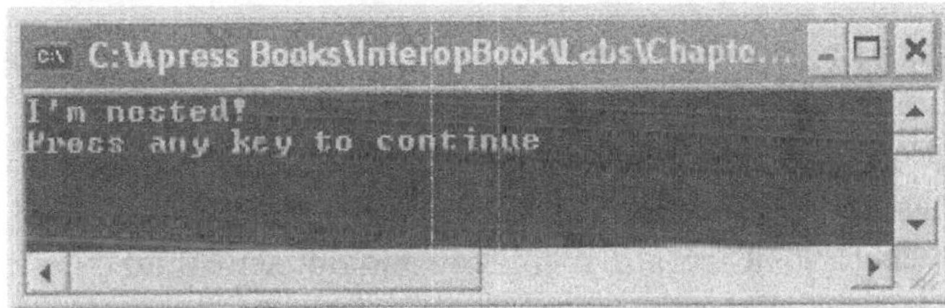

Figure 6-16. Invoking a member using late binding

As you might guess, MethodInfo.Invoke() has also been overloaded a number of times to allow you to qualify the member you wish to invoke. For example, many of the overloaded signatures allow you to define a set of flags that control the bind, using the BindingFlags enumeration (I'll assume you will check out online Help for full commentary). Do note that this enum takes the place of the COM IDispatch binding flags such as DISPATCH_METHOD, DISPATCH_PROPERTYGET, and DISPATCH_PROPERTYPUT.

```
// Binding Flags.
public enum System.Reflection.BindingFlags
{
   CreateInstance,
   DeclaredOnly,
   Default,
   ExactBinding,
   FlattenHierarchy,
```

```
    GetField,
    GetProperty,
    IgnoreCase,
    IgnoreReturn,
    Instance,
    InvokeMethod,
    NonPublic,
    OptionalParamBinding,
    Public,
    PutDispProperty,
    PutRefDispProperty,
    SetField,
    SetProperty,
    Static,
    SuppressChangeType
}
```

Invoking Parameterized Methods

The Invoke() method also allows you to specify the set of parameters that should be sent (where "null" signifies a method with no parameters). Now, for the sake of argument, assume that TheNestedClass also defines an additional method (ShowMessage()) that takes two parameters:

```
// The updated nested type.
public class TheNestedClass
{
...
   public void ShowMessage(string m, short numbOfTimes)
   {
      string message = "";
      for(short i = 0; i < numbOfTimes; i++)
      {
         message += m;
         message += " ";
      }
      MessageBox.Show(message);
      }
   }
}
```

To invoke this member using late binding, you would need to build an array of System.Object types to send in place of the null parameter of MethodInfo.Invoke():

```
// Invoke method with parameters.
short numbOfTimes = 5;
// 'Oi' Is a UK punk rocker vocative chant…
object[] theParams = {"Oi!", numbOfTimes};
mi = t.GetMethod("ShowMessage");
mi.Invoke(obj, theParams);
```

This would yield the output shown in Figure 6-17.

Figure 6-17. Invoking parameterized members

Binding Late to Shared Assemblies

The first example illustrated how to bind to a private assembly, which requires a local copy of the ComplexTypeLibrary.dll assembly. As you would expect, you are also able to bind to an assembly placed into the GAC. To do so requires specifying the strong name of the assembly, or if you prefer, a partial strong name of the assembly. Consider the following code:

```
// Construct a partial strong name
// (assume you are using the default culture).
string strongName = "System.Windows.Forms,";
strongName += "PublicKeyToken=b77a5c561934e089, Version=1.0.3300.0";
// Load from GAC.
Assembly asm2 = Assembly.LoadWithPartialName(strongName);
// Get OpenFileDialog type in the assembly.
Type t2 = asm2.GetType("System.Windows.Forms.OpenFileDialog");
object obj2 = Activator.CreateInstance(t2);

// Get info for ShowDialog().
MethodInfo mi2 = t2.GetMethod("ShowDialog", new Type[0]);
// Launch the dialog!
mi2.Invoke(obj2, null);
```

As you would guess, when this application is launched, the OpenFileDialog is displayed on the screen (again, totally on the fly at runtime). Notice that you have made use of an overloaded version of the MethodInfo.GetMethod() member. The optional second parameter is an array of Type objects that represents the parameters of the given method. Understand that the array of Types does not literally contain values to send into the method, but rather the signature of the method to invoke! Given that ShowDialog() has been overloaded twice:

```
// Shows the form as a modal dialog box with no owner window.
public DialogResult ShowDialog();
// Shows the form as a modal dialog with the specified owner.
public DialogResult ShowDialog(IWin32Window owner);
```

you are specifying that you are interested in obtaining a parameter-less variation using an empty array of Type types.

CODE *The LateBinder project is included under the Chapter 6 subdirectory.*

Contrasting COM and .NET Late-Binding Syntax

So then as you can see, the .NET platform still supports the ability to bind to a type at runtime. Depending on your comfort level with COM late binding, you may have noticed a very similar pattern between the two architectures. For example, under COM you are required to package a DISPPARAMS structure that holds the arguments to pass to the member specified by IDispatch::Invoke(). Under .NET, this idea is expressed as an array of System.Object types.

To further illustrate the syntactic similarities between each approach, assume you wish to invoke a method named Add() that returns the summation of two integers. Under the COM model, a late-bound C++ client would obtain the summation using IDispatch as follows:

```
// Once again, a C++ late bound client.
void main()
{
   CoInitialize(NULL);
   IDispatch* pDisp = NULL;
   CLSID clsid;
   DISPID dispid;
```

```
    // Go look up the CLSID from the ProgID.
    CLSIDFromProgID(OLESTR("ATLAddServer.Calc"),&clsid);
    LPOLESTR str = OLESTR("Add");
    // Create object and get IDispatch.
    CoCreateInstance(clsid, NULL, CLSCTX_SERVER, IID_IDispatch,
                          (void**)&pDisp);
    // Get DISPID from object.
    pDisp->GetIDsOfNames(IID_NULL, &str,1,
                               LOCALE_SYSTEM_DEFAULT, &dispid);
    // Build dispatch parameters.
    VARIANT args[2];
    VariantInit(&args[0]);
    args[0].vt = VT_I2;
    args[0].intVal = 10;
    VariantInit(&args[1]);
    args[1].vt = VT_I2;
    args[1].intVal = 51;
    DISPPARAMS myParams = { args, 0, 2, 0};
    VARIANT result;
    VariantInit(&result);
    // Call Add() using Invoke().
    pDisp->Invoke(dispid, IID_NULL, LOCALE_SYSTEM_DEFAULT,
       DISPATCH_METHOD, &myParams, &result, NULL, NULL);
    cout << "10 + 51 is " << result.intVal << endl;
    // COM clean up.
    pDisp->Release();
    CoUninitialize();
}
```

If you had a C# application that defined a class supporting a similar Add() method, you would find the following client-side code:

```
static void Main(string[] args)
{
    Assembly asm = Assembly.Load("CSharpAddServer");
    // Get type in the assembly.
    Type t = asm.GetType("CSharpAddServer.Calc");

    // Create the Calc class on the fly.
    object obj = Activator.CreateInstance(t);

    // Get info for Add.
    MethodInfo mi = t.GetMethod("Add");
    // Invoke method.
    object[] theParams = {10, 51};
    object retval = mi.Invoke(obj, theParams);
    Console.WriteLine("10 + 51 is {0}", ((int)retval).ToString());
}
```

As you can see from the code comments, the basic operation of late binding has remained intact. In either architecture, you are required to specify a string name of the member you wish to invoke and an array of items that represent the parameter set. Under COM, you make use of VARIANTs, IDispatch, and the DISPPARAMS structure. Under .NET, you are provided the more OO-aware System.Object and System.Type data types as well as the System.Reflection namespace.

Well, that wraps up the investigation of the .NET and COM type systems. If you have been reading this book from the beginning (and I hope this is the case) you should now feel quite familiar with how each architecture defines, represents, and contends with the almighty notion of "type." The remainder of this text dives headlong into the details of building bridges between these completely unrelated architectures.

Summary

The .NET type system is an extremely unified model when contrasted to that of classic COM. First and foremost, the base class System.Object ensures that all types maintain a shared polymorphic interface. As you have seen, you are able to override a number of these methods in your custom types to build intelligent user-defined types.

As far as the data type system of .NET is concerned, this chapter also examined how language-specific keywords map to a particular member of the System namespace. In addition to the core intrinsic data types, the CTS also documents how to construct the various members of the .NET type system—classes, interfaces, enumerations, and structures—to ensure symmetrical access of these types from any managed language.

The System.Reflection namespace is a key aspect to understanding the .NET type system. Using the members of this namespace (in conjunction with the System.Type class), you are able to obtain a complete runtime description of the characteristics of a given assembly, type, member, or parameter.

Closely related to the topic of reflection is the use of attribute-based programming. Unlike COM IDL, custom metadata is expressed under the .NET platform by creating class types that derive from System.Attribute. Finally, you wrapped up by making use of .NET reflection services to achieve client-side late binding. Next up, it's time to examine the basic details of .NET-to-COM interoperability.

CHAPTER 7

.NET-to-COM Interoperability—The Basics

The previous five chapters have exposed you to the core characteristics of the COM and .NET type systems. The remainder of this book addresses how these types can be expressed and manipulated across architectural boundaries. In this chapter, you are exposed to the key .NET-to-COM interoperability issues you are likely to encounter on a day-to-day basis (with some more exotic topics thrown in for good measure). For example, you investigate a number of ways to build interoperability assemblies (including "primary" interop assemblies), examine core IDL to .NET data type mappings, and understand how key COM data structures (interfaces, coclasses, enumerations) are expressed in terms of .NET. Along the way, you take a more detailed look at the types contained in the System.Runtime.InteropServices namespace (first introduced in Chapter 1). As you might expect, the materials presented here work as the backbone for more advanced topics found in the remainder of the text.

A High-Level Overview of .NET-to-COM Interoperability

As you have seen in Chapters 5 and 6, languages targeting the .NET runtime satisfy each pillar of object-oriented technology. For example, when you build an assembly using a given managed language, you are able to create classes that support any number of constructors, overloaded methods, and overridden members, and implement any optional interfaces. As well, the .NET platform makes use of a runtime garbage collector, which is responsible for freeing an object from the managed heap when it is no longer rooted in a given application.

In stark contrast, as you have seen in Chapters 2 through 4, COM types do not adhere to each and every pillar of OOP in the classic sense of the topic. For example, COM types are not created using class constructors, but rather using the

IClassFactory interface. In addition, COM classes are not allowed to define overloaded methods and cannot function as a base class to other COM types (as COM has no support for classical inheritance). As far as lifetime management of a coclass is concerned, COM does not make use of a garbage-collected heap, but employs a strict reference counting scheme provided courtesy of IUnknown.

Given the fact that COM and .NET types have so little in common, you may have deep-rooted fears regarding interoperability issues. Ideally, a .NET client should be able to use a COM type with no concern for the mechanics of COM. For example, a managed client should be able to create the COM type using constructor semantics, derive new types from the COM wrapper class (given that .NET supports classic inheritance), and should not be required to obtain or release interface references (given that .NET does not demand the use of interface references). In a nutshell, as far as a .NET client is concerned, manipulating a COM type should look identical to the act of manipulating a native .NET type. For example:

```
// COM classes should appear as .NET types.
MyComClass c = new MyComClass();
c.SomeMethod("Hello", 12);
```

Obviously, this cannot be achieved unless you have an intermediary that stands between the .NET client and the existing COM type. In short, what we need is a proxy that is in charge of transparently handling .NET-to-COM communications. To be sure, whenever a .NET application makes use of a legacy COM type, a proxy is created by the .NET runtime. Formally, this proxy is termed a Runtime Callable Wrapper (RCW).

In a similar vein, a COM client should be able to make use of a .NET type without concern for the mechanics of .NET. For example, COM clients should be able to activate a .NET class using CoCreateInstance(); directly call the members of IUnknown, IDispatch, and IClassFactory; and should assume the type is maintaining an internal reference count. When unmanaged code communicates with managed .NET types, a different sort of proxy called a COM Callable Wrapper (CCW) is used to translate COM requests into terms of .NET. Chapters 10 through 12 examine the process of COM-to-.NET interoperability. For the time being, let's concentrate on the role of the RCW.

Understanding the Role of the RCW

The RCW is a .NET object that is in charge of marshaling calls between a managed unit of code and a given COM type. While a managed client is making calls to a given COM type, the RCW intercepts each invocation, translates each incoming argument into terms of IDL data types, and invokes the coclass method. Likewise, if the coclass returns any information to the caller (via [out] or [out, retval] IDL parameters) the RCW is responsible for translating the IDL type(s) into the appropriate .NET type(s). As you would hope, there is a fixed set of translation rules used to map between IDL and .NET atoms (demonstrated throughout the remainder of this text).

In addition to marshaling data types to and fro, the RCW also attempts to fool the .NET client into believing that it is communicating directly with a native .NET type. To do so, the RCW hides a number of low-level COM interfaces from view (IClassFactory, IUnknown, IDispatch, and so forth). Thus, rather than forcing the .NET client to make manual calls to CoCreateInstance(), the client is free to use the activation keyword of its code base (e.g., new, New, and so on). And rather than forcing the managed client to manually call QueryInterface(), AddRef(), or Release(), the client is able to perform simple casting operations to obtain a particular interface and is never required to release interface references.

It is important to understand that a single RCW exists for each coclass the client interacts with, regardless of how many interfaces have been obtained from the type. In this way, an RCW is able to correctly manage the identity and reference count of the COM class. For example, assume a C# Windows Forms application has created three coclasses residing in various COM servers. If this is the case, the runtime creates three RCW proxy types to facilitate the communication (Figure 7-1).

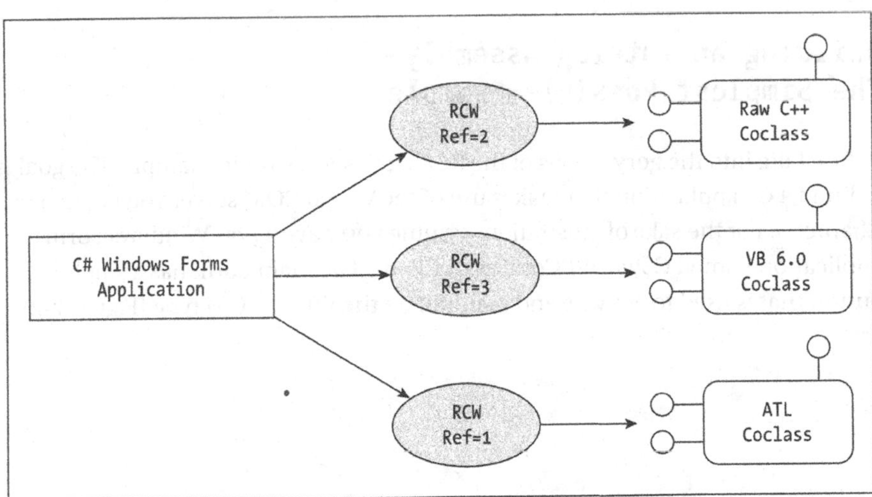

Figure 7-1. A single RCW exists for each coclass.

Notice how each RCW maintains an internal reference count for the corresponding object. A given RCW maintains a cache of interface pointers on the COM object it wraps and releases these references when the RCW is no longer used by the caller (and therefore garbage collected). In this way, the managed client is able to simply "new" the COM wrapper and is blissfully unaware of COM interface–based reference counting. Also, given that the RCW will not release the referenced interfaces until it is garbage collected, you can rest assured that a given coclass is alive as long as the .NET client is making use of the related RCW.

Understand, of course, that the RCW is responsible for more than simply mapping .NET types into COM atoms. As you see later in this text, the RCW is also responsible for mapping COM error objects (that is, IErrorInfo, ICreateErrorInfo) into managed exceptions. In this way, if a coclass throws a COM error, the .NET client is able to handle the problem using standard try, catch, and finally keywords. The RCW is also responsible for mapping COM event handling primitives (that is, IConnectionPointContainer, IConnectionPoint) into terms of managed delegates.

One question that may pop up at this point is "Where does an RCW come from in the first place?" As you will see, RCWs are .NET class types that are dynamically created by the runtime. The exact look and feel of an RCW will be based on the information contained within a related *interop assembly*. These assemblies contain metadata that is used specifically to bridge the gap between managed and unmanaged code. The good news is that you are not required to manually create interop assemblies by hand (though you could). Rather, you more typically make use of the tlbimp.exe tool that ships with the .NET SDK or the Visual Studio .NET IDE.

Building an Interop Assembly— The Simplest Possible Example

Before I dig into the gory details of the RCW, let's see a simple example. The goal is to build a C# application that makes use of the VB 6.0 COM server you created in Chapter 3. For the sake of illustration, assume you have a new Windows Forms application named CSharpVBComServerClient. The main Form has a single button that is used to activate and manipulate the VB 6.0 COM type (Figure 7-2).

Figure 7-2. The C# client application

To generate an interop assembly using VS .NET could not be any simpler. To do so, launch the Add Reference dialog box and select the COM tab. If your COM server has been registered correctly, you will find it listed alphabetically (Figure 7-3).

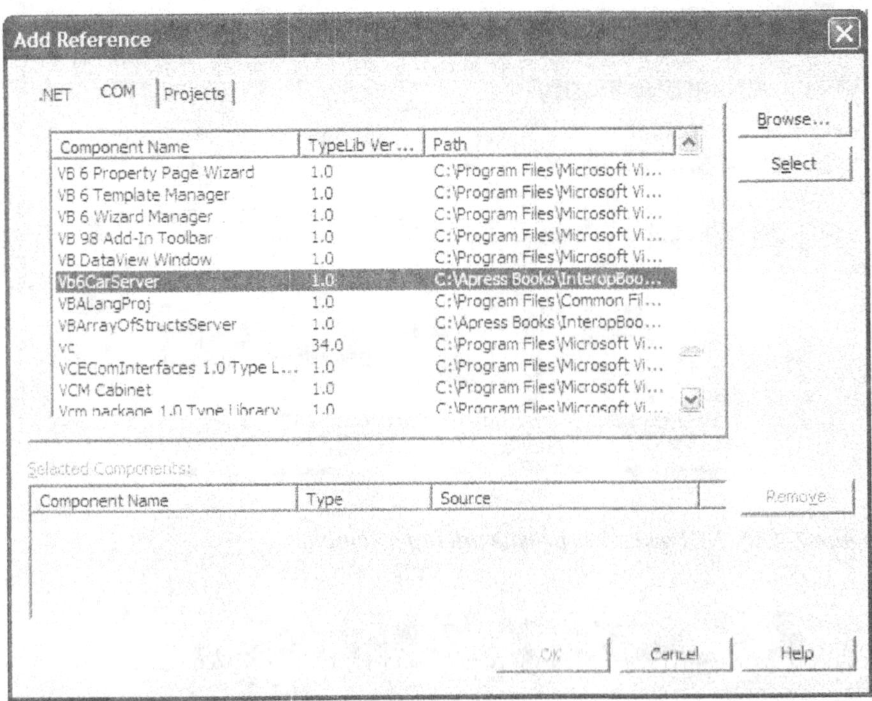

Figure 7-3. Referencing a COM server using Visual Studio .NET

Once you select the Vb6CarServer COM binary and click the OK button, check out the application directory of the C# client (Figure 7-4). You will find a new private assembly has been generated automatically. Also note that the name of this assembly has been prefixed with "Interop." to clearly mark the role of this binary. This is only a convention, however. An interop assembly can be named in any way you so choose.

If you examine the binary using the VS .NET Object Browser, you find that the interop assembly contains a single namespace that contains managed equivalents of each COM type documented in the COM type library (Figure 7-5).

Figure 7-4. VS .NET generates private interop assemblies.

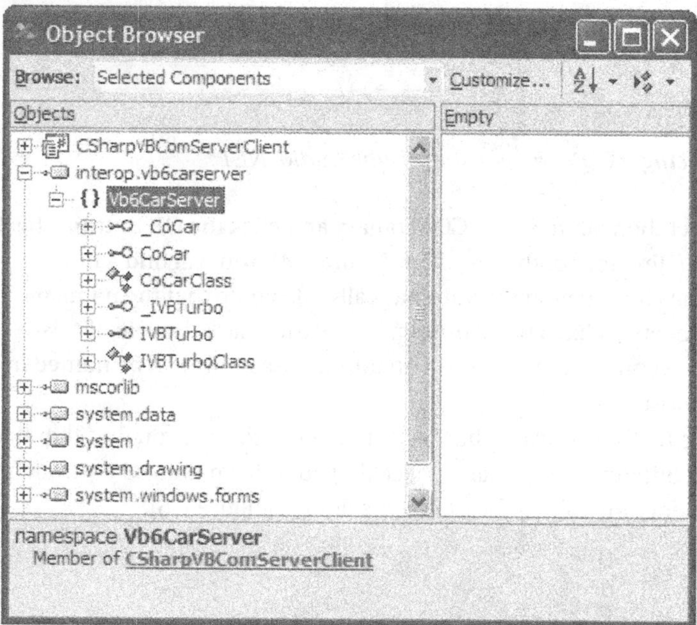

Figure 7-5. Peeking into the generated interop assembly

You examine the details of the conversion process soon enough, so for now, let's simply add the following code to the C# Windows Forms application to activate and exercise the VB 6.0 COM class:

```
// Need to reference namespace!
...
using Vb6CarServer;
namespace CSharpVBComServerClient
{
    public class MainForm : System.Windows.Forms.Form
    {
        ...
        // Button Click event handler.
        private void btnUseVb6ComCar_Click(object sender,
        System.EventArgs e)
        {
            // Use the COM class.
            CoCarClass vbComCar = new CoCarClass();
            vbComCar.TurboBlast();
            vbComCar.Speed = 20;
            MessageBox.Show(vbComCar.Speed.ToString(),
            "Speed is:");
        }
    }
}
```

As you can see, the C# client is completely hidden from the mechanics of COM. If you were to run the application, you would find that the COM type is activated (via the new keyword) and manipulated accordingly. Under the hood, of course, the RCW makes a call to the COM API function CoCreateInstance(). Although VS .NET makes the process of using existing COM types quite intuitive, you may have noticed a few items of interest. For example, notice that the name of the .NET wrapper (CoCarClass) is not identical to the COM type (CoCar). Also notice that the managed client is able to access the members of each interface (_CoCar and IVBTurbo) from what appears to be an instance of the coclass. You come to understand the details in the remainder of this chapter, so don't sweat the details for now.

A Visual Basic .NET Client

As you would expect, you can make use of any managed language to interact with legacy COM types. For example, if you make use of a VB .NET Windows Forms application (rather than C#), you find an almost identical code base:

```
' Reference the generated namespace.
Imports Vb6CarServer

Public Class MainForm
    Inherits System.Windows.Forms.Form
...
    ' VB .NET Button Click event handler.
    Private Sub btnUseVb6ComType_Click(ByVal sender As _
      System.Object, ByVal e As System.EventArgs) _
        Handles btnUseVb6ComType.Click
        ' Make the VB 6.0 coclass.
        Dim vbComCar As New CoCarClass()
        vbComCar.TurboBlast()
        vbComCar.Speed = 20
        MessageBox.Show(vbComCar.Speed.ToString(), "Speed is:")
    End Sub
End Class
```

So far, so good! Using Visual Studio .NET, you are able to work with the existing COM servers with minimum fuss and bother. In fact, using the basic information presented here, you can build managed solutions that leverage legacy COM types. As is always the case, however, the devil is in the details.

CODE *The CSharpVBComServerClient and VBDotNetVBComServerClient applications are included under the Chapter 7 subdirectory.*

Converting Between COM IDL Data Types and Managed Data Types

Now that you have seen the basics of using an existing COM type from managed code, it's time to dig deeper into the role of the RCW. As previously stated, a primary role of the RCW is to translate between IDL COM types and managed equivalents. I have already alluded to some of these translation rules (for example, BSTR to System.String). Table 7-1 documents the complete picture.

Table 7-1. COM-to-.NET Data Type Mappings

COM IDL Data Type	Managed .NET Data Type
bool, bool *	System.Int32
char, char * small , small *	System.SByte
short, short *	System.Int16
long, long * int , int *	System.Int32
hyper, hyper *	System.Int64
unsigned char, unsigned char *,	
byte, byte *	System.Byte
wchar_t, wchar_t * unsigned short, unsigned short *	System.UInt16
unsigned long, unsigned long * unsigned int, unsigned int *	System.UInt32
unsigned hyper unsigned hyper *	System.UInt64
float, float *	System.Single
double, double *	System.Double
VARIANT_BOOL VARIANT_BOOL *	System.Boolean
void *, void **	System.IntPtr
HRESULT, HRESULT *	System.Int16 or System.IntPtr
SCODE, SCODE *	System.Int32
BSTR, BSTR *	System.String
LPSTR or [string, ...] char * LPSTR *	System.String
LPWSTR or [string, ...] wchar_t * LPWSTR *	System.String
VARIANT, VARIANT *	System.Object
DECIMAL, DECIMAL * CURRENCY, CURRENCY *	System.Decimal
DATE, DATE *	System.DateTime
GUID, GUID *	System.Guid
IUnknown *, IUnknown **	System.Object
IDispatch *, IDispatch **	System.Object
SAFEARRAY(type) SAFEARRAY(type) *	type[] (i.e., a managed array deriving from System.Array)

As you may be able to tell, Table 7-1 is not exclusively confined to [oleautomation]-compatible IDL data types. For example, although the hyper, char*, and wchar_t* IDL data types can be expressed by a managed .NET base type, these items are not VARIANT compliant. Given this factoid, I do not discuss these mappings during the remainder of this chapter.

As far as the [oleautomation]-compatible types are concerned, note that IUnknown-and IDispatch-derived interfaces are mapped into the .NET System.Object data type. Although any COM interface can be represented by System.Object, do understand that the COM/.NET conversion process will generate managed equivalents for named COM interfaces. Thus, if your COM type library defines an interface named ICar, the conversion process generates a managed equivalent of the same name.

Also notice that COM BSTRs are mapped into the friendly System.String type, while COM SAFEARRAYs are mapped (by default) into System.Array. Later in this text, I examine a number of array-centric details, but for the time being it is safe to assume that arrays of COM IDL types map into a managed System.Array. Beyond these notable exceptions, most of the COM-to-.NET data type conversions should provoke no raised eyebrows.

Working with Managed GUIDs (System.Guid)

As you have also noticed from Table 7-1, the .NET base class libraries also supply a managed GUID equivalent. System.Guid provides a small number of members that allow you to manipulate the underlying GUID structure. In addition to overloading the equality and nonequality operators, System.Guid also provides the static (shared) NewGuid() method. For example, ponder the following C# code (as you may suspect, NewGuid() simply makes a call to CoCreateGuid() on your behalf).

```
// Get a GUID via System.Guid.NewGuid()
Guid myGuid = Guid.NewGuid();
Console.WriteLine(myGuid.ToString());
```

It is also useful to know that the Guid.ToString() method has been overloaded to support an incoming string parameter. This argument allows you to specify any of the following format characters:

```
// N format: ba5767980b834b7db8701b2e0377f58c
Console.WriteLine("N format {0}", myGuid.ToString("N"));
// D format: ba576798-0b83-4b7d-b870-1b2e0377f58c
Console.WriteLine("D format {0}", myGuid.ToString("D"));
// B format: {ba576798-0b83-4b7d-b870-1b2e0377f58c}
Console.WriteLine("B format {0}", myGuid.ToString("B"));
// P format: (ba576798-0b83-4b7d-b870-1b2e0377f58c)
Console.WriteLine("P format {0}", myGuid.ToString("P"));
```

Here, you find that the "N" format produces a raw 32-digit number, "D" makes use of a hyphen delimiter, and "B" and "P" make use of brackets and parentheses, respectively. As you will see later in this text, when an interop assembly is generated by a given tool, the GUIDs documented within a COM type library will be preserved and embedded into the interop assembly's metadata. Given this, you typically will not need to directly create a GUID from a managed client; however, we will see its usefulness where necessary.

Blittable and Non-Blittable Data Types

Technically speaking, the .NET data types listed previously in Table 7-1 can be broken down into two broad categories: blittable and non-blittable. The so-called blittable types listed in Table 7-2 are entities that are represented identically (under the hood) in both managed and unmanaged environments, and therefore do not require any special translations when marshaled between .NET and COM boundaries.

Table 7-2. The Blittable Types

Unmanaged Blittable Data Type	Managed Blittable Data Type	Meaning in Life
unsigned char, unsigned char *, byte, byte *	System.Byte	Represents an 8-bit unsigned integer
char, char *s small , small *	System.SByte	Represents an 8-bit signed integer, and is *not* CLS compliant
short, short *	System.Int16 integer	Represents a 16-bit signed
wchar_t, wchar_t * unsigned short, unsigned short *	System.UInt16	Represents a 16-bit signed integer, and is *not* CLS compliant
long, long *int , int *	System.Int32	Represents a 32-bit signed integer
unsigned long, unsigned long * unsigned int, unsigned int *	System.UInt32	Represents a 32-bit unsigned integer, and is *not* CLS compliant
hyper, hyper *	System.Int64	Represents a 64-bit signed integer, and is *not* CLS compliant
void *, void **	System.IntPtr	A platform-specific type that is used to represent a pointer or a handle

Given this information, it should be clear that if you have the following IDL interface description:

```
// COM IDL data type.
interface IAmSimple : IUnknown
{
   HRESULT Add([in] long x);
};
```

the resulting blittable type is System.Int32:

```
// .NET blittable data type.
void Add(int x);
```

In addition to stand-alone blittable types, arrays of blittable items and structures that contain blittable fields are themselves considered blittable. Thus, if you create a fixed array of IDL longs, you will find a managed array of System.Int32 types.

The Non-Blittable Data Types

On the other end of the data type spectrum, there are non-blittable data types. As the name suggests, non-blittable types are *not* represented identically between the COM and .NET architectures. Check out the core non-blittable types listed in Table 7-3.

Table 7-3. The Non-Blittable Data Types

Managed Non-Blittable Data Type	Meaning in Life
System.Array	Represents a managed version of a C-style array or a SAFEARRAY
System.Boolean	Converts to a 1, 2, or 4-byte value with true as 1 or –1
System.Char	Represents a Unicode or ANSI character
System.Object	Represents a VARIANT or an interface
System.String	Represents a managed version of a null-terminated string or BSTR
System.ValueType	Converts to a structure with a fixed memory layout (details to come)
System.Multicast Delegate	Converts COM connection points into managed delegates (details to come)

Non-blittable types do indeed require translations by the RCW to seamlessly map information between architectural boundaries. For example, passing BSTRs, COM interface pointers, and COM SAFEARRAYs between architecture boundaries forces the RCW to make calls to the COM library to properly handle these complex types. Again, the good news is that the RCW proxy type generally hides this internal goo from view. Thus, if you have the following COM IDL interface definition:

```
// COM IDL data type.
interface IAmMoreComplex : IUnknown
{
    HRESULT Speak([in] BSTR msg);
};
```

the non-blittable BSTR is translated into System.String automatically by the RCW:

```
// .NET non-blittable data type mapping.
void Speak(string msg);
```

Perhaps somewhat obviously, if you have a data type that contains non-blittable members (such as a structure containing BSTR fields) or an array of non-blittable types, the data structure in question is also non-blittable and requires translation by the RCW.

Interfaces Consumed by the RCW

In addition to mapping primitive data types, the RCW is also responsible for consuming a number of low-level COM interfaces from the .NET client, to make the COM type behave well within a managed environment. Specifically speaking, an RCW may consume any of the COM interfaces listed in Table 7-4 (depending on which interfaces the COM type supports).

Table 7-4. COM Interfaces Hidden from a Managed Client

Consumed COM Interface	Meaning in Life
IDispatch	The RCW implements IDispatch to allow the .NET client to activate the type using late binding, as well as to allow the COM type to be examined using .NET reflection services (System.Reflection).
IErrorInfo	As you see in detail later in this text, COM types are able to send COM error objects to a calling COM client. The IErrorInfo interface allows the client to obtain a textual description of the error, its source, a Help file, Help context, and the GUID of the interface that defined the error (always GUID_NULL for .NET classes). The RCW intercepts this information and exposes it to the .NET client via structured exception handling.

Table 7-4. COM Interfaces Hidden from a Managed Client (continued)

Consumed COM Interface	Meaning in Life
IProvideClassInfo	If the COM object being wrapped implements IProvideClassInfo (which is always the case when building VB 6.0 COM servers), the RCW extracts the type information from this interface to provide stronger type identity.
IUnknown	The RCW hides the functionality provided by IUnknown (object identity, type coercion, and lifetime management). Given this, a .NET client never directly calls AddRef(), Release(), or QueryInterface().
IConnectionPoint and IConnectionPointContainer	If the COM type sends COM-based events, the RCW implements these interfaces to map COM connection point events into .NET delegate-based events.
IDispatchEx	The IDispatchEx interface is an extension of the IDispatch interface that, unlike IDispatch, enables enumeration, addition, deletion, and case-sensitive calling of members. If the class implements IDispatchEx, the RCW implements IExpando.
IEnumVARIANT	Enables COM types that support enumerations to be treated as .NET style collections (specifically, be traversed using foreach syntax).

By way of a simple example, assume you have created a scriptable coclass that implements a single [dual] interface, fires events to the connected client, and exposes a set of subobjects using a COM collection (Figure 7-6). Note that the managed client is not exposed to these low-level interfaces.

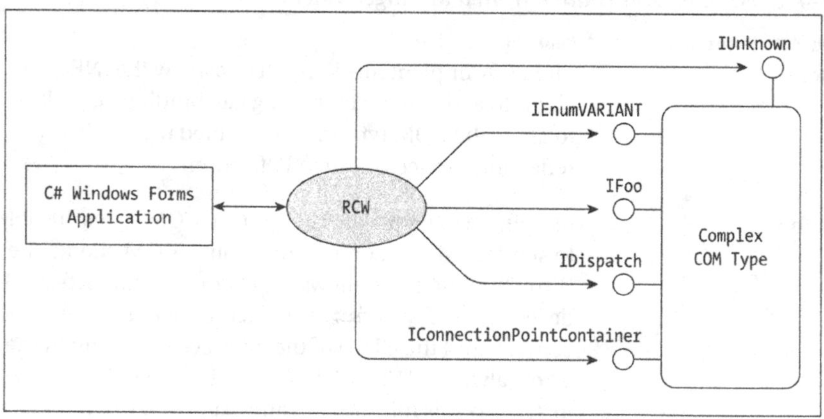

Figure 7-6. The RCW hides low-level COM interfaces from view.

Of course, these key COM interfaces are used indirectly by the managed client where necessary. For example, if a C# client were to intercept a COM event, the RCW will interact with IConnectionPointContainer and IConnectionPoint behind the scenes. Likewise, if a managed client wishes to activate a COM type using late binding, IDispatch is manipulated automatically.

Options to Obtain an Interop Assembly

Clearly, the RCW is a critical part of the .NET-to-COM interoperability puzzle. As you have already seen, VS .NET makes the process of generating interop assemblies quite painless. You do, however, have other options. For example, while it is possible to build a custom interop assembly using your managed language of choice and the types defined within the System.Runtime.InteropServices namespace, you seldom (if ever) need to do so. In Chapter 9, you examine the process of creating your own custom IDL-to-.NET interop assembly conversion utility. Until that point, you make use of the following more practical alternatives:

- Use the command line tool tlbimp.exe.
- Use the Add Reference | COM tab provided by VS .NET.

To be sure, the functionality provided by VS .NET fits the bill most of the time (as seen in the first example of this chapter). However, there are times when you need to drop down to the command line and interact with tlbimp.exe explicitly. As with most command line tools, the benefit of doing so is that you have much more control over how the interop assembly will be generated. For example, using various command line flags, you can specify a custom name of the generated namespace, configure a strongly named interop assembly, and so forth. Given this, let's get to know how to manipulate the raw command line utility.

Using the tlbimp.exe Command Line Utility

The Type Library Importer utility (tlbimp.exe) is a command line tool that reads COM type information (typically contained in *.tlb, *.dll or *.exe files) and generates a corresponding .NET interop assembly. In its simplest form, all you are required to specify is the name of the COM server you wish to convert. However, Table 7-5 documents the core flags used to build an interop assembly that does not support a strong name (you will examine this aspect of tlbimp.exe a bit later in the text).

Table 7-5. Core Options of tlbimp.exe

Core tlbimp.exe Flag	Meaning in Life
/asmversion:	Specifies the version number of the assembly to produce. By default, the assembly's version is based on the [library] attribute of the COM type library.
/namespace:	Specifies the namespace in which to produce the assembly. If not specified, the namespace is based on the name of the output file.
/sysarray:	Specifies that COM SAFEARRAYs should map into a managed System.Array.
/out:	Specifies the name of the output file, assembly, and namespace in which to write the metadata definitions.

If you do not specify the /out flag, tlbimp.exe writes the metadata to a file with the same name as the actual type library defined within the input file and assigns it a .dll file extension. If this action were to result in a name clash, tlbimp.exe generates an error.

Building an Interoperability Assembly with Tlbimp.exe

To illustrate the use of tlbimp.exe, let's build an interop assembly for the AtlCarServer.dll COM server you created in Chapter 3. Open a command window and navigate to the location of your ATL COM server. In keeping with the recommended naming convention, the name of the resulting interop assembly consists of an "Interop." prefix. Assuming the location of your COM server is located on the root C drive, you can issue the following command:

```
C:\tlbimp AtlCarServer.dll /out:Interop.AtlCarServer.dll
```

If you now check the C drive, you will see your new interop assembly is present and accounted for (Figure 7-7).

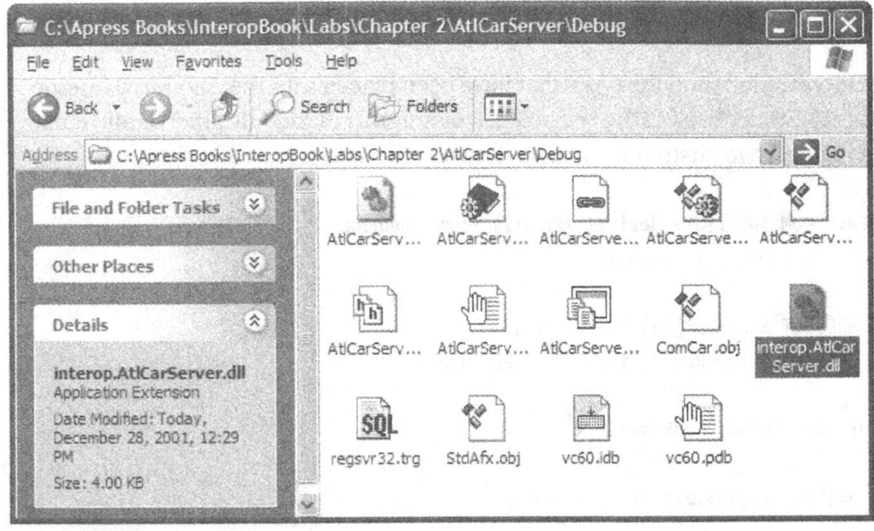

Figure 7-7. The generated interop assembly

When you open this new .NET assembly using ILDasm.exe, you will be pleased to find .NET types that represent the unmanaged COM atoms (Figure 7-8).

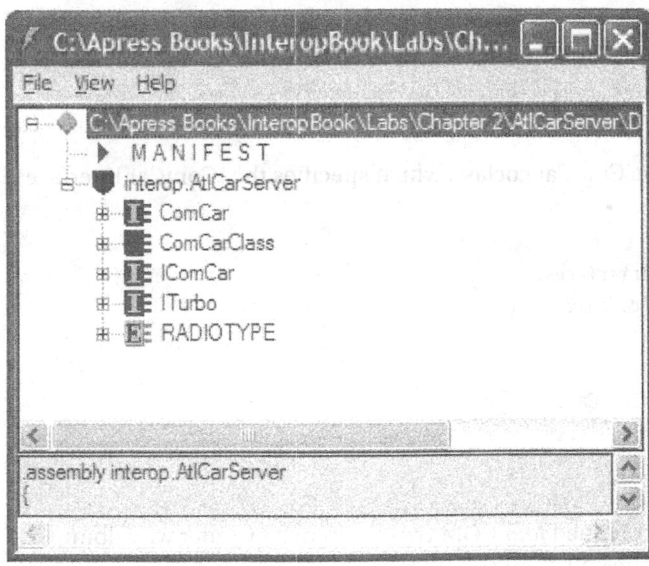

Figure 7-8. The managed COM wrapper types

Examining the Generated .NET Types

To better understand the types that have been placed into the generated interop assembly, think back to the original IDL definitions of the AtlCarServer.dll. First, you defined two custom IUnknown derived interfaces:

```
// Each COM interface derives directly from IUnknown.
interface IComCar : IUnknown
{
    HRESULT SpeedUp([in] long delta);
    HRESULT TurnOnRadio([in] RADIOTYPE make);
};
interface ITurbo: IUnknown
{
    HRESULT TurboBlast();
};
```

Recall that the IComCar::TurnOnRadio() method used a custom IDL enumeration, RADIOTYPE:

```
// The COM IDL enumeration.
typedef enum RADIOTYPE
{
    EIGHT_TRACK, CD,
    AM_RADIO, FM_RADIO
} RADIOTYPE;
```

Finally, you have the ComCar coclass, which specifies the IComCar interface as the [default]:

```
// ComCar supports two interfaces,
// where IComCar is the default.
coclass ComCar
{
    [default] interface IComCar;
    interface ITurbo;
};
```

Given that you have defined *four* COM types, you may wonder why tlbimp.exe generated metadata for *five* .NET entities. To begin to understand the translation process, examine Table 7-6.

Table 7-6. Types Generated for the AtlCarServer.dll COM Server

Generated Managed Type	Meaning in Life
ComCar	Tlbimp.exe generates a type that has the same name as the [default] interface, minus the "I-" prefix (ex: IFoo becomes Foo). This type is creatable, but you will only be able to access the members explicitly defined by this interface.
IComCar ITurbo	Tlbimp.exe always generates managed equivalents for each interface found within the COM type library. As you would expect, managed interfaces are not creatable.
ComCarClass	Each coclass listed in the IDL library statement is represented by a managed .NET class type and always takes a "-Class" suffix (e.g., MyComClass becomes MyComClassClass). These .NET types are directly creatable and support the members of each and every implemented COM interface.
RADIOTYPE	COM IDL data types are mapped to .NET types that extend System.Enum.

Manipulating COM Types Using Generated "-Class" Types

Let's see these types in action. Assume you have a new C# Console application (CSharpAtlComServerClient) that has already set a reference to the generated interop assembly using the Add Reference dialog box (use the Browse button of the .NET tab to navigate to the Interop.AtlCarServer.dll).

To illustrate the simplest way to manipulate the ATL ComCar, begin by creating an instance of the generated ComCarClass type as follows:

```
using System;
using interop.AtlCarServer;

namespace CSharpAtlComServerClient
{
    class CSharpATLClient
    {
        [STAThread]
        static void Main(string[] args)
        {
```

```
            // Use the ATL Car using the ComCarClass
            // type. Recall!  '-Class' types allow you
            // to call any member of each supported
            // interface.
            ComCarClass c = new ComCarClass();
            c.TurnOnRadio(RADIOTYPE.EIGHT_TRACK);
            c.SpeedUp(10);
            c.TurboBlast();
        }
    }
}
```

When you create a new instance of generated "-Class" types, the object instance (c, in this case) supports each member of each supported interface. This is a good thing, of course, given that .NET does not demand that types implement interfaces whatsoever, and therefore the C# client should not be forced to ask for an interface before interacting with the type. Using ComCarClass, you can make use of the functionality defined by IComCar and ITurbo from what seems to be a simple .NET object reference.

Manipulating COM Types Using Discrete Interfaces

Recall that tlbimp.exe generates managed equivalents for each IDL interface. Thus, if you wish, you are able to interact with the ATL ComCar using discrete interface references. Understand, of course, that you will not make use of QueryInterface() to obtain an interface reference, but will do so using C#-specific techniques (explicit casting, or using the is or as keywords). VB .NET clients would make use of the CType() casting function. For example:

```
// Now make use of explicit interfaces (C#).
IComCar itfComCar = new ComCarClass();
itfComCar.TurnOnRadio(RADIOTYPE.FM_RADIO);
try
{
    // QueryInterface() triggered via explicit cast.
    ITurbo itfTurbo = (ITurbo)itfComCar;
    itfTurbo.TurboBlast();
}
catch(InvalidCastException e)
{Console.WriteLine(e.Message); }

' Now make use of explicit interfaces (VB .NET).
Dim itfComCar As IComCar = New ComCarClass()
itfComCar.TurnOnRadio(RADIOTYPE.FM_RADIO)
```

```
Try
    Dim itfTurbo As ITurbo = CType(itfComCar, ITurbo)
    itfTurbo.TurboBlast()
Catch ex As InvalidCastException
    Console.WriteLine(ex.Message)
End Try
```

Leveraging Managed Interfaces

When you make use of managed interfaces to interact with COM types, things tend to look a bit more like classic COM. This is the case because you are now only able to make use of members supported on a particular interface. Even though working directly with the "-Class" generated types entails less effort on your part, the generated managed interfaces still come in quite handy. For example, assume that the AtlCarServer.dll COM binary supported another coclass that also supported ITurbo:

```
// Another ITurbo compatible coclass.
coclass JetPlane
{
    [default] interface IJet;
    interface ITurbo;
}
```

If you wish to build a managed method that can manipulate ComCars as well as JetPlanes, you could construct the following:

```
class CSharpATLClient
{
    [STAThread]
    static void Main(string[] args)
    {
        // Create some jets and comcars.
        ComCarClass c3 = new ComCarClass();
        JetPlaneClass j = new JetPlaneClass();
        XCelerate(c3);
        XCelerate(j);
    }
    // Turbo boost each COM type.
    public static void XCelerate(ITurbo itfTurbo)
    {
        itfTurbo.TurboBlast();
    }
}
```

Given that the generated .NET interfaces behave like any other .NET interface type, you are also allowed to make use of these interfaces from within managed code (this topic is examined in greater detail in Chapter 12). For example, you could build a custom C# class that implements ITurbo as follows:

```
// A C# class deriving from the COM ITurbo interface.
class UFO : ITurbo
{
    public void TurboBlast()
    { Console.WriteLine("UFOs are always at warp speed...");}
}
```

And make use of it using the XCelerate() method:

```
class CSharpATLClient
{
    [STAThread]
    static void Main(string[] args)
    {
        // Create some jets, UFOs and ComCars.
        ComCarClass c3 = new ComCarClass();
        JetPlaneClass j = new JetPlaneClass();
        UFO u = new UFO();
        XCelerate(c3);
        XCelerate(j);
        XCelerate(u);
    }
    // Turbo each COM type.
    public static void XCelerate(ITurbo itfTurbo)
    {
        itfTurbo.TurboBlast();
    }
}
```

As you would expect, you can use generated interfaces to perform other interface-based programming tricks. Assume you want to build an array of ITurbo interfaces, where each member points to some type (COM-based or otherwise) that supports the ITurbo interface. Once you have done so, you could loop over the array and trigger each TurboBoost() implementation:

```
// Managed interface types may point to
// managed or unmanaged entities!
// (as long as they support the correct interface).
```

```
ITurbo[] fastVehicles = {new ComCarClass(),     // COM type.
                         new UFO(),             // .NET type.
                         new JetPlaneClass()}; // COM type.
foreach(ITurbo i in fastVehicles)
    i.TurboBlast();
```

Manipulating COM Types Using the [Default] Interface Type

In addition to creating a "-Class" suffixed type that provides access to the members of each implemented COM interface, tlbimp.exe also generates a type that provides access to the members defined by the [default] interface of the coclass. The name of this type is always the same name as the [default] interface itself, minus the capital "I" prefix. For example, given that your ATL ComCar marked IComCar as the [default], you are able to make use of your COM type as follows:

```
// Now using 'default interface' type.
ComCar c2 = new ComCar();
c2.TurnOnRadio(RADIOTYPE.AM_RADIO);
```

Understand, of course, that when you manipulate a COM type using the [default] class type, you are only able to call members defined by the interface itself. If you attempt to access members of other interfaces, you are greeted by a compile time error:

```
// Ack!  TurboBoost() not defined by IComCar!
c2.TurboBoost(); // Compiler error!
```

To get at the members of other auxiliary interfaces, you need to make use of language-specific interface casting:

```
ITurbo itfTurbo2 = (ITurbo)c2;
itfTurbo2.TurboBlast();
```

You may be wondering exactly why tlbimp.exe generates these rather limited types in the first place. My hunch is that it is because Visual Basic 6.0 COM programmers typically created COM classes that supported a single [default] interface. Given that VB 6.0 is far and away the most popular COM language mapping out there, this gives VB .NET programmers the benefit of creating wrapper types that have the same name as the underlying COM type. In short, the default interface types are another bit of syntactic sugar.

CODE *The CSharpAtlComServerClient application is included under the Chapter 7 subdirectory.*

So there you have it! At this point, you have seen how to create and manipulate COM types using the wrappers contained in a given interop assembly. What you have not yet done is examine the specific rules that are used to map COM types into terms of managed equivalents. To do so requires a deeper understanding of the members found within the System.Runtime.InteropServices namespace.

Select Members of the System.Runtime.InteropServices Namespace

Before I dig too much more deeply into the world of COM/.NET interop, you need to be aware of the key members of the System.Runtime.InteropServices namespace that help facilitate the translation process. These types are used in two specific circumstances. First, when you generate a given interop assembly, the assembly metadata contains numerous references to the types found in this namespace, which are used to document bits of information regarding the original COM IDL definitions. Second, be aware that when you create .NET types that need to be exposed to COM (examined later in this text), you are making *direct* use of these same types to control how a .NET atom is exposed to COM.

As you would guess, the members of System.Runtime.InteropServices can be grouped by semantic similarity. In general, members of this namespace are used to describe the following information:

- How to configure type libraries and interop assemblies
- How to expose and marshal types between architectures
- How to describe classes, interfaces, methods, events, and parameters
- How to express error information between architectures
- How to represent arrays and structures across architectures

Rather than dump out a single huge table of each and every member, let's take some time to check out the members that can be logically grouped together. To begin, Table 7-7 lists the members that are specifically geared to the description of COM type libraries and .NET interop assemblies.

Table 7-7. Type Library/Interop Assembly–Centric Members of System.Runtime.InteropServices

Type Library/Interop Assembly-Centric Member	Meaning in Life
TypeLibConverter	Provides a set of services that allows you to programmatically convert a managed assembly to a COM type library and vice versa.
TypeLibFuncAttribute	Contains the FUNCFLAGS that were originally imported for this method from the COM type library. Used in conjunction with the TypeLibFuncFlags enumeration.
TypeLibTypeAttribute	Contains the TYPEFLAGS that were originally imported for this type from the COM type library. Used in conjunction with the TypeLibTypeFlags enumeration.
TypeLibVarAttribute	Contains the VARFLAGS that were originally imported for this field from the COM type library. Used in conjunction with the TypeLibVarFlags enumeration.
ImportedFromTypeLibAttribute	Indicates that the types defined within an assembly were originally defined in a COM type library.
PrimaryInteropAssemblyAttribute	Indicates that the attributed assembly is a primary interop assembly.

Closely related to the process of documenting COM type libraries and interop assemblies is the process of documenting how these entities are registered and how their internal types are exposed to the target architecture (Table 7-8).

Table 7-8. Registration/Visibility-Centric Members of System.Runtime.InteropServices

Registration/Visibility-Centric Member	Meaning in Life
ComRegisterFunctionAttribute	Specifies the method to call when you register an assembly for use from COM. This allows the execution of user-written code during the registration process.

Table 7-8. Registration/Visibility-Centric Members of System.Runtime.InteropServices (continued)

Registration/Visibility-Centric Member	Meaning in Life
ComUnregisterFunctionAttribute	Specifies the method to call when you unregister an assembly for use from COM. This allows for the execution of user-written code during the unregistration process.
RegistrationServices	Provides a set of services for registering and unregistering managed assemblies for use from COM.
ComImportAttribute	Indicates that the attributed type was previously defined in COM.
ComVisibleAttribute	Controls COM visibility of an individual type, member, or all types in an assembly.

As you would guess, classes, interfaces, methods, and parameters are also represented by various attributes of the System.Runtime.InteopServices namespace. Tables 7-9, 7-10, and 7-11 document the items of interest.

Table 7-9. Class-Centric Members of System.Runtime.InteropServices

Class-Centric Member	Meaning in Life
ExtensibleClassFactory	Enables customization of managed objects that extend from unmanaged objects during creation
ProgIdAttribute	Allows the user to specify the ProgId of a .NET class when exposed to COM

Table 7-10. Interface-Centric Members of System.Runtime.InteropServices

Interface-Centric Member	Meaning in Life
ClassInterfaceAttribute	Indicates the type of class interface that will be generated for a class, if at all. Used in conjunction with the ClassInterfaceType enumeration.
DispIdAttribute	Specifies the COM DISPID of a method, field, or property.

Table 7-10. Interface-Centric Members of System.Runtime.InteropServices (continued)

Interface-Centric Member	Meaning in Life
IDispatchImplAttribute	Indicates which IDispatch implementation the common language runtime uses when exposing dual interfaces and dispinterfaces to COM. Used in conjunction with the IDispatchImplType enumeration.
InterfaceTypeAttribute	Indicates whether a managed interface is exposed to COM as a dual, IDispatch-, or IUnknown-based interface. This attribute is used in conjunction with the ComInterfaceType enumeration.
AutomationProxyAttribute	Specifies whether the type should be marshaled using the Automation Marshaler (oleaut32.dll) or a custom proxy and stub DLL.

Table 7-11. Method and Parameter-Centric Members of System.Runtime.InteropServices

Method- and Parameter-Centric Member	Meaning in Life
InAttribute	Indicates that data should be marshaled from the caller to the callee.
OptionalAttribute	Indicates that a parameter is optional.
OutAttribute	Indicates that data should be marshaled from callee back to caller.
ComAliasNameAttribute	Indicates the COM alias for a parameter or field type.
LCIDConversionAttribute	Indicates that a method's unmanaged signature expects an LCID parameter.
PreserveSigAttribute	Indicates that the HRESULT or retval signature transformation that takes place during COM interop calls should be suppressed.
DllImportAttribute	Indicates that the attributed method is implemented as an export from an unmanaged DLL. Used in conjunction with the CallingConvention *and* CharSet enumerations.

There are two types used to document GUID-centric attributes, as shown in Table 7-12.

Table 7-12. GUID-Centric Members of System.Runtime.InteropServices

GUID-Centric Member	Meaning in Life
CoClassAttribute	Identifies the class ID of a coclass imported from a type library
GuidAttribute	Supplies an explicit GUID when an automatically generated GUID is undesirable

Finally, it is worth pointing out that System.Runtime.InteropServices defines a class type that can be used to obtain information about the .NET runtime itself (Table 7-13).

Table 7-13. .NET Runtime–Centric Members of System.Runtime.InteropServices

General .NET Utility-Centric Member	Meaning in Life
RuntimeEnvironment	Provides a collection of static (shared in Visual Basic) methods that return information about the common language runtime environment. The FromGlobalAccessCache() method can also be used to determine if a given assembly in located in the GAC.

An Interesting Aside: System.Runtime.InteropServices.RuntimeEnvironment

The RuntimeEnvironment type is helpful when you want to discover basic traits regarding how the target machine has configured the .NET runtime. For example, consider the following class:

```
class RuntimeSpy
{
    [STAThread]
    static void Main(string[] args)
    {
        // Check out the runtime...
        Console.WriteLine("Runtime Directory is:\n-->{0}\n",
            RuntimeEnvironment.GetRuntimeDirectory());
```

```
        Console.WriteLine("System Version is:\n-->{0}\n",
            RuntimeEnvironment.GetSystemVersion());

        Console.WriteLine(@"Location of system
                            config file is:\n-->{0}\n",
              RuntimeEnvironment.SystemConfigurationFile);
    }
}
```

The output can be seen in Figure 7-9.

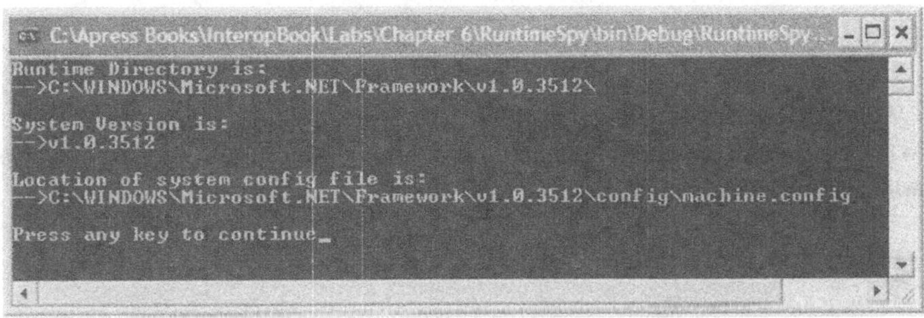

Figure 7-9. The .NET Runtime spy

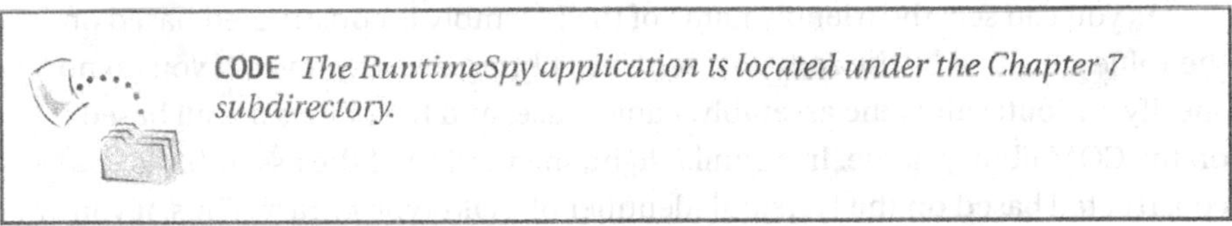

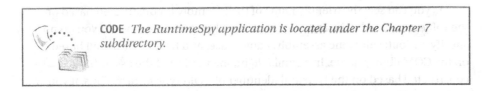

CODE *The RuntimeSpy application is located under the Chapter 7 subdirectory.*

COM Library Statement to .NET Assembly Statement Conversion Rules

Now that you have a better idea of the key types that lurk within an interop assembly, you can dig into the specifics. Begin by running tlbimp.exe and specify the *.tlb file of the RawComServer.dll you created in Chapter 2. Given that you did not embed the *.tlb file directly into the *.dll, you get an error if you attempt to specify the *.dll itself. The following command does the trick:

```
C:\ tlbimp RawComCar.tlb /out:interop.RawComCarLib.dll
```

As you may recall, COM type libraries maintain a special section termed the *library statement*. At minimum, COM type libraries must be adorned with a [uuid] attribute (which identified the LIBID). In addition, a well-behaved type library statement should support a [version] attribute and may support the [lcid] attribute to mark the locale of the type library itself. For example, ponder the following library statement for the RawComCar.dll COM server:

```
// The Raw Car Library.
[uuid(D679F136-19C9-4868-B229-F338AE163656), version(1.0)]
library RawComCarLib
{
    ...
}
```

When an interop assembly is generated, the information found in the COM type library statement is used to build the [.assembly] description statement of the assembly manifest. For example:

```
.assembly interop.RawComCarLib
{
  ... GuidAttribute...
    ... ImportedFromTypeLibAttribute...
  .ver 1:0:0:0
}
```

As you can see, the friendly name of the assembly is constructed based on the value specified by the /out: flag sent into tlbimp.exe. However, if you do not specify an /out: value, the assembly, namespace, and file names are all based on the COM library name. In a similar light, the version of the assembly is constructed based on the [version] identifier of COM type library. Thus, if you update the library version as follows:

```
[uuid(D679F136-19C9-4868-B229-F338AE163656), version(3.5)]
library RawComCarLib
{
    ...
}
```

the generated interop assembly would now be marked as version 3.5.0.0:

```
.assembly interop.RawComCarLib
{
    ...
  .ver 3:5:0:0
}
```

In addition to building the assembly's friendly name and version identifier, the generated [.assembly] statement also documents the fact that this assembly was generated from an existing COM type library using the ImportedFromTypeLibAttribute type as well as the GUID value of the LIBID itself using the GuidAttribute type.

Recall that the ImportedFromTypeLibAttribute type is used to indicate that the types contained within the assembly were generated using COM type information. Therefore, any assembly that contains this marker in its assembly manifest can be correctly identified as an interop assembly. Here is the complete [.assembly] statement for the generated interop assembly manifest (slightly reformatted for ease of reading):

```
.assembly Interop.RawComCarLib
{
  .custom instance void
  [mscorlib]System.Runtime.InteropServices.
  ImportedFromTypeLibAttribute
  ::.ctor(string) =
 ( 01 00 0C 52 61 77 43 6F 6D 43 61 72 4C 69 62 00  00 )
// ...RawComCarLib.

.custom instance void [mscorlib]System.Runtime.InteropServices.GuidAttribute
::.ctor(string) = ( 01 00 24 64 36 37 39 66 31 33 36 2D 31 39 63 39
2D 34 38 36 38 2D 62 32 32 39 2D 66 33 33 38 61
65 31 36 33 36 35 36 00 00 )
// d679f136-19c9-4868-b229-f338ae163656
  .hash algorithm 0x00008004
  .ver 1:0:0:0
}
```

Notice that the value passed into the constructor of the ImportedFromTypeLibAttribute is the name of the original COM type library (RawComCarLib), while the value passed into the GuidAttribute is the original LIBID (D679F136-19C9-4868-B229-F338AE163656).

Programmatically Controlling the Namespace Definition

The default behavior of tlbimp.exe is to create a namespace that is based on the name of the COM library statement. Although this is most likely exactly what you require, you are able to instruct tlbimp.exe to generate an alternative name using the /namespace or /out flags. However, the Visual Studio .NET IDE builds the generated namespace verbatim. When you wish to generate an alternative namespace for an interop assembly, you must make use of tlbimp.exe directly.

Alternatively, if you wish to ensure that a generated namespace will always take a particular form (regardless of the tool used to build the interop assembly), you can retrofit the COM type library to support a [custom] IDL attribute with the name 0F21F359-AB84-41e8-9A78-36D110E6D2F9 (see Chapter 4 for a discussion of building custom IDL attributes). The value of this custom IDL attribute is a literal string that is used to generate the name of the generated assembly. To illustrate, assume that you reengineered (and recompiled) the RawComCar library statement as follows:

```
[uuid(D679F136-19C9-4868-B229-F338AE163656), version(1.0),
custom(0F21F359-AB84-41e8-9A78-36D110E6D2F9,
"Intertech.RawComCarLib")]
library RawComCarLib
{
    ...
}
```

Once the interop assembly is regenerated, you would find the namespace definition shown in Figure 7-10.

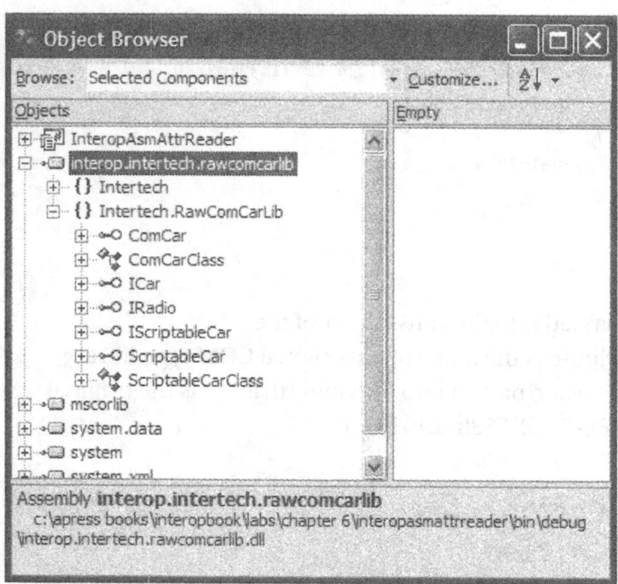

Figure 7-10. Creating custom namespace names

Understand, of course, that the chances are slim to none that you will import a legacy COM server that supports this custom IDL attribute, simply because most COM servers were created well before the release of .NET and had no foreknowledge of this predefined GUID. If you wish to change the name of the generated namespace using this technique, you need to update the underlying IDL of the original COM server. The only reason you may want to do so is to establish a nested namespace definition (which requires the use of the dot notation). As you may be aware, IDL [library] statements do not support the use of the dot notation when creating the friendly name of a COM type library.

So much for this examination of converting COM type library statements into .NET assembly definitions. Next up, let's check out how the core COM types are mapped into managed equivalents.

COM Types to .NET Types Conversion Rules

As you are well aware, a COM library statement contains numerous type definitions. Simply put, COM interfaces become managed interfaces, coclasses become .NET class types (which do indeed derive from System.Object), and COM enums become System.Enum derived types. Of course, there is much more to the story than meets the eye. To begin, let's check out the conversion of COM interface types.

COM Interface Conversion

When a COM interface is translated into a managed equivalent, the conversion process purposely strips away all members of IUnknown and, if necessary, IDispatch, from the managed type. For example, the RawComCar.dll COM server defined three custom interfaces, two of which (ICar and IRadio) derived directly from IUnknown, while the other (IScriptableCar) was configured as a [dual] interface and therefore derived from IDispatch. Here is the original IDL:

```
// The ICar interface
[uuid(710D2F54-9289-4f66-9F64-201D56FB66C7), object]
interface ICar : IUnknown
{
    HRESULT SpeedUp([in] long delta);
    HRESULT CurrentSpeed([out, retval] long* currSp);
};

// The IRadio interface
[uuid(3B6C6126-92A8-47ef-86DA-A12BFFD9BC42), object]
interface IRadio : IUnknown
{
    HRESULT CrankTunes();
};
```

```
// The IScriptableCar interface
[uuid(DBAA0495-2F6A-458a-A74A-129F2C45B642), dual, object]
interface IScriptableCar : IDispatch
{
    [id(1), propput] HRESULT Speed([in] long currSp);
    [id(1), propget] HRESULT Speed([out, retval] long* currSp);
    [id(2)] HRESULT CrankTunes();
};
```

Much like the LIBID assigned to the COM type library, IID values are encoded into .NET metadata using the GuidAttribute type. In addition, IUnknown-derived interfaces (meaning, interfaces that have not been configured as [dual] or raw dispinterfaces) are also adorned with the InterfaceTypeAttribute. The underlying value assigned to the InterfaceTypeAttribute is one of the following members of the ComInterfaceType enumeration, as seen in Table 7-14.

Table 7-14. Values of the ComInterfaceType Enumeration

ComInterfaceType Member Name	Description
InterfaceIsDual	Indicates the interface was configured as a dual interface
InterfaceIsIDispatch	Indicates the interface was configured as a dispinterface
InterfaceIsIUnknown	Indicates the interface was defined as an IUnknown-derived interface (as opposed to a dispinterface or a dual interface)

For example, if you examine the IL behind the IRadio interface, you find the following IL (again, slightly reformatted for readability):

```
.class interface public abstract auto ansi import IRadio
{
  .custom instance void[mscorlib]
  System.Runtime.InteropServices.GuidAttribute::
  .ctor(string) =
( 01 00 24 33 42 36 43 36 31 32 36 2D 39 32 41 38
2D 34 37 45 46 2D 38 36 44 41 2D 41 31 32 42 46
46 44 39 42 43 34 32 00 00 )
  // ..$3B6C6126-92A8-47EF-86DA-A12BF FD9BC42
  .custom instance void[mscorlib]
  System.Runtime.InteropServices.InterfaceTypeAttribute::
  .ctor(int16) =
( 01 00 01 00 00 00 )
} // end of class IRadio
```

The ICar interface has similar attributes. However, when tlbimp.exe encounters a [dual] interface, the underlying IL does not record an InterfaceTypeAttribute, but rather the TypeLibTypeAttribute type to document the TYPEFLAGS that were originally imported for this type from the COM type library. Recall from Chapter 4 that the TYPEFLAGS enumeration contains fields that identify if the entity is hidden, creatable, an application object, and so forth. For example, here is the IL definition of IScriptableCar:

```
.class interface public abstract auto ansi import IScriptableCar
{
  .custom instance void [mscorlib]
  System.Runtime.InteropServices.TypeLibTypeAttribute::
  .ctor(int16) =
( 01 00 40 10 00 00 )
  .custom instance void [mscorlib]
  System.Runtime.InteropServices.GuidAttribute::
  .ctor(string) =
( 01 00 24 44 42 41 41 30 34 39 35 2D 32 46 36 41
2D 34 35 38 41 2D 41 37 34 41 2D 31 32 39 46 32
43 34 35 42 36 34 32 00 00 )
// ..$DBAA0495-2F6A-458A-A74A-129F2 C45B642
} // end of class IScriptableCar
```

Importing COM Interface Hierarchies

A very standard technique in COM is to build new interface definitions based on existing interfaces (this is also a common design pattern within the .NET universe). When programmers make use of this approach, they are in effect "versioning" an interface. Despite the usefulness of this technique, Visual Basic 6.0 does not allow you to follow this pattern, given that VB 6.0 does not support any form of inheritance. Therefore, assume that you have a new ATL COM server (ATLVersionedInterfaceServer) that defines the following interface hierarchy:

```
interface IFoo : IUnknown
{
    [helpstring("method A")] HRESULT A();
};

interface IFoo2 : IFoo
{
    [helpstring("method B")] HRESULT B();
};

interface IFoo3 : IFoo2
{
    [helpstring("method C")] HRESULT C();
};
```

Each of these interfaces is implemented by a single coclass named (of course) Foo:

```
// The Foo coclass supports each versioned interface.
coclass Foo
{
    [default] interface IFoo;
    interface IFoo2;
    interface IFoo3;
};
```

When tlbimp.exe reads the underlying COM type information, it applies a very simple rule: When building a managed interface, derived interfaces support the members of their base interfaces. For example, the managed version of IFoo3 supports methods C(), B(), and A(). Likewise, the managed version of IFoo2 supports methods B() and A(). If you create an interop assembly for this ATL server and load it into ILDasm.exe, you find what appears in Figure 7-11.

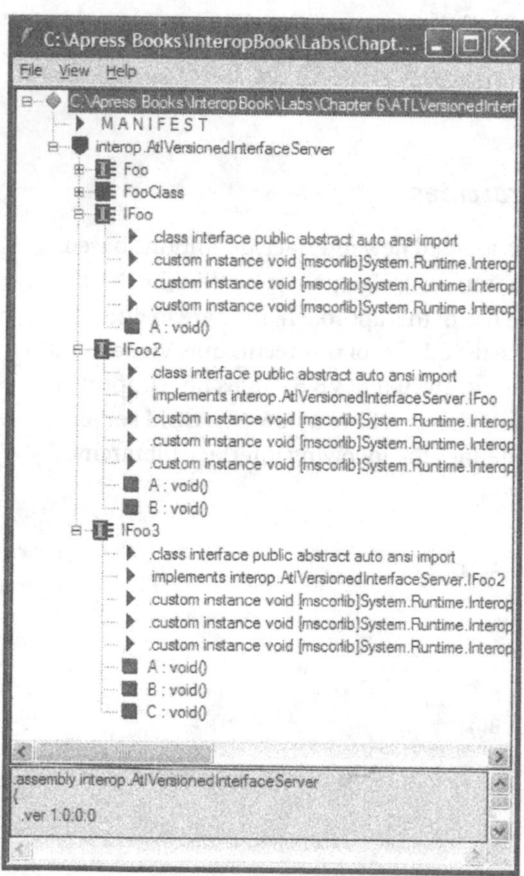

Figure 7-11. Imported COM interface hierarchies

CODE *The ATLVersionedInterfaceServer application is included under the Chapter 7 subdirectory.*

COM Interface Members to .NET Method Conversion Rules

A COM interface may contain any number of methods or the syntactic sugar you know as COM properties (recall that a COM property always maps to a pair of hidden functions). When an unmanaged member (that is, methods and properties) is mapped into a .NET equivalent, things are mostly what you would expect.

Consider the transformation of COM interface methods. Recall that COM interface methods return a standard HRESULT to signal the success or failure of the method invocation. When converting a COM method, the underlying HRESULT is hidden by the RCW. As you may be aware, there are many (many) predefined COM HRESULTs that are used to document the reason for a failure. Later in this text, when you examine COM/.NET error handling, you see how to handle failed HRESULT values within a managed client. For the time being, assume the world is a happy place, and all COM methods return S_OK.

COM properties, however, deserve special mention. Assume that you have created the following property (using VB 6.0):

```
' A simple COM property
' supported by the VB 6.0 PropClass coclass.
Private mName As String

Public Property Get Name() As String
    Name = mName
End Property

Public Property Let Name(ByVal rhs As String)
    mName = rhs
End Property
```

Under the hood, the VB 6.0 compiler generates the following IDL:

```
interface _PropClass : IDispatch
{
    [id(0x68030000), propget]
    HRESULT Name([out, retval] BSTR* );

    [id(0x68030000), propput]
    HRESULT Name([in] BSTR* );
};
```

Once you create an interop assembly, you are able to see (using ILDasm.exe) that [propput] methods are mapped to a hidden method named set_X(), whereas [propget] methods are mapped to a hidden get_X() method. In addition, the property itself is preserved by name. Check out Figure 7-12.

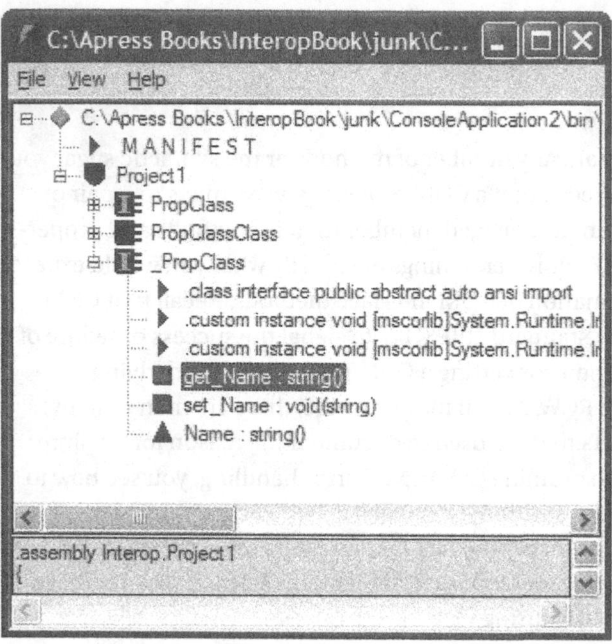

Figure 7-12. Mapping COM properties

The underlying IL for the get_X() and set_X() methods is quite interesting:

```
.method public hidebysig newslot specialname virtual abstract
    instance string  marshal( bstr)
    get_Name() runtime managed internalcall
{
...
} // end of method _PropClass::get_Name

.method public hidebysig newslot specialname virtual abstract
    instance void  set_Name([in] string  marshal( bstr) A_1)
    runtime managed internalcall
{
...
} // end of method _PropClass::set_Name
```

Note that each get_X() and set_X() member is marked using the [internalcall] directive that marks a call to a method implemented within the common language runtime itself. Translated into English, this simply means that [internalcall] methods are not typically called directly by a managed client. This begs the question of how these members are triggered. The answer can be found within the IL describing the managed Name property:

```
.property string Name()
{
...
  .get instance string Project1._PropClass::get_Name()
  .set instance void Project1._PropClass::set_Name(string)
} // end of property _PropClass::Name
```

As you can see, the Name property maintains the name of the [internalcall] member to "hit" based on the calling syntax. The [.get instance] directive is used to document the correct accessor method while [.set instance] marks the corresponding mutator. Given this, ponder the following C# client code:

```
// C# COM property manipulation.
PropClassClass c = new PropClassClass();
// Triggers Project1._PropClass::set_Name(string).
c.Name = "Fred"
// Triggers .get instance string Project1._PropClass::get_Name().
Console.WriteLine(c.Name);
```

So, as you can see, mapping methods and properties to managed equivalents isn't so bad. To spice things up a bit, let's check out parameterized members.

COM Method Parameters to .NET Method Parameters Conversion Rules

As you may recall from the first section of this text, COM parameters take attributes to document the direction of travel between coclass and client. When you create IDL definitions by hand, you have direct control over when parameters receive which attributes. However, when using Visual Basic 6.0, these IDL attributes are assigned behind the scenes when you use the ByVal and ByRef keywords.

While the managed definition of COM IDL parameters is not documented within the interop assembly's metadata, these IDL attributes do configure the calling conventions used by the managed client. C# clients make use of the ref and out keywords, while VB .NET clients use the familiar ByRef and ByVal keywords. For example, if you have the following IDL method definition:

```
// Some interface method.
HRESULT SomeMethod([in] int theIn,
    [out] int* theOut,
    [in, out] int* theInOut,
    [out, retval] int* theReturnValue);
```

Which has been implemented in an ATL coclass as follows:

```
STDMETHODIMP CFoo::SomeMethod(int theIn,
    int *theOut,
    int *theInOut,
    int *theReturnValue)
{
    // Fill [out] and change [in, out].
    *theOut = 100;
    *theInOut = 666;
    *theReturnValue = 777;
    return S_OK;
}
```

A C# client would call the member using the out and ref keywords:

```
FooClass theObj = new FooClass();
int x;    // No need to assign output parameters before use.
int y = 10;
int answer = theObj.SomeMethod(10, out x, ref y);
Console.WriteLine("X = {0}, Y = {1}, Answer = {2}", x, y, answer);
```

The results are seen in Figure 7-13.

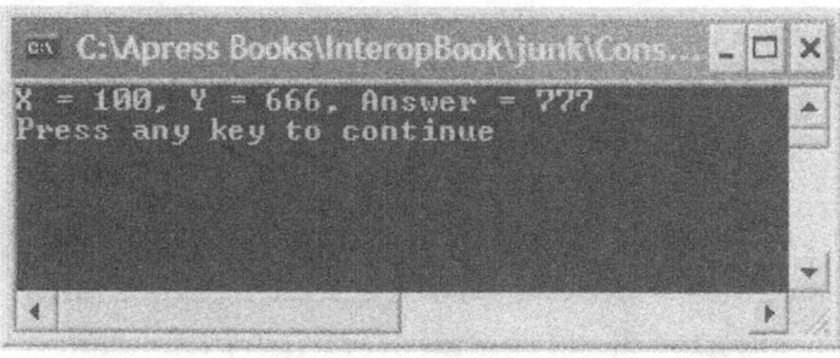

Figure 7-13. Interacting with COM parameters

It is also important to recall that the System.Runtime.InteropServices namespace defines a set of managed attributes that can be used to control how .NET parameters should be exposed to COM (the subject of a later chapter). Table 7-15 illustrates the relationship between these key players:

Table 7-15. Parameter Conversions

COM IDL Parameter Attribute	VB 6.0/VB .NET Keyword	C# Calling Convention	System.Runtime.InteropServices Attribute
[in]	ByVal	No language-specific keyword	InAttribute
[out]	n/a	C# out keyword	OutAttribute
[in, out]	ByRef	C# ref keyword	No managed attribute; simply supply the InAttribute and OutAttribute types on the same parameter.
[out, retval]	Standard VB 6.0 Function return value	IDL [out, retval] parameters are mapped as a physical return value from the function call.	No managed attribute; simply define a function return value.

VB 6.0 Parameter Conversions—An Annoying Aside

Visual Basic 6.0 is perhaps the only modern language in use that defaults parameters as being passed *by reference* rather than by value (in contrast, VB .NET defaults to by value parameter passing). For the sake of argument, if you define the previous Name property as follows:

```
' Note the lack of ByVal in the
' Property Let…
Private mName As String

Public Property Get Name() As String
    Name = mName
End Property

Public Property Let Name(rhs As String)
    mName = rhs
End Property
```

the underlying IDL would represent this COM interface as the following (note the presence of the [in, out] IDL attributes):

```
interface _PropClass : IDispatch
{
    [id(0x68030000), propget]
    HRESULT Name([out, retval] BSTR* );
```

```
    [id(0x68030000), propput]
    HRESULT Name([in, out] BSTR* );
};
```

While this does not seem too problematic, recall that managed clients must call a COM method by adhering to the same directional attributes. For example, although you might assume you could manipulate the Name property in C# as follows:

```
// This is the way the property should work…
PropClass p = new PropClass();
p.Name = "Hello";
Console.WriteLine("Name is: {0}", p.Name);
```

you will be issued some rather frustrating compiler errors such as these:

```
"C:\Apress Books\InteropBook\junk\ConsoleApplication2\
Class1.cs(25): Property, indexer,
or event 'Name' is not supported by the language;
try directly calling accessor methods
'Project1._PropClass.get_Name()' or 'Project1._PropClass.set_Name(ref string)'
```

The reason has to do with the fact that the VB 6.0 property definition has implicitly made use of the ByRef keyword during the construction of the [propput] method. This forces the C# client to directly call the hidden get_Name() and set_Name() methods:

```
// Yuck…
PropClass p = new PropClass();
string name = "Hello";
p.set_Name(ref name);
Console.WriteLine("Name is: {0}", p.get_Name());
```

If you make use of the ByVal keyword as follows:

```
' One more time, using ByVal.
Public Property Let Name(ByVal rhs As String)
    mName = rhs
End Property
```

you are able to call the property as expected. As an interesting corollary, understand that when a property has been correctly configured to make use of the ByVal keyword, the hidden get_X() and set_X() methods are unavailable. If you attempt to reference them within the client's code base, you are issued the following compiler error:

```
C:\Apress Books\InteropBook\junk\ConsoleApplication2\Class1.cs(28):
'Project1._PropClass.Name.set': cannot explicitly call operator or accessor
```

The annoying aspect of this behavior is the fact that you are likely to find many COM servers (written in VB 6.0) that make use of the default ByRef parameter attribute (most likely by accident). Unless you are willing to crack open the code base and apply the ByVal attribute, you may need to trigger the underlying get_X() and set_X() members to interact with the VB 6.0 COM property.

Handling Optional and Default Parameters

COM IDL supports the definition of parameters which are attributed by the [optional] and [defaultvalue] keywords. The semantics of these keywords are just as you would hope. Optional arguments may be omitted by the caller, and optional arguments marked with the [defaultvalue] keyword will make use of a hard-coded value if the item in question is omitted by the caller.

For the most part, optional/default parameters are only realized in the VB 6.0 COM language mapping and are not guaranteed to be honored by other COM-aware programming languages. Given that the current COM server under examination does not have members which support these IDL constructs, assume that you have a brand new VB 6.0 COM server which defines a single coclass (CoOptParams) that populates its [default] interface as so:

```
Public Function AddTwoOrThreeNumbers(ByVal x As Integer, _
ByVal y As Integer, _
Optional ByVal z As Integer) As Integer
    Dim ans As Integer
    ans = x + y
    ' Did they send the optional param?
    If Not IsMissing(x) Then
        ans = ans + z
    End If
    AddTwoOrThreeNumbers = ans
End Function

Public Function AddWithDefaults(Optional ByVal x As Integer = 2, _
Optional ByVal y As Integer = 2) As Integer
    ' No need to check if args
    ' are missing, as we always
    ' have 2+2.
    AddWithDefaults = x + y
End Function
```

The resulting IDL is as so:

```
interface _CoOptParams : IDispatch {
    [id(0x60030000)]
    HRESULT AddTwoOrThreeNumbers(
        [in] short x,
        [in] short y,
        [in, optional] short z,
        [out, retval] short* );
    [id(0x60030001)]
    HRESULT AddWithDefaults(
        [in, optional, defaultvalue(2)] short x,
        [in, optional, defaultvalue(2)] short y,
        [out, retval] short* );
};
```

Now, just as the [optional] and [defaultvalue] keywords are not guaranteed to be honored in every COM-aware programming language, these IDL keywords are not guaranteed to usable in every .NET-aware programming language. While it is true that the Common Type System (CTS) does describe how these programming constructs can be represented in terms of IL and .NET metadata, optional and default parameters are *not* CLS compliant! As you might expect, VB .NET does allow for the use of optional and default arguments, however C# does *not*. Given this fact, if you generate an interop assembly for a COM server which makes use of these IDL keywords, the manner in which you need to programming against theses COM atoms will depend on your choice of managed language.

Assume you have created an interop assembly for the VbOptParamsServer. The generated metadata for the AddTwoOrThreeNumbers() method would look like so (note the [opt] metadata keyword):

```
.method public hidebysig newslot virtual abstract
    instance int16  AddTwoOrThreeNumbers([in] int16 x,
    [in] int16 y, [in][opt] int16 z)
runtime managed internalcall
{
  .custom instance void[mscorlib]System.Runtime.InteropServices.
  DispIdAttribute::.ctor(int32) = ( 01 00 00 00 03 60 00 00 )
  // .....`..
} // end of method _CoOptParams::AddTwoOrThreeNumbers
```

As for the AddWithDefaults() method, notice that the default values of each parameter are hard-coded interop assembly (via the .param tag).

```
.method public hidebysig newslot virtual abstract
    instance int16  AddWithDefaults([in][opt] int16 x,
    [in][opt] int16 y) runtime managed internalcall
```

```
{
  .custom instance void [mscorlib]System.Runtime.InteropServices.
  DispIdAttribute::.ctor(int32) = ( 01 00 01 00 03 60 00 00 )
// .....`..
  .param [1] = int16(0x0002)
  .param [2] = int16(0x0002)
} // end of method _CoOptParams::AddWithDefaults
```

Now, if you were to make use of the CoOptParams COM type using VB .NET, things would look much like a classic VB 6.0 client. Thus, we could write the following:

```
Imports VbOptParamsServer

Module Module1
    Sub Main()
        Dim c As New CoOptParamsClass()
        Dim i As Integer

        ' work with optional params.
        i = c.AddTwoOrThreeNumbers(20, 20)
        Console.WriteLine("20 + 20 is {0}", i)

        i = c.AddTwoOrThreeNumbers(10, 20, 40)
        Console.WriteLine("10 + 20 + 40 is {0}", i)

        ' Work with default params.
        i = c.AddWithDefaults()
        Console.WriteLine("2 + 2 is {0}", i)

        i = c.AddWithDefaults(3)
        Console.WriteLine("3 + 2 is {0}", i)

        i = c.AddWithDefaults(4, 2)
        Console.WriteLine("4 + 2 is {0}", i)
    End Sub
End Module
```

As you can see, VB .NET clients are happy to honor the [defaultvalue] and [optional] IDL keywords. However, if you had a C# client which exercised the exact same coclass, you would *not* be able to work with any of the previous logic other than the following:

```
static void Main(string[] args)
{
    CoOptParamsClass  c = new CoOptParamsClass();
    int i;
```

```
        // Must specify all args in C#.
        i = c.AddTwoOrThreeNumbers(10, 20, 40);
        Console.WriteLine("10 + 20 + 40 is {0}", i);

        // Can't use defaults in C#.
        i = c.AddWithDefaults(4, 2);
        Console.WriteLine("4 + 2 is {0}", i);
}
```

As you can plainly see, C# demands that all optional parameters are accounted for, therefore, all default values are lost. This can be a bit of a bother for the C# developer, especially if the COM server being programmed against makes substantial use of either of these IDL keywords.

The System.Type.Missing Read-Only Field

The last thing to be aware of when programming against the [optional] and [defaultvalue] IDL keywords has to do with the VARIANT type (discussed in greater detail in Chapter 8). Technically speaking, if a C# client attempts to call a COM method which takes an optional VARIANT, they are required to supply an empty System.Object (given that VARIANTs map into System.Object types). Assume we have the following VB 6.0 method definition:

```
' Remember!  C# will always ignore default values,
' VARIANT or not.
Public Sub UseThisOptionalThing(ByVal msg As String, _
Optional ByVal x As Variant = "Again")
        MsgBox msg, , "The message"

        ' Show the thing.
        If Not IsMissing(x) Then
            MsgBox x, , "Optional Variant is:"
        End If
End Sub
```

When a C# client wishes to call a method taking optional VARIANTs, it is still responsible for passing an argument (even though it has been marked as [optional]). However if it were to send in an new instance of System.Object as the second parameter like so:

```
// Optional VARIANT? Nope…
object objMissing = new object();

// Displays "Hello" and then "System.Object"
c.UseThisOptionalThing("Hello", objMissing);
```

you would find that the allocated System.Object is indeed passed to the method as a valid argument. Given this, you will trigger two message boxes, the second of which displays "System.Object". When you want to indicate that you wish to pass in 'nothing' as the optional VARIANT parameter, make use of the Type.Missing field like so:

```
// Optional VARIANTs? Yes!
object objMissing = Type.Missing;

// Only displays "Hello"
c.UseThisOptionalThing("Hello", objMissing);
```

With this syntax, the call will only trigger one message box that displays "Hello". Again, do note that in both cases the [defaultvalue] IDL keyword is ignored.

As you might expect, VB .NET clients can forgo the Type.Missing syntax and simply omit the optional VARIANT parameter just as if it were an optional simple data type (strings, integers, and what not).

CODE *The VbOptParamsServer, VbNetOptParamsClient and CSharpOptParamClient programs are located under the Chapter 7 subdirectory.*

COM Coclass Conversion

As you have seen, tlbimp.exe generates two creatable types for each IDL coclass definition: the "-Class" suffixed type and the default interface class type. Obviously, each type must somehow document the interface(s) that it implements. Not surprisingly, the underlying IL makes use of the [implements] directive. For example, here is the (abbreviated) IL definition for the ComCarClass type:

```
.class public auto ansi import ComCarClass
       extends [mscorlib]System.Object
       implements Intertech.RawComCarLib.ICar,
                  Intertech.RawComCarLib.ComCar,
                  Intertech.RawComCarLib.IRadio
{
    // ClassInterfaceAttribute...
    // GuidAttribute...
    // TypeLibTypeAttribute...
} // end of class ComCarClass
```

Notice that the obvious interfaces, ICar and IRadio, are present and accounted for. However, also notice that the default interface class type interface ComCar is also listed as an implemented interface (explained shortly).

Within the body of the managed class definition are three .NET attributes: ClassInterfaceAttribute, GuidAttirbute, and TypeLibTypeAttribute. The GuidAttribute value maps to the GUID of the IDL [coclass] definition. As seen earlier in this chapter, the ClassInterfaceAttribute and TypeLibTypeAttribute types contain the ComInterfaceType value (of the [default] interface) and the TYPEFLAGS for the coclass.

As for the IL definition for the ComCar entity, you find the following:

```
.class interface public abstract auto ansi import ComCar
       implements Intertech.RawComCarLib.ICar
{
    // GuidAttribute…
    // CoClassAttribute…
} // end of class ComCar
```

Notice that the default interface class types maintain the GUID of the coclass that marks them as a [default] interface via the CoClassAttribute. If you check out the complete listing, you find that the CoClassAttribute also marks the friendly name of the associated coclass:

```
.class interface public abstract auto ansi import ComCar
       implements Intertech.RawComCarLib.ICar
{
 .custom instance void
[mscorlib]System.Runtime.InteropServices.CoClassAttribute::
.ctor(class[mscorlib]System.Type) =
  ( 01 00 22 49 6E 74 65 72 74 65 63 68 2E 52 61 77
43 6F 6D 43 61 72 4C 69 62 2E 43 6F 6D 43 61 72
43 6C 61 73 73 00 00 )
// .."Intertech.RawComCarLib.ComCarClass..
…
}
```

As you might expect, the value of the GuidAttribute is identical to that of the related COM interface definition (IComCar in this case). Given these insights, it should be clear how the following managed code is permissible:

```
// Really creates the ComCarType
// and returns a reference to the
// [default] interface.
ComCar c = new ComCar();
```

Mapping [noncreatable] and [appobject] Coclasses

As you recall from Chapter 4, a COM coclass may be defined as [noncreatable], which prevents the COM type from being created directly by the calling client (a common technique used when building object models). For example:

```
[uuid(752545ED-C4F7-42FB-92A8-F8BF32A61E2F),
helpstring("NoCreate Class"), noncreatable]
coclass NoCreate
{
    [default] interface INoCreate;
};
```

When tlbimp.exe encounters such a COM type, the generated wrapper supports a *private* default constructor. This should make sense, given that the type was never intentionally created. Therefore, the following is illegal:

```
// Can't create [noncreatable] types!
NoCreate wontWork = new NoCreate(); // Error!
```

Also seen in Chapter 4, coclasses may be marked using the [appobject] IDL attribute. When an unmanaged COM wants to make use of an application, it is able to call members of its default interface without needing to directly create an instance of the class type. However, when tlbimp.exe encounters [appobject]-configured COM classes, this attribute is effectively ignored. Managed clients are required to make instances of [appobject] types before calling type members.

One possible workaround to this problem is to create a managed wrapper that exposes the members of the [appobject] coclass through the use of static members. Furthermore, to ensure that the contained coclass is created automatically, you are able to "new" the type using a static constructor. To illustrate, recall that you defined the GlobalObject type in Chapter 4 as follows:

```
interface IGlobalObject : IUnknown
{
    [helpstring("method SomeMethod")] HRESULT SomeMethod();
};
[
    uuid(138B91B9-C70A-49C3-9768-C5202B50E708),
    helpstring("GlobalObject Class"), appobject
]
coclass GlobalObject
{
    [default] interface IGlobalObject;
};
```

If you have a C# application that has set a reference to the defining COM server, you would be able to build the following class, which simulates the IDL [appobject] attribute:

```
public class ManagedGlobalObjectClass
{
    private static GlobalObjectClass theCOMAppObject;
    static ManagedGlobalObjectClass()
    { theCOMAppObject = new GlobalObjectClass();}

    public static void SomeMethod()
    { theCOMAppObject.SomeMethod();}
}
```

With this shim class, the C# application can make use of the underlying [appobject] as follows:

```
// Make use of the [appobject] wrapper.
ManagedGlobalObjectClass.SomeMethod();
```

So, is this a hack? You bet! However, given that tlbimp.exe ignores [appobject] attributed coclasses, if you wish to preserve the semantics of this IDL attribute in terms of managed code, this is about as close as you can get.

Cataloging COM DISPIDs

Cataloging COM DISPIDs might seem to be a slightly out-of-context topic at this point in the text, but hold tight. As you know, when a COM interface wants to be discovered and exercised at runtime, it must be configured as a [dual] or raw dispinterface. In addition, each interface member is marked with a token (termed a DISPID) that uniquely identifies a given member within the coclass implementation. The RawComCar.dll COM server defines the following [dual] interface:

```
[uuid(DBAA0495-2F6A-458a-A74A-129F2C45B642), dual, object]
interface IScriptableCar : IDispatch
{
    [id(1), propput] HRESULT Speed([in] long currSp);
    [id(1), propget] HRESULT Speed([out, retval] long* currSp);
    [id(2)] HRESULT CrankTunes();
};
```

Regardless of the fact that COM DISPIDs are recorded on a per interface level, managed equivalents embed a member's DISPID within the definition of the generated "-Class" type. The managed IL definition of the ScripableCarClass type documents the underlying DISPID of each member of the scriptable COM interface. Consider the IL behind the CrankTunes() member:

```
.method public hidebysig newslot virtual
        instance void CrankTunes() runtime managed internalcall
{
  .custom instance void[mscorlib]
  System.Runtime.InteropServices.DispIdAttribute::
  .ctor(int32) =( 01 00 02 00 00 00 00 00 )
  .override Intertech.RawComCarLib.IScriptableCar::CrankTunes
} // end of method ScriptableCarClass::CrankTunes
```

As you see later in this chapter, when you make use of .NET late-binding to activate a managed COM wrapper, the embedded DISPID value is obtained under the hood to invoke the correct member of the dispinterface.

Additional Coclass to .NET Class Infrastructure

In addition to listing the set of interfaces supported by a given COM type, the tlbimp.exe utility also (a) creates a default constructor for each coclass and (b) derives each coclass from System.Object. Looking at the underlining IL, you find the following [.extends] directive for each "-Class" type:

```
.class public auto ansi import ComCarClass
       extends [mscorlib]System.Object
       implements Intertech.RawComCarLib.ICar,
                  Intertech.RawComCarLib.ComCar,
                  Intertech.RawComCarLib.IRadio
{
  …
} // end of class ComCarClass
```

As all COM wrappers derive from System.Object, you are able to call any of the virtual members. For example:

```
// Trigger inherited System.Object members.
ComCarClass theCar = new ComCarClass();
  ComCarClass otherCar = new ComCarClass();
Console.WriteLine("ToString: {0}", theCar.ToString());
Console.WriteLine("Hash: {0}", theCar.GetHashCode().ToString());
Console.WriteLine("theCar = otherCar? : {0} ", theCar.Equals(otherCar).ToString());
Type t = theCar.GetType();
Console.WriteLine(t.Assembly.FullName);
```

Although I assume the semantics of the virtual Object members are no surprise to you at this point, Table 7-16 documents how these members are realized with regard to RCWs.

Table 7-16. Inherited System.Object Members

Inherited Member of System.Object	Meaning in COM
ToString()	When applied to a COM type, ToString() returns the fully qualified name.
GetHashCode()	As expected, this member returns a hash code for the COM type.
Equals()	Compares two .NET COM wrappers using value-based semantics.
GetType()	Returns a System.Type object that fully describes the underlying COM type.

You examine details of the Type information you can obtain from a RCW wrapper type later in this text. At this point, however, you should feel comfortable understanding how COM coclasses are translated into corresponding .NET types.

Extending COM Types

Classic COM types were unable to be extended using classic is-a inheritance. However, when you have created an interop assembly based on a given COM server, the managed client is able to build new .NET class types that are based on existing COM coclasses. Given the seamless mappings provided by the RCW, it should be clear that when you derive a new .NET class from an existing "-Class" type, you are able to override any supported interface member as well as trigger the base class implementation. To illustrate, assume the following C# class definition:

```
// Derive a new .NET type from the
// managed ComCarClass.
class DotNetCar : ComCarClass
{
    // Override the COM interface method!
    public override void CrankTunes()
    {
        Console.WriteLine("It's .NET from here baby!");
        // Call base class impl.
        base.CrankTunes();
    }
}
```

Here, you have a new .NET class type that derives from the managed ComCarClass type. As you have seen, ComCarClass implements the ICar and IRadio (and the generated ComCar) interfaces. Thus, DotNetCar is free to override the CurrentSpeed(), SpeedUp(), and CrankTunes() methods as necessary (in addition to the virtual members of System.Object). Furthermore, if the derived method wishes to trigger the base class implementation, simply use the correct language-specific keyword (base in C#, MyBase in VB .NET, the scope resolution operator in managed C++, and so on).

When you combine the ability to derive .NET types from COM wrappers as well as implement (and extend!) unmanaged interfaces on .NET types, you are able to achieve an extremely high level of interoperability. By way of simple math, consider the fact that classic COM was realistically supported by four core languages (VB 6.0, C++, Delphi, and J++) and the current state of .NET supports over 30 managed languages under development: Java classes deriving from C++ classes, APL.NET classes implementing interfaces defined in Delphi, PL1.NET classes extending VB 6.0 classes, and so on.

COM Enum Conversion

COM enums are simple entities. They exist to map programming constants to numerical values. The RawComCar.dll type does not define any custom IDL enumerations, so turn your attention to the AtlComCar.dll server created in Chapter 3. Recall the following IDL definition:

```
typedef enum RADIOTYPE
{
   EIGHT_TRACK, CD,
   AM_RADIO, FM_RADIO
} RADIOTYPE;
```

When COM IDL enums are mapped into managed equivalents, the managed type derives from System.Enum. Given this fact, you are able to investigate the underlying type information of a COM enum using any of the static members of System.Enum. For example:

```
// Exercise the enum!
RADIOTYPE rt = RADIOTYPE.AM_RADIO;
string[] names = Enum.GetNames(rt.GetType());
foreach(string s in names)
{
   Console.WriteLine("Name: {0}", s);
}
```

Cool! At this point, you have dug into the details of converting COM type libraries, coclasses, interfaces, members, parameters, and enumerations into managed equivalents. This information will serve as a firm foundation for more advanced issues that you see in the remainder of this text. Next, let's examine the options you have to deploy an interop assembly.

Deploying Interop Assemblies

When you build interop assemblies using VS .NET, you typically receive a private assembly. As you recall from Chapter 5, private assemblies typically do not have a strong name and are certainly not placed into the GAC. When managed clients are using a private interop assembly to communicate with a classic COM server, they are free to make use of an application configuration file to instruct the .NET runtime where to probe during the discovery process. For example, if you create a subdirectory named InteropAsms under the application directory of a given client, you could build the following *.config file:

```
<configuration>
    <runtime>
        <assemblyBinding xmlns="urn:schemas-microsoft-com:asm.v1">
            <probing privatePath="InteropAsms"/>
        </assemblyBinding>
    </runtime>
</configuration>
```

But what if you wish to place a given interop assembly into the GAC to allow any number of managed clients to have access to the wrapped COM types? Given what you already know about shared assemblies (see Chapter 5), you are correct to assume that you will need to generate a *.snk file using the sn.exe utility. When you wish to bind this file into the interop assembly, you must make use of the tlbimp.exe utility and specify the /keyfile: flag. At this point, the interop assembly may be placed into the GAC.

As a simple illustration, assume you have created a brand-new VB 6.0 COM server (LameVbComServer) that contains a single coclass named Hello. Here is the [default] public interface:

```
Public Sub SayHello()
    MsgBox "Hi there"
End Sub
```

Next, assume that you have generated a new *.snk file (named theKey.snk) using sn.exe. To build a strongly named interop assembly, you would issue the following command:

```
C:\ >tlbimp LameVbComServer.dll /out: SharedLameServer.dll /keyfile: thekey.snk
```

If you check out the manifest of the SharedLameServer.dll, you will find that the binary has been configured with a [.publickey] and can thus be installed into the GAC (Figure 7-14).

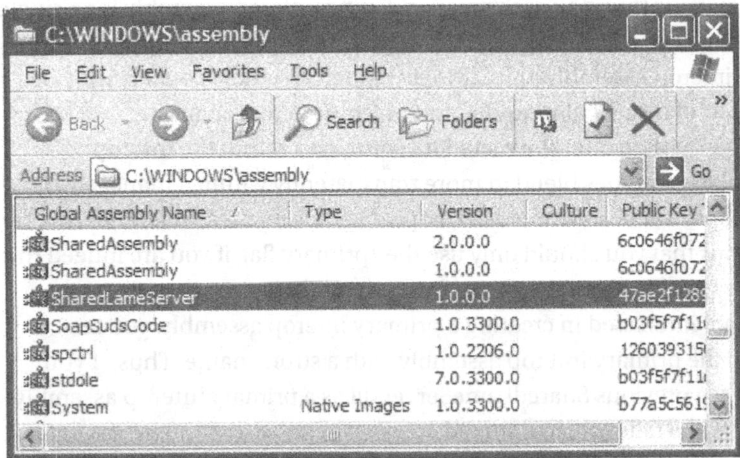

Figure 7-14. A shared interop assembly

At this point, you are able to build any number of managed clients that make use of this shared assembly.

Creating a Primary Interop Assembly

As you have seen, tlbimp.exe allows you to build an interop assembly from any registered COM server. This is typically a good thing. However, assume for a moment that you are in the business of building COM class libraries for purchase by external vendors. Ideally, these vendors trust your work, your company, and (most important) your code. Now assume that you wish to create an "official" interop assembly for each of your legacy COM libraries for use by your client base. While you could simply run tlbimp.exe and ship the .NET binary, you may wish to place your mark on the assembly using the /primary flag.

The /primary flag is used to produce what is known as a *primary interop assembly* for a specified COM type library. When you apply this flag, metadata is added to the interop assembly indicating that the publisher of the COM type library is identical to the publisher of the interop assembly. In this way, you are able to differentiate the official publisher's assembly from any other assemblies that are created from the type library using tlbimp.exe.

Creating a primary interop assembly can be useful for a number of reasons. Perhaps the most practical reason for building an interop assembly is to reduce the possible cluttering of numerous interop assemblies generated from the same COM server. For example, it is possible that numerous developers, departments, and system administrators may each create a distinct interop assembly for a single COM server using tlbimp.exe. However, if you as the component vendor were to ship a primary interop assembly, this strongly named assembly could simply be placed in the GAC of a particular production machine at the client site.

Also, you may wish to alter the metadata contained within the interop assembly to make your types blend in more transparently within a managed environment (this topic will be examined in Chapter 12). Given these scenarios, it should be obvious that you should only use the /primary flag if you are indeed the publisher of the type library of the COM library that is being converted.

When you are interested in creating a primary interop assembly, you are required to sign the primary interop assembly with a strong name. Thus, if you want to rework the previous SharedLameServer.dll as a primary interop assembly, you could specify the following command:

```
tlbimp LameVbComServer.dll
/out: PrimarySharedLameServer.dll
/keyfile: thekey.snk /Primary
```

If you now check the manifest of the PrimarySharedLameServer.dll, you find that the PrimaryInteropAssemblyAttribute type is now documented in the manifest in addition to the ImportedFromTypeLibAttribute and GuidAttribute types:

```
.assembly PrimarySharedLameServer
{
…ImportedFromTypeLibAttribute
… GuidAttribute

  .custom instance void
[mscorlib]System.Runtime.InteropServices.
   PrimaryInteropAssemblyAttribute::.ctor
   (int32, int32) = ( 01 00 01 00 00 00 00 00 00 00 00 00 )

  .publickey = (00 24 00 00 04 80 00 00 94 00 00 00 06 02 00 00
  // .$..
  00 24 00 00 52 53 41 31 00 04 00 00 01 00 01 00   //
  .$..RSA1.......
  91 8F AE D3 2F 1B E6 D5 A8 24 27 46 99 71 67 2C   //
  ..../....$'F.qg,
  0C 23 C0 BD 3D 32 C2 B6 09 35 32 20 A1 DE 86 38   // .#..=2...52
  ...8
  26 56 BB DF B2 71 CA CE 0C 88 56 CD F8 DB 5F C8   //
  &V...q....V..._.
```

```
  4E 2E 7A 64 0B A6 0F 10 FA 91 83 48 5C 08 F2 98   //
  N.zd.......H\...
  BB C1 9B 62 AE ED 54 22 BA 47 30 B1 CC 4F 2A 1A   //
  ...b..T".G0..O*.
  A3 73 A1 DA E3 F3 41 C5 72 5B CB 63 AF 2A 03 8B   //
 .s....A.r[.c.*..
 02 02 21 77 7E 8C F8 99 08 61 BF B5 82 98 5A 99   //
 ..!w~....a....Z.
 DE 46 84 2B EA 2E 44 43 02 0B E9 60 AD 33 B0 C8 ) //
 .F.+..DC...`.3..
 .hash algorithm 0x00008004
 .ver 1:0:0:0
}
```

Once this .NET interop assembly has been tagged with the PrimaryInteropAssembly attribute, the client is able to set references to this binary as usual (using the .NET tab of the Add Reference dialog box). However, as an optional step, primary interop assemblies can be further configured on a given machine to ease the development process. As you will see beginning in Chapter 10, the .NET SDK ships with a tool named regasm.exe. Typically, this tool is used to configure a .NET assembly to be accessible from a classic COM client. In addition to this functionality, this same tool can be used to "register" a primary interop assembly. To see the end result, assume you have entered the following command:

```
Regasm PrimarySharedLameServer.dll
```

Once you register a primary interop assembly, the system registry is updated with a value under HKCR\TypeLib\{<your LIBID>}, which records a value that documents the fully qualified name of your assembly (Figure 7-15).

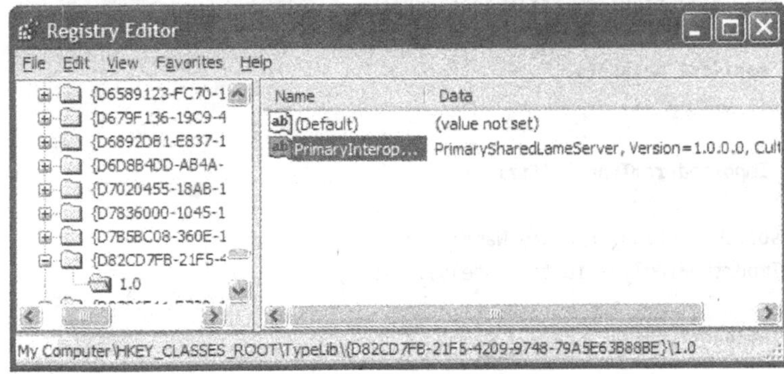

Figure 7-15. Registered primary interop assemblies are cataloged under HKCR\TypeLib.

Because the primary interop assembly is cataloged in the system registry, when tools such as Visual Studio .NET are told to add a reference to a given .NET interop assembly, they will automatically consult the registry to see if there is a valid primary interop assembly to use. If this is the case, VS .NET will not generate a new interop assembly. Assuming the primary interop assembly has been installed into the GAC, clients can rest assured that they are interacting with the "official" interop binary.

Reflecting on Interop Assembly Attributes

As you have seen over the course of this chapter, when an interop assembly is generated using tlbimp.exe, the assembly's metadata is colored by numerous members of the System.Runtime.InteropServices namespace. Given that these attributes are nothing more than standard .NET types, you can make use of reflection services to scrape out their values at runtime.

For example, assume you wish to load an interop assembly from the GAC and determine if it has been configured as a primary interop assembly. In addition, what if you wish to extract the values of the GuidAttribute and ImportedFromTypeLibAttribute type? The following code does the trick:

```
static void Main(string[] args)
{
    // Load the assembly from the GAC and see if it is
    // a primary interop assembly.
    string strongName = "PrimarySharedLameServer,";
    strongName += @"PublicKeyToken=47ae2f12896460f7,
    Version=1.0.0.0";

    // Load from GAC.
    Assembly asm = Assembly.LoadWithPartialName(strongName);
    object[] atts = asm.GetCustomAttributes(true);

    // Dump out manifest metadata.
    foreach(object o in atts)
    {
        if(o is ImportedFromTypeLibAttribute)
        {
            Console.WriteLine("Library Name: {0}",
             ((ImportedFromTypeLibAttribute)o).Value);
        }
        if(o is GuidAttribute)
        {
            Console.WriteLine("LIBID: {0}",
                ((GuidAttribute)o).Value);
        }
        if(o is PrimaryInteropAssemblyAttribute)
        {
```

```
            Console.WriteLine
           ("This is a primary interop assembly!");
            Console.WriteLine("COM Major {0}\nCOM Minor {1}",
                ((PrimaryInteropAssemblyAttribute)o).MajorVersion,
                ((PrimaryInteropAssemblyAttribute)o).MinorVersion);
        }
    }
}
```

Of course, you can also make use of .NET reflection services to read out attributes for a managed interface, class, method, or parameter. For example, if you wish to read metadata that describes the TYPEFLAGS value (see Chapter 4) and CLSID for the HelloClass type, the process would appear as follows:

```
// Get attributes for HelloClass type.
Type t = asm.GetType("PrimarySharedLameServer.HelloClass");
object[] moreAtts = t.GetCustomAttributes(true);
foreach(object o in moreAtts)
{
    // Get TYPEFLAGS for HelloClass.
    if(o is TypeLibTypeAttribute)
    {
        Console.WriteLine("TYPEFLAGS: " +
            ((TypeLibTypeAttribute)o).Value);
    }
    if(o is GuidAttribute)
    {
        Console.WriteLine("CLSID: " +
            ((GuidAttribute)o).Value);
    }
}
```

And just for good measure, read out the attributes that describe the SayHello() method (the DISPID in this case):

```
// Get attributes for SayHello method.
object[] evenMoreAtts = mi.GetCustomAttributes(true);
Console.WriteLine("\n***** SayHello metadata *****\n");
foreach(object o in evenMoreAtts)
{
    if(o is DispIdAttribute)
    {
        Console.WriteLine("DISPID of SayHello: {0}",
            ((DispIdAttribute)o).Value);
    }
}
```

The final output can be seen in Figure 7-16.

Figure 7-16. Reflecting on interop assembly metadata

Obtaining Type Information for a COM Wrapper Type

Needless to say, all managed COM wrappers can return type information using the inherited System.Object.GetType() method. To illustrate, ponder the following code:

```
// Get type information for HelloClass.
Console.WriteLine("***** HelloClass type info *****\n");
Type helloTypeInfo = Type.GetType("PrimarySharedLameServer.HelloClass");
Console.WriteLine("Base type {0}", t.BaseType);
Console.WriteLine("GUID {0}", t.GUID);
Console.WriteLine("COM Object? {0}", t.IsCOMObject);
Console.WriteLine("Defining Namespace {0}", t.Namespace);
```

Of course, you can invoke any member of the Type class (see Chapter 6 for further details). Figure 7-17 shows the output of the previous code block.

Figure 7-17. Reading type information for a COM wrapper

The Role of System.__ComObject

Take a closer look at Figure 7-17. As you can see, the base class of the HelloClass wrapper is a hidden, inaccessible, and undocumented type named System.__ComObject. This class is the direct base class of any COM interop wrapper type. The formal definition is as follows:

```
public class __ComObject : MarshalByRefObject
{ .
    public virtual System.Runtime.Remoting.ObjRef
        CreateObjRef(Type requestedType);
    public virtual bool Equals(object obj);
    public virtual int GetHashCode();
    public virtual object GetLifetimeService();
    public Type GetType();
    public virtual object InitializeLifetimeService();
    public virtual string ToString();
}
```

The key role of __ComObject is to ensure that all COM types are marshaled across process boundaries using by reference passing semantics (thus the derivation from MarshalByRefObject). In addition to this aspect, __ComObject overrides the virtual members of System.Object to behave appropriately for a COM wrapper type. Again, for the most part you can forget about the fact that COM wrapper types derive from __ComObject and simply assume the logical parent type is System.Object.

CODE *The LameVbComServer and InteropAsmAttrReader applications are located under the Chapter 7 subdirectory.*

Interacting with Well-Known COM Servers

As mentioned at the opening of this chapter, the process of accessing custom COM servers from managed code is identical to the process of interacting with well-known COM types. Thus, to wrap up this chapter, let's check out the process of making use of an existing (and quite well-known) COM object library: Microsoft Active Data Objects (classic ADO). ADO is a COM object model that allows programmers to connect to a wide variety of database management systems using a small handful of coclasses. Although this is not the place to drill through the full details of ADO, I can most certainly address the process of using this COM server from managed code. If you wish to follow along, create a new C# Windows Forms application and set a reference (via the COM tab of the Add References dialog box) to classic ADO (Figure 7-18).

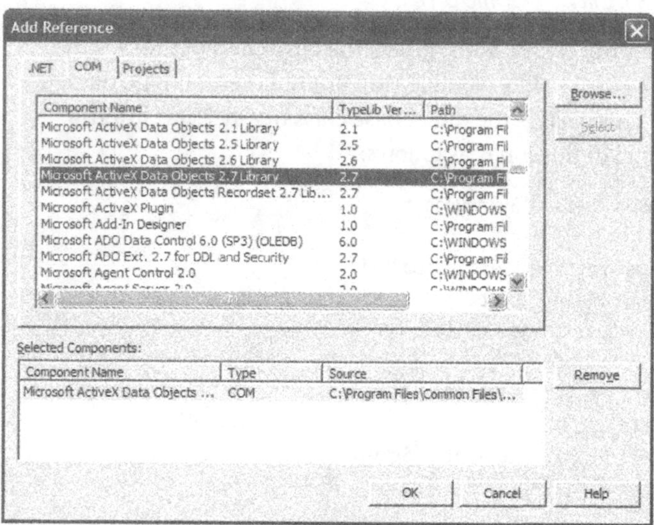

Figure 7-18. Accessing ADO from a managed application

Assume you have placed a Windows Forms DataGrid type on the main Form using the design-time editor. The goal is to open a connection to your local machine and read out the records from the Authors table of the Pubs database. As you may already know, the ADO Connection type is used to represent a given session with a given DBMS, while the ADO Recordset is used to contain the results of a given SQL query. To read back all of the values in the Authors table, you could begin with the following logic (contained within the Form's Load event handler):

```
private void mainForm_Load(object sender, System.EventArgs e)
{
   // First make use of an ADO Connection type.
   ConnectionClass cn = new ConnectionClass();
   cn.Open(
   "Provider=SQLOLEDB.1;data source=.;initial catalog=pubs;",
     "sa", "", -1);

   // Now make use of an ADO Recordset.
   RecordsetClass rs = new RecordsetClass();
   rs.Open("Authors", cn, CursorTypeEnum.adOpenKeyset,
      LockTypeEnum.adLockOptimistic, -1);
}
```

Assuming the previous code has executed without error, you now have a Recordset filled with all of the entries of the Authors table. At this point, you can make use of the Recordset's Fields collection to iterate over each entry. Ideally, you would like to bind directly this Recordset to Windows Forms DataGrid type using the DataSouce property:

```
// Sorry, nice try through!
theDataGrid.DataSouce = rs;
```

As you can tell from the code comment, this is not permitted. Even though a .NET DataGrid type does not know how to bind directly to an ADO Recordset, it is equipped to bind to an ADO.NET System.Data.DataTable type. The trick, therefore, is to build a DataTable type that is constructed using the records contained in the ADO Recordset. The following logic will do the trick:

```
private void mainForm_Load(object sender, System.EventArgs e)
{
    // Same ADO logic as before...

    // Using the recordset, construct a DataTable
    // which will be bound to the DataGrid widget.
    DataTable theTable = new DataTable();

    // Fill in column names.
    for(int i = 0; i < rs.Fields.Count; i++)
      theTable.Columns.Add(new DataColumn(
         rs.Fields[i].Name, typeof(string)));

    // Fill in rows.
    while(!rs.EOF)
    {
        DataRow currRow;
        currRow = theTable.NewRow();
        for(int i = 0; i < rs.Fields.Count; i++)
            currRow[i] = rs.Fields[i].Value.ToString();
        theTable.Rows.Add(currRow);
        rs.MoveNext();
    }

    // Now bind to the DataGrid.
    theDataGrid.DataSource = theTable;

    // Close up ADO.
    rs.Close();
    cn.Close();
}
```

Once you have filled the DataTable type with the data contained within the classic ADO Recordset, you are able to see the data grid shown in Figure 7-19 upon running the application.

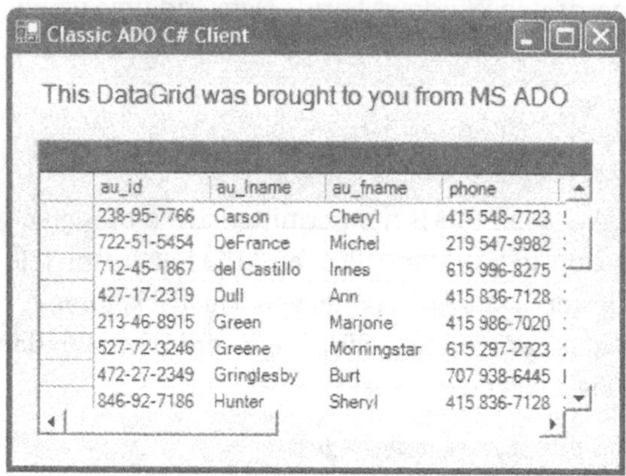

Figure 7-19. Interacting with msado15.dll using managed code

CODE *The CSharpUsingClassicADO application is located under the Chapter 7 subdirectory.*

Summary

This chapter presented the core .NET-to-COM interoperability issues you are likely to encounter on a day-to-day basis. The RCW is a .NET proxy class that is responsible for mapping .NET data types into COM IDL, returning values from a COM method invocation, and concealing a number of low-level COM interfaces from view. In a nutshell, the RCW exists to fool a managed client into thinking it is communicating with a standard .NET type rather than a legacy COM type.

As you have seen, the tlbimp.exe utility is the key to creating an interop assembly based on COM type information. While using tlbimp.exe in the raw is critical in some circumstances (building a primary interop assembly, configuring a shared assembly, and so forth), VS .NET automates the process using the Add Reference dialog box. Regardless of the tool you use to build an interop assembly, the resulting binary will contain numerous attributes defined in the System.Runtime.InteropServices namespace to document the information found in the original COM type library.

Now that you have a solid basis, Chapter 8 drills into further details of the .NET-to-COM communication process.

CHAPTER 8

.NET-to-COM Interoperability—Intermediate Topics

In the previous chapter you examined the core aspects of COM-to-.NET type conversions (data types, parameters, interfaces, coclasses, and whatnot). This chapter builds upon your current foundation by examining how a number of more exotic COM patterns are realized in terms of managed code. In addition to addressing the topics of handling COM VARIANTs, structures, and SAFEARRAYs, you also learn how to interact with custom COM collections, HRESULTs, and COM error objects. I wrap up this chapter by examining how COM connection points are mapped into the .NET delegate architecture and address the issue of debugging COM servers within Visual Studio .NET. If you like, consider this chapter a potpourri of useful .NET-to-COM interoperability tidbits.

Handling the COM VARIANT

The COM VARIANT data type is one of the most useful (and most hated) constructs of classic COM. The VARIANT structure is useful in that it is able to assume the identity of any [oleautomation]-compliant IDL type, which may be reassigned after the initial declaration. VARIANTs are hated for much the same reason, given that these dynamic transformations take time. Nevertheless, you are bound to run into a coclass that makes use of this type, and you would do well to understand how it maps into terms of .NET.

As you recall from Chapter 2, the VARIANT structure maintains a field (vt) that identifies the underlying [oleautomation] data type as well as a union representing the values of each possibility (bstrVal, lVal, and so forth). In VB 6.0 these details are hidden from view using the intrinsic Variant data type:

```
' vt field and corresponding value field set automatically.
Dim v as Variant
v = "I am a BSTR"
v = True
v = 43.444
Set v = New SomeCoClass
```

In raw C++, you are forced to establish this information manually:

```
// Make a VARIANT a la C++.
VARIANT v;
VariantInit(&v);
v.vt = VT_BSTR;
v.bstrVal = SysAllocString(L"I am also a BSTR");
```

Under .NET, a COM VARIANT can be generically represented as a System.Object data type. However, if you make use of a strongly typed data type (System.String, System.Byte, and so on), the RCW will set the vt and value fields automatically (much like the behavior of VB 6.0). Table 8-1 documents the relationship between intrinsic .NET types and the underlying VARIANT VT_XXX flag.

Table 8-1 .NET Data Types Used to Set the vt Field of COM VARIANTs

Type Assigned to System.Object Variable	Raw COM VARIANT VT_XXX Flag (Assigned to the vt Field)
Null object reference.	VT_EMPTY
System.DBNull	VT_NULL
ErrorWrapper	VT_ERROR
System.Reflection.Missing	VT_ERROR
DispatchWrapper	VT_DISPATCH
UnknownWrapper	VT_UNKNOWN
CurrencyWrapper	VT_CY
System.Boolean	VT_BOOL
System.SByte	VT_I1
System.Byte	VT_UI1
System.Int16	VT_I2
System.UInt16	VT_UI2
System.Int32	VT_I4
System.UInt32	VT_UI4
System.Int64	VT_I8
System.UInt64	VT_UI8
System.Single	VT_R4
System.Double	VT_R8
System.Decimal	VT_DECIMAL
System.DateTime	VT_DATE
System.String	VT_BSTR
System.IntPtr	VT_INT
System.UIntPtr	VT_UINT
System.Array	VT_ARRAY

Do understand that when you create and manipulate a System.Object data type exclusively using managed code, the object variable type does *not* contain VARIANT-centric information. The correct VARIANT flag is set only by the RCW when marshaling System.Object variables between managed and unmanaged code.

Building a VARIANT-Centric COM Server

To illustrate the interplay between the .NET System.Object type and the COM VARIANT, assume you have created a VB 6.0 COM DLL named VbVariantServer. This COM server contains a single coclass (VariantObj) that defines the following initial method (note that the VB line-feed constant, vbLf, maps into the C# "\n" string token):

```
' This function takes a VARIANT and returns
' a string describing the underlying structure.
Public Function CheckThisVariant(ByVal v As Variant) As String
    Dim s As String
    s = "Type name: " + TypeName(v) + vbLf + _
        "Value: " + CStr(VarType(v))
    CheckThisVariant = s
End Function
```

The role of CheckThisVariant() is to return a string that documents the name of an incoming VARIANT data type. As you might guess, the VB 6.0 TypeName() function checks the underlying VT_XXX flag on your behalf and maps the numerical value to a textual equivalent (for example, VT_BSTR becomes "String"). Also note that CheckThisVariant() embeds the numerical value of the VT_XXX flag as part of the return value using the VB 6.0 VarType() method.

Another common use of the VARIANT is to simulate overloaded methods in COM. As you know, managed languages such as C# and VB .NET (as well as most modern day OO languages) allow class types to define numerous versions of a single method, as long as the number or type of parameters is unique for each version. Classic COM, however, does not support overloaded members on interface types. To circumvent this limitation, it is possible to create a single function that takes some set of VARIANT data types. Given that a VARIANT can contain any [oleautomation]-compatible data type, you have effectively provided a way for the caller to pass in varying data types! This being said, let's add another member to the default interface of VariantObj:

```
' Add two VARIANTs (if they are the same type and
' are not interfaces, structs, arrays, or data access objects).
Public Function AddTheseVariants(ByVal v1 As Variant, _
  ByVal v2 As Variant) As Variant
    Dim answer As Variant

    If (VarType(v1) = VarType(v2) _
      And (VarType(v1) <> vbObject _
      And VarType(v1) <> vbUserDefinedType _
      And VarType(v1) <> vbDataObject _
      And IsArray(v1) = False) Then
            answer = v1 + v2
    Else
        answer = "Bad data!"
    End If

    AddTheseVariants = answer
End Function
```

AddTheseVariants() does just what it says. Given two identical variant types (thus the initial VarType() logic), as long as the underlying VARIANT type is not an interface reference, COM structure, or SAFEARRAY, you return the summation of the types. Although you certainly could retrofit this function to handle adding these sorts of COM types (provided it made sense to do so), here you will focus on returning the sum of more generic data points (numerical and string data).

Once you compile this VB COM server, you can use oleview.exe to examine the generated COM type information. The IDL definition is as you would expect:

```
interface _VariantObj : IDispatch
{
    [id(0x60030000)]
    HRESULT CheckThisVariant([in] VARIANT v,
        [out, retval] BSTR* );
    [id(0x60030001)]
    HRESULT AddTheseVariants([in] VARIANT v1,
        [in] VARIANT v2, [out, retval] VARIANT* );
};
```

CODE *The VbVariantServer project is included under the Chapter 8 subdirectory.*

Exercising COM VARIANTs from Managed Code

Say you have created a new C# console application and have set a reference to the VbVariantServer.dll COM server. If you open the integrated object browser and view the definitions of the managed members, you will indeed see that each COM VARIANT has been mapped into a System.Object (Figure 8-1).

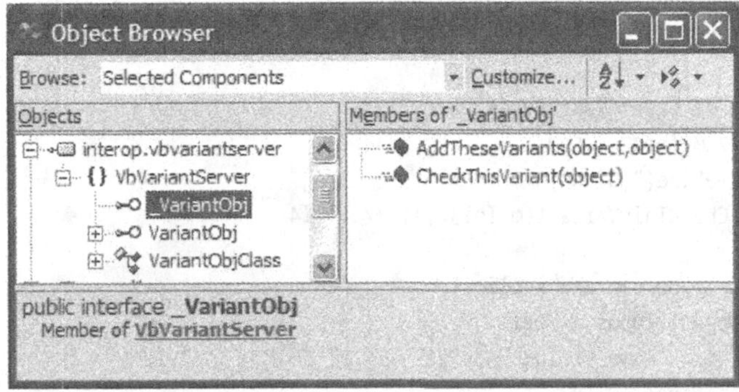

Figure 8-1. COM VARIANTs map to System.Object

First, let's exercise the CheckThisVariant() method. Given that everything "is-a" object under the .NET architecture, you are free to pass in intrinsic C# data types, the equivalent base type alias, or a direct System.Object. For example.

```
using System;
using VbVariantServer;

namespace CSharpVariantClient
{
    class VariantClient
    {
        [STAThread]
        static void Main(string[] args)
        {
            // Fun with VARIANTs.
            VariantObjClass varObj = new VariantObjClass();

            // Make use of implicit data types.
            Console.WriteLine("{0}\n",
                varObj.CheckThisVariant("Hello"));  // VT_BSTR
            Console.WriteLine("{0}\n",
                varObj.CheckThisVariant(20));       // VT_I4
            Console.WriteLine("{0}\n",
```

```
            varObj.CheckThisVariant(999999)); // VT_I4
        Console.WriteLine("{0}\n",
            varObj.CheckThisVariant(true));     // VT_BOOL
        Console.WriteLine("{0}\n",
            varObj.CheckThisVariant(9.876));    // VT_R8

        int[] theStuff = {12,22,33};
        // VT_ARRAY | VT_I4
        Console.WriteLine("{0}\n",
            varObj.CheckThisVariant(theStuff));

        // Make use of base class types.
        System.Int32 myInt32 = 500;
        Console.WriteLine("{0}\n",
            varObj.CheckThisVariant(myInt32)); // VT_I4

        // Of course, you can use explicit
        // System.Object types as well.
        object theObj = "Some string data";     // VT_BSTR
        Console.WriteLine("{0}\n",
            varObj.CheckThisVariant(theObj));
    }
}
```

The bulk of this code makes use of implicit data types (meaning 20 rather than an explicit int data type). Given that raw numerical values always map to System.Int32 and floating-point numbers always map to System.Double, you are free to cast the raw data as required. For example, to force the underlying VT_XXX flag to be set to VT_I2 you could write:

```
// Cast if necessary...
Console.WriteLine("{0}\n",
    varObj.CheckThisVariant((byte)5));    // VT_I2
```

The process of calling AddTheseVariants() is more or less identical. Note in the following code block that I am attempting to pass in two managed arrays (which are mapped into a COM SAFEARRAY) to AddTheseVariants(). Recall that the implementation of this method explicitly tests for the VT_ARRAY bit flag, and if found, returns a textual error message.

```
// Add some variants.
Console.WriteLine("Summation: {0}",
    varObj.AddTheseVariants("Hello", "There"));
Console.WriteLine("Summation: {0}",
    varObj.AddTheseVariants(4, 4));
Console.WriteLine("Summation: {0}",
    varObj.AddTheseVariants(54.33, 98.3));

// Remember your truth tables!
// True + False = False (-1).
Console.WriteLine("Summation: {0}",
    varObj.AddTheseVariants(false, true));

// This will not be processed by the coclass!
// (theStuff is an array of ints declared previously…)
Console.WriteLine("Summation: {0}",
    varObj.AddTheseVariants(theStuff, theStuff));
```

The VARIANT Wrappers

The System.Runtime.InteropServices namespace defines four types used to handle VARIANTs that are not explicitly represented by managed code (VT_ERROR, VT_DISPATCH, VT_UNKNOWN, and VT_CY). ErrorWrapper, DispatchWrapper, UnknownWrapper, and CurrencyWrapper allow you to control how a managed type should be marshaled via System.Object. You will learn how to pass IUnknown- and IDispatch-derived types in Chapter 9. However, by way of example, assume you wish to pass an unmanaged type as a COM CURRENCY type. Given that the .NET libraries do not support this type, you are free to use CurrencyWrapper as follows (recall that under .NET, the Currency type has been replaced with System.Decimal):

```
// Pass a value as a VARIANT of type VT_CURRENCY.
Console.WriteLine("{0}\n",
    varObj.CheckThisVariant(new CurrencyWrapper(new Decimal(75.25))));
```

The output of your C# console application can be seen in Figure 8-2.

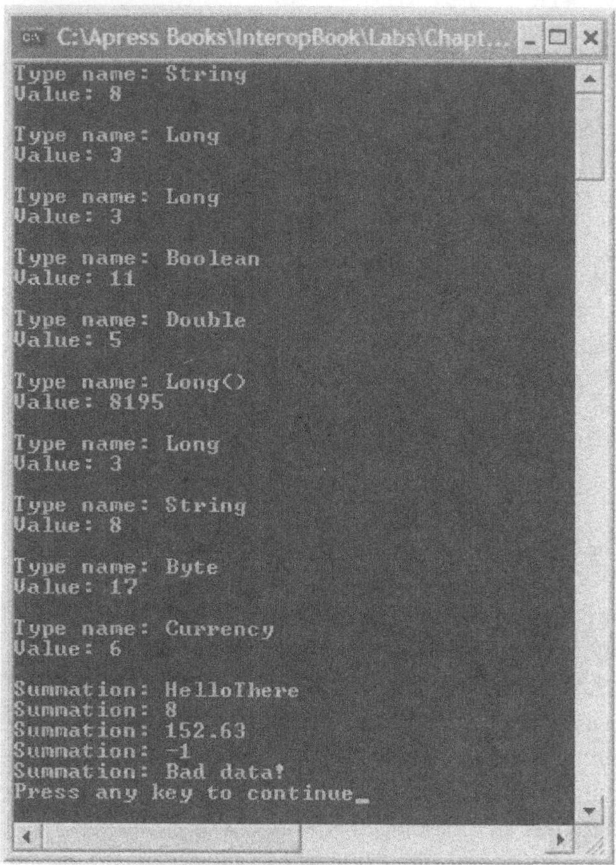

C:\Apress Books\InteropBook\Labs\Chapt...
Type name: String
Value: 8
Type name: Long
Value: 3
Type name: Long
Value: 3
Type name: Boolean
Value: 11
Type name: Double
Value: 5
Type name: Long()
Value: 8195
Type name: Long
Value: 3
Type name: String
Value: 8
Type name: Byte
Value: 17
Type name: Currency
Value: 6
Summation: HelloThere
Summation: 8
Summation: 152.63
Summation: -1
Summation: Bad data!
Press any key to continue

Figure 8-2. Interacting with VariantObj

CODE *The CSharpVariantClient project is included under the Chapter 8 directory.*

Handling COM SafeArrays

COM interfaces can most certainly contain parameters that represent an array of types. As you have already seen in Chapter 4, the ideal manner to represent arrays in COM is using the SAFEARRAY structure (as opposed to C-style arrays). Recall that a COM SAFEARRAY is a self-describing type that includes not only the underlying data, but also other important bits of information such as the upper and lower bounds of each dimension.

As you also have seen in Chapter 4, working with a COM SAFEARRAY using C++ is a bit on the verbose side. Therefore, let's say you have created a new ActiveX DLL workspace (VbSafeArrayServer) using Visual Basic 6.0 that contains a single coclass named SafeArrayObj. The default interface (_SafeArrayObj) defines the following array-centric members:

```
' This method receives an array of Strings.
Public Sub SendMeAnArrayOfStrings(strs() As String)
    Dim upperBound As Integer
    upperBound = UBound(strs)

    Dim strStats As String
    ' +1 to account for zero.
    strStats = "You gave me " & (upperBound + 1) _
        & " Strings" & vbLf

    Dim i As Integer
    For i = 0 To upperBound
        strStats = strStats + "-> " & strs(i) & vbLf
    Next
    MsgBox strStats, , "Client supplied strings"
End Sub

' This method returns an array of 10 Integers.
Public Function GiveMeAnArrayOfInts() As Integer()
    Dim intArray(9) As Integer
    Dim i As Integer
    For i = 0 To 9
        intArray(i) = i * 100
    Next
    GiveMeAnArrayOfInts = intArray
End Function
```

As you can see, these first two methods simply receive and return arrays of varying types (Strings and Integers). To make things a bit more interesting, let's also assume that this same project defines an additional coclass named TestObject. Here is the formal definition of the TestObject class:

```
' The simple TestObject.cls definition.
Private strData As String

Public Property Let StringData(ByVal s As String)
    strData = s
End Property
Public Property Get StringData() As String
    StringData = strData
End Property
```

Now, let's add two new methods to the _SafeArrayObj interface that make use of this type:

```
' This method returns an array of VARIANTS,
' one of which is a _TestObject interface.
Public Function GiveMeAnArrayOfVariants() As Variant()
    Dim variantArray(4) As Variant
    variantArray(0) = "String data"
    variantArray(1) = True
    variantArray(2) = 23.4
    Set variantArray(3) = New TestObject
    variantArray(3).StringData = "Hey buddy!  You found me!"
    variantArray(4) = 8
    GiveMeAnArrayOfVariants = variantArray
End Function

' This method returns an array of _TestObject interfaces.
Public Function GiveMeAnArrayOfCoClasses() As TestObject()
    Dim objArray(4) As TestObject
    Set objArray(0) = New TestObject
    Set objArray(1) = New TestObject
    Set objArray(2) = New TestObject
    Set objArray(3) = New TestObject
    Set objArray(4) = New TestObject

    ' Set state of each object.
    objArray(0).StringData = "Hello"
    objArray(1).StringData = "there"
    objArray(2).StringData = "from"
    objArray(3).StringData = "VB"
    objArray(4).StringData = "6.0!"
    GiveMeAnArrayOfCoClasses = objArray
End Function
```

Once you compile this COM server, you will be able to view the following IDL definition (using oleview.exe, of course):

```
// IDL definition of the _SafeArrayObj interface.
interface _SafeArrayObj : IDispatch
{
    [id(0x60030000)] HRESULT
    SendMeAnArrayOfStrings([in, out]SAFEARRAY(BSTR)* strs);
    [id(0x60030001)] HRESULT
    GiveMeAnArrayOfInts([out, retval]SAFEARRAY(short)* );
    [id(0x60030002)] HRESULT
    GiveMeAnArrayOfVariants([out, retval]SAFEARRAY(VARIANT)* );
    [id(0x60030003)] HRESULT
    GiveMeAnArrayOfCoClasses([out, retval]SAFEARRAY(_TestObject*)* );
};
```

You can see here that VB 6.0 always represents arrays of types as a COM SAFEARRAY, which you recall is defined in IDL using the SAFEARRAY(<type>) syntax.

CODE *The VbSafeArray project is located under the COM Servers\VBArrayServer subdirectory.*

Exercising COM SAFEARRAYs from Managed Code

If you create a new C# console application (CSharpSafeArrayClient) and set a reference to VbSafeArrayServer.dll, you will find that each of the SAFEARRAY types (parameters and return values) have been mapped to a System.Array reference (Figure 8-3).

It is important to note that the .NET System.Array class defines a number of instance-level and class-level members that make the process of sorting, reversing, and altering array data painfully simple (in stark contrast to the dozens of C++ SAFEARRAY API functions). Table 8-2 lists some of the more interesting members of System.Array.

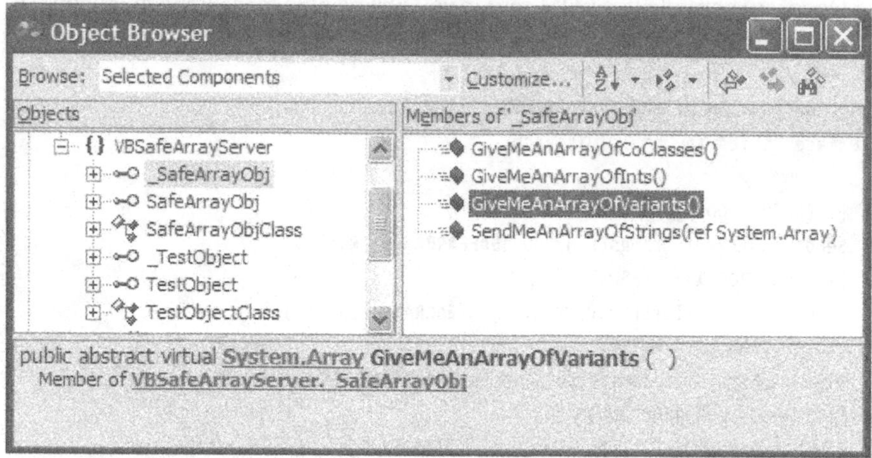

Figure 8-3. COM SAFEARRAYs map to System.Array

Table 8-2. A (Very) Partial List of the Members of System.Array

Select Member of System.Array	**Meaning in Life**
Array.Clear()	This static member cleans out the contents of the array.
Array.CreateInstance()	This static member creates a new instance of System.Array.
Array.Reverse()	This static member reverses the items in the array.
Array.Sort()	This static member sorts items alphabetically or numerically (based on data type). If the array contains object-implementing IComparable, the type is sorted according the defined semantics.
GetLength() Length	These members return the length of the array.
GetLowerBound() GetUpperBound()	As you would expect, these members return the bounds of the array.
GetValue() SetValue()	These members get or set a value in the array.

When you wish to pass an array into an unmanaged COM object, you may use one of two approaches. First, you may create a new instance of System.Array using the static CreateInstance() method and populate the type using the instance level SetValue() method:

```
static void Main(string[] args)
{
    // Interact with the SAFEARRAY functions.
    SafeArrayObjClass saObj = new SafeArrayObjClass();

    // Send in strings (take one).
    Array strData = Array.CreateInstance(typeof(string), 4);
    strData.SetValue("Hello", 0);
    strData.SetValue("there", 1);
    strData.SetValue("from", 2);
    strData.SetValue("C#!", 3);
    saObj.SendMeAnArrayOfStrings(ref strData);
...
}
```

Although this is a valid approach, you are more likely to make use of the array syntax of your language of choice. Do note, however, that COM methods requiring a SAFEARRAY expect to be passed in a strongly typed System.Array, not the language-specific shorthand. This being said, ponder the following functionally equivalent code:

```
// Send in strings (take two).
Console.WriteLine("Calling SafeArrayObjClass.SendMeAnArrayOfStrings()");
string[] theStringData = {"Hello", "there", "from", "C#!"};
Array temp = theStringData;
saObj.SendMeAnArrayOfStrings(ref temp);
```

Here, you begin by creating a managed string array using the familiar C# [] syntax. The critical step is to assign this array to a System.Array object variable *before* passing it into the interop assembly for transformation. If you attempt to write either of the following:

```
// Bad!  Compile time errors.
string[] moreStrs = {"too", "bad", "this", "bombs..."};
saObj.SendMeAnArrayOfStrings(ref moreStrs);
saObj.SendMeAnArrayOfStrings(ref (System.Array)moreStrs);
```

you will be presented with a handful of compile time errors. However, when you send in a System.Array type, you are presented with the appropriate message box (Figure 8-4).

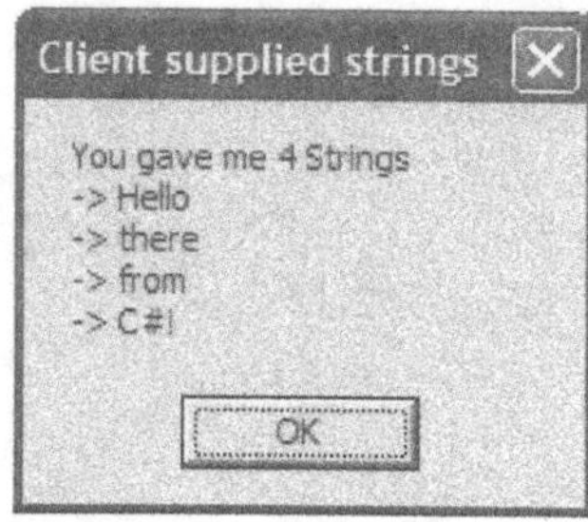

Figure 8-4. SendMeAnArryOfStrings() output

Receiving SAFEARRAYs

Recall that the unmanaged SafeArrayObj coclass defined a set of methods that return an array to the caller. On the simple end of the spectrum, you have GiveMeAnArrayOfInts(). Once you obtain the System.Array from the interop assembly, you are free to call any members of the managed System.Array type to manipulate the contents. For example, the following code results in the output shown in Figure 8-5.

```
// Get the ints from the coclass.
Array theInts = saObj.GiveMeAnArrayOfInts();
for(int i = 0; i < theInts.Length; i++)
    Console.WriteLine("Int data {0} is {1}", i,
    theInts.GetValue(i));

// Reverse elements.
Console.WriteLine("Reversed Int array!\n");
Array.Reverse(theInts);
for(int i = 0; i < theInts.Length; i++)
    Console.WriteLine("Int data {0} is {1}", i,
    theInts.GetValue(i));

// Sort elements.
Console.WriteLine("Sorted Int array!");
Array.Sort(theInts);
for(int i = 0; i < theInts.Length; i++)
    Console.WriteLine("Int data {0} is {1}", i,
    theInts.GetValue(i));
```

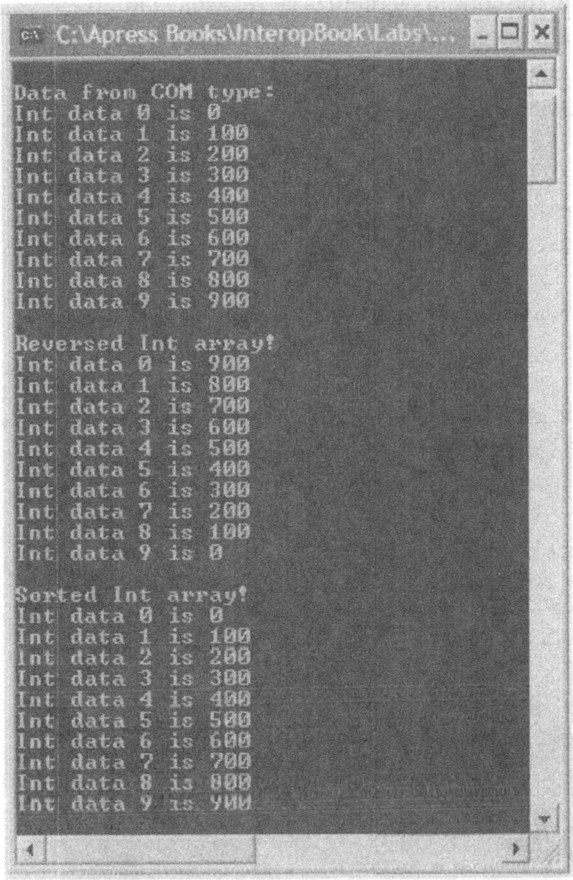

Figure 8-5. Manipulating the System.Array

Calling GiveMeAnArrayOfCoClasses() is also quite simple. Recall that this function returns a set of _TestObject interfaces. Because the interfaces are contained within a System.Array type, accessing the StringData property requires an explicit cast as shown here:

```
// Get array of _TestObject interfaces!
Array theTestobjects = saObj.GiveMeAnArrayOfCoClasses();
for(int i = 0; i < theTestobjects.Length; i++)
Console.WriteLine("Test object {0}'s string data: {1}", i,
    ((TestObjectClass)theTestobjects.GetValue(i)).StringData);
```

And finally you have GiveMeAnArrayOfVariants(). This method is the most interesting of the lot, given that the managed client is responsible for filtering through the System.Array in order to determine exactly what is contained in the array of objects. If you find that the current element is a _TestObject interface, you will trigger the StringData property to extract out the textual data. As you may recall from Chapter 5, RTTI support under the .NET Framework is realized using System.Type. Ponder the following (Figure 8-6 shows the final output):

```
// Get the VARIANTs.
Array theVariants = saObj.GiveMeAnArrayOfVariants();
for(int i = 0; i < theVariants.Length; i++)
{
    Console.WriteLine("VARIANT number {0}'s data: {1}", i,
      theVariants.GetValue(i));

    // Do we have a _TestObject interface?
    if(theVariants.GetValue(i).GetType() ==
      typeof(VBSafeArrayServer.TestObjectClass))

    Console.WriteLine("  -> Data of object is {0}",
      ((TestObjectClass)theVariants.GetValue(i)).StringData );
}
```

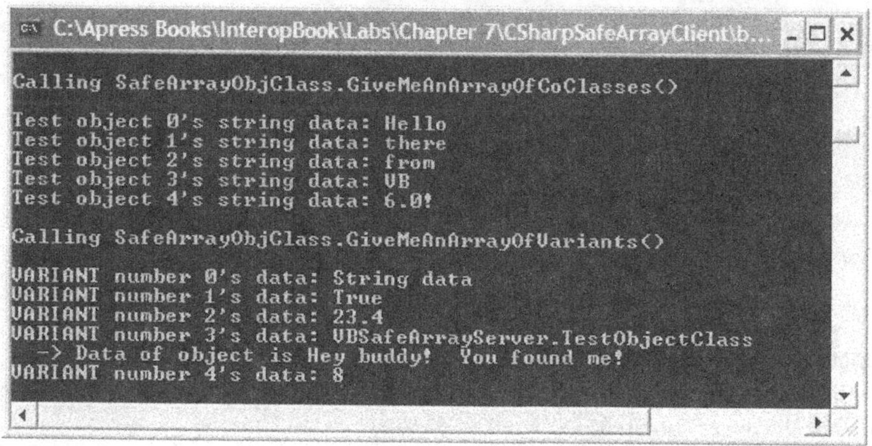

Figure 8-6. Manipulating SAFEARRAYs of COM interfaces and COM VARIANTs

CODE *The CSharpSafeArray project is included under the Chapter 8 directory.*

Handling C-Style Arrays

In a perfect world, all COM objects would make exclusive use of the SAFEARRAY, given that it is the one array type that can be understood by all COM language mappings. However, C and C++ COM programmers may occasionally make use of traditional C-style arrays as an alternative. In a nutshell, COM IDL allow you to define three core C-style arrays:

- Fixed-length arrays
- Varying arrays
- Conformant arrays

To illustrate each possibility, you need to make use of ATL (as VB 6.0 arrays are always expressed as COM SAFEARRAYs). Assume you have a Simple Object that supports the following interface:

```
interface ICoCStyleArrayObject : IUnknown
{
    // Fixed arrays define a constant capacity.
    HRESULT MethodWithFixedArray([in] int myArrayOfInts[10]);

    // Varying arrays allow the developer
    // to pass in a chuck of an array.
    HRESULT MethodWithVaryingArray
      ([in, length_is(len)] int myArrayOfInts[1000],
       [in] long len);

    // Conformant arrays can have varying
    // capacities, which are identified
    // using the [size_is()] IDL keyword.
    HRESULT MethodWithConformantArray
      ([in, size_is(cnt)] int* myInts, [in] long cnt);
};
```

If you were to run this COM server through tlbimp.exe, you would find that each of the IDL C-style-centric keywords (size_is(), length_is(), and so on) are completely ignored. Thus, as far as the .NET is concerned, COM methods that make use of varying or conformant arrays are exposed as methods that employ vanilla-flavored fixed arrays. Furthermore, in the case of conformant arrays, the parameter attributed with the [size_is()] IDL attribute is represented as a System.IntPtr.

Given these facts, consider the .NET metadata that describes the MethodWithFixedArray() method:

```
.method public hidebysig newslot virtual abstract
    instance void  MethodWithFixedArray([in] int32[]
    marshal([10]) myArrayOfInts)
    runtime managed internalcall
{
} // end of method ICoCStyleArrayObject::MethodWithFixedArray
```

As you can see, the method is adorned with the MarshalAsAttribute, which preserves the maximum upper limit of the IDL definition. The .NET metadata descriptions of the MethodWithVaryingArray() and MethodWithConformantArray() methods are as follows:

```
.method public hidebysig newslot virtual abstract
    instance void  MethodWithVaryingArray([in] native
    int myArrayOfInts,
    [in] int32 len) runtime managed internalcall
{
} // end of method ICoCStyleArrayObject::MethodWithVaryingArray

.method public hidebysig newslot virtual abstract
    instance void  MethodWithConformantArray([in] int32& myInts,
    [in] int32 cnt) runtime managed internalcall
{
} // end of method ICoCStyleArrayObject::MethodWithConformantArray
```

Handling COM Param Arrays

The final array-centric topic I will address is the transformation of COM "parameter arrays." As you may know, COM IDL provides the [vararg] attribute, which is used to mark a parameter that can be represented by varying number of arguments. No, that was not a typo. The IDL [vararg] keyword allows you to pass in a varying number of arguments that are logically grouped as a single entity. To illustrate, assume that you have created the following VB 6.0 method definition (supported by some class type):

```
' This method can take any number of items,
' of various types.
Public Sub Foo(ParamArray items() As Variant)
    ' Do stuff with the array.
End Sub
```

The generated IDL is defined as follows:

```
interface _ParamArrayClass : IDispatch {
    [id(0x60030000), vararg]
    HRESULT Foo([in, out] SAFEARRAY(VARIANT)* items);
};
```

If you were to build an interop assembly for this VB 6.0 COM server, you would find that the .NET metadata description of Foo() preserves the [vararg] IDL attribute using the ParamArrayAttribute type:

```
.method public hidebysig newslot virtual abstract
    instance void  Foo([in][out] object[]&
    marshal( safearray variant) items) runtime managed internalcall
{
  .custom instance void
  [mscorlib]System.Runtime.InteropServices.DispIdAttribute::
  .ctor(int32) = ( 01 00 00 00 03 60 00 00 )
  .param [1]
  .custom instance void
  [mscorlib]System.ParamArrayAttribute::.ctor() = ( 01 00 00 00 )
} // end of method _ParamArrayClass::Foo
```

When this interop assembly is used from C#, the Foo() method is realized using the intrinsic params keyword. VB .NET clients would make use of the familiar ParamArray keyword (just as with Visual Basic 6.0). Understand that the use of the System.ParamArrayAttribute type is not CLS compliant. Therefore, if a given COM server is used in a .NET language that does not honor its usage, the method is not invokible.

Handling COM Structures

Back in Chapter 3, you created a COM interface method (using ATL) that operated on a COM structure (see the WidgetServer project). The DrawALine() method was defined to take two MYPOINT structures by reference (a requirement for passing structures).

```
typedef struct
{
    long xPos;
    long yPos;
}MYPOINT;

interface IDraw : IUnknown
{
    [helpstring("method DrawALine")]
    HRESULT DrawALine([in, out] MYPOINT* p1,
        [in, out] MYPOINT* p2);
};
```

When tlbimp.exe encounters an unmanaged COM structure, it maps the type into a managed value type (of the same name). Recall that .NET value types derive from the System.ValueType base class, which can be verified in C# as follows:

```
// Declare a COM MYPOINT structure.
MYPOINT pt1;
pt1.xPos = 100;
pt1.yPos = 100;

// Validate base class (System.ValueType).
MessageBox.Show(pt1.GetType().BaseType.ToString());
```

Given what you already know about parameter transformations (see Chapter 7), you are correct in assuming that a managed client will need to pass the managed MYPOINT structure using the C# ref keyword. For example, if you set a reference to the WidgetServer.dll, you will find the mapping shown in Figure 8-7.

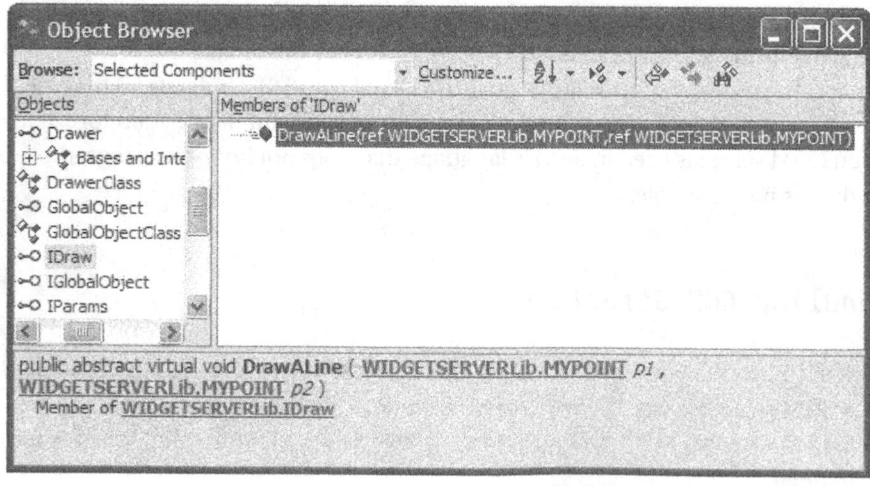

Figure 8-7. Mapping COM structures of System.ValueTypes

Calling DrawALine() is straightforward:

```
private void btnDrawLine_Click(object sender, System.EventArgs e)
{
    MYPOINT pt1;
    MYPOINT pt2;
    pt1.xPos = 100;
    pt1.yPos = 100;
    pt2.xPos = 400;
    pt2.yPos = 400;

    DrawerClass draw = new DrawerClass();
    draw.DrawALine(ref pt1, ref pt2);
}
```

Building a VB 6.0 Structure Server

To further illustrate the process of managed clients manipulating COM structures, imagine you have created a new VB 6.0 project named VBStructsServer. The [default] interface of the VBStructObject coclass defines the following members:

```
Option Explicit
' A simple COM structure.
Public Type WidgetStruct
    ID As Integer
    stringName As String
End Type
' This method returns an array of COM structures to the
' caller.
Public Function UseThisArrayOfStructs() As WidgetStruct()
    Dim structs(2) As WidgetStruct
    structs(0).ID = 1
    structs(0).stringName = "Fred"
    structs(1).ID = 2
    structs(1).stringName = "Mary"
    structs(2).ID = 3
    structs(2).stringName = "Billy"
    UseThisArrayOfStructs = structs
End Function

' This method changes the values of an incoming structure.
Public Sub ChangeThisStruct(w As WidgetStruct)
    w.ID = 99
    w.stringName = "FooFoo"
End Sub
```

Obviously, UseThisArrayOfStructs() revisits the notion of COM SAFEARRAYs. If you examine the underlying IDL for this member, you will find the following COM type information:

```
struct tagWidgetStruct
{
    [helpstring("ID")] short ID;
    [helpstring("stringName")] BSTR stringName;
} WidgetStruct;

interface _VBStructObject : IDispatch
{
    [id(0x60030000)]
    HRESULT
    UseThisArrayOfStructs([out, retval]
        SAFEARRAY(WidgetStruct)* );
    [id(0x60030001)]
    HRESULT ChangeThisStruct([in, out] WidgetStruct* w);
};
```

CODE *The VbStructServer is located under the COM Servers\ VBStructsServer directory.*

Exercising COM Structures from Managed Code

For a change of pace, let's build a Windows Forms application to manipulate the _VBStructObject interface (and if you wish, the ATL WidgetServer.dll). The UI (Figure 8-8) will allow the user to obtain the array of structures that are displayed inside the Form's ListBox type. In addition, the Change a Struct button will be used to display a WidgetServer structure before and after calling ChangeThisStruct().

Figure 8-8. The Windows Forms GUI

As you would expect, the majority of the code is found behind the Button Click event handler. Here is the relevant code:

```
private void btnGetArrayOfStructs_Click(object sender, System.EventArgs e)
{
    // Get the SAFEARRAY from the COM object.
    VBStructObjectClass  c = new VBStructObjectClass();
    Array s = c.UseThisArrayOfStructs();

    // Loop over each member in the array
    // and scrape out the structure data.
    foreach(WidgetStruct ws in s)
    {
        string str = String.Format("Number: {0} Name: {1}",
            ws.ID.ToString(),
            ws.stringName);

        // Plop into Form's listbox.
        lstStructs.Items.Add(str);
    }
}

private void btnChangeStruct_Click(object sender,
 System.EventArgs e)
{
    // Make and show a WidgetStruct.
    WidgetStruct w;
    w.ID = 9;
    w.stringName = "Fred";
    string str = String.Format("Number: {0} Name: {1}",
        w.ID.ToString(), w.stringName);
    MessageBox.Show(str, "WidgetStruct as created");

    // Now pass it in.
    VBStructObjectClass  c = new VBStructObjectClass();
    c.ChangeThisStruct(ref w);

    // Check out the new values.
    str = String.Format("Number: {0} Name: {1}",
        w.ID.ToString(), w.stringName);
    MessageBox.Show(str, "After call");
}
```

CODE *The CSharpComStructClient application is located under the Chapter 8 directory.*

Handling COM Collections

A very common pattern in COM is that of a custom collection. COM collection objects are simply coclasses that contain references to other (somehow related) coclasses. To illustrate the collection pattern, you will create the collection shown in Figure 8-9.

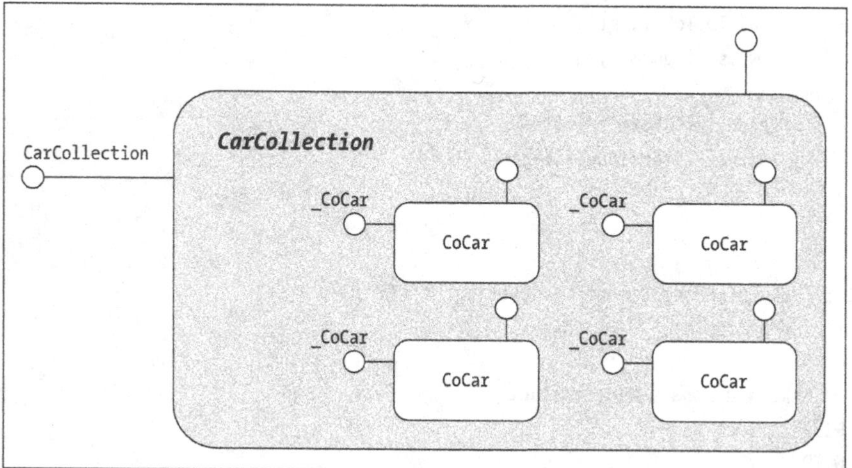

Figure 8-9. A COM collection

If you wish to follow along, fire up VB 6.0 and create a new ActiveX DLL named VbCollectionServer and change the name of your initial class to CoCar. The CoCar coclass defines a small set of private data members (which should be looking very familiar by this point) that are accessible using standard COM properties (one of which will be designed as read only). Also, CoCar defines a custom creation method (as VB 6.0 does not support parameterized constructors). Here is the complete code:

```
' The CoCar
Option Explicit

' Private data.
Private mColor As String
Private mMake As String
Private mPetName As String
Private mCarID As Integer

' Custom creation method.
Public Sub Create(ByVal Color As String, ByVal Make As String, _
  ByVal PetName As String, ByVal id As Integer)
    mColor = Color
    mPetName = PetName
    mMake = Make
    mCarID = id
End Sub

' CoCar supports the following COM properties.
Public Property Let Color(ByVal s As String)
    mColor = s
End Property
Public Property Get Color() As String
    Color = mColor
End Property

Public Property Let Make(ByVal s As String)
    mMake = s
End Property
Public Property Get Make() As String
    Make = mMake
End Property

Public Property Let PetName(ByVal s As String)
    mPetName = s
End Property
Public Property Get PetName() As String
    PetName = mPetName
End Property

' Read only (set using Create()).
Public Property Get CarID() As Integer
    CarID = mCarID
End Property
```

A common approach used when building COM collections is to explicitly prevent inner classes from being directly created by the caller. The idea behind this tactic is to force the user to obtain interface references of the inner types from the container (and only the container). As you learned in Chapter 4, the IDL [noncreatable] keyword can be used for this very purpose. The problem is that with VB 6.0 you are unable to directly edit the underlying COM type information. You can, however, instruct VB 6.0 to add the [noncreatable] keyword by setting a coclass' Instancing property to PublicNotCreatable (Figure 8-10).

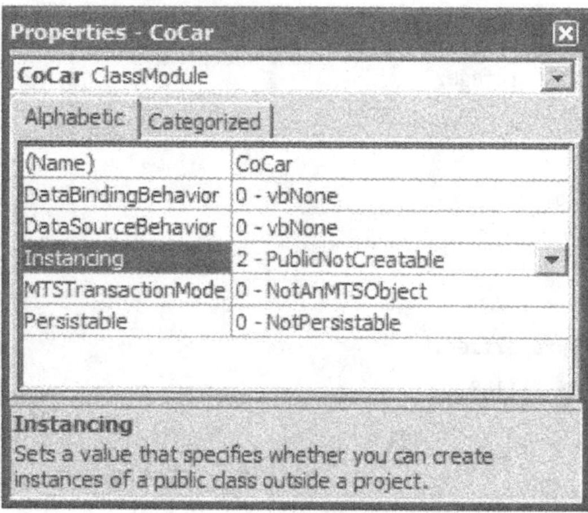

Figure 8-10. Preventing a VB COM Type from being directly created

If you examine the generated IDL (after compiling the server), you will find the following definition of CoCar (as an interesting side note, oleview.exe will not let you expand the VbCollectionServer.CoCar node, given that this type is now not creatable!):

```
[ uuid(44D7497B-D086-4BB0-AE79-5F9C0A9DD259),
  version(1.0), noncreatable]
coclass CoCar {
    [default] interface _CoCar;
};
```

Now that you have created the inner CoCar, you need to build the containing coclass. Insert a new VB 6.0 class type named CarCollection. To allow the outside world to interact with the internal set, programmers populate the [default] interface of the containing object with a well-known set of members (Table 8-3).

Table 8-3. Typical Members of a COM Collection

COM Collection Member	Meaning in Life
Add()	The collection's Add method allows the user to insert a new coclass into the COM collection.
Remove()	Obviously, this member allows the outside world to remove an item from the collection.
Item()	This member is much like a C# indexer method in that it allows access to a particular item in the collection.
Count	This member returns the number of items in the collection.
_NewEnum()	This hidden member is typically not directly called by the COM client, but rather internally by VB 6.0 when using the For Each iteration syntax. Under the hood, this method returns the standard IEnumVARIANT interface.

Of course, you are *not* required to name your container's members identically to the items listed in Table 8-3. Thus, if you would rather name your insertion method AddThisNewCarToTheCollection(), you are free to do so. The semantics of these members, however, should be identical.

If you were building a custom COM collection using ATL, you might make use of an STL vector to hold the inner interface references. Under the VB 6.0 model, you have a less syntactically strenuous option: the intrinsic Collection class. The VB 6.0 Collection type is a predefined type that supports the Add(), Remove(), Count, Item(), and _NewEnum() members.

However, the raw Collection type allows you to insert any possible item into the collection! When you wish to restrict exactly what can be inserted (or removed) from the coclass, you will want to build a strongly typed collection that leverages the functionality of the Collection type. The first step, therefore, is to add a private Collection member variable to the CarCollection type and fill it with some initial data points:

```
' The CarCollection.
Option Explicit
Private mCarColl As Collection

Private Sub Class_Initialize()
    Set mCarColl = New Collection
    ' Add some initial cars to the collection.
    AddCar "Red", "Viper", "Fred", 1
    AddCar "Yellow", "SlugBug", "Pippy", 2
```

```
    AddCar "Black", "BMW", "Buddha", 3
    AddCar "Gold", "Colt", "Goldy", 4
    AddCar "Pink", "Caravan", "Illness", 5
End Sub
```

Your insertion method, AddCar(), allows the user to send in the individual data points that constitute a new CoCar. Following convention, once AddCar() has inserted the new object, you return its reference to the caller:

```
Public Function AddCar(ByVal Color As String,
 ByVal Make As String, _
    ByVal PetName As String, ByVal id As Integer) As CoCar
    ' Make a new car and add it to the collection.
    Dim c As CoCar
    Set c = New CoCar
    c.Create Color, Make, PetName, id
    mCarColl.Add c
    Set AddCar = c
End Function
```

The indexer method, GetCar(), is a stylized version of Item() that is implemented as follows:

```
Public Function GetCar(ByVal index As Integer) As CoCar
    ' Get a car from collection.
    Set GetCar = mCarColl.Item(index)
End Function
```

The variation of Count() is a no-brainer. Simply ask the private Collection for its current number of items:

```
Public Function NumberOfCars() As Integer
    ' Return number of cars.
    NumberOfCars = mCarColl.Count()
End Function
```

The removal method is also very straightforward:

```
Public Sub RemoveCar(ByVal index As Integer)
    ' Remove a car.
    mCarColl.Remove (index)
End Sub
```

The implementation of RemoveCar() could be much more extravagant. You could, for example, allow the user to pass in the ID of the car he or she is interested in obtaining, and search for the correct member in the Collection. If you were to design the CarCollection in this manner, you would do better to make use of the VB 6.0 Dictionary type rather than the Collection entity. For the purposes of this example, the current implementation will do just fine.

Last but not least, you have the hidden _NewEnum() method. As noted, the COM client does not directly call this method. However, under the hood, Visual Basic will invoke this member whenever the client makes use of the For . . . Each syntax. Good enough, but what exactly does _NewEnum() do? In a nutshell, this method returns an IUnknown interface to the client (VB in this case) that will use it to query the type for its IEnumVARIANT interface. This standard interface (defined in oaidl.idl) allows a client to interact with the contained items using four members:

```
// IEnumVARIANT interface.
interface IEnumVARIANT : IUnknown
{
    // This method returns a set of VARIANTs.
    HRESULT Next( [in] ULONG celt,
        [out, size_is(celt),
          length_is(*pCeltFetched)] VARIANT* rgVar,
        [out] ULONG * pCeltFetched);

    // This method skips over some number of items.
    HRESULT Skip( [in] ULONG celt);

    // Set the internal pointer back to the beginning.
    HRESULT Reset();

    // Allows a client to obtain a carbon copy of the
    // current enumerator.
    HRESULT Clone( [out] IEnumVARIANT ** ppEnum);
}
```

C++ programmers who build COM classes in the raw (or using ATL) may be aware of the mythical IEnumXXXX interface. This enumeration interface offers a design pattern by which a collection object allows access to a set of internal items. These internal items may be anything at all: a set of integers, VARIANTs, BSTRs, or even the interfaces of custom coclasses.

However, rather than allowing each and every developer to define the members that provide access to the contained types, the COM specification offers the fictional IEnumXXXX interface. This interface is not literally defined in a given type library. Rather, IEnumXXXX is a recommended pattern to follow when building the container object. Simply replace "XXXX" with the type of inner item you are allowing access to (for example, IEnumVARIANT, IEnumFrogs, IEnumURLs, and so forth). Because a VB 6.0 Collection type can hold anything at all, it stands to reason that its enumerator interface is IEnumVARIANT. With this brief backgrounder out of the way, here is the implementation of the _NewEnum() member (recall that the [] notation allows you to call hidden members):

```
' Required to support For Each iteration.
Public Function NewEnum() As IUnknown
    Set NewEnum = mCarColl.[_NewEnum]
End Function
```

Now, when you make use of the For . . . Each syntax, VB does not invoke _NewEnum() by name, but rather by indirectly invoking the member via it's DISPID. Note for example that the CarCollection's _NewEnum() member is named simply NewEnum() (without the underscore). In fact, you could have called this method GiveMeIEnumVARIANT(). To associate your method (whatever its name) with the correct DISPID, you will need to use the Procedure Attributes dialog box (located under the Tools menu of the VB 6.0 IDE). What is the magic number you ask? It's –4 (note the Procedure ID edit box seen in Figure 8-11). While you're at it, mark this member as hidden (via the check box).

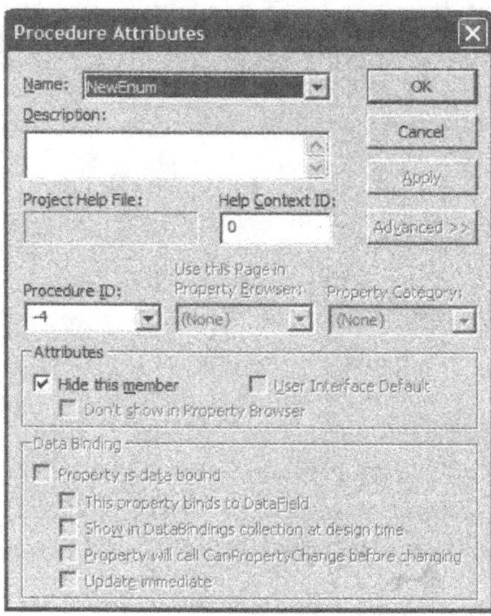

Figure 8-11. Setting the correct DISPID

If you are interested, the value –4 maps to a predefined const named DISPID_NEWENUM (found in oaild.idl).

```
// DISPID reserved for the standard "NewEnum" method.
const DISPID DISPID_NEWENUM = -4;
```

Once you compile your VB server, you will see that the correct hexadecimal value of –4 has been added to your NewEnum() method:

```
interface _CarCollection : IDispatch
{
    [id(0x60030000)]
    HRESULT AddCar([in] BSTR Color,
        [in] BSTR Make, [in] BSTR PetName,
        [in] short id, [out, retval] _CoCar** );
    [id(0x60030001)]
    HRESULT GetCar( [in] short index,
        [out, retval] _CoCar** );
    [id(0x60030002)]
    HRESULT NumberOfCars([out, retval] short* );
    [id(0x60030003)]
    HRESULT RemoveCar([in] short index);

    // 0xfffffffc = DISPID_NEWENUM (-4)
    [id(0xfffffffc), hidden]
    HRESULT NewEnum([out, retval] IUnknown** );
};
```

With this, your VB 6.0 COM collection is complete! Now let's see how to manipulate it using managed code.

CODE *The VbCollectionServer is located under the Chapter 8 subdirectory.*

Exercising the COM Collection from Managed Code

Now you'll take your COM collection out for a spin via a new C# console application (CSharpComCollectionClient). First off, the application object defines a static method named PrintCarCollection() that will iterate over each item in the collection and dump out the contents:

```
namespace CSharpComCollectionClient
{
    class COMCollectionUser
    {
        static void PrintCarCollection(CarCollection coll)
        {
            // DISPID_NEWENUM triggered here!
            foreach(CoCarClass car in coll)
            {
                Console.WriteLine(@"ID: {0} Make: {1}
                  Color: {2} PetName: {3}",
                  car.CarID, car.Make, car.Color, car.PetName);
            }
        }
        [STAThread]
        static void Main(string[] args)
        {
        }
    }
}
```

As you can see from the code comment, just like the VB 6.0 For Each syntax, the C# foreach keyword demands that the type being traversed support an enumeration mechanism. Recall that your CarCollection coclass defined a hidden method with the DISPID of –4. When the tlbimp.exe utility finds this value, it will automatically build in support for the System.Collections.IEnumerable interface:

```
// A COM class that defines a member with DISPID -4
// will support this interface.
public interface System.Collections.IEnumerable
{
    System.Collections.IEnumerator GetEnumerator();
}
```

This interface simply returns another interface to the caller (IEnumerator), which allows the type's internal sub objects to be iterated over. System.Collection.IEnumerator is defined as follows:

```
// A managed variation of the COM IEnumXXXX interface.
public interface System.Collections.IEnumerator
{
    object Current { get; }
    bool MoveNext();
    void Reset();
}
```

If you check out the managed type using the IDE's integrated Object Browser (Figure 8-12), you'll see the CarCollectionClass does indeed support IEnumerable (which again provides access to IEnumerator).

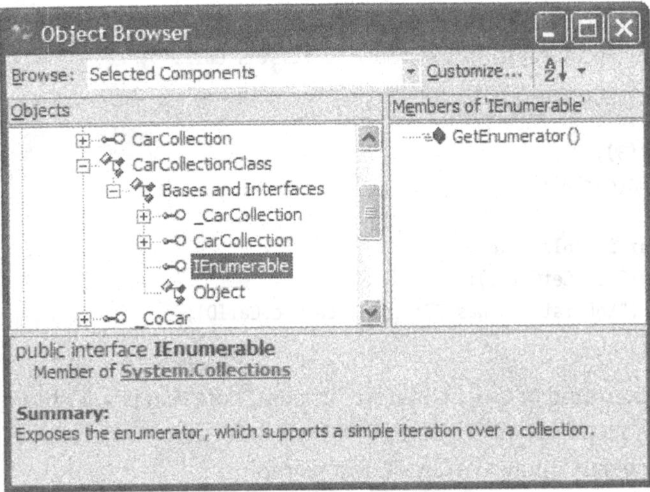

Figure 8-12. Supporting DISPID_NEWENUM results in the implementation of the IEnumerable interface.

If you did not assign DISPID_NEWENUM to a given member of the COM collection, the generated class type would not support IEnumerable. Rather, you are presented with the following compile time error:

```
foreach statement cannot operate on variables of type
'VbCollectionServer.CarCollection' because
'VbCollectionServer.CarCollection' does not contain a definition
for 'GetEnumerator', or it is inaccessible
```

Now, to illustrate interaction with the CarCollectionClass type, ponder the following updated Main() method that calls AddCar(), RemoveCar(), and GetCar():

```
static void Main(string[] args)
{
    // Make the COM collection.
    CarCollectionClass carColl = new CarCollectionClass();
    Console.WriteLine("Number of cars in initial collection: {0}",
        carColl.NumberOfCars());

    // Iterate over initial collection.
    PrintCarCollection(carColl);
```

```
        // Add a car.
        CoCar newCar = carColl.AddCar("White", "Jetta", "Chucky", 55);
        Console.WriteLine("\nCollection after adding a car.");
        PrintCarCollection(carColl);

        // Now remove the first 3 cars.
        Console.WriteLine("\nCollection after removing first 3 cars:");
        carColl.RemoveCar(1);
        carColl.RemoveCar(2);
        carColl.RemoveCar(3);
        PrintCarCollection(carColl);

        // Get first CoCar in collection.
        CoCar carOne = carColl.GetCar(1);
        Console.WriteLine("\nFirst Car has ID: {0}", carOne.CarID);
}
```

If you have a background in C++ COM development, note that if you obtain the IEnumerator interface from an imported COM collection, you are in effect interacting with the coclass' IEnumVARIANT. For example:

```
// Now using raw enumerator.
IEnumerator itfEnum = carColl.GetEnumerator();
itfEnum.Reset();
itfEnum.MoveNext();
CoCarClass c = (CoCarClass)itfEnum.Current;
Console.WriteLine("ID: {0} Make: {1} Color: {2} PetName: {3}",
    c.CarID, c.Make, c.Color, c.PetName);
```

Figure 8-13 illustrates the complete output.

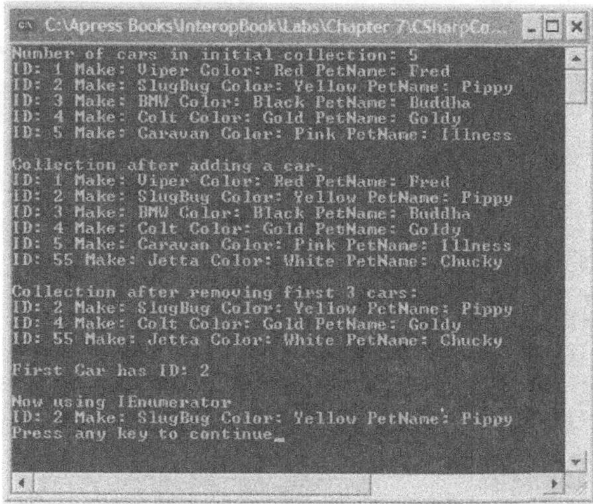

Figure 8-13. Interacting with the COM enumerator

CODE *The CSharpComCollectionClient is located under the Chapter 8 subdirectory.*

A Brief Review of COM Connection Points (COM Events)

Now that you have examined the COM collection pattern (and the role of COM enumeration interfaces), let me turn your attention to the consumption of COM events from a managed environment. However, before you build a sample COM event server, let's take some time to briefly review the core concepts of the connection point architecture. In classic COM, the ability for one object to send events to another object requires four key ingredients:

- A connection point container
- A connectable object (or possibly a set of them) maintained by the container
- An outbound interface (aka source interface) defined in the server's type library
- The client's implementation of the source interface (aka client-side sink).

Understanding IConnectionPointContainer

The first piece of the puzzle is the *connection point container*. To be honest, this is just a fancy name for a collection coclass that implements the standard COM interface named (surprise, surprise) IConnectionPointContainer. The role of IConnectionPointContainer is to allow the client to investigate the set of connectable objects it is maintaining. A *connectable object* is a COM class that understands how to send a predefined set of events (more details in a moment). The official definition of this standard COM interface can be found inside ocild.idl:

```
// Implemented by the connection point container.
interface IConnectionPointContainer : IUnknown
{
    // Allows client to enumerate over the inner objects.
    HRESULT EnumConnectionPoints(
        [out] IEnumConnectionPoints ** ppEnum);
    // Allows the client to ask for a connection point by name.
    HRESULT FindConnectionPoint( [in] REFIID riid,
        [out] IConnectionPoint ** ppCP);
}
```

The first way a client may obtain an internal connection point is to call EnumConnectionPoints(), which returns a standard COM enumeration interface named IEnumConnectionPoints. Using IEnumConnectionPoints, the client can iterate over each of the contained subobjects in the same manner as IEnumVARIANT. The second (and more common) approach is to ask for a specific connectable object by name using FindConnectionPoint(), which allows a client to ask for a specific connection point by name.

Understanding IConnectionPoint

Regardless of which technique the client uses to view the container's inner objects, the end result is a reference to the connectable object's IConnectionPoint interface. In fact, by definition, a connectable object is a coclass that implements the members of IConnectionPoint. This interface defines a set of methods that allows the external client to connect and disconnect from the connectable object (among other chores). IConnectionPoint is also defined within ocidl.idl as follows:

```
// Internal connectable objects must implement IConnectionPoint.
interface IConnectionPoint : IUnknown
{
   // Get the GUID of the outbound interface
   // this object makes calls upon.
   HRESULT GetConnectionInterface( [out] IID * pIID);
   // Get pointer back to the container.
   HRESULT GetConnectionPointContainer(
       [out] IConnectionPointContainer ** ppCPC);
   // Allows external client to hook into this connectable object.
   HRESULT Advise( [in] IUnknown * pUnkSink,
       [out] DWORD * pdwCookie);
   // Allows external client to detach
   // from this connectable object.
   HRESULT Unadvise( [in] DWORD dwCookie);
   // Allows client to determine all other
   // connections to this connectable
   // object.
   HRESULT EnumConnections( [out] IEnumConnections ** ppEnum);
}
```

Of all the methods of IConnectionPoint, Advise() and Unadvise() are by far the most interesting. Using these methods, an external client is able to inform the connection point object that it is interested in receiving incoming events by passing in a reference to the client-side sink (represented as an IUnknown*) via the Advise() method. The connectable object holds onto each client-side sink reference and makes calls on each sink when a given event occurs. As you might assume, each connectable object maintains an array of IUnknown* interfaces that represent a given connected client. Unadvise(), on the other hand, allows the client to terminate the connection by passing back the connection cookie received as an output parameter from the Advise() method.

Understanding the Outbound Interface

Next you have the entity known as the *outbound interface.* A given connectable object is only able to make calls against a particular set of methods. Formally speaking, this set of methods is known as an outbound interface, which is defined in IDL using the [source] keyword. [source] interfaces are defined in the server's type information *but implemented by the client* in a given sink object. Also understand that outbound interfaces are defined as dispinterfaces (by convention) to ensure that late-bound clients (such as a Web browser) can intercept the incoming events. Here is a simple IDL definition of an outbound interface:

```
library MYEVENTSERVERLib
{
    importlib("stdole32.tlb");
    importlib("stdole2.tlb");

    // Event interfaces are defined in the server's IDL,
    // but implemented by the client. The underscore is a
    // convention that marks the interface as hidden.
    [uuid(17B8B6D5-887C-46B4-9B4D-554954863CD8)]
    dispinterface _ICoEventObjectEvents
    {
        properties:
        methods:
        [id(1), helpstring("method TheEvent")] HRESULT TheEvent();
    };

    [uuid(F94E0935-7DE1-46CC-9E3C-BFDE8998A80B)]
    coclass CoEventObject
    {
        [default] interface ICoEventObject;
        [default, source] dispinterface _ICoEventObjectEvents;
    };
};
```

Although it is possible that a COM server may define multiple source interfaces (and therefore multiple connection points), 99.9 percent of all connection point containers define a single connectable object and a single [default, source] interface that defines *all* the events for a given container.

All Together Now...

To be sure, the connection point architecture is a bit on the complex side. To help solidify the role of each entity, let's see a concrete example. Figure 8-14 illustrates yet another CoCar, this time containing two connectable objects. EngineCP is a COM type that only knows how to communicate with a sink that implements _EngineEvents. RadioCP is another connectable object that only knows how to communicate with a sink implementing the members of _RadioEvents. Recall that the IDL definition of outbound [source] interface is located within the server's type library but implemented by a given client-side sink.

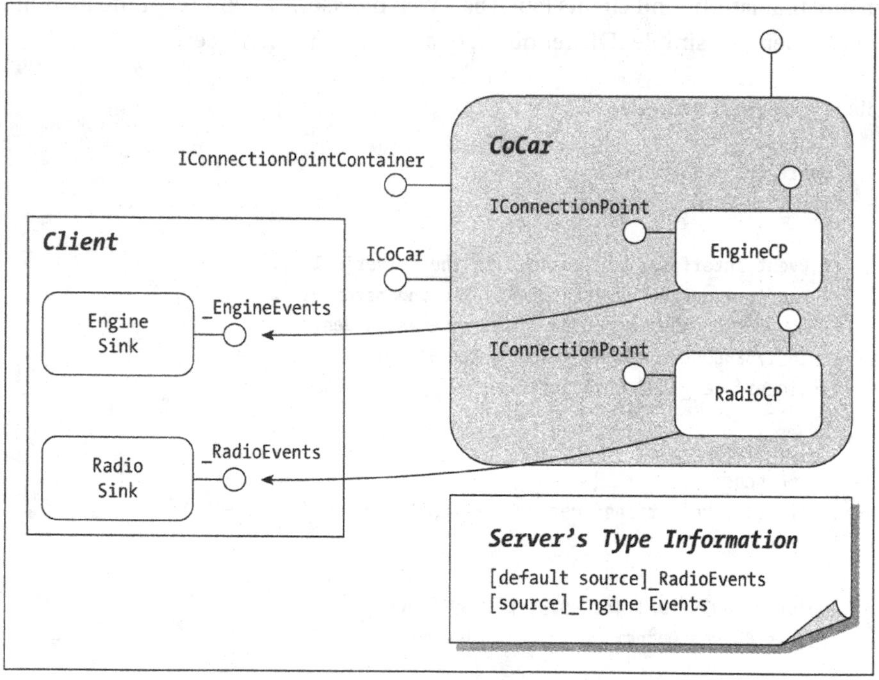

Figure 8-14. The complexity that is COM connection points

Building a Connectable COM Type

To be sure, if you were to build a connectable coclass using raw C++ and IDL, you would have quite a chore ahead of you. To keep things focused on interoperability issues (rather than on the gory details of constructing connectable objects), you will once again make use of Visual Basic 6.0. The VBComEventsServer.dll defines a single coclass named CoCar. This COM type is able to send out two events to a connected client (based on the value of its current rate of speed). The beautiful thing about defining and sending events using VB 6.0 is that the IConnectionPointContainer and IConnectionPoint interfaces are implemented behind the scenes automatically. All you are required to do is this:

- Define the events using the Event keyword.
- Fire the event (under the correct conditions) using the RaiseEvent keyword.

Here, then, is this iteration of the CoCar type (CoCar.cls):

```
Option Explicit
' Class constant.
Const MAXSPEED = 200

' Simple state data.
Private mCurrSpeed As Integer

' The CoCar can send two events.
Public Event AboutToBlow()
Public Event Exploded()

' The sole member of the [default] interface.
Public Function SpeedUp() As Integer
    mCurrSpeed = mCurrSpeed + 10
    If (MAXSPEED - mCurrSpeed) = 10 Then
        RaiseEvent AboutToBlow
    End If
    If mCurrSpeed >= MAXSPEED Then
        RaiseEvent Exploded
    End If
    ' Return current speed
    SpeedUp = mCurrSpeed
End Function
```

Once you compile this server, examine the set of supported interfaces using oleview.exe. As you can see, VB has indeed supplied the necessary infrastructure (Figure 8-15).

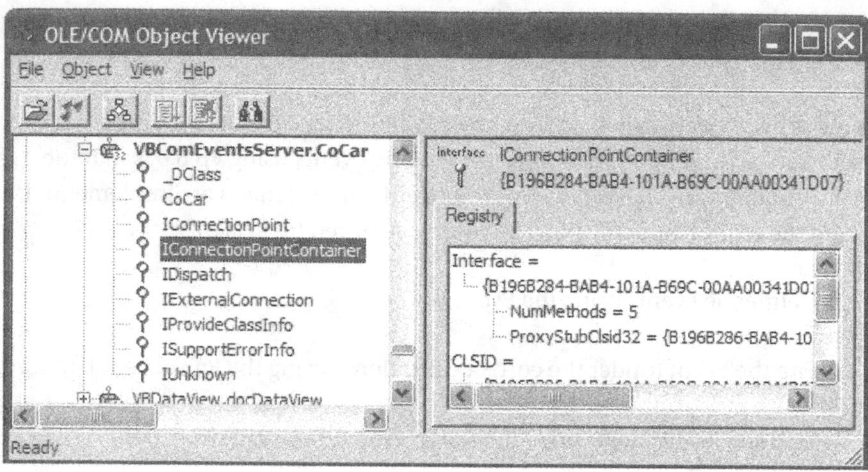

Figure 8-15. VB 6.0 coclasses automatically support COM event atoms.

If you examine the generated COM type information, you will find that a single [default, source] interface has been defined and populated with each event you declared using the VB 6.0 Event keyword (note that by convention, [source] interfaces are typically defined as dispinterfaces to allow late-bound clients to receive the outgoing events):

```
[uuid(C2112F74-9C98-435E-8304-7735421F3C23),
  version(1.0), hidden, nonextensible]
dispinterface __CoCar {
    properties:
    methods:
        [id(0x00000001)]
        void AboutToBlow();
        [id(0x00000002)]
        void Exploded();
};
```

CODE *The VBComEventServer project is included under the Chapter 8 subdirectory.*

A Brief Review of .NET Delegates

As you might expect, COM connection points are mapped into terms of the .NET delegate architecture. By way of a quick review, recall that a delegate is a type that represents a pointer to some function, much like a traditional C-style callback (see Chapter 1). The key difference, however, is that a .NET delegate is a class that derives from System.MulticastDelegate.

This base class defines a number of members that maintain core information about the method(s) it is responsible for invoking. Using the inherited Combine() and Remove() methods, the delegate type adds or removes function pointers to the internal linked list it is maintaining.

Because a delegate is indeed a class type, it can be directly created and manipulated, like any class type you may pass in, as a constructor argument you pass in the name of the method that will be invoked. For example, ponder the following code (note the similarity to the PInvoke callback example described in Chapter 1):

```
namespace SimpleCSharpDelegate
{
    // This delegate knows how to call
    // methods that take no arguments and returns nothing.
    public delegate void DoneAddingDelegate();

    class Adder
    {
        public int Add(int x, int y)
        { return x + y; }

        // The delegate target.
        // (Note this method matches the calling conventions of the
        // DoneAddingDelegate delegate).
        public void AddingComplete()
        {
           Console.WriteLine("The adder is done...");
        }

        [STAThread]
        static void Main(string[] args)
        {
            // Create an adder.
            Adder a = new Adder();

            // Assign a method to the delegate.
            DoneAddingDelegate del =
                new DoneAddingDelegate(a.AddingComplete);
```

```
            Console.WriteLine("Delegate target: {0}",
                del.Target.ToString());
            Console.WriteLine("Delegate method name: {0}",
                del.Method.Name);

            // Trigger the method maintained by the delegate.
            Console.WriteLine("Sum of 10 and 10 is: {0}",
                a.Add(10, 10));
            del.DynamicInvoke(null);
        }
    }
}
```

Here, the DoneAddingDelegate delegate has been defined to invoke methods that take no arguments and return nothing. Notice that when you create the delegate (within the Main() method), you are passing in the name of a function to call (which, of course, matches the calling conventions of the DoneAddingDelegate delegate).

After you print some basic stats about the delegate (via the inherited Target and Method properties), you invoke the member using DynamicInvoke(). The output can be seen in Figure 8-16.

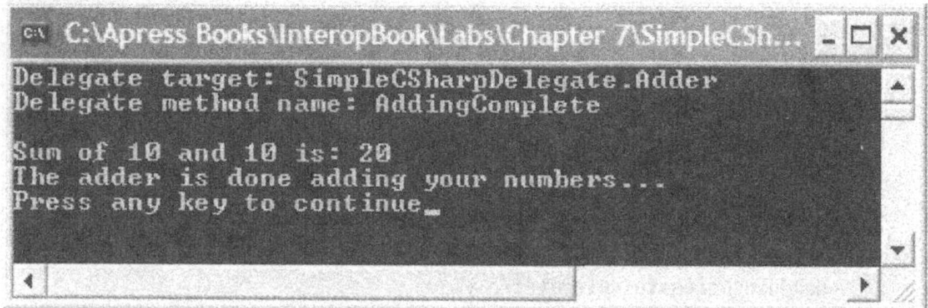

Figure 8-16. The DoneAddingDelegate type in action

If you view the generated assembly using ILDasm.exe, you will find that the delegate keyword does indeed expand to a class deriving from System.MulticastDelegate (Figure 8-17).

CODE *The SimpleCSharpDelegate application is included under the Chapter 8 directory.*

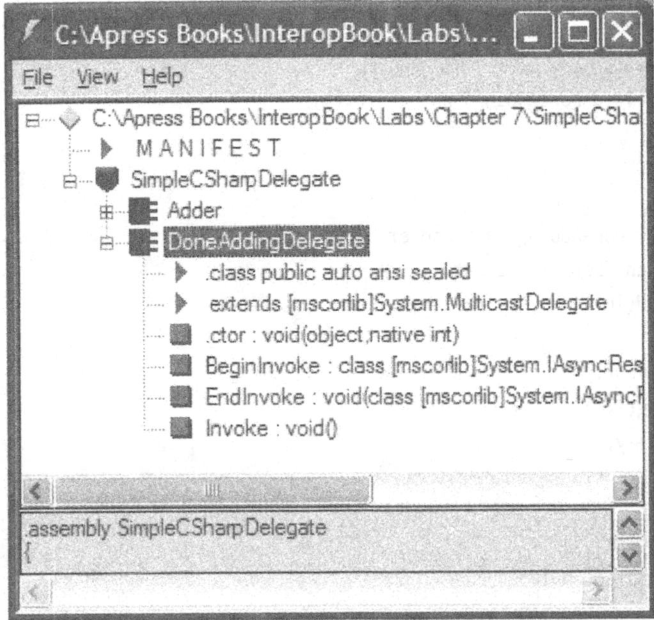

Figure 8-17. Delegates derive from System.MulticastDelegate.

A Brief Review of .NET Events

Although .NET delegates can be used as independent agents, it is more common to leverage delegates to create custom events. A C# event is defined using the following syntax (assume you have already defined a delegate named NameOfDelegate):

```
// C# Event declaration.
public event NameOfDelegate NameOfEvent;
```

As you can see, an event is simply a named class member that knows how to communicate with a set of methods matching the corresponding delegate. Once a class type has defined some number of events, you are able to assign delegate targets using the convenient += syntax; likewise, if you wish to remove a member from the list maintained by the delegate, you may make use of the -= syntax. And finally, when you want the class to fire the event (thereby calling each method contained within the delegate), simply call the event by name. To showcase the .NET event architecture, here is a new C# console application that retrofits the previous SimpleCSharpDelegate application to make use of a custom event.

```
namespace SimpleCSharpEvent
{
    // The delegate.
    public delegate void DoneAddingEventHandler();
  class Adder
  {
      // The event.
        public event DoneAddingEventHandler DoneAdding;
      // Method which fires the event.
      public int Add(int x, int y)
      {
          // Fire event.
          DoneAdding();
          return x + y;
      }

      // The event sink.
      public void AddingComplete()
      {
        Console.WriteLine("The adder is done...");
      }

      [STAThread]
      static void Main(string[] args)
      {
          // Create an adder.
          Adder a = new Adder();

          // Assign a method to the event.
          a.DoneAdding +=
           new DoneAddingEventHandler(a.AddingComplete);

          // Trigger the event.
          Console.WriteLine("Sum of 10 and 10 is: {0}",
            a.Add(10, 10));
      }
  }
}
```

Although the output is identical to the previous delegate, the underlying metadata is quite unique (Figure 8-18).

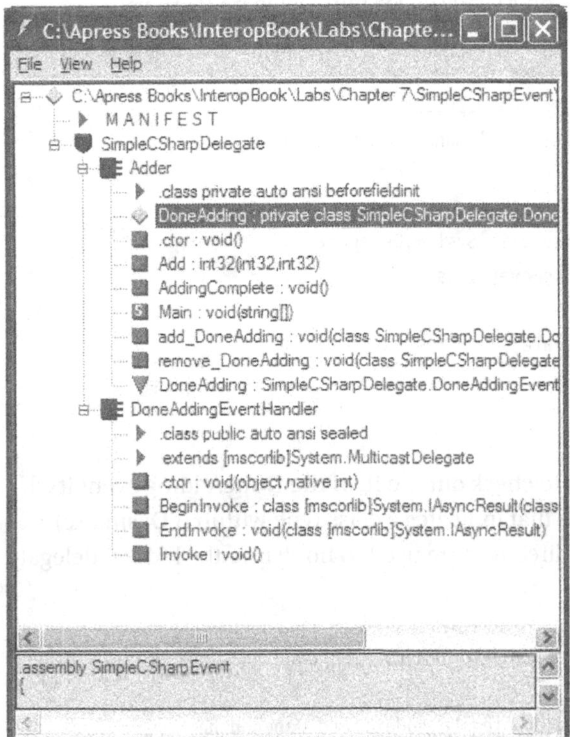

Figure 8-18. The underbelly of .NET events

Notice that the Adder class type now defines two additional members, add_DoneAdding() and remove_DoneAdding(). These members are called behind the scenes when you make use of the += and -= operators. The crux of their usefulness is to hide the raw delegate manipulation from view. For example, if you check out the IL for add_DoneAdding(), you will find that System.Delegate::Combine() is called on your behalf:

```
method public hidebysig specialname instance void
add_DoneAdding(class
 SimpleCSharpDelegate.DoneAddingEventHandler 'value')
cil managed synchronized
{
...
  IL_0008:  call       class [mscorlib]System.Delegate
    [mscorlib]System.Delegate::Combine(class
    [mscorlib]System.Delegate,
    class [mscorlib]System.Delegate)
...
}
```

Likewise, remove_DoneAdding() will call System.Delegate.Remove():

```
.method public hidebysig specialname instance void
     remove_DoneAdding(class SimpleCSharpDelegate.
    DoneAddingEventHandler 'value') cil managed synchronized
{
...
  IL_0008:  call       class [mscorlib]System.Delegate
    [mscorlib]System.Delegate::Remove(class
    [mscorlib]System.Delegate,
    class [mscorlib]System.Delegate)
...
}
```

The last point of interest is to check out the IL of the DoneAdding event itself (identified by the green triangle that indicates a class type within ILDasm.exe). The [.addon] and [.removeon] directives are used to hook into the hidden delegate members:

```
 event SimpleCSharpDelegate.DoneAddingEventHandler DoneAdding
{
  .addon instance void SimpleCSharpDelegate.Adder::add_DoneAdding
    (class SimpleCSharpDelegate.DoneAddingEventHandler)
  .removeon instance void
  SimpleCSharpDelegate.Adder::remove_DoneAdding
    (class SimpleCSharpDelegate.DoneAddingEventHandler)
}
```

CODE *The SimpleCSharpEvent project is included under the Chapter 8 directory.*

Examining the Interop Assembly

Now that you have seen how to work with .NET delegates and events in and of themselves, you should have no problem intercepting COM events. When you generate an interop assembly for a COM server making use of the connection point architecture, tlbimp.exe will generate a number of additional types beyond the XXXClass, [default] interface class type, and managed interface. Check out Figure 8-19.

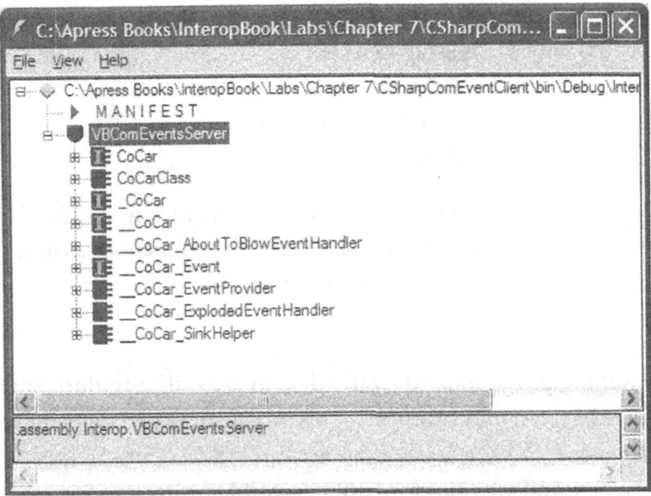

Figure 8-19. Event-centric generated types

Table 8-4 documents the meaning of each member of the interop.vbcomeventserver.dll assembly (note that the XXX_EventProvider and XXX_SinkHelper types are private to the interop assembly and not directly usable from a managed client).

Table 8-4. Generated Event-Centric Types

Generated Type	Meaning in Life
CoCarClass, CoCar, _CoCar	As you would expect, the interop assembly contains managed class and interface types (as described in Chapter 6).
__CoCar	Tlbimp.exe generates a managed inbound interface for each [source] interface. Typically this interface can be ignored; however, you can make use of it to manually build a managed event sink.
__CoCar_Event	Tlbimp.exe also generates a managed outbound interface for each [source] interface. Again, this member can typically be ignored.
__CoCar_AboutToBlowEventHandler __CoCar_ExplodedEventHandler	Tlbimp.exe generates a managed delegate for each method defined in the COM [source] interface.

Table 8-4. Generated Event-Centric Types (continued)

Generated Type	Meaning in Life
__CoCar_EventProvider	This internal class type is used by the RCW to map COM connection points to .NET delegates.
__CoCar_SinkHelper	This internal class implements the members of the outbound interface and functions as a default client side sink object.

Although quite a few types are generated by the tlbimp.exe utility, understand that the only items you are likely to make direct use of are the managed delegates. Furthermore, two of the types (__XXXX_EventProvider and __XXXX_SinkHelper) are declared as internal types, and are therefore not accessible from outside of the interop assembly. In a nutshell, the RCW uses these two types internally to map COM connection points to the correct .NET delegate. For example, if you were to peek inside the underlying IL for these types, you would find that the __CoCar_EventProvider type maintains a System.Collections.ArrayList type to hold onto the client-side sinks. Again, given that you are unable to directly use these types, I'll focus exclusively on the remaining members.

Examining the Generated Delegates

The most critical members generated by tlbimp.exe are the managed delegates. Recall that the VB 6.0 [default, source] interface defines two event members:

```
dispinterface __CoCar {
    properties:
    methods:
        [id(0x00000001)] void AboutToBlow();
        [id(0x00000002)] void Exploded();
};
```

This results in the following .NET delegates:

```
public sealed delegate __CoCar_AboutToBlowEventHandler
    : System.MulticastDelegate
{…}

public sealed delegate __CoCar_ExplodedEventHandler
    : System.MulticastDelegate
{…}
```

The name given to each .NET delegate is based on a very specific pattern:

```
<NameOfTheSourceInterface>_<NameOfTheEvent>EventHandler
```

Thus, if you had a [source] interface named MyEvents that defined a single method called TheEvent, the generated delegate would be named MyEvents_TheEventEventHandler. As you will see in just a moment, these generated delegates are used just like any .NET delegate type.

Examining the Generated __CoCar and __CoCar_Event Interfaces

When tlbimp.exe encounters a [source] interface in the COM server's type information, it will automatically generate two managed interfaces. The first interface defines each member as an inbound interface. In this example, the __CoCar defines the AboutToBlow() and Exploded() members as shown in Figure 8-20.

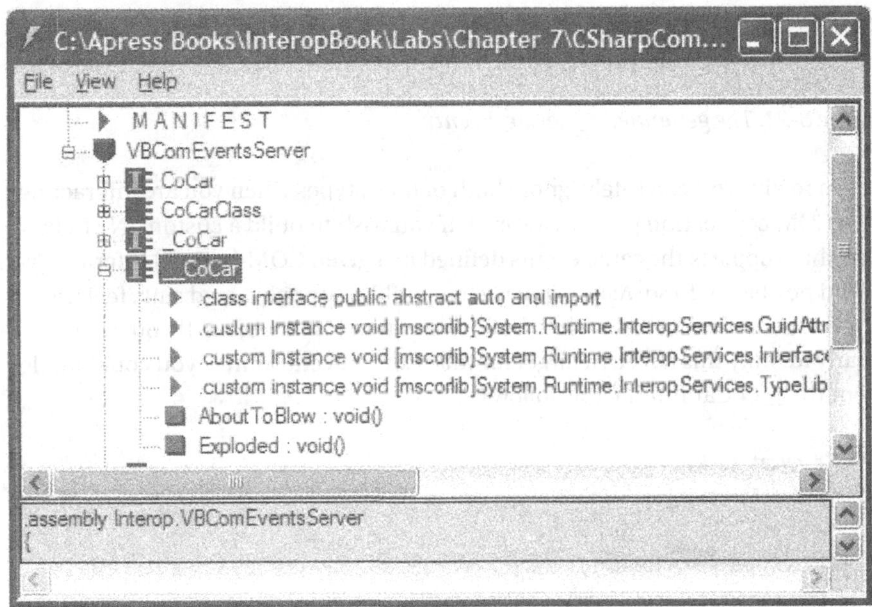

Figure 8-20. The generated __CoCar interface

The generated __CoCar_Event interface defines the same members as an outbound interface (that is, an interface defining the AboutToBlow() and Exploded() events). As you can see from Figure 8-21, the __CoCar_Event interface also defines the related add_XXX() and remove_XXX() members.

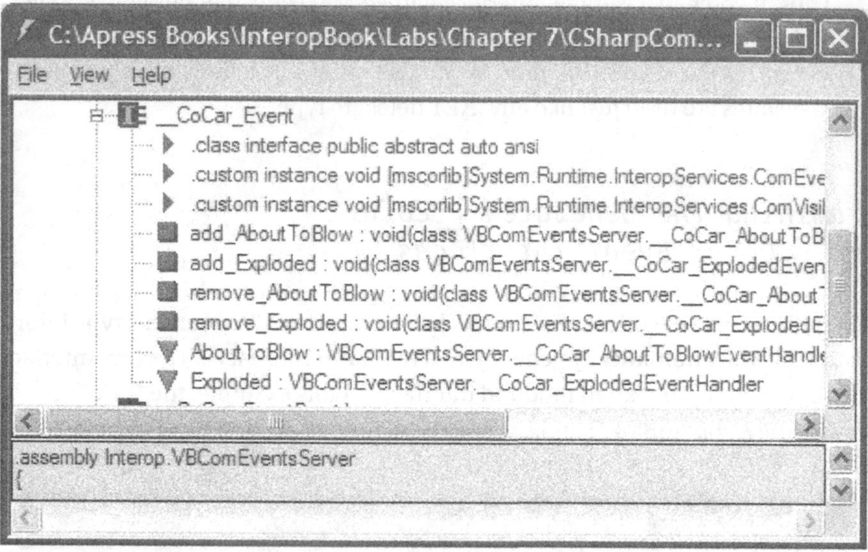

Figure 8-21. The generated __CoCar_Event

In reality, you can safely ignore both of these types when you are interacting with COM connection points. However, if you wish to build a custom .NET class type that supports the same events defined in a given COM [source] interface, you would be able to do so. Also, if you wish to build a strongly typed sink, feel free.

For example, say you wish to build a client-side sink object. If you wish to clearly identify this sink as a target for the _CoCar event source, you could implement the __CoCar interface as follows:

```
// A C# event sink.
class CSharpEventSink : __CoCar
{
    public void AboutToBlow()
    { Console.WriteLine("->Dude!  Slow down!");}

    public void Exploded()
    {Console.WriteLine("->You're toast...");}
}
```

You are *not* required to implement the generated managed [source] interface. However, you are free to build a .NET sink using any valid .NET syntactic constructs (a class defining static members, a class that does not implement the managed [source] interface, and so forth).

As far as the __CoCar_Event interface is concerned, this type simply supports each event in terms of managed code. As you may know, .NET interfaces can define any number of properties, methods, *and events*. Thus, if you wish to build a .NET class type that supports the same events as the COM CoCar, you would be able to inherit support for the AboutToBlow and Exploded events as demonstrated here:

```
// This .NET class supports the same events
// as defined in the COM type information
// for the VB CoCar.
class ExampleDotNetEventType : __CoCar_Event
{
    // Inherited events from the __CoCar_Event interface.
    public event __CoCar_AboutToBlowEventHandler AboutToBlow;
    public event __CoCar_ExplodedEventHandler Exploded;

    public void FireTheEvents()
    {
        ...
    }
}
```

So the bottom line is that tlbimp.exe generates two .NET interface definitions to allow you to build custom .NET types that either (a) support the methods of a given [source] interface or (b) support the same events of a given [source] interface. As noted, unless you wish to build custom types that mimic existing COM event objects (or strongly typed sinks), you can safely ignore these generated types.

Examining the Managed CoClass

Like any interop assembly, tlbimp.exe will define a managed class type for each coclass. Check out the following type definition:

```
.class public auto ansi import CoCarClass
       extends [mscorlib]System.Object
       implements VBComEventsServer._CoCar,
                  VBComEventsServer.CoCar,
                  VBComEventsServer.__CoCar_Event
{
...
}
```

As you can see, CoCarClass implements the __CoCar_Event interface, and therefore supports the AboutToBlow and Exploded events. To handle the firing of these events, you will find the type also supports a unique add_XXX() and remove_XXX() method for each event (Figure 8-22).

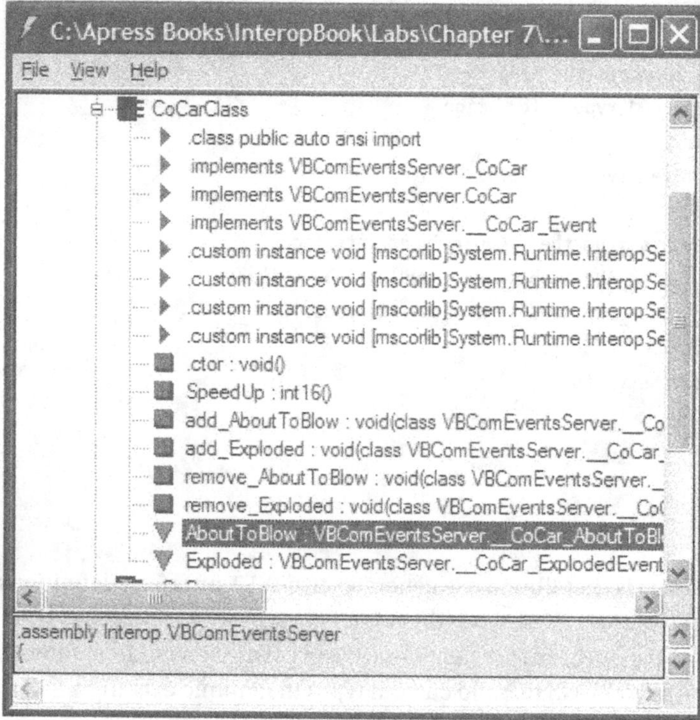

Figure 8-22. The generated class type supports events of the [source] interface.

And as you would expect, each event definition will make use of the [.addon] and [.removeon] directives to map the events to the correct delegate method (just like in the previous SimpleCSharpEvent application). For example:

```
.event VBComEventsServer.__CoCar_AboutToBlowEventHandler AboutToBlow
{
  .addon instance void
  VBComEventsServer.CoCarClass::add_AboutToBlow(class
  VBComEventsServer.__CoCar_AboutToBlowEventHandler)
  .removeon instance void
  VBComEventsServer.CoCarClass::remove_AboutToBlow(class
  VBComEventsServer.__CoCar_AboutToBlowEventHandler)
}
```

Receiving the COM Events (C#)

Now that you have checked out the core generated types, you are in the position to build a C# application that intercepts the incoming COM events. Assume you have a new C# console application (CSharpComEventClient) and have set a reference to VbComEventServer.dll. The process is identical to intercepting a native .NET event:

```
using System;
using VBComEventsServer;

namespace CSharpComEventClient
{
    // Helper sink class.
    class CSharpEventSink
    {
        public static void AboutToDie()
        { Console.WriteLine("->Dude!  Slow down!");}

        public static void Exploded()
        {Console.WriteLine("->You're toast...");}
    }
    class CSharpEventClient
    {
        [STAThread]
        static void Main(string[] args)
        {
            // First, create the CoCar.
            CoCarClass car = new CoCarClass();

            // Now hook the events to the correct sink method.
            car.AboutToBlow += new

            __CoCar_AboutToBlowEventHandler(
             CSharpEventSink.AboutToDie);
            car.Exploded += new
            __CoCar_ExplodedEventHandler(
             CSharpEventSink.Exploded);

            // Finally, work the car and trigger the events.
            for(int i = 0; i < 20; i++)
                Console.WriteLine("Current speed: {0}",
                 car.SpeedUp());
        }
    }
}
```

Notice that your sink object has not implemented the generated __CoCar_Event interface (as this is optional). Figure 8-23 shows the output.

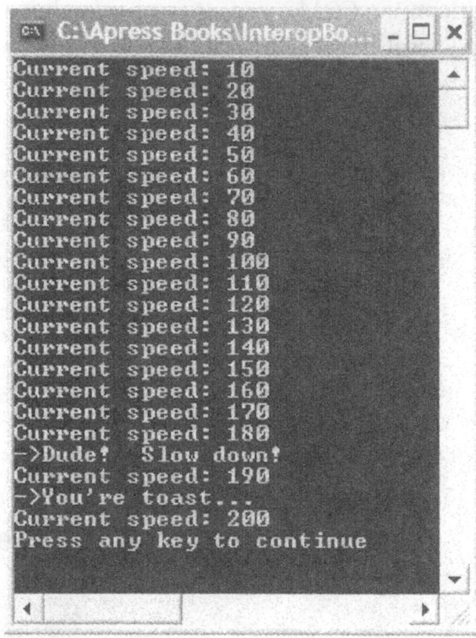

Figure 8-23. Managed output

As you can see, the complexity of COM connection points is completely hidden from view. Given that tlbimp.exe has already generated the correct delegates based on the [source] interfaces found in the COM type library, all you are required to do is provide a target for the delegate and associate it to the coclass' events.

CODE *The CSharpComEventClient project is included under the Chapter 8 directory.*

Receiving the COM Events (VB .NET)

Although VB .NET developers are also able to make direct use of .NET delegates, the language does simplify the process by supplying the WithEvents (which should be very familiar to VB 6.0 developers) and Handles keywords. To illustrate, here is a VB .NET client making use of VbComEventServer.dll.

```
Imports VBComEventsServer
Module Module1
    ' We want the events...
    Public WithEvents car As New CoCarClass()

    Sub Main()
        ' Speed things up.
        Dim i As Integer
        For i = 0 To 19
            Console.WriteLine("Current speed: {0}", car.SpeedUp())
        Next
    End Sub
    ' Sinks.
    Public Sub car_AboutToBlow() Handles car.AboutToBlow
        Console.WriteLine("Dude!  Slow down!")
    End Sub

    Public Sub car_Exploded() Handles car.Exploded
        Console.WriteLine("You're toast...")
    End Sub
End Module
```

Here, the VB .NET client application declares a CoCarClass type WithEvents. This keyword takes care of creating the correct delegates on your behalf. The Handles keyword is the VB .NET analogy of the "myType.Event +=" syntax.

CODE *The VbNetComEventClient project is included under the Chapter 8 directory.*

Handling COM Types with Multiple [source] Interfaces

When you create event-centric coclasses using VB 6.0, you are always confined to working with a single [default, source] interface. Of course, this fact means that your connection point container maintains a single connection point. The truth of the matter is, even though the connection point architecture allows a container to support numerous connection points, few developers make use of this feature. The reason is simple: Most client applications (such Microsoft IE and VB 6.0) are only able to receive events from the [default, source] interface. In fact, under classic COM, the only language that is sophisticated enough to interact with additional connection points is C++.

However, let's assume that you have a legacy ATL type that does indeed define multiple event sources. The IDL might look something like this:

```
library ATLMULTIPLESOUCEINTERFACESSERVERLib
{
    importlib("stdole32.tlb");
    importlib("stdole2.tlb");

    [uuid(B972F07E-D620-4A76-BEA9-2C3B02D5214A)]
    dispinterface _DefaultEventSet
    {
        properties:
        methods:
        [id(1), helpstring("method FirstEvent")]
        HRESULT FirstEvent();
    };

    [uuid(86B73A3E-83CF-49ee-A7DE-CCE2EBFCEB62)]
    dispinterface _ExtraEventSet
    {
        properties:
        methods:
        [id(1), helpstring("method SecondEvent")]
        HRESULT SecondEvent();
    };

    [uuid(A628B861-5CD4-4EEA-87B1-ABCB7942EF4D)]
    coclass ComplexCPContainer
    {
        [default] interface IComplexCPContainer;
        [default, source] dispinterface _DefaultEventSet;
        [source] dispinterface _ExtraEventSet;
    };
};
```

As you may recall from the previous chapter, when a COM class implements multiple interfaces, the tlbimp.exe utility creates a .NET class type that is a union of each interface member. In the same exact way, if you import a COM class type that supports multiple [source] interfaces, tlbimp.exe will simply define the class type to support the events of each [source] interface (and generate a the necessary delegate). Figure 8-24 shows the truth of the matter via the IDE's object browser.

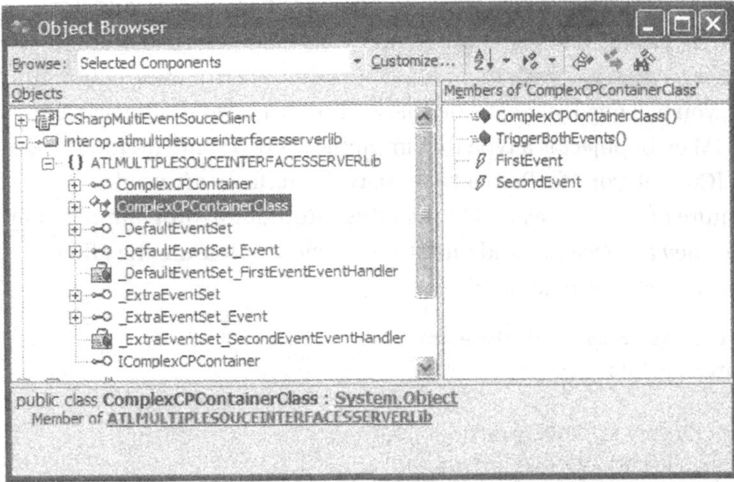

Figure 8-24. Multiple [source] interfaces are bound to a single class.

Handling COM Error Objects

And now on to the next topic of this chapter: bugs. In a perfect world, software would perform without failure. Networks would always be online, memory would exist without bounds, and data points would never exceed their limits. Of course, this is fantasyland. To deal with the unknown, classic COM provides two very specific mechanisms to report error information to the caller: HRESULTs and error objects.

First and foremost, every COM interface method is required to return an HRESULT value that informs the client if the current method invocation succeeded or failed. The COM APIs define numerous well-known HRESULTs that describe the result in question. The most beloved of all HRESULTs is S_OK, which provides the client with the proverbial thumbs up (that is, the method succeeded without error). The most generic form of a failed HRESULT is E_FAIL. Between the range of S_OK and E_FAIL are dozens (if not hundreds) of predefined HRESULTs (many of which are defined in winerror.h) that you can make use of in your custom applications. For example, consider the following ATL coclass method implementation:

```
STDMETHODIMP CAtlComClass::SomeMethod()
{
    // Assume DoSomeWork() is a method returning a Boolean.
    if( DoSomeWork() )
        return S_OK;
    else
        return E_FAIL;
}
```

Although COM HRESULTs can help the calling code base understand the basics of what (if anything) failed, it is often more helpful to return additional details to the caller. When you wish to return more verbose error information from a COM coclass, you will need to create, define, and send a *COM error object*. By definition, a COM error object is a type that implements two standard interfaces: IErrorInfo and ICreateErrorInfo. Basically, these two interfaces are used to describe the nature of the error as well as read this information programmatically (in other words, they are accessor and mutator interfaces). Here are the official IDL definitions for each (see oaidl.idl):

```
// Used by the coclass to document the error.
interface ICreateErrorInfo: IUnknown
{
    HRESULT SetGUID([in] REFGUID rguid);
    HRESULT SetSource([in] LPOLESTR szSource);
    HRESULT SetDescription([in] LPOLESTR szDescription);
    HRESULT SetHelpFile([in] LPOLESTR szHelpFile);
    HRESULT SetHelpContext([in] DWORD dwHelpContext);
}
// Used by the client to obtain the details of the error.
interface IErrorInfo: IUnknown
{
    HRESULT GetGUID([out] GUID * pGUID);
    HRESULT GetSource([out] BSTR * pBstrSource);
    HRESULT GetDescription([out] BSTR * pBstrDescription);
    HRESULT GetHelpFile([out] BSTR * pBstrHelpFile);
    HRESULT GetHelpContext([out] DWORD * pdwHelpContext);
}
```

As you can see, these interfaces allow you to document numerous details beyond a single HRESULT. Table 8-5 outlines the supported functionality.

Table 8-5. Aspects of the COM Error Object

Aspect of COM Error Object	Meaning in Life
SetGuid() GetGuid()	Provides a way to identify the GUID of the interface that caused the error
SetSource() GetSource()	Provides a way to identify the source of the error (typically the ProgID of the server)
SetDescription() GetDescription()	Allows you to create a custom textual message that documents the error (for example, "Sorry, server is down," "You don't have access rights to this method," "Go away, I'm busy," and so on)
SetHelpFile() GetHelpFile() SetHelpContext() GetHelpContext()	Allows you to use a COM error object to point the caller to a specific help file

Manipulating COM Error Objects in COM

Different COM language mappings have different ways to create a COM error object. If you were to use the raw COM APIs, you could simply call CreateErrorInfo() and make use of the returned ICreateErrorInfo interface:

```
// Creating a COM error object
// via the COM API.
ICreateErrorInfo *pCreateErrorInfo;
HRESULT hr;
hr = CreateErrorInfo(&pCreateErrorInfo);
pCreateErrorInfo ->SetDescription(L" Houston, we have a problem…");
…
```

Throwing the error back to the client is a job for the SetErrorInfo() COM library function. Recall that the IErrorInfo interface is what the client needs to extract the details of the error object, thus you must first obtain said interface:

```
// Now throw it back to the client.
…
IErrorInfo* pErrorInfo;
PCreateErrorInfo->QueryInterface(IID_IErrorInfo,
  (void**)&pErrorInfo);
SetErrorInfo(NULL, pErrorInfo);
…
```

The ATL framework hides the details of directly working with ICreateErrorInfo by supplying a set of overloaded Error() members defined by CComCoClass. As you would expect, the parameters you send into a given Error() method will be shuffled into the respective methods of ICreateErrorInfo. Furthermore, the Error() methods will automatically throw the error before exiting. Thus, in ATL the previous logic could be simplified as follows:

```
// Creating a COM error object via ATL.
Error("Houston, we have a problem…");
```

Visual Basic 6.0 takes a similar approach by supplying the intrinsic Err object. This object implements the ICreateErrorInfo and IErrorInfo interfaces. Therefore, this single object can be used to create a COM error as well as extract the information.

```
' Creating and sending COM error via VB 6.0
' (using an arbitrary error ID).
Public Sub BadDeal()
    Err.Raise 6666, " Houston, we have a problem..."
End Sub
```

The Role of ISupportErrorInfo

Before you learn how managed code processes COM error objects (as well as raw HRESULTs), you have one final error-centric interface to contend with: ISupportErrorInfo.

```
// This interface is implemented by the coclass
// and allows the client to verify that the error
// they are looking at came from the interface
// that triggered the error.
interface ISupportErrorInfo: IUnknown
{
    HRESULT InterfaceSupportsErrorInfo([in]  REFIID riid);
}
```

The role of ISupportErrorInfo is to allow the client to verify that the current error object it is investigating has indeed come from the correct interface. Implementing this interface's sole method is done automatically using ATL (and VB 6.0), but it can be done using raw C++ as follows (note that *you* are the one in charge of determining which interfaces of your coclass return rich error information):

```
STDMETHODIMP CTheBrokenObject::InterfaceSupportsErrorInfo(
  REFIID riid)
{
    static const IID* arr[] =
    {&IID_ITheBrokenObject};

    for (int i=0; i < sizeof(arr) / sizeof(arr[0]); i++)
    {
        if (InlineIsEqualGUID(*arr[i],riid))
        return S_OK;
    }
    return S_FALSE;
}
```

Building a Simple ATL Error Server

For the sake of discussion, assume you have created a new in-proc COM server using ATL and inserted a single coclass (TheBrokenObject) that has explicitly added support for the ISupportErrorInfo interface (Figure 8-25). This option will add ISupportErrorInfo to your class' inheritance chain and update the COM_MAP, as well as provide a default implementation of ISupportErrorInfo.InterfaceSupportsErrorInfo().

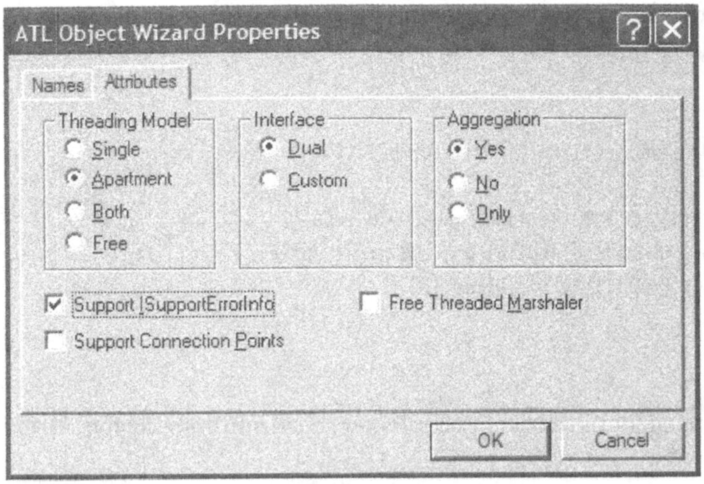

Figure 8-25. Supporting ISupportErrorInfo using ATL

This ATL coclass defines two painfully simple methods, which as luck would have it always fail. First you have ReturnFailedHRESULT(), which returns a standard COM HRESULT informing the caller that this entity is not a COM collection:

```
STDMETHODIMP CTheBrokenObject::ReturnFailedHRESULT()
{
    // Return a failed HRESULT.
    // DISP_E_NOTACOLLECTION is a standard HR which
    // informs the caller that a given item is
    // not a COM collection.
    // Of course, returning this HR is semantically
    // out of whack for this method, but it is
    // more interesting than a simple E_FAIL.

    return DISP_E_NOTACOLLECTION;
}
```

Of course returning DISP_E_NOTACOLLECTION is a bit of a stretch for your current ATL coclass; however, it is a bit more interesting than a vanilla-flavored E_FAIL. DISP_E_NOTACOLLECTION is defined in winerror.h as follows (take note of the textual description):

```
// MessageId: DISP_E_NOTACOLLECTION
// MessageText:
//  Does not support a collection.
#define DISP_E_NOTACOLLECTION
```

ReturnComErrorObject() will make use of the inherited Error() method to return a custom description of the current failure (albeit not a very helpful description):

```
STDMETHODIMP CTheBrokenObject::ReturnComErrorObject()
{
    // The ATL Error() methods (defined in CComCoClass)
    // hide the gory details of building a COM error object.
    Error("This is a reallllly bad error");
    return E_FAIL;
}
```

That's all you need for the current example. Go ahead and compile the server.

CODE *The AtlComErrorServer project is included under the Chapter 8 subdirectory.*

The .NET Error Handling Mechanism

Managed objects do not make use of HRESULTs or COM error objects. Rather, the .NET platform makes use of a tried-and-true error handling technique known as *structured exception handling* (SEH). Although a given managed language (C#, VB .NET, MC++, and so forth) may have a unique syntax to represent SEH, all managed languages make use of the following concepts:

- A class type that represents a given exception. Under .NET, all exceptions derive from a common parent class (System.Exception).
- A "try" block that marks a set of code, which may trigger an exception.
- A "catch" block (or possibly multiple catch blocks) that will handle a specific exception.
- An optional "finally" block that *always* executes, regardless of error.

In terms of C#, typical SEH logic might look like the following:

```
try
{
    // Code that may cause an exception.
}
catch (Exception ex)
{
    // Handle this exception.
}
finally
{
    // This code will always execute.
}
```

Notice that the catch block specifies the generic System.Exception type. Because this class is the base class for all .NET exceptions, your catch block can handle any possible error generated by the try block. Of course, the .NET base class libraries define numerous derived exceptions that can be used in place of a generic System.Exception.

In any case, once an error has been trapped by a given catch block, what sort of information can you obtain? Table 8-6 documents some of the interesting members of System.Exception.

Table 8-6. Select Members of System.Exception

Member of System.Exception	Meaning in Life
HelpLink	Gets or sets a link to the help file associated with this exception
InnerException	Gets the Exception instance that caused the current exception
Message	Gets a message that describes the current exception
Source	Gets or sets the name of the application or the object that causes the error
StackTrace	Gets a string representation of the frames on the call stack at the time the current exception was thrown
TargetSite	Gets the method that throws the current exception

The COMException Type

The System.Runtime.InteropServices namespace defines a derived exception type used to trap COM error information sent to the managed client by the RCW. COMException is responsible for exposing the data found in a given COM error object using the familiar .NET SEH mechanism. Table 8-7 illustrates how information exposed via IErrorInfo is mapped to the members of System.Runtime.InteropServices.COMException.

Table 8-7. Mapping IErrorInfo to a Managed COMException

Member of COMException	Source of Information from COM
ErrorCode	HRESULT returned from call.
HelpLink	If IErrorInfo.HelpContext is nonzero, the string is formed by concatenating IErrorInfo.GetHelpFile and "#" and IErrorInfo.GetHelpContext. Otherwise the string is returned from IErrorInfo.GetHelpFile.
InnerException	Always null.
Message	String returned from IErrorInfo.GetDescription().
Source	String returned from IErrorInfo.GetSource().
StackTrace	The stack trace.
TargetSite	The name of the method that returned the failing HRESULT.

Handling COM Error Information from Managed Code

Now that you have an understanding of how COM error information is mapped into the COMException type, the following client-side code should be straightforward:

```
using System;
using ATLCOMERRORSERVERLib;
using System.Runtime.InteropServices;

namespace CSharpComErrorClient
{
    class ComErrorClient
    {
```

```
        // Helper function.
        static void ReportCOMError(COMException e)
        {
            Console.WriteLine("*********************");
            Console.WriteLine("Raw HRESULT: {0}", e.ErrorCode);
            Console.WriteLine("Message: {0}", e.Message);
            Console.WriteLine("Source of error: {0}", e.Source);
            Console.WriteLine("Method Name: {0}", e.TargetSite);
            Console.WriteLine("**********************\n");
        }

        [STAThread]
        static void Main(string[] args)
        {
            // Create the ATL coclass.
            TheBrokenObjectClass b = new TheBrokenObjectClass();

            // Trigger the errors.
            try
            {
                b.ReturnFailedHRESULT();
            }
            catch(COMException comEx)
            {
                ReportCOMError(comEx);
            }
            try
            {
                b.ReturnComErrorObject();
            }
            catch(COMException comEx)
            {
                ReportCOMError(comEx);
            }
        }
    }
}
```

Simply put, this client-side code triggers each error and catches the COMException returned by the RCW. The ReportCOMError() helper function prints out the statistics held by the COM error object. Figure 8-26 shows the output.

```
C:\Apress Books\InteropBook\Labs\Chapter 7\CSharpComErrorClient\bi...
*************************************
Raw HRESULT: -2147352559
Message: Does not support a collection.
Source of error: Interop.ATLCOMERRORSERVERLib
Method Name: Void ReturnFailedHRESULT()
*************************************

*************************************
Raw HRESULT: -2147467259
Message: This is a realllllly bad error
Source of error: AtlComErrorServer.TheBrokenObject.1
Method Name: Void ReturnComErrorObject()
*************************************

Press any key to continue
```

Figure 8-26. Processing COM errors from managed code

CODE *The CSharpComErrorClient project can be found under the Chapter 8 subdirectory.*

Debugging COM Servers Using VS .NET

The final topic of this chapter has to do with the process of debugging a COM server that is used from a managed environment. It is no secret that Visual Studio .NET has a fantastic integrated debugging engine. However, it may not be as well known that the IDE supports a special mode termed *mixed mode debugging*. Specifically, this mode allows you to step into the code base of a classic COM server from a managed environment. Although this feature is disabled by default (given the performance penalty that you inherit), you are able to activate it by bringing up the Property page for your managed project, selecting the Debugging node under the Configuration Properties folder, and enabling the option Enable Unmanaged Debugging.

Assuming this is done, the next mandatory step is to ensure that the COM server in question has an accompanying *.pdb file. If the COM server was developed using ATL (or C++ in general), you will receive a *.pdb file by default. However, if the COM server was created in VB 6.0, you will need to explicitly request this file by checking the Create Symbolic Debug Info option located under the Compile tab of the Project Properties dialog box.

For the sake of illustration, assume you wish to debug the VbVariantServer.dll COM server created at the beginning of this chapter. First, request the *.pdb file (Figure 8-27) and recompile the project.

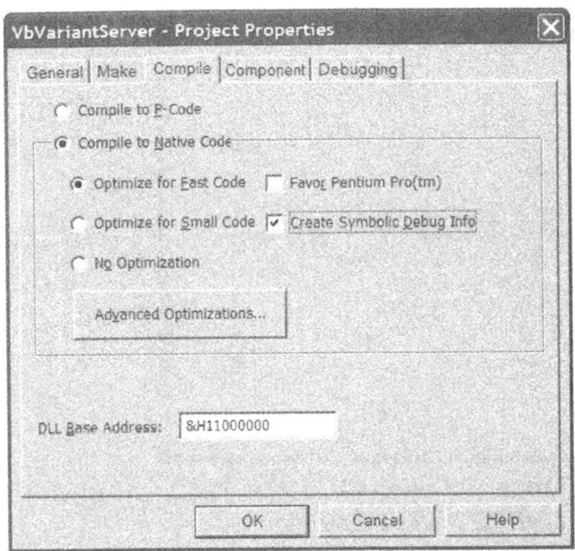

*Figure 8-27. Generating a *.pdb file for a VB 6.0 COM server*

As long as the C# client project has enabled mixed-mode debugging, simply set a break point at the desired location (Figure 8-28).

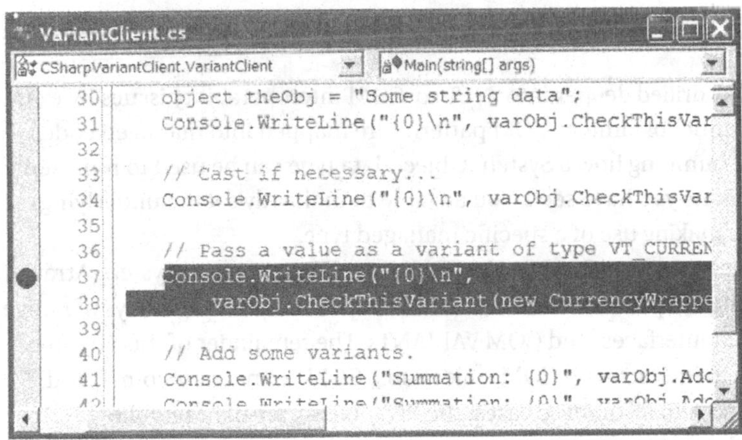

Figure 8-28. Preparing to step into the VB 6.0 COM server

If you begin a debug session (and twiddle your thumbs for just a bit), you are able to step into this line of code, and lo and behold, you are now in the guts of the VB 6.0 CheckThisVariant() method (Figure 8-29).

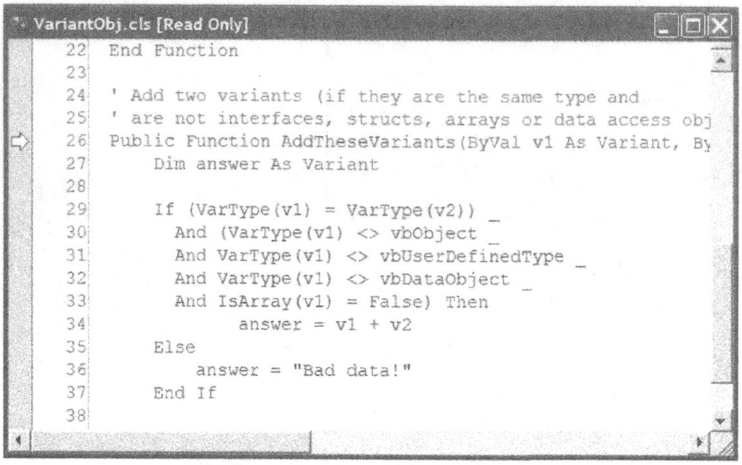

VariantObj.cls [Read Only]

```
End Function

' Add two variants (if they are the same type and
' are not interfaces, structs, arrays or data access obj
Public Function AddTheseVariants(ByVal v1 As Variant, By
    Dim answer As Variant

    If (VarType(v1) = VarType(v2)) _
      And (VarType(v1) <> vbObject _
      And VarType(v1) <> vbUserDefinedType _
      And VarType(v1) <> vbDataObject _
      And IsArray(v1) = False) Then
            answer = v1 + v2
    Else
        answer = "Bad data!"
    End If

```

Figure 8-29. Behold, the power of mixed-mode debugging.

Sweet! So, at this point you have drilled into the key .NET-to-COM interop issues you are likely to encounter on a day-to-day basis. The next chapter will examine a number of advanced topics you may need to make occasional use of. After this point, I switch gears and examine the topic of COM-to-.NET interop.

Summary

This chapter has drilled deeper into .NET-to-COM interoperability issues by examining how a number of familiar COM patterns are mapped into managed code. You began by examining how a System.Object data type can be used to represent COM VARIANTs. As you have seen, you are able to indirectly set the underlying VT_XXX flag by making use of a specific managed type.

Next, you learned how COM SAFEARRAYs map into managed System.Array types and during the process learned how to handle manipulating arrays of native data types, COM interfaces, and COM VARIANTs. The remainder of this chapter examined how to interact with COM collections, COM connection points, and COM error objects. In all of these cases, the RCW takes care of hiding the underbelly of the COM infrastructure and exposes these atoms as simple .NET equivalents.

Great! Having completed this chapter, you are now ready to import your favorite COM type libraries (classic ADO, SQL DMO, DirectX, or what have you) and make use of the contained types. The next chapter completes my discussion of .NET-to-COM communications by addressing some advanced topics such as handling custom IDL attributes and building custom type library importer utilities.

CHAPTER 9

.NET-to-COM Interoperability—Advanced Topics

This chapter wraps up your examination of building managed applications that make use of legacy COM types. Here, you will find a handful of advanced .NET to COM interoperability topics, which (to be sure) you may not have to contend with on a daily basis. Nevertheless, in these pages you come to learn how a COM coclass can implement .NET interfaces to achieve type compatibility with other like-minded .NET types. For example, you see how to implement the IComparable interface to allow a COM class to be sorted when contained within a .NET System.Collections.ArrayList type.

The next topic of this chapter illustrates how to import existing ActiveX controls for use by managed Windows Forms applications. During the process, you learn how to customize the generated ActiveX interop assembly to make up for shortcomings in the conversion process. On a related note, this chapter also demonstrates how to directly modify (and recompile) the contents of an interop assembly to alter the contained metadata. This entails the topic of handling [custom] IDL attributes from managed code. You wrap up by leaning how to import COM type information at runtime using the TypeLibConverter class. Once you have completed this chapter, you should have all the skills you need to successfully make use of COM types from managed code.

Revisiting the Marshal Class

As you have already seen, when a managed application makes use of a classic COM type, the low-level mechanics of AddRef(), Release(), and QueryInterface() are completely hidden from view. This is a good thing, as the primary role of the RCW is to hide such low-level details from view, allowing the .NET client to interact with the COM type as one of its own. As you may recall from Chapter 1, however, the Marshal type defines a small number of static members that allow you to get a bit closer to the action (if you so choose). Before you see some select examples, Table 9-1 reiterates the members in question.

Table 9-1. COM-Centric Members of the Marshal Type

General COM-Centric Member of the Marshal Type	Meaning in Life
AddRef()	Increments the reference count on the specified interface
BindToMoniker()	Gets an interface pointer identified by the specified moniker
GenerateGuidForType()	Returns the GUID for the specified type, or generates a GUID using the algorithm employed by the Type Library Exporter (tlbexp.exe)
GenerateProgIdForType()	Returns a ProgID for the specified type
GetActiveObject()	Obtains a running instance of the specified object from the Running Object Table (ROT)
GetComInterfaceForObject()	Returns an IUnknown pointer representing the specified interface for an object
GetIDispatchForObject()	Returns an IDispatch interface from a managed object
GetIUnknownForObject()	Returns an IUnknown interface from a managed object
GetObjectForNativeVariant()	Converts a COM VARIANT to an object
GetObjectsForNativeVariants()	Converts an array of COM VARIANTs to an array of objects
GetNativeVariantForObject()	Converts an object to a COM VARIANT
IsComObject()	Indicates whether a specified object represents an unmanaged COM object
IsTypeVisibleFromCom()	Indicates whether a type is visible to COM clients
QueryInterface()	Requests a pointer to a specified interface from an existing interface
Release()	Decrements the reference count on the specified interface
ReleaseComObject()	Decrements the reference count of the supplied Runtime Callable Wrapper (RCW)

Directly Interacting with IUnknown

One interesting use of the Marshal class is to directly obtain a pointer to any coclass' IUnknown interface. Of course, the .NET platform does not supply you with a managed definition of this core COM interface; however, you are able to represent this type using a generic System.IntPtr. To illustrate, assume you have created a new C# console application and set a reference to the RawComCar.tlb file created in Chapter 2. The following code illustrates how Marshal may be used to directly trigger the member of IUnknown:

```
using System;
using Intertech.RawComCarLib;
using System.Runtime.InteropServices;

namespace LowLevelManagedClient
{
    class DownAndDirtyClient
    {
        [STAThread]
        static void Main(string[] args)
        {
            // Make a raw COM car.
            ComCarClass c = new ComCarClass();

            // See if this guy is a COM object...
            Console.WriteLine("Am I a COM object? {0}",
                Marshal.IsComObject(c).ToString());

            // Get IUnknown of object.
            IntPtr itfUnknownPtr =
                Marshal.GetIUnknownForObject(c);

            // Manually AddRef() and Release()
            // using the IUnknown pointer.
            for(int i = 0; i < 5; i++)
            {
                Console.WriteLine("AddReffing! Count: {0}",
                    Marshal.AddRef(itfUnknownPtr));
                Console.WriteLine("Releasing! Count: {0}",
                    Marshal.Release(itfUnknownPtr));
            }

            // Manually call QueryInterface().
            IntPtr itfRadioPtr;
            Guid IIDRadio =
                Marshal.GenerateGuidForType(typeof(IRadio));
```

```
                Marshal.QueryInterface(itfUnknownPtr,
                    ref IIDRadio, out itfRadioPtr);

                // Convert raw IntPtr to IRadio and
                // manually crank tunes.
                IRadio itfRadio =
                    (IRadio)Marshal.GetObjectForIUnknown(itfRadioPtr);
                itfRadio.CrankTunes();
            }
        }
    }
```

Here, you begin by creating a new RawComCar as usual. However, rather than call members using the generated "-Class" type, you instead obtain the type IUnknown interface using Marshal.GetIUnknownForObject(). Using the returned System.IntPtr, you can then influence the coclass' reference count using Marshal.AddRef() and Marshal.Release(). To make things a bit more interesting, notice the logic used to trigger the type's QueryInterface() implementation. The Marshal.QueryInterface() method requires the same three points of information as the unmanaged definition, specifically, an interface used to make the call (itfUnknownPtr), the IID, and a place to store the pointer. To obtain the IID of IRadio, you make a call to Marshal.GenerateGuidForType(), which despite its name returns the GUID of the type based on the referenced interop assembly. Finally, once you have the IntPtr representing IRadio, you are able to obtain a strongly typed equivalent (via Marshal.GetObjectForIUnknown()) and crank some tunes.

Now, understand of course that the chances that you will need to drop down to this level are extremely low. Nevertheless, it is enlightening to see how to interact with these COM primitives from a managed environment.

Manually Destroying a COM Object

As discussed in Chapter 7, an RCW is in charge of caching references to a given COM class. When the managed wrapper (ComCarClass in our case) is no longer referenced by the client, the interfaces are released on the COM type as the managed type is garbage collected. While this is all well and good, sometimes it is useful to destroy a COM class at a time of your choosing, rather than waiting for the .NET garbage collector to do so. The Marshal.ReleaseComObject() method can be used to force the RCW to release *all* references held on the underlying coclass. Once this has been done, the __ComObject-derived class is then unusable. If this type is used after a call to Marshal.ReleaseComObject(), a NullReference exception is thrown:

```
// This releases ALL interfaces
// held by the RCW.
ComCarClass c2 = new ComCarClass();
Console.WriteLine("Ref Count after calling Marshal.ReleaseComObject(c2): {0}",
  Marshal.ReleaseComObject(c2));

// This will throw an error.
try
{
    c2.CrankTunes();
}
catch(NullReferenceException ex)
{
    Console.WriteLine(ex.Message);
}
```

CODE *The LowLevelManagedClient project is included under the Chapter 9 subdirectory.*

COM Coclasses Implementing .NET Interfaces

As you will see in Chapter 10, when you want to build a COM client that can make use of the types contained within a .NET assembly, you need to generate the appropriate COM type information using a tool named tlbexp.exe (Type Library Exporter). Understand, however, that a select number of .NET assemblies (such as mscorlib.dll) have already been converted into a corresponding COM type library (i.e., mscorlib.tlb) for your convenience. Also understand that the designer of a given .NET assembly always has the option of hiding a given type (or type member) using the ComVisible attribute (also described in Chapter 10). Given this, you need to be aware that a .NET-centric type library (such as mscorlib.tlb) may not account for each and every type contained in the original assembly.

In any case, when a given assembly chooses to expose an item as "COM visible," COM programmers can make use of these types in a manner (more or less) identical to that of a native COM entity. As you are most likely aware, mscorlib.dll defines a large number of general interfaces (ICloneable, IComparable, IDisposable, and whatnot) that allow a given .NET type to support a specific behavior. In fact, most .NET assemblies contain some number of interface definitions that are semantically related to the defining namespace (for example, System.Data defines data-centric interfaces, System.Windows.Forms defines GUI-centric interfaces, and so on).

Given the fact that a .NET assembly can be expressed in terms of COM type information, one very interesting possibility is the act of implementing .NET interfaces on an unmanaged COM type to improve the integration of the coclass in a managed environment. When a given COM type does implement .NET interfaces, it is said to be *type compatible* with the native .NET types supporting the same interface.

Building a Comparable COM Class

To illustrate the process of a building .NET type compatible COM class, let's create a simple example. The System.IComparable interface provides a standard manner by which identical objects can be compared based on a specific point of reference. The sole method of this interface, CompareTo(), takes a single parameter of type System.Object (which therefore represents any possible .NET class or structure):

```
// This .NET interface allows an object to
// compare itself with other objects of its type.
public interface IComparable
{
  int CompareTo(object obj);
}
```

When implementing this interface on a COM (or .NET) type, you need to determine the data point that will serve as the point of comparison. For example, if you were building a Car type, you might compare two Cars based on a numerical ID. Two Person types might be compared based on their social security numbers (and so on). Once you have identified the basis of the comparison, CompareTo() should return 0 if the two values are identical, –1 if the current object is less than the value of the incoming object, and +1 if the current object is greater than the value of the incoming object.

To illustrate, assume you have created a brand-new VB 6.0 ActiveX DLL named ComparableComObj, and you have set a reference to the Common Language Runtime type library using the Project | References menu selection (Figure 9-1).

Now that you have access to mscorlib.tlb, the implementation of IComparable for a trivial VB 6.0 Car class might look like this:

```
Option Explicit
Private mCarID As Integer

' The VB 6.0 Car class is
' comparable via its carID.
Implements IComparable

' Remember! System.Object is mapped into a COM VARIANT.
Private Function IComparable_CompareTo(ByVal obj As Variant) _
```

```
 As Long
  If obj.GetCarID = Me.GetCarID Then
    IComparable_CompareTo = 0
  ElseIf obj.GetCarID < Me.GetCarID Then
    IComparable_CompareTo = 1
  Else
    IComparable_CompareTo = -1
  End If
End Function
' Yes, you could use a COM property here too…
Public Sub SetCarID(ByVal id As Integer)
  mCarID = id
End Sub
Public Function GetCarID() As Integer
  GetCarID = mCarID
End Function
```

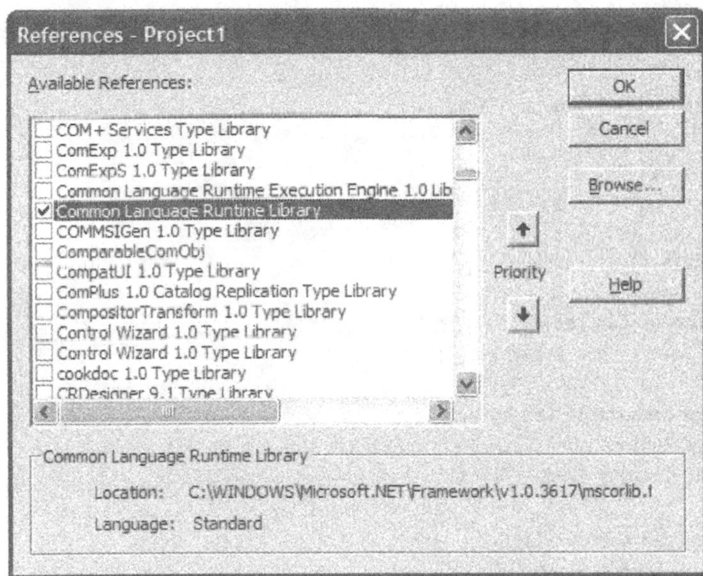

Figure 9-1. A COM client referencing mscorlib.tlb

Here, the Car type has implemented IComparable using an internal numerical identifier (mCarID) to represent the point of comparison. CompareTo() simply tests the value of the incoming Car (expressed as a COM VARIANT) against its own mCarID value and returns –1, 0, or +1 accordingly. Now that you have a COM class that is type compatible with the .NET IComparable interface, you can take this type out for a test drive.

CODE *The ComparableComObj project is included under the Chapter 9 subdirectory.*

Using the Comparable COM Object

Assume you have created a new C# Console application (ComparableComObjClient) that has set a reference to the ComparableComObj.dll COM server (via the Add References dialog). The Main() method begins by creating a new ArrayList type to hold a group of COM cars that are each assigned a random ID using the System.Random type. Once the ArrayList has been populated, you will print out the ID of each Car. Here is the story thus far:

```
using System;
using ComparableComObj;
using System.Collections;

namespace ComparableComObjClient
{
  class ComparableCarClient
  {
    [STAThread]
    static void Main(string[] args)
    {
      // A collection of COM cars.
      ArrayList carArray = new ArrayList();

      // Create some comparable COM cars.
      Random r = new Random();
      for(int i = 0; i < 10; i++)
      {
        carArray.Add(new CarClass());
        int newID = r.Next(50)+100;
        ((CarClass)(carArray[i])).SetCarID((short)newID);
      }

      // Print cars as is...
      Console.WriteLine("***** The unordered COM cars *****");
      for(int i = 0; i < carArray.Count; i++)
      {
        Console.WriteLine("Car #{0} has ID {1}", i,
          ((CarClass)(carArray[i])).GetCarID());
      }
    }
  }
}
```

Now, to interact with the IComparable interface, ask the ArrayList type to sort its contents. As you may know, the Sort() method automatically calls CompareTo() under the hood as it sorts the contained subobjects. Once you have sorted the ArrayList, you will print out the contents again. If the COM Car's implementation of IComparable is correct, you should now see each Car ordered by numerical value (which you do).

```
// Now sort the COM objects.
Console.WriteLine("***** The ordered COM cars *****");
carArray.Sort(); // IComparable obtained here!

// Print sorted cars...
for(int i = 0; i < carArray.Count; i++)
{
  Console.WriteLine("Car #{0} has ID {1}", i,
    ((CarClass)(carArray[i])).GetCarID());
}
```

Figure 9-2 shows the result.

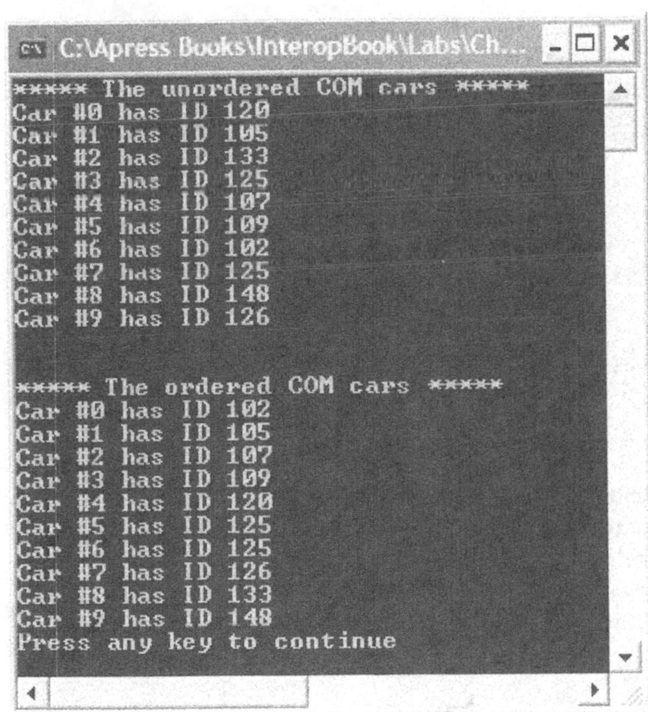

Figure 9-2. Sorting the COM types via IComparable

CODE *The VbCloneableObjectServer project is located under the Chapter 9 subdirectory.*

Building a Cloneable COM Type

Let's take a look at a second example of building .NET type compatible COM objects. The goal here is to implement the .NET ICloneable interface on a VB 6.0 coclass named CoPoint. CoPoint supports a [default] interface that defines two COM properties. The implementation of the ICloneable.Clone() method creates a new CoPoint that is configured to look exactly like the object that was asked to supply the copy. Assuming you have set a reference to mscorlib.tlb, here is the complete code:

```
Option Explicit
Implements ICloneable

Private xPos As Integer
Private yPos As Integer

Public Property Let X(ByVal rhs As Integer)
    xPos = rhs
End Property
Public Property Get X() As Integer
    X = xPos
End Property
Public Property Let Y(ByVal rhs As Integer)
    yPos = rhs
End Property
Public Property Get Y() As Integer
    Y = yPos
End Property

Private Function ICloneable_Clone() As Variant
    ' Make a new point which
    ' is identical to 'me'
    Dim newPt As CoPoint
    Set newPt = new CoPoint
    newPt.X = Me.X
    newPt.Y = Me.Y

    ' Return (VB will automatically
    ' package as VARIANT)
    Set ICloneable_Clone = newPt
End Function
```

Recall that the ICloneable.Clone() method is formally defined in terms of managed code as returning a System.Object. When the .NET metadata is transformed into a COM type definition, this parameter is realized as a COM VARIANT. The nice thing about using VB 6.0 (with regard to VARIANTs) is the fact that VB takes charge of the process of building the raw VARAINT under the hood. Thus, when you return the CoPoint type, the default interface is bundled into a COM VARIANT on your behalf.

CODE *The VbCloneableObjectServer project is located under the Chapter 9 subdirectory.*

Using the Cloneable COM Object

To test your coclass, let's simply update the previous ComparableComObjClient application to make use of the VB 6.0 CoPoint. Once you have set a reference to the COM type information, update the Main() method with the following C# code:

```
// Test the clone!
CoPointClass p1 = new CoPointClass();
p1.X = 100;
p1.Y = 100;
Console.WriteLine("P1.x = {0} P1.x = {1}", p1.X, p1.Y);

// Make a clone.
CoPointClass p2 = (CoPointClass)p1.Clone();
// Also prints out 100, 100.
Console.WriteLine("P2.x = {0} P2.x = {1}", p2.X, p2.Y);
```

When you run this application, you will find that both CoPoints are configured with X = 100, Y = 100. Given that a correctly designed clone should be a standalone copy of the original type, if you change the value of p2.X, p1 is unaffected.

Building .NET Type Compatible Coclasses Using ATL 3.0

Of course, any COM-aware programming language is able to build .NET type compatible COM types. However, when you attempt to do so with ATL 3.0, there are a few glitches to be aware of. Assume you were to implement ICloneable on an ATL Simple Object named CoRectangle. First, you need to obtain the IDL description of this .NET type via the Implement Interface Wizard. To activate this tool, simply right-click your CCoRectangle class via the Class View tab (Figure 9-3).

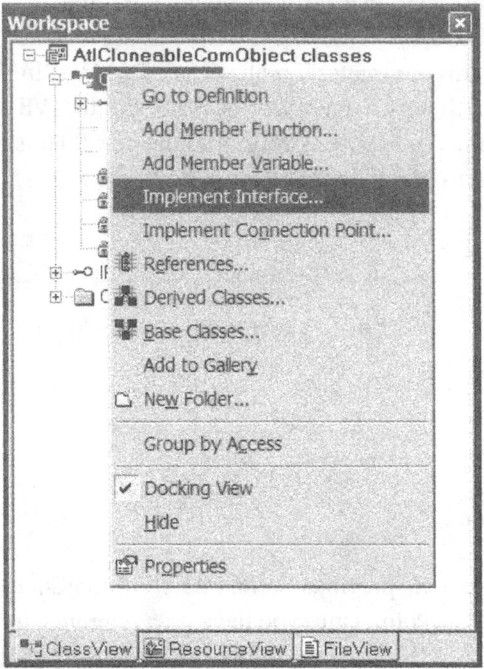

Figure 9-3. Implementing an interface

From the resulting dialog box, click the Add TypeLib button and locate the Common Language Runtime Library (Figure 9-4).

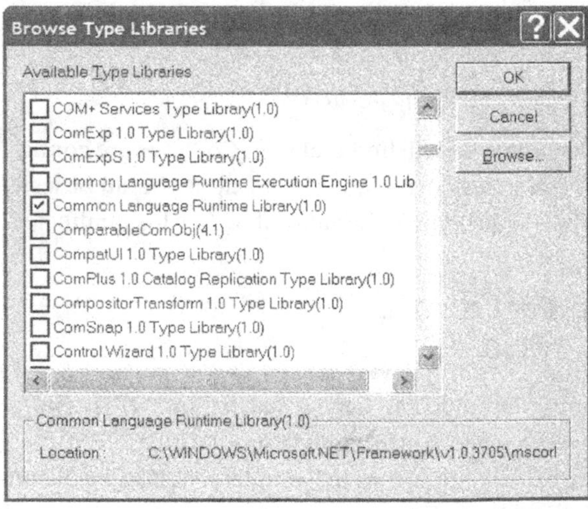

Figure 9-4. Using mscorlib.tlb from C++

Finally, once you click OK, locate the ICloneable interface (Figure 9-5).

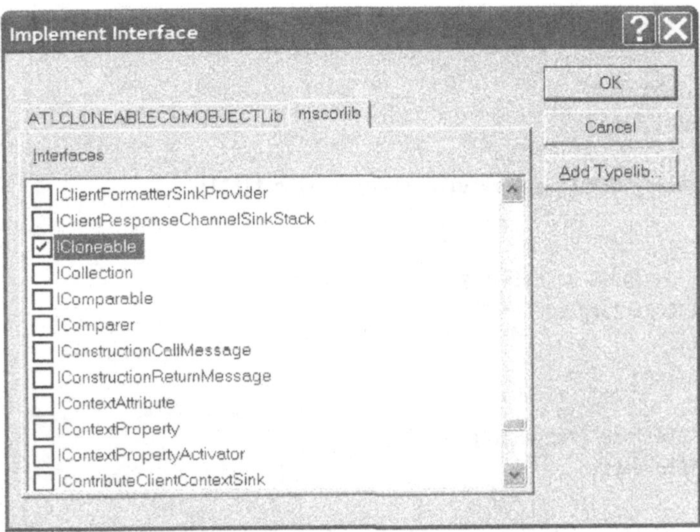

Figure 9-5. Specifying support for ICloneable

Once you have finished, you will find that the CCoRectangle.h file has been updated with a VC 6.0 #import statement that will be used to generate smart pointers for each COM visible type found in mscorlib.tlb. However, if you compile this application as is right now, you would be issued two errors and two warnings. The reason is that the ATL 3.0 framework declares a global instance of the CComModule helper class named _Module. Likewise, mscorlib.tlb defines a type named _Module (which is the default interface of the System.Reflection.Module class type). Thus, the compiler is terribly confused because it sees a _Module definition that is not in line with the ATL framework (no assigned GUID). The simplest way to resolve this name clash is to modify the generated #import statement to rename the _Module type of mscorlib.tlb to a unique definition:

```
#import "C:\WinNT\Microsoft.NET\Framework\v1.0.3705\mscorlib.tlb" \
  raw_interfaces_only, raw_native_types, no_namespace, \
named_guids, rename("_Module", "_SystemReflectionModule")
```

Updating the COM IDL

Assuming you have provided a valid implementation of ICloneable, you should tidy up the COM type information to advertise that your CoRectangle indeed implements this .NET type. This must be done manually because the ATL

Implement Interface tool does not automatically do so. Here are the relevant IDL updates:

```
library ATLCLONEABLECOMOBJECTLib
{
    importlib("stdole32.tlb");
    importlib("stdole2.tlb");
    importlib
    ("C:\WinNT\Microsoft.NET\Framework\v1.0.3705\mscorlib.tlb");

    [
        uuid(DBBEFF2D-3490-4C72-A41E-8530977D3AF7),
        helpstring("CoRectangle Class")
    ]
    coclass CoRectangle
    {
        [default] interface IRectangle;
        interface ICloneable;
    };
};
```

Cool! At this point you have created some COM classes that are tightly integrated with the .NET type system. Understand, of course, that a COM programmer is able to implement similar .NET interfaces in an identical manner (should the occasion arise). For example, you could implement IDisposable to allow your COM types to be treated like a managed .NET class. Furthermore, if you have created a .NET assembly that defines custom interfaces, the COM developer is able to support these behaviors as well. Before that can be done, however, you need to convert the defining .NET assembly to the equivalent COM type information. Chapter 10 describes this process in detail, so just put this idea on the back burner for now.

Guidelines for Building .NET Type Compatible COM Classes

Now that you have seen the process of building a .NET type compatible coclass, it is important to point out that just because you *can* implement .NET interfaces on COM classes does not mean you always *should*. As you would expect, there are some commonsense best practices that help guide the way. Key points to be aware of are discussed in the next sections.

Guideline #1: Don't Indirectly Implement the Same Interface Twice

First, understand that a given RCW automatically simulates a small handful of .NET interfaces depending on the composition of the coclass. Specifically,

- IEnumerable will be supported for COM classes that support a member with the DISPID of –4 (i.e., the DISPID_NEWENUM value used when building COM collections).
- IExpando will be supported for coclasses implementing IDispatchEx.
- IReflect will be supported for objects implementing ITypeInfo.

Given that the RCW will simulate such interfaces without effort on your part, it makes sense that you should never manually implement the same interface on a given COM type. In fact, if you do, the interop assembly incorrectly implements the same interface twice (causing massive chaos). The truth of the matter is, few COM programmers directly implement IDispatchEx or ITypeInfo in the first place, so this should not be too much of an issue. However, do make sure that when you build a COM collection you don't implement the .NET IEnumerable interface on the same type.

Guideline #2: Don't Implement .NET Class Interfaces

The second commonsense guideline has to do with implementing autogenerated "class interfaces." As you will see in greater detail beginning with the next chapter, when a .NET type is converted to a corresponding COM type definition, a class may make use of a class interface to establish a [default] interface for the type. Simply put, a *class interface* is the summation of each public member on the .NET class (as well as each public member up the chain of inheritance). By convention, class interfaces are always named _NameOfTheClass. For example, the class interface of System.Object is _Object. MyCoolDotNetClass produces a class interface named _MyCoolDotNetClass and so on.

Understand that you gain nothing if you implement an autogenerated class interface on a given COM class because the .NET type system does not honor the definition or use of class interfaces in the first place! If you implement a class interface on a given COM type, it would *not* be type compatible with original .NET type. By way of a simple example, assume that you have the following .NET class definition:

```
using System;
using System.Runtime.InteropServices;

namespace MyClassInterfaceLibrary
{
  [ClassInterface(ClassInterfaceType.AutoDual)]
  public class DotNetClass
  {
    public DotNetClass(){}
    public void Foo(){}
  }
}
```

Without getting too bogged down in the details at this point, simply understand that the ClassInterfaceAttribute type is used to instruct how to expose a .NET class to COM. By specifying ClassInterfaceType.AutoDual, you are instructing tlbexp.exe to expose this class type as a [dual] COM interface named _DotNetClass. Once this assembly is converted into a related COM type library (via tlbexp.exe), you find the following IDL definition:

```
interface _DotNetClass : IDispatch
{
  // Inherited System.Object members removed for clarity…
  HRESULT Foo();
};
…
coclass DotNetClass
{
  [default] interface _DotNetClass;
  interface _Object;
};
```

As you can see, the generated coclass supports the class interface _DotNetClass as the [default], and therefore a VB 6.0 COM client could call the Foo() method as follows:

```
' VB 6.0 calling Foo() on a .NET class.
Dim f as DotNetClass
Set f = New DotNetClass
f.Foo
```

Now, what if the same VB 6.0 application implemented this class interface on a given COM type? It could be done given that _DotNetClass has been published into the COM type information. Assume you have a coclass named CoIWannaBeLikeYou, which is defined as follows (recall that VB 6.0 hides underscore prefixes):

```
' Inherited System.Object members removed for clarity…
Option Explicit
Implements DotNetClass
```

```
Private Sub DotNetClass_Foo()
  ' Stuff...
End Sub
```

Here's the million-dollar question: "Could a managed client application treat the original .NET DotNetClass type and the VB 6.0 CoIWannaBeLikeYou identically?" The answer is a resounding "No." When a managed client creates the native .NET type, it is working with a direct object reference (the class interface is nonexistent). When the managed client creates an instance of the COM class, it is pointing to an interface named _DotNetClass. Thus, if the managed client defined a method such as

```
public void WorkWithDotNetClass(DotNetClass x)
{ x.Foo();}
```

the two types could *not* be treated polymorphically, given that the _DotNetClass interface is not the same as a DotNetClass object reference! The bottom line is that class interfaces are only meaningful by an unmanaged COM client. If a coclass implements a class interface, it is most certainly not type compatible with the .NET class that produced it (so don't bother to do so).

Guideline #3: Take Care When Implementing Interface Hierarchies

Next, understand that if a COM class implements a .NET interface that has been derived from a base interface, any reference to the base interface is lost during the .NET to COM conversion process. Again, you will drill into the details of exposing .NET types to COM in the next chapter. For the sake of argument, however, assume you are building the following .NET interface hierarchy:

```
// A C# interface hierarchy.
public interface IBaseInterface
{
  void MethodA();
}

public interface IDerivedInterface : IBaseInterface
{
  void MethodB();
}
```

If a .NET class type wished to support the functionality of IDerivedInterface, it would be responsible for implementing MethodA(), given that members in a base interface are automatically inherited by the derived interface:

```
// Implementing derived interfaces
// entails supporting each member up
// the chain of inheritance.
public class Foo : IDerivedInterface
{
  public Foo(){}
  public void MethodB(){}
  public void MethodA(){}
}
```

However, if these interfaces were published to a COM type library, you would find that both are expressed as dual interfaces deriving from IDispatch. This is because there is no way to instruct tlbexp.exe to make use of a custom interface when defining a base interface. Thus:

```
// .NET interface hierarchies do not
// preserve base interface relationships when
// converted to COM IDL!
interface IBaseInterface : IDispatch {
  [id(0x60020000)]
  HRESULT MethodA();
};

interface IDerivedInterface : IDispatch {
  [id(0x60020000)]
  HRESULT MethodB();
};
```

Given this behavior, it would be possible to implement IDerivedInterface on a COM type *without* accounting for the intended base functionality! This would, of course, be a huge problem to a .NET client using the COM type. If the managed client obtains a reference to IDerivedInterface, it assumes MethodA() is present and accounted for:

```
// Assume this COM object has only
// implemented IDerivedInterface...
NotReallyTypeCompatibleObj ack =
  new NotReallyTypeCompatibleObj();
ack.MethodA(); // Bomb!
```

When you attempt to build a .NET type compatible COM object that requires the use of derived interfaces, you should always explicitly implement the interfaces up the chain of inheritance, as seen in the following VB 6.0 coclass definition:

```
Option Explicit
Implements IBaseInterface
Implements IDerivedInterface
```

```
Private Sub IBaseInterface_MethodA()
  ' Something interesting…
End Sub

Private Sub IDerivedInterface_MethodB()
  ' Something even more interesting…
End Sub
```

If this is the case, the managed client is now able to interact with the base members using an explicit IBaseInterface reference:

```
// Better.
TypeCompatibleObj better = new TypeCompatibleObj();
IBaseInterface theBase = (IBaseInterface)better;
theBase.MethodA();
```

Guideline #4: VB 6.0 Has a Key Limitation (Imagine That . . .)

This final guideline is more of a heads-up than a true design consideration. Visual Basic 6.0 has a rather annoying behavior when it comes to the act of implementing interfaces: It is unable to implement interfaces that contain members named using an underbar (for example, My_Method(), My_Other_Method(), HereAreThreeUnderbars___(), and so on). Assume a COM interface defined in IDL as follows:

```
interface IFoo : IDispatch
{
    [id(1), helpstring("method Hello_There")]
    HRESULT Hello_There();
};
```

If you implement the IFoo interface on a VB 6.0 coclass, you would *not* be able to provide programming logic for Hello_There() given the presence of the dreaded underbar (in fact, you couldn't even compile).

While it might not be the case that you will ever build a COM method using this rather old-fashioned naming convention, recall that when tlbimp.exe encounters a type that defines overloaded methods, it disambiguates each version using an underbar (i.e., Method_1(), Method_2(), and so on). Given these facts, understand that you cannot build a .NET type compatible COM class using VB 6.0 if the interface in question defines overloaded members.

So, with these guidelines in mind, you should be able to build .NET type compatible COM types if the need arises. Doing so can make your coclasses appear a bit more "natural" from a managed client's perspective, but make sure you have good reason for doing so in the first place.

Consuming ActiveX Controls from Managed Code

Let's shift gears now and check out how a managed Windows Forms application can make use of legacy COM-based ActiveX controls. These COM types are just like any other COM types in that they support some number of COM interfaces (including the mandatory IUnknown). The key difference is the fact that many of the interfaces supported by an ActiveX control are used exclusively for graphical rendering and host interaction.

Building a fully functional ActiveX control is quite an art, given that you are basically constructing a mini-window that supports any number of properties, methods, and events (typically using a single [default] inbound interface and a single [default] source interface). Rather than diving into the details of building a production-level custom control, you will construct a trivial ActiveX control using VB 6.0. Once you have created the COM type, you will import it into a C# Windows Forms application (of course, the process of importing more exotic controls would be identical).

Building an Example ActiveX Control

To begin, launch VB 6.0 and select a new ActiveX Control project workspace named SimpleVb6AxCtrl. Your trivial control (named LameColorControl) provides two properties (TheText and TheBackGroundColor) that allow the outside world to configure the color used to render the control as well as a string to be displayed in a Label object. The control also defines a single event (TextChanged) that will be fired when the user calls the underlying put_TheText() method (recall that all COM properties resolve to two hidden methods). Finally, the control's surface contains three Button objects that allow the user to select from three predefined color values at runtime. Figure 9-6 shows the design time GUI.

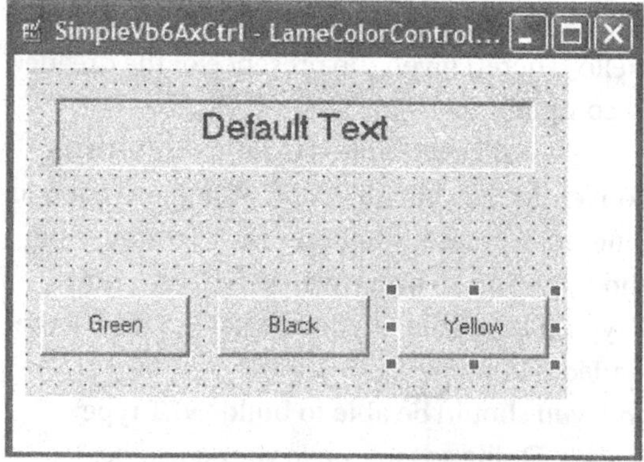

Figure 9-6. The GUI of your ActiveX control

The code behind the UserControl type is very straightforward (even for those with no formal exposure to building ActiveX controls with VB 6.0). Here is the complete listing:

```
' Private data.
Private mBkColor As OLE_COLOR
Private mText As String

' A single event
Public Event TextChanged()

' Public properties.
Public Property Get TheText() As String
  TheText = mText
End Property
Public Property Let TheText(ByVal newText As String)
  mText = newText
  txtLabel = mText
  RaiseEvent TextChanged ' Fire event!
End Property
Public Property Get BackGroundColor() As OLE_COLOR
  BackColor = mBkColor
End Property
Public Property Let BackGroundColor(ByVal newColor As OLE_COLOR)
  mBkColor = newColor
End Property

' Button click handlers.
Private Sub btnBlack_Click()
  mBkColor = vbBlack
  BackColor = mBkColor
End Sub
Private Sub btnGreen_Click()
  mBkColor = vbGreen
  BackColor = mBkColor
End Sub
Private Sub btnYellow_Click()
  mBkColor = vbYellow
  BackColor = mBkColor
End Sub
Private Sub UserControl_Initialize()
  mBkColor = vbRed
  BackColor = mBkColor
End Sub
```

Before you compile your ActiveX control, you will update the underlying IDL with some [helpstring] attributes (this step is important later in this chapter). As you are most likely aware, the [helpstring] attribute allows you to provide textual documentation that describes how a given property is to be used. Under VB 6.0, you are not able to directly edit the underlying IDL, but [helpstring] values can be set by accessing the Tools | Procedure Attributes menu selection (be sure your code window is the active window before you launch this tool). Figure 9-7 shows the [helpstring] value for the BackGroundColor property (add a similar value for the TheText property).

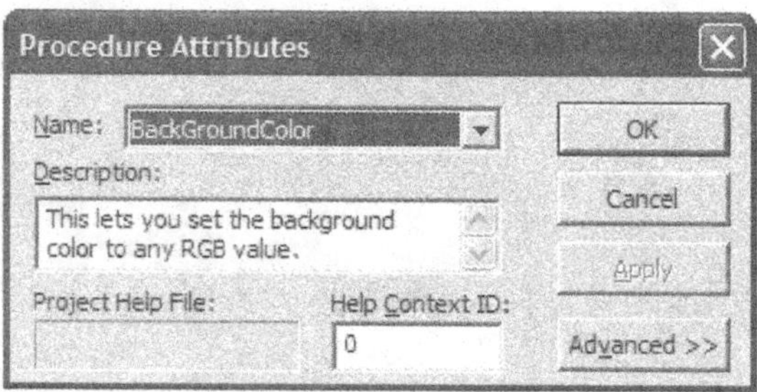

Figure 9-7. Applying IDL [helpstring]s in VB 6.0

Finally, to integrate the custom BackGroundColor property more fully into an IDE's Properties window, click the Advanced button and link this custom attribute to the standard BackColor DISPID (Figure 9-8). Once you have done so, compile your control and close the project workspace.

CODE *The SimpleVb6AxControl project is included under the Chapter 9 subdirectory.*

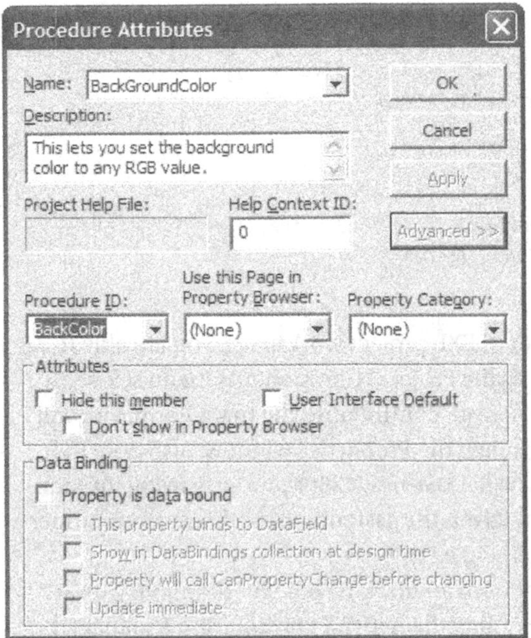

Figure 9-8. Setting DISPID_BACKCOLOR in VB 6.0

Viewing the Generated IDL

Now, using oleview.exe, locate your control under the Control category and view the underlying IDL. As you can see, each [helpstring] is documented in the COM type information (also note that the BackGroundColor property has been assigned the predefined DISPID, DISPID_BACKCOLOR, 0xfffffe0b, or –501), given your Procedure ID setting:

```
 [ odl,
 uuid(F4BB1CE2-2A68-4292-AE71-8895E6FD8A9A),
 version(1.0), hidden, dual,
 nonextensible, oleautomation ]
interface _LameColorControl : IDispatch {
  [id(0x68030000), propget,
  helpstring(
  "This sets the text which is to be displayed in the label.")]
  HRESULT TheText([out, retval] BSTR* );

  [id(0x68030000), propput,
  helpstring(
  "This sets the text which is to be displayed in the label.")]
  HRESULT TheText([in, out] BSTR* );
```

```
    [id(0xfffffe0b), propget,
    helpstring(
    "This lets you set the background color to any RGB value.")]
    HRESULT BackGroundColor([out, retval] OLE_COLOR* );

    [id(0xfffffe0b), propput,
    helpstring(
    "This lets you set the background color to any RGB value.")]
    HRESULT BackGroundColor([in, out] OLE_COLOR* );
};
```

If you build a new VB 6.0 Standard EXE project workspace, you are able to set a reference to your control type (using the Project | Components menu selection). Once you place an instance of the ActiveX control onto the main Form, you will find your help strings are visible through the Properties window. Also note that you are able to select the value of the BackGroundColor property using the standard color selection drop-down list (given the assignment of this custom property to DISPID_BACKCOLOR). Check out Figure 9-9.

So much for using your control from an unmanaged environment. Now it's time to turn your attention to consuming the ActiveX control from a managed Windows Forms application.

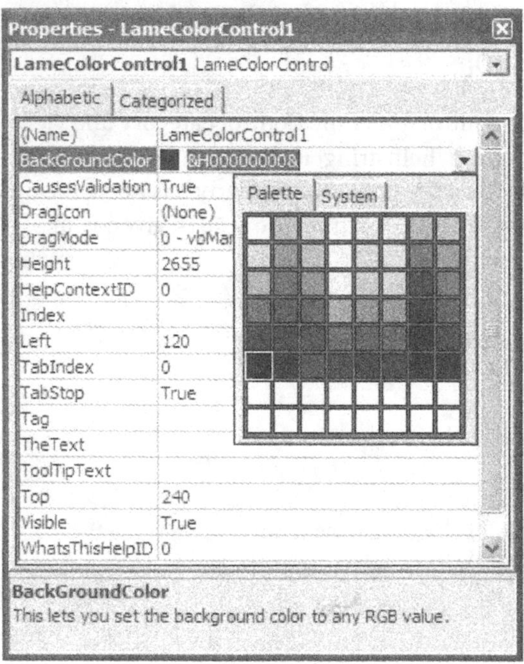

Figure 9-9. DISPID_BACKCOLOR in action

Options for Consuming ActiveX Controls from Managed Code

Much like a traditional COM server, before a .NET application can make use of an ActiveX control, the COM metadata must be converted into terms of .NET metadata. As you may suspect, you do have options:

- Make use of the Visual Studio .NET Customize Toolbox dialog box.
- Run the AxImp.exe command line utility.

You examine both options in turn the next several pages. Understand, of course, that regardless of which option you choose, you end up with *two* new .NET assemblies (explained shortly).

Consuming an ActiveX Control Using the VS .NET IDE

Assume you have created a brand-new C# Windows Forms application that wishes to make use of the VB 6.0 LameColorControl (and who wouldn't?). To do so, simply right-click the Toolbox and select Customize Toolbox (Figure 9-10).

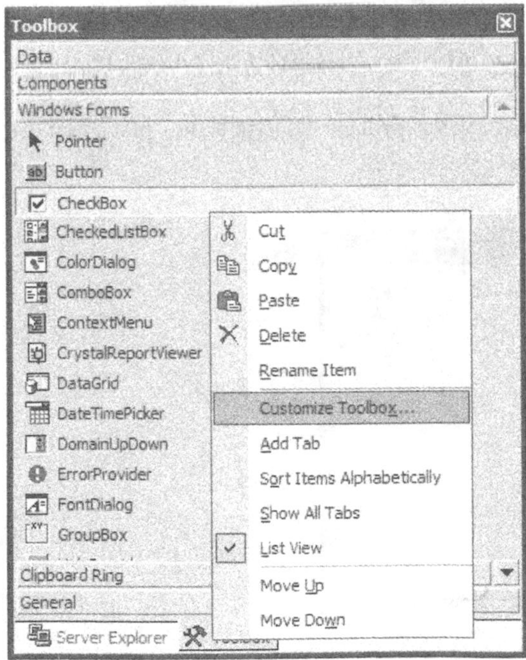

Figure 9-10. Referencing ActiveX controls from managed code begins here.

From the resulting dialog box, select the control you are interested in (Figure 9-11).

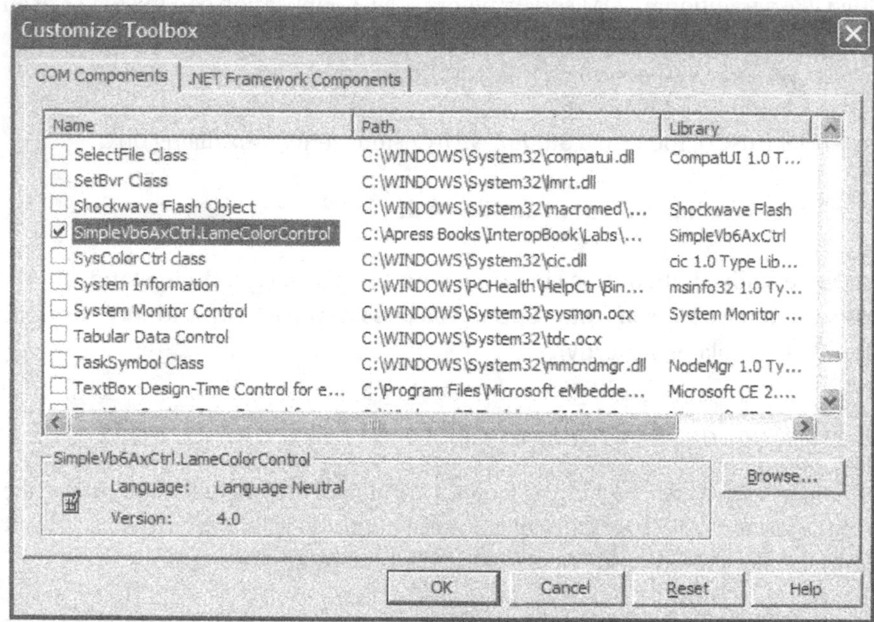

Figure 9-11. All registered controls are listed under the COM Components tab.

Once you have selected the control, you will see its icon is now placed on the Windows Forms tab of the Toolbox (Figure 9-12).

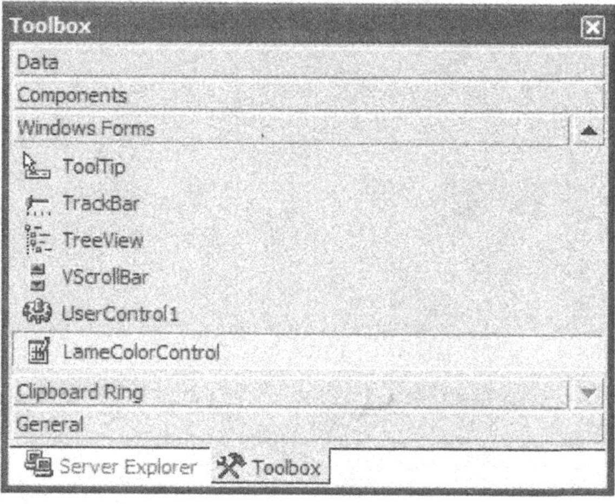

Figure 9-12. The LameColorControl icon

Once you place an instance of this control onto the C# Form-derived type, check out the Solution Explorer. You will find that you have been given references to two new .NET assemblies (Figure 9-13).

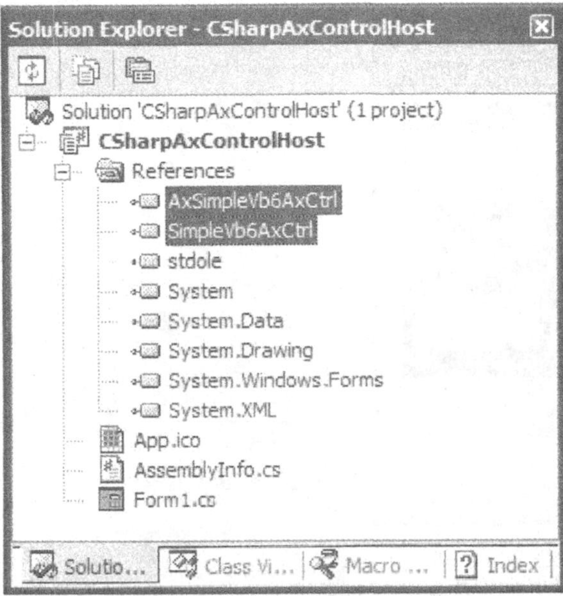

Figure 9-13. Using an imported ActiveX control results in two new interop assemblies.

You will check out the internals of these generated assemblies in just a moment. However, the short answer is that the content of the interop assembly (SimpleVb6AxCtrl) is as you would expect: It contains .NET metadata that was constructed based on the original COM type library.

The other assembly (taking an "Ax-" prefix) is a helper assembly that wraps the ActiveX control with various Windows Forms bells and whistles, to ensure that the legacy ActiveX type can be treated identically to a native .NET Windows Forms Control. Formally speaking, the "Ax-"-prefixed assembly generated for a given ActiveX control is termed an *ActiveX interop assembly.*

Understand that the managed client must be able to locate and manipulate both of these assemblies to correctly expose the ActiveX control type from a managed environment. Given this, also understand that when you deploy the .NET application, you need to ensure that each of these *.dlls is present and accounted for.

In any case, at this point you are free to build a C# GUI that interacts with the ActiveX type. Like a native Windows Forms Control, you are able to manipulate the control's properties and events using the IDE's Properties window (VB .NET applications are able to interact with the widget's event using the code window). Thus, if you design a simple UI that allows the user to input a text string, things might shape up as shown in Figure 9-14.

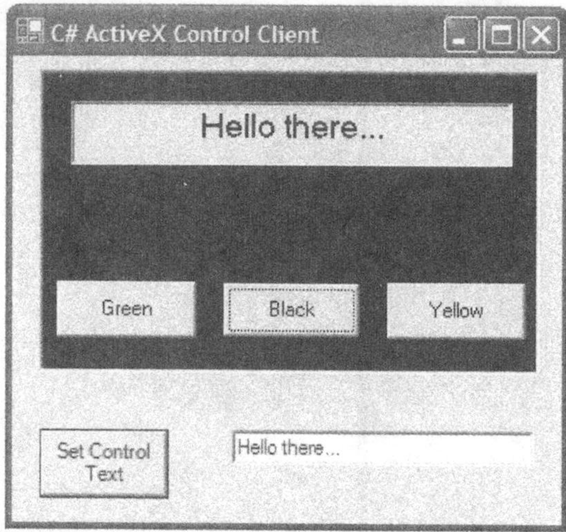

Figure 9-14. The ActiveX control in action

As you can see, the process of interacting with legacy ActiveX controls from a managed environment is quite straightforward. The code behind this C# Form is simple enough, so much so that I do not bother to list it here. When you place a LameColorControl onto the Form, you are able to interact with its properties, methods, and events in an identical manner as any other Windows Forms control.

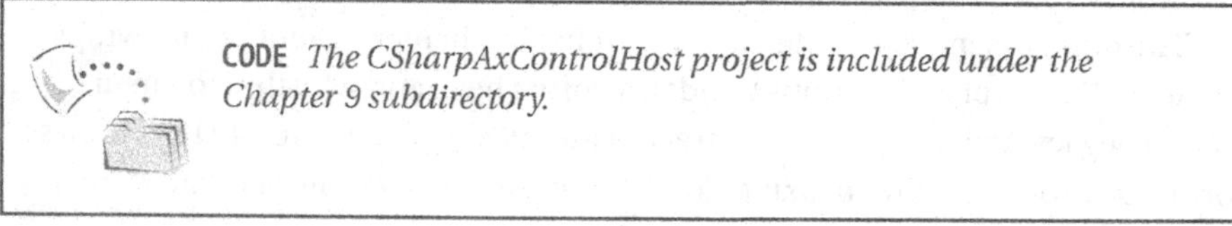

CODE *The CSharpAxControlHost project is included under the Chapter 9 subdirectory.*

Examining the Generated Assemblies

Now that you have created a managed client, let's check out the details of the two generated assemblies. The interop assembly (interop.SimpleVb6AxCtrl.dll) is identical in purpose to any other interop assembly in that it simply contains .NET metadata based on the original COM type information. If you check out the content of the generated interop assembly using ILDasm.exe, you find no big surprises. For example, the LameColorControl coclass is still represented by the LameColorControl, LameColorControlClass, and _LameColorControl types. The interop assembly still contains the required event helper types, and the assembly manifest is still composed based on the information found in the COM type library statement.

The additional generated assembly is unique. The role of the ActiveX interop assembly (AxInterop.SimpleVb6AxCtrl.dll) is to expose the raw ActiveX control as a true blue Windows Forms Control equivalent. This is accomplished by deriving the raw ActiveX control from the System.Windows.Forms.AxHost base class. The reason for deriving the COM type from AxHost is simple: Windows Forms can only host Windows Forms controls (classes ultimately deriving from System.Windows.Forms.Control).

The AxHost .NET class type defines a large number of properties that mimic the corresponding standard ActiveX members (such as BackColor and Text) as well as a number of additional properties and methods that allow the ActiveX type to behave like a native .NET control. In this way, the .NET host is able to provide a symmetrical treatment of COM-based and .NET-based GUI widgets.

Given this definition of the AxHost base class, ponder the following .NET metadata for the derived type (AxLameColorControl):

```
.class public auto ansi beforefieldinit AxLameColorControl
   extends [System.Windows.Forms]System.Windows.Forms.AxHost
{
 .custom instance void[System]System.ComponentModel.
DesignTimeVisibleAttribute::.ctor(bool) = ( 01 00 01 00 00 )
 .custom instance void[System]System.ComponentModel.
DefaultEventAttribute::.ctor(string)
 = ( 01 00 10 54 65 78 74 43 68 61 6E 67 65 64 45 76  //
 ...TextChangedEv
65 6E 74 00 00 )                    // ent..
 .custom instance void[System.Windows.Forms]System.Windows.
 Forms.AxHost/ClsidAttribute::.ctor(string) =
( 01 00 26 7B 62 66 65 62 62 35 35 30 2D 37 33 33
// ..&{bfebb550-733
65 2D 34 32 62 65 2D 38 62 65 35 2D 38 65 30 39
// e-42be-8be5-8e09
33 64 32 35 39 38 34 65 7D 00 00 )
// 3d25984e}..
} // end of class AxLameColorControl
```

As you can see, the derived type is the same name as the initial ActiveX control, with an "Ax" prefix. In fact, when you place an instance of the

ActiveX control onto the design time Form, you are in fact creating a member variable of the AxHost-derived type, not the raw ActiveX type:

```
public class mainForm: System.Windows.Forms.Form
{
  private System.Windows.Forms.TextBox txtMessage;
  private System.Windows.Forms.Button btnSetCtrlText;
  private AxSimpleVb6AxCtrl.AxLameColorControl axLameColorControl1;
...
}
```

As you might suspect, the AxHost-derived type is populated with the public properties, methods, and events of the original COM type (Figure 9-15).

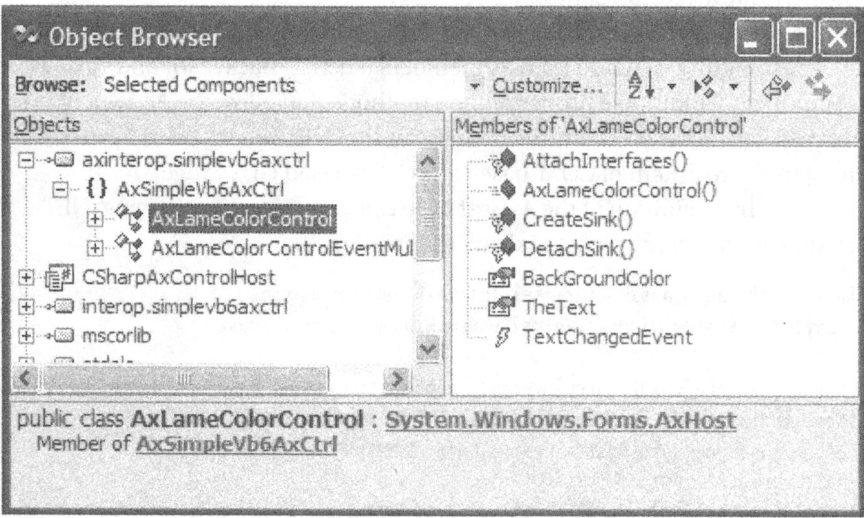

Figure 9-15. The "Ax-"-prefixed class supports all members of the raw COM type.

Finally, understand that the ActiveX interop assembly and the literal interop assembly are quite intertwined. This should make sense, given that the ActiveX interop assembly needs to read the metadata of the related COM server. If you examine the manifest of axinterop.simplevb6axctrl.dll, you find a specific [.assembly extern] tag that identifies its dependency on interop.simplevb6axctrl.dll:

```
.assembly extern Interop.SimpleVb6AxCtrl
{
 .ver 1:0:0:0
}
```

Now that you have a better idea of the role of each generated assembly, let's take a tour of the process of generating these binaries at the command line using AxImp.exe (and see why you might wish to do so).

Importing ActiveX Controls Using AxImp.exe

In addition to making use of the VS .NET IDE, you are able to generate the necessary .NET assemblies manually using the AxImp.exe utility. Like other command line tools, AxImp.exe does support a small set of optional arguments, most of which allow you to assign a strong name to the output assemblies. Additionally, AxImp.exe provides a very interesting flag named /source. As you might guess, this flag makes use of System.CodeDOM to generate the code on the fly (see Chapter 6):

```
aximp simplevb6axctrl.ocx /source
```

Just like VS .NET, AxImp.exe generates a traditional interop assembly as well as the assembly containing the AxHost-derived type. When the /source flag is specified, you also receive a C# code file that defines the types within the "Ax-"-prefixed assembly (to date, there is no way to specify VB .NET source code). If you opened this file, you would indeed find that the generated AxLameColorControl class type derives from AxHost and has been attributed with various Windows Forms–centric attributes that qualify how this widget should be viewed at design time.

The constructor of the AxHost-derived type also passes the CLSID of the registered ActiveX control up to its base class, to create the COM type via CoCreateInstance(). Finally, note that the AxHost-derived type maintains a member variable named "ocx" that represents the [default] interface of the COM type. The overridden AttachInterfaces() function assigned this variable using the base class GetOcx() method. Here is the story thus far:

```
[System.Windows.Forms.AxHost.ClsidAttribute
("{bfebb550-733e-42be-8be5-8e093d25984e}")]
[System.ComponentModel.DesignTimeVisibleAttribute(true)]
[System.ComponentModel.DefaultEvent("TextChangedEvent")]
public class AxLameColorControl : System.Windows.Forms.AxHost
{
  private SimpleVb6AxCtrl._LameColorControl ocx;
  ...
  public AxLameColorControl() :
    base("bfebb550-733e-42be-8be5-8e093d25984e") {}
  ...
  protected override void AttachInterfaces()
  {
    try {
      this.ocx =
```

```
        ((SimpleVb6AxCtrl._LameColorControl)(this.GetOcx()));
      }
      catch (System.Exception ) {}
    }
  }
```

The C# source code file also defines each member of the original ActiveX type in terms of managed code. Once a member has been checked for possible runtime exceptions, the wrapper methods make use of the valid "ocx" member variable (which, you recall, points to the [default] interface of the COM type) to call the correct COM member. In the following code block for the custom BackGroundColor property, notice that the DispIdAttribute has been assigned the correct value of DISPID_BACKCOLOR (–501) to ensure that you are able to set this value using the VS .NET design time Properties window (even better, note that the raw OLE_COLOR variable has been mapped into a System.Drawing.Color type):

```
[System.ComponentModel.DesignerSerializationVisibility
(System.ComponentModel.DesignerSerializationVisibility.Hidden)]
[System.Runtime.InteropServices.DispIdAttribute(-501)]
[System.Runtime.InteropServices.ComAliasNameAttribute(
 "System.UInt32")]
public virtual System.Drawing.Color BackGroundColor
{
  get
  {
    if ((this.ocx == null)) {
    throw new InvalidActiveXStateException("BackGroundColor",
      System.Windows.Forms.AxHost.ActiveXInvokeKind.PropertyGet);
    }
    return GetColorFromOleColor(
    ((System.UInt32)(this.ocx.BackGroundColor)));
  }

  set
  {
    if ((this.ocx == null)) {
    throw new InvalidActiveXStateException("BackGroundColor",
      System.Windows.Forms.AxHost.ActiveXInvokeKind.PropertySet);
    }
    this.ocx.BackGroundColor = (
    (System.UInt32)(GetOleColorFromColor(value)));
  }
}
```

The code behind the TheText property is more or less identical. The remaining code found in this autogenerated C# code file establishes the logic that maps any incoming COM events into terms of managed code.

CODE *The AxSimpleVb6AxCtrl.cs code file is located under the Chapter 9 subdirectory.*

Limitations of the AxImp.exe Utility

In most cases, the COM-to-.NET utilities that ship with the .NET SDK (tlbimp.exe and AxImp.exe) do a fine job of converting COM type information into terms of .NET metadata. However, both tools completely ignore two rather useful IDL attributes:

- IDL [helpstring] annotations
- Custom IDL attributes

For example, if you host the LameColorControl on a Windows Form and select this widget at design time, you would find the [helpstring] values you assigned to the ActiveX control do *not* appear in the VS .NET IDE (Figure 9-16).

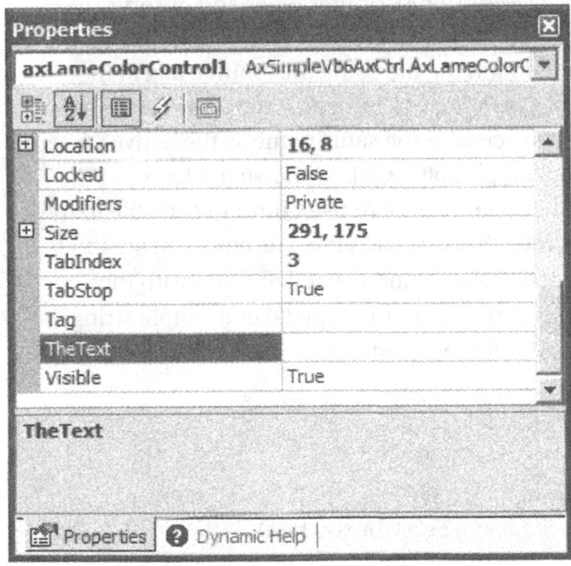

Figure 9-16. Hmm . . . the [helpstring] values are absent.

It is unfortunate that AxImp.exe fails to account for IDL [helpstring] values, given that the .NET class libraries do supply a managed class that is roughly analogous: System.ComponentModel.DescriptionAttribute. This type, which is specifically designed to represent a textual description for a given member of a Windows Forms Control, is the attribute read by the VS .NET Properties window to display the helpful string message.

Modifying the Code for the AxHost-Derived Type

If you want to ensure that imported ActiveX controls are able to display their original IDL [helpstring] values within the VS .NET IDE, your tasks are as follows:

- Edit the generated C# source code file to support any number of DescriptionAttribute types.
- Compile the *.cs file back into an ActiveX interop assembly.
- Distribute the updated assembly with the Windows Forms client application.

To illustrate the process, let's update the C# source code file generated by AxImp.exe to support three new DescriptionAttributes types and observe the result. First and foremost, understand that you are only able to directly edit the underlying C# source code if you obtain the file using the /source flag of the AxImp.exe command line utility. Assuming you have generated the C# file, create a new C# code library project workspace with the same name as the ActiveX interop assembly (in this case, AxInterop.SimpleVb6AxCtrl, as shown in Figure 9-17).

Next, copy the contents of the generated C# ActiveX interop code file to the clipboard and paste it into the project's initial class file. The edits you are interested in making are to update each property and event definition with the DescriptionAttributes type. The constructor of this type takes a simple string that is read at design time by the Properties window.

```
public class AxLameColorControl : System.Windows.Forms.AxHost
{
...
  [System.ComponentModel.Description
  ("This sets the text which is to be displayed in the label.")]
  public virtual string TheText {...}

  [System.ComponentModel.Description
  ("This lets you set the background color to any RGB value.")]
  public virtual System.Drawing.Color BackGroundColor {...}
```

```
  [System.ComponentModel.Description
   ("This Event is fired when the text is changed (duh!).")]
  public event System.EventHandler TextChangedEvent;
...
}
```

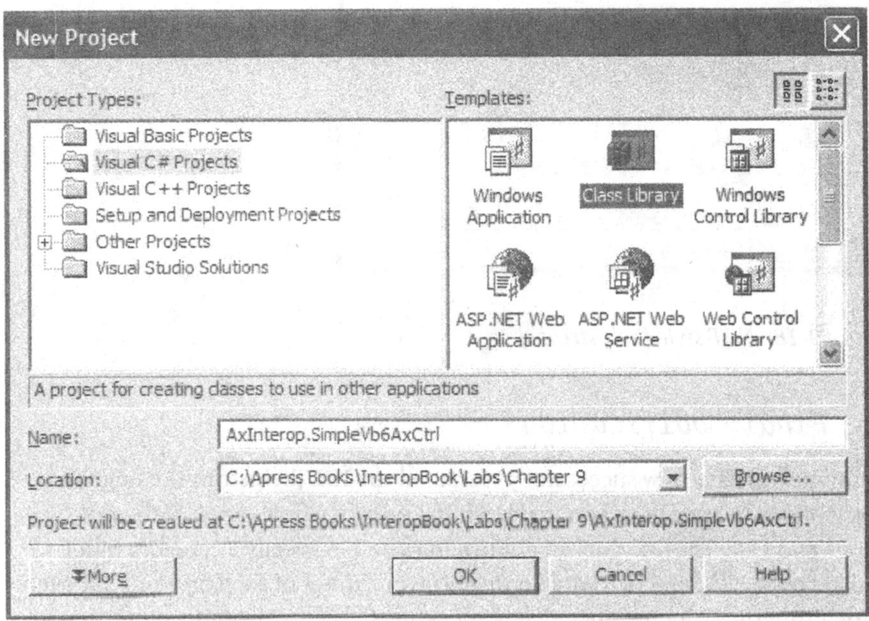

Figure 9-17. A new Class Library to hold the source of the ActiveX interop assembly

At this point, the ActiveX interop assembly project can be recompiled. If you now build a new C# Windows Forms application and set a reference to this specific interop assembly (rather than the original COM server, which would generate a new interop assembly), you will find that when you select this type from the design time template and view the Properties window, the helpful text messages are pleasingly present (Figure 9-18).

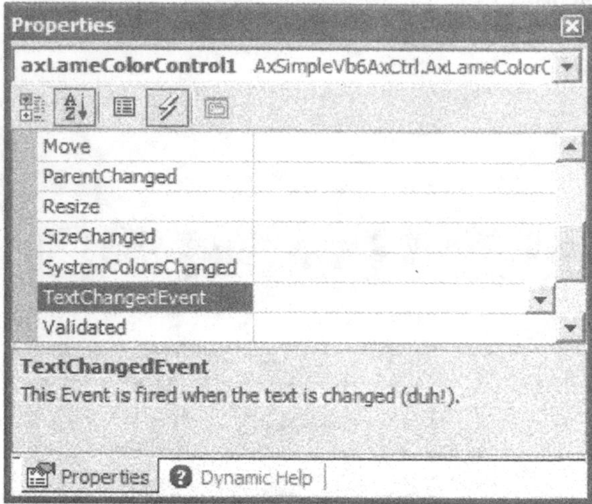

Figure 9-18. .NET-style [helpstrings]

One Final Modification

Although you have now successfully recreated the IDL [helpstrings] using the DescriptionAttribute type, you may wish to perform a final tweak of the raw C# source code file. The CategoryAttribute allows you to specify a category name to be used by the VS .NET IDE when it displays the names of each property (or event) in the Properties window. Specifically speaking, CategoryAttribute allows you to assign your properties and events to any of the categories in Table 9-2.

Table 9-2. Possible Categories for Control Members

Possible Category	Meaning in Life
Action	Properties regarding available actions
Appearance	Properties affecting how an entity appears
Behavior	Properties affecting how an entity acts
Data	Properties concerning data
Design	Properties that are available only at design time
DragDrop	Properties about drag-and-drop operations
Focus	Properties pertaining to focus
Format	Properties affecting format
Key	Properties affecting the keyboard
Layout	Properties concerning layout
Mouse	Properties pertaining to the mouse
WindowStyle	Properties affecting the window style of top-level forms

If these predefined categories don't fit the bill, you are also free to craft one more to your liking. For example, let's say you want to ensure that when the properties of the LameColorControl are viewed by category, each of them appears under a heading named "Lame Stuff." You could do so by updating the C# code as follows:

```
public class AxLameColorControl : System.Windows.Forms.AxHost
{
  ...
  [System.ComponentModel.Description
  ("This sets the text which is to be displayed in the label."),
  System.ComponentModel.Category("Lame Stuff")]
  public virtual string TheText
  {...}

  [System.ComponentModel.Description
  ("This lets you set the background color to any RGB value."),
  System.ComponentModel.Category("Lame Stuff")]
  public virtual System.Drawing.Color BackGroundColor
  {...}

  [System.ComponentModel.Description
  ("This Event is fired when the text is changed (duh!)."),
  System.ComponentModel.Category("Lame Stuff")]
  public event System.EventHandler TextChangedEvent;
...
}
```

The result of this final modification is seen when a new Windows Forms application selects the LameColorControl and examines the Properties window (Figure 9-19).

The act of editing the C# code behind an arbitrary ActiveX assembly simply for the sake of doing so is not required. However, assume you are in the business of building (and selling) ActiveX controls. If you wish to generate a primary interop assembly (see Chapter 7) for your client base, taking this time to simulate COM [helpstring] values gives your final product a more polished look and feel.

That wraps up your formal investigation of making use of legacy ActiveX controls from managed code. At this point, you should have a solid understanding of the default conversion process and understand how you are able to modify the metadata contained within an ActiveX interop assembly using the generated C# source code.

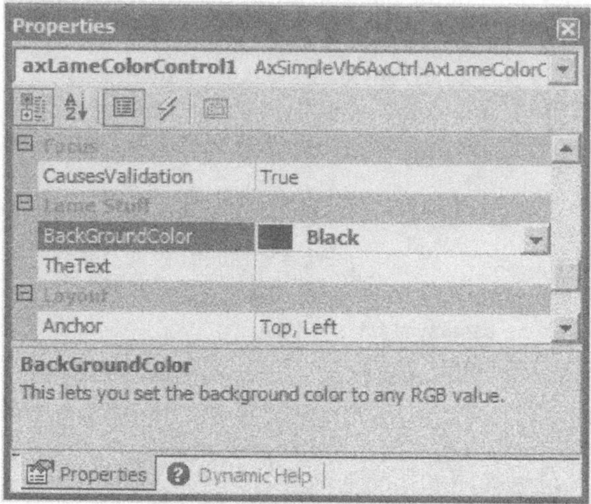

Figure 9-19. Assigning the control's members to a custom category

Manually Modifying Interop Assemblies

Another fairly advanced topic is the manual modification of previously generated interop assemblies. Not the source code, mind you (as in the previous example), but the raw .NET metadata. As you have seen during the last few chapters, the tlbimp.exe utility does a fine job of mapping COM types (interfaces, coclasses, enums, and structures) into terms of managed code. In fact, the conversion process is so seamless that in many cases you are able to simply make use of the Visual Studio. NET Add Reference dialog box and program against the generated interop assembly without any further consideration. Recall, however, that both AxImp.exe and tlbimp.exe ignore

- IDL [helpstring] annotations
- Custom IDL attributes

As previously illustrated, if the coclass in question is an ActiveX control, you can specify the /source flag to AxImp.exe to obtain the C# source code. Once you make your custom modifications, you can recompile and distribute the ActiveX interop assembly and make everything right with the world.

Tlbimp.exe does not supply a similar flag. If you want to simulate [helpstring] information in an interop assembly produced from a server containing a more traditional COM coclass (i.e., not an ActiveX control), you need to disassemble the binary and modify the metadata by hand. Similarly, if you wish to account for any orphaned custom IDL attributes, editing the interop assembly is your most direct option. Before you decide to re-create IDL [helpstring] and [custom] attributes, be aware that the VS .NET IDE only displays DescriptionAttribute values for GUI-based .NET types. Thus, even if you crack open an interop assembly and insert the correct metadata to mimic [helpstring] data (as well as [custom] IDL attributes), you need to build a custom tool that can read this information (using .NET reflection services).

In addition to accounting for [helpstring] and [custom] IDL attributes, there could be other reasons you want to edit the contents of an interop assembly. For example, you may wish to alter how a C-style array is exposed to a .NET client, add information that instructs the runtime to make use of a custom marshaler when transforming COM types to .NET types (and vice versa), or manually insert DISPIDs for a COM server that does not natively define them. In a nutshell, as long as you stay within the syntax constraints of .NET metadata, you are able to update an interop assembly in any way you see fit.

Again, understand that if the original COM server made use of [oleautomation]-compliant data types, the chances are extremely good that you will never need to alter the generated interop assembly in the first place. Nevertheless, let's check out the process firsthand (just for the sake of knowledge). If you are interested in examples beyond the one shown here, check out online Help (do a search for the topic "Customizing Runtime Callable Wrappers"). Once you understand the example presented in this chapter, you will have no problem making other modifications to an interop assembly.

Building an Example COM Server

To illustrate the process of manually editing an interop assembly, assume that you have created a COM server (usingATL) named AtlHelpCustomAttsServer that defines a single coclass, implementing a single interface, which supports a single method. Being a kindhearted COM programmer, you also took the time to document the coclass using a [helpstring] attribute. Furthermore, being a COM programmer under a deadline, you added a custom ToDo attribute (as seen in Chapter 4). Here is the IDL under discussion:

```
import "oaidl.idl";
import "ocidl.idl";
[ object,
uuid(EC7C1641-4031-45EA-8B61-7AAAD04A0BA7),
dual, pointer_default(unique) ]
interface IAdd : IDispatch
{
  [id(1)]
  HRESULT Add([in] int x, [in] int y,
```

```
  [out, retval] int* answer);
};

[uuid(85CE5F31-AAD7-4C43-93F4-12841414C822),
version(1.0)]
library ATLHELPCUSTOMATTSSERVERLib
{
  importlib("stdole32.tlb");
  importlib("stdole2.tlb");

  [ uuid(4C3DB474-61BF-49BF-979B-68A5FB53E43B),
  helpstring("This class adds two numbers"),
  custom(1403B3A5-38FE-4ba9-94E2-54577F712E7A,
   "ToDo: Add subtraction functionality...")]
  coclass AtlAdder
  {
    [default] interface IAdd;
  };
};
```

CODE *The AtlHelpCustomAttsServer project is included under the Chapter 9 subdirectory.*

Understanding the Interop Editing Process

Before you go and modify the interop assembly for the HelpfulAtlServer.dll COM server, you need to get your bearings and understand the general steps involved in manually editing a .NET assembly. The first obvious step is to have access to the interop assembly that was generated from a valid COM type library. To do so, you may manually run the tlbimp.exe utility or make use of VS .NET.

Once you have the interop assembly at your disposal, your next task is to disassemble its contents to obtain an *.il (Intermediate Language) file that contains the assembly's metadata descriptions. As you might have guessed, ildasm.exe provides an option to dump the contents of a loaded assembly to file (you will see this shortly).

Armed with this *.il file, you are now able to manually update the contents using whichever text editor suits your fancy. Of course, this step in the process does demand that you are aware of the basic syntax of IL and .NET metadata descriptions. The good news is that interop assemblies actually contain very little (if any) actual IL code. The only time in which you are likely to encounter IL of any notable length is if the interop assembly has mapped COM connections into terms of .NET delegates. Beyond this specific case, most interop assemblies contain nothing by metadata, which is quite easy on the eyes.

Last but not least, after you have applied any edits to the *.il file, you need to recompile the code into a valid interop assembly using the ilasm.exe utility (Intermediate Language assembler) and distribute the modified assembly. To solidify the sequences of events, ponder Figure 9-20.

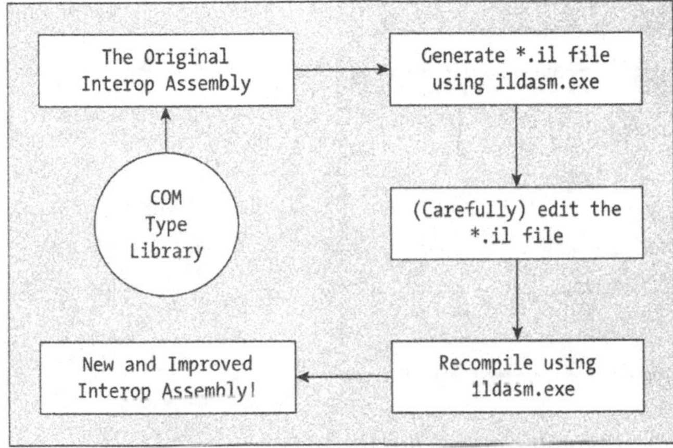

Figure 9-20. The flow of the IL editing process

Generating the Initial Interop Assembly

Now that you see the big picture (and hopefully have some idea when this technique is helpful), let's walk through each step and update the interop assembly for the AtlHelpCustomAttsServer.dll COM server to simulate the [helpstring] and [custom] IDL attributes that were ignored by tlbimp.exe. The journey begins by creating the interop assembly to be modified:

```
tlbimp AtlHelpCustomAttsServer.dll /out: interop.AtlHelpCustomAttsServer.dll
```

CODE *The original interop.AtlHelpCustomAttsServer.dll interop assembly can be found under the \Initial interop.AtlHelpCustomAttsServer directory.*

*Obtaining the *.il File for interop.HelpfulATLServer.dll*

As mentioned, ILDasm.exe supports a special command that allows you to dump the contents of a given .NET assembly into an *.il file. Assuming you have loaded the interop.AtlHelpCustomAttsServer.dll assembly into ildasm.exe, select the File | Dump menu option (Figure 9-21).

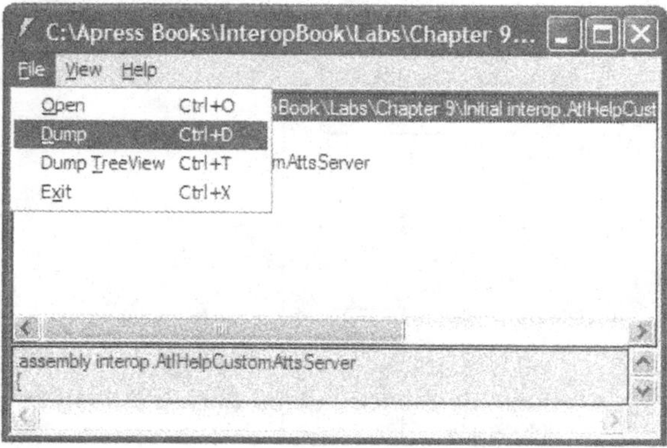

Figure 9-21. Dumping the assembly contents to a file

This will launch a (rather odd-shaped) dialog box that allows you to configure how the underlying *.il file is to be written to file (the default settings are fine for your current purposes). When you click OK, you are asked for the location to save the file via a standard File Save dialog box. Once you save your *.il file to a convenient location, you will find that two files have been generated (Figure 9-22).

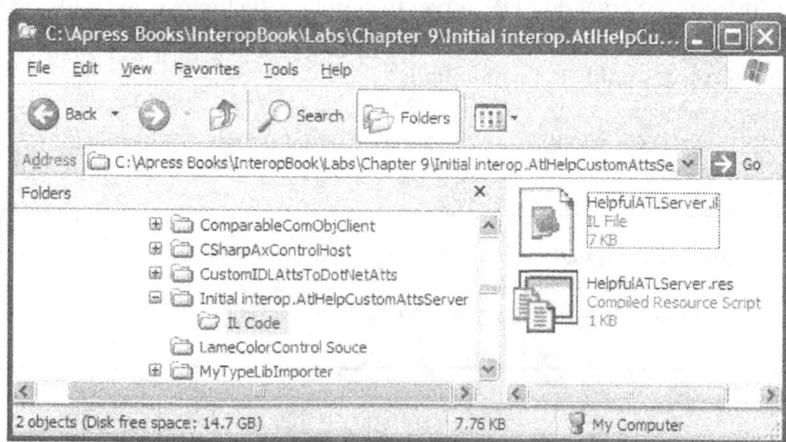

Figure 9-22. Dumping an assembly to a file results in two new files.

When you dump an interop assembly to a file, you will always receive (in addition to the *.il file) a Win32 *.res file that contains general file-centric information obtained from the original type library. If you open this file using Visual Studio .NET, you find the information that appears in Figure 9-23.

HelpfulATLServer.res (1 - Version)

Key	Value
FILEVERSION	1, 0, 0, 0
PRODUCTVERSION	1, 0, 0, 0
FILEFLAGSMASK	0x3fL
FILEFLAGS	0x0L
FILEOS	VOS__WINDOWS32
FILETYPE	VFT_DLL
FILESUBTYPE	VFT2_UNKNOWN
Block Header	Language Neutral (007f04b0)
Comments	
CompanyName	
FileDescription	
FileVersion	1.0.0.0
InternalName	interop.HelpfulATLServer
LegalCopyright	
LegalTrademarks	
OriginalFilename	interop.HelpfulATLServer.dll
PrivateBuild	
ProductName	Assembly imported from type library HELPFULATLSERVERLib
ProductVersion	1.0.0.0
SpecialBuild	

*Figure 9-23. The *.res file*

Understand that this is *not* the information you are attempting to edit. You do, however, need to specify this file as a command line parameter to ilasm.exe (using the /resource flag) when recompiling your *.il back into a valid interop assembly.

CODE *The original *.il and *.res files are located under the \Initial interop.AtlHelpCustomAttsServer\IL Code subdirectory.*

Viewing the Original IL/Metadata Definitions

Before you augment the IL code to take into account the orphaned IDL [helpstring] and [custom] attributes, let's check out the unaltered IL dump. The very first section of the IL file documents any required external .NET assemblies (interop assemblies always need to reference mscorlib.dll) as well as an [.assembly] statement that is constructed based on the metadata of the COM type information.

Recall that tlbimp.exe makes use of the ImportedFromTypeLibAttribute and GuidAttribute types to document the LIBID of the COM type library used to generate the interop assembly. Given your understanding of .NET assemblies, this initial section of the *.il file should ring a bell! You are basically looking at the raw manifest definition:

```
.assembly extern mscorlib
{
 .publickeytoken = (B7 7A 5C 56 19 34 E0 89 ) // .z\V.4..
 .ver 1:0:3300:0
}
.assembly interop.HelpfulATLServer
{
 .custom instance void[mscorlib]System.Runtime.
InteropServices.ImportedFromTypeLibAttribute::.ctor(string) =
( 01 00 13 48 45 4C 50 46 55 4C 41 54 4C 53 45 52  // ...HELPFULATLSER
56 45 52 4C 69 62 00 00 )            // VERLib..
 .custom instance void[mscorlib]System.Runtime.
InteropServices.GuidAttribute::.ctor(string) =
( 01 00 24 65 63 36 33 65 36 39 30 2D 61 33 38 35
// ..$ec63e690- a385
2D 34 31 66 39 2D 39 61 30 39 2D 35 34 36 39 65
// -41f9-9a09-5469e
66 36 63 32 64 38 62 00 00 )
// f6c2d8b..
 .hash algorithm 0x00008004
 .ver 1:0:0:0
}
.module HELPFULATLSERVERLib.dll
// MVID: {DC7BFAF6-CAC1-478F-87C1-BA4F3D6E0616}
.imagebase 0x00400000
.subsystem 0x00000003
.file alignment 512
.corflags 0x00000001
```

After the manifest definition, you have a section termed the *class structure declaration*. Here you find the skeletal prototype of each .NET type in the assembly, devoid of any members. Given that the COM type information for the HelpfulATLServer.dll defined two COM types (the IAdd interface and AtlAdder coclass) you end up with three .NET type declarations (recall that tlbimp.exe always creates a "-Class"-suffixed type that represents a union of all interface members). In the following IL metadata, note that the [.namespace] tag is used to document the .NET namespace, while [.class] is a generic way to define any .NET type:

```
// ==== CLASS STRUCTURE DECLARATION ====
//
.namespace interop.HelpfulATLServer
{
 .class public auto ansi import AtlAdderClass
     extends [mscorlib]System.Object
     implements interop.HelpfulATLServer.IAdd,
          interop.HelpfulATLServer.AtlAdder
 {} // end of class AtlAdderClass

 .class interface public abstract auto ansi import AtlAdder
     implements interop.HelpfulATLServer.IAdd
 {} // end of class AtlAdder

 .class interface public abstract auto ansi import IAdd
 {} // end of class IAdd
} // end of namespace interop.HelpfulATLServer
```

After the structural definition of each type, the remaining metadata definitions document the members of each type. First and foremost, you have the members of the AtlAdderClass type:

```
.namespace interop.HelpfulATLServer
{
 .class public auto ansi import AtlAdderClass
     extends [mscorlib]System.Object
     implements interop.HelpfulATLServer.IAdd,
          interop.HelpfulATLServer.AtlAdder
 {
  .custom instance void[mscorlib]System.Runtime.
  InteropServices.GuidAttribute::.ctor(string) =
  ( 01 00 24 33 43 37 42 44 35 42 46 2D 32 44 39 45
   // ..$3C7BD5BF-2D9E
   2D 34 39 36 30 2D 41 39 37 45 2D 36 35 44 42 35
   // -4960-A97E-65DB5
   45 42 38 45 32 34 39 00 00 )        // EB8E249..

  .custom instance void[mscorlib]System.Runtime.
  InteropServices.ClassInterfaceAttribute::
  .ctor(int16) = ( 01 00 00 00 00 00 )
  .custom instance void[mscorlib]System.Runtime.
  InteropServices.TypeLibTypeAttribute::
```

```
.ctor(int16) = ( 01 00 02 00 00 00 )
.method public specialname rtspecialname
    instance void .ctor() runtime managed internalcall
{} // end of method AtlAdderClass::.ctor
.method public hidebysig newslot virtual
    instance int32 Add([in] int32 numb1,
    [in] int32 numb2) runtime managed internalcall
{
 .override interop.HelpfulATLServer.IAdd::Add
} // end of method AtlAdderClass::Add
} // end of class AtlAdderClass
```

Notice how the members of the AtlAdderClass type do not contain any literal IL instructions, but rather various bits of metadata that describe characteristics of the related COM type. The AtlAdder class (which as you recall only supports members of the [default] interface) looks quite similar:

```
.class interface public abstract auto ansi import AtlAdder
    implements interop.HelpfulATLServer.IAdd
{
 .custom instance void[mscorlib]System.Runtime.
InteropServices.GuidAttribute::.ctor(string) =
( 01 00 24 35 30 36 41 35 43 42 31 2D 31 44 30 44
// ..$506A5CB1-1D0D
2D 34 41 41 32 2D 38 31 43 45 2D 41 41 37 46 39
// -4AA2-81CE-AA7F9
39 32 38 31 30 42 42 00 00 )
// 92810BB..

 .custom instance void[mscorlib]System.Runtime.
InteropServices.CoClassAttribute::.ctor(class [mscorlib]System.Type) =
( 01 00 26 69 6E 74 65 72 6F 70 2E 48 65 6C 70 66
// ..&interop.Helpf
75 6C 41 54 4C 53 65 72 76 65 72 2E 41 74 6C 41
// ulATLServer.AtlA
64 64 65 72 43 6C 61 73 73 00 00 )
// dderClass..
} // end of class AtlAdder
```

Finally, you have the metadata description of the members of the IAdd interface:

```
.class interface public abstract auto ansi import IAdd
{
 .custom instance void[mscorlib]System.Runtime.
InteropServices.TypeLibTypeAttribute::.ctor(int16) =
( 01 00 00 01 00 00 )

 .custom instance void[mscorlib]System.Runtime.
InteropServices.GuidAttribute::.ctor(string) =
```

```
 ( 01 00 24 35 30 36 41 35 43 42 31 2D 31 44 30 44
 // ..$506A5CB1-1D0D
 2D 34 41 41 32 2D 38 31 43 45 2D 41 41 37 46 39
 // -4AA2-81CE-AA7F9
 39 32 38 31 30 42 42 00 00 )
// 92810BB..

  .custom instance void[mscorlib]System.Runtime.
InteropServices.InterfaceTypeAttribute::
.ctor(int16) = ( 01 00 01 00 00 00 )
  .method public hidebysig newslot virtual abstract
      instance int32 Add([in] int32 numb1,
               [in] int32 numb2) runtime managed internalcall
  {}
  } // end of method IAdd::Add
```

Now that you have seen what is contained within your interop assembly, you are just about ready to hack away. But first, a few words about how .NET attributes are represented in terms of raw metadata.

Dissecting the Layout of Attribute Metadata

Recall that all custom .NET attributes derive from the System.Attribute base class. By default, a .NET attribute can be applied to any aspect of a C# code file using the bracket notation (much like COM IDL). Also recall that a given .NET attribute is able to restrict its usage by being defined with the AttributeUsageAttribute type and the related AttributeTargets enumeration. However, when a .NET attribute is defined in terms of raw IL metadata (regardless of what it is attributing), it will always have the following format (attribute-specific values are seen inside bold curly brackets):

```
.custom instance void {fully qualified name}::


.ctor({ctor data type}) = ({ctor args})
```

For example, in Chapter 7 you created the following C# custom attribute:

```
// The custom attribute.
[AttributeUsage(AttributeTargets.Class |
 AttributeTargets.Interface |
 AttributeTargets.Enum |
 AttributeTargets.Struct)]
public class ToDoAttribute : System.Attribute
{
  private string toDoComment;
```

```
  public ToDoAttribute(string comment)
  { toDoComment = comment;}

  public string Comment
  {get {return toDoComment;}}
}
```

The ToDoAttribute type was attributed to the following enum:

```
[ToDo("This enum stinks!")]
public enum TheEnum
```

If you check out the IL metadata for TheEnum using ILDasm.exe, you find the following description:

```
.class public auto ansi sealed TheEnum
    extends [mscorlib]System.Enum
{
.custom instance void ComplexTypeLibrary.ToDoAttribute::.ctor(string) =
( 01 00 11 54 68 69 73 20 65 6E 75 6D 20 73 74 69
// ...This enum sti
6E 6B 73 21 00 00 )                            // nks!..
} // end of class TheEnum
```

As you can see, the string passed into the constructor of the ToDoAttribute ("This enum stinks!") is represented by its hexadecimal equivalent. However, the value you are viewing (01 00 11 54 68 69 73 20 65 6E 75 6D 20 73 74 69 6E 6B 73 21 00 00) contains a bit more information than the literal string tokens. Specifically speaking, the value can be parsed into three basic segments. First, all .NET attributes begin with 01. The next four bytes (in this case 00 11) mark the size of the data that follows. The data itself can be arbitrarily long, depending on what exactly was passed into the constructor of the custom attribute type. Here, the hexadecimal of your string is realized as the following:

```
54 68 69 73 20 65 6E 75 6D 20 73 74 69 6E 6B 73 21
T  h  i  s     e  n  u  m     s  t  i  n  k  s  !
```

Finally, every custom attribute ends with 4 bytes that mark the number of named properties supported by the attribute. Given that ToDoAttribute does not contain such information, the value 00 00 is present and accounted for.

So (you may be asking), what does this have to do with the process of updating an interop assembly to describe orphaned IDL attributes? Everything! If you wish to insert custom .NET metadata that qualifies a given IDL [helpstring], you need to insert metadata that describes a DescriptionAttribute type. This alone is not a problem, but as you can guess, it would be a tremendous drag to build the hexadecimal representation of "This class adds two numbers." While you could manually calculate the correct value, you will do well (and save time) to simply build a temporary .NET assembly that sends in the correct string to the constructor of the DescriptionAttribute type and grabs the correct hex via ILDasm.exe.

Building a "Scratch" Assembly

To illustrate, let's create a scratch assembly named ScratchAssembly to generate the hex values of the correct textual data on your behalf. Obviously, it really makes no difference what the names of these temporary types are (and they most certainly don't have to do anything). All you need is a set of .NET classes that make use of the DescriptionAttribute type for each string you are interested in obtaining:

```
using System;
using System.ComponentModel;

namespace TempHelpStringAsm
{
  [DescriptionAttribute("This class adds two numbers")]
  public class AtlAdderClass{}
}
```

Once you compile and open this assembly with ildasm.exe, you are able to find the correct hexadecimal values for each string. For example:

```
.class public auto ansi beforefieldinit AtlAdderClass
    extends [mscorlib]System.Object
{
 .custom instance void [System]System.ComponentModel.DescriptionAttribute
  ::.ctor(string) =
 ( 01 00 1B 54 68 69 73 20 63 6C 61 73 73 20 61 64
 // ...This class ad
64 73 20 74 77 6F 20 6E 75 6D 62 65 72 73 00 00 )
// ds two numbers..
} // end of class AtlAdderClass
```

Creating a .NET [custom] Wrapper

At this point, you have the correct hex values for the two strings you are attempting to insert into the interop assembly. If you were simply annotating the metadata with the DescriptionAttribute class, you would be ready to update the *.il and move on. However, recall that one of your tasks was to account for the [custom] IDL attribute. Although the .NET class libraries do not have a type that directly mimics the IDL [custom] attribute, nothing is preventing you from rolling your own. Recall that a [custom] IDL attribute is represented by a GUID/BSTR pair. If you build a custom .NET attribute that mimics the IDL [custom] attribute, you could add the following information to the scratch assembly:

```
using System;
using System.ComponentModel;

namespace ScratchAssembly
{
  // Generate correct metadata for the .NET version of "ToDo".
  [IDLCustomAttribute("1403B3A5-38FE-4ba9-94E2-54577F712E7A",
  "ToDo: Add subtraction functionality...")]
  public class CustomAttString{}

  [DescriptionAttribute("This class adds two numbers")]
  public class AtlAdderClass{}

  // This is a class type which is a .NET
  // representation of the IDL [custom] attribute.
  public class IDLCustomAttribute : Attribute
  {
    public string theGuidName;
    public string theStringValue;
    public IDLCustomAttribute(string g, string s)
    {
      theGuidName = g;
      theStringValue = s;
    }
  }
}
```

Now, if you dump the contents of this scratch assembly to an *.il file using ILDasm.exe (which will be important in an upcoming step), you will be happy to see that this type has been expressed in terms of .NET metadata:

```
.class public auto ansi beforefieldinit IDLCustomAttribute
     extends [mscorlib]System.Attribute
{
} // end of class IDLCustomAttribute

...

.class public auto ansi beforefieldinit IDLCustomAttribute
     extends [mscorlib]System.Attribute
{
  .field public valuetype [mscorlib]System.Guid theGuidName
  .field public string theStringValue
```

```
  .method private hidebysig specialname rtspecialname
      instance void .ctor(valuetype [mscorlib]System.Guid g,
                 string s) cil managed
  {
   // Code size    21 (0x15)
   .maxstack 2
   IL_0000: ldarg.0
   IL_0001: call    instance void [mscorlib]System.Attribute::.ctor()
   IL_0006: ldarg.0
   IL_0007: ldarg.1
   IL_0008: stfld   valuetype [mscorlib]System.Guid
   ScratchAssembly.IDLCustomAttribute::theGuidName
   IL_000d: ldarg.0
   IL_000e: ldarg.2
   IL_000f: stfld   string ScratchAssembly.IDLCustomAttribute::theStringValue
   IL_0014: ret
  } // end of method IDLCustomAttribute::.ctor
} // end of class IDLCustomAttribute
```

Given that you applied the IDLCustomAttribute type to a scratch class, you have the definition you need to update the interop assembly:

```
.custom instance void ScratchAssembly.IDLCustomAttribute::.ctor(string,
string) = ( 01 00 24 31 34 30 33 42 33 41 35 2D 33 38 46 45
// ..$1403B3A5-38FE
2D 34 62 61 39 2D 39 34 45 32 2D 35 34 35 37 37
// -4ba9-94E2-54577
46 37 31 32 45 37 41 26 54 6F 44 6F 3A 20 41 64
// F712E7A&ToDo: Ad
64 20 73 75 62 74 72 61 63 74 69 6F 6E 20 66 75
// d subtraction fu
6E 63 74 69 6F 6E 61 6C 69 74 79 2E 2E 2E 00 00 )
// nctionality.....
```

Understand that you need to copy *all* of this information into the *.il file of the initial interop assembly, given that you are attempting to insert a new type definition into the interop assembly.

CODE *The ScratchAssembly project (and related *.il file) is included under the Chapter 9 subdirectory.*

Updating the Interop Assembly

Now that you have the correct hex values for each string and an IL description of the IDLCustomAttribute type, you are finally ready to edit the metadata of the IL initial interop assembly. First, add back the [helpstring] for the related coclass. Understand that you must account for a reference to the external system.dll assembly, given that it contains the definition of DescriptionAttribute:

```
.assembly extern mscorlib
{
 .publickeytoken = (B7 7A 5C 56 19 34 E0 89 )  // .z\V.4..
 .ver 1:0:3300:0
}

// ****** Need to add this to get DescriptionAttribute! ******
.assembly extern System
{
 .publickeytoken = (B7 7A 5C 56 19 34 E0 89 )  // .z\V.4..
 .ver 1:0:3300:0
}
...
 .class public auto ansi import AtlAdderClass
      extends [mscorlib]System.Object
      implements interop.AtlHelpCustomAttsServer.IAdd,
           interop.AtlHelpCustomAttsServer.AtlAdder
{
     ...
  // ******Added this. ******
  .custom instance void [System]System.ComponentModel.
 DescriptionAttribute::.ctor(string) =
( 01 00 1B 54 68 69 73 20 63 6C 61 73 73 20 61 64
// ...This class ad
64 73 20 74 77 6F 20 6E 75 6D 62 65 72 73 00 00 )
// ds two numbers..
...
} // end of class AtlAdderClass
```

Here, you simply added the metadata description of the DescriptionAttribute to the AtlAdderClass type by copying the code from the *.il file of the scratch assembly. To account for the orphaned [custom] IDL attribute, you begin by defining the IDLCustomAttribute type in the class structure declaration section:

```
// ==== CLASS STRUCTURE DECLARATION ====
//
.namespace interop.AtlHelpCustomAttsServer
{
 .class public auto ansi import AtlAdderClass
```

```
    extends [mscorlib]System.Object
    implements interop.AtlHelpCustomAttsServer.IAdd,
        interop.AtlHelpCustomAttsServer.AtlAdder
{
} // end of class AtlAdderClass
  ...
// ****** Added this. ******
.class public auto ansi beforefieldinit IDLCustomAttribute
    extends [mscorlib]System.Attribute
{
} // end of class IDLCustomAttribute
} // end of namespace interop.AtlHelpCustomAttsServer
```

In the member definition section, you define the implementation of IDLCustomAttribute (which again, you simply copy from the *.il file of the scratch assembly). Do be aware, however, that you need to change the fully qualified ScratchAssembly.IDLCustomAttribute to interop.AtlHelpCustomAttsServer.IDLCustomAttribute, given that you are copying the definition from the ScratchAsembly namespace!

```
// ====CLASS MEMBERS DECLARATION ====
.namespace interop.AtlHelpCustomAttsServer
{
...
// ****** Added this. ******
.class public auto ansi beforefieldinit IDLCustomAttribute
    extends [mscorlib]System.Attribute
{
  .field public string theGuidName
  .field public string theStringValue
  .method public hidebysig specialname rtspecialname
      instance void .ctor(string g,
                  string s) cil managed
  {
   // Code size    21 (0x15)
   .maxstack 2
   IL_0000: ldarg.0
   IL_0001: call    instance void
  [mscorlib]System.Attribute::.ctor()
   IL_0006: ldarg.0
   IL_0007: ldarg.1
   IL_0008: stfld   string
   interop.AtlHelpCustomAttsServer.IDLCustomAttribute::theGuidName
   IL_000d: ldarg.0
   IL_000e: ldarg.2
   IL_000f: stfld   string
   interop.AtlHelpCustomAttsServer.IDLCustomAttribute::theStringValue
```

```
  IL_0014: ret
 } // end of method IDLCustomAttribute::.ctor
} // end of class IDLCustomAttribute
} // end of namespace interop.AtlHelpCustomAttsServer
```

And finally, now that you have the metadata description of the IDLCustomAttribute type, inside the HelpfulATLServer.il file you can apply the attribute to the AtlAdderClass definition:

```
.class public auto ansi import AtlAdderClass
    extends [mscorlib]System.Object
    implements interop.AtlHelpCustomAttsServer.IAdd,
         interop.AtlHelpCustomAttsServer.AtlAdder
{
...
  // Added this.
  .custom instance void[System]
  System.ComponentModel.DescriptionAttribute::.ctor(string) =
( 01 00 1B 54 68 69 73 20 63 6C 61 73 73 20 61 64  // ...This class ad
64 73 20 74 77 6F 20 6E 75 6D 62 65 72 73 00 00 ) // ds two numbers..

  .custom instance void
  interop.AtlHelpCustomAttsServer.IDLCustomAttribute
::.ctor(string,
string) = ( 01 00 24 31 34 30 33 42 33 41 35 2D 33 38 46 45  // ..$1403B3A5-38FE
2D 34 62 61 39 2D 39 34 45 32 2D 35 34 35 37 37
// -4ba9-94E2-54577
46 37 31 32 45 37 41 26 54 6F 44 6F 3A 20 41 64
// F712E7A&ToDo: Ad
64 20 73 75 62 74 72 61 63 74 69 6F 6E 20 66 75
// d subtraction fu
6E 63 74 69 6F 6E 61 6C 69 74 79 2E 2E 2E 00 00 )
// nctionality.....
...
} // end of class AtlAdderClass
```

Whew! That was interesting, huh? At this point you are ready to recompile the IL code into an interop assembly.

Recompiling the IL

Ilasm.exe is the tool that compiles raw IL code into a .NET assembly. While this tool contains numerous command line parameters, all that is required for this example is to specify the name of the input files. Recall that when an interop assembly is disassembled, ildasm.exe generates a *.res file that can be referenced using the /resource flag. Because ilasm.exe names the assembly based on the name of the *.il file, you should make appropriate use of the /output flag.

```
ilasm /dll /output:interop.AtlHelpCustomAttsServer.dll HelpfulATLServer.il
/resource:HelpfulATLServer.res
```

Now, if you going through the bother of manually editing the metadata in an interop assembly, the chances are good that you are indeed a component vendor who is attempting to produce a primary interop assembly. If this is the case, understand that ilasm.exe also supports a /keyfile flag to allow you to pass in the *.snk file. You don't need to do so for the example here, but the parameter to ilasm.exe would look like this:

```
ilasm /dll /output:interop.AtlHelpCustomAttsServer.dll HelpfulATLServer.il
/resource:HelpfulATLServer.res /keyfile:theKey.snk
```

In any case, as long as all your ducks are in a row, you can now open the modified interop assembly using ildasm.exe and find the IDLCustomAttribute has been accounted for (Figure 9-24) and applied to the AtlAdderClass (Figure 9-25).

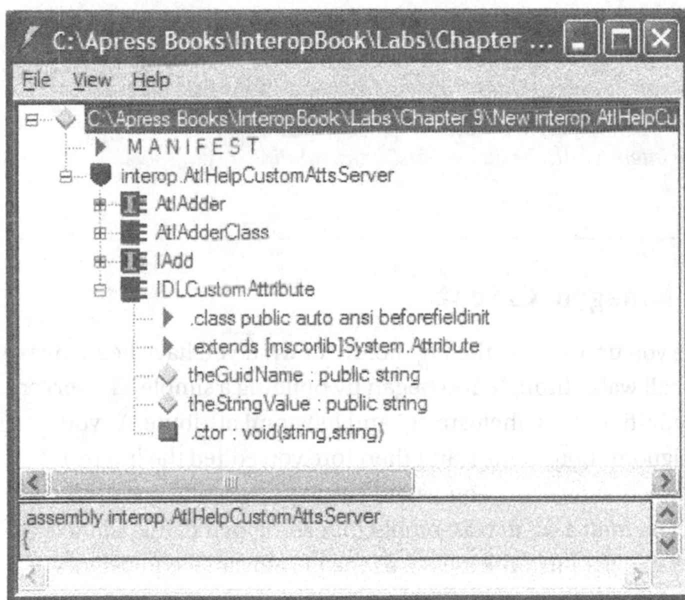

Figure 9-24. The custom System.Attribute-derived type

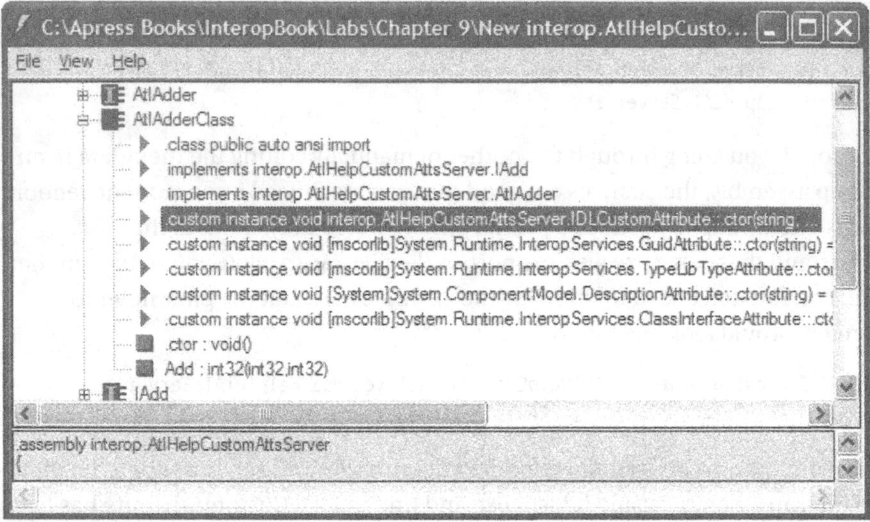

Figure 9-25. Applying the custom System.Attribute-derived type

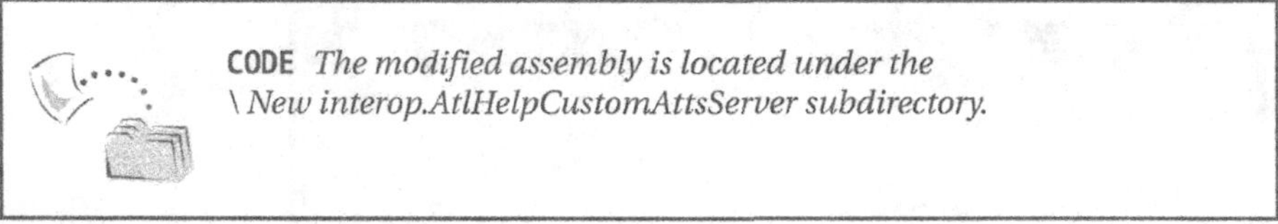

CODE *The modified assembly is located under the \New interop.AtlHelpCustomAttsServer subdirectory.*

Building the Managed Client

So, just to make sure you understand the big picture of what you have been investigating, let's do a small walk-through. You began by building a simple ATL server that contains IDL definitions for a [helpstring] and [custom] attribute. As you learned, tlbimp.exe ignores both values, and therefore you edited the interop assembly in such a way that the .NET equivalents were present and accounted for. During the process, you built a scratch assembly that contained IL metadata definitions for your custom .NET attribute as well as the hexadecimal equivalents of the string data.

So, did it work? Ponder the following C# console application and see for yourself (of course, this client wants to set a reference to the *new* interop assembly you edited, not the original interop assembly). The output can be seen in Figure 9-26.

```
using System;
using interop.AtlHelpCustomAttsServer;
using System.ComponentModel;
using System.Reflection;
```

```
namespace CustomInteropAsmClient
{
  class TheClient
  {
    [STAThread]
    static void Main(string[] args)
    {
      // Trigger functionality.
      AtlAdderClass c = new AtlAdderClass();
      Console.WriteLine("10 + 10 is {0}", c.Add(10, 10));

      // Get all the custom atts.
      object[] theAtts =
        c.GetType().GetCustomAttributes(false);

      // Which attribute do we have?
      foreach(object o in theAtts)
      {
        if(o is DescriptionAttribute)
          Console.WriteLine("Helpstring: {0}",
            ((DescriptionAttribute)o).Description);
        if(o is IDLCustomAttribute)
        {
          Console.WriteLine("Guid: {0}",
            ((IDLCustomAttribute)o).theGuidName);
          Console.WriteLine("Value: {0}",
            ((IDLCustomAttribute)o).theStringValue);
        }
      }
    }
  }
}
```

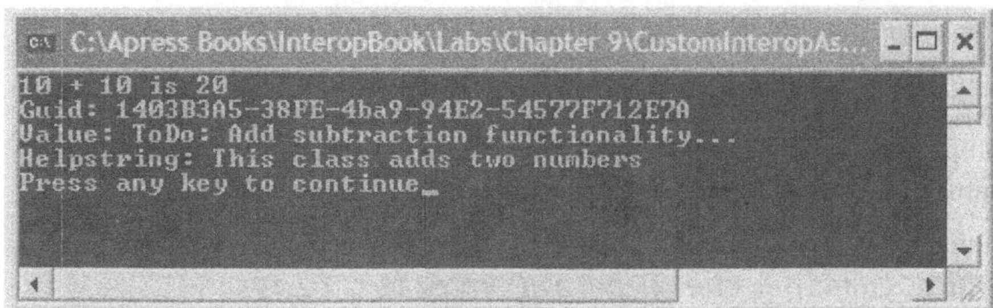

Figure 9-26. Reading the manually inserted .NET metadata

Sweet. As you can see, it is entirely possible (although somewhat clumsy) to edit an interop assembly to account for details tlbimp.exe may have ignored. Now that you have walked through a complete example of how to do so, you should be able to modify interop assemblies as you see fit.

CODE *The CustomInteropAsmClient project is located under the Chapter 9 subdirectory.*

Building a Custom Type Library Importer Utility

The final topic regarding .NET-to-COM interoperability is that of programmatically converting a COM type library into a .NET assembly using the TypeLibConverter class type defined within the System.Runtime.InteropServices namespace. Before you dive into the details, let me just say that you are never required to build custom utilities that dynamically generate a .NET interop assembly from a COM type library. To be honest, most of the time you will simply make use of the Add Reference dialog box of Visual Studio .NET. As far as working with the raw tlbimp.exe utility, you will typically opt for this choice when you (as a component vendor) wish to generate a primary interop assembly for your client base. However, as you may suspect, both of these tools make use of the TypeLibConverter class type. Given this, it is very illuminating to take a low-level look at the work being done on your behalf.

Building a custom type library importer may come in handy when you wish to customize exactly how an interop assembly is named, versioned, or deployed. For example, you may wish to ensure that each interop assembly created by your company has an accompanying log file that lists the name of each imported COM type. This (as well as any other possible customization) could be achieved through a custom COM-to-.NET conversion utility. As you might imagine, a customized type library importer could be as simple or as complex as necessary. The tool in question could be a Windows-, console-, or Web-based application. To keep focused on the raw conversion process (rather than the additional complexities of GUI-based development), you build a console application (named MyTypeLibImporter) that illustrates the key points of interest.

Understanding the TypeLibConverter Class

The .NET platform provides the System.Runtime.InteropServices.TypeLibConverter type for those times when you need to customize the type library importing process. As you see later in this book, this very same class can be used to convert a .NET assembly into COM type information (for .NET-to-COM interoperability). As you can see from the formal C# definition, this type (despite its powerful features) supplies only a handful of members:

```
public sealed class TypeLibConverter : object, ITypeLibConverter
{
  public TypeLibConverter();

  // Build COM type library based on .NET assembly.
  public virtual object ConvertAssemblyToTypeLib(Assembly assembly,
    string strTypeLibName, TypeLibExporterFlags flags,
    ITypeLibExporterNotifySink notifySink);

  // Two ways to build a .NET assembly based on COM type lib.
  public virtual AssemblyBuilder ConvertTypeLibToAssembly(
    object typeLib,
    string asmFileName, TypeLibImporterFlags flags,
    ITypeLibImporterNotifySink notifySink, byte[] publicKey,
    StrongNameKeyPair keyPair,
    string asmNamespace, Version asmVersion);

  public virtual AssemblyBuilder ConvertTypeLibToAssembly(
    object typeLib, string asmFileName,
      int flags, ITypeLibImporterNotifySink notifySink,
    byte[] publicKey, StrongNameKeyPair keyPair,
    bool unsafeInterfaces);

  // Used to see if a primary interop assembly is already
  // registered for a given COM type library.
  public virtual bool GetPrimaryInteropAssembly(Guid g,
    int major, int minor, int lcid, ref String asmName,
    ref String asmCodeBase);

  public virtual bool Equals(object obj);
  public virtual int GetHashCode();
  public Type GetType();
  public virtual string ToString();
}
```

Notice that this type implements the ITypeLibConverter interface (also defined in the System.Runtime.InteropServices namespace). If you check out this interface using wincv.exe, you see that it defines the CovertAssemblyToTypeLib(), ConvertTypeLibToAssembly(), and GetPrimaryInteropAssembly() members.

Given this, it is conceivable that you *could* build your own class type that manually transforms entities across architectural boundaries, but why bother?

The fact that TypeLibConverter implements the ITypeLibConverter interface is helpful if you build a custom type library importer using unmanaged code. For example, a COM client could obtain the ITypeLibConverter interface via COM-to-.NET interop and interact with the canned implementation of each method. I leave that task for the interested reader.

Building the Main Shell

Now that you have been introduced to the functionality of the TypeLibConverter class, you are in the position to begin building the MyTypeLibImporter application. The basic flow of this application is as follows:

1. The user is prompted to specify the path to the COM type library to be converted.
2. The *.tlb file is then loaded into memory via PInvoke.
3. Finally, the assembly is dynamically generated and saved to file.

First, you simply create the logic for prompting the user for the correct path to the COM type information. To make things a bit more interesting, your application supports a command line flag named -NOGUI, which instructs the program to obtain the path of the COM type library at the command prompt. By default, however, a Windows Forms OpenFileDialog type is displayed to allow the user to quickly locate the correct file (and minimize the required number of keystrokes).

```
using System;
using System.Runtime.InteropServices;
using System.Reflection;
using System.Reflection.Emit; // For AssemblyBuilder.
using System.Windows.Forms;

namespace MyTypeLibImporter
{
  class MyTlbImpApp
  {
    static void Main(string[] args)
    {
      // Check for -NOGUI switch.
      bool usingGUI = true;
      for(int i = 0; i < args.Length; i++)
      {
        if(args[i] == "-NOGUI")
        usingGUI = false;
      }
```

```
      // Gather user input.
      string pathToComServer = "";
      if(!usingGUI)
      {
        Console.WriteLine("Please enter path to COM type info.");
        Console.WriteLine(@"Example: C:\Stuff\MyComServer.dll");
        Console.Write("Path: ");
        pathToComServer = Console.ReadLine();
      }
      else
      {
        Console.WriteLine("Pick a COM server...");
        OpenFileDialog d = new OpenFileDialog();
        if(d.ShowDialog() == DialogResult.OK)
        pathToComServer = d.FileName;
      }

      // Show path to COM server.
      Console.WriteLine("Path: {0}\n", pathToComServer);
      Console.WriteLine("All done!");
    }
  }
}
```

If you run the application as is, you will find that you are able to obtain the path to a given COM type library (which may, of course, be embedded within a COM *.dll) via the command line or a Windows Forms open dialog box. The only point of interest is the pathToComServer string type, which is local to the Main() method. This value is used to load the COM type info into memory (speaking of which . . .).

Programmatically Loading the COM Type Information

As you recall from Chapter 5, when a .NET application wants to load COM type information programmatically, it requires PInvoke (given that there is no managed equivalent to the LoadTypeLibEx() API). This COM library function, defined in oleaut32.dll, will load (and optionally register) COM type information and return a runtime representation of the *.tlb file via the ITypeLib interface.

The System.Runtime.InteropServices namespace does provide a managed version of ITypeLib to make use of within a managed environment. However, the related REGKIND enumeration must be re-created in terms of C# syntax, given that you are not provided with a managed equivalent. This being said, here are the code updates:

```
namespace MyTypeLibImporter
{
  internal enum REGKIND
  {
    REGKIND_DEFAULT = 0,
    REGKIND_REGISTER = 1,
    REGKIND_NONE = 2
  }

  class MyTlbImpApp
  {
    // Need to leverage the LoadTypeLibEx() API
    // to do our dirty work.
    // Param 3: UCOMITypeLib is the .NET version of ITypeLib.
    [DllImport("oleaut32.dll", CharSet = CharSet.Unicode)]
    private static extern void LoadTypeLibEx(string strTypeLibName,
      REGKIND regKind, out UCOMITypeLib TypeLib);

    static void Main(string[] args)
    {
      // Same prompting logic as before…

      // Load the COM type library using helper function.
      UCOMITypeLib theTypeLib = LoadCOMTypeInfo(pathToComServer);
      if(theTypeLib == null)
        return;
    }
  }
}
```

The LoadCOMTypeInfo() helper function does the dirty work of loading the type information and returning the UCOMITypeLib interface. In addition, this helper method prints out some relevant stats about the library definition using ITypeLib.GetDocumentation() (as seen in Chapter 5):

```
public static UCOMITypeLib LoadCOMTypeInfo(string pathToComServer)
{
  // Load type information for COM server.
  UCOMITypeLib typLib = null;
  try
  {
    LoadTypeLibEx(pathToComServer,
      REGKIND.REGKIND_NONE, out typLib);

    string strName, strDoc, strHelpFile;
    int helpCtx;
    Console.WriteLine("COM Library Description:");
```

```
      typLib.GetDocumentation(-1, out strName,
        out strDoc, out helpCtx, out strHelpFile);
      Console.WriteLine("->Name: {0}", strName);
      Console.WriteLine("->Doc: {0}", strDoc);
      Console.WriteLine("->Help Context: {0}", helpCtx.ToString());
      Console.WriteLine("->Help File: {0}", strHelpFile);
    }
    catch
    { Console.WriteLine("ugh...can't load COM type info!");}
      return typLib;
}
```

At this point, you are able to load a COM type library and print out the information contained in the formal library statement. For example, if you load the WidgetServer.dll created in Chapter 5, you would find the output shown in Figure 9-27.

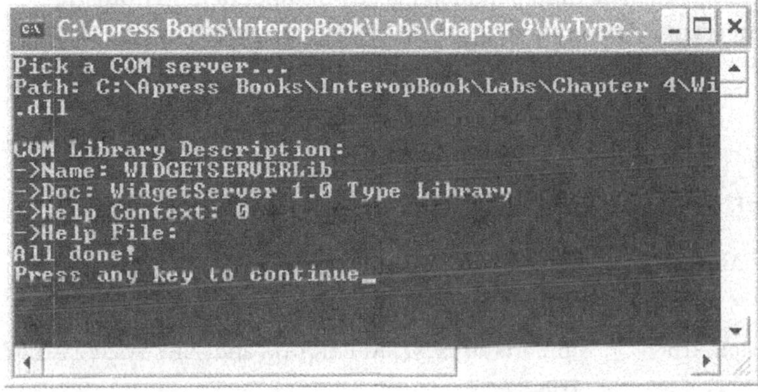

Figure 9-27. Extracting [library] COM type information

Dissecting the TypeLibConverter.ConvertTypeLibToAssembly() Method

The final task of your application is to perform the literal conversion of the COM type library into a .NET assembly using the TypeLibConverter class. On the surface, your task is quite simple: Call ConvertTypeLibToAssembly(). However, the parameters of this method entail that you define an additional custom class type that implements an interface named ITypeLibImporterNotifySink (defined in a moment). Generically speaking, calling ConvertTypeLibToAssembly() breaks down to the following:

```
// This method returns an AssemblyBuilder type
// which is used to save the assembly to file.
TypeLibConverter tlc = new TypeLibConverter();

AssemblyBuilder asmBuilder = tlc.ConvertTypeLibToAssembly(
  (UCOMITypeLib)typLib,     // ITypeLib interface.
  "interop.MyAssembly.dll",   // Name of assembly to be created.
  TypeLibImporterFlags.SafeArrayAsSystemArray, // Flags.
  sink,  // ITypeLibImporterNotifySink compatible helper class.
  null,  // If you have a strong name: keyPair.PublicKey,
  null,  // If you have a strong name: keyPair
  typeLibName, // Name of the .NET namespace.
  new Version(1, 0, 0, 0)); // Version of the assembly.
```

Well, calling the method is simple enough, it's specifying the parameters that takes a little elbow grease. First, you need to pass in a valid ITypeLib interface that points to the loaded COM type information, followed by the name of the assembly that will be saved to file. The third parameter is any number of flags from the TypeLibImporterFlags enumeration, the most common of which are defined in Table 9-3.

Table 9-3. TypeLibImporterFlags

TypeLibImporterFlags Member Name	Meaning in Life
PrimaryInteropAssembly	Generates a primary interop assembly. This option demands that a valid keyfile (*.snk) must be specified.
SafeArrayAsSystemArray	Imports all COM SAFEARRAYs and .NET System.Array types.

The fourth parameter is the real point of interest, given that it represents a custom class that will be called whenever the conversion process generates an error (thus giving you a chance to generate report information) or when the converter encounters a reference to another COM type library (via the importlib() IDL keyword) within the current type library. When this occurs, the ItypeLibImporterNotifySink-compatible helper object is required to generate an additional assembly for the contained COM type library (more details in a moment).

The final parameters to ConvertTypeLibToAssembly() allow you to specify the namespace, an optional key file (if you happen to be building a strongly named assembly, such as a primary interop assembly), as well as the version of the assembly itself.

Ideally, it would be nice if your custom type library importer application were intelligent enough to generate the name and version information based on the information contained in the COM type library. You inject such intelligence into your tool in just a bit, but first let's flesh out the code behind the helper sink object.

Building the Helper Sink

The ITypeLibImporterNotifySink interface defines two members that all sink objects are therefore required to contend with:

```
public interface ITypeLibImporterNotifySink
{
  void ReportEvent(ImporterEventKind eventKind,
    int eventCode, string eventMsg);
  Assembly ResolveRef(object typeLib);
}
```

The ReportEvent() method is called by the TypeLibConverter type when (and if) it encounters any errors during the process of converting metadata. The ImporterEventKind parameter is used to identify the type of error, and it can be any of the values listed in Table 9-4.

Table 9-4. Members of the ImporterEventKind Enumeration

ImporterEventKind Member Name	Meaning in Life
ERROR_REFTOINVALIDTYPELIB	This property is not supported in version 1.0 of the .NET Framework; however, in the future it will represent the converter encountered an invalid type library.
NOTIF_CONVERTWARNING	Event is invoked when a warning occurred during conversion.
NOTIF_TYPECONVERTED	Event is invoked when a type has been imported if the /verbose flag is specified.

While ReportEvent() is helpful, the ResolveRef() method is critical. As you are aware, COM type libraries can most certainly import additional type libraries. In terms of IDL, this is expressed using the [importlib] attribute. When TypeLibConverter is transforming the initial *.tlb file, it will call ResolveRef() to obtain an Assembly based on the incoming object parameter. This parameter (while typed as a System.Object) is in reality a reference to the UCOMITypeLib interface that describes a nested *.tlb reference.

The implementation of your sink class can be painfully simple or painfully complex, based on a number of design considerations. For example, do you want your ResolveRef() method to take into consideration the use of primary interop assemblies? Do you want to allow the returned Assembly reference to be assigned a strong name? If so, how to do want to obtain the correct *.snk file? To keep things simple, your implementation of ResolveRef() will *not* deal with primary interop assemblies or strong names. In fact, your version of ResolveRef() simply passes the incoming System.Object to a static helper method defined by the MyTlbLibApp class:

```
internal class ImporterNotiferSink : ITypeLibImporterNotifySink
{
  public void ReportEvent(ImporterEventKind eventKind,
    int eventCode, string eventMsg)
  {
    // We don't really care which kind of error is
    // sent. Just print out the information.
    Console.WriteLine("Event reported: {0}", eventMsg);
  }
  public Assembly ResolveRef(object typeLib)
  {
    // Delegate to helper function.
    Assembly nestedRef = Assembly.Load(
      MyTlbImpApp.GenerateAssemblyFromTypeLib
      ((UCOMITypeLib)typeLib));
    return nestedRef;
  }
}
```

Implementing MyTlbImpApp.GenerateAssemblyFromTypeLib()

The implementation of MyTlbImpApp.GenerateAssemblyFromTypeLib() is quite straightforward. Note that you are building the name of the assembly dynamically using Marshal.GetTypeLibName(). Notice too that the ConvertTypeLibToAssembly() function allows you to pass in null for the version. When you do so, the version will be based on the version of the type library's [version] attribute (typeLibMajor.typeLibMinor.0.0). Once the assembly is saved to disk, you return the name of the dynamically created assembly (which will be helpful for the ResolveRef() method of your sink type).

```
public static string GenerateAssemblyFromTypeLib(UCOMITypeLib typLib)
{
  // Need a sink for the TypeLibConverter.
```

```
  ImporterNotiferSink sink = new ImporterNotiferSink();
  TypeLibConverter tlc = new TypeLibConverter();

  // Generate name of the assembly.
  string typeLibName = Marshal.GetTypeLibName(typLib);
  string asmName = "interop." + typeLibName + ".dll";

  // Now make the assembly based on COM type information.
  AssemblyBuilder asmBuilder = tlc.ConvertTypeLibToAssembly(
    typLib,
    asmName,
    TypeLibImporterFlags.SafeArrayAsSystemArray,
    sink,
    null, // If you have a strong name: keyPair.PublicKey,
    null, // If you have a strong name: keyPair
    typeLibName, // Namespace name is same as file name.
      null); // null = (typeLibMajor.typeLibMinor.0.0)

    // Save the assembly in the app directory!
    asmBuilder.Save(asmName);

    // return name of assembly which was created.
    return asmName;
}
```

And finally, you update Main() to call GenerateAssemblyFromTypeLib() after obtaining the UCOMITypeLib interface.

```
static void Main(string[] args)
{
  // Same prompting logic as before…

  // Load the COM type library using helper function.
  UCOMITypeLib theTypeLib = LoadCOMTypeInfo(pathToComServer);
  if(theTypeLib == null)
    return;

  // Generate the assembly.
  GenerateAssemblyFromTypeLib(theTypeLib);
}
```

So, there you have it. When you run the application, you will be greeted with a Windows Forms open dialog box. Once you select a COM *.tlb file, the result is a new interop assembly, which is placed in the same directory of the original COM server. Figure 9-28 shows the output of importing the RawComCar server you created in Chapter 3.

```
C:\Apress Books\InteropBook\Labs\Chapter 9\MyTypeLibImporter\...
Pick a COM server...
Path: C:\Apress Books\InteropBook\Labs\Chapter 2\RawComCar\De

COM Library Description:
->Name: RawComCarLib
->Doc:
->Help Context: 0
->Help File:
Event reported: Type ComCar imported.
Event reported: Type ICar imported.
Event reported: Type IRadio imported.
Event reported: Type ScriptableCar imported.
Event reported: Type IScriptableCar imported.
All done!
Press any key to continue_
```

Figure 9-28. MyTypeLibImporter in action

CODE *The MyTypeLibImporter project is included under the Chapter 9 subdirectory.*

Summary

The point of this chapter has been to round out your understanding of using COM types from managed code. As you have seen, COM types can make use of .NET types if (and only if) the .NET assembly is expressed in terms of COM type information. While this process is formalized beginning with Chapter 10, here you looked at the process of implementing .NET interfaces on COM types to achieve type compatibility with other like-minded .NET types.

The bulk of this chapter, however, looked at manually updating the metadata contained within a .NET interop assembly. As you have seen, this technique can be helpful when the type library importer tools (tlbimp.exe, aximp.exe) fail to produce an interop assembly that fits your needs. In the examples, you explored the process of inserting the .NET equivalents of IDL [helpstring] and [custom] attributes. Finally, the chapter wrapped up with an examination of building a customized type library importer utility using the TypeLibConverter type.

Now that you have drilled into the details of .NET-to-COM interoperability, Chapter 10 begins to examine the opposite scenario: COM objects talking to .NET types.

CHAPTER 10

COM-to-.NET Interoperability—The Basics

The previous three chapters drilled into the process of interacting with COM types from .NET applications. This chapter begins to look at the inverse proposition: COM applications making use of .NET types. Even though we developers may wish to bid a fond farewell to classic COM and focus exclusively on .NET development, chances are quite good that many of us will be forced to develop software using both architectures for some time to come. As such, it is important to understand how a COM type can make use of the functionality contained in a given .NET assembly.

I begin by describing the core techniques used to expose .NET entities to the COM runtime and come to terms with a number of basic design rules (such as the class interface) and command line utilities used during the process. Along the way, you will come to understand how to influence the generation of COM type information using various .NET attributes, as well as understand the process of updating the registry with the appropriate information. Once these basic building blocks are out of the way, the conclusion of this chapter addresses the process of interacting with .NET types from Visual Basic 6.0, C++, and VBScript COM clients.

The Role of the CCW

As you have seen during the previous three chapters, when a .NET client wishes to communicate with a legacy COM type, a proxy known as a *Runtime Callable Wrapper* (RCW) is used to transform .NET requests into terms of COM. In a very similar manner, when a COM client wishes to communicate with a shiny new .NET type, the runtime creates a different sort of proxy called a *COM Callable Wrapper* (CCW). To understand the big picture, ponder Figure 10-1.

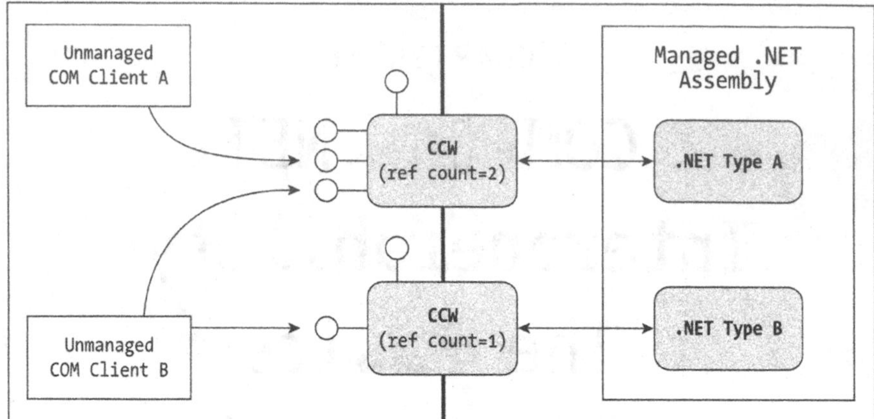

Figure 10-1. COM Clients communicate with .NET types using a CCW.

In contrast to the RCW, the CCW is in charge of making the COM client (which of course may be a coclass in a *.dll as well as a traditional *.exe) believe it is chatting with a "normal" COM type. As you can see from Figure 10-1, a single CCW is shared among multiple COM clients for a given .NET type. In addition to acting as a proxy for some number of COM clients, the CCW performs the following critical tasks:

- The CCW transforms COM data types into .NET equivalents.
- The CCW provides canned implementation of standard COM interfaces.
- The CCW simulates COM reference counting and type coercion for the .NET type.

All in all, the CCW exists to seamlessly marshal COM requests to an existing .NET type. To begin to understand the process, let's check out how intrinsic data types are transformed between architectural boundaries.

The CCW: Mapping .NET Data Types into COM IDL Data Types

Given your work in the previous chapters, you should be well aware how a particular .NET data type translates into COM (for example, System.String to BSTR, System.Object to VARIANT, and so forth). When translating COM IDL data types into .NET system types, the CCW simply reverses the process (for example, BSTR to System.String, VARIANT to System.Object, and so forth). Although you have already investigated the conversions of intrinsic data type in Chapter 6, Table 10-1 reiterates the specifics for your convenience.

Table 10-1. Default .NET-to-COM IDL Data Type Conversions

Managed .NET Data Type	COM IDL Data Type
System.Int32	bool, bool *
System.SByte	char, char * small, small *
System.Int16	short, short *
System.Int32	long, long * int, int *
System.Int64	hyper, hyper *
System.Byte	unsigned char, unsigned char *, byte, byte *
System.UInt16	wchar_t, wchar_t * unsigned short, unsigned short *
System.UInt32	unsigned long, unsigned long * unsigned int, unsigned int *
System.UInt64	unsigned hyper unsigned hyper *
System.Single	float, float *
System.Double	double, double *
System.Boolean	VARIANT_BOOL VARIANT_BOOL *
System.IntPtr	void *, void **
System.Int16 or System.IntPtr	HRESULT, HRESULT *
System.Int32	SCODE, SCODE *
System.String	BSTR, BSTR *
System.String	LPSTR or [string, …] char * LPSTR *
System.String	LPWSTR or [string, …] wchar_t * LPWSTR *
System.Object	VARIANT, VARIANT *
System.Decimal	DECIMAL, DECIMAL * CURRENCY, CURRENCY *
System.DateTime	DATE, DATE *

Table 10-1. Default .NET-to-COM IDL Data Type Conversions (continued)

Managed .NET Data Type	COM IDL Data Type
System.Guid	GUID, GUID *
System.Object	IUnknown *, IUnknown **
System.Object	IDispatch *, IDispatch **
type[] (that is, a managed array deriving from System.Array)	SAFEARRAY(type) SAFEARRAY(type) *

As you may have inferred from the title of Table 10-1, the CCW is prewired to transform a specific .NET type to a specific COM type using a default mapping. However, as you will see in Chapter 12, the MarshalAs attribute can be used to alter these default .NET-to-COM data mappings.

The CCW: Simulating Implemented COM Interfaces

The next major duty of the CCW is to simulate the implementation of core COM interfaces. To fool the COM client into believing that the CCW proxy is a true blue COM object, the CCW always implements the interfaces listed in Table 10-2.

Table 10-2. COM Interfaces That Are Always Simulated by the CCW

Interface Exposed by the CCW	Meaning in Life
IDispatch	The CCW supplies an implementation of IDispatch to allow COM-style late binding.
ISupportErrorInfo IErrorInfo	All .NET exceptions are exposed as COM error objects (detailed in Chapter 8), and therefore the CCW provides a default implementation of ISupportErrorInfo and expresses the .NET exception as a COM type implementing IErrorInfo.
IProvideClassInfo	Enables COM clients to gain access to the ITypeInfo interface describing a managed class.
ITypeInfo	As you learned in Chapter 4, ITypeInfo allows a COM client to discover the type's type information at runtime. The CCW returns the ITypeInfo interface to allow COM-style RTTI.
IUnknown	Of course, IUnknown is implemented by the CCW to allow the COM client to reference count and query the .NET type in the rules consistent with the COM specification.

In addition to these key COM interfaces, a given CCW may (or may not) implement various other standard COM interfaces, based on the composition of the .NET type. As you will see over the course of the next few chapters, .NET developers can apply various attributes (defined in the System.Runtime.InteropServices namespace) to their types to instruct the CCW to simulate the interfaces shown in Table 10-3.

Table 10-3. COM Interfaces That May Be Simulated by the CCW

Possible Interface Exposed by the CCW	Meaning in Life
The .NET type's "class interface"	As you will see in just a bit, .NET types can define a class interface that exports the public members of a .NET class as a [default] COM interface.
IConnectionPoint IConnectionPointContainer	.NET delegates (and the related events) are exposed as COM connection points, therefore the CCW will simulate the required COM event interfaces.
IDispatchEx	Classic COM defines an interface named IDispatchEx, which allows a client to manipulate a coclass' dispinterface at runtime. Under .NET this same behavior is supported by an interface named IExpando. If the .NET type supports IExpando, it will be exposed to a COM client as IDispatchEx.
IEnumVARIANT	Any .NET type that implements IEnumerable (for example, a .NET collection object) will expose its contents to COM via IEnumVARIANT (see Chapter 8).

The CCW: Simulating COM Identity

The final major task of the CCW is to simulate COM reference counting and type coercion for the .NET class. Simply put, this facility of the CCW ensures that the COM client is able to directly call AddRef(), Release(), and QueryInterface() against the underlying .NET type (regardless of the fact that a .NET class could care less about these methods).

Unlike the .NET type wrapped by the CCW, the CCW uses reference counting in traditional COM fashion. Thus, when the reference count on the CCW reaches zero, it releases its reference on the managed object and self-destructs. If the managed object has no remaining references, it is reclaimed during the next garbage-collection cycle. At that point, the GC will call the object's overridden System.Object.Finalize() method (if the type has chosen to override said method).

To illustrate, assume you have created a .NET type that has been correctly configured to interact with the COM runtime (which you will of course learn to do during this chapter). A VB 6.0 client is able to interact with this type just as with any native COM type (you will examine various COM clients in detail later in this chapter):

```
Public Sub SomeVb6Function()
    ' Assume you have set a reference to
    ' the correct type library…
    Dim netObj as MyDotNetObject
    ' VB queries for default interface
    ' which addrefs the object.
    Set netObj = New MyDotNetObject
    netObj.DoThis

    ' Get other interface from type.
    Dim itfOtherInterface as IOtherInterface

    ' VB queries for other interface
    ' (which addrefs the object again).
    Set itfOtherInterface = netObj
    itfOtherInterface.ToThat

    ' Release() called when references drop
    ' out of scope, which destroys the CCW.
    ' .NET object is then GC-ed.
End Sub
```

Core Requirements for COM-to-.NET Communications

Now that you have a feel for the role of the CCW, you need to understand the basic steps used to expose .NET types to COM. When you wish to configure a .NET assembly to be accessible by the COM runtime, you have two major tasks ahead of you (in addition to the process of building the assembly itself):

- Generate a COM type library that describes the types within the .NET assembly in terms of COM IDL.

- Update the system registry with the information needed to fool the COM runtime.

Generating COM Type Definitions

The need for the first task should be rather self-explanatory. You are already well aware that COM type libraries are the key to allowing various COM-aware languages to interact with types contained in a distinct binary. However, as you are also well aware, .NET metadata has no syntactic relationship to COM IDL! What you need is a tool that reads .NET metadata and writes the information into a corresponding *.tlb file. Once this has been accomplished, a COM client can reference the *.tlb file to program against the .NET entities using early binding (technically speaking, if you only wish to communicate with a .NET type using late binding, you don't require a type library). The .NET SDK provides a number of options for generating COM type information based on a .NET assembly:

- The tlbexp.exe command line utility
- The regasm.exe command line utility
- Programmatically using the TypeLibConverter type
- The regsvcs.exe command line utility

This chapter concerns itself with the first two options, given that the regsvcs.exe utility is typically only used when you wish to install a .NET code library into a specific COM+ application (you get a chance to examine COM+ interoperability in Chapter 13). The process of building a custom .NET-to-COM metadata converter via TypeLibConverter is discussed in Chapter 12.

As you can guess, a number of transformations must occur to expose .NET types as COM types. The vast majority of this chapter documents these specific conversion rules; however, for the time being simply make a mental note that you need to have access to a *.tlb file in order to interact with .NET types using early binding.

Registering the .NET Assembly with COM

The reason for the second task should be clear based on the information presented in Chapter 2. As you recall, the COM runtime makes considerable use of the system registry to locate, load, and marshal COM types. However, .NET assemblies are not registered in the system registry (which presents an obvious problem). As you will see, .NET developers make use of regasm.exe for this very reason (more details to come).

One thing to be aware of from the outset is that when you wish to expose .NET types to COM, you will be forced to contend with command line utilities. At the time of this writing, the core COM development environments (such as VB 6.0 and Visual C++) do not support an integrated wizard that will automatically generate COM type information and configure the system registry. Doing so is not terribly difficult, however, and future versions of these products may support such functionality. In fact, once you have completed the next three chapters, you may be inspired to build your own IDE snap-in utility that does this very thing!

Using the tlbexp.exe Utility

Now that you have the big picture in mind, you can begin checking out one very helpful utility. The Type Library Exporter utility (tlbexp.exe) is a command line tool that generates a COM type library (*.tlb) based on a .NET assembly (in contrast with the tlbimp.exe utility, which creates an interop assembly based on a COM type library). You may be surprised to learn that this tool has very little by way of command line flags, given that you programmatically control the resulting type library using a number of .NET attributes. In fact, the command line flags recognized by tlbexp.exe are for the most part useless (unless you want to see a display of the generally useless flags using the /help flag). Therefore, all you need to do to run the tool is specify the name of the .NET assembly you wish to convert into a COM type library:

```
tlbexp.exe myDotNetAssembly.dll
```

Actually, you may be interested in two of the flags. The /names flag allows you to specify a *.txt file that contains a set of strings used to indicate how to capitalize the names of the COM types (by default, the COM types are capitalized exactly as defined in the .NET metadata). I will assume that you are happy with the capitalization dictated by the .NET type definitions, so check online Help if you require further information on the /names directive.

The /out flag is a bit more useful, as it allows you to control the name of the resulting *.tlb file. If you do not make use of the /out flag, the name of the *.tlb file will be identical to the name of the assembly (for example, myDotNetAssembly.dll results in myDotNetAssembly.tlb). To change this default behavior, run tlbexe.exe as follows:

```
tlbexp.exe myDotNetAssembly.dll /out:typeInfoForMyAsm.tlb
```

Here, you are passing in the .NET assembly (myDotNetAssembly.dll) to receive typeInfoForMyAsm.tlb as output. In any case, the end result of running tlbexp.exe is a *.tlb file that contains binary IDL definitions for the assembly's type metadata. Just like any *.tlb file, this entity can be referenced from a COM client to view the internal types. Of course, you are not quite ready to activate these types, given that you have not yet configured the system registry to recognize the .NET assembly. You will see how to do so in just a bit. For the time being, however, let's address some basic .NET-to-COM design principles.

General Guidelines for Building COM-Aware .NET Types

The COM and .NET architectures are wildly different beasts. Under .NET, you are free to build class types that derive from other types and support some number of parameterized constructors, overloaded methods, static members, and whatnot. Many of these programming constructs are simply not supported under classic COM. Thus, when you are building a .NET assembly that you wish to expose to a COM client, you need to take greater care (and forethought) when designing the contained types.

Before you pound out some more elaborate C# code, let's drill into the baseline rules that you should make use of all the time. If you wish to follow along, create a brand-new C# code library named MySimpleDotNetServer. As you read over the remainder of this chapter, I assume you will run the .NET assemblies through tlbexp.exe and check the underlying IDL using oleview.exe without further prompting.

Establishing Type Visibility

First and foremost, if a managed type (class, interface, enum, or structure) is to be accessed by COM, it must be defined as a *public* entity. If a given namespace contains type definitions that are declared as internal (realized as "Friend" under VB .NET), these entities will *not* be published to the COM type library. For example, ponder the following namespace definition of the MySimpleDotNetServer.dll assembly:

```
namespace MySimpleDotNetServer
{
    // This will be placed in the *.tlb file.
    public class Foo{}

    // This will NOT be placed in the *.tlb file.
    internal interface IBar{}
}
```

Establishing Type Member Visibility

Closely related to this rule is the other (rather obvious) rule that members of a .NET type (fields, properties, methods, and events) must be declared as public if they are to be published in the COM type library. Thus, if the Foo class seen previously defines the following set of members:

```
public class Foo
{
    // These will be published.
    public void A(){}
    public int B(int x){ return x++;}

    // These will not.
    private void HelperFunction(){}
    protected void HelperFunctionForDerivedTypes(){}
}
```

the only members that will be published to the COM *.tlb file are the A() and B() methods (as they are public). Do note that protected members (as well as private members) are not placed into the COM type library definition (ever).

Controlling Type and Member Visibility Using the ComVisible Attribute

Now, what if you have a set of type members that needs to be declared as public for a .NET client, but should be hidden from view from a given COM client? Furthermore, what if you have a number of public types that need to be hidden from the lurking eye of a COM client? Obviously, it would be a huge bother if you were required to define members as private or types as internal to accomplish this task (as the .NET clients would be unable to make use of them!). Luckily for you, the System.Runtime.InteropServices namespace defines an attribute that explicitly controls COM visibility.

Recall that by default all public types and public type members are visible by COM. When you need to restrict the visibility of a public type or public members of a public type, apply the ComVisibleAttribute as follows:

```
namespace MySimpleDotNetServer
{
    public class Foo
    {
        // This will be published.
        public void A(){}
```

```
        // This will NOT be published.
        [ComVisible(false)]
        public int B(int x){ return x++;}

        // These will never be published.
        private void HelperFunction(){}
        protected void HelperFunctionForDerivedTypes(){}
    }

    // This will not be placed in the *.tlb file,
    // but is visible to other .NET assemblies.
    [ComVisible(false)]
    public interface IBar{}
}
```

Understand that the ComVisibleAttribute type is ultimately used to instruct tools such as tlbexp.exe how *you would like* to expose .NET types to a COM type library. This means that if a given .NET type was been formally declared as public (despite the fact that the author of the type marked it as COM invisible), it would be possible to build a unique .NET assembly that exposes the invisible member to COM via standard containment/delegation. However, when you as a COM developer reference a *.tlb file describing a .NET assembly, you should assume that the .NET entities that are exposed are there for a reason. Typically, .NET entities that are COM invisible are marked as such given that they don't translate well into terms of COM in the first place. That being said, if a .NET type (or member) was not published to a COM *.tlb file, don't use it.

Translating Constructors and C#-Style Destructors

Now that you have a namespace that defines a small set of .NET types (of varying visibility), you can drill into some specific details of building the class itself. First and foremost, .NET class types exposed to COM must support a *public default constructor*. In fact, even if a .NET type has been declared as COM visible, a COM client cannot activate it if the type lacks a default class constructor.

Recall that a .NET class type will always receive a freebie default constructor. However, as soon as the class type does define additional constructors, the default is silently removed (and must be reinserted if you wish to support it). Because the Foo class does not define any custom constructors, the type automatically supports a default constructor and may be activated by COM. However, you are also permitted to explicitly define the no argument constructor as well (and you must redefine it if your class supports additional custom constructors):

```
public class Foo
{
    // Creatable COM visible types must
    // support a default constructor.
    public Foo(){}

    public void A(){}
    [ComVisible(false)]
    public int B(int x){ return x++;}

    private void HelperFunction(){}
    protected void HelperFunctionForDerivedTypes(){}
}
```

Understand that it is sometimes useful (if not mandatory) to define a COM-visible class type that does *not* support a default constructor. For example, say you wish to build a managed version of the VB 6.0 CarCollection constructed in Chapter 7. If you want to ensure that the contained Car types are not directly creatable from a COM client, simply define a private default constructor (or add custom constructors and don't bother to resupply the default). Defining a class type with a private constructor is in effect the .NET equivalent of the VB 6.0 approach of assigning the PublicNotCreatable value to the Instancing property. For example, the following C# class definition:

```
public class Foo
{
    // Visible, but not directly creatable.
    private Foo(){}
    ...
}
```

results in the following (partial) COM type definition:

```
[uuid(CE6BCA78-808F-3C00-AA67-BE19EEC2BF37),
  noncreatable, …]
coclass Foo
{
    ...
};
```

Now, what if you have a custom C# class type that defines a set of overloaded constructors? Given that classic COM does not activate COM types using constructor syntax, it should stand to reason that constructors of any sort will not be published to the generated COM type library. The same holds true for C#-style destructors (the VB .NET equivalent of overriding the Finalize() method). Recall that System.Object.Finalize() is a protected method, and like any protected member, it will not be placed into a COM type library.

Because COM clients never interact with COM types using OO-based constructors or destructors in the first place, it should make perfect sense that these entities will never end up in a COM type library. Rather, when a C++ client calls CoCreateInstance() (or New via VB 6.0), the CCW will automatically trigger the default constructor of the .NET type. Likewise, when the COM client releases all references to the CCW, the .NET type is a candidate for .NET garbage collection.

Translating Abstract Base Classes

Closely related to the previous design consideration is the fact that abstract base classes should never be published to a COM type library. By default, if you declare a COM-visible abstract class, the IDL definition will identify it as a [noncreatable] entity. However, given that abstract types should never be creatable in any programming architecture, you should explicitly set the ComVisible attribute to false for each abstract type:

```
// Abstract types should not be listed in a COM type library!
[ComVisible(false)]
public abstract class TheAbstractBaseClass
{
    public TheAbstractBaseClass(){}
    ...
}
```

Translating Overridable Members

Abstract base classes tend to define some number of virtual (or abstract) members in order to provide a polymorphic interface for the derived types. By way of a simple review, recall the following:

- Overridable members define a default implementation of the method in question that *may* be overridden by the derived type.
- Abstract members do *not* define a default implementation whatsoever. Abstract base classes define abstract members to enforce the polymorphic interface on all derived types.

Of course, classic COM does not allow any form of "is-a" relations. The obvious question, therefore, is what the IDL code will look like if you expose a derived type to COM. To illustrate, assume the following C# parent/child class dependency:

```
[ComVisible(false)]
public abstract class TheParentClass
{
    public abstract void YouMustDealWithThis();
```

```
    public virtual void YouCanChangeThis()
    { MessageBox.Show("Default impl of YouCanChangeThis()");}
}

[ClassInterface(ClassInterfaceType.AutoDual)]  // Defined soon.
public class DerivedClass : TheParentClass
{
    public override void YouMustDealWithThis()
    { MessageBox.Show("Fine...happy now?");}

    public override void YouCanChangeThis()
    {
        MessageBox.Show("I added this functionality!");
        base.YouCanChangeThis();
    }
}
```

From a managed C# client, you can simply leverage the inherited functionality (as well as conform to the polymorphic demands of your parent class) as follows:

```
// Simple C# client.
DerivedClass dc = new DerivedClass();
dc.YouCanChangeThis();
dc.YouMustDealWithThis();
```

As you would assume, when the managed client calls YouCanChangeThis(), two message boxes are displayed on the screen because you explicitly trigger your parent's functionality via the C# base keyword.

Now assume you have run the MySimpleDotNetServer.dll assembly through the tlbexp.exe utility. When you open the resulting *.tlb file using oleview.exe, you will find the following definition of the DerivedClass interface:

```
interface _DerivedClass : IDispatch
{
    [id(00000000), propget,
        custom({54FC8F55-38DE-4703-9C4E-250351302B1C}, "1")]
    HRESULT ToString([out, retval] BSTR* pRetVal);
    [id(0x60020001)]
    HRESULT Equals( [in] VARIANT obj,
        [out, retval] VARIANT_BOOL* pRetVal);
    [id(0x60020002)]
    HRESULT GetHashCode([out, retval] long* pRetVal);
    [id(0x60020003)]
    HRESULT GetType([out, retval] _Type** pRetVal);
    [id(0x60020004)]
    HRESULT YouMustDealWithThis();
    [id(0x60020005)]
    HRESULT YouCanChangeThis();
};
```

As you can see, the members of a derived type are expressed in terms of COM IDL as a union of all abstract and virtual members of the parent classes. For example, given that TheParentClass defines an abstract and virtual member, the _DerivedType interface accounts for each function. However, also note that the _DerivedType interface contains definitions for the overridable members of System.Object! This should make sense, because the .NET DerivedType derives from TheParentClass, which in turn derives from System.Object.

Inheriting Public Members

The union of inherited methods flows up the chain of inheritance as far as possible. Thus, if the most derived class has five base classes, every virtual and abstract member will be placed into the COM interface definition. The same holds true for a simple public member of a base class type. For example, if TheParentClass defines a set of concrete COM-visible public members as follows:

```
[ComVisible(false)]
public abstract class TheParentClass
{
    [ComVisible(false)]
    public abstract void YouMustDealWithThis();

    public virtual void YouCanChangeThis()
    { MessageBox.Show("Default impl of YouCanChangeThis()");}

    // Basic inheritable members.
    public void A(){}
    public void B(){}
    public void C(){}
    public void D(){}
}
```

the IDL of the _DerivedClass interface will support direct access to each public member (cool, huh?):

```
interface _DerivedClass : IDispatch
{
    ...
    [id(0x60020005)]
    HRESULT A();
    [id(0x60020006)]
    HRESULT B();
    [id(0x60020007)]
    HRESULT C();
    [id(0x60020008)]
    HRESULT D();
};
```

So to recap, any public member (abstract, virtual, or concrete) defined in a .NET base class will be accessible to the generated COM coclass definition. Although this is not quite a pure "is-a" relationship, it does honor the semantics of a base and derived type.

Translating Static and Constant Members

Finally, if a given class type contains static (Shared in VB .NET) or constant members, they will not be published to the COM type information (regardless of the assigned visibility). Thus, the following members are not accessible by a COM client:

```
// Static data / static methods are not reachable from COM.
[ComVisible(true)]
public class Foo
{
    ...
    // Not published to the generated type library.
    public static int fooObjCounter = 0;
    public static int GetNumbOfFooObjs()
    { return fooObjCounter;}

    // Also not published to the generated type library.
    public const double PI = 3.14;
}
```

So much for learning what cannot be expressed in terms of COM. Next up, let's examine some basic .NET-to-COM conversion rules.

Critical .NET-to-COM Conversion Details

Assume you have created a new C# class type that defines a .NET property, field set, and various methods taking input, output, and reference parameters (recall that public entities are COM visible automatically):

```
[ClassInterface(ClassInterfaceType.AutoDual)]  // Defined soon.
public class BasicTypeMembers
{
    private string mStrValue;
    // .NET Property.
    public string StringValue
    {
        get{return mStrValue;}
        set{mStrValue = value;}
    }
```

```
    // .NET Fields.
    public int mIntField;
    public bool mBooleanField;

    // .NET Methods.
    public void A(){}
    public int B(int x){return x++;}
    public void C(ref int x){x++;}
    public void D(out int x){x = 1000;}
}
```

Now, run this updated assembly through the tlbexp.exe utility and let's check out the results.

Converting Method Signatures

All parameters in COM must be defined using the [in], [out], [in, out], or [out, retval] IDL keywords. Under C# .NET, these same semantics are expressed using the ref and out keywords (input parameters are the assumed directory of travel). Based on the initial chapters of this text, which dove into the specifics of the COM and .NET types, the following mappings should not raise any eyebrows:

```
// Based on: public void A(){}
[id(0x60020006)]
HRESULT A();

// Based on: public int B(int x){return x++;}
[id(0x60020007)]
HRESULT B([in] long x, [out, retval] long* pRetVal);

// Based on: public void C(ref int x){x++;}
[id(0x60020008)]
HRESULT C([in, out] long* x);

// Based on: public void D(out int x){x = 1000;}
[id(0x60020009)]
HRESULT D([out] long* x);
```

A few points of interest. First of all, realize that by default all .NET methods will map to IDL methods that return the mandatory HRESULT. Furthermore, if the .NET method returns void (the equivalent of a VB subroutine), the IDL method signature will not support an [out, retval] parameter. Just to be sure that the relationship between IDL, C#, and VB .NET parameter modifiers are fixed in your mind, Table 10-4 provides a handy summary.

Table 10-4. Parameter Modifier Decoder

C# Parameter Modifier	Visual Basic .NET Parameter Modifier	IDL Attribute Parameter Modifier
Input parameters (no C#-specific keyword)	ByVal (default)	[in]
ref	ByRef	[in/out]
out	No equivalent	[out]

The InAttribute and OutAttribute Types

It is worth noting that the System.Runtime.InteropServices namespace defines two managed types that can be used to explicitly control how a .NET parameter is mapped into an IDL method definition: InAttribute and OutAttribute. To illustrate, if you rework the logic of methods B(), C(), and D(), you could write the following:

```
// Explicitly mark IDL [in].
public int B2([In]int x){return x++;}

// Explicitly mark IDL [in, out].
public void C2([In][Out]ref int x){x++;}

// Explicitly mark IDL [out].
public void D2([Out]out int x){x = 1000;}
```

Again, making use of the InAttribute and OutAttibute types is optional, given that the C# out and ref keywords will automatically map to the appropriate IDL. However, if ever you wish to expose a method to COM in a manner that is different from the way it is expressed to .NET, you are able to do so using these two managed attributes.

Converting .NET Properties

.NET property syntax maps perfectly into the property syntax of COM. Thus, for each read/write .NET property, you will find a [propput] and [propget] IDL method definition. When you expose a read-only (or write-only) .NET property to COM, the related [propput] and [propget] member will be removed as required. Given the previous StringValue property, you will find the following IDL definition:

```
// Based on: get{return mStrValue;}
[id(0x60020004), propget]
HRESULT StringValue([out, retval] BSTR* pRetVal);

// Based on: set{mStrValue = value;}
[id(0x60020004), propput]
HRESULT StringValue([in] BSTR pRetVal);
```

Converting .NET Fields

Classic COM does not support class-level public data points, given that all communications must flow through a valid interface reference. Thus, if you have a .NET type that defines a set of public fields, it stands to reason that tlbexp.exe will generate a corresponding IDL *property* definition as follows:

```
// Based on: public int mIntField;
[id(0x6002000a), propget]
HRESULT mIntField([out, retval] long* pRetVal);
[id(0x6002000a), propput]
HRESULT mIntField([in] long pRetVal);

// Based on: public bool mBooleanField;
[id(0x6002000c), propget]
HRESULT mBooleanField([out, retval] VARIANT_BOOL* pRetVal);
[id(0x6002000c), propput]
HRESULT mBooleanField([in] VARIANT_BOOL pRetVal);
```

So, at this point you have learned how to configure the visibility of .NET types and .NET members as well as a number of basic conversion details (constructors, parameters, properties, and fields). Now that you understand the basic rules of building .NET class types that are COM visible, you can formally tackle the topic of the class interface.

CODE *The MySimpleDotNetServer project is included under the MySimpleDotNetServer Chapter 10 subdirectory.*

Understanding the Class Interface

As you are well aware, .NET class types are never required to support interfaces of any kind. This poses a problem for the COM client, because COM demands all communications take place using an interface reference. Now, as you have seen in numerous places in this text, VB 6.0 attempts to simplify the process of creating and accessing COM types by defining a [default] interface for each coclass. The rule is simple: If a VB 6.0 *.cls file defines a public member, it is published to the [default] interface automatically.

When exposing a .NET type to COM, you can take a similar approach. The ClassInterfaceAttribute type (defined in the System.Runtime.InteropServices namespace) is an attribute that you apply at the class level to define how COM-visible class members should be configured in the generated COM type library.

As you may recall, a COM interface can be defined as an IUnknown-derived (that is, custom) interface, a [dual] interface, or a raw dispinterface (whose members are only accessible via IDispatch). Although the ClassInterfaceAttribute type does not allow you to specify class interfaces deriving directly from IUnknown, you are able to specify [dual] and dispinterfaces using the closely related ClassInterfaceType enumeration:

```
// This enum is used in conjunction
// with the ClassInterface attribute.
public enum ClassInterfaceType
{
    AutoDispatch,
    AutoDual,
    None
}
```

Table 10-5 documents the meaning of each member of the ClassInterfaceType enumeration.

Table 10-5. The ClassInterfaceType Enumeration

ClassInterfaceType Member	Meaning in Life
AutoDispatch	This is the default setting for ClassInterfaceAttribute and is used to indicate that the public members of a class are only accessible using IDispatch. To preserve the requirements of COM versioning, tlbexp.exe will not assign specific DISPIDs to the public members, to prevent client applications from caching the dispinterface members.
AutoDual	Indicates that public members are placed in a dual interface and can thus be accessed from late-bound and early-bound clients. In this case, DISPIDs are assigned by tlbexp.exe.
None	Indicates that the .NET class does not support a class interface. If you do not explicitly define and implement interfaces for the .NET type, the members will only be reachable using COM-style late binding.

Establishing a .NET Class Interface

To illustrate the use of these values, let's say you have a new C# code library (named DotNetMathServer) that defines the following class type:

```
using System;
using System.Runtime.InteropServices;

namespace DotNetMathServer
{
    public class DotNetCalc
    {
        public DotNetCalc(){}

        public int Add(int x, int y)
        { return x + y;}

        public int Subtract(int x, int y)
        { return x - y;}
    }
}
```

If you run this type through the tlbexp.exe utility as is, you will find that you have been provided with an empty [default] dual interface:

```
[odl, uuid(BDD31E6C-07D6-33E8-AC86-BC3A23C91544),
hidden, dual, oleautomation,
custom({0F21F359-AB84-41E8-9A78-36D110E6D2F9},
" DotNetMathServer.DotNetCalc")]
interface _DotNetCalc : IDispatch
{
};

[…]
coclass DotNetCalc
{
    [default] interface _DotNetCalc;
    interface _Object;
};
```

Recall that by default tlbexp.exe will always generate an AutoDispatch class interface unless you say otherwise. In fact, if you explicitly assign the ClassInterface attribute the value of ClassInterfaceType.AutoDispatch, you will find an identical IDL definition, as shown in this example:

```
[ClassInterface(ClassInterfaceType.AutoDispatch)]
public class DotNetCalc
{…}
```

When a .NET class is defined without the ClassInterface attribute or using the ClassInterfaceType.AutoDispatch value, the COM client is forced to access the members using late binding *exclusively*. Also note that the resulting COM type information does not catalog the DISPIDs of the members of the dispinterface. The reason for this seemingly odd behavior will be examined in the "The Case Against the Class Interface" section.

Now assume you want to establish the ClassInterface attribute as ClassInterfaceType.AutoDual:

```
[ClassInterface(ClassInterfaceType.AutoDual)]
public class DotNetCalc
{…}
```

You would now find that the generated class interface is populated with the custom Add() and Subtract() methods, as well as the public members inherited from your base class, System.Object:

```
[odl, uuid(524EBD3B-334E-3E04-AA82-998BDEA7F2FB),
hidden, dual, nonextensible, oleautomation,
custom({0F21F359-AB84-41E8-9A78-36D110E6D2F9},
" DotNetMathServer.DotNetCalc")]
interface _DotNetCalc : IDispatch
{
    [id(00000000), propget,
    custom({54FC8F55-38DE-4703-9C4E-250351302B1C}, "1")]
      HRESULT ToString([out, retval] BSTR* pRetVal);
    [id(0x60020001)]
    HRESULT Equals( [in] VARIANT obj,
       [out, retval] VARIANT_BOOL* pRetVal);
    [id(0x60020002)]
      HRESULT GetHashCode([out, retval] long* pRetVal);
    [id(0x60020003)]
    HRESULT GetType([out, retval] _Type** pRetVal);
    [id(0x60020004)]
    HRESULT Add( [in] long x,  [in] long y,
      [out, retval] long* pRetVal);
    [id(0x60020005)]
    HRESULT Subtract( [in] long x,  [in] long y,
    [out, retval] long* pRetVal);
};
```

Finally, you have ClassInterfaceType.None, which results in a coclass definition that does not support a class interface of any type. As a result, your coclass definition supports the generated _Object interface, which again defines the inherited members of System.Object. Do note, however, that when you specify

ClassInterfaceType.None, _Object is marked as the [default] interface of the type! This would, of course, be quite confusing to a COM client, given that they would not expect to trigger this .NET-centric behavior off the cuff. Later you will see how to combine ClassInterfaceType.None with strongly typed .NET interfaces to gain a more usable COM coclass. Nevertheless, here is the end result of the story so far:

```
// The result of ClassInterfaceType.None.
coclass DotNetCalc
{
   [default] interface _Object;
};
```

The Custom IDL Attribute: {0F21F359-AB84-41E8-9A78-36D110E6D2F9}

If you've carefully read the generated COM type information for the various .NET class interfaces, you no doubt noticed that each variation supports a custom IDL attribute with the name {0F21F359-AB84-41E8-9A78-36D110E6D2F9} (see Chapter 4 for coverage of custom IDL attributes). The predefined .NET attribute is used to document the ProgID of the COM type that defines the interface in question. In fact, when tlbexp.exe generates any COM type (coclass, interface, enum, or structure), the IDL definition will always make use of {0F21F359-AB84-41E8-9A78-36D110E6D2F9}. For example:

```
[…custom({0F21F359-AB84-41E8-9A78-36D110E6D2F9},
" DotNetMathServer.DotNetCalc")]
interface _DotNetCalc : IDispatch
{};
```

Understand that this custom attribute is completely ignored by COM clients, unless you explicitly build a COM solution that is on the lookout for this name/value pair. Furthermore, the .NET runtime ignores the custom IDL attribute as well. This begs the following obvious question: What good is an attribute that is ignored by both architectures?

The truth of the matter is, if you were to build a COM IDL file by hand and explicitly make use of this custom IDL attribute, the tlbimp.exe (reread: Type Library *Importer*) utility will create a .NET type with the specified name. Thus, if you were to define the following COM IDL definition:

```
[…custom({0F21F359-AB84-41E8-9A78-36D110E6D2F9},
"TheNameSpaceIWant.TheClassIWant")]
coclass CoFoo
{};
```

you would find the following definition in the generated interop assembly:

```
namespace TheNameSpaceIWant
{
    public class TheClassIWant{…}
}
```

To be honest, you will seldom need to instruct tlbimp.exe to generate a name that is unique from the COM type definition in this manner. Nevertheless, this custom IDL attribute does allow you to do so. In most situations, this IDL annotation is basically ignored.

Understanding the _Object Interface

Another aspect of the assembly-to-type library conversion process you may have noticed is the definition of a specific interface named _Object. As you certainly know, all .NET types ultimately derive from the mighty System.Object. When tlbexp.exe encounters a type that derives from a given base class, it will automatically create a new COM interface that is the summation of all COM-visible members defined in the parent class. Given that the DotNetCalc type implicitly derives from System.Object, you are offered a COM interface that defines the equivalent functionality. Table 10-6 lists the IDL definitions of each inherited member.

Table 10-6. Members of the _Object Interface

_Object Interface Member Name	Meaning in Life
HRESULT ToString([out, retval] BSTR* pRetVal);	Maps to the .NET type's implementation of ToString() to a default COM property (read-only) of the same name
HRESULT Equals([in] VARIANT obj, [out, retval] VARIANT_BOOL* pRetVal);	Maps to the .NET type's implementation of Equals()
HRESULT GetHashCode([out, retval] long* pRetVal);	Maps to the .NET type's implementation of GetHashCode()
HRESULT GetType([out, retval] _Type** pRetVal);	Maps to the .NET type's implementation of GetType()

Exactly how a generated coclass supports the members of _Object will depend on how you configured the type's class interface, specifically:

- The AutoDual option will expose the members of the _Object interface as part of the generated class interface.
- An AutoDispatch class interface (the default) or a class interface defined as None will expose the members of _Object as members of the generated dispinterface.

Transforming System.Object.ToString()

While the transformation of Object.GetType(), Object.Equals(), and Object.GetHashCode() into terms of COM IDL is quite straightforward, the handling of Object.ToString() requires a second look. By default, when tlbexp.exe accounts for the ToString() method, it will expose this member as a read-only COM property:

```
// System.Object.ToString() is exposed as a COM property.
[id(00000000), propget,
custom({54FC8F55-38DE-4703-9C4E-250351302B1C}, "1")]
HRESULT ToString([out, retval] BSTR* pRetVal);
```

Note that the DISPID of the ToString() property is zero, which marks this member as the default property of the coclass. Given this, a VB 6.0 COM client may display the state data of a .NET type as follows:

```
' ToString() is the default property, thus…
MsgBox myDotNetObject
' Which is the same as…
MsgBox myDotNetObject.ToString
```

Also note that the ToString() property has been assigned with yet another [custom] IDL attribute named 54FC8F55-38DE-4703-9C4E-250351302B1C. This is used to ensure that if this COM *.tlb file is reimported into terms of .NET metadata, ToString() is correctly configured back into the expected method definition.

You will see examples of accessing the members of _Object a bit later in this chapter. For the time being, I'll turn your attention to why you would typically *not* wish to define a class interface in the first place.

The Case Against Class Interfaces

Although the concept of a class interface makes the process of exposing public class members to a COM client very simple, this approach is not without its drawbacks. In fact, the official word on the streets (according to the online documentation) is that you should avoid defining a class interface on your .NET types and make explicit use of ClassInterface.None. In place of a class interface, you are encouraged to make use of strongly typed custom interfaces.

So, why is the class interface considered evil? The reason has to do with the dreaded type versioning problem. Under COM, the general rule used during interface development is that once an interface has been placed into production code, its definition should never, ever change. If you somehow alter a COM interface after it has been deployed (for example, add a method, remove a method, or change the signature of a method), you run the risk of breaking existing clients (not to mention the polymorphic nature of COM itself).

Given that a .NET class type does not necessarily need to adhere to this strict versioning scheme, AutoDual class interfaces may quickly become out of sync with the underlying .NET type. Furthermore, as an AutoDispatch interface demands late binding, COM clients are bound to be unhappy. Given these realities, the recommended pattern is as follows:

```
// Class interface?  Just say no…
[ClassInterface(ClassInterfaceType.None)]
public class DotNetCalc {…}
```

Exposing Custom .NET Interfaces to COM

To illustrate the benefits of making use of explicit interfaces (as opposed to class interfaces), let's rework the logic of the current DotNetCalc type to implement an interface named IBasicMath. Before you do, however, you need to come to terms with the InterfaceType attribute.

When defining a .NET interface that needs to be exposed to COM, you should always qualify the type by applying the InterfaceTypeAttribute type, which is used in conjunction with the ComInterfaceType enumeration. As you would guess, the ComInterfaceType attribute is used to control whether the interface is recorded in the type library as IUnknown derived (which is not possible using a class interface), a dual interface, or a raw dispinterface (Table 10-7).

Table 10-7. ComInterfaceType Values

ComInterfaceType Member Name	Description
InterfaceIsDual	Indicates the interface needs to be exposed to COM as a dual interface
InterfaceIsIDispatch	Indicates an interface needs to be exposed to COM as a dispinterface
InterfaceIsIUnknown	Indicates an interface needs to be exposed to COM as an IUnknown-derived interface, as opposed to a dispinterface or a dual interface

For example, if you wish to expose IBasicMath as an IUnknown-derived interface, you could write the following .NET interface definition:

```
// A strongly typed interface for use by COM.
[InterfaceType(ComInterfaceType.InterfaceIsIUnknown)]
public interface IBasicMath
{
    int Add(int x, int y);
    int Subtract(int x, int y);
}
```

This results in the following IDL:

```
 [odl,uuid(30C6D943-D332-3E24-90DC-589A8579E33B),
 version(1.0), oleautomation,
 custom({0F21F359-AB84-41E8-9A78-36D110E6D2F9},
" DotNetMathServer.IBasicMath")]
interface IBasicMath : IUnknown
{
    HRESULT _stdcall Add( [in] long x,  [in] long y,
    [out, retval] long* pRetVal);

    HRESULT _stdcall Subtract( [in] long x,  [in] long y,
    [out, retval] long* pRetVal);
};
```

When you specify ComInterfaceType.InterfaceIsIUnknown, the IDL interface definition is automatically configured with the [oleautomation] attribute. This is a very good thing, given that the IBasicMath interface is now ready to be marshaled using the universal marshaler (oleaut32.dll) rather than a custom stub/proxy DLL. Although it is possible to specify an alternative stub/proxy DLL to marshal your interfaces (as shown later in this chapter), there really is no reason to do so.

If you make use of ComInterfaceType.InterfaceIsDual when defining IBasicMath, you will find tlbexp.exe generates a [dual] interface with autogenerated DISPIDs:

```
[odl, uuid(30C6D943-D332-3E24-90DC-589A8579E33B),
version(1.0), dual, oleautomation,
custom({0F21F359-AB84-41E8-9A78-36D110E6D2F9},
"DotNetMathServer.IBasicMath")]
interface IBasicMath : IDispatch
{
    [id(0x60020000)]
    HRESULT Add( [in] long x,  [in] long y,
    [out, retval] long* pRetVal);
    [id(0x60020001)]
    HRESULT Subtract( [in] long x,  [in] long y,
    [out, retval] long* pRetVal);
};
```

And obviously, ComInterfaceType.InterfaceIsIDispatch generates a raw dispinterface:

```
[uuid(30C6D943-D332-3E24-90DC-589A8579E33B),
version(1.0),
custom({0F21F359-AB84-41E8-9A78-36D110E6D2F9},
"DotNetMathServer.IBasicMath")]
dispinterface IBasicMath
{
    properties:
    methods:
    [id(0x60020000)]
    long Add( [in] long x,  [in] long y);
    [id(0x60020001)]
    long Subtract( [in] long x,  [in] long y);
};
```

Controlling IID and DISPID Generation

As you know, the runtime automatically assigns unique DISPIDs to a given member at runtime. Also, the tlbexp.exe utility automatically assigns GUIDs to each .NET type (as seen in the COM type library). If you wish to make use of fixed, unchangeable IID and DISPID values, you are free to apply the GuidAttribute and DispIdAttribute types as follows (of course, DISPIDs will be ignored if you make use of them with an interface defined as ComInterfaceType.InterfaceIsIUnknown):

```
// An even stronger typed interface for use by COM.
[InterfaceType(ComInterfaceType.InterfaceIsDual)]
[Guid("B3D938A2-0B47-469f-BECE-DBD35008EAD8")]
public interface IBasicMath
{
    [DispId(1)] int Add(int x, int y);
    [DispId(2)] int Subtract(int x, int y);
}
```

Note the resulting IDL definition:

```
[uuid(B3D938A2-0B47-469F-BECE-DBD35008EAD8)…]
interface IBasicMath : IDispatch
{
    [id(0x00000001)]
    HRESULT Add(…);

    [id(0x00000002)]
    HRESULT Subtract(…);
};
```

Implementing Explicit Interfaces

Now that you have fully defined the IBasicMath interface, you are ready to implement it on a given C# class type:

```
// This class does NOT support a class interface.
[ClassInterface(ClassInterfaceType.None)]
public class DotNetCalcWithInterface : IBasicMath
{
    public DotNetCalcWithInterface(){}
    public int Add(int x, int y)
    {return x + y;}
    public int Subtract(int x, int y)
    {return x - y;}
}
```

As you would expect, you are also able to implement an explicit COM-visible interface using explicit interface implementation. Recall that this would force the .NET client to interact with the members of IBasicMath from an interface reference exclusively.

Controlling the Generated ProgID

Before moving on to the task of registering and accessing your .NET assemblies, you have a few additional basic points of interest to contend with. The first is altering the generated COM ProgID. By default, tlbexp.exe automatically generates a ProgID for each .NET class type found in the input assembly using the following naming convention:

```
<NamespaceName.ClassName>
```

Thus, given a namespace named MyDotNetAssembly and a COM-visible class type named MyClass, the resulting ProgID is MyDotNetAssembly.MyClass. Most of the time, this default naming convention will fit the bill. However, if you wish to programmatically control the ProgID for a given class type, you may apply the ProgIdAttribute:

```
// Customizing the generated ProgId.
[ClassInterface(ClassInterfaceType.None)]
[ProgId("COM2NetExample.DotNetCalcWithInterface")]
public class DotNetCalcWithInterface : IBasicMath
{
    ...
}
```

Although you have no need to alter the ProgID value for this current example, specifying a custom ProgID for a class type can be more useful than you might first suspect. As you may already know, a ProgID has a limit of 39 characters. If you have a class type defined in a nested namespace (for example, IntertechInc.AndrewsNamespace.CurrentProject.TheClassIAmBuilding), you may have a ProgId that exceeds this limit. In this case, making use of the ProgIdAttribute type will be a necessary fix.

Controlling the COM Library Definition

Another basic point of interest is that you are able to (optionally) control the name of the generated type library statement. When the tlbexp.exe utility is building the COM library statement, it does so using the following translation rules:

- The LIBID is generated based on the friendly name of the assembly and (optional) [.publickeytoken]. If the assembly is not strongly named (and therefore does not have a [.publickeytoken] value), the LIBID is randomly generated.
- The [version] is based on the <major>.<minor> values of an assemblies version.
- The [helpstring] of the library is based on the AssemblyDescription value (if any).

As you would expect, you are able to alter this information using a number of assembly-level attributes found in the System.Runtime.InteropServices namespace. Thus, if you apply the following assembly-level attributes (typically within the assemblyinfo.* file):

```
// Assume your assemblyinfo.cs file defines the following.
[assembly: AssemblyDescription("C# Math Library")]
[assembly: AssemblyVersion("9.2.0.0")]
[assembly: Guid("B33D5B5E-7D33-4d86-85C4-FD62D270DADF")]
```

you will find the following library statement:

```
[
    uuid(B33D5B5E-7D33-4D86-85C4-FD62D270DADF),
    version(9.2),
    helpstring("C# Math Library")
]
library DotNetMathServer
{…}
```

Of course, you really don't need to version your COM type library in this manner, so I'll assume you simply set the AssemblyVersion attribute to 1.0.0.0.

Handling Overloaded Methods

Another point of interest at this stage of the game is how a COM client is able to handle overloaded members of a .NET type. Recall that when a type "overloads" members, it defines a set of members of the same exact name, each of which differ by the number of (or type of) parameters. For example, assume that the DotNetCalc type defines an overloaded version of the Add() method:

```
[ClassInterface(ClassInterfaceType.AutoDual)]
[Guid("46933500-E958-48e2-89DA-018A12A43881")]
public class DotNetCalc
{
    public DotNetCalc(){}
    public int Add(int x, int y)
    {return x + y;}
    public double Add(double x, double y)
    {return x + y;}
    public int Subtract(int x, int y)
    {return x - y;}
}
```

Now, as you are well aware, classic COM does *not* allow developers to build interfaces that support overloaded members. Therefore, when tlbexp.exe encounters a type with various versions of a single method, it employs a clever hack. Observe:

```
interface _DotNetCalc : IDispatch {
...
    [id(0x60020004)]
    HRESULT Add( [in] long x,  [in] long y,
        [out, retval] long* pRetVal);
    [id(0x60020005),
    custom({0F21F359-AB84-41E8-9A78-36D110E6D2F9}, "Add")]
    HRESULT Add_2( [in] double x,  [in] double y,
        [out, retval] double* pRetVal);
...
};
```

As you can see, the first version of the overloaded method (which takes two integers) is named as expected. Subsequent versions, however, add a numerical suffix to the method name (Add_2). If DotNetCalc defined four versions of Add(), you would indeed see Add_3() and Add_4() as well. It is important to point out that tlbexp.exe will add these numerical suffixes based on the order of the members in the original .NET class definition. This behavior can lead to long-term versioning problems.

Assume, for example, that you have added yet another overloaded Add() method to the DotNetClac class, and you have chosen to do so directly in between the initial versions:

```
public class DotNetCalc
{
    public DotNetCalc(){}
    public int Add(int x, int y)
    {return x + y;}
    public long Add(long x, long y)
    {return x + y;}
    public double Add(double x, double y)
    {return x + y;}
    public int Subtract(int x, int y)
    {return x - y;}
}
```

If you do not regenerate the related *.tlb file for DotNetCalc, the COM client suddenly has incorrect type definitions! In this case, what was previously called Add_2() has now been renamed as Add_3(). To be as safe as possible, you may wish to make all overloaded members COM invisible and expose uniquely named members in their place (for example, AddInts(), AddFloats(), and AddDoubles()).

Although this numerical suffixing may not seem like the most elegant solution, it's really all that can be done. COM does not allow overloaded members, so tlbexp.exe is forced to generate unique names for each variation of the Add() method.

Importing mscorlib.tlb

The final point I need to address before moving on to using your .NET calculator from COM is to ponder the meaning of the following always-present IDL import:

```
[
  uuid(B33D5B5E-7D33-4D86-85C4-FD62D270DADF),
  version(1.0),
  helpstring("C# Math Library")
]
library DotNetMathServer
{
    // TLib : Common Language Runtime Library :
    //{BED7F4EA-1A96-11D2-8F08-00A0C9A6186D}
    importlib("mscorlib.tlb");
...
}
```

All type libraries that are generated from a .NET assembly will contain an IDL importlib() directive to ensure that the core .NET type definitions are included with your custom types. You have already seen a need for this in the COM version of the System.Object.GetType() method. Given that this method returns a System.Type, it stands to reason that the Type class needs to be defined in terms of COM IDL. As seen previously in Chapter 9, given that the types defined within mscorlib.dll are expressed in COM-centric terms, you are indeed able to build COM applications that make use of critical .NET types! For example, you could build a VB 6.0 application that makes use of System.String, System.Collections.ArrayList, System.IO.FileInfo, or any other entity defined in the vast number of namespaces contained within mscorlib.dll. To see the big picture, consider Figure 10-2.

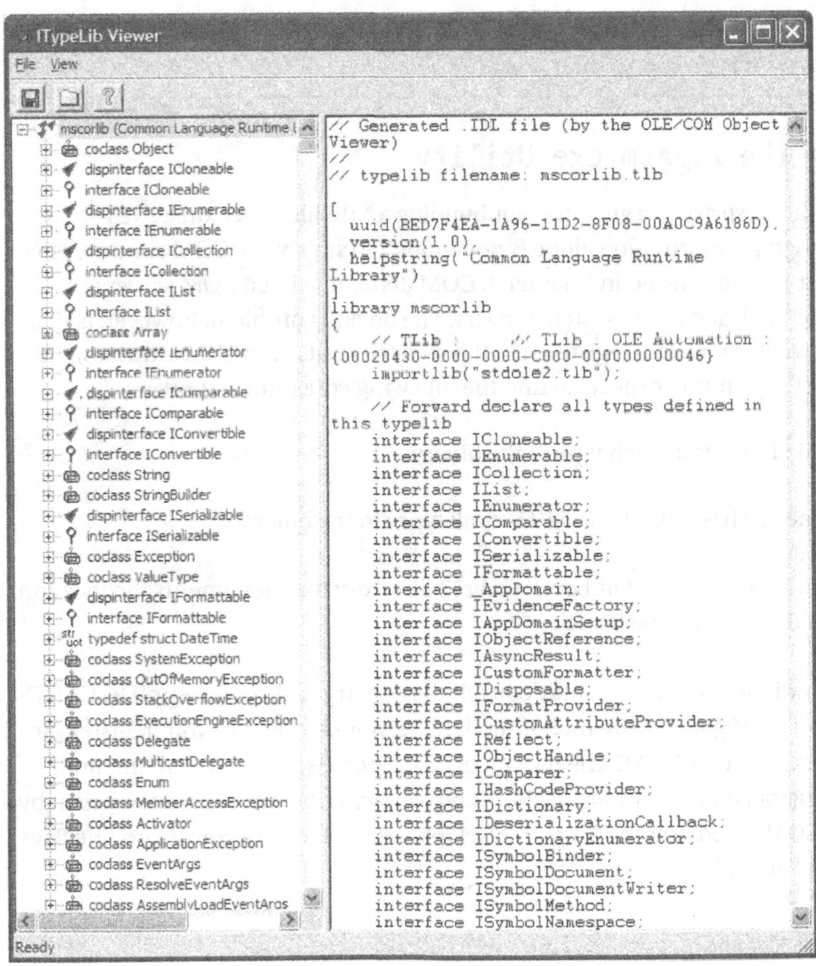

Figure 10-2. Mscorlib.dll presented in terms of classic COM

You will make use of mscorlib.tlb a bit later in this chapter when you build your COM clients. While it is enticing to envision building COM applications that leverage .NET types, understand that many key .NET assemblies (such as System.Xml.dll) have been configured entirely as *COM invisible*.

That wraps up the initial examination of expressing a .NET type in terms of COM IDL. In the next chapter you learn how to expose more elaborate .NET patterns to an interested COM client (delegates, class hierarchies, and whatnot). To wrap up this chapter, however, let's examine how to register and deploy the COM-aware .NET assembly and build a number of clients that make use of the DotNetMathServer.

CODE *The DotNetMathServer project is included under the Chapter 10 subdirectory.*

Using the regasm.exe Utility

Although tlbexp.exe is a great tool for building a *.tlb file based on a .NET assembly, type information alone is not enough to satisfy the COM runtime environment. As you learned in Chapter 2, COM demands that a COM server is correctly cataloged in the system registry. The obvious problem, however, is that .NET assemblies are *not* registered in the registry whatsoever! Nevertheless, the classic COM runtime expects to find the following core information:

- The ProgIDs of each type in the binary
- The CLSIDs, LIBIDs, and IIDs of all types in the binary
- An InprocServer32 or LocalServer32 directory that documents the location of the binary to be loaded

In addition, the runtime may consult the registry to discover AppIDs, CATIDs, and other COM goo. So, the million-dollar question is, how can you "register" an assembly for use by COM? The regasm.exe (register assembly) command line utility is a tool that updates a machine's registry with the information required by classic COM based on a .NET assembly. First, regard the core command line flags presented in Table 10-8.

Table 10-8. Key Flags of regasm.exe

regasm.exe Command Line Flag	Meaning in Life
/codebase	As you will see during your examination of deploying .NET assemblies for use by COM, assemblies are typically placed in the GAC. However, if you would rather not do so, this flag adds a CodeBase entry in the registry to map an assembly to an arbitrary directory location.
/regfile [:regFile]	Generates the specified .reg file for the assembly, which contains the necessary registry entries. Specifying this option does not change the registry. You cannot use this option with the /u or /tlb options.
/tlb [:typeLibFile]	Generates a type library from the specified assembly containing definitions of the accessible types defined within the assembly. The /tlb file also registers the type library in question.
/unregister or /u	Unregisters the creatable classes from the system registry.

The first flag of direct interest is /tlb. Using regasm.exe, you are able to generate a standalone *.tlb file for a given assembly in addition to installing the correct information in the system registry. Given this factoid, you are correct in assuming that the tlbexp.exe utility is not mandatory when exposing a .NET type to COM. If you would rather make use of a single tool to (a) generate COM type information and (b) register the assembly with COM, you can enter the following command:

```
regasm simpledotnetserver.dll /tlb
```

As you would hope, the generated simpledotnetserver.tlb file contains the same IDL definitions as you'd get using the tlbexp.exe utility. If you wish to remove the inserted registry information, simply use the /u flag:

```
regasm simpledotnetserver.dll /u
```

Another very helpful command line flag is /regfile. Recall from Chapter 2 that a *.reg file can be used to install COM registry information on a given machine via a simple double-click. When you specify the /regfile flag, you are instructing regasm.exe to generate a *.reg file that contains all the necessary information for a given .NET assembly. Also understand that specifying the /regfile flag will not update the current registry! This option simply spits out a new file in the application directory (Figure 10-3).

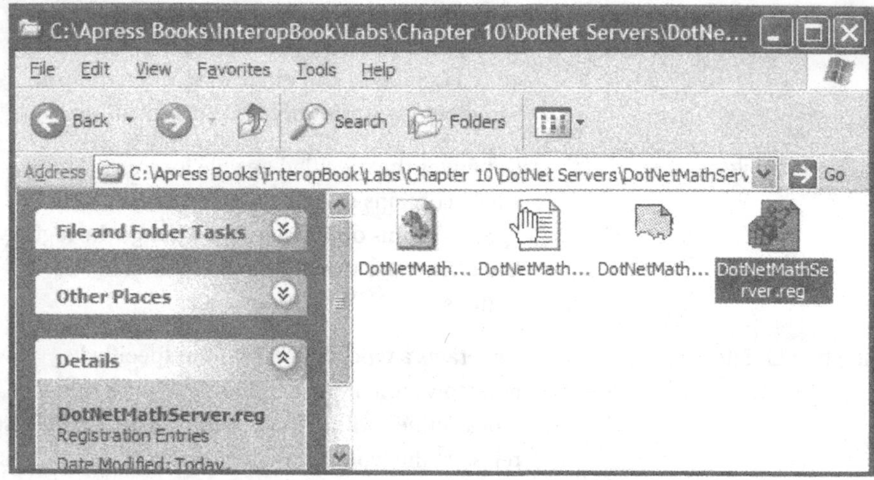

*Figure 10-3. The generated *.reg file*

Finally, you have the /codebase flag. Recall from Chapter 5 that it is possible to place a .NET assembly at an arbitrary location on your machine (or some other connected machine) by specifying a codebase element in the application configuration file. In the same light, if you make use of the /codebase flag, the InprocServer32 directory is updated with a CodeBase value that points to the location of the registered .NET assembly. Although this can be helpful during the development phase, .NET assemblies that are to be used by COM clients are typically deployed to the GAC. Given this, I'll ignore the use of the /codebase flag and allow you to check it out at your leisure.

Examining the Updated Entries

Let's check out the generated registration entries entered by the regasm.exe utility (of course, this same information is contained within the *.reg file). Recall that the DotNetMathServer.dll assembly contains two class types (DotNetCalc and DotNetCalcWithInterface) as well as a single interface named IBasicMath. To keep things simple, you will trace the generated entries for DotNetCalc, given that the registration information will be identical (modulo GUIDs) for DotNetCalcWithInterface.

The ProgID Entry

First of all, regasm.exe has entered the correct ProgID for DotNetCalc, which may be found directly under HKCR (Figure 10-4).

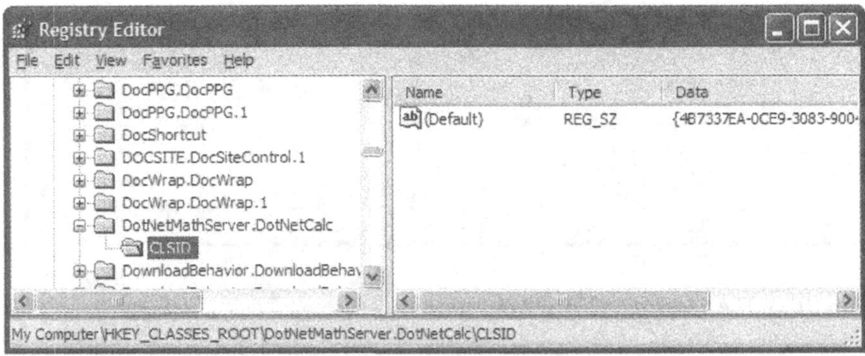

Figure 10-4. The ProgID

Like any COM ProgID, the generated listing will contain a \CLSID subdirectory that maps to the CLSID of the coclass. As mentioned, if you adorn your .NET classes with the GuidAttribute type, you are able to specify a hard-coded GUID value. If not, regasm.exe/tlbexp.exe generates one automatically.

To generate a CLSID, tlbexp.exe/regasm.exe obtains a hash code using the fully qualified name of the .NET class as well as the identity (version, friendly name, and the public key value) of the assembly in which it resides. In this way, if two different .NET assemblies define a class of the exact same name, they will be recorded as two different CLSIDs (which is a good thing).

The HKCR\CLSID Entry

The next stop on your journey is to check out the generated information contained under the HKEY_CLASSES_ROOT\CLSID\<your GUID> subdirectory (Figure 10-5).

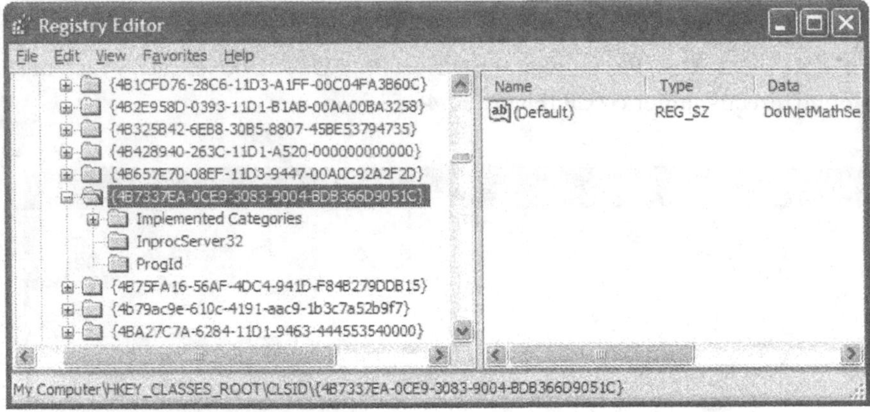

Figure 10-5. The necessary CLSID information

Although you can't see each critical bit of information from the previous screen shot, rest assured (and validate for yourself) that the various subdirectories have been populated based on the following registration script:

```
[HKEY_CLASSES_ROOT\DotNetMathServer.DotNetCalc\CLSID]
@="{4B7337EA-0CE9-3083-9004-BDB366D9051C}"

[HKEY_CLASSES_ROOT\CLSID\
{4B7337EA-0CE9-3083-9004-BDB366D9051C}]
@="DotNetMathServer.DotNetCalc"

[HKEY_CLASSES_ROOT\CLSID\
{4B7337EA-0CE9-3083-9004-BDB366D9051C}\InprocServer32]
@="C:\WINDOWS\System32\mscoree.dll"
"ThreadingModel"="Both"
"Class"="DotNetMathServer.DotNetCalc"
"Assembly"="DotNetMathServer, Version=9.2.0.0, Culture=neutral,
PublicKeyToken=3a7bb5f335af01f2"
"RuntimeVersion"="v1.0.3617"

[HKEY_CLASSES_ROOT\CLSID\{4B7337EA-0CE9-3083-9004-BDB366D9051C}\ProgId]
@="DotNetMathServer.DotNetCalc"

[HKEY_CLASSES_ROOT\CLSID\
{4B7337EA-0CE9-3083-9004-BDB366D9051C}\
Implemented Categories\{62C8FE65-4EBB-45E7-B440-6E39B2CDBF29}]
```

Beyond the expected ProgID subdirectory, the most interesting aspect of the .NET assembly registration process is discovered by examining the value listed under the InProcServer32 subdirectory. Recall from Chapter 2 that the COM runtime will examine the contained value to locate the requested COM DLL. However, when a .NET assembly is registered, the (Default) value is, in fact, mscoree.dll (Figure 10-6).

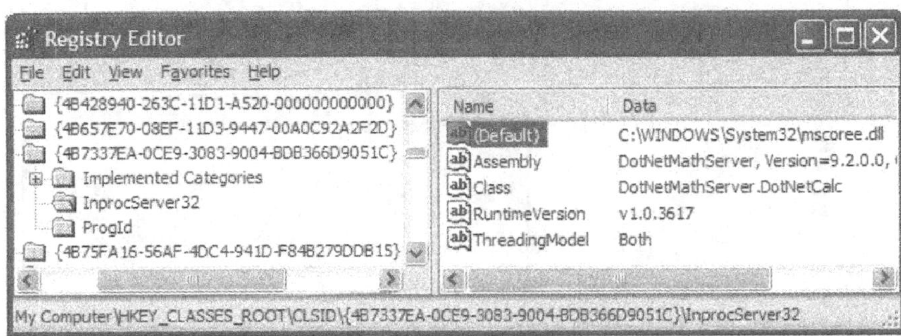

Figure 10-6. A coclass' InProcServer32 value points to the .NET runtime engine.

As you may suspect, when a COM client attempts to load a .NET type via the generated type information, the COM runtime ends up loading the .NET runtime! Also notice that each creatable type is registered with a Class value that documents the fully qualified name of the type within the .NET assembly. This value is passed (automatically) into mscoree.dll to specify the name of the type it is to create for the COM client. At this point, the same search heuristics described in Chapter 5 take over the show. Therefore, if the .NET assembly is located in the same folder as the COM client (aka a private assembly), the search is finished. As you will see in the next section, however, .NET assemblies that are COM aware are typically deployed as a shared assembly and tend to be located in the GAC.

Enlisting .NET Types into a Specific COM Category

The last point of interest regarding the registered values under HKCR\CLSID\<your guid> is a specific COM category of the value {62C8FE65-4EBB-45E7-B440-6E39B2CDBF29}. As you may know, classic COM allows developers to assign a given COM class to a particular numerical category (termed a *CATID*). CATIDs can be discovered at runtime by a given COM client to discover all coclasses that belong to a specific CATID.

This can be very helpful when you are attempting to group similar COM objects into a well-known category. For example, assume you are building a C++ COM client that needs to place the names of all COM classes belonging to the CATID {40FC6ED4-2438-11CF-A3DB-080036F12502}. This CATID is used to mark your old friend the ActiveX Control. In fact, if you open up the oleview.exe utility and examine the Grouped by Component Category folder, you will find all members belonging to the Control CATID (Figure 10-7).

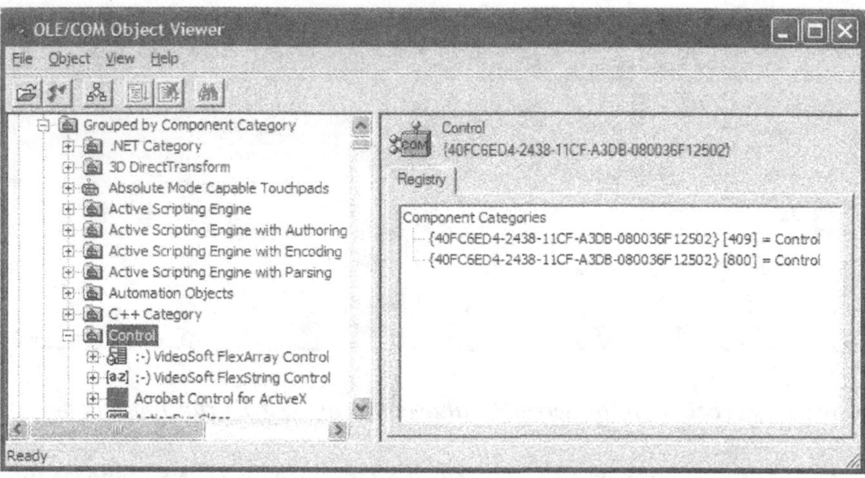

Figure 10-7. A well-known COM CATID

With the advent of .NET, Microsoft created a new CATID ({62C8FE65-4EBB-45E7-B440-6E39B2CDBF29}) that identifies all .NET class types that have been exposed to COM. As you have just seen, when you make use of regasm.exe, your .NET classes are automatically enlisted in this COM category. Thus, if you view the .NET Category folder, you will find your .NET math types (Figure 10-8).

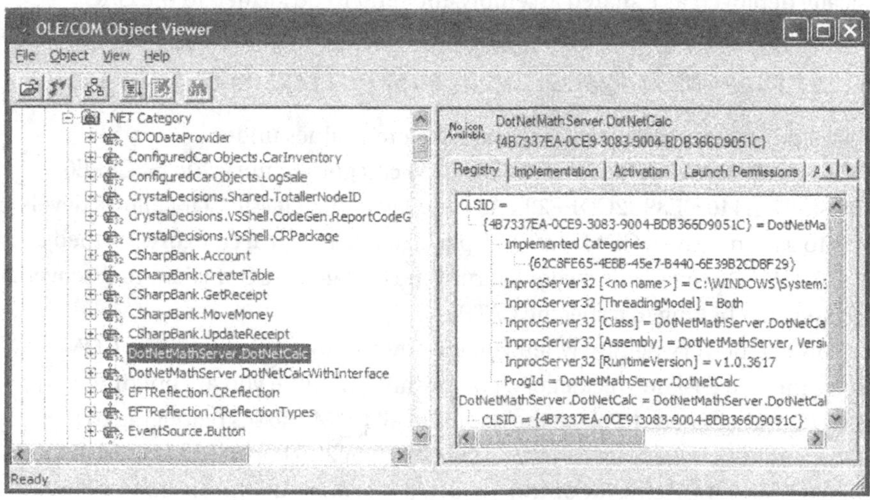

Figure 10-8. The regasm.exe utility assigns your .NET types to the .NET Category.

One question you may have at this point is, where exactly are these CATIDs logged in the system registry in the first place? The answer: in the HKCR\Component Categories (Figure 10-9).

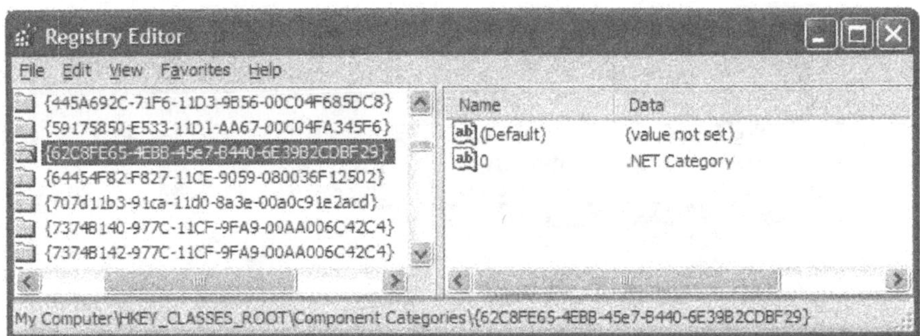

Figure 10-9. HKCR\Component Categories

Finally, in addition to the registration information I have just presented, regasm.exe also documents the version of the .NET runtime that the .NET assembly was compiled against (via the RuntimeVersion value) as well as the friendly name, version, cultural information, and public key token of the assembly itself for each class type.

Registering the Exposed Interfaces

Under classic COM, when you intend a given interface to be accessed across a process boundary (such as one *.exe using an object in another *.exe), that interface must be explicitly registered in the system registry under HKCR\Interfaces\<your guid>. The ProxyStubClsid32 subdirectory contains a value that identifies the CLSID of the object that understands how to marshal your interfaces between apartment, process, or machine boundaries. Using this CLSID value, the COM runtime is able to locate the correct stub/proxy *.dll to build a bridge between the two interested parties.

Although C++ developers are always able to build custom stub and proxy *.dlls using various midl.exe-generated files, they are seldom in the position of absolutely having to do so. The reason is that the COM runtime supplies a default stub and proxy *.dll (oleaut32.dll) that goes by the friendly name "the universal marshaler." Using your registered COM type information, the universal marshaler is able to build stub and proxies on the fly as long as each exposed type is [oleautomation] compliant.

The regasm.exe utility takes the lead of Visual Basic 6.0 and automatically configures each exposed interface (including class interfaces) to make use of the universal marshaler. Thus, if you locate the GUID for IBasicMath under HKCR\Interfaces (Figure 10-10), you will find that the ProxyStubClsid32 subdirectory contains the CLSID of the universal marshaler ({00020420-0000-0000-C000-000000000046}).

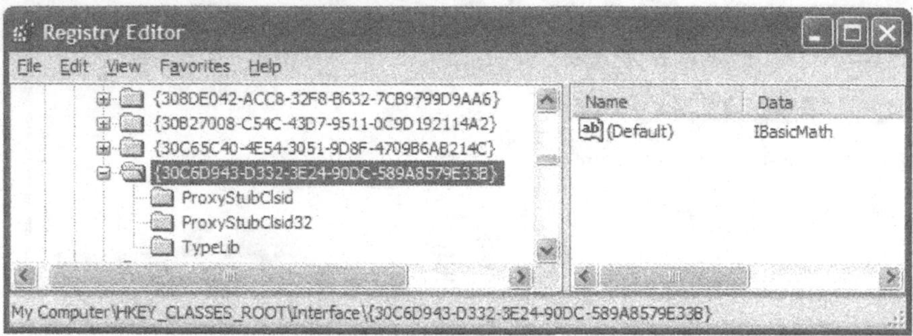

Figure 10-10. Custom .NET interfaces are registered to make use of universal marshaling.

As mentioned, if your .NET class types define a class interface (as was done for the DotNetCalc type), the autogenerated interface (_DotNetCalc) is also registered to make use of the universal marshaler (Figure 10-11).

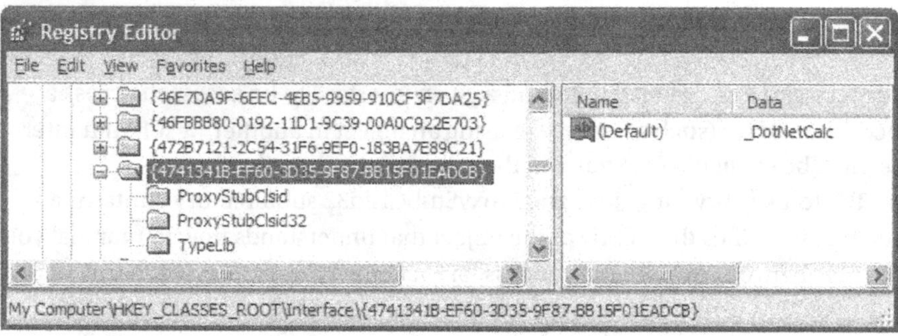

Figure 10-11. Class interfaces are also registered to make use of universal marshaling.

If you follow the bouncing ball and look up {00020420-0000-0000-C000-000000000046} under HKCR\CLSID, you will indeed find that both IBasicMath and _DotNetCalc are marshaled via oleaut32.dll (Figure 10-12).

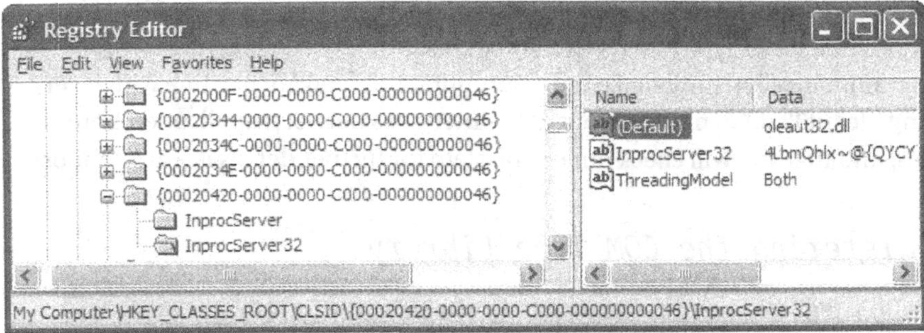

Figure 10-12. The universal marshaler

When generating a GUID for a given COM-visible interface, tlbexp.exe/regasm.exe will again construct a hash value, this time based on the type's fully qualified name in addition to the signature (but not the name) of each member of the interface. In this way, if you add or (heaven forbid) remove a member from an interface, this will result in a new IID. Again, to take full control over GUID generation for your interfaces, apply the GuidAttribute type to each exposed .NET type.

One final point to be very aware of is that if you were to shutter (reorder) the members of a COM-visible interface, the previous *.tlb file will now be hopelessly out of order. Given this, treat COM-visible interfaces with the same care you would give to an IDL interface definition (and don't reorder the members).

Specifying an Alternative Stub and Proxy DLL

As you may suspect, it is possible to configure your exposed COM-visible interfaces to make use of an alternative stub/proxy *.dll. Now, let me reiterate that the *only* reason that a programmer may choose to build and distribute a custom stub/proxy *.dll is if the COM interfaces to be marshaled expose data types that cannot be represented by a COM VARIANT (such as fixed array of C-style unions, char* style strings, and other C-isms).

If you are in the unfortunate position of exposing a non–[oleautomation]-compliant COM interface from a managed .NET application (which should seldom if ever be the case), you can apply the AutomationProxyAttribute type to prevent your interfaces from being automatically configured to point to oleaut32.dll:

```
// This attribute can also be applied at the
// assembly level to deny all interfaces
// access to the universal marshaler.
[AutomationProxy(false)]
public interface IDontUseTheUniversalMarshaler{…}
```

If you enable this behavior, you of course need to specify the CLSID of the custom marshaler type and register things accordingly (via regsvr32.exe or programmatically). I will make the assumption that you are just fine with leveraging oleaut32.dll to marshal your .NET interfaces between application boundaries, and that you will check out online Help for further details if you so choose.

Registering the COM Type Library

The final registration entry you need to examine is the information used to describe the *.tlb file itself. Recall from Chapter 3 that HKCR\TypeLib\<your guid> holds the version, locale, and physical location of your *.tlb file. Thus, if you hunt down the GUID of your *.tlb (which you hard coded using an assembly-level GuidAttribute type), you will see the registered COM type library shown in Figure 10-13.

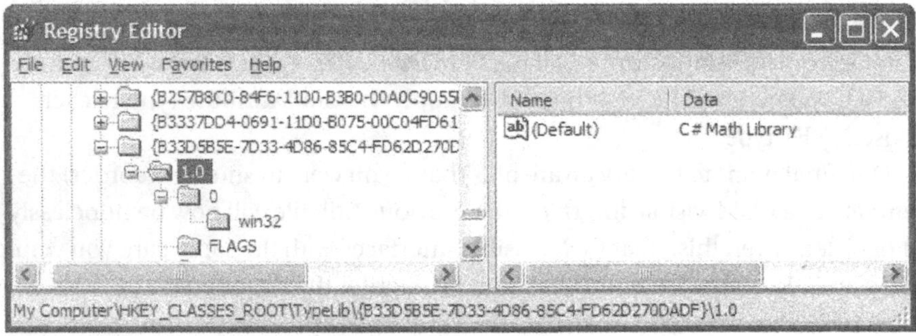

Figure 10-13. The registered COM type library

Do remember that the only way to ensure that your *.tlb file is registered is to specify the /tlb flag using regasm.exe (tlbexp.exe will *not* do so).

Of course, when you expose a .NET assembly to classic COM, you are now playing by the rules of COM. Thus, if you rename or relocate your generated *.tlb file, you need to register the COM type information using regasm.exe.

Deploying the .NET Assembly

At this point, the DotNetMathServer.dll has been expressed in terms of COM type information and registered with COM. You now have one final task before you are able to build a set of COM clients. As you have seen, the value assigned to HKCR\CLSID\{<guid>}\InProcServer32 is not the name of the .NET assembly, but mscoree.dll. When a COM client activates a registered .NET type, the following steps occur:

1. The COM runtime resolves the CLSID of the type.
2. The COM runtime reads the value listed under \InProcServer32 (mscoree.dll).
3. The value specified by the Class listing is passed into mscoree.dll.
4. The .NET runtime then searches for the assembly as expected (see Chapter 4).

Given the flow of events, you should be aware that the .NET assembly could be deployed as a private assembly (in which case it will need to be located in the application directory), as a shared assembly (in which case it will need to be strongly named and placed in the GAC), or at an arbitrary location via a specified codebase. Note that once the .NET runtime takes over, it will make use of its own brand of assembly resolution heuristics. Thus, if you wish to make use of XML configuration files, you are free to do so.

The truth is that the most common way to deploy a COM-aware .NET assembly is to assign it a strong name and install it in the GAC. Given this, let's assume you have a valid *.snk file and have placed the DotNetMathServer.dll into the GAC (Figure 10-14).

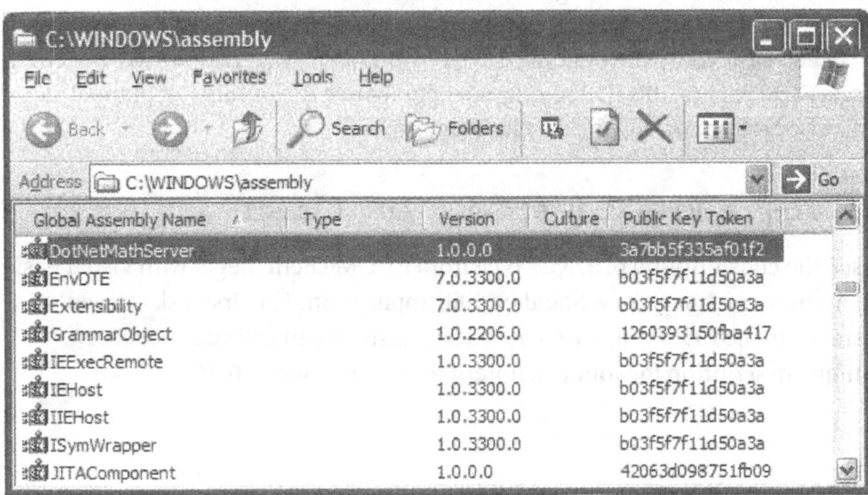

Figure 10-14. .NET assemblies used by COM are typically deployed as shared binaries.

Leveraging the Visual Studio .NET IDE

At this point in the chapter, you have seen how to make use of two key command line tools (tlbexp.exe and regasm.exe) that you must employ when exposing a .NET assembly to COM clients. While running regasm.exe (typically using the /tlb flag) is not that difficult, do be aware that Visual Studio .NET provides some IDE support that will run regasm.exe automatically.

If you activate the Properties window for your current project and select the Configuration Properties | Build node from the tree view, you will find an option named Register for COM Interop (which is disabled by default). If you enable this setting, each time you build the .NET code library, regasm.exe is run automatically with the following set of flags:

```
regasm.exe yourDotNetAsm.dll / tlb /codebase
```

One potential problem with the support offered by VS .NET is the /codebase flag cannot be omitted. As mentioned earlier in this chapter, this flag will add a CodeBase value under the InprocServer32 subdirectory for each class type that will point to the arbitrary location of your .NET *.dll. The good news is, if you later place this assembly into the GAC (as you should), mscoree.dll will continue to probe for the assembly even if the value specified by the /codebase flag is out of sync. Given this, it is safe to regard the CodeBase value as a "hint" to the runtime where it should begin its search (rather than an indisputable fact).

In any case, if you are building a .NET assembly that you intend to be used by classic COM clients, this IDE setting can help reduce the number of manual steps you must perform during the development cycle.

Building a Visual Basic 6.0 COM Client

To see the consumption of a .NET type from a COM client, begin with Visual Basic 6.0. Assume you have a new Standard EXE application. The first task is to set a reference to the COM *.tlb file created a la regasm.exe (recall you specified a unique description for your IDL library, as seen in Figure 10-15).

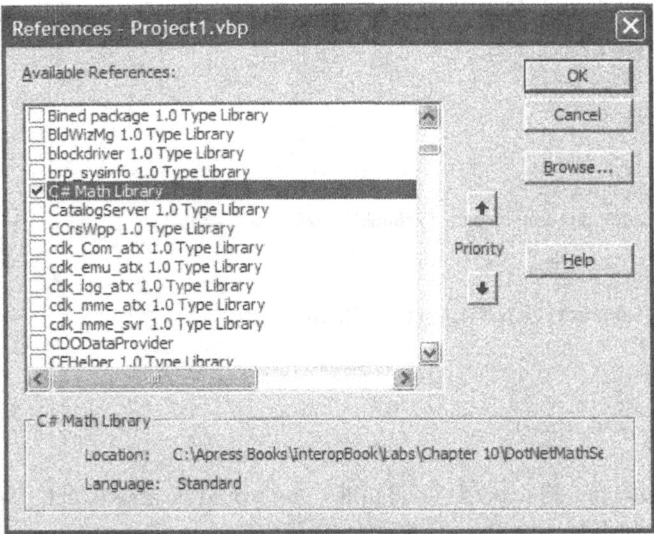

Figure 10-15. Referencing your .NET assembly via VB 6.0

The UI of the main form will simply allow the user to add two numbers (Figure 10-16).

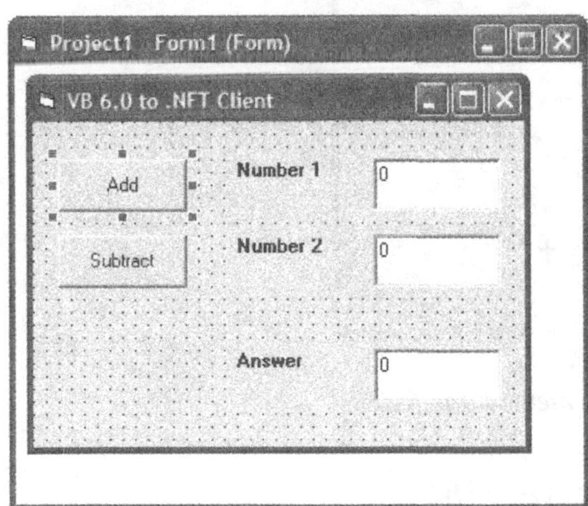

Figure 10-16. The simple GUI

The code behind this form is identical to the process of accessing a traditional COM type, courtesy of the CCW:

```
Option Explicit
Private c As DotNetCalc

Private Sub btnAdd_Click()
    txtAnswer.Text = c.Add(txtNumb1.Text, txtNumb2.Text)
End Sub
Private Sub btnSub_Click()
    txtAnswer.Text = c.Subtract(txtNumb1.Text, txtNumb2.Text)
End Sub
Private Sub Form_Load()
    Set c = New DotNetCalc
End Sub
```

Of course, if you wish to add two VB 6.0 Doubles, you would be able to call the generated Add_2() method (as suggested in Figure 10-17).

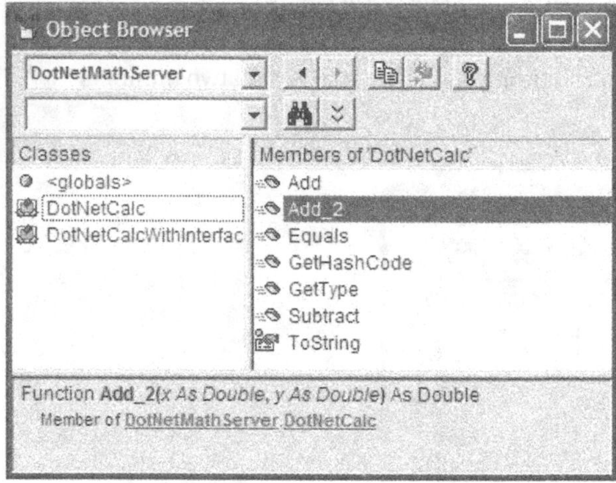

Figure 10-17. The overloaded Add() method and friends

Interacting with Mscorlib.tlb

Recall that all generated COM *.tlb files will have an importlib() statement that references the COM type information describing mscorlib.dll. A COM client (such as VB 6.0) is therefore able to interact with predefined .NET types. If you wish to do so from a VB 6.0 COM client, your first step is to set a reference to the preregistered Common Language Runtime Library COM type information (Figure 10-18).

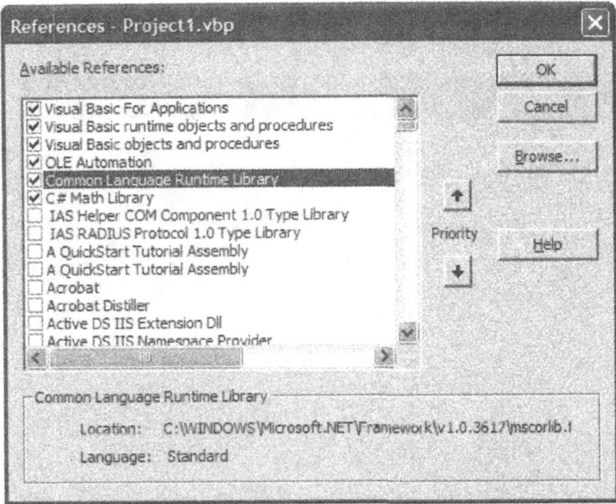

Figure 10-18. Referencing mscorlib.tlb

Now that you have an unmanaged definition of the System.Type class, let's trigger some of the inherited members of System.Object. Assume your VB 6.0 form has an additional Button widget that performs the following logic:

```
Private Sub btnObj_Click()
    ' Call ToString property / GetHashCode()
    MsgBox c.ToString, , "ToString() says..."
    Dim s As String
    Dim t As mscorlib.Type
    Set t = c.GetType()
    MsgBox c.GetHashCode(), , "GetHashCode() says..."

    ' Get some stats about the DotNetCalc.
    s = "Is this a COM object? : " & t.IsCOMObject & vbLf
    s = s + "Assembly stats? : " & t.Assembly.FullName & vbLf
    s = s + "Is this a Class? : " & t.IsClass & vbLf
    s = s + "Base type? : " & t.BaseType.FullName & vbLf
    s = s + "Abstract class? : " & t.IsAbstract & vbLf & vbLf

    ' List all methods of the DotNetCalc class.
    Dim mi() As MethodInfo
    mi = t.GetMethods_2()
    Dim i As Integer
    For i = 0 To UBound(mi)
        s = s + "Method " & i & ": " & mi(i).Name & vbLf
    Next

    MsgBox s, , "Select info ala System.Type"
End Sub
```

The final message box can been seen in Figure 10-19.

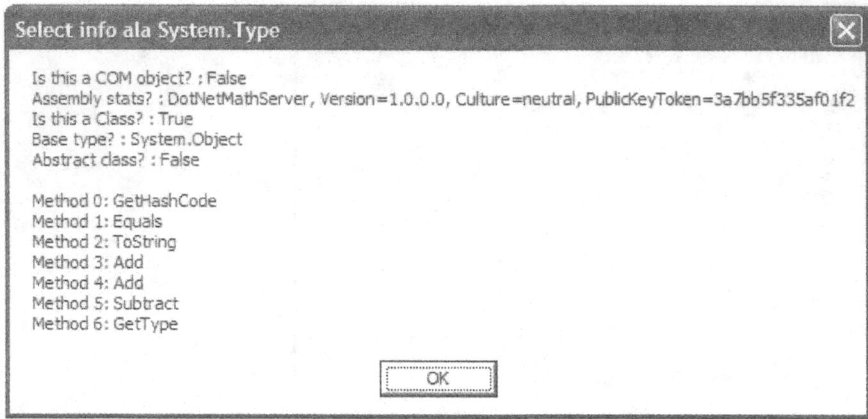

Figure 10-19. Accessing System.Type from a COM client

This logic echoes the same managed reflection logic discussed in Chapter 5. Notice, for example, that you are able to obtain an array of MethodInfo types that can be interrogated by a given COM client. Also note that you are able to investigate the details of the .NET assembly that contains the native DotNetCalc class type.

Understand that you are able to access ToString() and GetHashCode() directly from an instance of DotNetCalc because you defined an AutoDual class interface. If you define an empty class interface (ClassInterfaceType.None) or a raw dispinterface (ClassInterfaceType.AutoDispatch), you will need to explicitly query for _Object (represented in VB 6.0 as an mscorlib.Object data type).

```
' Using the explicit DotNetCalcWithInterface type.
Private Sub btnSolid_Click()
    Dim objItf As mscorlib.Object
    Dim c As DotNetCalcWithInterface
    Set c = New DotNetCalcWithInterface
    MsgBox c.Add(100, 43), , "Adding 100 + 43"

    ' Get _Object.
    Set objItf = c
    MsgBox objItf.ToString(), , "My fully qualified name..."
End Sub
```

On a final VB 6.0–centric note, understand that if you were to deploy a given .NET assembly as a private assembly for use by a given VB 6.0 COM client, the *incorrect* way to do so is to place the *.dll in the directory of the current VB project.

If you do so and run the application, you will receive a load type exception. The reason is that during development, VB 6.0 considers the active application directory to be the directory containing VB6.exe! You could circumvent this problem by compiling the VB client and running the compiled application from the Windows Explorer. However, it will be far simpler to place the .NET type into the GAC.

CODE *The Vb6DotNetMathClient application can be found under the Chapter 10 subdirectory.*

Building a C++ COM Client

When you wish to access a .NET type from a C++ COM client, you need to understand that the tlbexp.exe and regasm.exe command line utilities do not trigger the classic COM midl.exe compiler. Therefore, you are *not* provided with an *_i.c or *.h file that describes the .NET types in terms of C++. Therefore, your only option is to either (a) copy the IDL from oleview.exe and run the midl.exe compiler directly (yuck) or (b) make use of the Visual C++ #import directive (see Chapter 3). This being said, consider the following C++ COM client that is making use of the DotNetCalcWithInterface type:

```
#include "stdafx.h"
#include <iostream.h>

// For ATL conversion macros.
#include <atlbase.h>
#include <atlconv.h>

// Adjust your paths accordingly!
#import "C:\WinNT\Microsoft.NET\Framework\v1.0.3617\mscorlib.tlb" \
no_namespace named_guids
#import "C:\ DotNetMathServer.tlb" \
no_namespace named_guids

int main(int argc, char* argv[])
{
    CoInitialize(NULL);
    USES_CONVERSION;

    IBasicMathPtr pBM(__uuidof(DotNetCalcWithInterface));
    cout << "50 + 50 is: " << pBM->Add(50, 50) << endl;
```

```
    // Use _Object interface.
    _ObjectPtr ptrObj = pBM;
    cout << "ToString vlaue: " << W2A(ptrObj->ToString) << endl;
    cout << "Hash vlaue: " << ptrObj->GetHashCode() << endl;

    _TypePtr ptrType = ptrObj->GetType();
    cout << "Base Type of _Object: "
         << W2A(ptrType->BaseType->FullName) << endl;

    pBM = NULL;
    ptrType = NULL;
    ptrObj = NULL;
    CoUninitialize();
    return 0;
}
```

The output can be seen in Figure 10-20.

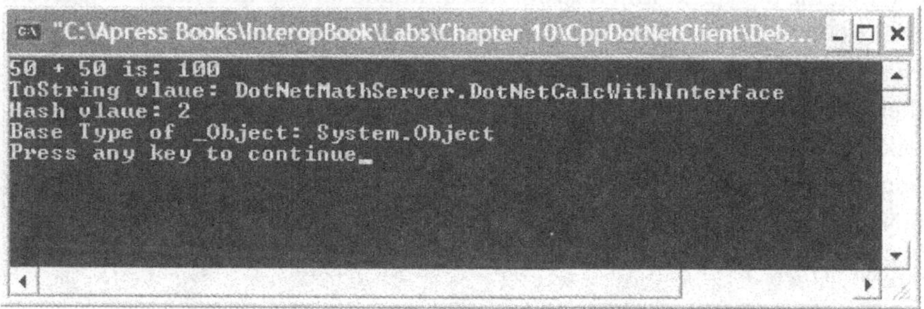

Figure 10-20. Accessing a .NET assembly from a C++ COM client

CODE *The CppDotNetClient application can be found under the Chapter 10 subdirectory.*

Building a VBScript COM Client

As you may recall, the CCW will simulate the IDispatch interface to allow the COM client to interact with the type using late binding. Although you could quite easily call the VB 6.0 CreateObject() function or query for IID_IDispatch from C++, let's check out how to access the DotNetCalc type using VBScript. Assume you have created a new *.htm file and authored the following VBScript code:

```
<HTML>
<HEAD>
    <TITLE>HTML code making use of .NET!</TITLE>
</HEAD>
<BODY>
<!-- A bit of late binding -->
<SCRIPT language = VBScript>
    dim calcObj
    Set calcObj = CreateObject("DotNetMathServer.DotNetCalc")
    MsgBox calcObj.Add(10, 10)
    MsgBox calcObj.Subtract(50, 900)
    MsgBox calcObj.Add_2(20.3, 44.9)
</Script>
</BODY>
</HTML>
```

If you open this HTML file from IE, you will first be presented with the dreaded "safe for scripting" error dialog box. To mark your .NET assemblies safe for scripting, you would need to add the correct registration entries to the system registry. Chapter 12 examines the process of interacting with the registration of a .NET assembly. However, once you dismiss the warning dialog box, three message boxes pop up displaying the results of your scripting logic.

CODE *The DotNetCalcScriptClient.htm file is located under the VBScript Client subdirectory.*

Summary

When you wish to build a .NET assembly that will be accessed by a classic COM client, you have two major options. On the simple end of the spectrum, you just expose all public members as a class interface and walk away. However, on the other end of the spectrum, you need to take the preferred approach and adorn your .NET types with various interop-centric attributes (Guid, Dispid, ComVisible, and so on).

As you have seen, once your .NET assembly has been constructed with the appropriate .NET attributes, you are required to generate COM type information (using tlbexp.exe or regasm.exe) as well as register the assembly for use by COM. As far as deployment of the assembly, you will find that installing the .NET binary into the GAC is the simplest option.

Finally, when building COM clients using your language of choice (VB 6.0, C++, VBScript), the process will look identical to that of accessing and manipulating a native COM coclass. As an interesting byproduct, also recall that mscorlib.dll (as well as other core .NET assemblies) already have a corresponding *.tlb that you are able to leverage from a COM client.

So then! At this point you should feel comfortable with the process of building .NET types that are COM aware. The next chapter builds on your foundation by examining how to expose .NET events and collections to COM clients (as well as additional advanced COM-to-.NET interop details).

CHAPTER 11

COM-to-.NET Interoperability—Intermediate Topics

In the previous chapter you were presented with the key tidbits of information required to expose a .NET type to COM. In this chapter, you build on these basics and examine how to expose .NET enumerations and custom UDTs (System.ValueTypes) to unmanaged COM clients. As well, this chapter examines how more elaborate .NET patterns, such as delegates, collections, and custom exceptions, are mapped into terms of classic COM. You wrap up by examining further details of exposing .NET interfaces and interface hierarchies to unmanaged COM clients.

Do note that many of these examples make use of the dreaded "class interface" to expose the COM-visible members of a .NET class to a COM client. The reason is simply to minimize the length of the code samples and focus squarely on the .COM-to-.NET translation at hand.

Converting .NET Enums to COM Enums

The previous chapter illustrated how .NET class types and stand-alone .NET interface types are mapped into terms of classic COM. As you recall from Chapter 6, the .NET type system also supports custom enumerations, structures, and delegates in addition to classes and interfaces. Given this, your initial task in this chapter is to check out how .NET enumerations map into COM IDL. Assume you have a new C# class library (DotNetEnumServer) that defines a custom enumeration that is manipulated by an appropriate class type:

```
namespace DotNetEnumServer
{
    public enum CarMake
    {BMW, Dodge, Saab, VW, Yugo}

    [ClassInterface(ClassInterfaceType.AutoDual)]
    [Guid("F64F79EA-DF4C-48d3-97AF-534A7F197EDD")]
    public class Car
    {
        public Car(){}
        private CarMake mCarMake = CarMake.BMW;
        public CarMake CarMake
        {
            get{return mCarMake;}
            set{mCarMake = value;}
        }
    }
}
```

When you run this .NET assembly through the regasm.exe (specifying the /tlb flag) or tlbexp.exe utility, you find that .NET enums map quite naturally to COM IDL:

```
typedef [uuid(FE6915B0-B42D-346C-BCE4-12EBE64D29A0), version(1.0),
custom({0F21F359-AB84-41E8-9A78-36D110E6D2F9},
"DotNetEnumServer.CarMake")]
enum {
    CarMake_BMW = 0,
    CarMake_Dodge = 1,
    CarMake_Saab = 2,
    CarMake_VW = 3,
    CarMake_Yugo = 4
} CarMake;
```

Notice that the naming convention used to specify the IDL enumeration entails prefixing the name of the .NET enumeration (CarMake_) to each discrete value (Yugo). Also notice how each member of the CarMake enumeration has been assigned a default numerical value (zero-based). Under .NET, you have the option to assign alternative numerical values to each individual field (if you do not, .NET field values also begin at zero and follow an n+1 incrementation):

```
public enum CarMake
{
    BMW = 10, Dodge = 20,
    Saab = 30, VW = 40,
    Yugo = 0
}
```

If you examine the resulting COM IDL, you find that the custom values of each field have been accounted for:

```
enum {
    CarMake_BMW = 10,
    CarMake_Dodge = 20,
    CarMake_Saab = 30,
    CarMake_VW = 40,
    CarMake_Yugo = 0
} CarMake;
```

Regardless of how you configure the numerical values of the enum's members, COM interface methods that make use of the enum type look identical to those of a native COM enumeration. Consider the following (partial) class interface definition for the current Car type:

```
interface _Car : IDispatch {
...
    [id(0x60020004), propget]
    HRESULT CarMake([out, retval] CarMake* pRetVal);
    [id(0x60020004), propput]
    HRESULT CarMake([in] CarMake pRetVal);
};
```

Given this, a VB 6.0 COM client would be able to make use of this enumeration as follows:

```
Private Sub btnUseEnum_Click()
    ' The Car type.
    Dim c As Car
    Set c = New Car

    ' Set and get the car make.
    c.CarMake = CarMake_Yugo
    MsgBox c.CarMake

    ' Make use of a CarMake variable.
    Dim e As CarMake
    e = CarMake_BMW
    c.CarMake = e
    MsgBox c.CarMake
End Sub
```

Altering the Underlying Field Storage

Recall that .NET enumerations allow you to specify an alternative storage type for the contained values. By default, all .NET enumerations use a System.Int32 type. If, however, you wish to specify System.Byte as the underlying storage, you are able to write:

```
public enum CarMake : byte
{
    BMW = 10, Dodge = 20,
    Saab = 30, VW = 40,
    Yugo = 0
}
```

If you refresh the COM IDL, you see that the IDL definition of the CarMake enum is identical to the previous definition. In fact, you will not find any trace of the byte storage, as COM enumerations always use a 32-bit storage type (in fact, if the underlying storage/values are set to a type larger than a System.Int32, tlbexp.exe/regasm.exe issues a processing error).

However, if you now to look at the CarMake property of the Car class, you find that the [in] and [out, retval] data types are no longer a strongly typed CarMake enumeration, but rather (surprise, surprise) an unsigned char (the unmanaged equivalent of System.Byte):

```
interface _Car : IDispatch {
...
    [id(0x60020004), propget]
    HRESULT CarMake([out, retval] unsigned char* pRetVal);
    [id(0x60020004), propput]
    HRESULT CarMake([in] unsigned char pRetVal);
};
```

Luckily, this does not demand a reconfiguration of the VB 6.0 client. Thus, although the unsigned char has been mapped into a VB 6.0 Byte (Figure 11-1) you are able to program against the Car.CarMake property in the same way.

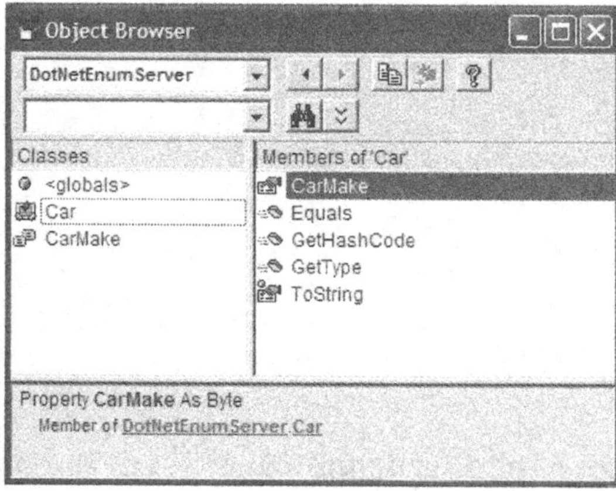

Figure 11-1. Realizing the underlying enum type

Leveraging System.Enum?

Recall that all .NET enumerations alias the System.Enum base class type. Using various static members (such as Parse(), GetNames(), and so forth) managed clients are able to extract relevant details of the underlying enumeration. In addition, all .NET enumerations inherit the virtual members of System.Object. For example, under .NET, you are able to extract the underlying name of an enumeration type using ToString() as follows:

```
// C# client code.
CarMake m = CarMake.BMW;
Console.WriteLine("Make is: {0}", m.ToString());
```

However, as you have already learned from the previous chapter, static members are never published to a COM type library. Furthermore, notice that the virtual object-level members of System.Enum (such as ToString()) are *not* present in the COM IDL because COM enumerations are represented as simple name/value pairs. Thus, if you examine the DotNetEnumServer.dll from the VB 6.0 Object Browser, you will find what you see in Figure 11-2.

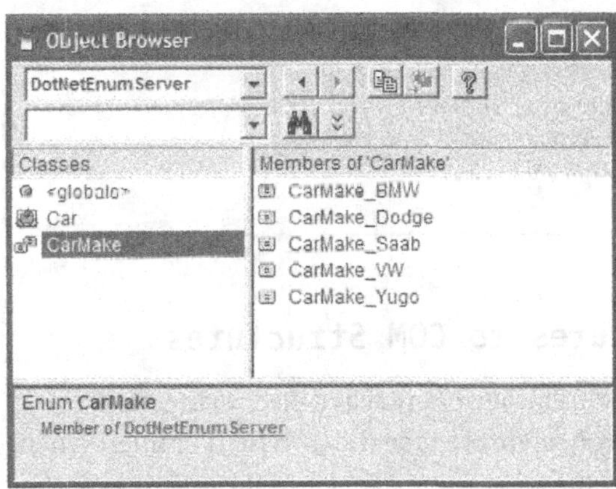

Figure 11-2. .NET enumerations are mapped to COM as simple name/value pairs.

So, given that static members cannot be expressed into COM IDL, you have no practical way to interact with the members of System.Enum from an unmanaged COM client. However, you are able to send an unmanaged enum back to a .NET type to leverage the managed functionality:

```
[ClassInterface(ClassInterfaceType.AutoDual)]
[Guid("F64F79EA-DF4C-48d3-97AF-534A7F197EDD")]
public class Car
{
```

```
    ...
    public void DisplayCarMake(CarMake car)
    {
        MessageBox.Show(car.ToString(), "This car is a:");
    }
}
```

Given this new method, you are able to send in an unmanaged CarMake to the DisplayCarMake() method, as the CCW automatically converts the raw IDL enumeration into a type referring to System.Enum (Figure 11-3 shows a possible output).

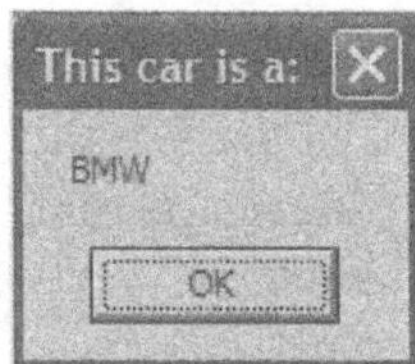

Figure 11-3. Identifying the COM enum

CODE *The DotNetEnumServer and Vb6EnumClient projects are included under the Chapter 11 subdirectory.*

Converting .NET Structures to COM Structures

As you learned in Chapter 6, the .NET Framework makes a clear distinction between value type (stack-based) and reference type (heap-based) entities. When you wish to create a custom .NET value type, you make use of the C# struct or the VB .NET Structure keyword. For example, assume you want to build a C# structure that describes a simple (*x*, *y*) coordinate:

```
// .NET structures always derive from System.ValueType.
public struct MYPOINT
{
    public int xPos;
    public int yPos;
}
```

As you may expect, the resulting IDL is as follows:

```
typedef [uuid(CBEFC9B8-7A1F-34FE-BBE8-EFFC9DE89F0C), version(1.0),
custom({0F21F359-AB84-41E8-9A78-36D110E6D2F9}, "DotNetStructServer.MYPOINT")
]
struct tagMYPOINT {
    long xPos;
    long yPos;
} MYPOINT;
```

Recall that under the .NET Framework, it is perfectly legal to define structures that support any number of events, properties, and methods (as well as some set of implemented interfaces). Understand, however, that when tlbexp.exe encounters a System.ValueType-derived type, these members are stripped from the IDL definition. Thus, if you update the POINT structure with the following functionality:

```
public struct MYPOINT
{
    // These are now private!
    private int xPos;
    private int yPos;

    // Add some members to the MYPOINT struct.
    public void SetPoint(int x, int y)
    { xPos = x; yPos = y;}
    public void DisplayPoint()
    {MessageBox.Show(String.Format("X: {0} Y: {1}", xPos, yPos));}
}
```

the SetPoint() and DisplayPoint() members would be completely absent from the COM type definition. Furthermore, also understand that *all* structure field data (public or private) will be exported to COM IDL as public members (as COM structures do not support encapsulation services):

```
struct tagMYPOINT {
    long xPos;
    long yPos;
} MYPOINT;
```

At this point, you may assume that all COM clients are able to make use of this structure in a manner identical to a native COM structure. Well, you are partially correct. For example, if you load this type library into a new VB 6.0 project workspace and check out the Object Browser (Figure 11-4) things appear to be going well on the surface.

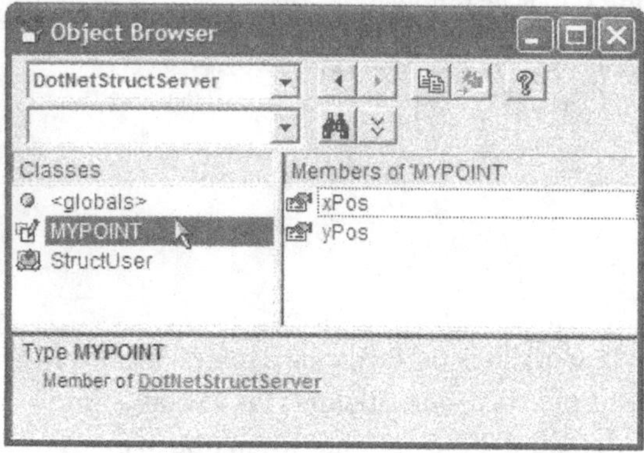

Figure 11-4. .NET UDTs map directly to COM IDL structures.

But assume that the C# code library also defines a class with members that manipulate the MYPOINT type:

```
[ClassInterface(ClassInterfaceType.AutoDual)]
public class StructUser
{
    public StructUser(){}

    // Pass in a MYPOINT.
    public void DisplayPointInfo(MYPOINT pt)
    {
        pt.PrintPoint();
    }

    // Return a MYPOINT.
    public MYPOINT PointFactory()
    {
        MYPOINT pt = new MYPOINT();
        pt.SetPoint(100, 8);
        return pt;
    }
}
```

The IDL definition also seems to indicate that the MYPOINT structure is ready for manipulation:

```
interface _StructUser : IDispatch {
...
    [id(0x60020004)]
    HRESULT DisplayPointInfo([in] MYPOINT pt);
    [id(0x60020005)]
    HRESULT PointFactory([out, retval] MYPOINT* pRetVal);
};
```

Now, assume your VB 6.0 COM client wishes to obtain a new MYPOINT via the PointFactory() member (in response to a given Button click):

```
Private Sub btnStructMe_Click()
    Dim pt As MYPOINT

    Dim o As StructUser
    Set o = New StructUser
    pt = o.PointFactory()
    MsgBox "X: " & pt.xPos & " Y: " & pt.yPos, , "The MYPOINT is:"
End Sub
```

The good news is that you are indeed returned a new, properly configured MYPOINT type, as shown in Figure 11-5.

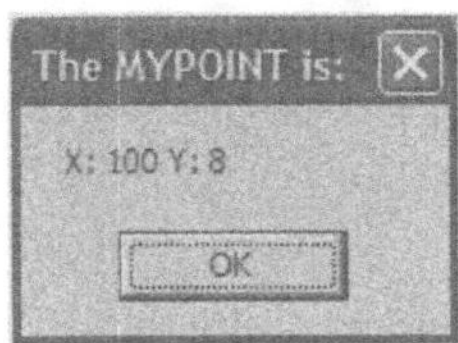

Figure 11-5. Receiving a .NET structure

However, what if the VB 6.0 COM client wishes to send in a MYPOINT structure to the managed DisplayPointInfo() method as follows:

```
Private Sub btnUseStruct_Click()
    Dim pt As MYPOINT
    pt.xPos = 99
    pt.yPos = 8
    Dim o As StructUser
    Set o = New StructUser
    o. DisplayPointInfo pt
End Sub
```

Sadly, during compilation VB 6.0 issues the error you see in Figure 11-6.

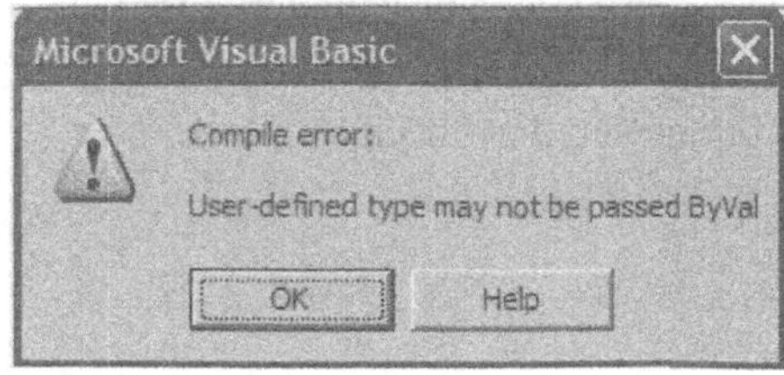

Figure 11-6. VB 6.0 does not allow structures to be passed by value.

Given what you already know of COM IDL, this error should indicate that tlbexp.exe has defined the MYPOINT parameter of the DisplayPointInfo() method as an [in] parameter. Indeed this is the case:

```
// The MYPOINT was passed by value to
// the DisplayPointInfo() method.
HRESULT DisplayPointInfo([in] MYPOINT pt);
```

Understand right here and now that Visual Basic 6.0 has never been able to handle passing user-defined types (aka structures) by value, and this inconvenience has nothing to do with .NET-to-COM interoperability.

To rectify the problem, you are forced to return to the C# implementation of DisplayPointInfo() and pass the MYPOINT by reference as follows:

```
// Pass by ref to attempt to appease VB 6.0.
public void DisplayPointInfo(ref MYPOINT pt)
{
    pt.PrintPoint();
}
```

With this update, you are able to find the correct IDL definition of the DisplayPointInfo() method:

```
// This looks better…
HRESULT DisplayPointInfo([in, out] MYPOINT* pt);
```

which will appease VB 6.0 just fine (as shown in Figure 11-7).

Figure 11-7. Passing a structure (by reference)

So then, here is the golden rule: When you build a .NET method that takes a .NET structure type, it must be *passed by reference* if it is to be called by a VB 6.0 COM client. Again, this limitation of VB 6.0 was present long before the release of .NET. As you might guess, C++ clients are not restricted by this limitation.

Exposing a .NET Structure As an IDL Union

The final topic regarding exposing .NET structures to COM has to do with the StructLayout attribute. Recall from Chapter 1 that a .NET structure can be configured as LayoutKind.Auto, LayoutKind.Sequential, or LayoutKind.Explicit. Typically, you do not need to adorn your .NET structures with the StructLayout attribute in the first place, given that the marshaler will always translate a structure exactly as defined in the .NET type. It is interesting, however, to know that if you define a .NET structure as LayoutKind.Explicit, it is possible to produce an IDL union! The one caveat is that each member must have an offset of zero. For example, the following C# structure:

```
[StructLayout(LayoutKind.Explicit)]
public struct MyUnion
{
    [FieldOffset(0)] int a;
    [FieldOffset(0)] int b;
}
```

maps to the following IDL definition:

```
typedef [uuid(4F617950-2D1D-3235-B1A2-79B40C310799), version(1.0),
custom({0F21F359-AB84-41E8-9A78-36D110E6D2F9}, "DotNetStructServer.MyUnion")
]
union tagMyUnion {
    long a;
    long b;
} MyUnion;
```

Understand that COM unions are not [oleautomation]-compliant, and thus can really only be used by a C or C++ COM client. Given this, you seldom need to expose a .NET structure as LayoutKind.Explicit (unless you know for sure the only COM client that will ever use the exported is of the C[++] variety). LayoutKind.Auto is never an acceptable way to configure a .NET structure exposed to COM, given that the runtime reserves the right to reorder the discrete fields as it sees fit (which would be an obvious problem for COM).

CODE *The DotNetStructServer and VbStructClient projects are both included under the Chapter 11 subdirectory.*

Converting .NET Delegates to COM Connection Points

.NET class types can support any number of events, which, as you recall, are defined in conjunction with a particular delegate type. Assume that you have created a C# class that defines and fires a single event as follows:

```
namespace DotNetEventServer
{
    public class DotNetEventSender
    {
        public DotNetEventSender(){}
        public delegate void MyEventTarget(string msg);
        public event MyEventTarget TheEvent;

        public void FireTheEvent()
        {
            TheEvent("Hello from the DotNetEventSender");
        }
    }
}
```

The question is, how can this class type expose the TheEvent event in terms of COM connection points? To understand the solution to this dilemma, recall what a COM client must do when it wants to link to a given COM event source:

- The COM client must implement the server's event interface in a given sink object.
- The COM client must be able to determine which event interface the coclass can make calls on and pass the correct sink reference to the connectable COM object.

Both of these requirements can be expressed in terms of COM IDL. Recall that a COM event interface is typically defined in terms of IDL as a raw dispinterface. In fact, if you want to ensure that VB 6.0 and scripting clients can intercept incoming COM events, the event interface must be defined as a raw dispinterface ([dual] or IUnknown-derived interfaces will not be accessible by VB 6.0/script clients). Also recall that the supporting coclass marks its support for an event interface using the IDL [source] keyword. As you would guess, there are specific attributes that can be applied to a .NET class type to correctly configure the underlying IDL. In a nutshell, .NET programmers must perform two key steps when they wish to expose .NET events as COM connection points:

- First, define a managed interface that represents the raw event dispinterface.

- Second, map the event interface to a given .NET class type using the ComSourceInterfaces attribute type.

Creating the Event Interface

Creating the COM event interface is quite straightforward. Begin by building a managed interface (using the ComInterfaceAttribute type) that defines the set of methods that are to be implemented by the client-side sink. (In keeping with COM naming conventions, I have defined the event interface to take a _D prefix, but this is not mandatory.)

Also, be aware that you should always explicitly assign DISPIDs to each member of the event interface (each of which must be greater than zero). The reason again has to do with VB 6.0 compatibility. Given that a VB 6.0 COM client may choose to handle a subset of event members (rather than all members), VB 6.0 must be able to identify the correct DISPID at runtime to invoke the correct event handler. If you do not define explicit DISPIDs for each member of your event interface, the VB 6.0 COM client must implement each and every member, or else the VB runtime will return a failed HRESULT (DISP_E_UNKNOWNNAME)! The short answer is, always provide unique DISPIDs for your event interfaces if you expect them to be consumed correctly by a VB COM client. That being said, here is your event interface:

```
// This is the name of the event interface to be
// implemented by the client-side sink.
[InterfaceType(ComInterfaceType.InterfaceIsIDispatch)]
[Guid("3289316F-0B19-44f1-B33B-8673D6FAF057")]
public interface _DEventInterface
{
    [DispId(1)] void TheEvent(string msg);
}
```

When the type library is generated using tlbexp.exe, you will find that your managed interface is expressed in terms of COM IDL as follows:

```
[
  uuid(3289316F-0B19-44F1-B33B-8673D6FAF057),
  version(1.0),
  custom({0F21F359-AB84-41E8-9A78-36D110E6D2F9},
  "DotNetEventServer._DEventInterface")]
dispinterface _DEventInterface
{
    properties:
    methods:
        [id(0x60020000)]
        void TheEvent([in] BSTR msg);
};
```

Understand again that the purpose of defining this interface is to provide the *COM client* with an interface to implement in a given client-side sink object. Therefore, this interface never needs to be implemented by a .NET type. However, you make use of this interface by name when you mark it as a [source] interface of a given .NET type.

Specifying the Event Interfaces (a la ComSourceInterfacesAttribute)

When you wish to mark a particular interface as a [source] interface for a given .NET class, you make use of the ComSourceInterfaces attribute (yes, it is plural). For example, if you wish to associate _DEventInterface as a [source] for the DotNetEventSender, you can update the definition as follows (also note that you have marked the managed delegate as COM-invisible, as the COM client could care less about this type):

```
// The DotNetEventSender .NET class defines
// DEventInterface as the [default, source].
[ComSourceInterfaces(typeof(_DEventInterface))]
[ClassInterface(ClassInterfaceType.AutoDual)]
[Guid("24F279CB-D9BA-4ca4-95CD-2F2338443088")]
public class DotNetEventSender
{
    public DotNetEventSender(){}
    // No need to show this delegate to COM
    [ComVisible(false)]
    public delegate void MyEventTarget(string msg);
    public event MyEventTarget TheEvent;
    public void FireTheEvent()
    {
        TheEvent("Hello from the DotNetEventSender");
    }
}
```

Do note that the ComSourceInterfaces attribute also supplies a constructor that allows you to identify the name of the event interface as a string name. In any case, given this update, you find the resulting IDL definition:

```
[
  uuid(24F279CB-D9BA-4CA4-95CD-2F2338443088),
  version(1.0),
  custom({0F21F359-AB84-41E8-9A78-36D110E6D2F9},
    "DotNetEventServer.DotNetEventSender")
]
coclass DotNetEventSender {
    [default] interface _DotNetEventSender;
    interface _Object;
    [default, source] dispinterface _DEventInterface;
};
```

Establishing Multiple [source] Interfaces

As the name of the ComEventInterfaces attribute suggests, you are able to define multiple [source] interfaces for a single .NET class type (just as you can in classic COM). However, recall that this is seldom done, as the only COM-aware language that is able to communicate the [source] interfaces beyond the [default, source] is C++. Given this fact, you will tend to interact with the ComEventInterfaces attribute as seen previously (by specifying the type of a single event interface). Nevertheless, if you do need to expose multiple [source] interfaces from a single .NET class type, you can specify up to five event interfaces using the following overloaded constructor:

```
[InterfaceType(ComInterfaceType.InterfaceIsIDispatch)]
[Guid("FEBB2E08-7F6D-415d-AD90-B8C4C03A7B4B")]
public interface _DEventInterfaceOne
{[DispId(1)] void EventA ();}

[InterfaceType(ComInterfaceType.InterfaceIsIDispatch)]
[Guid("5941D9A2-1149-4daf-88EA-EB5B04B9B85B")]
public interface _DEventInterfaceTwo
{[DispId(1)] void EventB ();}

[InterfaceType(ComInterfaceType.InterfaceIsIDispatch)]
[Guid("333E8C06-04AC-4677-8AE2-3AAEF2E046DC")]
public interface _DEventInterfaceThree
{[DispId(1)] void EventC ();}

[ComSourceInterfaces(typeof(_DEventInterfaceOne),
    typeof(_DEventInterfaceTwo),
    typeof(_DEventInterfaceThree))]
[ClassInterface(ClassInterfaceType.AutoDual)]
[Guid("58E48229-9FFF-42fb-B987-8096B27B6B19")]
public class DotNetMultiEventSourceClass
{
    public DotNetMultiEventSourceClass(){}
    [ComVisible(false)]
    public delegate void MyEventTarget();
    public event MyEventTarget EventA;
    public event MyEventTarget EventB;
    public event MyEventTarget EventC;

    // Fire events in various methods...
}
```

This would result in an unmanaged definition of each event interface, as well as the following coclass statement (note that the first listed interface functions as the [default] source interface):

```
 [
  uuid(58E48229-9FFF-42FB-B987-8096B27B6B19),
  version(1.0),
  custom({0F21F359-AB84-41E8-9A78-36D110E6D2F9},
    "DotNetEventServer.DotNetMultiEventSourceClass")
]
coclass DotNetMultiEventSourceClass {
    [default] interface _DotNetMultiEventSourceClass;
    interface _Object;
    [default, source] dispinterface _DEventInterfaceOne;
    [source] dispinterface _DEventInterfaceTwo;
    [source] dispinterface _DEventInterfaceThree;
};
```

CODE *The DotNetEventServer project is included under the Chapter 11 subdirectory.*

Building a .NET Event Server Using VB .NET

Although I have chosen to make use of C# almost exclusively during the creation of the example .NET code libraries, it is worth pointing out how to expose .NET events from the VB .NET programming language. Reason? Using the Event and RaiseEvent keywords, a VB .NET programmer is able to avoid the process of manually defining a managed delegate (and thus make the whole process of defining class events a wee bit easier). That being said, here is the VB .NET equivalent of the previous C# DotNetEventServer project:

```
Imports System.Runtime.InteropServices

' This is the name of the event interface to be generated.
<InterfaceType(ComInterfaceType.InterfaceIsIDispatch), _
Guid("68E53BB4-48F9-45cc-96C6-72033295E26A")> _
Public Interface _DEventInterface
    <DispId(1)> Sub TheEvent(ByVal msg As String)
End Interface
```

```
<ClassInterface(ClassInterfaceType.AutoDual), _
Guid("7D6A1F10-0224-4fbf-8C17-B7A4B707372A"), _
ComSourceInterfaces(GetType(_DEventInterface))> _
Public Class VbDotNetEventSender
    Public Event TheEvent(ByVal msg As String)
    Public Sub FireTheEvent()
        RaiseEvent TheEvent("Hello from the DotNetEventSender")
    End Sub
End Class
```

Notice that the VB .NET Event keyword automatically generates and associates a related delegate behind the curtains. Beyond this one simplification, the process of applying the ComSourceInterfaces attribute is the same. And, of course, the generated COM IDL definitions are identical to the IDL generated from the previous C# code base.

CODE *The VbDotNetEventServer project is included under the Chapter 11 subdirectory.*

Building a Visual Basic 6.0 Event Client

When the runtime creates the related CCW for a .NET event source, it takes care of the nasty details of mapping .NET delegates to COM connection points. To prove the fact, if you deploy the DotNetEventServer as a shared assembly and investigate the type using oleview.exe, you see that the CCW simulates the IConnectionPointContainer interface automatically (Figure 11-8).

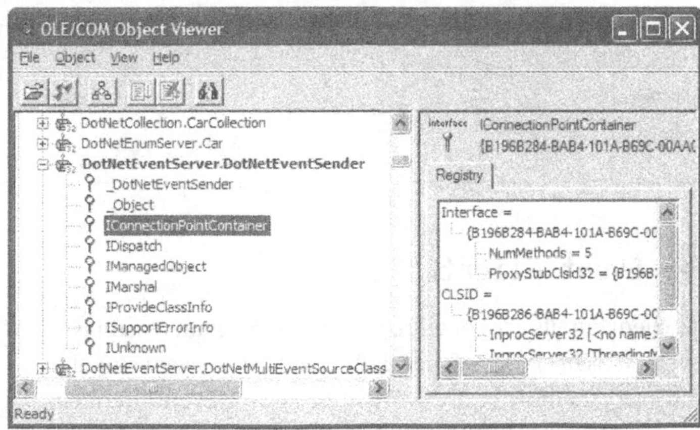

Figure 11-8. .NET delegates are mapped into COM connection points.

Using IConnectionPointContainer, a C++ client is able to manually obtain a given IConnectionPoint interface and call Advise() to pass in the sink object that implements the correct [source] interface, and (eventually) receive the incoming events. To keep things simple, let's first build a VB 6.0 Standard EXE application that handles the incoming event of the DotNetEventSouce type (VB will kindly create the sink object on your behalf):

```
Option Explicit
Private WithEvents eventObj As DotNetEventSender

Private Sub btnDoIt_Click()
    eventObj.FireTheEvent
End Sub

Private Sub eventObj_TheEvent(ByVal msg As String)
    MsgBox msg, , "Message from event object"
End Sub

Private Sub Form_Load()
    Set eventObj = New DotNetEventSender
End Sub
```

Not too much to say here. The VB 6.0 client, as always, begins the event-handling process by declaring the type using the WithEvents keyword. At this point, the IDE allows you to select the events from a given source using the drop-down lists mounted atop the code window. Once you do, the event handler is automatically written on your behalf (eventObj_TheEvent() in your case). Like many VB COM endeavors, sinking with an event source is painfully simple (which is a good thing). Next up, let's see how to receive the incoming event notifications from C++.

CODE *The Vb6EventClient project is included under the Chapter 11 subdirectory.*

Building a C++ Event Client

Building a C++ event client entails a lot of work (honest). The main reason is because the C++ developer is in charge of manually building an event sink that implements each and every member of the event interface (_DEventInterface).

At first glance, you may wonder why this would be problematic, given that _DEventInterface defines a single method:

```
[InterfaceType(ComInterfaceType.InterfaceIsIDispatch)]
[Guid("3289316F-0B19-44f1-B33B-8673D6FAF057")]
public interface _DEventInterface
{
    [DispId(1)]void TheEvent(string msg);
}
```

The key to the complexity is that most event interfaces are declared raw dispinterfaces (thus the ComInterfaceType.InterfaceIsIDispatch interface configuration), which means that the sink object is required to implement a grand total of *eight* methods (that's four from IDispatch, three from IUnknown, and [finally] TheEvent() itself). Once the sink class has been created, the C++ developer is then required to manually do the following:

- Query the type for IConnectionPointContainer (ICPC).
- Use the given ICPC interface to obtain the correct IConnectionPoint (ICP) interface.
- Call Advise() on the given ICP interface, passing in a valid sink reference.
- Eventually call Unadvise() on the ICP interface to detach from the event source.

While you can most certainly do such manual tasks by yourself, the chances are quite good that you would rather make use of a C++ COM library (such as ATL) to help with the mundane details. Given this assumption, let's check out how to build a simple C++ console application that makes use of various ATL helper templates, types, and magic macros. Understand that this is not the place to dig into each and every detail of the Active Template Library, so be sure to keep your favorite reference manual close by if you require further details.

Building the Client-Side Sink

First up, you need to build the client-side sink object, which is in charge of implementing the _DEventInterface event interface. Rather than contend with each inherited member, you use the ATL helper template, IDispEventSimpleImpl<>, and the related sink map (which simply routes the DISPID of a given event method to a particular event handler). Also note that the constructor and destructor of the sink object calls the inherited DispEventAdvise() and DispEventUnadvise() methods to handle the connection to and disconnection from the event source. Sadly, the only *real* method of interest is OnTheEvent(), which will be called by the .NET type when the custom TheEvent event is fired. The rest of the sink is just the necessary grunge that is raw C++ COM.

```
// This mess describes the layout of the event handler,
// and is required by the ATL sink map.
_ATL_FUNC_INFO OnTheEventInfo =
    {CC_STDCALL, VT_EMPTY, 1, {VT_BSTR}};

// The sink object implements the .NET _DEventInterface type.
class CEventSink : public IDispEventSimpleImpl<1, CEventSink,
    &DIID__DEventInterface>
{
public:
    BEGIN_SINK_MAP(CEventSink)
        SINK_ENTRY_INFO(1, DIID__DEventInterface,
            1, OnTheEvent, &OnTheEventInfo)
    END_SINK_MAP()

    void __stdcall OnTheEvent(BSTR msg)
    {
        USES_CONVERSION;
        cout << "The message is: " << W2A(msg) << endl;
        SysFreeString(msg);
    }

    // Set up advisory connection...
    CEventSink(_DotNetEventSender* pObj)
    {
        pDotNetObject = pObj;
        pDotNetObject->AddRef();
        DispEventAdvise((IUnknown*)pDotNetObject);
    }

    // Detach from event source.
    ~CEventSink()
    {
        pDotNetObject->Release();
        DispEventUnadvise((IUnknown*)pDotNetObject);
    }

private:
    _DotNetEventSender* pDotNetObject;
};
```

Now that you have the client-side event sink, the core logic is not too hard on the eyes. Recall that when building a C++ COM client, you typically make use of the #import directive to obtain the required GUID constants. For a change of pace, however, I have used the raw COM library (rather than the C++ smart pointers) to (I hope) clarify what the C++ client is doing under the hood. That said, ponder the following C++ COM to .NET main() function:

```
#include "stdafx.h"
#include <atlbase.h>
CComModule _Module;  // Explained below…
#include <atlcom.h>
#include <iostream.h>

// ****Adjust import paths if needed!! **** //
// Note that the _Module type within mscorlib.tlb is renamed
// to _NETModule to avoid the ATL _Module variable.
#import "C:\WINDOWS\Microsoft.NET\Framework\v1.0.3617\mscorlib.tlb" \
no_namespace named_guids rename("_Module", "_NETModule")

#import "C:\ DotNetEventServer.tlb" \
no_namespace named_guids

int main(int argc, char* argv[])
{
    USES_CONVERSION;
    CoInitialize(NULL);

    // Create the dot net class.
    _DotNetEventSender *pDotNetEventSender = NULL;
    CoCreateInstance(CLSID_DotNetEventSender, NULL, CLSCTX_SERVER,
        IID__DotNetEventSender, (void**)&pDotNetEventSender);

    // Make instance of the sink.
    CEventSink theSink((_DotNetEventSender*)pDotNetEventSender);

    // Trigger the event!!
    pDotNetEventSender->FireTheEvent();

    // COM clean up.
    pDotNetEventSender->Release();
    CoUninitialize();
    return 0;
}
```

The main() function is straight C++ COM code. You begin by creating the DotNetEventSender coclass (via CoCreateInstance()) and obtain a reference to the [default] interface. Notice that when you create the sink object, you pass in your reference to the [default] interface as a constructor parameter. As shown in the previous sink implementation logic, this pointer is passed into the DispEventAdvise() method that automatically polls the object for IConnectionPointContainer, obtains the correct IConnectionPoint interface, and calls Advise() on your behalf.

The only other odd block of code is nestled within the myriad #includes. Note that I have created a global instance of the ATL 3.0 helper class, CComModule, which is named _Module. The reason for doing this is that the ATL framework demands that every project making use of ATL types define a single instance of CComModule that *must* be named _Module. Given this strict demand, the renaming of the _Module type found in mscorlib.tlb to _NETModule can be found in the second #import (if you are a VB 6.0 COM programmer, feel free to stop laughing at any time . . .). Nevertheless, Figure 11-9 shows the result.

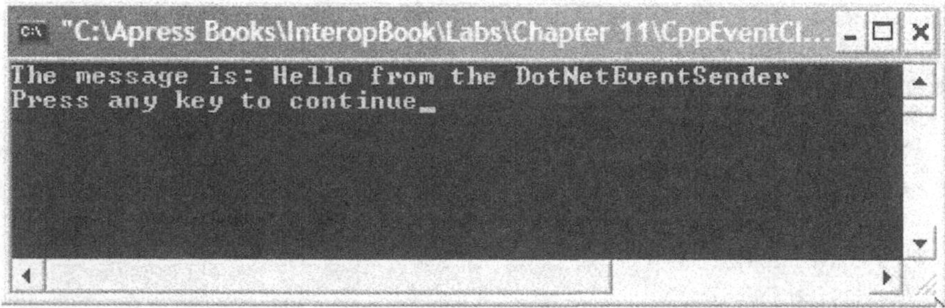

Figure 11-9. Receiving the .NET event from a C++ COM client

CODE *The CppEventClient project is included under the Chapter 11 subdirectory.*

Exposing Custom .NET Collections

Collections, in any architecture, are extremely helpful entities. When a programmer creates a strongly typed collection, he or she typically makes use of the containment/delegation model. The model is used to wrap and expose an internal data structure that is responsible for holding the individual subitems. Building such a container using C++/COM was a very painful and complex process, as you were forced to contend with explicit IUnknown logic for each inner item. Given this, many COM programmers made use of Visual Basic and the intrinsic Collection or Dictionary types. Even with VB 6.0, however, some of the COM grunge was exposed to the developer, such as the dreaded "set the method that returns the hidden IEnumVARIANT to DISPID –4" nonsense to ensure the collection worked with VB's For Each iteration.

Under .NET (regardless of your language of choice), the process of building a custom collection is quite painless, given the types found in the System.Collections namespace. To ensure that managed and unmanaged languages can iterate over the contained subitems using For Each–like iteration (foreach in C#, For Each in VB 6.0/VB .NET), programmers can simply implement the System.Collections.IEnumerable interface. This interface defines a single method (GetEnumerator()), which in fact returns IEnumerator to the caller. Under the hood, the For Each syntaxes of the world call the members of IEnumerator to pull over the internal types.

To ensure this method is recognized by VB 6.0's For Each syntax, the IDL definition of IEnumerable sets the DISPID of GetEnumerator() to the mandatory –4 (0xfffffffc). Also note the .NET IEnumerable interface returned from GetEnumerator() is represented as a COM IEnumVARIANT:

```
[
  odl,
  uuid(496B0ABE-CDEE-11D3-88E8-00902754C43A),
  version(1.0), dual, oleautomation,
  custom({0F21F359-AB84-41E8-9A78-36D110E6D2F9},
    "System.Collections.IEnumerable")
]
interface IEnumerable : IDispatch {
    [id(0xfffffffc)]
    HRESULT GetEnumerator([out, retval] IEnumVARIANT** pRetVal);
};
```

To illustrate the process of consuming a .NET custom collection from an unmanaged COM client, assume you have a new C# code library named DotNetCollection. As you would expect, you are going to build a custom container that holds onto individual Car types:

```
[ClassInterface(ClassInterfaceType.AutoDual)]
[Guid("98B815E2-D3A8-455d-82EA-0D8F82D16CC8")]
public class Car
{
    private string make;
    private string color;
    private string petName;

    public Car(){}
    public Car(string m, string c, string pn)
    { make = m; color = c; petName = pn;}
```

```
    public void SetCarState(string m, string c, string pn)
    { make = m; color = c; petName = pn;}

    public string GetCarState()
    {
        return string.Format("Make: {0} Color: {1} PetName: {2}",
        make, color, petName);
    }
}
```

The container (CarCollection) uses a System.Collection.ArrayList type to hold individual Cars. The public members of CarCollection provide a manner to insert, remove, and obtain a given Car, as well as empty the internal ArrayList. Furthermore, CarCollection implements IEnumerable to ensure that the caller can use the For Each–style traversal of the inner Car objects.

```
// This class implements IEnumerable.
[ClassInterface(ClassInterfaceType.AutoDual)]
[Guid("7802A4A0-9F7F-401a-B7A0-80B65DE2E107")]
public class CarCollection : IEnumerable
{
    public CarCollection()
    {
        ar.Add(new Car("Ford", "Red", "Joe"));
        ar.Add(new Car("BMW", "Silver", "Fred"));
        ar.Add(new Car("Yugo", "Rust", "Clunker"));
    }

    // List of items.
    private ArrayList ar = new ArrayList();

    public IEnumerator GetEnumerator()
    {return ar.GetEnumerator();}
    public void AddCar(Car c)
    {ar.Add(c);}
    public void RemoveCar(int index)
    {ar.RemoveAt(index);}
    public void ClearCars()
    {ar.Clear();}
}
```

Note that the constructor of the CarCollection automatically inserts three new Car types into the container, just to give the COM client something to investigate. Also notice how you can leverage the fact that the ArrayList type implements IEnumerator and simply returns its canned support. Now, strongly name, compile, register, and deploy this assembly into the GAC. Next up: a VB 6.0 client.

CODE *The DotNetCollection project can be found under the Chapter 11 subdirectory.*

A VB 6.0 .NET Collection Client

Assuming you have a new Standard EXE project workspace (and have set a reference to the COM type information describing the DotNetCollection types), construct a simple GUI that allows the user to list each car in the collection as well as add, remove, and clear the set of automobiles. Figure 11-10 shows one such UI.

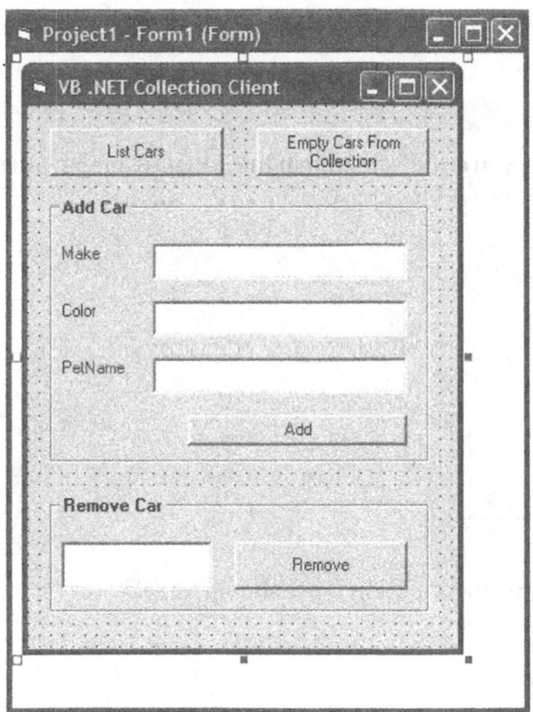

Figure 11-10. The VB 6.0/.NET collection client GUI

Now, recall from the previous chapter that when a .NET type implements the IEnumerable interface (and therefore returns access to IEnumerable), the CCW simulates the COM equivalent, IEnumVARIANT. Although you do not see this directly in the generated IDL, whenever a caller attempts to make use of For Each, IEnumVARIANT is automatically requested by the COM runtime. The generated

CCW intercepts this request and returns a simulated reference via the managed IEnumerable interface. Thus, if the user clicks the List Cars button, you can display the current list like this:

```
Option Explicit
Private coll As DotNetCollection.CarCollection

Private Sub Form_Load()
    Set coll = New CarCollection
End Sub

Private Sub btnListCars_Click()
    Dim s As String
    Dim temp As Car
    For Each temp In coll
        s = s + temp.GetCarState() & vbLf
    Next
    MsgBox s, , "The Cars"
End Sub
```

Once you run the application, you are able to obtain the initial set of Car types (Figure 11-11).

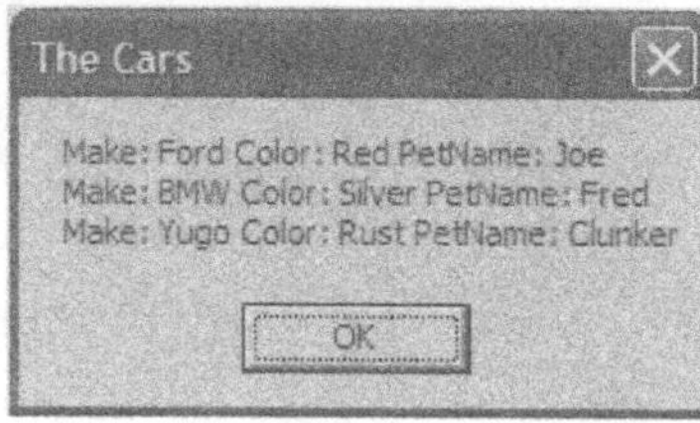

Figure 11-11. Iterating over the Car types

The code behind the remaining VB 6.0 Button types should be self-explanatory:

```
' Insert a Car into the collection.
Private Sub btnAddCar_Click()
    Dim c As New Car
    c.SetCarState txtMake.Text, txtColor.Text, txtPetName.Text
    coll.AddCar c
End Sub

' Clear out all cars.
Private Sub btnClearCars_Click()
    coll.ClearCars
End Sub
```

```
' Remove a specific Car.
Private Sub btnRemoveCar_Click()
On Error GoTo OOPS
    coll.RemoveCar CInt(txtCarToRemove.Text)
    Exit Sub
OOPS:
    MsgBox Err.Description, , Err.Source
End Sub
```

CODE *The Vb6CollectionClient project is included under the Chapter 11 subdirectory.*

Exposing .NET Exceptions

If you were looking closely at the previous VB 6.0 client, you noticed that the btnRemoveCar_Click() subroutine was making use of standard VB 6.0–style error handling (ick) to trap any errors that might occur during the removal of a Car type. This brings up the obvious question of how a .NET object is able to return error information to the COM caller. As you learned previously in this text, COM error objects allow COM parties to send and receive rich error information using a small set of COM interfaces (ISupportErrorInfo, IcreateErrorInfo, and IErrorInfo). Under .NET of course, these interfaces are seen as legacies, and in their place you have strongly typed exception objects.

Recall that all .NET exceptions are indeed objects, which derive from the System.Exception base class. And as you would expect, the CCW automatically maps .NET exceptions in terms of COM error objects. For example, let's return to your existing DotNetCollection project and ponder the ArrayList.RemoveAt() method that is triggered by CarCollection.RemoveCar():

```
public void RemoveCar(int index)
{ar.RemoveAt(index);}
```

As seen previously, the CarCollection type starts life with three internal Car types. Now, what if the VB 6.0 client attempts to remove item number 777 from the container? The ArrayList.RemoveAt() method responds by throwing an IndexOutOfRange exception to the caller, which is trapped by the VB 6.0 On Error Goto syntax. The result is seen in Figure 11-12.

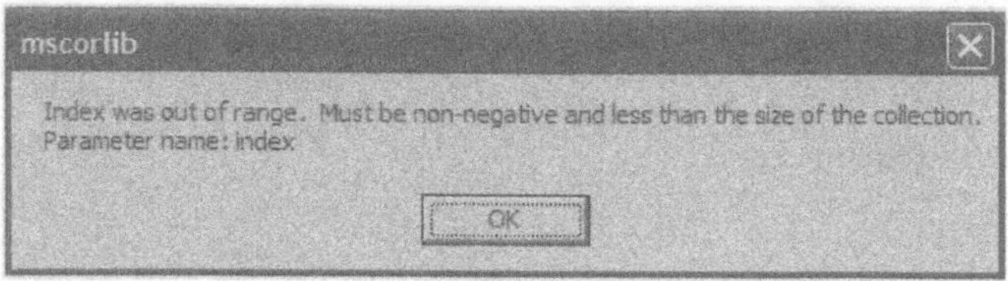

Figure 11-12. Trapping a .NET exception

As you can see, the IndexOutOfBounds exception thrown from ArrayList.RemoveAt() contains a helpful text string (via System.Exception.Message). This is mapped into IErrorInfo.GetDescription(), which is expressed in terms of VB 6.0 as Err.Description (see Chapter 8 for a complete mapping of System.Exception members to and from IErrorInfo members).

Throwing Custom .NET Exceptions

Assume you want to equip the CarCollection.RemoveCar() method to throw out a custom .NET exception, rather than using the prefabricated IndexOutOfRange type. For example:

```
// Custom exceptions are of little
// use to COM, as they will be
// mapped into IErrorInfo equipped
// COM error object.
[ComVisible(false)]
public class BoneHeadUserException
    : System.Exception
{
    public override string Message
    {
        get { return "Hey bonehead, count your cars first!";}
    }
}

public class CarCollection : IEnumerable
{
    …
    public void RemoveCar(int index)
    {
        try
        {
            ar.RemoveAt(index);
        }
        catch
        { throw new BoneHeadUserException();}
    }
}
```

Notice that you have explicitly prevented the custom COM exception from being published into the COM type information, given that this is of little use to a classic COM client. Beyond this one small design step, the remaining logic is straightforward COM exception handling.

Now, when the CCW translates the custom exception into terms of COM, the intrinsic VB 6.0 Err object is able to not only display the custom message, but also to identify the DotNetCollection type as the sender of the error (rather than mscorlib.dll). Check out Figure 11-13.

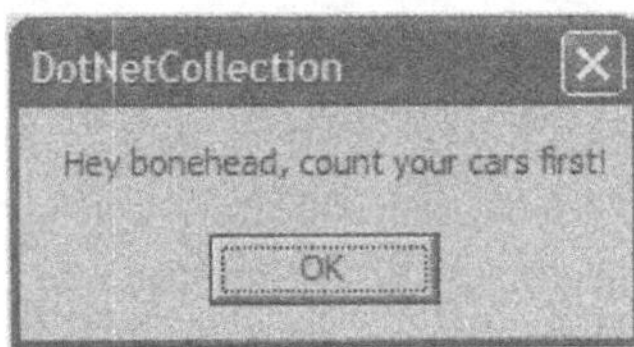

Figure 11-13. Trapping a custom .NET exception

Exercising Your DotNetCollection Assembly from C++

Just to keep the C++ folks out there happy, I'll walk you through the process of interacting with .NET exceptions and collections from the world of C++ COM. Recall that when a .NET class type implements IEnumerable, the CCW simulates support for the standard COM interface, IEnumVARIANT. Given that C++ does not have a native "for each"–style iteration syntax, C++ programmers instead make direct use of the following members:

```
// The classic COM enumerator interface
interface IEnumVARIANT : IUnknown
{
    virtual HRESULT Next(unsigned long celt,
              VARIANT FAR* rgvar,
              unsigned long FAR* pceltFetched) = 0;
    virtual HRESULT Skip(unsigned long celt) = 0;
    virtual HRESULT Reset() = 0;
    virtual HRESULT Clone(IEnumVARIANT FAR* FAR* ppenum) = 0;
};
```

The only member that requires special comment for your purposes is the Next() method. Notice that the first and second parameters allow you to specify the number of items in the VARIANT array. The strange thing about this method is that it is totally possible for the COM client to request more contained items than the container actually contains! For example, the DotNetCollection type begins life by creating three internal Car types. If the client asks for the next 60 Cars, you have an obvious problem. Thus enters the final parameter of

IEnumVARIANT.Next(), pceltFetched, which holds the value of the number of items actually returned.

So, how exactly does a COM client obtain the .NET type's enumerator? Well, contrary to what you may be thinking, you do *not* directly query for IID_IEnumVARIANT, but instead call IEnumerable.GetEnumerator(). Rather than returning a .NET-centric IEnumerator, the CCW transforms this type into IEnumVARIANT automatically. Consider the following C++ COM client code:

```
#include <iostream.h>

// Adjust your paths accordingly...
#import "C:\WINDOWS\Microsoft.NET\Framework\v1.0.3617\mscorlib.tlb" \
    no_namespace named_guids
#import "C:\Apress Books\InteropBook\Labs\Chapter
11\DotNetCollection\bin\Debug\DotNetCollection.tlb" \
no_namespace named_guids

int main(int argc, char* argv[])
{
    CoInitialize(NULL);

    // Create collection and get enumerator.
    _CarCollectionPtr pColl(__uuidof(CarCollection));
    IEnumVARIANTPtr pEnum;
    pEnum = pColl->GetEnumerator();

    // Ask for three cars.
    VARIANT theCars[3];
    ULONG numberReturned = 0;
    pEnum->Next(3, theCars, &numberReturned);
    cout << "You got back " << numberReturned << " cars." << endl;

    // Print out each car.
    for(ULONG i = 0; i < numberReturned; i++)
    {
        _CarPtr temp = theCars[i].punkVal;
        cout << temp->GetCarState() << endl;
        temp = NULL;
    }
    pColl = NULL;
    CoUninitialize();
    return 0;
}
```

Here, you again make use of the generated smart pointers (via the #import statement). Understand that from the _CarCollectionPtr type, you are able to call any member of the CarCollection type (AddCar(), RemoveCar(), and whatnot). In this example, you are simply calling GetEnumerator() and iterating over the contained Car types.

As far as trapping .NET exceptions, the #import statement allows C++ programmers to handle COM error objects using the _com_error type in conjunction with standard try/catch exception handling. Given that _com_error is simply a canned implementation of IErrorInfo, consider this type the C++ equivalent of the VB 6.0 Err object. Thus:

```
// Trigger .NET exception and
// map to COM error object.
try
{
    pColl->RemoveCar(888);
}
catch(_com_error &e)
{
    cout << "Error from: " << e.Source() <<
    endl << "Message: " << e.Description() << endl;
}
```

The output can be seen in Figure 11-14.

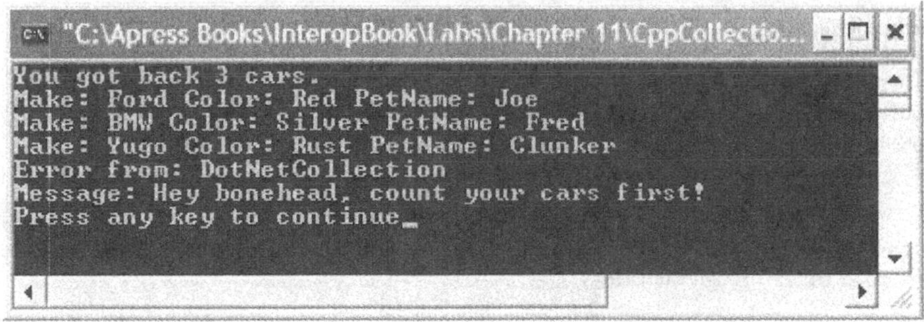

Figure 11-14. .NET collections (and exceptions) handled via C++ COM

CODE *The CppCollectionClient project can be found under the Chapter 11 subdirectory.*

Converting .NET Interface with Multiple Base Interfaces

Under classic COM, a given COM interface is required to have exactly one (and only one) parent interface, which is often IUnknown itself. However, under .NET, a given interface can be configured to derive from multiple base interfaces. This ability gives us the power to describe very rich behaviors in an abstract manner. To illustrate, assume you have created two stand-alone .NET interfaces that describe a basic automobile as well as a more feature-rich four-wheeler:

```
[InterfaceType(ComInterfaceType.InterfaceIsIUnknown)]
[Guid("294D6CDE-25AE-4948-8D2E-CE8A39EAA781")]
public interface ICar
{
    void Start();
    void Stop();
}

[InterfaceType(ComInterfaceType.InterfaceIsIUnknown)]
[Guid("070E86D9-64AF-4f39-A640-2EE690478141")]
public interface ISportsCar
{
    void TurboBoost();
}
```

Now, if you wish to define a new behavior that leverages each of these behaviors, you are able (under .NET) to do the following:

```
[InterfaceType(ComInterfaceType.InterfaceIsIUnknown)]
[Guid("ABBF550F-DD00-4eb5-A031-AD74D41F0861")]
public interface IJamesBondCar : ICar, ISportsCar
{
    void Fly();
    void DiveUnderWater();
    void DrillThroughMountain();
}
```

If you visualize the relationships of these three interfaces, you would see something like what is shown in Figure 11-15.

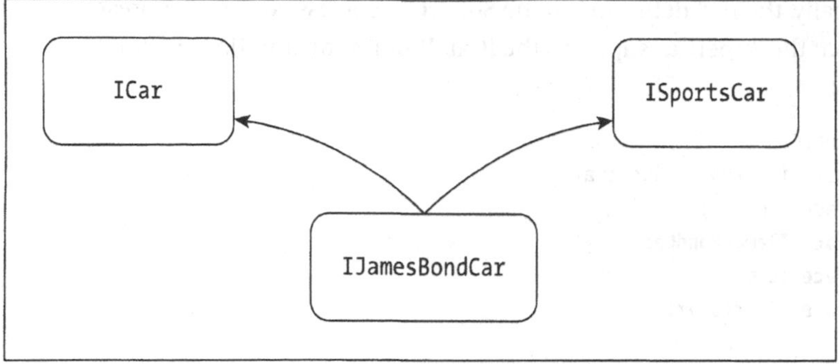

Figure 11-15. .NET interfaces can have multiple base interfaces.

Also assume that you have a given C# class type that implements IJamesBondCar in some way (you really don't care exactly how for this example):

```
[ClassInterface(ClassInterfaceType.AutoDual)]
[Guid("9776534F-55E7-419d-BE7D-36C993DF6ECF")]
public class SuperCar : IJamesBondCar
{
    public SuperCar(){}
    // Some impl...
    public void Start(){}
    public void Stop(){}
    public void TurboBoost(){}
    public void Fly(){}
    public void DiveUnderWater(){}
    public void DrillThroughMountain(){}
}
```

The question, of course, is how would the IJamesBondCar be represented in terms of COM IDL? One might expect that tlbexp.exe would simply suck in the methods of the members of each base interface to populate the members of IJamesBondCar. Sadly, you find the following IDL:

```
// Ug!  We are now derived from IUnknown
// and lost the members of ICar and ISportsCar!
interface IJamesBondCar : IUnknown {
    HRESULT _stdcall Fly();
    HRESULT _stdcall DiveUnderWater();
    HRESULT _stdcall DrillThroughMountain();
};
```

Ironically, the IDL definition of the SuperCar coclass correctly represents the fact that the SuperCar supports the ICar, ISportsCar, and IJamesBondCar interfaces:

```
coclass SuperCar {
    [default] interface _SuperCar;
    interface _Object;
    interface IJamesBondCar;
    interface ICar;
    interface ISportsCar;
};
```

Clearly, however, tlbexp.exe shot for the lowest common denominator (IUnknown) when defining the base class of IJamesBondCar. If you wish to ensure that a .NET interface supports the members of each base interface, the most straightforward approach is to explicitly re-list the inherited members in the derived type. If you were to blindly retype the definitions exactly as shown, you would effectively hide the base interface members! To prevent this from occurring, you must explicitly mark the re-listed members as new to prevent the automatic shadowing. For example:

```
[InterfaceType(ComInterfaceType.InterfaceIsIUnknown)]
[Guid("ABBF550F-DD00-4eb5-A031-AD74D41F0861")]
public interface IJamesBondCar : ICar, ISportsCar
{
    // From ICar.
    new void Start();
    new void Stop();

    // From ISportsCar
    new void TurboBoost();

    void Fly();
    void DiveUnderWater();
    void DrillThroughMountain();
}
```

If you refresh the COM IDL definitions, you would now find the following correct unmanaged representation of this complex behavior:

```
interface IJamesBondCar : IUnknown {
    HRESULT _stdcall Start();
    HRESULT _stdcall Stop();
    HRESULT _stdcall TurboBoost();
    HRESULT _stdcall Fly();
    HRESULT _stdcall DiveUnderWater();
    HRESULT _stdcall DrillThroughMountain();
};
```

A VB 6.0 COM client could now interact with all members of the supported interfaces using a valid IJamesBondCar interface reference:

```
Dim c as SuperCar
Set c = New SuperCar
Dim ijbcItf as IJamesBondCar
Set ijbcItf = c
ijbcItf.Start
ijbcItf.TurboBoost
ijbcItf.DrillThroughMountain
```

As you would expect, each interface is also recognized as an individual entity (Figure 11-16).

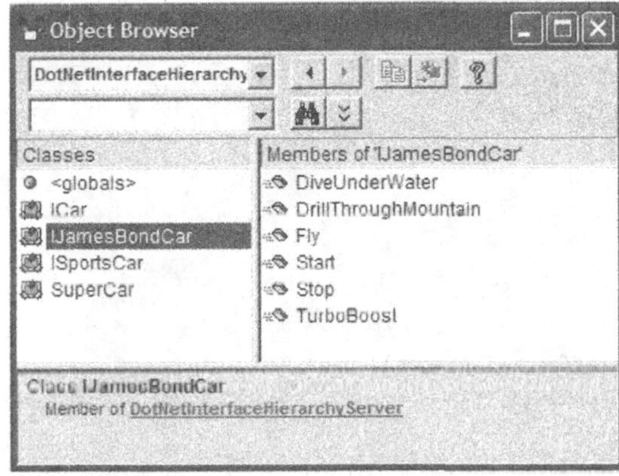

Figure 11-16. Simulating .NET interface inheritance

Converting .NET Interface Hierarchies

The previous iteration of the IJamesBondCar interface hierarchy employed the technique of deriving a single interface from multiple base interfaces. Although .NET supports this very helpful design pattern, most programmers tend to stick to a traditional single-based design. For example, assume that you crafted the IJamesBondCar type as shown in Figure 11-17.

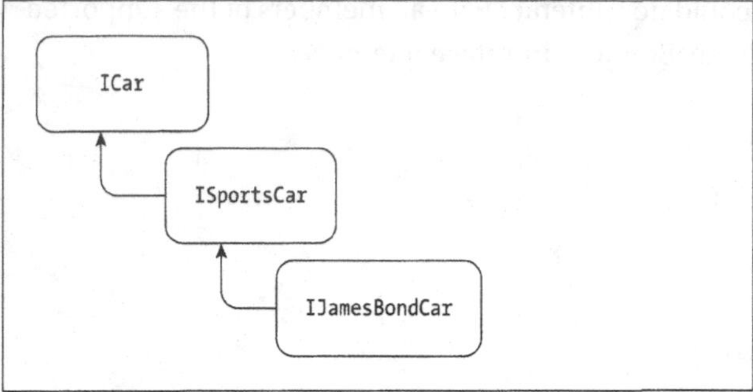

Figure 11-17. A more traditional interface hierarchy

This time, through, these three interfaces are arranged in a single inheritance model, which can be represented by the following C# code:

```
[InterfaceType(ComInterfaceType.InterfaceIsIUnknown)]
[Guid("294D6CDE-25AE-4948-8D2E-CE8A39EAA781")]
public interface ICar
{
    void Start();
    void Stop();
}

[InterfaceType(ComInterfaceType.InterfaceIsIUnknown)]
[Guid("070E86D9-64AF-4f39-A640-2EE690478141")]
public interface ISportsCar : ICar
{
    void TurboBoost();
}

[InterfaceType(ComInterfaceType.InterfaceIsIUnknown)]
[Guid("ABBF550F-DD00-4eb5-A031-AD74D41F0861")]
public interface IJamesBondCar : ISportsCar
{
    void Fly();
    void DiveUnderWater();
    void DrillThroughMountain();
}
```

Now, if you run this .NET assembly through tlbexp.exe (or regasm.exe), you would find that, once again, the derived interfaces do *not* provide support for the inherited members of the base interface(s):

```
[...]
 interface ICar : IUnknown {
    HRESULT _stdcall Start();
    HRESULT _stdcall Stop();
};
```

```
[…]
interface ISportsCar : IUnknown {
    HRESULT _stdcall TurboBoost();
};

[…]
interface IJamesBondCar : IUnknown {
    HRESULT _stdcall Fly();
    HRESULT _stdcall DiveUnderWater();
    HRESULT _stdcall DrillThroughMountain();
};
```

Now, when you consider how each interface was defined under .NET, you made use of ComInterfaceType.InterfaceIsUnknown. It is important to recall that this enumeration defines exactly three possible values—and only three possible values. Given this fact, understand that the InterfaceTypeAttribute type does not allow you to specify a custom .NET interface as the base interface type:

```
// Illegal .NET code!
// This will NOT work!
[InterfaceType(typeof(ICar))]  // No! (Nice try though…)
[Guid("070E86D9-64AF-4f39-A640-2EE690478141")]
public interface ISportsCar : ICar
{
    void TurboBoost();
}
```

The cold, hard fact is that assembly-to-type library conversion is able to create interfaces that derive directly from IUnknown or IDispatch (i.e., a [dual] interface or as a raw dispinterface). However, just as you did in the previous iteration of the IJamesBondCar interface, you are able to explicitly re-list inherited members using the new keyword. Thus:

```
[InterfaceType(ComInterfaceType.InterfaceIsIUnknown)]
[Guid("54E46D63-C1E7-4f62-9EE2-939B17394D9E")]
public interface ICar
{
    void Start();
    void Stop();
}

[InterfaceType(ComInterfaceType.InterfaceIsIUnknown)]
[Guid("C04D9BBE-AF00-473d-93E8-1F04E3AF197E")]
public interface ISportsCar : ICar
{
```

```
    // From ICar
    new void Start();
    new void Stop();

    void TurboBoost();
}

[InterfaceType(ComInterfaceType.InterfaceIsIUnknown)]
[Guid("07482652-2B4F-40da-B8A1-CFA9AAB51D64")]
public interface IJamesBondCar : ISportsCar
{
    // From ICar.
    new void Start();
    new void Stop();

    // From ISportsCar
    new void TurboBoost();

    void Fly();
    void DiveUnderWater();
    void DrillThroughMountain();
}
```

This generates the IDL you expect. Again, the use of the new keyword when defining a derived interface is not the ideal approach. Unfortunately, when you wish to ensure that a COM interface definition explicitly inherits base members, this is your only option.

CODE *The DotNetInterfaceHierarchyServer project is included under the Chapter 11 subdirectory.*

Summary

At this point, you have seen how members of the .NET type system (classes, interfaces, enums, structures, and delegates) are mapped into terms of classic COM. As you have seen, .NET enumerations translate almost directly into unmanaged IDL equivalents. The same holds true for System.ValueType-derived .NET types (i.e., structures). Perhaps the most drastic conversion occurs when exposing a .NET delegate into terms of COM connection points. When you wish to do so, you need to define a managed version of a given source interface and mark its support by a given .NET class type using the ComSourceInterfaces attribute. As for the remaining topics examined here (.NET collections and .NET exceptions), remember that in a nutshell the .NET IEnumerable interface is mapped into a COM IEnumVARIANT, while .NET exceptions are mapping into COM error objects.

Given the materials presented in the last two chapters, you now have the skills you need to make your .NET assemblies COM aware. The next chapter wraps up your investigation of .NET-to-COM interoperability by examining a set of more advanced topics, such as building custom .NET-to-COM conversion utilities and COM-compatible .NET types.

CHAPTER 12

COM-to-.NET Interoperability—Advanced Topics

The point of this chapter is to round out your knowledge of exposing .NET types to COM applications by examining a number of advanced techniques. The first major topic is to examine how .NET types can implement COM interfaces to achieve binary compatibility with other like-minded COM objects (a topic first broached in Chapter 7). Closely related to this topic is the process of defining COM types directly using managed code. Using this technique, it is possible to build a binary-compatible .NET type that does not directly reference a related interop assembly (and is therefore a bit more lightweight). As for the next major topic, you examine the process of building a customized version of tlbexp.exe while also addressing how to programmatically register interop assemblies at runtime. Finally, you wrap up by taking a deeper look at the .NET runtime environment and checking out how a COM client can be used to build a custom host for .NET types. In addition to being a very interesting point of discussion, you will see that a custom CLR host can simplify COM-to-.NET registration issues.

Changing Type Marshaling Using MarshalAsAttribute

Before digging into the real meat of this chapter, let's examine yet another interop-centric attribute. As you have seen, one nice thing about the tlbexp.exe utility is that it will always ensure the generated type information is [oleautomation] compatible. When you build COM interfaces that are indeed [oleautomation] compatible, you are able to ensure that all COM-aware languages can interact with the .NET type (as well as receive a free stub/proxy layer courtesy of the universal marshaler). Typically, if you have created a COM interface that is not [oleautomation] compatible, you have either (a) made a mistake, (b) are building a COM server you only intend to use from C++, or (c) wish to define a custom stub and proxy DLL for performance reasons.

Nevertheless, if you wish to create a managed method that is exposed to COM as a non–oleautomation-compatible entity, you are able to apply the MarshalAsAttribute type. The MarshalAs attribute can also be helpful when a single .NET type has the ability to be represented by multiple COM types. For example, a System.String could be marshaled to unmanaged code as a LPSTR, LPWSTR, LPTSTR, or BSTR. While the default behavior (System.String to COM BSTRs) is typically exactly what you want, the MarshalAsAttribute type can be used to expose System.String in alternative formats.

This attribute may be applied to a method return type, type member, and a particular member parameter. Applying this attribute is simple enough; however, the argument that is specified as a constructor parameter (UnmanagedType) is a .NET enumeration that defines a *ton* of possibilities. To fully understand the scope of the MarshalAs attribute, let's check out some core values of this marshal-centric enumeration. First up, Table 12-1 documents the key values of UnmanagedType that allow you to expose a System.String in various formats.

Table 12-1. String-Centric Values of UnmanagedType

String-Centric UnmanagedType Member Name	Meaning in Life
AnsiBStr	ANSI character string that is a length-prefixed single byte.
BStr	Unicode character string that is a length-prefixed double byte.
LPStr	A single-byte ANSI character string.
LPTStr	A platform-dependent character string, ANSI on Windows 98, Unicode on Windows NT. This value is only supported for Platform Invoke, and not COM interop, because exporting a string of type LPTStr is not supported.
LPWStr	A double-byte Unicode character string.

To illustrate, assume you have a small set of .NET members that are defined as follows:

```
[ClassInterface(ClassInterfaceType.AutoDual)]
public class MyMarshalAsClass
{
    public MyMarshalAsClass(){}

    // String marshaling.
    public void ExposeAsLPStr
        ([MarshalAs(UnmanagedType.LPStr)]string s){}
    public void ExposeAsLPWStr
        ([MarshalAs(UnmanagedType.LPWStr)]string s){}
}
```

Once processed by tlbexp.exe, you find the following COM IDL:

```
interface _MyMarshalAsClass : IDispatch
{
    [id(0x60020004)]
    HRESULT ExposeAsLPStr([in] LPSTR s);
    [id(0x60020005)]
    HRESULT ExposeAsLPWStr([in] LPWSTR s);
};
```

Table 12-2 documents the key values of UnmanagedType that are used to expose System.Object types as various flavors of COM types.

Table 12-2. System.Object-Centric Values of UnmanagedType

Object-Centric UnmanagedType Member Name	Meaning in Life
IDispatch	A COM IDispatch pointer
IUnknown	A COM IUnknown pointer

If you extend the MyMarshalAsClass type to support the following members:

```
// Object marshaling.
public void ExposeAsIUnk
    ([MarshalAs(UnmanagedType.IUnknown)]object o){}
public void ExposeAsIDisp
    ([MarshalAs(UnmanagedType.IDispatch)]object o){}
```

you find the following COM type information:

```
 [id(0x60020006)]
HRESULT ExposeAsIUnk([in] IUnknown* o);
[id(0x60020007)]
HRESULT ExposeAsIDisp([in] IDispatch* o);
```

UnmanagedType also provides a number of values that are used to alter how a .NET array is exposed to classic COM. Again, remember that by default, .NET arrays are exposed as COM SAFEARRAY types, which is typically what you require. For the sake of knowledge, however, Table 12-3 documents the key array-centric member of UnmanagedType.

Table 12-3. Array-Centric Value of UnmanagedType

Array-Centric UnmanagedType Member Name	**Meaning in Life**
LPArray	A C-style array

As you would guess, the following C# member definition:

```
// Array marshaling.
public void ExposeAsCArray
    ([MarshalAs(UnmanagedType.LPArray)]int[] myInts){}
```

results in the following IDL:

```
[id(0x60020008)]
HRESULT ExposeAsCArray([in] long* myInts);
```

Finally, UnmanagedType defines a number of members that allow you to expose intrinsic .NET data types in various COM mappings. While many of these values are used for generic whole numbers, floating-point numbers, and whatnot, one item of interest is UnmanagedType.Currency. As you recall, the COM CURRENCY type is not supported under .NET and has been replaced by System.Decimal. Table 12-4 documents the key data-centric types.

Table 12-4. Data-Centric Values of UnmanagedType

Data Type-Centric UnmanagedType Member Name	**Meaning in Life**
AsAny	Dynamic type that determines the Type of an object at runtime and marshals the object as that Type.
Bool	4-byte Boolean value (true != 0, false = 0).
Currency	Used on a System.Decimal to marshal the decimal value as a COM currency type instead of as a Decimal.
I1	1-byte signed integer.
I2	2-byte signed integer.
I4	4-byte signed integer.
I8	8-byte signed integer.
R4	4-byte floating-point number.
R8	8-byte floating-point number.

Table 12-4. Data-Centric Values of UnmanagedType (continued)

Data Type-Centric UnmanagedType Member Name	Meaning in Life
SysInt	A platform-dependent signed integer. 4 bytes on 32-bit Windows, 8 bytes on 64-bit Windows.
SysUInt	Hardware natural-size unsigned integer.
U1	1-byte unsigned integer.
U2	2-byte unsigned integer.
U4	4-byte unsigned integer.
U8	8-byte unsigned integer.
VariantBool	2-byte OLE-defined Boolean value (true = -1, false = 0).

Again, the most useful of these data type-centric members of the UnmanagedType enumeration is the UnmanagedType.Currency value, given that .NET no longer supports the COM CURRENCY type. However, given that a System.Decimal provides the same storage, you can apply MarshalAs as follows:

```
// Exposing Decimal and Currency.
public void ExposeAsCURRENCY
    ([MarshalAs(UnmanagedType.Currency)]Decimal d){}
```

This results in the following IDL:

```
[id(0x60020008)]
HRESULT ExposeAsCURRENCY([in] CURRENCY d);
```

So, now that you have seen the various ways that the MarshalAsAttribute type can be configured, you may be wondering exactly when (or why) you may wish to alter the default interop marshaler. In reality, you typically won't need to alter the default marshaling behavior. The only time it might be beneficial on a somewhat regular basis is when you wish to expose .NET System.Objects as a specific COM interface type (IUnknown or IDispatch) or expose a System.Decimal as a legacy COM CURRENCY type.

CODE *The MyMarshalAsLibrary project is included under the Chapter 12 subdirectory.*

.NET Types Implementing COM Interfaces

Recall from Chapter 9 that if a COM coclass implements a COM-visible .NET interface, the coclass in question is able to achieve type compatibility with other like-minded .NET objects. The converse of this scenario is also true: .NET types can implement COM interfaces to achieve binary compatibility with other like-minded COM types. When a .NET programmer chooses to account for COM interfaces in his or her type implementations, there are two possible choices:

- Implement a *custom* COM interface.
- Implement a *standard* COM interface.

As you recall from Chapter 2, although a COM interface always boils down to the same physical form (a collection of pure virtual functions identified by a GUID), standard interfaces are predefined types (published by Microsoft). Furthermore, standard interfaces are already defined in terms of COM IDL, have a predefined GUID, and are recorded in the system registry. Custom interfaces, on the other hand, are authored by a COM developer during the course of a software development cycle. In this case, the programmer is the one in charge of describing the item in terms of COM IDL and registering the resulting type library (all of which is done automatically when using VB 6.0). When a .NET type implements a custom COM interface, the result is that a given COM client is able to interact with the .NET type as if it were a coclass adhering to a specific binary format.

On the other hand, if a .NET type implements a standard interface (such as IDispatch, IConnectionPointContainer, or ITypeInfo), it will be used as a customized *replacement* for the equivalent interface implemented by the CCW. To be sure, the chances that you will need to provide a customized implementation of an interface supported by the CCW are slim to none. Given this likelihood, I focus solely on the process of defining managed versions of custom COM interfaces.

Defining Custom COM Interfaces

Before you can examine how to implement custom COM interfaces on a .NET type, you first need the IDL descriptions of the interfaces themselves. As you will see later in this chapter, it is possible to build a binary-compatible .NET type without a formal COM type description; however, for this example, assume you have created an ATL in-proc COM server (AnotherAtlCarServer). This COM server defines a coclass (CoTruck) by implementing two simple interfaces named

IStartable and IStoppable. Here is the relevant IDL (if you need a refresher on building COM servers with ATL, see Chapter 3):

```
[object,
uuid(7FE41805-124B-44AE-BEAE-C3491E35372B),
oleautomation,
helpstring("IStartable Interface"),
pointer_default(unique)]
interface IStartable : IUnknown
{ HRESULT Start(); };

[object,
uuid(B001A308-8D66-4d23-84A4-B67615646ABB),
oleautomation,
helpstring("IStartable Interface"),
pointer_default(unique)]
interface IStoppable : IUnknown
{ HRESULT Break();};

[uuid(7B69AEB6-F0B7-46BB-8AD4-1CACD1EA5AE9),
version(1.0),
helpstring("AnotherAtlCarServer 1.0 Type Library")]
library ANOTHERATLCARSERVERLib
{
    importlib("stdole32.tlb");
    importlib("stdole2.tlb");

    [uuid(862C5338-8AD7-43A3-A9A7-F21B145D61D0),
    helpstring("CoTruck Class")]
    coclass CoTruck
    {
        [default] interface IStartable;
        interface IStoppable;
    };
};
```

The implementation of the CoTruck::Start() and CoTruck::Break() methods simply triggers a Win32 MessageBox() API to inform the caller which object has been told to do what:

```
STDMETHODIMP CCoTruck::Start()
{
    MessageBox(NULL, "The truck as started.",
        "CoTruck::Start() Says:", MB_OK);
    return S_OK;
}
```

```
STDMETHODIMP CCoTruck::Break()
{
    MessageBox(NULL, "The truck as stopped.",
        "CoTruck::Start() Says:", MB_OK);
    return S_OK;
}
```

That's it. Go ahead and compile this ATL project to ensure that this COM server is properly recorded in the system registry.

CODE *The AnotherAtlCarServer project can be found under the Chapter 12 subdirectory.*

Building and Deploying the Interop Assembly

Now that you have a COM server defining a set of custom interfaces, you need to transform the COM type information into terms of .NET metadata. Thus, assuming you have a valid *.snk file, configure a strongly named interop assembly using tlbimp.exe as follows:

```
tlbimp AnotherAtlCarServer.dll /out:interop.AnotherAtlCarServer.dll
/keyfile:theKey.snk
```

Finally, deploy this interop assembly into the GAC (Figure 12-1).

C:\WINDOWS\assembly

File Edit View Favorites Tools Help

Back Search Folders

Address C:\WINDOWS\assembly Go

Global Assembly Name	Type	Version	Culture	Public Key Token
IEExecRemote		1.0.3300.0		b03f5f7f11d50a3a
IEHost		1.0.3300.0		b03f5f7f11d50a3a
IIEHost		1.0.3300.0		b03f5f7f11d50a3a
interop.AnotherAtlCarServer		1.0.0.0		3a7bb5f335af01f2
ISymWrapper		1.0.3300.0		b03f5f7f11d50a3a
JITAComponent		1.0.0.0		42063d098751fb09
LoanLib		1.0.0.0		1d12ee7b52e0a2fa
math		1.0.0.0		4b33a370f199aacc

Figure 12-1. Another machine-wide interop assembly

CODE *The interop assembly for AnotherAltCarServer.dll is included under the Chapter 12 subdirectory.*

Building a Binary-Compatible C# Type

To illustrate building a binary-compatible .NET type, let's create a new C# Code Library that defines a simple class (DotNetLawnMower) that supports both interfaces. First, add a reference to interop.AnotherAtlCarServer.dll, and for simplicity, configure this type to be exposed to COM as an AutoDual class interface:

```
namespace BinaryCompatibleDotNetTypeServer
{
    // This .NET class supports two COM interfaces.
    [ClassInterface(ClassInterfaceType.AutoDual)]
    public class DotNetLawnMower: IStartable, IStoppable
    {
        public DotNetLawnMower(){}
    }
}
```

Now that DotNetLawnMower has defined support for IStartable and IStoppable, and you are obligated to flesh out the details of the Start() and Break() methods. While you could manually type the definitions of each inherited member, you do have a shortcut. The Visual Studio .NET IDE supports an integrated wizard that automatically generates stub code for an implemented interface. However, the manner in which you interact with this tool depends on your language of choice. Here, in your C# project, you activate this tool by right-clicking a supported interface using Class View (Figure 12-2).

Again, the implementation of each member is irrelevant for this example, so just set a reference to System.Windows.Forms.dll and call MessageBox.Show() in an appropriate manner:

```
public void Start()
{
    MessageBox.Show("Lawn Mower starting..." ,
        "DotNetLawnMower says:");
}
public void Break()
{
    MessageBox.Show("Lawn Mower stopping..." ,
        "DotNetLawnMower says:");
}
```

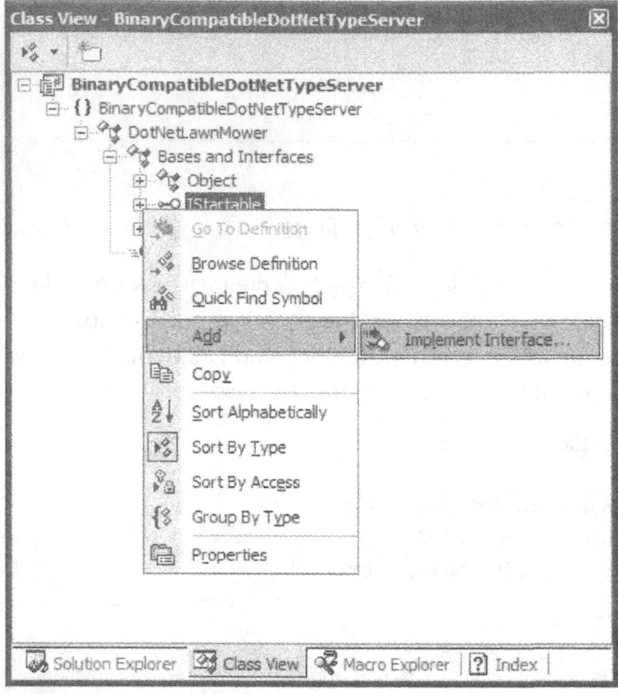

Figure 12-2. The C# IDE Implement Interface Wizard

Because this .NET class library is to be used by a classic COM client, you will want to deploy this binary as a shared assembly. Thus, be sure to set the assembly's version (1.0.0.0 will do) and specify a valid *.snk file. Once you have done so, deploy this assembly to the GAC.

CODE *The BinaryCompatibleDotNetTypeServer project is included under the Chapter 12 subdirectory.*

Building a Binary-Compatible VB .NET Type

Any managed language has the ability to implement COM interfaces, provided they have access to the interface descriptions. To further highlight the process, assume you have a VB .NET Code Library that defines a type named UFO. The UFO type is able to be started and stopped (presumably) and thus wishes to implement the COM interfaces defined in the ATL server. Once you set a reference to the interop assembly and define support for each interface (via the Implements keyword), the VB .NET IDE provides a simple shortcut to automatically build stubs for each method. Simply select the name of the supported interface from the left drop-down list and the name of the method from the right drop-down list (Figure 12-3).

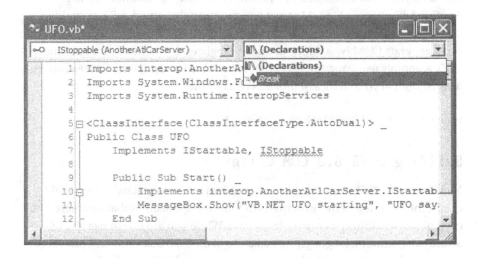

Figure 12-3. The VB .NET IDE Implement Interface Wizard

Here is the complete VB .NET definition of UFO, which also makes use of an AutoDual class interface (again, be sure to assign a strong name to the assembly and deploy this assembly to the GAC):

```
<ClassInterface(ClassInterfaceType.AutoDual)> _
Public Class UFO
    Implements IStartable, IStoppable
    Public Sub Start() _
        Implements ANOTHERATLCARSERVERLib.IStartable.Start
        MessageBox.Show("VB.NET UFO starting", "UFO says:")
    End Sub
    Public Sub Break() Implements ANOTHERATLCARSERVERLib.IStoppable.Break
        MessageBox.Show("VB.NET UFO stopping", "UFO says:")
    End Sub
End Class
```

CODE *The BinaryCompatibleVbNetTypeServer project is included under the Chapter 12 directory.*

Registering the .NET Assemblies with COM

So, to recap the story thus far, at this point you have three objects (CoTruck, LawnMower, and UFO). Each has been created in a specific language (C++, C#, or VB .NET) using two different architectures (COM and .NET) that implement the same two COM interfaces. Furthermore, the interop assembly for the AnotherAtlCarServer.dll COM server and the strongly named .NET assemblies have been deployed to the GAC. Like any COM-to-.NET interaction, however, you must generate COM type information (and register the contents) for each native .NET assembly using regasm.exe. Thus, from the command line, run regasm.exe against both of your .NET assemblies. For example:

```
regasm BinaryCompatibleVbNetTypeServer.dll /tlb
```

Building a VB 6.0 COM Client

Now that each .NET assembly has been configured to be reachable by a COM client, the final step of this example is to build an application that interacts with each object in a binary-compatible manner. While you are free to use any COM-aware programming language, I'll make use of a VB 6.0 Standard EXE project that interacts with each type. The big picture is illustrated in Figure 12-4.

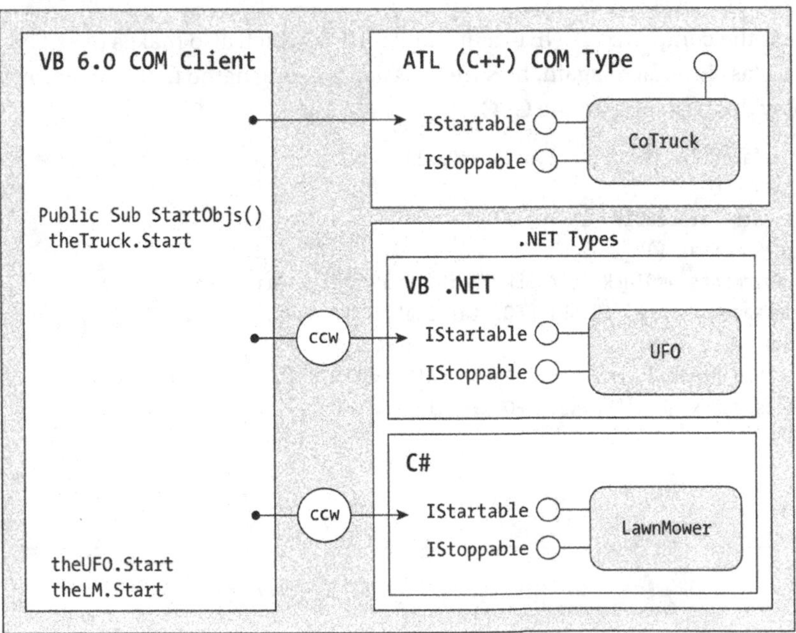

Figure 12-4. Behold, the power of interface-based programming.

The first step (of course) is to set a reference to each type library (Figure 12-5).

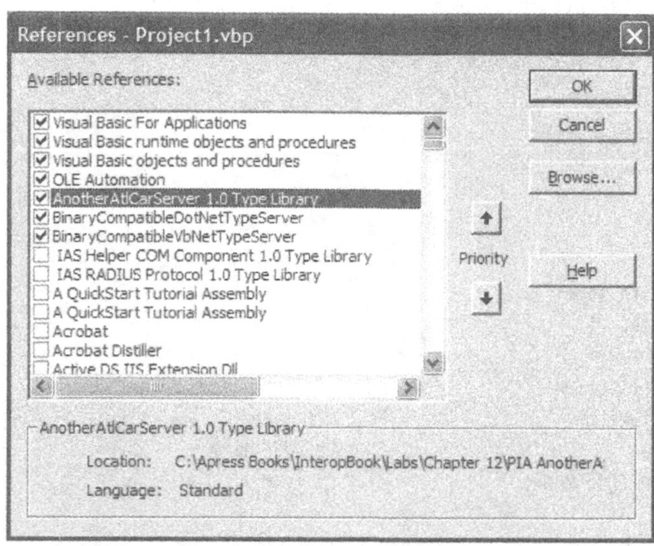

Figure 12-5. Referencing the COM type information

Just to keep things interesting, you will add one additional refinement to the scenario suggested by Figure 12-4. Rather than declaring three Form-level member variables of type UFO, LawnMower, and CoTruck, let's make use of a VB 6.0 Collection type to contain each item (as this will better illustrate the interface-based polymorphism of semantically gluing the types together). Thus, if the main Form has two Button types that start and stop each item in the collection, you are able to author the following VB 6.0 code:

```
Option Explicit
Private theObjs As Collection

' Loop through the collection
' and start everything using IStartable.
Private Sub btnStartObjs_Click()
    Dim temp As IStartable
    Dim i As Integer
    For i = 0 To theObjs.Count - 1
        Set temp = theObjs(i + 1)
        temp.Start
    Next
End Sub
```

```
' Loop through the collection and
' stop everything using IStoppable.
Private Sub btnStopObjs_Click()
    Dim temp As IStoppable
    Dim i As Integer
    For i = 0 To theObjs.Count - 1
        Set temp = theObjs(i + 1)
        temp.Break
    Next
End Sub

' Fill the collection with some
' binary compatible types.
Private Sub Form_Load()
    Set theObjs = New Collection
    theObjs.Add New CoTruck                    ' ATL type.
    theObjs.Add New UFO                        ' VB .NET type.
    theObjs.Add New DotNetLawnMower            ' C# type
End Sub
```

Notice that you are able to communicate with each type using the custom COM interfaces defined in the original ATL server (thus the binary compatibility nature of the example). If you were to run the client application, you would see a series of message boxes pop up as the types in the collection were manipulated.

CODE *The Vb6COMCompatibleClient project is included under the Chapter 12 subdirectory.*

Defining COM Interfaces Using Managed Code

Although the previous example did indeed allow the .NET types to implement existing COM interfaces, you had to jump through a few undesirable hoops during the process. First, each .NET code library was required to obtain the type information of IStoppable and IStartable via tlbimp.exe. This of course results in an [.assembly extern] listing in each assembly manifest. Given this, each .NET assembly now depends on the presence of the interop assembly on the target machine. If the interop assembly is not present and accounted for, the .NET consumer is unable to find the correct metadata and it becomes woefully binary-*incompatible* with other like-minded COM types.

When you think about it, the C# LawnMower and VB .NET UFO types never needed to directly interact with the CoTruck. All these projects required were the managed definitions of the raw COM interfaces. To simplify the process, you could have defined IStartable and IStoppable (using managed code) directly within the .NET assemblies. In this way, your .NET assemblies are no longer tied to an interop assembly and are still binary compatible!

To illustrate, let's see a simple example. Assume you have yet another C# Code Library (ManagedComDefs) that contains a simple class named DvdPlayer. Given that DVD players are also startable and stoppable, our goal is to achieve binary compatibility with the CoTruck, UFO, and LawnMower types, *without* referencing the interop.AnotherAltCarServer.dll assembly.

When you define COM interfaces directly within managed code, each and every interface must be attributed with the ComImportAttribute, GuidAttribute, and InterfaceTypeAttribute types. Therefore, all your managed interfaces look something like the following:

```
// Some binary compatible COM interface
// defined in managed code.
[ComImport, Guid("<IID>"),
InterfaceType(ComInterfaceType.<type of COM interface>)]
public interface SomeBinaryCompatibleInterface
{ // Members…}
```

The ComImportAttribute type is simply used to identify this type as a COM entity when exposed to a COM client. Obviously, the value of the GuidAttribute type must be identical to the original IDL IID. As for the InterfaceTypeAttribute, you are provided with the following related enumeration to mark the representation of the COM interface you are describing:

```
public enum System.Runtime.InteropServices.ComInterfaceType
{
    InterfaceIsDual,
    InterfaceIsIDispatch,
    InterfaceIsIUnknown
}
```

The ComInterfaceType value passed into the InterfaceTypeAttribute is used by the .NET runtime to determine how to build the correct vtable for the unmanaged COM interface (more on this tidbit in just a moment). Recall that the IStartable and IStoppable interfaces were defined in IDL as follows:

```
[object,
uuid(7FE41805-124B-44AE-BEAE-C3491E35372B),
oleautomation,
helpstring("IStartable Interface"),
pointer_default(unique)]
interface IStartable : IUnknown
{ HRESULT Start(); };
```

```
[object,
uuid(B001A308-8D66-4d23-84A4-B67615646ABB),
oleautomation,
helpstring("IStartable Interface"),
pointer_default(unique)]
interface IStoppable : IUnknown
{ HRESULT Break();};
```

Looking at these interface types, it should be clear that the COM-to-.NET data type, type, and type member conversion rules still apply (for example, System.String becomes BSTR and whatnot). In this case, you are happy to find that Start() and Break() take no parameters, and therefore can be defined in terms of C# in a rather straightforward manner. Here is the complete code behind the binary-compatible DvdPlayer:

```
using System;
using System.Runtime.InteropServices;
using System.Windows.Forms;

namespace ManuallyInterfaceDefsServer
{
    // Managed definition of IStartable.
    [ComImport,
    Guid("7FE41805-124B-44AE-BEAE-C3491E35372B"),
    InterfaceType(ComInterfaceType.InterfaceIsIUnknown)]
    interface IStartable { void Start(); };

    // Managed definition of IStoppable.
    [ComImport,
    Guid("B001A308-8D66-4d23-84A4-B67615646ABB"),
    InterfaceType(ComInterfaceType.InterfaceIsIUnknown)]
    interface IStoppable { void Break();};

    // A binary compatible DVD player!
    [ClassInterface(ClassInterfaceType.AutoDual)]
    public class DvdPlayer : IStartable, IStoppable
    {
        public DvdPlayer(){}
        public void Start()
        { MessageBox.Show("Staring movie...", "DvdPlayer");}

        public void Break()
        {MessageBox.Show("Stopping movie...", "DvdPlayer");}
    }
}
```

Once you compile this .NET assembly, if you (a) deploy this assembly into the GAC and (b) export the metadata to a COM *.tlb file via regasm.exe, you would be able to set a reference to the exported *.tlb file and update the VB 6.0 COM client as follows:

```
' Add a DVD player into the mix.
Private Sub Form_Load()
    Set theObjs = New Collection
    theObjs.Add New CoTruck
    theObjs.Add New UFO
    theObjs.Add New DotNetLawnMower
    theObjs.Add New DvdPlayer
End Sub
```

Sure enough, you are able to make use of IStartable and IStoppable of the DvdPlayer as expected (Figure 12-6).

Figure 12-6. Using the binary-compatible DvdPlayer

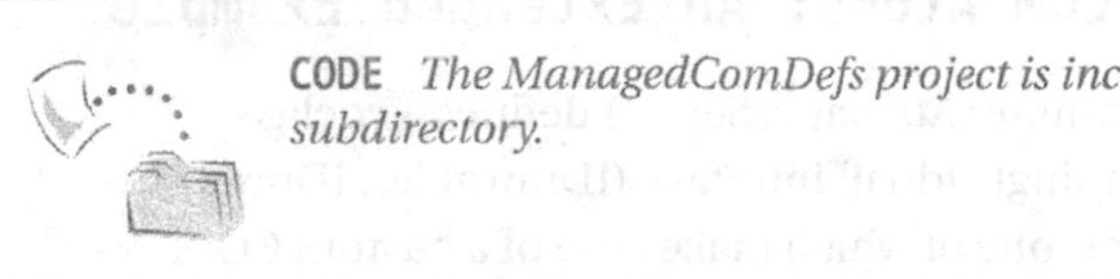

CODE *The ManagedComDefs project is included under the Chapter 12 subdirectory.*

Selected Notes on Manually Defining COM Interfaces Using Managed Code

The previous example was quite straightforward, given that the interfaces you defined were IUnknown-derived entities (thus no DISPIDs) and contained methods with no parameters (thus no [in], [out], or [out, retval] attributes to worry about). As you might expect, if you attempt to manually pound out the details of more complex COM interfaces, you need to apply additional .NET attributes. Furthermore, it is possible (although not altogether likely) that you might need to define other COM types (enums, structures, coclasses) in terms of managed code. To be sure, if the COM type you are attempting to become binary-compatible with has been defined in terms of COM IDL, you will never need to manually define COM types other than the occasional interface. Even then, if the dependency on a related interop assembly is acceptable, you will not need to bother to do this much.

However, there may be some (hopefully) rare cases in which you will need to manually define COM interfaces via managed code. For example, in C++, it is possible to build a COM class supporting a set of COM interfaces without the use of IDL. Given that the midl.exe compiler simply regards IDL interfaces as a collection of C++ pure virtual functions, a C++ developer could choose to define the pure virtual functions directly in terms of C++. The obvious downfall to this approach is that the programmer has effectively created a COM server that can only be used by other C++ clients. If a .NET programmer wished to build a binary-compatible type using an interface described in raw C++, it would demand creating a managed definition of the COM type, given that the COM type library (and thus the interop assembly) doesn't exist!

The process of manually defining a COM type in terms of managed code can be very helpful if you require only a subset of items defined in the type library, or if you need to somehow modify the COM type to work better from a managed environment. As you may recall from Chapter 9, it is possible to crack open an interop assembly and tweak the internal metadata. The same result can often be achieved by directly implementing the COM types using managed code (not to mention, it can be achieved in a much simpler manner). Given these possibilities, let's walk through an extended example.

Manually Defining COM Atoms: An Extended Example

The next COM server you examine (AtlShapesServer) defines a coclass (CoHexagon) that supports a single [dual] interface (IDrawable). IDrawable defines a small set of methods, one of which makes use of a custom COM enumeration. Here is the complete IDL:

```
typedef enum SHAPECOLOR
{
    RED, PINK, RUST
}SHAPECOLOR;

[object,
uuid(B1691C03-7EA8-4DAB-86CC-7D6CD859671A),
dual,
pointer_default(unique)]
interface IDrawable : IDispatch
{
    [id(1), helpstring("method Draw")]
    HRESULT Draw([in] int top, [in] int left, [in] int bottom, [in] int right);
```

```
    [id(2), helpstring("method SetColor")]
    HRESULT SetColor([in] SHAPECOLOR c);
};

[uuid(95FBF6E3-1B03-4904-A5D3-C77A02785F9A),
version(1.0)]
library ATLSHAPESSERVERLib
{
    importlib("stdole32.tlb");
    importlib("stdole2.tlb");
    [uuid(204F9A4B-4D22-451B-BE2F-338F2917E7F5)]
    coclass CoHexagon
    {
        [default] interface IDrawable;
    };
};
```

Defining the Dual Interface (and SHAPECOLOR Enum) Using C#

When you describe a [dual] interface in terms of managed code, you obviously need to supply ComInterfaceType.InterfaceIsDual to the InterfaceTypeAttribute constructor (given the IDL definition). Additionally, you are required to supply the correct DISPID values for each member. This alone is not too earth-shattering. However, recall that the IDrawable interface defines two members:

```
interface IDrawable : IDispatch
{
    [id(1)]
    HRESULT Draw([in] int top, [in] int left, [in] int bottom, [in] int right );
    [id(2)] HRESULT SetColor([in] SHAPECOLOR c);
};
```

Now, as you are aware, COM interfaces are used to construct a vtable for the implementing coclass. A vtable is little more than a listing of addresses that point to the correct function implementation. Given that COM is so dependent on a valid vtable, you must understand that it is *critical* that you define the methods of a managed COM interface in the same order as found in the original IDL (or C++ header file). If you do not, you are most certainly not binary-compatible. Given this, here is the definition of IDrawable (and the related SHAPECOLOR enum) in terms of C#:

```
// Defining COM enums in managed
// code is painless.
public enum SHAPECOLOR
{ RED, PINK, RUST };
```

```
// The managed version of IDrawable.
[ComImport,
Guid("B1691C03-7EA8-4DAB-86CC-7D6CD859671A"),
InterfaceType(ComInterfaceType.InterfaceIsDual)]
interface IDrawable
{
    [DispId(1)]
    void Draw([In] int top, [In] int left,
            [In] int bottom, [In] int right);
    [DispId(2)]
    void SetColor([In] SHAPECOLOR c);
};
```

Here, you are making use of the DispIdAttribute type to define the DISPIDs of each interface. As you are most likely able to figure out, it is critical that the values supplied to each DispIdAttribute match the values of the original COM IDL. If you build a .NET type that is binary compatible with the IDrawable interface, you might author the following:

```
[ClassInterface(ClassInterfaceType.AutoDual)]
public class Circle: IDrawable
{
    public Circle(){}
    public void Draw(int top, int left, int bottom, int right)
    {
        MessageBox.Show(String.Format("Top:{0} Left:{1} Bottom:{2} Right{3}",
            top, left, bottom, right));
    }

    public void SetColor(SHAPECOLOR c)
    {
        MessageBox.Show(String.Format("Shape color is {0}", c.ToString()));
    }
}
```

If you view the .NET metadata descriptions of the IDrawable interface using ILDasm.exe, you find that the ComImportAttribute type is not listed directly with the GuidAttribute and InterfaceType values. The essence of the ComImport attribute is cataloged, however, using the [import] tag on the interface definition:

```
.class interface private abstract auto ansi import IDrawable
{
...
} // end of class IDrawable
```

Assuming you have processed this .NET assembly using regasm.exe, you would now be able to build an unmanaged COM client that interacts with the ATL CoHexagon and C# Circle type in a binary-compatible manner (using either early or late binding).

So, to wrap up the topic of building binary-compatible .NET types, understand that just because you can define COM interfaces in managed code does not mean you have to. Typically speaking, you simply set a reference to the correct interop assembly. However, if you are building a managed application that needs to communicate to a COM class using an interface for which there is no interop assembly, it is often necessary to manually define the type in terms of managed code (recall, for example, your C# COM type library viewer in Chapter 4).

Interacting with Interop Assembly Registration

As you recall from Chapter 2, a COM in-process server defines two function exports that are called by various installation utilities (regsvr32.exe) to register or unregister the necessary registry entries. As well, when a .NET assembly is to be used by COM, the system registry must be updated using regasm.exe to effectively fool the COM runtime. As you have seen, regasm.exe catalogs the correct entries automatically. What happens, however, if you want to insert custom bits of information into the registry during the default process performed by regasm.exe?

The System.Runtime.InteropServices namespace defines two attributes for this very reason. To illustrate, assume you have a new C# code library (CustomRegAsm) that defines some number of types. When you want to allow regasm.exe to trigger a custom method during the registration process, simply define a static (or Shared in VB .NET) method that is adorned with the ComRegisterFunctionAttribute. Likewise, if you wish to provide a hook for the unregistration process, define a second static member that supports the ComUnregisterFunctionAttribute. For example:

```
public class SomeClass
{
    public SomeClass(){}

    // This method will be called when
    // regasm.exe is run against this assembly.
    [ComRegisterFunction()]
    private static void CustomReg(Type t)
    {
        MessageBox.Show(String.Format("Registering {0}",
            t.ToString()));
    }
```

```
    // This method will be called when
    // regasm.exe is run against this
    // assembly using the /u flag.
    [ComUnregisterFunction()]
    private static void CustomUnReg(Type t)
    {
        MessageBox.Show(String.Format("Registering {0}",
            t.ToString()));
    }
}
```

As you can see, the target methods must provide a single argument of type System.Type, which represents the current type in the assembly being registered for use by COM. As you might guess, regasm.exe passes in this parameter automatically.

Inserting Custom Registration Information

So, when might you need to interact with the assembly's registration process? Assume that you wish to record the date and time on which a given .NET assembly has been registered on a given user's machine. To do this, you can make use of the Microsoft.Win32 namespace, which contains a small number of types that allow you to programmatically read from and write to the system registry. For example, the CustomReg() and CustomUnReg() methods could be retrofitted as follows:

```
[ComRegisterFunction()]
private static void CustomReg(Type t)
{
    RegistryKey k =
        Registry.CurrentUser.CreateSubKey(@"Software\Intertech\CustomRegAsm");
    k.SetValue("InstallTime", DateTime.Now.ToShortTimeString());
    k.SetValue("InstallDate", DateTime.Now.ToShortDateString());
    k.Close();
}

[ComUnregisterFunction()]
private static void CustomUnReg(Type t)
{
    Registry.CurrentUser.DeleteSubKey(@"Software\Intertech\CustomRegAsm");
}
```

When you register this .NET assembly via regasm.exe, you find the following information inserted under HKEY_CURRENT_USER\Software\Intertech\CustomRegAsm (Figure 12-7).

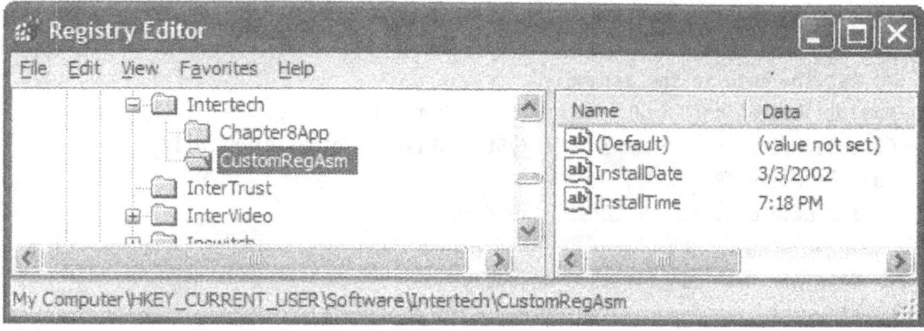

Figure 12-7. Getting involved with assembly registration

If you specify the /u flag, the information is correctly removed from the same subkey.

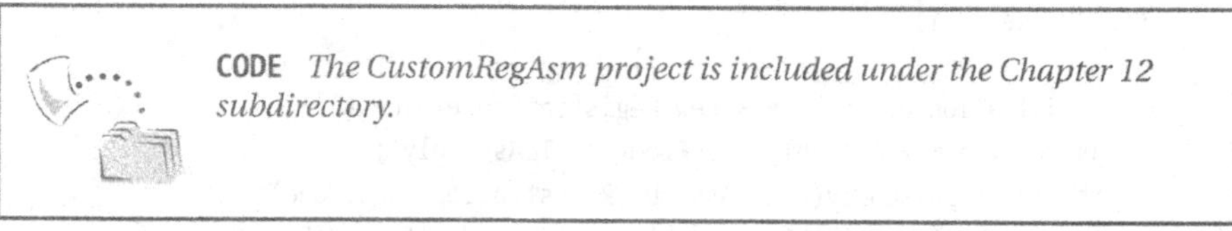

CODE *The CustomRegAsm project is included under the Chapter 12 subdirectory.*

Programmatically Converting Assemblies to COM Type Information

Recall from Chapter 9 that the System.Runtime.InteropServices.TypeLibConverter type allows you to programmatically convert COM *.tlb files into .NET interop assemblies. As mentioned at that time, this same class provides the ability to convert .NET assemblies into COM type information programmatically. Given this, let's examine the process of building a customized version of the tlbexp.exe command line utility (which as you will see looks much like the customized tlbimp.exe utility).

To begin, assume that you have a new C# console application named MyTypeLibExporter. The goal here is to allow the user to enter the path to a given .NET assembly and, using TypeLibConverter, to build a corresponding COM type library. The application's Main() method prompts for the assembly to export and passes this string into a static helper function named GenerateTLBFromAsm().

Once the *.tlb file has been generated (and stored in the application directory), the user is again prompted to determine if the .NET assembly should be registered for use by COM. If the user wishes to do so, make use of the System.Runtime.InteropServices.RegistrationServices type. Here then, is the complete implementation behind Main():

```
static void Main(string[] args)
{
    // Get the path to the assembly.
    Console.WriteLine("Please enter the path to the .NET binary");
    Console.WriteLine(@"Example: C:\MyStuff\Blah\myDotNetServer.dll");
    Console.Write("Path: ");
    string pathToAssembly = Console.ReadLine();

    // Generate type lib for this assembly.
    UCOMITypeLib i = GenerateTLBFromAsm(pathToAssembly);

    // Ask if user wants to register this server with COM.
    int regValue;
    Console.WriteLine("Would you like to register this .NET library with COM?");
    Console.Write("1 = yes or 0 = no ");
    regValue = Console.Read();

    if(regValue == 1)
    {
        RegistrationServices rs = new RegistrationServices();
        Assembly asm = Assembly.LoadFrom(pathToAssembly);
        rs.RegisterAssembly(asm, AssemblyRegistrationFlags.None);
        Console.WriteLine(".NET assembly registered with COM!");
    }
}
```

As you can see, the real workhorse of this application is the GenerateTLBFromAsm() helper function. Like the custom tlbimp.exe application you created earlier in this text, the TypeLibConverter.ConvertAssemblyToTypeLib() method requires you to pass in an instance of a class that will be called by the TypeLibConverter type to resolve references to additional assemblies as well as general reporting information. In this case, however, the class type is required to adhere to the behavior defined by ITypeLibExporterNotifySink:

```
public interface ITypeLibExporterNotifySink
{
    void ReportEvent(ExporterEventKind eventKind,
        int eventCode, string eventMsg);
    object ResolveRef(System.Reflection.Assembly assembly);
}
```

Much like the ITypeLibImporterNotifySink interface seen in Chapter 9, the implementation of ITypeLibExporterNotifySink delegates the work of resolving the referenced assembly to the static MyTypeLibExporter.GenerateTLBFromAsm() helper function:

```
// The callback object.
internal class ExporterNotiferSink : ITypeLibExporterNotifySink
{
    public void ReportEvent(ExporterEventKind eventKind,
        int eventCode, string eventMsg)
    {
         Console.WriteLine("Event reported: {0}", eventMsg);
    }

    public object ResolveRef(System.Reflection.Assembly assembly)
    {
        // If the assembly we are converting references another assembly,
        // we need to generate a *tlb for it as well.
        string pathToAsm;
        Console.WriteLine("MyTypeLibExporter encountered an assembly");
        Console.WriteLine("which referenced another assembly...");
        Console.WriteLine("Please enter the location to {0}", assembly.FullName);
        pathToAsm = Console.ReadLine();
        return MyTypeLibExporter.GenerateTLBFromAsm(pathToAsm);
    }
}
```

Before you see the details behind MyTypeLibExporter.GenerateTLBFromAsm(), you need to define some low-level COM types in terms of managed code. As you may recall from Chapter 4, when you create a custom COM type library generation tool, you need to call ICreateTypeLib.SaveAllChanges() to commit the type information to file. The trouble, however, is that the System.Runtime.InteropServices namespace does not define a managed equivalent of this method. Thus, using the tricks presented in this chapter, here is a makeshift version. It is makeshift in that I am representing the ICreateTypeInfo interface returned from the CreateTypeInfo() method (also recall from Chapter 4 that the ICreateTypeInfo interface is *huge*).

```
[ComImport,
GuidAttribute("00020406-0000-0000-C000-000000000046"),
InterfaceTypeAttribute(ComInterfaceType.InterfaceIsIUnknown),
ComVisible(false)]
internal interface UCOMICreateTypeLib
{
    // IntPtr is a hack to avoid having
    // to define ICreateTypeInfo (which is HUGE).
    IntPtr CreateTypeInfo(string name, TYPEKIND kind);
    void SetName(string name);
    void SetVersion(short major, short minor);
    void SetGuid(ref Guid theGuid);
    void SetDocString(string doc);
```

```
    void SetHelpFileName(string helpFile);
    void SetHelpContext(int helpCtx);
    void SetLcid(int lcid);
    void SetLibFlags(uint flags);
    void SaveAllChanges();
}
```

Now that you have a managed definition for use by the GenerateTLBFromAsm() method, you can flesh out the details as follows:

```
public static UCOMITypeLib GenerateTLBFromAsm(string pathToAssmebly)
{
    UCOMITypeLib managedITypeLib = null;
    ExporterNotiferSink sink = new ExporterNotiferSink();

    // Load the assembly to convert.
    Assembly asm = Assembly.LoadFrom(pathToAssmebly);
    if (asm != null)
    {
        try
        {
            // Create name of type library based on .NET assembly.
            string tlbname = asm.GetName().Name + ".tlb";

            // Convert the assembly.
            ITypeLibConverter TLBConv = new TypeLibConverter();
            managedITypeLib = (UCOMITypeLib)
                TLBConv.ConvertAssemblyToTypeLib(asm, tlbname, 0, sink);

            // Save the type library to file.
            try
            {
                UCOMICreateTypeLib managedICreateITypeLib =
                    (UCOMICreateTypeLib)managedITypeLib;
                managedICreateITypeLib.SaveAllChanges();
            }
            catch (COMException e)
            {
                throw new Exception("Error saving the type lib : "
                    + e.ErrorCode.ToString("x"));
            }
        }
        catch (Exception e)
        {
            throw new Exception("Error Converting assembly" + e);
        }
    }
    return managedITypeLib;
}
```

I'd bet the details of this method are not too shocking by this point in the text. Basically, you load the assembly based on the incoming string parameter and define a name for the type library you are creating using the assembly's name as a base. Once you have an Assembly reference, you call ConvertAssemblyToTypeLib() and specify the reference to the loaded assembly, the name of the type library to create, any additional flags (or in our case, a lack thereof), and an instance of the sink implementing ITypeLibExporterNotifySink.

The System.Object that is returned from ConvertAssemblyToTypeLib() actually represents a reference to the in-memory representation of the COM type information, which is to say, an UCOMITypeLib interface. Once you cast this type into your version of the unmanaged ICreateTypeLib type, you are able to call SaveAllChanges() to commit the information to file.

Do note that your GenerateTLBFromAsm() helper function returns the UCOMITypeLib interface to the caller. You really don't need to do so. Using this type, however, you could interact with the internal COM types defined by this type library (as illustrated in Chapter 4). In any case, this wraps up the implementation of your custom tlbexp.exe utility. Figure 12-8 shows a test drive by importing the CSharpCarLibrary.dll assembly created in Chapter 6.

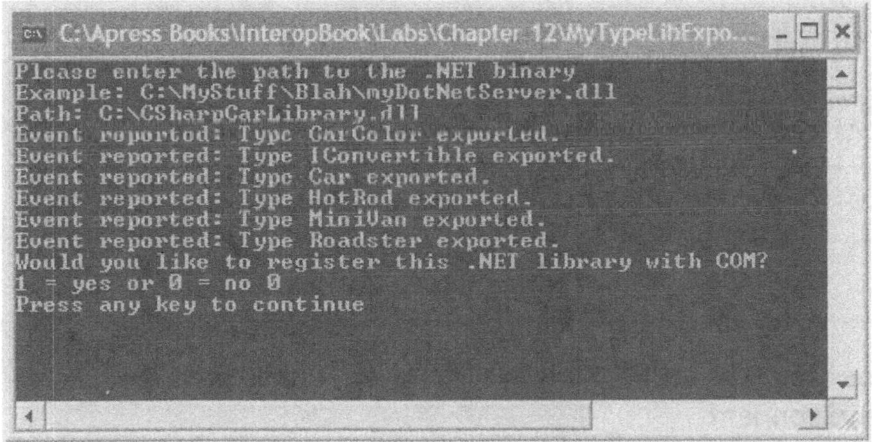

Figure 12-8. Exporting CSharpCarLibrary.dll

If you opened the generated *.tlb file using oleview.exe, you would find the COM definitions for each .NET type (Figure 12-9).

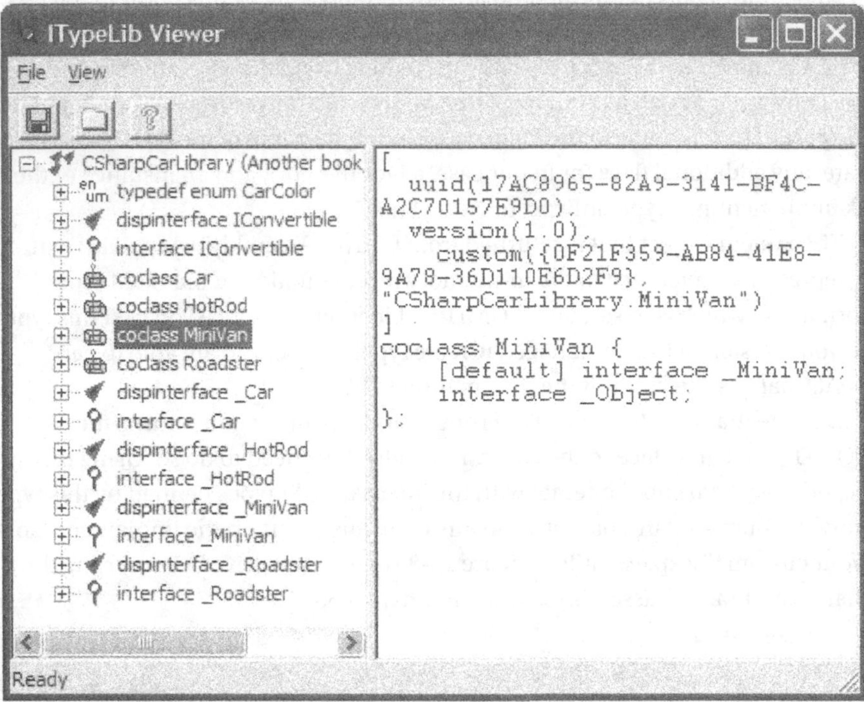

*Figure 12-9. The exported *.tlb file*

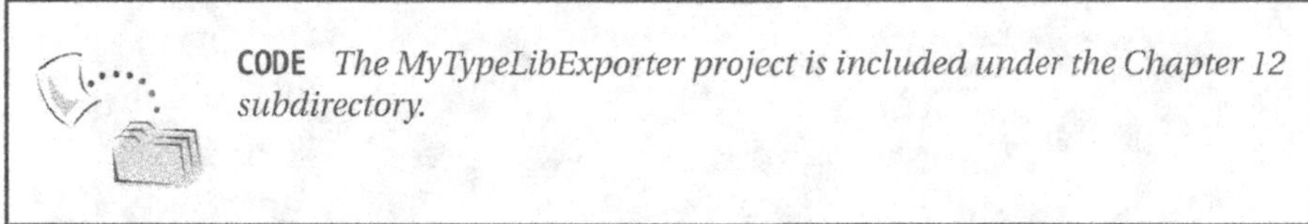

CODE *The MyTypeLibExporter project is included under the Chapter 12 subdirectory.*

Hosting the .NET Runtime from an Unmanaged Environment

The final topic of this chapter is a rather intriguing one: building a custom host for the .NET runtime (aka the CLR). Like all things under the .NET platform, the runtime engine is accessible using a set of managed types. In this case, the assembly in question is mscoree.dll (where "ee" stands for execution engine). It may surprise you to know that when you install the .NET platform, you receive a corresponding *.tlb file for mscoree.dll (mscoree.tlb) that has been properly configured in the system registry.

Because the content of mscoree.dll has been expressed in terms of COM metadata, it is possible to build a custom host using any COM-aware programming language (within the realm of the language's limitations). Do understand that regardless of which COM language you choose, when you make use of mscoree.tlb, you are also required to reference the related mscorlib.tlb file. For the example that follows, assume that you have created a new Standard EXE application using VB 6.0. This assumption aside, set a reference to each *.tlb file using the IDE's Project | References menu option (see Figure 12-10).

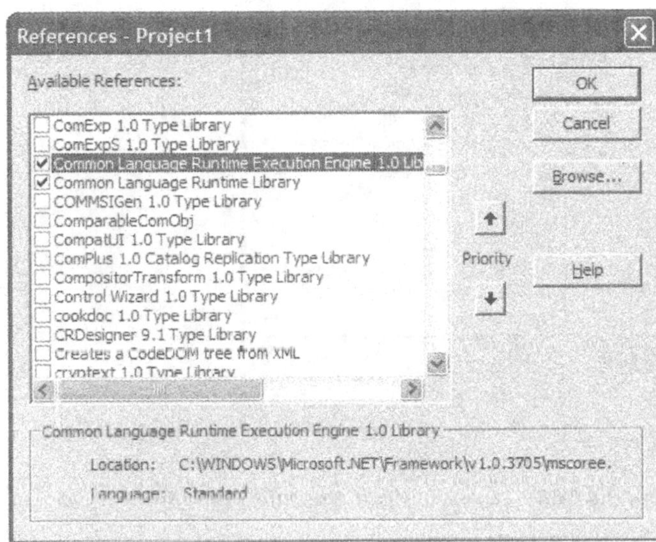

Figure 12-10. Referencing mscoree.tlb/mscorelib.tlb

Various chapters of this text have already examined some types contained within mscorlib.tlb, but what of mscoree.tlb? Like any loaded type library, the VB 6.0 Object Browser allows you to view the contained types. As you can see from Figure 12-11, despite the exotic nature of this exported assembly, mscoree.tlb defines a surprisingly small number of items.

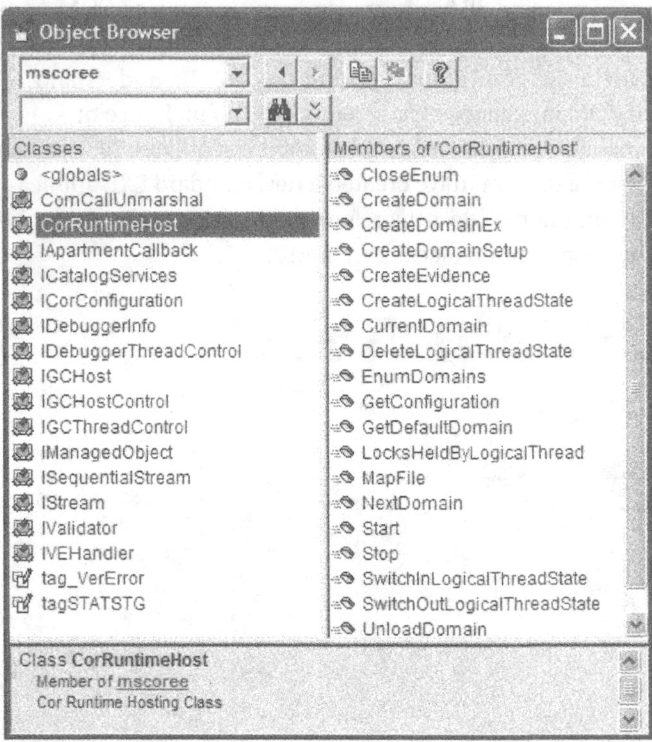

Figure 12-11. The crux of the CLR in terms of COM type information

A full treatment of each and every type defined in mscoree.dll is beyond the scope of this text. Luckily, you are able to build a custom CLR host using a single type: CorRuntimeHost. This single .NET class type implements a set of interfaces (also defined within mscoree.tlb) that provide the following functionality:

- The ability to load and unload .NET application domains
- The ability to manipulate the .NET garbage collector
- The ability to validate code within a given .NET assembly
- The ability to interact with a given debugger attached to the current process

So, given that mscoree.tlb defines the types you need to build a custom CLR host, the next logical question is when you might want to do this. Besides the fact that building a custom host is extremely interesting in its own right, there is a practical reason to do so. When you build a custom host from unmanaged code, you are able to dynamically load .NET assemblies for use by COM, without having to register the assembly using regasm.exe.

Building a Custom Host

The first detail of your VB 6.0 host is to establish a valid application domain to host the loaded assemblies. As you may know, under the .NET platform an application domain is a unit of isolated execution within a Win32 process (similar in function to the apartment architecture of classic COM). Just as a process may contain numerous application domains, a given application domain may contain numerous .NET assemblies. You are able to represent a given application domain using the System.AppDomain type.

Given this, the Form_Load() event handler creates an instance of CorRuntimeHost. Once the host has started, obtain a valid AppDomain via CorRuntimeHost.GetDefaultDomain(). The Form_Unload() event handler shuts down the CLR via the aptly named CorRuntimeHost.Stop(). Here is the story thus far:

```
' The types we need to host the CLR.
Private myAppDomain As AppDomain
Private myCLRHost As CorRuntimeHost

' Load the CLR and set app domain.
Private Sub Form_Load()
    Set myCLRHost = New CorRuntimeHost
    myCLRHost.Start
    myCLRHost.GetDefaultDomain myAppDomain
End Sub

' Unload the CLR.
Private Sub Form_Unload(Cancel As Integer)
    myCLRHost.Stop
End Sub
```

Now assume that the main Form has three VB 6.0 Button types. The Click event handler of the first button (btnListLoadedAsms_Click()) obtains and displays the list of each assembly currently hosted by the default application domain. To do this, you are able to obtain an array of Assembly types from the GetAssemblies() method of the AppDomain type. To display the name of each assembly, you are able to simply make use of the Assembly.FullName property:

```
' List all the loaded assemblies.
Private Sub btnListLoadedAsms_Click()
    Dim loadedAsms() As Assembly
    loadedAsms = myAppDomain.GetAssemblies()
```

```
    Dim theAsms As String
    Dim i As Integer
    For i = 0 To UBound(loadedAsms)
        theAsms = theAsms + loadedAsms(i).FullName + vbLf
    Next
    MsgBox theAsms
End Sub
```

The next Button type is responsible for loading the System.Collections.dll assembly from the GAC to exercise the ArrayList type. Note how the CreateInstance() method requires you to send in (a) the friendly name of the assembly containing the type and (b) the fully qualified name of the type itself. What is returned from AppDomain.CreateInstance() is an ObjectHandle type, which provides the ability to obtain the underlying type using the Unwrap() method:

```
' Load a type from the GAC.
Private Sub btnLoadFromGAC_Click()
    Dim arLst As ArrayList
    Dim obj As ObjectHandle
    Set obj = myAppDomain.CreateInstance("mscorlib",
        "System.Collections.ArrayList")
    Set arLst = obj.Unwrap

    arLst.Add "Hello there!"
    arLst.Add 12
    arLst.Add True

    Dim items As String
    items = items + arLst(0) + vbLf
    items = items + CStr(arLst(1)) + vbLf
    items = items + CStr(arLst(2)) + vbLf

    MsgBox items
End Sub
```

If you run the application at this point, once you load System.Collection.dll, you find the message displayed in Figure 12-12.

Figure 12-12. Interacting with System.Collections.dll

The final button of your VB 6.0 Form type is responsible for loading a private, and unregistered, .NET assembly. To ensure that this example illustrates the point of loading unregistered .NET binaries, assume you have the following trivial C# class definition, defined in an assembly named (of course) UnregisteredAssembly:

```
using System;
using System.Runtime.InteropServices;

namespace UnregisteredAssembly
{
    [ClassInterface(ClassInterfaceType.AutoDual)]
    public class AnotherAdder
    {
        public AnotherAdder(){}
        public int Add(int x, int y)
        { return x + y;}
    }
}
```

Now, although you do not need to register this assembly, you still need to generate type information for your VB 6.0 client. Thus, run tlbexp.exe against this binary, and place the *.tlb and UnregisteredAssembly.dll files in the same directory as the current VB 6.0 project (Figure 12-13).

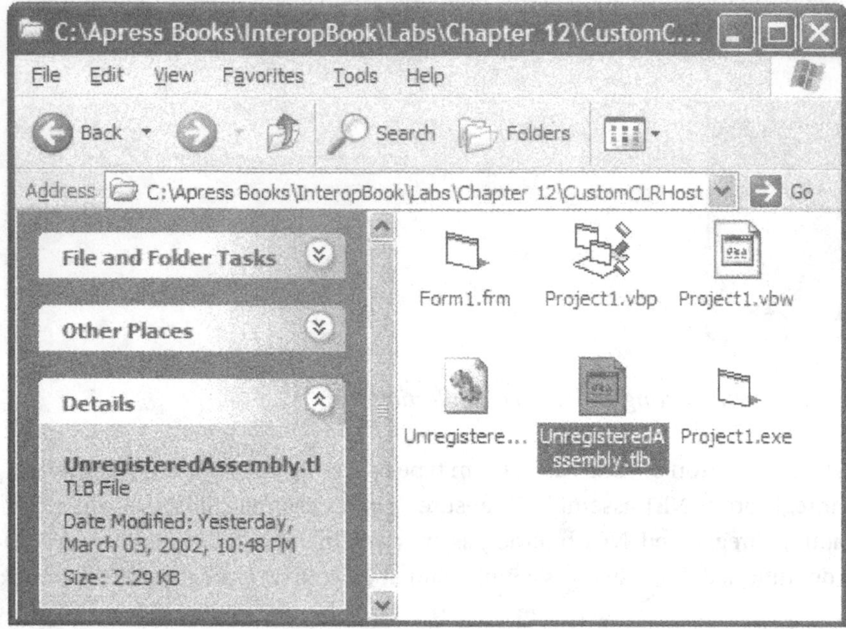

*Figure 12-13. Configuring the unregistered assembly and related *.tlb file*

Now that you have a private assembly, you are able to write the following event handler for the Form's final Button type:

```
' NOTE!!!  Because VB projects do not directly
' run from the application directory within
' the IDE, you will
' need to run the EXE to use this function.
Private Sub btnLoadFromPrivateAsm_Click()
    Dim adder As AnotherAdder
    Dim obj As ObjectHandle
    Set obj = myAppDomain.CreateInstance("UnregisteredAssembly", _
        "UnregisteredAssembly.AnotherAdder")
    Set adder = obj.Unwrap
    MsgBox adder.Add(99, 3)
End Sub
```

As you can gather from the lengthy code comment, before you can test this final bit of functionality, you need to build the VB 6.0 application (File | Make) and run the application outside the VB IDE. Once you have built the EXE, simply double-click the executable file. If you loaded UnmanagedAssembly.dll and System.Collections.dll via the correct Button types, you would now find the results shown in Figure 12-14 when you click on the "list all loaded assemblies" Button type.

Figure 12-14. Documenting loaded assemblies

With your custom host complete, you come to the end of Chapter 12. As illustrated by this example, when you build a custom host for the CLR, you are able to avoid the process of registering .NET assemblies prior to building COM clients that consume them. If you want to dive into further details of the functionality of mscoree.dll, be sure to check out the tool-builders documents included with the .NET SDK (installed by default under C:\Program Files\Microsoft Visual Studio .NET\FrameworkSDK\Tool Developers Guide\docs).

CODE *The UnmanagedAssembly and CustomCLRHost projects are located in the Chapter 12 subdirectory.*

Summary

The chapter wraps up your investigation of COM-to-.NET interoperability issues. As you have seen, just as a COM type can implement .NET interfaces to achieve type compatibility, a .NET type can implement COM interfaces to achieve binary compatibility with related coclasses. Using managed code, you are able to build managed representations of COM types to avoid creating a dependency with a related interop assembly.

Another key aspect of this chapter illustrated how you are able to build a customized version of tlbexp.exe. While you may never be in the position of needing to do so, this should solidify your understanding of what this tool does on your behalf. The final major topic presented here illustrated how you can interact with the CLR via mscoree.tlb to build a custom host from unmanaged code.

At this point in the text, you have drilled quite deeply into the COM and .NET type systems, and you have seen numerous aspects of the interoperability layer. Before I wrap things up, the next (and final) chapter addresses the topic of building COM+ types (i.e., configured components) using managed code.

CHAPTER 13

Building Serviced Components (COM+ Interop)

The .NET platform provides a specific assembly, System.EnterpriseServices.dll, which allows you to build managed code libraries that can leverage the services provided by the COM+ runtime. Thus, using C#, VB .NET, or any other managed language, you are able to build types that can support the same behaviors (for example, automated transactions, JITA, role-based security, and whatnot) as a classic COM+ type. The point of this chapter is to provide an overview of the key features of COM+, as well as to dig into the details of building configured components under the .NET platform. As you will see, building COM+-aware .NET types is similar to the process of exposing .NET types to a classic COM client (as described in Chapters 10 through 12).

Now, to be sure, a single chapter cannot cover every possible detail of building serviced components. However, by the time you have completed this material, you will have written a three-tier application that illustrates the core services provided by the COM+ runtime and will be in a perfect position to explore additional features of COM+ within the world of managed code.

The MTS, COM+, Component Services Name Game

Microsoft-centric developers are without a doubt aware of the role of Microsoft Transaction Server (MTS). MTS was, in essence, an application server designed to host classic COM servers in the middle tier under Windows NT. Using MTS, developers were able to create highly scalable systems complete with numerous bells and whistles. However, the infrastructure of MTS was incomplete at the time of its release (for example, no support for object pooling) and was not fully integrated with COM proper. In effect, MTS was a subsystem, living side-by-side with classic COM, that produced some rather inelegant constructs (competing registry entries among the most notable).

With the release of Windows 2000, MTS was integrated with COM itself and renamed COM+ 1.0. In addition to streamlining the underlying programming model, COM+ also introduced further services for objects in the middle tier. For example, under COM+, coclasses can support object constructor strings, participate in an object pool, make use of loosely coupled events (LCEs), as well as leverage an object-oriented wrapper (Queued Components) around the raw MSMQ protocol.

Windows XP has further upgraded the set of services provided by the COM+ runtime by introducing COM+ 1.5 (which by the way, is fully compatible with COM+ 1.0). Some of these new features include the ability to disable and pause applications and components, configure private components, as well as expose a configured application as an NT service or XML Web service. Although the screen shots shown in this chapter all make use of COM+ 1.5 dialog boxes, I mainly focus on the services that are common to both COM+ 1.0 and 1.5 (with COM+ 1.5-specific features clearly noted).

Now, with the advent of .NET, COM+ is more commonly referred to as *Component Services*, because it is possible to build .NET code libraries that can also be placed under the loving arms of the COM+ runtime layer. Like a classic COM type, a .NET type is also able to make use of just-in-time activation (JITA), object constructor strings, object pooling, and automatic transactions. In short, anything that could be done using a classic COM object can now be done using managed code (and much more easily I might add).

Given that .NET has nothing to do with classic COM, the shift from "COM+" to "Component Services" is a justifiable name change. During this chapter, keep in mind that when discussing the topic of COM+-aware .NET types, I am really describing Component Services (although I will typically use the term "COM+" for easy reading). Now that you have a handle on the current terminology, let's review exactly what Component Services (aka COM+) brings to the table.

Recapping Component Services

As mentioned, COM+ (Component Services) is an application server that provides the ability to host classic COM and .NET types in a manner fitting for an enterprise-level, n-tier environment. For example, assume you have created a classic COM binary that is in charge of connecting to a data source (perhaps using classic ADO) to update a number of related tables. Once this COM server has been installed under Component Services, it inherits a number of core traits, such as support for declarative transactions, JIT activation/ASAP deactivation (to increase scalability), as well as a very nice role-based security model.

For a given object to make use of the services provided by the Component Services runtime, it must be explicitly installed into a logical entity termed a *COM+ application*. The COM+ infrastructure makes use of a distinct registration database called (not surprisingly) the *COM+ Catalog*, which maintains all relevant settings for the COM+ applications (and their components) configured on a given machine. Once an object has been placed into a given COM+ application, the *.dll is referred to as a *configured component* as opposed to a *nonconfigured component*, which is a *.dll that is not logged within the COM+ Catalog.

All configured components have an associated context object used to represent any number of specific traits about how the object is being employed. For example, the context object may contain information about the security credentials of the caller, information regarding the object's transactional outcome (that is, the happy bit), and information regarding whether the object is ready to be reclaimed from memory (that is, the done bit). In addition to object-level context, COM+ supports *call-level context*, used to hold contextual information regarding the current method invocation. More on the topic of context in just a bit.

By and large, configured components are designed to be stateless entities. This simply refers to the fact that the object can be created and destroyed by the runtime (to reclaim scarce resources) without affecting the connected "base client" (the entity making calls to the COM+ runtime layer). In this light, configured components play the role of traditional business objects that perform a unit of work for the base client and quietly pass away. If the base client makes a call on the object that has been reclaimed, the COM+ runtime simply creates a new copy (thus the motivation for building stateless types). Formally speaking, this process is termed *just-in-time activation* (JITA), which is used in conjunction with ASAP deactivation. In addition to the pervious traits, here is a quick rundown of some additional COM+-specific behaviors:

- Enhanced support for declarative programming. COM+ builds on the declarative programming model used with classic COM and MTS. Using a declarative approach, programmers are able to change how a configured object responds at runtime by changing its settings at *design time* via a friendly user interface called the *Component Services Explorer*. In this way, you are not required to reengineer an existing code base when you wish to alter the functionality of a given type. As mentioned, the settings established using the Component Services Explorer are logged in the COM+ Catalog.

- Support for poolable objects. The COM+ runtime can maintain a collection of active objects that can be quickly handed off to the base client. This trait can help decrease the time the base client needs to wait to be returned an interface reference from the COM+ type.

- A new event model termed *loosely coupled events*, or LCEs. The LCE model of COM+ allows clients and COM+ types to communicate in a disconnected manner. This means that a given COM+ class can send out an event without any foreknowledge of who (if anyone) is listening. Also, a COM+ client can receive events without needing to be connected to (or aware of) the sender.

- Support for object construction strings. Given that classic COM does not allow the client to directly trigger class constructors, COM+ introduced a standard interface (IObjectConstruct) that gives the coclass the ability to receive any start-up parameters in the form of a COM BSTR (represented as a System.String in managed code).

- The ability to control the queuing behavior of a COM+ type in a declarative manner. As you may know, Microsoft Message Queue (MSMQ) is an enterprise-level messaging service that entails lots of boilerplate grunge. COM+ introduces Queued Components (QC), which hide much of this grunge from view.

As you can see, the services provide by COM+ can greatly simplify the development of distributed applications. The only problem is that these services were originally intended for use by classic COM objects. To allow .NET developers to obtain these same benefits, the base class libraries provide numerous .NET types defined in the System.EnterpriseServices namespace. For the time being, however, let's check out the COM+ runtime environment in greater detail.

Reviewing the COM+ Runtime Environment

The first thing to be aware of is that the COM+ runtime only hosts objects that have been packaged into a binary *.dll (objects contained within *.exe files cannot be hosted by the COM+ runtime). As you know, however, *.dll files must always be contained within a given process. Because COM+ is all about facilitating the development of distributed applications, you may wonder exactly who or what is in charge of hosting a configured *.dll on behalf of the remote base client. The short (incomplete) answer is that when a local or remote client creates an instance of a configured component, the COM+ runtime hosts the *.dll within a surrogate named dllhost.exe. The situation changes just a bit if the types have been configured as a library application (defined later in this chapter).

As you would guess, the COM+ runtime does a great deal more than simply place DLLs within an instance of dllhost.exe. Specifically, the COM+ runtime places an activated object within a given *context*. So what is context? Basically, a context is the runtime execution scope of a configured object. In even simpler terms, context is simply a place to store objects.

Reviewing Object Context

Each COM+ contextual boundary is represented by a runtime-generated object, called a *context object,* which implements four key interfaces. The first two interfaces, IObjectContext and IObjectContextActivity, are legacy MTS interfaces, supported for purposes of backward compatibility. Of these two MTS-centric interfaces, I would assume that IObjectContext is by far the most familiar. Here is the managed definition:

```
// This MTS style interface allows a
// configured component to interact with
// its context object.
interface IObjectContext
{
    object CreateInstance(Guid rclsid, Guid riid);
    void DisableCommit();
    void EnableCommit();
    bool IsCallerInRole(string role);
    bool IsInTransaction();
    bool IsSecurityEnabled();
    void SetAbort();
    void SetComplete();
}
```

The final two interfaces (IObjectContextInfo and IContextState) are only available under COM+, and mimic and enhance the behaviors found in the legacy MTS interfaces. Although it is possible to access the functionality of each of the four interfaces supported by the context object from managed code, you will most likely prefer the improved granularity of the COM+-specific interface types. This said, here are the managed definitions of IObjectContextInfo and IContextState:

```
// Used to obtain various statistics about the current state of affairs.
interface IObjectContextInfo
{
    Guid GetActivityId();
    Guid GetContextId();
    object GetTransaction();
    Guid GetTransactionId();
    bool IsInTransaction();
}

// Used to control object deactivation and transaction voting.
// Basically, this is a more granular representation of SetComplete()
// and SetAbort().
interface IContextState
{
```

```
    bool GetDeactivateOnReturn();
    System.EnterpriseServices.TransactionVote GetMyTransactionVote();
    void SetDeactivateOnReturn(bool bDeactivate);
    void SetMyTransactionVote(System.EnterpriseServices.TransactionVote txVote);
}
```

Using these interfaces, a configured component is able to read and set its contextual settings including transactional data, lifetime management data, and various security settings. If you are coming to .NET from a classic COM+ background, you are most likely aware that a configured classic COM+ type can obtain a reference to these interfaces using the CoGetObjectContext() API function. When you are building managed configured types, however, you do not use these interfaces directly (in fact, they are marked as internal types to the System.EnterpriseServices.dll assembly). Instead, you make use of various static members of the ContextUtil type that you will get to know shortly.

Reviewing Call Context

In addition to the context object, COM+ also supports a *call object* that is created each time a member is invoked on a configured component and is destroyed as soon as the method completes. The COM+ call object supports two interfaces, ISecurityCallContext and IServerSecurity, which provide information regarding the call-level security settings for a given method invocation. The managed definition of the key call-level interface, ISecurityCallContext, is as follows:

```
// Obtain call level security traits.
interface ISecurityCallContext
{
    int Count { get; }
    void GetEnumerator(ref System.Collections.IEnumerator pEnum);
    object GetItem(string name);
    bool IsCallerInRole(string role);
    bool IsSecurityEnabled();
    bool IsUserInRole(ref Object pUser, string role);
}
```

Again, if you have a background in classic COM+, you are aware that configured components may interact with the call object using the CoGetCallContext() API function. However, under .NET, similar call-level information may be obtained using various static members of the SecurityCallContext type. To summarize the story thus far, ponder Figure 13-1, which illustrates the basic relationship between these core items of the COM+ runtime (stubs and proxies removed for clarity).

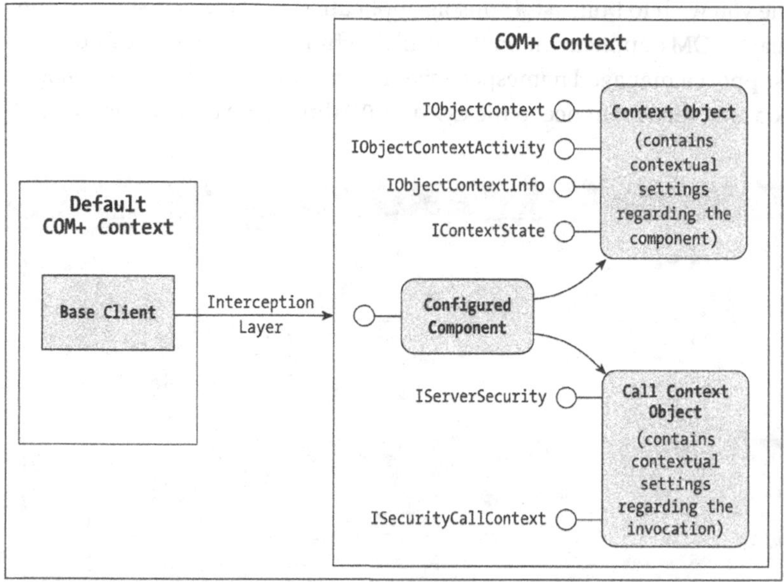

Figure 13-1. Clients, objects, and context

Note that under the COM+ model, *all* objects must belong to a context (such as the nonconfigured base client). Formally speaking, the contextual boundary that is used to host types that have not been listed in the COM+ Catalog is termed the *default context.*

The Role of the COM+ Catalog

Unlike classic MTS, contextual information for a configured component is not stored in the system registry. Rather, COM+ components maintain contextual information within the COM+ Catalog. As mentioned, the COM+ Catalog is a machine-wide database that is used to hold any and all information for every configured component on a given machine. As you may already be aware, you are not going to find a regedit.exe-like tool that allows you to edit the catalog directly. In fact, the exact name and location of the COM+ Catalog is officially undocumented.

When you wish to manipulate the COM+ Catalog, you will most likely make use of the Component Service Explorer to do so. Under the hood, however, this GUI-based tool makes use of a classic COM object model contained within ComAdmin.dll. Using this COM server, you are able to build applications that perform the same exact functions as the Component Services Explorer. Although this chapter does not describe the complete object model maintained by the ComAdmin.dll, let's see a simple example.

Assume you wish to build a C# console application capable of displaying the names of each COM+ application on the local machine. Given that .NET does not currently support a managed namespace that interacts with the COM+ Catalog, the first step is to set a reference to the COM+ 1.0 Admin type library (Figure 13-2).

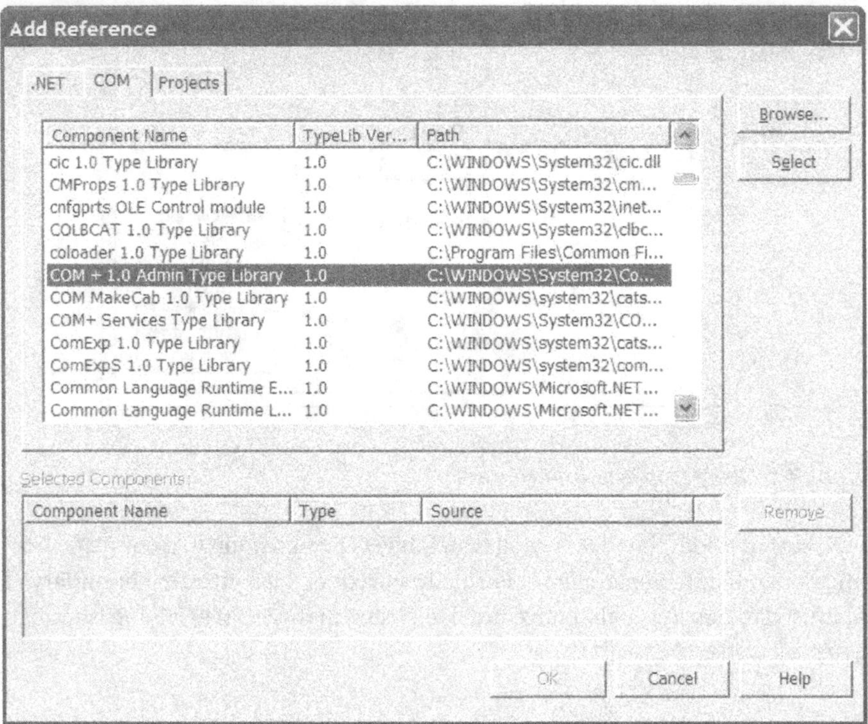

Figure 13-2. Referencing comadmin.dll

To take ComAdmin.dll out for a test drive, create a simple Main() loop that is responsible for obtaining a collection of all COM+ applications on the current machine using the generated COMAdminCatalogClass type. If you have never programmatically manipulated the COM+ Catalog, just understand that the COMAdminCatalog is the point of entry into the object model. The key method of this type is GetCollection(), which takes a string parameter used to identify the collection you are requesting ("Applications" in this case). Once the collection has been filled using the Populate() method, you are able to iterate over each member in the collection (using ICatalogObject) and display the relevant information. Consider the following code listing:

```
namespace ComPlusCatalogReader
{
    class ComPlusAppReader
    {
        [STAThread]
        static void Main(string[] args)
        {
            // Load all the COM+ apps into a COM collection.
            COMAdminCatalogClass comcat = new COMAdminCatalogClass();
            ICatalogCollection apps =
                (ICatalogCollection)comcat.GetCollection("Applications");
            apps.Populate();

            // Iterate over the collection.
            foreach(ICatalogObject app in apps)
            {
                // Print the name of the COM+ application.
                Console.WriteLine("COM+ App: {0}", app.Name.ToString());
            }
        }
    }
}
```

Figure 13-3 shows a possible test run. (Your application names will vary!)

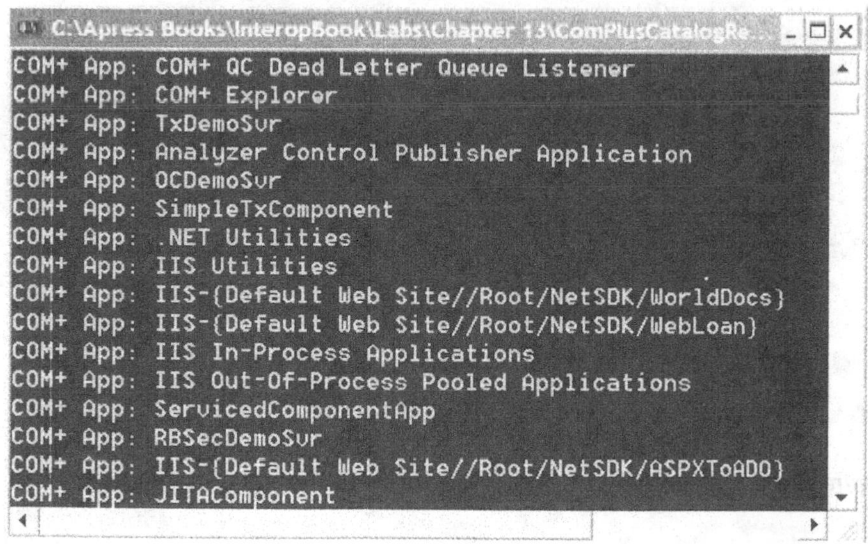

Figure 13-3. Programmatically interacting with the COM+ Catalog

CODE *The ComPlusCatalogReader application is located under the Chapter 13 subdirectory.*

The Component Service Explorer

To be sure, if you were to make direct use of ComAdmin.dll every time you wish to build and configure a new COM+ application, life would be unnecessarily complex. The Component Services Explorer (aka COM+ Explorer) is a GUI-based tool that is used to configure the serviced components on a given machine (including remote machines if you have the correct administrative privileges). Like most GUI-based configuration tools that ship with Windows 2000/Windows XP, the Component Services Explorer is yet another Microsoft Management Console (MMC) snap-in that can be launched from the Windows Control Panel. Simply open the Administrative Tools directory and double-click the Component Services icon (Figure 13-4).

Figure 13-4. The Component Service Explorer

Creating COM+ Applications

The most basic aspect of the Component Services Explorer is the ability to create new COM+ applications using the COM+ Application Install Wizard (Figure 13-5).

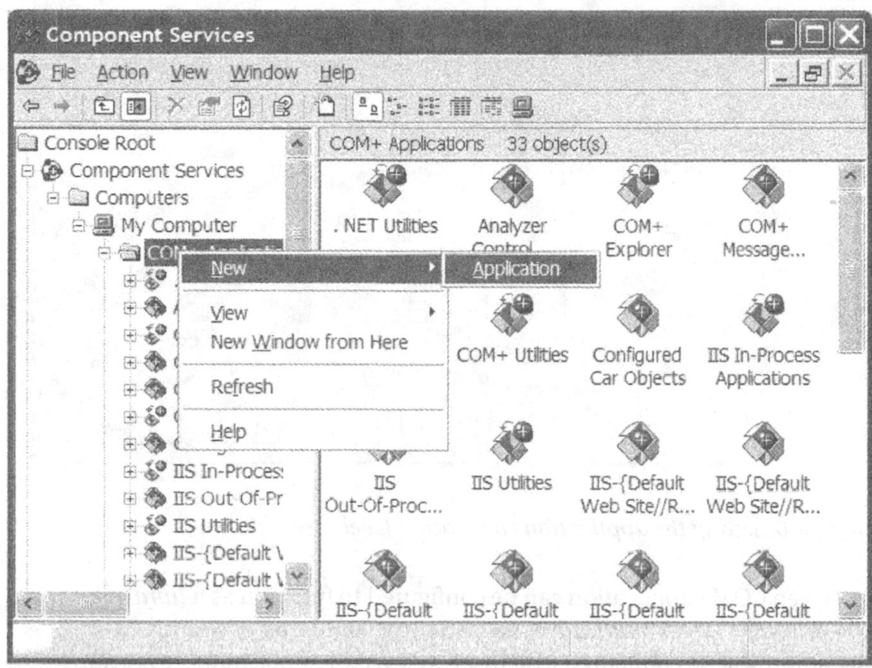

Figure 13-5. Declaratively creating a new COM+ application

The resulting wizard allows you to create a new empty COM+ application (as well as install existing COM+ applications) and establish the mode of activation and identity of the contained types. Assume you wish to create a new application named "COM+ Message Application". For the current discussion, the most important configuration detail is the activation mode (Figure 13-6).

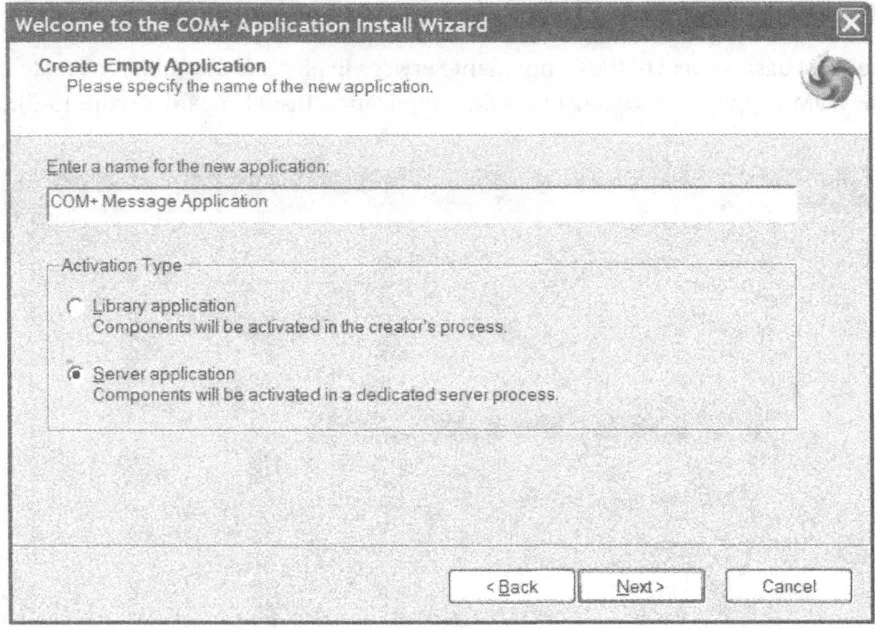

Figure 13-6. Setting the application's activation level

A given COM+ application can be configured to function as a *library application* or a *server application*. To be honest, almost all of your COM+ applications will be configured to activate as a server application. However, Table 13-1 illustrates the differences between each application type.

Table 13-1. Server Activation Modes

COM+ Application Activation Mode	**Meaning in Life**
Library applications	Library applications are loaded directly into the context of the calling application. This type of COM+ application cannot be accessed remotely and thus must be installed on the same machine as the calling client. Furthermore, library applications cannot make use of COM+ role-based security and cannot contain queued components.
Server applications	The most common (and useful) choice. Server applications run under dllhost.exe and may be accessed out of process. Also, server applications can participate in the COM+ role-based security model and may contain queued components.

Once you have finished creating the new COM+ application, you find a new application icon representing the package (Figure 13-7). Of course, the initial settings you established using COM+ Application Install Wizard can be changed after the fact by opening the property page for your new application (simply right-click the icon). In addition, this same property page allows you to establish additional details of your new COM+ application such as server shutdown, security settings, and whatnot (you will see specific details during the course of this chapter).

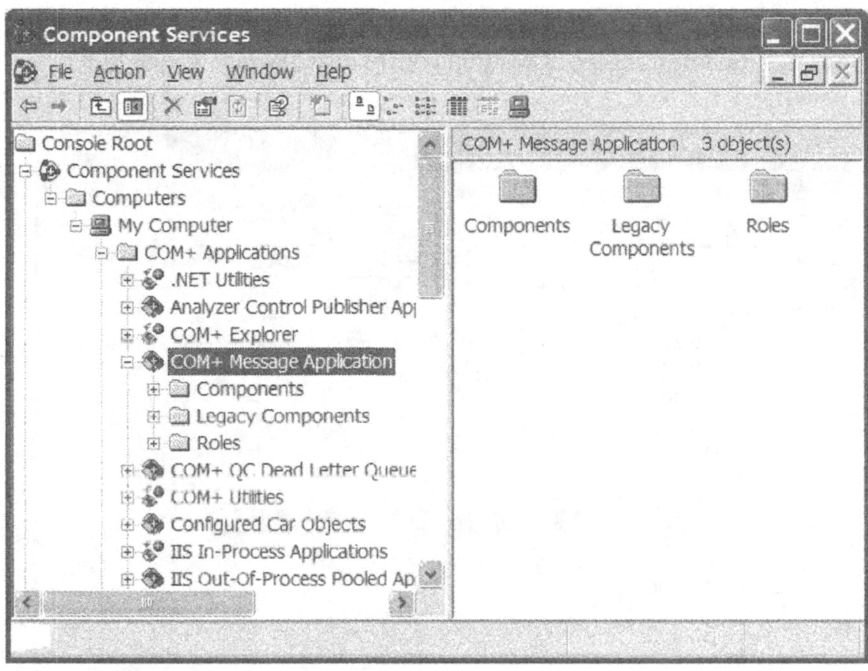

Figure 13-7. Your new COM+ application

In addition to creating a new COM+ application using the COM+ Application Install Wizard, you are also able to programmatically establish a new application using a set of COM types that directly allow you to manipulate the COM+ Catalog. Finally, and most important for .NET developers, COM+ applications can be configured using a command line tool named regsvcs.exe. You will get to know the functionality of this tool in just a bit. However, for the time being, let's build a classic COM type to install into your new COM+ application.

A Classic COM+ Example

By way of a simple example, assume you have launched VB 6.0 (or if you wish, ATL) and selected a new ActiveX DLL named ClassicVBComPlusServer. The only member of the [default] _MsgClass interface is the following public subroutine:

```
' _MsgClass member.
Public Sub DisplayMessage(ByVal s As String)
    MsgBox s, , "Client says:"
End Sub
```

Once compiled, the ClassicComPlusServer.dll can be placed under management of the COM+ runtime using the COM+ Component Install Wizard (Figure 13-8).

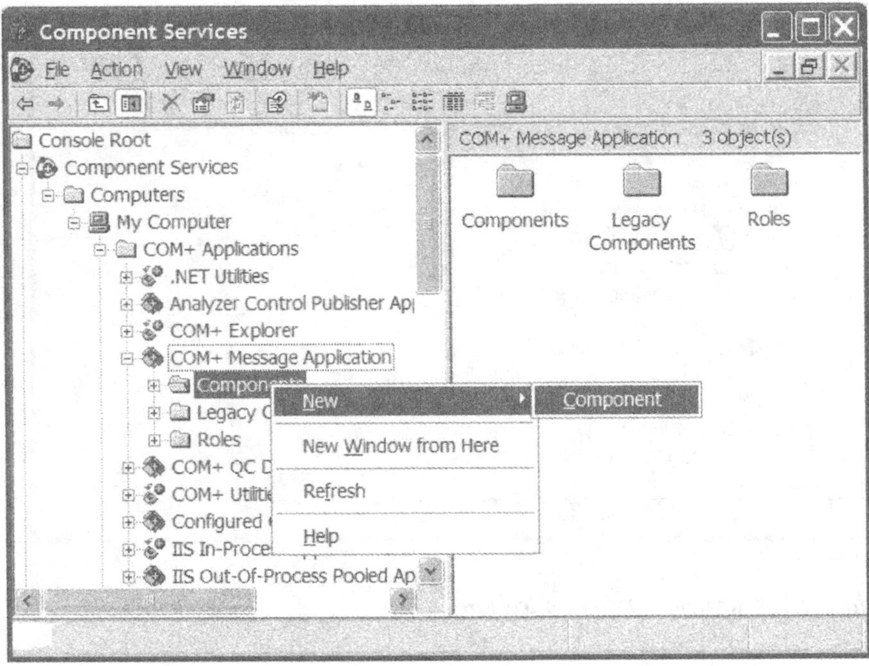

Figure 13-8. Installing configured components into a COM+ application

Once you skip past the welcome screen, you are asked to choose from one of three possible component types; for the current discussion select "Install new component(s)". Navigate to the location of your ClassicComPlusServer.dll COM server and install the component. If you now check out the Components subfolder of your COM+ application, you find the MsgClass coclass, its interfaces, and their methods are each listed under a related directory (Figure 13-9).

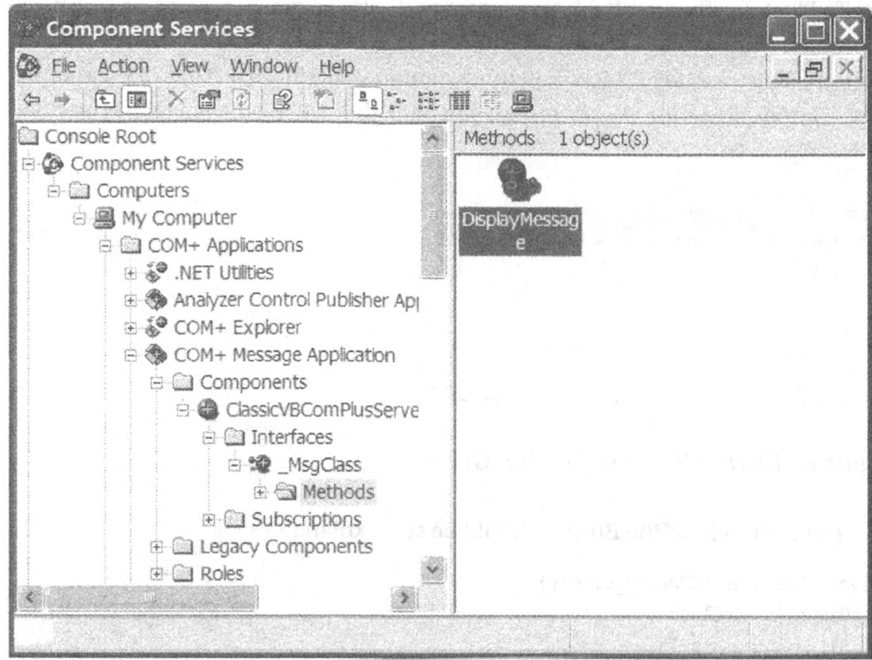

Figure 13-9. The installed COM+ type

Like a COM+ application, configured classes, interfaces, and methods each support a related property page to allow you to further configure the underlying characteristics of a given entity. Again, you will see details where necessary; however, for the time being let's build a simple VB 6.0 COM client to interact with the configured COM+ type.

CODE *The ClassicVBComPlusServer application is included under the Chapter 13 subdirectory.*

Building a VB 6.0 COM+ Client

Like classic COM, Component Services honors the trait of location transparency. When you are interacting with a configured type (COM based or .NET based), the base client is not required to perform any special processing to trigger the underlying members of the supported interfaces. In fact, the base client is completely encapsulated from the location and configuration details of the type, and has no clue that the type has been installed under COM+ management.

To illustrate, fire up VB 6.0 once again and select a new Standard EXE project workspace (named Vb6ClassicComPlusClient) and select the server's type information using the Add | Project References menu selection. The GUI of the main Form simply allows the user to enter a message that will be displayed by the COM+ type (Figure 13-10).

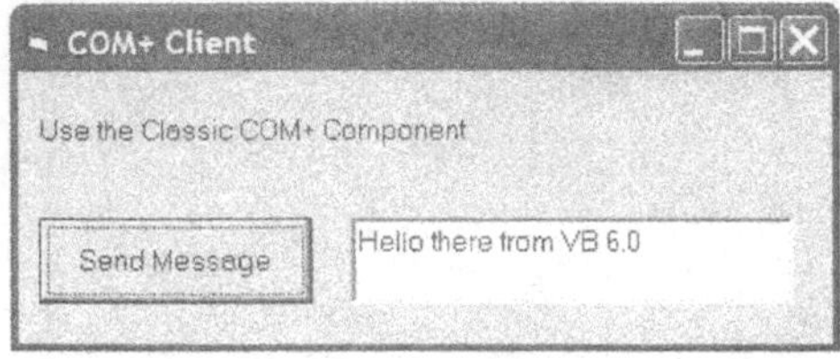

Figure 13-10. The VB 6.0 COM+ client GUI

The code behind the Button should be self-explanatory:

```
Private Sub btnSendMesage_Click()
    Dim o As MsgClass
    Set o = New MsgClass
    o.DisplayMessage txtMessage.Text
End Sub
```

When you run the application, you will be able to see that the configured type has been activated by investigating the Status view of the Components folder (Figure 13-11).

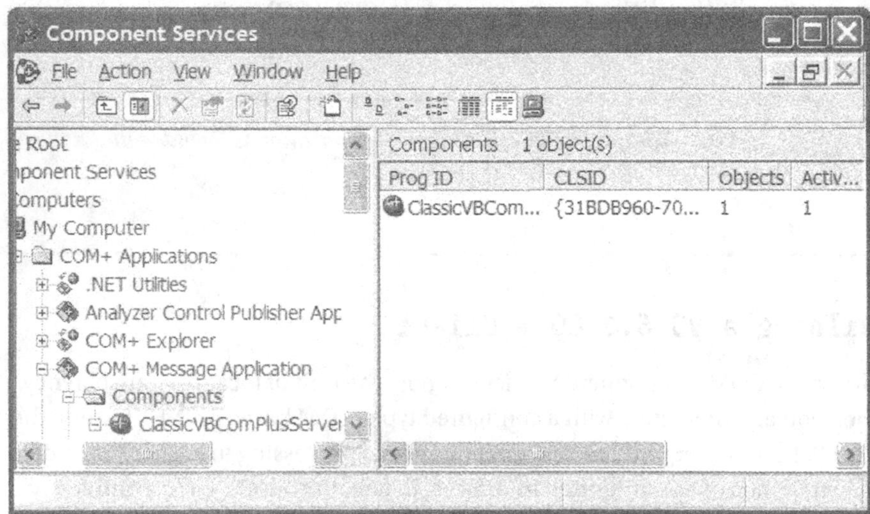

Figure 13-11. The activated COM+ type

As you can see, using classic COM, it is possible to install a vanilla-flavored COM server and have it run as a configured component. However, when you wish to build a .NET code library, you are required to add some supporting infrastructure using the types of the System.EnterpriseServices namespace. Before you check out this key group of .NET types, a brief word on deploying COM+ applications.

CODE *The VB6ClassicComPlusClient application is included under the Chapter 13 subdirectory.*

Deploying COM+ Applications

When you are testing and exploring component services from the comfort of your own home or office, the chances are good that you have a single machine that contains the base client as well as the configured types. However, when it comes time to deploy your COM+ application across the enterprise, the Component Service Explorer provides two key options, both of which are available using the Export command (Figure 13-12).

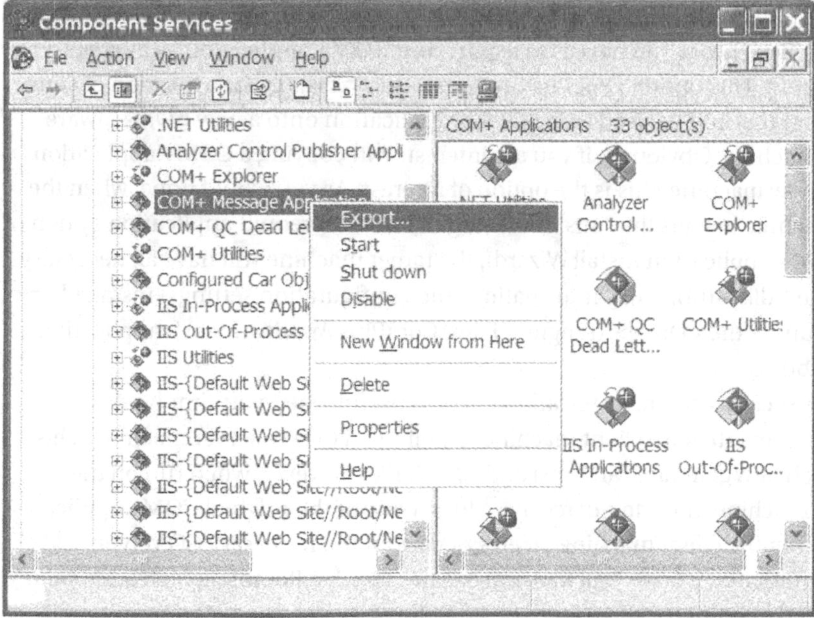

Figure 13-12. Exporting a COM+ application

The resulting wizard provides two major options (Figure 13-13).

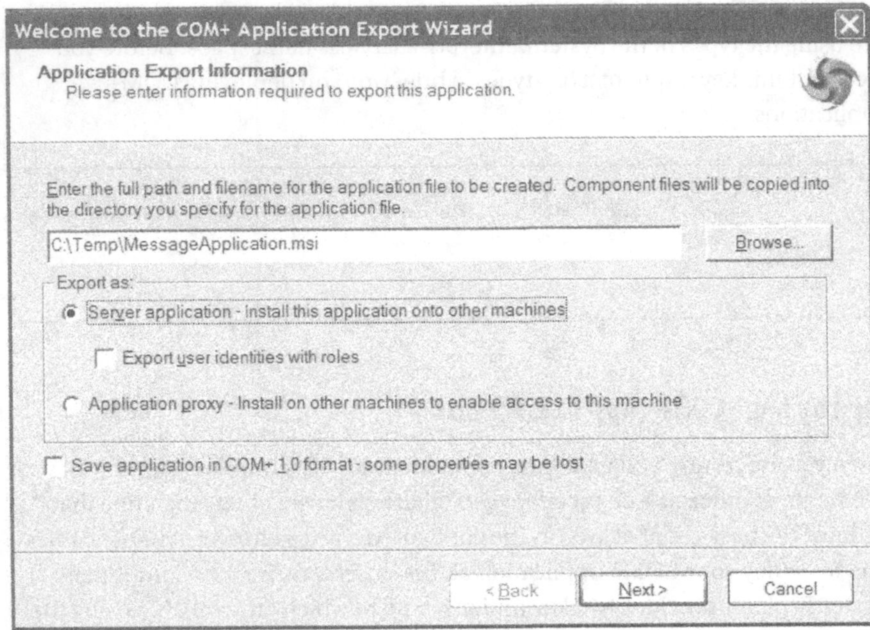

Figure 13-13. Deployment options

The first choice you have is to export your COM+ application as a server application. This option generates an *.msi and a *.cab file (at a location of your choosing) that can be used to install this application onto a new COM+-aware server machine. Obviously, if you are interested in copying a COM+ application onto a new machine, this is the option of interest. As you would hope, when the new machine installs the *.msi file (using the Install prebuilt application option of the COM+ Application Install Wizard), the target machine will have all necessary files (the *.dlls, stub/proxy information, and configuration settings) installed locally under the <Drive>:\Program Files\ComPlus Applications\{<application ID>} subdirectory.

The second option, Application Proxy, is useful when you simply wish to redirect a remote base client machine to point to a COM+ server machine. This approach also generates an *.msi and a *.cab file; however, when run on the client's machine, they do *not* receive a local copy of the original COM+ application, rather the client machine receives a copy of the necessary COM type information (the *.tlb or *.dll file) and has the AppID's RemoteServerName value retrofitted to point to the remote server. In this way, the client can simply reference the COM type information and program against the remote COM+ types as normal. At runtime, however, the client is redirected to the remote server via an intervening stub and proxy layer.

So, hopefully the previous pages have given you a better understanding of the role of COM+. Now as they say, on to the interesting stuff! The remainder of this chapter will now address how to construct .NET code libraries that are capable of leveraging the COM+ runtime layer.

The System.EnterpriseServices Namespace

As mentioned earlier in this chapter, when you wish to build configured types using a managed language, you must make use of the types found within the System.EnterpriseServices namespace. Table 13-2 documents the core types, grouped by related functionality.

Table 13-2. Core Types of the System.EnterpriseServices Namespace

Members of System.EnterpriseServices	Meaning in Life
ApplicationAccessControlAttribute ApplicationActivationAttribute ApplicationIDAttribute ApplicationNameAttribute ApplicationQueuingAttribute	These attributes are used to configure the core characteristics of the COM+ application itself (security access settings, activation mode, the identifying GUID, friendly name, and queuing behavior).
AutoCompleteAttribute	Marks a given method to automatically call SetComplete() upon successful completion.
ComponentAccessControlAttribute	Enables security checking on calls to a component.
ConstructionEnabledAttribute	Enables COM+ object construction support.
ContextUtil	Obtains information about the COM+ object context. If you have a background in classic COM+, this is basically an implementation of the IObjectContext (and related) interface(s).
DescriptionAttribute	Sets the description on an application, component, method, or interface. Values are viewable using the property page of the given item.
EventClassAttribute EventTrackingEnabledAttribute	These attributes are used when you wish to leverage the loosely coupled event (LCE) model of COM+.

Table 13-2. Core Types of the System.EnterpriseServices Namespace (continued)

Members of System.EnterpriseServices	Meaning in Life
JustInTimeActivationAttribute	This attribute turns just-in-time activation (JITA) on or off for a given class type.
ObjectPoolingAttribute	Enables and configures object pooling for a component.
PrivateComponentAttribute	Identifies a component as a private component that is only seen and activated by components in the same application. Supported only by COM+ 1.5–enabled machines.
RegistrationHelper	Allows you to programmatically install and configure assemblies in the COM+ Catalog.
SecurityCallContext SecurityCallers SecurityIdentity SecurityRoleAttribute	As you would expect, System.EnterpriseServices contains a number of types that allow you to interact with call context and the COM+ role-based security model.
ServicedComponent	Perhaps the most important type in the System.EnterpriseServices namespace. Represents the base class of all classes using COM+ services.
SharedProperty SharedPropertyGroup SharedPropertyGroupManager	System.EnterpriseServices also supports types that allow .NET objects to interact with the shared property manager (SPM) of COM+.

As you can see from Table 13-2, System.EnterpriseServices supports manipulation of the COM+ shared property manager (SPM). However, given that SPM has shown itself to hinder scalability, I do not address these types. If you have made use of SPM using classic COM, you will find the process just about identical.

Having pondered Table 13-2, the one thing that might strike you as odd is that COM+- (and MTS-) centric interfaces such as IObjectControl, IObjectContext, and IObjectConstruct are *not* visible members of the System.EnterpriseServices namespace. The reason is simple. As you already know, .NET does not demand that custom types support discrete interfaces. Thus, rather than forcing the .NET developer to implement or obtain interface references, they are able to override base class members and/or call any number of static methods of the ContextUtil and SecurityCallContext types.

Here's another key point to be mindful of: Many of the attribute types found in the System.EnterpriseServices namespace are used to ensure that when the component is installed under the management of COM+, the contained types are configured with an initial look and feel. Of course, you (or your local system administrator) are always free to alter the default values using the Component Services Explorer. In this light, understand that in many cases you are not required to apply these COM+-centric attributes to function correctly as a configured component.

The System.EnterpriseServices.ServicedComponent Type

Any .NET type that wishes to function under component services must derive (directly or indirectly) from System.EnterpriseServices.ServicedComponent, which in turn derives from ContextBoundObject. Like any .NET type, ServicedComponent supports the members of System.Object, as well as the following interfaces:

```
// The base class of all configured .NET types.
public abstract class System.EnterpriseServices.ServicedComponent :
    ContextBoundObject,
    System.EnterpriseServices.IRemoteDispatch,
    IDisposable,
    System.EnterpriseServices.IManagedObject,
    System.EnterpriseServices.IServicedComponentInfo
{…}
```

Table 13-3 documents the critical methods of the ServicedComponent type. Based on your current exposure to Component Services, you may notice that a number of the members defined by ServicedComponent echo the functionality of the standard COM+ interfaces IObjectControl and IObjectConstruct (both of which will be described shortly). Also note that types derived from ServicedComponent support two methods that allow the creator to explicitly destroy any resources held by the configured type (also described shortly).

Table 13-3. Select Members of System.EnterpriseServices.ServicedComponent

Member of ServicedComponent	Meaning in Life
Activate()	This method is called by the infrastructure when the object is created or allocated from a pool. Override this method to add custom initialization code to objects.
CanBePooled()	This method is called by the infrastructure before the object is put back into the pool. Override this method to vote on whether the object is put back into the pool.
Construct()	This method is called by the infrastructure just after the constructor is called, passing in the constructor string. Override this method to make use of the construction string value.
Deactivate()	This method is called by the infrastructure when the object is about to be deactivated. Override this method to add custom finalization code to objects when just-in-time (JIT) compiled code or object pooling is used.
Dispose()	Releases the resources used by the configured object.
DisposeObject()	This static (Shared under VB .NET) method finalizes the configured object and removes the associated COM+ reference.

The Simplest Possible Example

To illustrate the basic building blocks of creating a configured .NET type, let's construct a C# code library named ServicedDotNetLib that mimics the functionality of the previous Visual Basic 6.0 COM+ server. Given that this *.dll will contain a class deriving from System.EnterpriseServices.ServicedComponent, you need to explicitly set a reference to the containing assembly (Figure 13-14).

As you may recall, when you wish to expose members of a .NET type to COM (including COM+), you must establish the interface type using the ClassInterface attribute. The COM+ runtime will host any type of COM interface (custom, dual, or IDispatch based), so for the sake of ease, set your class interface to be AutoDual. Of course, if you do not wish to support a class interface on your .NET types, you are also free to implement any number of custom interfaces on the class itself.

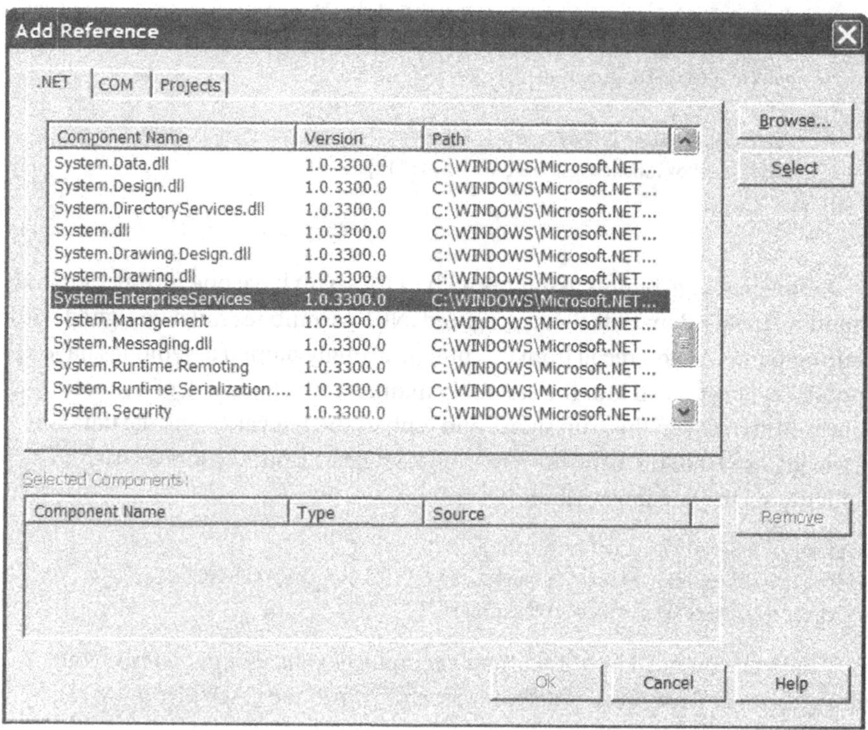

Figure 13-14. Referencing the System.EnterpriseServices.dll assembly

Another point I should make is that .NET classes that wish to function under the COM+ runtime must support a default (parameterless) constructor (as you might expect given the examination of exporting .NET class types to COM). Recall that although it is syntactically possible for configured .NET types to support additional parameterized constructors, they are not reachable by the calling base client. This being said, here is an initial crack at a managed, configured component:

```
using System;
using System.Runtime.InteropServices;
using System.EnterpriseServices;
using System.Windows.Forms;

namespace ServicedDotNetLib
{
    // Expose class members on the class interface
    // (_SimpleServicedType) as a [dual] interface.
    [ClassInterface(ClassInterfaceType.AutoDual)]
    public class SimpleServicedType : ServicedComponent
    {
```

```
        // Serviced Components must support a default
        // constructor.
        public SimpleServicedType(){}

        public void DisplayMessage(string msg)
        { MessageBox.Show(msg, "Client says:");}
    }
}
```

Before you register this assembly with COM+, you have one further detail to attend to. COM+ demands that configured .NET assemblies must be signed with a strong name. As you recall from Chapter 5, strongly named assemblies have a [.publickey] tag placed into the assembly manifest (the hallmark of a shared binary entity). Given this, run sn.exe and embed the relevant *.snk file data into ServicedDotNetLib.dll using the AssemblyKeyFile attribute (you may wish to explicitly set the version attribute as well).

```
[assembly: AssemblyVersion("1.0.0.0")]
[assembly: AssemblyKeyFile(@"C:\Apress Books\InteropBook\Labs\Chapter
13\ServicedDotNetLib\bin\Debug\thekey.snk")]
```

That's all you need for this current example. Go ahead and compile your library. Once you are done, place your assembly into the GAC (Figure 13-15).

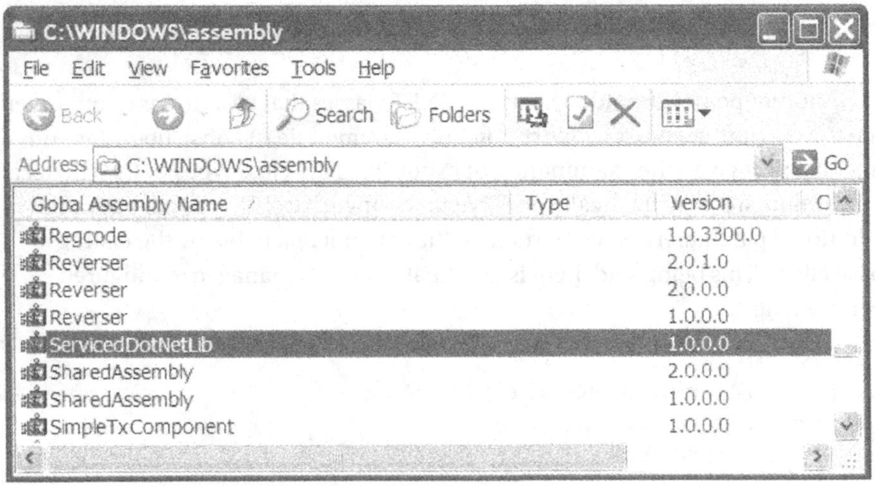

Figure 13-15. Serviced assemblies are typically placed into the GAC.

CODE *The ServicedDotNetLibrary application is included under the Chapter 13 subdirectory.*

Installing the Code Library

Now that you have a binary *.dll, you are in the position to install the contained types into a given COM+ application. Your first inclination may be to simply make use of the COM+ Component Install Wizard as you would for a classic COM-based *.dll. Sadly, if you attempt to do so, you get the error shown in Figure 13-16.

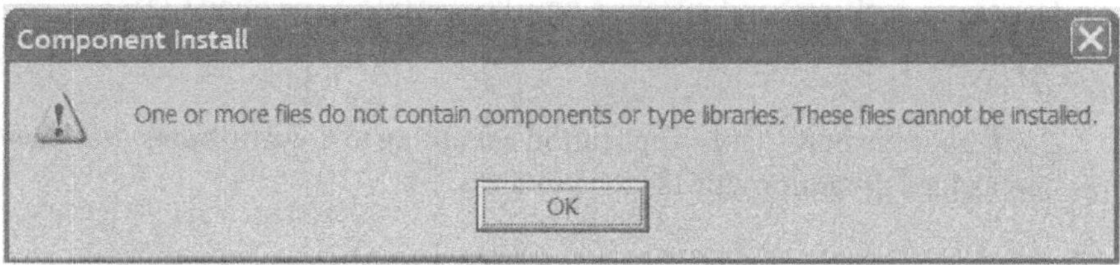

Figure 13-16. .NET assemblies cannot simply be imported into a COM+ application using the Component Install Wizard.

In the future, I'm sure that the COM+ Explorer will support the ability to install .NET components using the IDE, but not for now. So, the million-dollar question is, how do you install a managed *.dll under the care of COM+? Well, recall that the COM+ runtime demands that configured components are

- Described using a COM type library
- Cataloged in the system registry (HKCR)
- Accounted for in the COM+ Catalog

To automate each of these tasks, you are offered three equally valid possibilities:

- Make use of the command line tool named regsvcs.exe.
- Make use of a technique called *lazy registration*.
- Build a custom .NET application that makes use of the RegistrationHelper type.

You will get a chance to examine the final two approaches later in this chapter. For the time being, let's focus on the most common (and most practical) technique of running regsvcs.exe.

Using the regsvcs.exe Command Line Utility

Currently, the regsvcs.exe utility is only available at the command line. It is, however, quite possible that future versions of VS. NET will support this tool within the IDE. In general, this tool performs a number of actions in a single swoop:

- Registers an assembly for use by COM (HKCR)
- Generates, registers, and installs a type library into a specified COM+ application
- Configures the new COM+ application according to any attributes that have been added programmatically to your class

Like any command line tool, regsvcs.exe supports a number of command line flags that are used to instruct the utility how to create (or locate) the underlying COM+ application. Table 13-4 documents the key flags.

Table 13-4. Core Flags of regsvcs.exe

regsvcs.exe Utility Option	Meaning in Life
/appname:applicationName	Specifies the name of the COM+ application to either find or create
/c	Creates the target application
/componly	Configures components only; ignores methods and interfaces
/extlb	Uses an existing type library
/fc	Finds or creates the target application
/parname:name	Specifies the name or id of the COM+ application to either find or create
/reconfig	Reconfigures an existing target application
/tlb:typelibraryfile	Specifies the type library file to install
/u	Uninstalls the target application

In general, when you are attempting to install a .NET assembly into the COM+ runtime, you may choose to first build the COM+ application using the Component Services Explorer and then make use of the /fc flag. If the utility is able to locate the specified COM+ application in the COM+ Catalog, the types are installed into the exiting application.

On the other hand, if the specified COM+ application cannot be found, the /fc flag instructs regsvcs.exe to create a *new* listing in the COM+ Catalog. The /fc flag is the default behavior of regsvcs.exe, and as such, it is also acceptable to specify the /appname flag directly to locate or create a given COM+ application. In either case, navigate to the location of your ServicedDotNetLib.dll assembly and enter the following command:

```
regsvcs.exe /appname:MyDotNetComPlusApp ServicedDotNetLib.dll
```

Once you have issued a given request to regsvcs.exe, you are in a position to build a classic COM or .NET client application. Before you do so, however, let's check out exactly what regsvcs.exe has accomplished. As you will see, the process has a very similar look and feel to the process of exposing a .NET type to classic COM.

Viewing the Generated Type COM Information

The first task performed by regsvcs.exe is to generate and register COM type information (a *.tlb file) for the managed assembly (much like tlbexp.exe). If you examine the coclass definition using oleview.exe, you will find that the generated class interface has been listed as the [default], followed by a number of auxiliary .NET-centric interfaces:

```
// The generated coclass statement.
coclass SimpleServicedType
{
    [default] interface _SimpleServicedType;
    interface _Object;
    interface IRemoteDispatch;
    interface IDisposable;
    interface IManagedObject;
    interface System_EnterpriseServices_IServicedComponentInfo;
};
```

As you have already seen in Chapter 8, when a .NET type is exposed to COM, the type will support an interface named _Object that supports the members of System.Object. I assume you are already aware of the role of IDisposable and its single Dispose() method (however, you will revisit COM+ object lifetime later in this chapter). The remaining interfaces are used internally by the types of the

System.EnterpriseServices namespace and are not intended for use by your custom code base.

Given that you configured the class interface as AutoDual, you will find the following [dual] interface definition (with autogenerated DISPIDs and various inherited public members from the implemented interfaces):

```
interface _SimpleServicedType : IDispatch
{
   [id(00000000), propget,
     custom({54FC8F55-38DE-4703-9C4E-250351302B1C}, "1")]
   HRESULT ToString([out, retval] BSTR* pRetVal);
   [id(0x60020001)]
   HRESULT Equals( [in] VARIANT obj,
                   [out, retval] VARIANT_BOOL* pRetVal);
   [id(0x60020002)]
   HRESULT GetHashCode([out, retval] long* pRetVal);
   [id(0x60020003)]
   HRESULT GetType([out, retval] _Type** pRetVal);
   [id(0x60020004)]
   HRESULT GetLifetimeService([out, retval] VARIANT* pRetVal);
   [id(0x60020005)]
   HRESULT InitializeLifetimeService([out, retval] VARIANT* pRetVal);
   [id(0x60020006)]
   HRESULT CreateObjRef( [in] _Type* requestedType,
                         [out, retval] _ObjRef** pRetVal);
   [id(0x60020007)]
   HRESULT Dispose();
   [id(0x60020008)]
   HRESULT DisplayMessage([in] BSTR msg);
};
```

Acknowledging the Registration Entries

Much like the process of registering a .NET assembly with classic COM, regsvcs.exe updates the system registry with entries for the following:

- Each type's ProgID
- Each type's CLSID (and relevant information)
- Each interface's IID (and relevant information)
- The COM type library (and relevant information)

This process is identical to the one outlined in Chapter 10, so take a peek if you need a refresher. Finally, as you would expect, regsvcs.exe automatically generates GUID values for the classes and interfaces found in your .NET assembly. If you wish to assign specific GUID values to a given entity, simply apply the GuidAttribute type (as shown in Chapter 8).

And Finally, the COM+ Application Itself

The final task performed by regsvcs.exe is to update the COM+ Catalog based on any COM+-centric attributes located in the assembly's metadata. Because you have not yet added any COM+-centric attributes in the ServicedDotNetLib code base, regsvcs.exe makes use of a well-known set of default values as it configures the COM+ application and the contained components, interfaces, and methods. You will check out these default values (and how to change them) in just a bit. For now, here is the MyDotNetComPlusApp COM+ application (Figure 13-17).

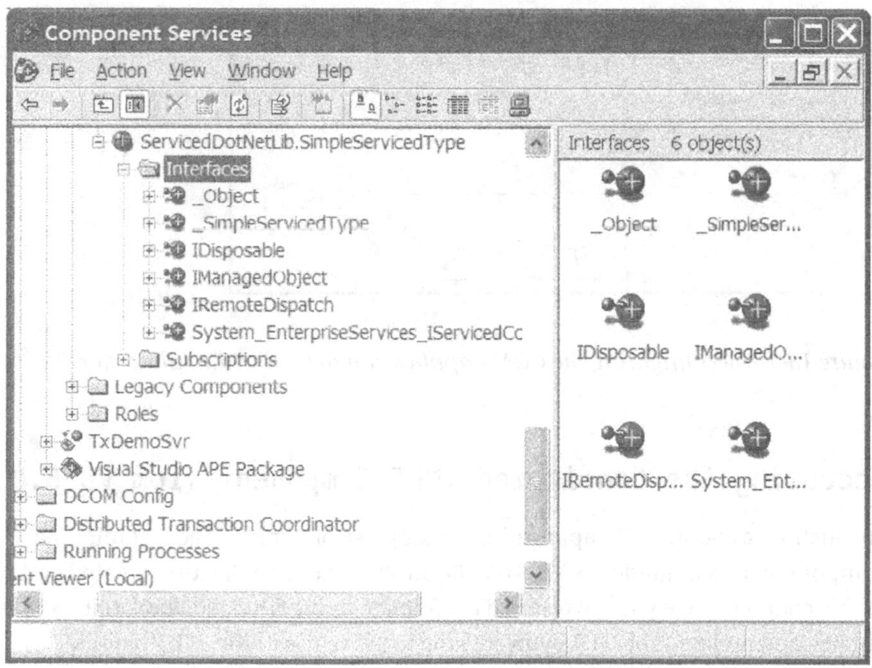

Figure 13-17. The new COM+ application

The only default value you absolutely must change before you are able to build a client application is the one assigned to the application activation setting. If you check out the property page of the new COM+ application, you will find that regsvcs.exe automatically configures a new application to run as a *library* application rather than a server application (you will see how to change this using .NET attributes a bit later in this chapter). Figure 13-18 shows the necessary update.

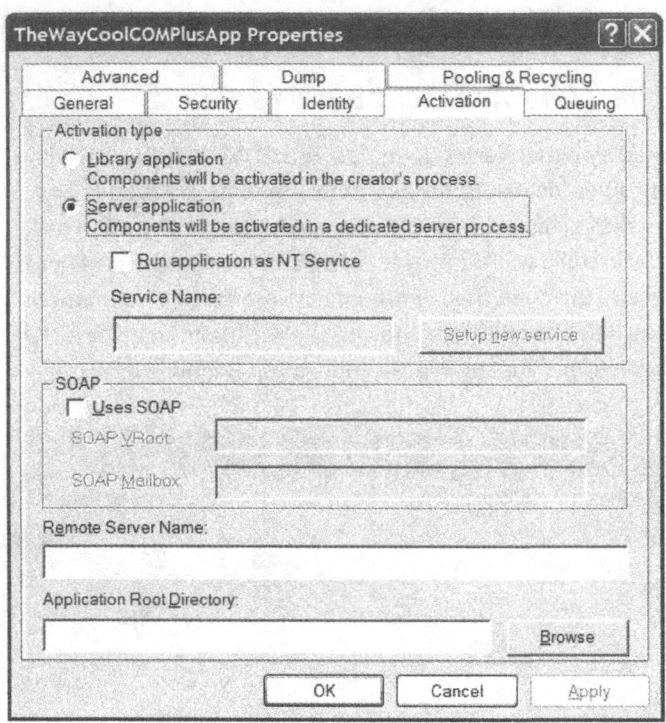

Figure 13-18. Reconfiguring the COM+ application to load within dllhost.exe

Accessing the Configured .NET Component from VB 6.0

To illustrate a classic COM application making use of our managed/configured component, let's upgrade the VB 6.0 VB6ComPlusClient application created earlier in this chapter. Once you have added a reference to the ServicedDotNetLib type library (and updated the GUI), you are able to make use of the .NET type as follows (notice of course that the process looks identical to manipulating the classic COM+ type):

```
Private Sub btnSendDotNetMesage_Click()
    Dim o As SimpleServicedType
    Set o = New SimpleServicedType
    o.DisplayMessage txtDotNetMsg.Text
End Sub
```

Accessing the Configured .NET Component from C#

As you would hope, you can also build managed clients that make use of managed/configured .NET types. To begin, assume you have a C# console application that sets a reference to the ServicedDotNetLib.dll assembly. In addition to setting a reference to the original .NET assembly, any managed client making use of a configured component *also* needs to set a reference to System.EnterpriseServices.dll. Mind you, your client code will not make direct references to these types; however, given that configured .NET types derive from ServicedComponent, your client-side code must be able to account for this type in its own code base. Once this is done, you could retrofit Main() as the following:

```
using System;
using ServicedDotNetLib;
using System.EnterpriseServices;

namespace CSharpComPlusClient
{
    class CSharpClient
    {
        [STAThread]
        static void Main(string[] args)
        {
            // Use the C# COM+ type.
            SimpleServicedType st = new SimpleServicedType();
            st.DisplayMessage("Hello from C#!");
        }
    }
}
```

CODE *The CSharpComPlusClient application is located under the Chapter 13 subdirectory.*

Enabling Component Statistics

One of the great joys of COM+ programming is seeing the hallmark of an activated type: the famed "spinning ball." Although this bit of eye candy is quite satisfying, it does place additional processing burden on the server machine. Given this, when you install an assembly into the COM+ Catalog, the configured components will not automatically support event and statistical information (and thus won't spin). To change this setting at design time, simply check off the "Component supports events and statistics" check box on the Activation tab for a given component (Figure 13-19).

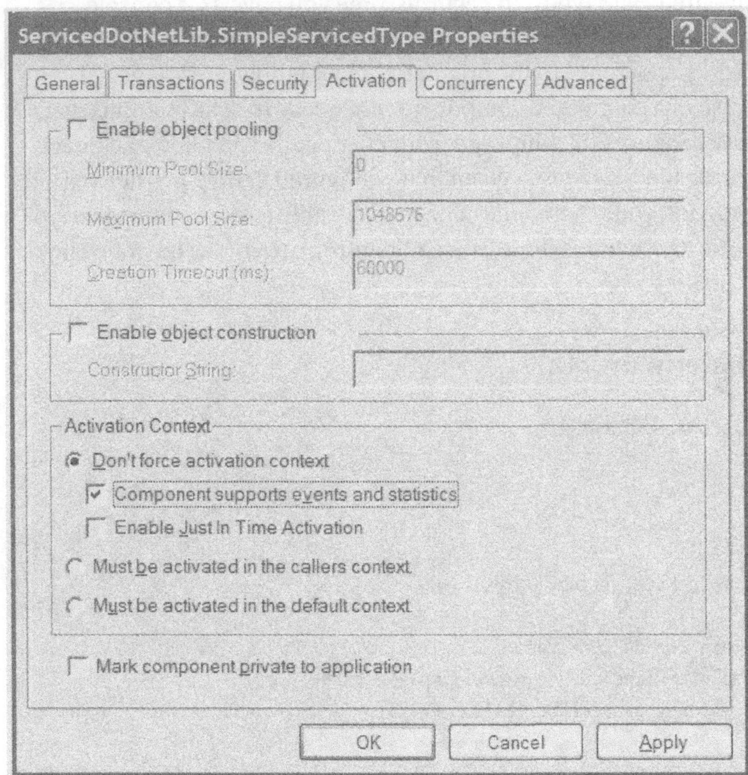

Figure 13-19. Enabling the famed spinning ball

If you wish to ensure that your .NET components automatically support this behavior, you are also able to apply the EventTrackingEnabled attribute for a given ServiceComponent derived type:

```
[EventTrackingEnabled(true)]
[ClassInterface(ClassInterfaceType.AutoDual)]
public class SimpleServicedType : ServicedComponent
{…}
```

A Brief Word on Lazy (Automatic) Registration

Recall that a .NET assembly may be registered with COM+ using one of three approaches. Although regsvcs.exe is the technique of champions, it is worth pointing out that .NET assemblies can also be automatically configured with

COM+ using *lazy registration*. The "lazy" aspect of this approach is due to you (or your system administrator) not being required to manually run regsvcs.exe. Rather, when a managed client references an assembly and creates a type derived from ServicedComponent, it automatically creates a new COM+ application that is named based on the friendly name of the assembly or using the attributes found within the assembly's metadata (just like regsvcs.exe). Although this approach may sound ideal, note the limitations of lazy registration.

- Assemblies must be deployed as private, strongly named binary (and cannot be placed into the GAC).
- Lazy registration will *only occur when accessed by .NET clients!* If a classic COM type attempts to access an assembly that has not been installed manually, the client will bomb at runtime.
- Once an assembly has been configured within the COM+ Catalog using lazy registration, it will not be reregistered unless you increment the assembly's version number each time you alter the contained types (or add new types).

Given these limitations, you should always prefer using regsvcs.exe to ensure that all clients (COM based and .NET based) are able to access your managed/configured types.

Working with the RegistrationHelper Type

The final way in which you may configure a .NET code library to function within the COM+ runtime environment is to do so programmatically using the RegistrationHelper type found within the System.EnterpriseServices namespace. This class provides two very simple (and overloaded) instance-level methods that allow you to install and uninstall a .NET assembly into the COM+ Catalog. InstallAssembly() requires you to specify the name of the assembly, generated *.tlb file, and name of the COM+ application to be created and any additional installation flags that echo the flags of regsvcs.exe. UninstallAssembly() requires similar information. Do note that each of these methods are defined by the IRegistrationHelper interface. Here is the formal definition:

```
public sealed class System.EnterpriseServices.RegistrationHelper :
    MarshalByRefObject,
    System.EnterpriseServices.IRegistrationHelper,
    System.EnterpriseServices.Thunk.IThunkInstallation
{
...
    public void InstallAssembly(string assembly, ref String application,
```

```
        string partition, ref String tlb,
        System.EnterpriseServices.InstallationFlags installFlags);

    public virtual void InstallAssembly(string assembly, ref String application,
        ref String tlb, System.EnterpriseServices.InstallationFlags installFlags);

    public virtual void UninstallAssembly(string assembly, string application);

    public void UninstallAssembly(string assembly,
        string application, string partition);
}
```

Let's see a simple example. Again, let's say you have a C# Console application that has set a reference to System.EnterpriseServices.dll. Also assume that this C# client has a strongly named assembly named FooServicedComp.dll in its application directory. These assumptions aside, the following code programmatically performs the same exact duties as regsvcs.exe (note that if the RegistrationHelper encounters an error, it throws a RegistrationException):

```
using System;
using System.EnterpriseServices;

namespace RegistrationHelperApp
{
    class MyRegHelper
    {
        [STAThread]
        static void Main(string[] args)
        {
            // Register a private, strongly named assembly.
            RegistrationHelper rh = new RegistrationHelper();
            try
            {
                string comPlusAppName = "NewComPlusApp";
                string typeLibName = "FooServicedComp.tlb";

                rh.InstallAssembly("FooServicedComp.dll",
                    ref comPlusAppName,
                    ref typeLibName,
                    InstallationFlags.FindOrCreateTargetApplication);
            }
            catch(RegistrationException rhex)
            {
                Console.WriteLine(rhex.Message);
            }
        }
    }
}
```

Upon successful completion, you will find the newly configured COM+ application viewable using the Component Services Explorer. Also, the generated COM type information will be fully accounted for under HKCR. All you have to do at this point is install the assembly into the GAC and code away.

CODE *The RegistrationHelperApp project is included under the Chapter 13 subdirectory.*

Configuring a Managed COM+ Application Using .NET Attributes

Now that you have seen how to install a .NET assembly using the default behavior of regsvcs.exe, let's check out the relevant attributes of the System.EnterpriseServices namespace that allow you to fine-tune the installation process (some of which you have already seen during the course of this chapter). Table 13-5 illustrates the assembly-level attributes that you can specify from your managed code libraries.

Table 13-5. COM+ Application-Specific Attributes

COM+ Application-Level Attribute	Value If Omitted	Meaning in Life
ApplicationAccessControl	False	Allows security configuration for a given COM+ application.
ApplicationActivation	Library	Server application or library? Used in conjunction with the ActivationOption enumeration.
ApplicationID (or simply the GuidAttribute type)	Autogenerated GUID	Specifies a fixed GUID for the application.
ApplicationName	Same as the assembly name.	Specifies a fixed friendly name of the application.
ApplicationQueuing	No default	Enables QC support for this application.
Description	No description.	Specifies a description string for this COM+ application.

For example, assume you (a) unregister the previous MyDotNetComPlusApp COM+ application using the /u flag of regsvcs.exe and (b) update the AssemblyInfo.cs file as follows:

```
using System.EnterpriseServices;

// COM+ Application configuration.
[assembly: ApplicationName("TheWayCoolCOMPlusApp")]
[assembly: ApplicationID("9F1DE1E4-EC11-4455-9A8E-3D35C71B03F4")]
[assembly: ApplicationActivation(ActivationOption.Server)]
[assembly: Description("My way cool COM+ application created with C#")]
```

When the assembly is reprocessed using regsvcs.exe, you are able to view the property page for the new TheWayCoolCOMPlusApp application and find your initial configuration settings. Understand, of course, that these values can be changed after the time of installation. As you may agree, the most useful application-level attribute is ApplicationActivation, given that the default behavior establishes your COM+ application as a library application.

Supporting Object Construction Strings

As mentioned, configured .NET types can only be created using a default constructor (given the requirements of COM(+)). However, as you may know, classic COM+ defines two standard interfaces (IObjectConstruct and IObjectConstructString) that can be used by the supporting coclass to receive an *object construction string*. Although these interfaces are hidden away as internal types of the System.EnterpriseServices.dll assembly, the same behavior can be supported by a .NET type by simply overriding the virtual protected Construct() method defined by the ServicedComponent base class. Assume you have updated your SimpleServicedType as follows:

```
[EventTrackingEnabled(true)]
[ClassInterface(ClassInterfaceType.AutoDual)]
public class SimpleServicedType : ServicedComponent
{
...
    // This type now supports an object constructor string.
    protected override void Construct(string ctorString)
    { MessageBox.Show(ctorString, "Object Constructor string is:");}
}
```

Here, for the sake of testing, you are simply grabbing an incoming System.String and placing the underlying value within a Windows Forms message box. An obvious question is, what might this value be? The answer is, literally, anything at all. The string passed into a given Construct() implementation may contain type-specific instance data, an ADO(.NET) connection string value (to allow dynamic resolution of a given data source), or anything else that may be of use to the object at hand. Regardless of what you decide the value of your type's object construction string will be, you are now able to unregister (/u) and reregister (/fc) the assembly using regsvcs.exe and enable construction string support using the component's property page (Figure 13-20).

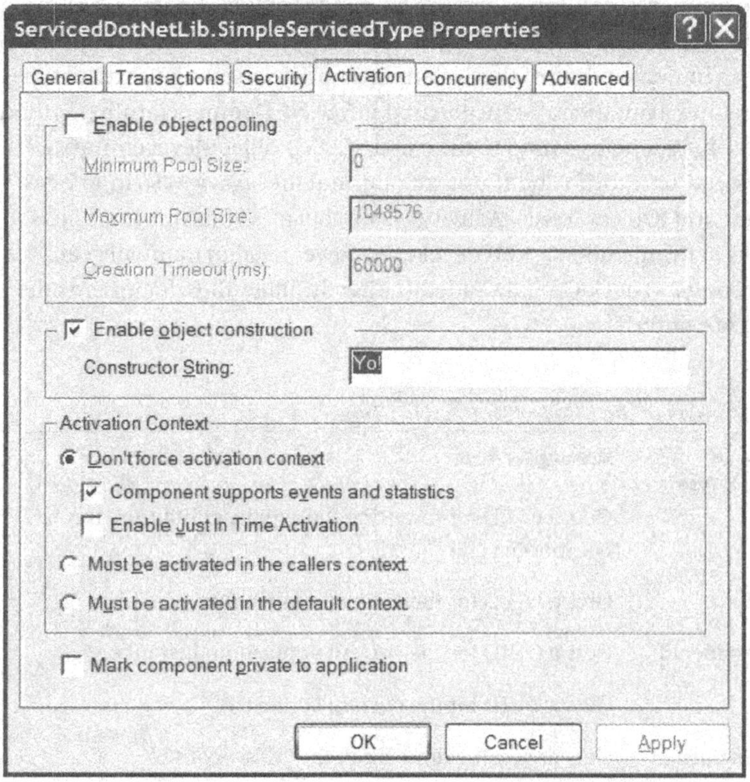

Figure 13-20. Enabling and configuring object constructor strings

If you would rather make use of .NET attributes to enable and configure an object construction string, you can make use of the ConstructionEnabled attribute and specify your configuration using named properties:

```
[EventTrackingEnabled(true)]
[ClassInterface(ClassInterfaceType.AutoDual)]
[ConstructionEnabled(Enabled = true, Default = "Yo!")]
public class SimpleServicedType : ServicedComponent
{
    ...
}
```

In this way, when your assembly is configured with COM+, it will have an initial value supplied as an object constructor string. Like any attribute value, this can always be changed after registration using the Component Services Explorer.

Examining the ContextUtil Type

Now that you have seen the basics of creating, installing, and accessing managed configured components, you can spend the remainder of this chapter examining the aspects of COM+ that you will leverage in an enterprise-level application. This task requires an understanding of the System.EnterpriseService.ContextUtil type. ContextUtil defines a number of static (Shared in VB .NET nomenclature) methods that expose the functionality found in the classic COM+ object-level contextual interfaces IObjectContextInfo and IContextState, and the legacy MTS interfaces IObjectContext and IObjectContextActivity. Given that all of this information is provided using static members, .NET developers never need to manually call CoGetObjectContext() or CoGetCallContext() directly. Table 13-6 documents the key members of ContextUtil.

Table 13-6. Members of the Mighty ContextUtil Type

Static Members of the ContextUtil Type	Meaning in Life
ActivityId	Gets a GUID representing the activity containing the component
ApplicationId	Gets a GUID for the current application
ApplicationInstanceId	Gets a GUID for the current application instance
ContextId	Gets a GUID for the current context
DeactivateOnReturn	Gets or sets the done bit in the COM+ context
IsInTransaction	Gets a value indicating whether the current context is transactional
IsSecurityEnabled	Gets a value indicating whether role-based security is active in the current context
MyTransactionVote	Gets or sets the happy bit in the COM+ context
Transaction	Gets an object describing the current COM+ transaction
TransactionId	Gets the GUID of the current transaction
DisableCommit()	Sets both the happy bit and the done bit to false in the COM+ context

Table 13-6. Members of the Mighty ContextUtil Type (continued)

Static Members of the ContextUtil Type	Meaning in Life
EnableCommit()	Sets the happy bit to true and the done bit to false in the COM+ context
IsCallerInRole()	Determines whether the caller is in the specified role
SetAbort()	Sets the consistent bit to false and the done bit to true in the COM+ context
SetComplete()	Sets the consistent bit and the done bit to true in the COM+ context

To illustrate how to use the ContextUtil type to scrape out some basic contextual information, assume you have updated your existing SimpleServiceType to support a new member named ShowObjCtxInfo():

```
public void ShowObjCtxInfo()
{
    StringBuilder sb = new StringBuilder();
    sb.AppendFormat("COM+ Application ID: {0}\n",
        ContextUtil.ApplicationId);
    sb.AppendFormat("Context ID: {0}\n",
        ContextUtil.ContextId);
    sb.AppendFormat("In a transaction? : {0}\n",
        ContextUtil.IsInTransaction.ToString());
    sb.AppendFormat("Security Enabled? : {0}\n",
        ContextUtil.IsSecurityEnabled);
    MessageBox.Show(sb.ToString(), "Object Level Contextual Information");
}
```

If you were to reinstall this configured component and activate the ShowObjCtxInfo() method, you would find the output shown in Figure 13-21.

Figure 13-21. Context in action

Now, even if you are unaware of the behavior of each member, don't sweat it. The point at this stage of the game is to be aware that ContextUtil is your key to accessing the meat of the COM+ runtime. You will see numerous details in the pages that follow. To begin the journey, let's check out the concept of just-in-time activation (JITA).

Understanding JITA

Two of the most compelling features of COM+ would have to be its support for declarative transaction processing and instance management of the objects it is responsible for hosting. You will examine transactional support later in this chapter and focus on instance management for the time being. As you have seen, base clients make use of a configured object in the same exact manner as a nonconfigured COM or .NET type. Assume for example that you have a VB 6.0 client application that creates a number of class-level variables upon the loading of the main window:

```
' Behold, the greedy client.
Private mObjA as SomeObject
Private mObjB as SomeOtherObject
Private mObjC as YetAnotherObject

' Get the objects when the form loads…
Private Sub Form_Load()
    Set mObjA = New SomeObject
    Set mObjB = New SomeOtherObject
    Set mObjC = New YetAnotherObject
End Sub

' Only release them when the form shuts down.
Private Sub Form_Unload(Cancel As Integer)
    Set mObjA = Nothing
    Set mObjB = Nothing
    Set mObjC = Nothing
End Sub
```

For the sake of argument, let's say that each of these objects obtains a connection to a remote database. If 100 client applications were launched, you would suddenly have dished out 300 database connections. Now assume that all 100 end users take a well-perceived lunch break (that lasts at least 2 hours) and never bother to shut down the running applications. Given that these three object variables have been declared in the [General] [Declarations] section, they are scoped at the *class level*, and will therefore be alive until the Form type has been unloaded from memory. Sadly, you now have 300 database connections that are held in memory but not actually in use (an obvious problem).

Ideally, some outside agent would be able to determine that the objects are finished with the current unit of work and could therefore be destroyed, thereby freeing the expensive data connections. When the end users return from their feast and begin using the application once again, this same agent would dynamically create a new object for the calling client. The beauty of this approach is the fact that the client's code base can be blissfully unaware that the objects they *think* they are always connected to are in fact being destroyed and re-created behind the scenes.

To enable this philosophy, COM+ provides an instance management technique termed *just-in-time activation* (JITA) and the closely related *as soon as possible* (ASAP) deactivation policy. Using JITA, COM+ is able to make an object available for use only during the duration of a method invocation. Specifically, the configured object is activated only at the exact point in which the base client makes a method call and is destroyed when the method call completes. At this point, any resources that have been acquired by the type are freed as quickly as possible.

This technique is exactly why configured types are typically created as stateless entities. Now, understand that a "stateless COM+ type" does *not* mean that you cannot have any number of private member variables defined in the class. It also does *not* mean that you cannot have a COM+ type that supports some number of properties to encapsulate this private data. What is does mean is that the configured object does not need to be in charge of maintaining the state data directly.

Rather, if a configured type must remember information between method invocations, it will either (a) not inform the runtime it is ready to be destroyed (described in the next section) or (b) inform the runtime it is ready to be destroyed and save its state data elsewhere (such as in a database, in-memory with the Shared Property Manager, or perhaps in another nonconfigured type). In a nutshell, what makes a COM+ type stateless is nothing more than the fact that the type will inform the runtime when it is finished with its current workload and is ready to be terminated.

The "Happy" and "Done" Bits

So, the big question at this point is, how does the COM+ runtime know when it is safe to destroy a given object? In a nutshell, a COM+ context object maintains two bits that are commonly referred to as the *happy* and *done* bits, both of which may be set to either true or false. A configured object sets the state of its happy and done bits to inform the runtime of two key points of information:

- Done bit: Can the current object be destroyed safely?
- Happy bit: Should I commit or abort the current database transaction (if any)?

By default, a configured object begins life busy and miserable (happy = false, done = false). During the course of an object's lifetime, these bits may be set using two separate interfaces of the context object. MTS applications make use of the SetComplete() and SetAbort() methods of the IObjectContext interface. Under COM+, a configured object is able to report the same information using the IContextState interface. The benefit of making use of IContextState lies in the capability of setting the values of these bits independently. Table 13-7 illustrates how each bit is set using the IObjectContext and IContextState interfaces, assuming a currently unhappy and preoccupied object.

Table 13-7. Approaches to Setting the Happy and Done Bits

Interface Method Invocation	Value of Happy Bit	Value of Done Bit
IObjectControl.SetComplete()	True	True
IObjectControl.SetAbort()	False	True
IObjectControl.DisableCommit()	False	False
IObjectControl.EnableCommit()	True	False
IContextState.SetDeactivateOnReturn(true)	False	True
IContextState.SetDeactivateOnReturn(false)	False	False
IContextState.SetMyTransactionVote(txCommit)	True	False
IContextState.SetMyTransactionVote(txAbort)	False	False

One final point to be aware of: Although the term "happy bit" makes the process of discussing COM+ much more user friendly, the more formal (that is, dry and boring) term is the "consistency bit," given that the happy bit is used to control the outcome of a given transaction (recall the ACID rules?). You will examine COM+ transactions in the next section. For now, let's see how to programmatically control the state of the done bit.

Enabling JITA/ASAP Deactivation

Given that the whole purpose is to keep an object alive only as long as the current method invocation, you will find that each member of a given configured component needs to set the done bit before exiting. Using the types within the System.EnterpriseServices namespace, you have three possible approaches. Also note that the COM+ Explorer allows you to enable or disable JITA processing for a given configured type using the Activation tab. Recall that by default, assemblies registered with the COM+ Catalog using regsvcs.exe *disable* this feature; be sure you *enable* this feature to make your types JITA aware (Figure 13-22).

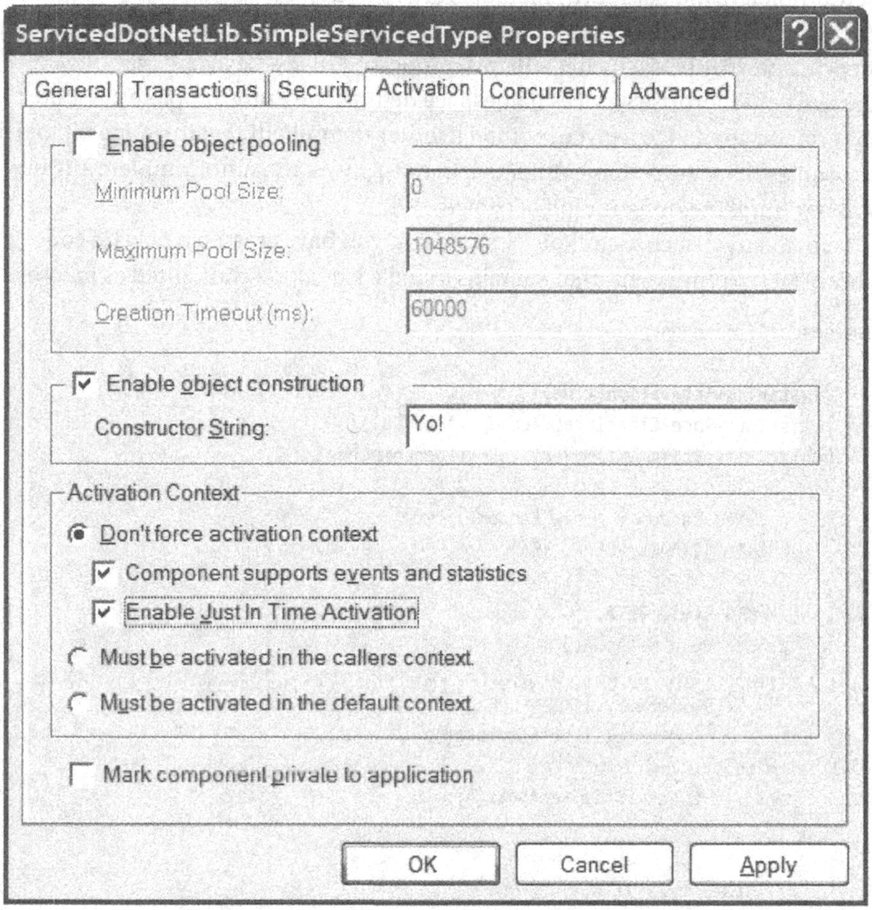

Figure 13-22. Enabling JITA for a given configured type

If you wish to ensure that JITA is always enabled during installation, you may make use of the JustInTimeActivation attribute:

```
[JustInTimeActivation(true)]
[ClassInterface(ClassInterfaceType.AutoDual)]
public class JITAAwareObject : ServicedComponent {…}
```

Controlling the Done Bit

Once JITA has been enabled, your first approach is to use the MTS-style SetComplete() and SetAbort() members of the ContextUtil class. If you would rather set the done bit independently of the happy bit, you need to use the static ContextUtil.DeactivateOnReturn property. Finally, be aware that the System.EnterpriseServices namespace defines the AutoComplete attribute that can be applied to a given method in order to implicitly set the done bit to true as soon as the method has completed. In most cases, the AutoComplete attribute will be your JITA configuration of choice.

To illustrate each technique, assume that you have created a new C# code library (JITAComponent) that contains a single class type configured as follows:

```
namespace JITAComponent
{
    [JustInTimeActivation(true)]
    [ClassInterface(ClassInterfaceType.AutoDual)]
    public class JITAAwareObject : ServicedComponent
    {
        private Random r = new Random();
        public JITAAwareObject(){}

        // MTS style JITA.
        public void MethodA()
        {
            if(DoSomeWork())
                ContextUtil.SetComplete();
            else
                ContextUtil.SetAbort();
        }

        // COM+ style JITA.
        public void MethodB()
        {
            if(DoSomeWork())
                ContextUtil.DeactivateOnReturn = true;
            else
                ContextUtil.DeactivateOnReturn = false;
        }

        // This will always set the done bit to true.
        [AutoComplete(true)]
        public void MethodC()
        {
            DoSomeWork();
        }
```

```
        // Work simulation...
        private bool DoSomeWork()
        {
            if(r.Next(1) == 0)
                return false;
            else
                return true;
        }
    }
}
```

Be aware that the AutoComplete attribute is simply a programmatic way to enable the "Automatically deactivate this object when this method returns" check box located on the General tab of a method's property page. As always, this initial value can be changed after the fact.

JITA and Implementing IObjectControl (So to Speak...)

Classic COM+ types that participate in JITA typically implement the IObjectControl interface. Understand that a given base client never obtains this interface! Rather, the COM+ runtime calls the members of IObjectControl on a configured object when the type is activated or deactivated based on its JITA configuration. This same interface is also used if the object has been configured as a "poolable" type (described in the next section). IObjectControl defines three methods: Activate(), Deactivate(), and CanBePooled():

```
// This is an internal type!
interface IObjectControl
{
    void Activate();
    bool CanBePooled();
    void Deactivate();
}
```

When you are building a .NET COM+ type, however, you do not directly implement this interface, but simply override the appropriate method of the ServicedComponent base class. For example:

```
[JustInTimeActivation(true)]
[ClassInterface(ClassInterfaceType.AutoDual)]
public class JITAAwareObject : ServicedComponent
{
    // IObjectControl members.
    protected override void Activate()
    {
        // Acquire any necessary resources...
```

```
        }
        protected override void Deactivate()
        {
            // Free any acquired resources...
        }
        protected override bool CanBePooled()
        {
            return false;  // This is the default implementation.
        }
...
}
```

Here, the JITAAwareObject class type has overridden each IObjectControl-centric method. When the type has been created (given that a base client is making a method invocation), Activate() is called automatically to give the object a chance to obtain any necessary resources. As soon as the object informs the COM+ runtime it has finished its current unit of work (by setting the done bit to true), Deactivate() is also called automatically to give the type a chance to clean up any allocated resource. This story changes just a bit if the type is poolable (as you will soon see).

JITA, IObjectControl, and the .NET Garbage Collector

As you are well aware, the .NET runtime makes use of a garbage collected heap to destroy its objects "at some time in the future." While this can greatly simplify your efforts in some regards (deleting allocated memory is no longer your problem), it does present a new problem: How can you ensure your object's acquired resources are freed up in a timely manner? Consider a typical COM+ type. The overridden Activate() method may attach to a given data source, while the overridden Deactivate() can be used to release said connection. This is a valid approach that still makes perfect sense when building managed components using .NET.

However, when is the memory allocated for the .NET type freed? The good news is that when you install .NET assemblies into the COM+ Catalog, the .NET runtime ensures that the overridden System.Object.Finalize() implementation is called automatically (expressed in C# using destructor syntax). In this way, you can ensure that when an object is deactivated, it is truly destroyed and removed from memory. Given this, here is the lifecycle of a nonpoolable object:

1. The default constructor of the configured type is called.
2. IObjectControl.Activate() is called.
3. [...the object is alive and eventually sets the done bit to true...]

4. IObjectControl.Deactivate() is called.
5. System.Object.Finalize() is called automatically!

CODE *The JITAComponent project is included under the Chapter 13 subdirectory.*

Configuring Poolable Objects

COM+ employs one additional instance-level activation technique termed *poolable objects*. In some regards, object pooling is a complement to ASAP deactivation, given that the goal of object pooling is to allocate a set of objects that can be kept in a ready (deactivate) state for use by calling clients. Distinct pools are maintained for distinct object types. Therefore, if you have a single COM+ application that contains four poolable objects, the COM+ runtime will create four separate pools.

Understand that an object never *has* to be configured as poolable. Typically pooling is an attractive option if the configured type requires significant start-up logic that can take a good deal of time. If a type needs to connect to multiple data sources, read initialization files, and call across the wire to obtain other bits of information, it would be quite time intensive to perform these actions in the Activate() event, due to the same lengthy operation needing to occur each time the object is placed in a ready state. To shave off time on the initialization of the type, a poolable object will perform this same sort of logic in the *default constructor*.

The lifetime management of a poolable object changes just a bit from a nonpoolable type. First of all, as with nonpoolable types, the default constructor and overridden Finalize() methods are called only once. However, Activate() and Deactivate() are called numerous times as the object comes out of and is placed into the pool. Once the COM+ application is unloaded (given that its timeout setting has expired), the destructors of each pooled type are called. The Component Services Explorer allows you to configure the poolability of a configured type using the component's property page. Notice in Figure 13-23 that you are also able to define the minimum and maximum size of the pool itself.

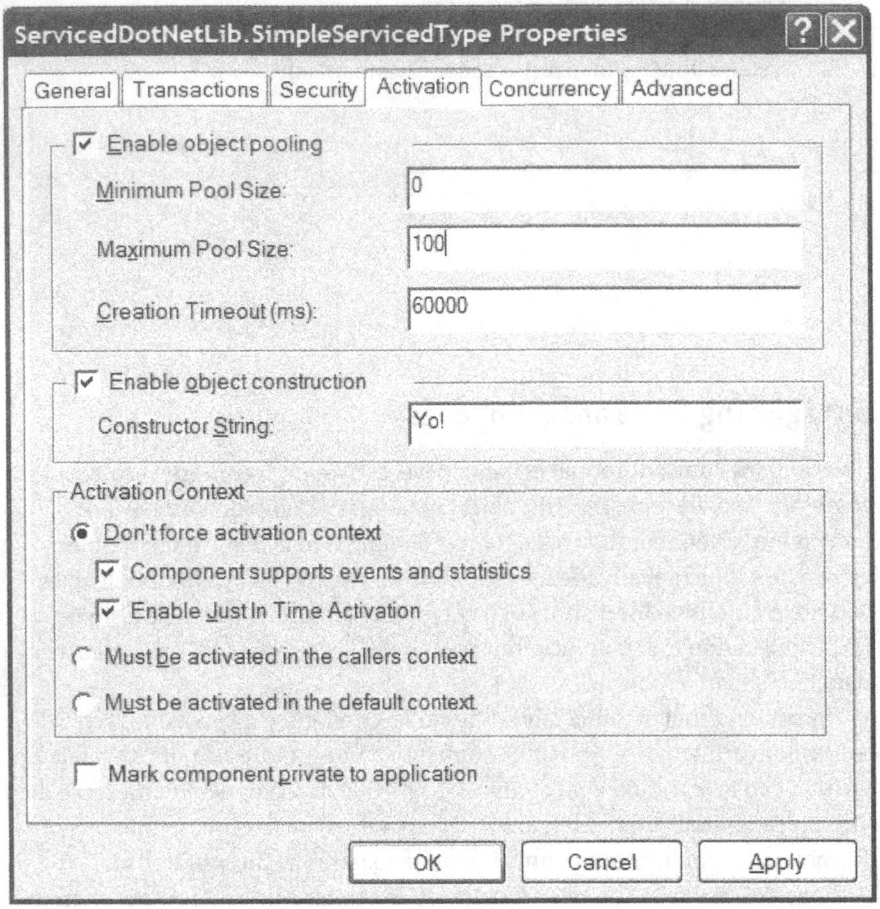

Figure 13-23. Configuring the poolability

When you wish to enable pooling programmatically using .NET attributes, simply adorn the class type as follows:

```
[JustInTimeActivation(true)]
[ClassInterface(ClassInterfaceType.AutoDual)]
[ObjectPooling(true, 10, 100)]
[EventTrackingEnabled(true)]
public class PoolableObject : ServicedComponent
{
...
    protected override bool CanBePooled()
  {
        return true;
    }
}
```

The ObjectPoolingAttribute defines a number of properties that may be configured using the type's overloaded constructor set. In the previous code block, you are enabling pooling for this type as well as establishing the minimum and maximum pool size.

CODE *The PoolableComponent is located under the Chapter 13 subdirectory.*

A Recap of Transactional Programming

The next major feature of COM+ is its automated transactional support. Before I dig into the details of building transactional components using managed code, a few words regarding transactions themselves are in order. A transaction may be simply defined as a group of operations that must either *all* succeed or *all* fail; there is no middle ground. Although transactions are helpful in areas outside of database manipulations, they are the driving agent that ensures a database transaction is Atomic, Consistent, Isolated, and Durable (that is, it meets the ACID test). Table 13-8 defines each aspect of the ACID acronym.

Table 13-8. The ACID Properties of a Transaction

Acidic Property (Pun Intended)	Meaning in Life
A is for *Atomic*	An atomic transaction ensures that if any one operation fails, all operations fail and the current transaction is aborted.
C is for *Consistent*	A consistent transaction ensures that when a transaction is aborted, any changes made to a data store are rolled back to its original state.
I is for *Isolated*	An isolated transaction ensures that if two transactions are manipulating the same data source, they should not see each other's work. Under SQL Server, COM+ isolation basically boils down to locking a data table while a transaction is in progress.
D is for *Durable*	A durable transaction is, well, durable. Once a transaction is committed (or while it is in progress), it is able to survive catastrophic failures such as a power outage. Typically, a database management system maintains a log file to keep transactions durable.

The entity that is in charge of monitoring the outcome of a given transaction is formally termed a *Transaction Processing Monitor* (TPM). As you would guess, COM+ is one of many possible TPMs. Although the process of configuring COM+ transactions is extremely simple on the surface, under the hood numerous complex entities are working to ensure your transactions adhere to the ACID test (the details of which you can be blissfully unaware of during the scope of this chapter).

In its simplest form, a COM+ transaction may consist of a single object. The lone configured component may contain a method that is responsible for updating a given table in some database (Figure 13-24).

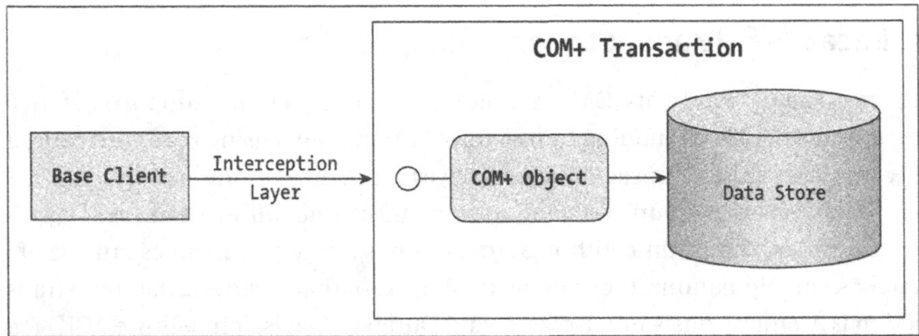

Figure 13-24. A single object transaction

While the operations are being carried out by the configured component, the TPM records all changes it is responsible for making. If the object successfully completes all its work (that is, it is happy), the transaction is committed. If, on the other hand, the object is unable to get its work done for any variety of reasons (can't find the database, ill-formed data, bad SQL query, or whatnot), the transaction aborts.

Root Objects, Secondary Objects, and COM+ Transactions

Although it is quite possible for a COM+ transaction to consist of a single object doing all the work for a base client, it is far more common for a group of objects to collaborate for a given base client. To examine this situation, you need to understand a key concept regarding COM+ transactional processing: the role of the *root object*. By definition, a root object is an object that marks the beginning of a COM+ transaction (as you may guess, root objects are typically created by a given base client). If a root object needs to enlist other objects into the current transaction, these are referred to as *secondary objects*.

For example, assume you have created a new COM+ application containing three configured components, all of which are responsible for performing a given unit of transactional work. Because all configured types are placed into a given context, each object has a chance to vote on the outcome of the current transaction by altering the state of their associated happy bit. When the root object is deactivated, the values of the happy bits are examined (by the runtime) for each object involved within the transaction. The transaction itself maintains a final bit termed the *doomed bit*, which marks the success or failure of the transaction itself. The rules that are used to calculate the doomed bit are quite simple:

- If all the objects are happy, the transaction is committed (that is, the transaction's doomed bit is set to false).
- If any of the enlisted objects are not happy, the transaction is aborted (the doomed bit is set to true), and any work performed by the enlisted objects is rolled back to its previous state.

Figure 13-25 illustrates the big picture.

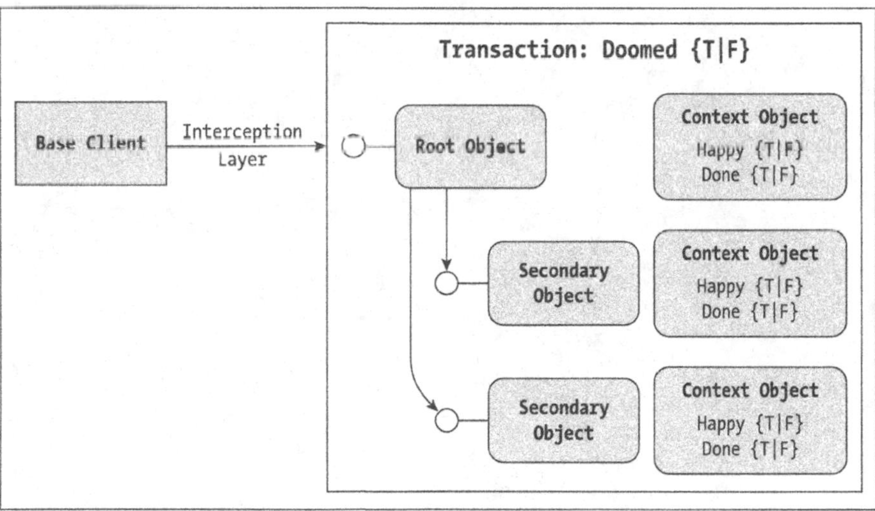

Figure 13-25. A transaction enlisting multiple objects

It is also educational to point out that under the hood, the COM+ runtime assigns a GUID to each transaction currently in progress. If each of the objects seen in Figure 13-25 supported a method that displayed the current transactional ID as follows:

```
public void ShowMyTxID()
{
    MessageBox.Show(ContextUtil.TransactionId.ToString(),
                                    "Tx ID is:");
}
```

you would be able to verify that each object is indeed in the same transaction.

Programming COM+ Transactions

The beautiful thing about the COM+ transaction model is that you do not need to write any transaction-centric code. Like most services provided by COM+, transactions are configured using a declarative model through the Transaction tab of an object's property page (Figure 13-26).

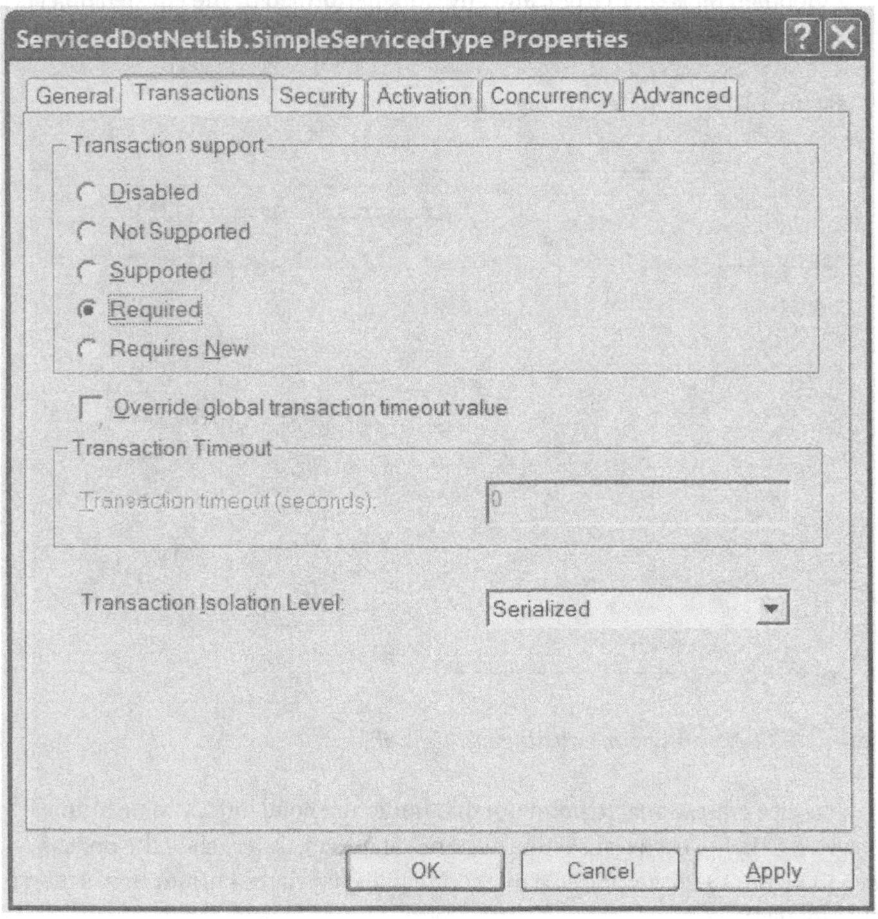

Figure 13-26. Declarative transactional settings

Basically, these five settings allow you to control how a configured component functions in a transactional setting (if at all) as well as whether the object is configured as a root object (if at all). Table 13-9 documents the various settings.

Table 13-9. Transactional COM+ Settings

COM+ Transactional Value	Meaning in Life
Disabled	The component does not care about, and will not participate in, a COM+ transaction.
Not Supported	The component does not care about, and will not participate in, a COM+ transaction. If it is within a transaction, its vote will not count.
Supported	The component will take on the transactional settings of the configured component that created it. Thus, if COM+ object A is in a transaction and creates COM+ object B, object B is enlisted into the current transaction.
Required	The component demands to be in a transaction. If the creating client is in a transaction, the object is enlisted. Also, if the creating client is *not* in a transaction, this component will be placed into a new transaction and will function as the root object.
Requires New	The component will always be placed in a brand-new transaction and function as the root object. Even if the object is created by another configured type that is already in a transaction, a new transaction will be created.

If you wish to ensure that your configured components are automatically set with a given transactional value when installed under the COM+ runtime, you are free to adorn your .NET class types with the Transaction attribute. This attribute works in conjunction with the TransactionOption enumeration:

```
// Transactional Options
public enum TransactionOption
{
    Disabled,
    NotSupported,
    Required,
    RequiresNew,
    Supported
}
```

By default, Transaction establishes the transaction support of a .NET class type as TransactionOption.Required by way of the default constructor. Also be aware that when you apply the Transaction property to your managed classes, JITA support is automatically enabled.

Setting the Happy Bit

As you have seen, the context object maintains the values of the happy and done bits for a given configured component. The done bit is simple to understand: The method has completed its unit of work for the base client and is prepared to be deactivated. But what of the happy bit? When exactly is a COM+ object happy with the current state of affairs? Simply put, a configured object is happy under two conditions:

- It is part of a COM+ database transaction.
- It has successfully completed its atomic measure of the current database transaction.

To set the happy bit for a given method invocation, you may make use of the static SetComplete() and SetAbort() methods of the ContextUtil type (which also affect the happy bit). Unlike classic COM, you do not test for failed HRESULTs to determine the value to assign the happy bit, but rather .NET exceptions. Consider the following C# class:

```
[ClassInterface(ClassInterfaceType.AutoDual)]
[Transaction(TransactionOption.Required)]
[EventTrackingEnabled(true)]
public class MyTxClass : ServicedComponent
{
    public MyTxClass(){}
    public void TryThisTransaction()
    {
        try
        {
            // Do the work here...
            …

            // Everything worked!  I'm happy and done.
            // Commit the transaction!
            ContextUtil.SetComplete();
        }
        catch
    {
```

```
            // Problem!  I'm done but not happy about it.
            // Abort the current transaction.
            ContextUtil.SetAbort();
        }
    }
}
```

If you would rather interact with the happy bit independently, use the COM+-style ContextUtil.MyTransactionVote property and the corresponding TransactionVote enumeration (the done bit can be set using the DeactivateOnReturn attribute):

```
public void TryThisOtherTransaction()
{
    try
    {
        // Do the work here...
        …
        // Happy!
        ContextUtil.MyTransactionVote = TransactionVote.Commit;
    }
    catch
    {
        // Unhappy.
        ContextUtil.MyTransactionVote = TransactionVote.Abort;
    }
    finally
    {
        // Done.
        ContextUtil.DeactivateOnReturn = true;
    }
}
```

The final way that you can interact with the happy bit is to make use of the AutoComplete attribute. As you may recall, this attribute sets the done bit to true once the method returns. However, this same attribute sets the happy bit to true as long as the method does not trigger any exceptions. Thus, if no exceptions are thrown, the transaction is committed automatically:

```
[AutoComplete]
public void YetAnotherTxMethod()
{
    // Do the work here...

    // Happy and done, if no exceptions are thrown.
}
```

Regardless of your preferred technique, understand that the essence of a configured component is to perform a discrete unit of work on behalf of the base client and be deactivated as quickly as possible (to release any acquired resources). By ensuring that each method of a given component informs its context of its transactional vote (the happy bit) and its deactivation status (the done bit), you enable the COM+ runtime to handle the instance in a scalable manner.

CODE *The SimpleTxComponent project is included under the Chapter 13 directory.*

A Complete Serviced Component Example

To pull together all the information presented thus far, let's now build a minimal and complete C# application that makes use of various configured .NET components. Your application will be a three-tiered application that is broken down as described in Table 13-10.

Table 13-10. The Design Notes

Application Tier	Meaning in Life
Presentation tier	The front end of your application will be a C# Windows Forms application (that is, base client) that will allow the end user to view a table of data as well as insert and delete new records (I'll also re-create this client using ASP.NET at the conclusion of this chapter).
Business tier	The middle tier will be a COM+ application that contains two configured types written with C#. These types will interact with a custom SQL Server database and participate under a COM+ transaction. The types are as follows: • CarInventory. This root object makes use of ADO.NET to insert and delete records as well as return a DataSet containing all records. • LogSale. This type will log a deleted car to a discrete table in the same database.
Data tier	The back end will be a custom SQL Server database named CarLot, which contains two custom Table objects: • Inventory. A list of records containing the columns CarMake, CarColor, and CarID. • CarsSold. A list of records that have been removed from the Inventory table, containing the columns CarID and DateSold.

Building the Custom Database

Your first step is to create the database itself. I make the assumption that you are well equipped to create a new database using SQL Server; however, here are some additional design notes.

The Inventory table maintains three columns that represent a given automobile on the car lot. As you might assume, CarID has been established as the primary key, while CarMake and CarColor are a represented by a fixed number of characters (Figure 13-27).

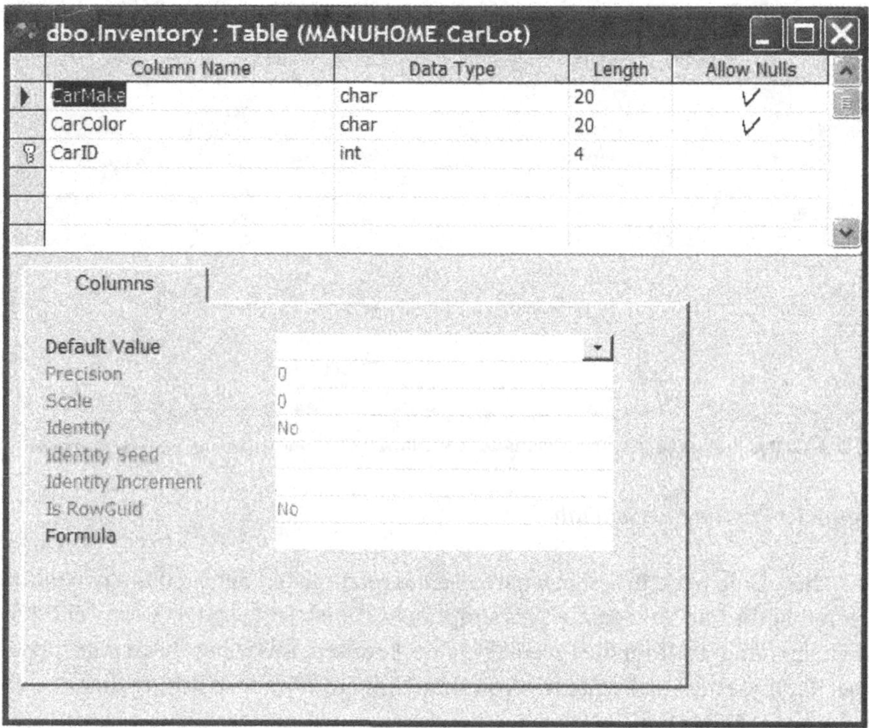

Figure 13-27. The Inventory table

The CarsSold table maintains two data columns (CarID and DateSold) as shown in Figure 13-28.

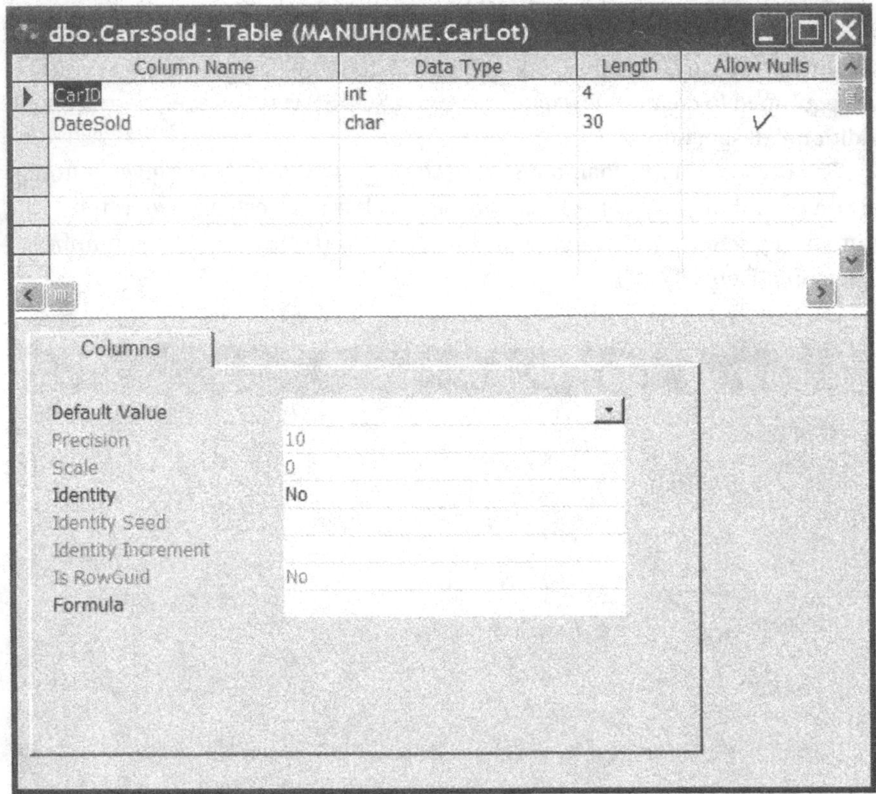

Figure 13-28. The CarsSold table

There is no need to assign a parent-child relationship between the two tables, given that the CarsSold database is simply a log book (so to speak) of any car that has been removed from the Inventory table. Granted, this is hardly an enterprise-level database design, but it gives you something to work with during the remainder of this chapter.

Building the C# Code Library

Now on to the managed code library itself (which I have called ConfiguredCarObjects). Given that the *.dll will contain two configured objects that both make calls to the CarLot database, begin by setting a reference to the System.Data.dll and System.EnterpriseServices.dll assemblies.

Building the LogSale Type

The first class to define is LogSale, which will be created by the root object (not the base client) to record a new sale to the CarsSold table of the CarLot database. As this will be a transaction-aware type, make use of the [Transaction] attribute to ensure that when your assembly is registered with the COM+ Catalog, it is initially configured as TransactionOption.Required. If you wish, you are free to configure the type to support an object constructor string; however, I have elected to hard code the connection string logic directly within the type (the CarInventory object will make use of an object constructor string).

All of the real work takes place in a single public method named Log(). Once the record has been constructed based on the incoming CarID, you calculate the current date (using the DateTime type) and update the CarsSold table. Finally, you alter the values of the happy and done bits using the MTS-style SetComplete() and SetAbort() methods of the ContextUtil type. Here is the complete code listing:

```
[ClassInterface(ClassInterfaceType.AutoDual)]
[Transaction(TransactionOption.Required)]
[EventTrackingEnabledAttribute(true)]
public class LogSale : ServicedComponent
{
  public LogSale(){}

  public void Log(int ID)
  {
     try
     {
        SqlConnection sqlConn = new SqlConnection
      ("Integrated Security=SSPI;Initial Catalog=CarLot;Data Source=localhost;");
      sqlConn.Open();

      // Build a SQL statement based on incoming params.
     string myInsertQuery =
        string.Format(@"INSERT INTO CarsSold (CarID, DateSold)
         Values('{0}', {1}'", ID, DateTime.Today);
      // Configure SqlCommand type.
      SqlCommand sqlCmd = new SqlCommand(myInsertQuery);
      sqlCmd.Connection = sqlConn;

      // Insert the record.
      sqlCmd.ExecuteNonQuery();
      sqlConn.Close();
      ContextUtil.SetComplete();
      }
      catch
      {
```

```
            ContextUtil.SetAbort();
        }
    }
}
```

Building the CarInventory Class Type

The root object, CarInventory, supports a number of the COM+ topics illustrated during the course of this chapter. First of all, this object supports an object constructor string that allows the declarative administration of the ADO.NET construction string. Also, the object (obviously) supports a COM+-style transaction (TransactionOption.Required) and event statistics. Here is the initial class definition:

```
[ClassInterface(ClassInterfaceType.AutoDual)]
[Transaction(TransactionOption.Required)]
[EventTrackingEnabledAttribute(true)]
[ConstructionEnabled(Default =
    "Integrated Security=SSPI;Initial Catalog=CarLot;Data Source=localhost;")]
public class CarInventory : ServicedComponent
{
    public CarInventory(){}

    // Instance data.
    private string connString;
    private SqlConnection sqlConn;
}
```

To receive the incoming constructor string, you override the Construct() method and cache the value in your private connString data member. To control the timely construction and destruction of your SqlConnection, you also override the IObjectControl-centric members. Here is the relevant update:

```
protected override void Construct(string ctorStr)
{connString = ctorStr;}
protected override void Activate()
{
    // Make connection to database.
    try
    {
        sqlConn = new SqlConnection(connString);
    }
    catch(SqlException ex)
    { throw ex;}
}
```

```
protected override void Deactivate()
{
    // Close connection to database.
    sqlConn.Close();
}

protected override bool CanBePooled()
{return false;}
```

The first client-reachable member of the CarInventory type is AddCar(), which as you would expect inserts a new record into the CarLot database and alters the values of its happy and done bits based on the outcome of the transaction, this time using the DeactivateOnReturn and MyTransactionVote properties of ContextUtil:

```
// Insert a new record and set the happy and done bits!
public void AddCar(string make, string color, int ID)
{
    // Always done.
    ContextUtil.DeactivateOnReturn = true;

   // Build a SQL statement based on incoming params.
   string myInsertQuery =
      string.Format(@"INSERT INTO Inventory (CarMake, CarColor, CarID)
                           Values('{0}', '{1}', '{2}'", make, color, ID);
    try
    {
        // Configure SqlCommand type.
        SqlCommand sqlCmd = new SqlCommand(myInsertQuery);
        sqlCmd.Connection = sqlConn;
        sqlConn.Open();

        // Insert the record.
        sqlCmd.ExecuteNonQuery();

        // Update our context.
        ContextUtil.MyTransactionVote = TransactionVote.Commit;
    }
    catch {ContextUtil.MyTransactionVote = TransactionVote.Abort;}
}
```

The public GetAllInventory() method populates and returns an ADO.NET DataSet to the base client, and sets the happy and done bits using the [AutoComplete] attribute (just for the heck of it).

```
[AutoComplete]
public DataSet GetAllInventory()
```

```
{
    // Fill a DataSet using a DataAdapter.
    SqlDataAdapter dAdapt;
    DataSet myDS = new DataSet("CarInventory");
    dAdapt = new SqlDataAdapter("SELECT * FROM Inventory", sqlConn);
    dAdapt.Fill(myDS, "Inventory");

    return myDS;
}
```

Finally, you have the BuyCar() member, which first creates a LogSale type that is automatically enlisted into the current transaction. Once the LogSale component has moved the moribund record into the CarsSold table, the listing is removed from the Inventory table:

```
public void BuyCar(int carID)
{
    // Build a SQL statement based on incoming params.
    string myInsertQuery =
        string.Format("DELETE FROM Inventory WHERE CarID = '{0}'", carID);
    try
    {
        // Log car to be purchased.
        LogSale log = new LogSale();
        log.Log(carID);
        log.Dispose();

        // Configure SqlCommand type.
        SqlCommand sqlCmd = new SqlCommand(myInsertQuery);
        sqlCmd.Connection = sqlConn;
        sqlConn.Open();

        // Delete the record.
        sqlCmd.ExecuteNonQuery();

        // Update our context.
        ContextUtil.SetComplete();
    }
    catch{ContextUtil.SetAbort();}
}
```

That does it for the business logic of the configured types. The final bits of work are purely administrative. First, be sure to assign a strong name to your assembly (using the AssemblyKeyFile attribute and a valid *.snk file). Next, insert a few additional assembly-level attributes to ensure that your application is activated as a server (not a library) application:

```
// COM+ Application configuration.
[assembly: ApplicationName("Configured Car Objects")]
[assembly: ApplicationID("11DF40BE-1C96-4e85-9551-3CE0DCC522DD")]
[assembly: ApplicationActivation(ActivationOption.Server)]
[assembly: Description("Did you really think I would not use cars?")]
```

Once the assembly has been compiled, install it in the GAC and make use of regsvcs.exe to update the COM Catalog. The end result of your labors can be seen in Figure 13-29.

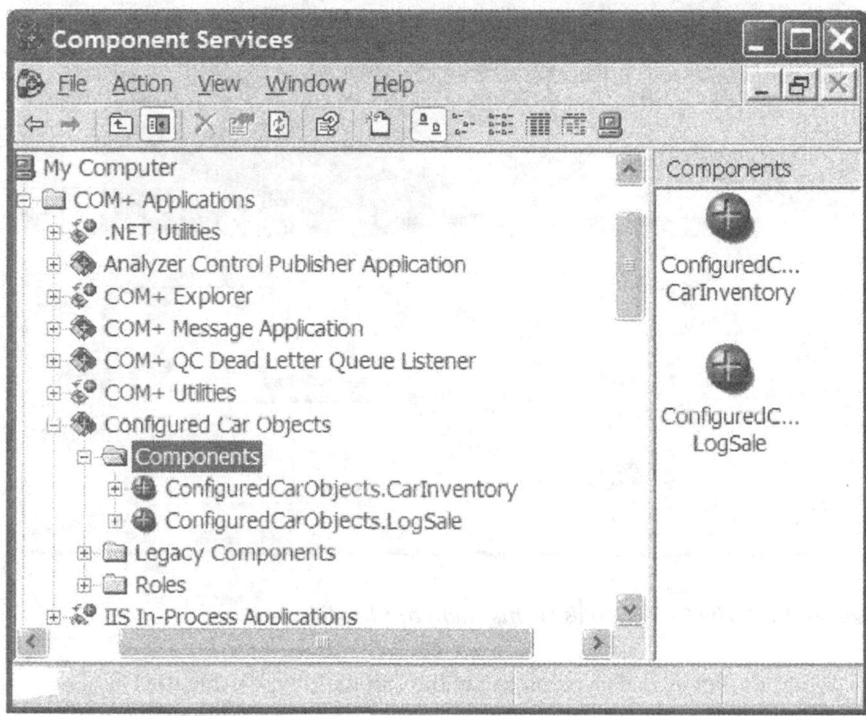

Figure 13-29. The configured car objects

CODE *The ConfiguredCarObjects project can be found under the Chapter 13 directory.*

Building the Windows Forms Front End

The main Form of the C# Windows Forms application will provide a minimal but complete UI that allows the end user to insert, remove, and view the cars currently within the Inventory table. Before you see the code, assume you have already set a reference to the ConfiguredCarObjects.dll assembly. Figure 13-30 shows the final product.

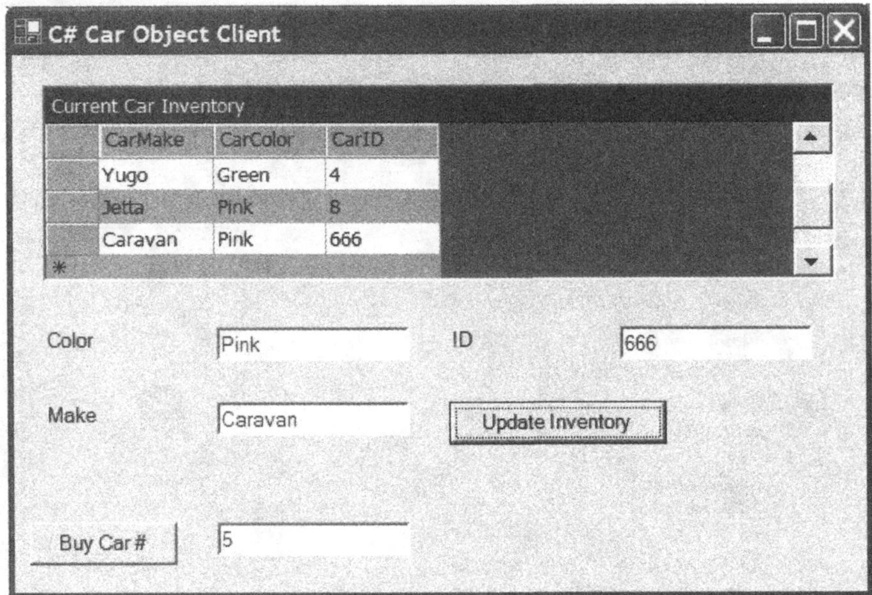

Figure 13-30. The C# Windows Forms client application

When the Form loads, you populate the DataGrid type using the DataSet returned from CarInventory.GetAllInventory(). The code behind the Update Inventory and Buy Car # buttons should be self-explanatory.

```
public class mainForm : System.Windows.Forms.Form
{
    CarInventory ci = new CarInventory();
...
    private void btnUpdate_Click(object sender, System.EventArgs e)
    {
        try
        {
            ci.AddCar(txtMake.Text, txtColor.Text, Int32.Parse(txtID.Text));
            UpdateGrid();
        }
```

```
        catch(Exception ex)
        { MessageBox.Show(ex.Message); }
    }
    private void btnBuyCar_Click(object sender, System.EventArgs e)
    {
        try
        {
            ci.BuyCar(Int32.Parse(txtBuyCarID.Text));
            UpdateGrid();
        }
        catch(Exception ex)
        { MessageBox.Show(ex.Message); }
    }
    private void Form1_Load(object sender, System.EventArgs e)
    { UpdateGrid(); }

    private void UpdateGrid()
    {
        carDataGrid.DataSource = ci.GetAllInventory().Tables["Inventory"];
    }
}
```

CODE *The CarObjectClient is included under the Chapter 13 directory.*

Creating Private Components (COM+ 1.5 Only)

Defining visibility is a key aspect of building intelligent object models. In classic COM, you were offered the [noncreatable] attribute. .NET simplifies the matter by allowing C# developers to define internal components. Now, with the advent of COM+ 1.5, you are provided with yet another way to control how your objects are exposed. When you create a COM+ 1.5 application, you may create *private components,* which cannot be activated outside of the current application (thus, the base client cannot directly create them). You may agree that the LogSale type is really of no use to external base clients, and therefore would be a good candidate for a private component. To do so declaratively, access the Activation tab of a given COM+ component (Figure 13-31).

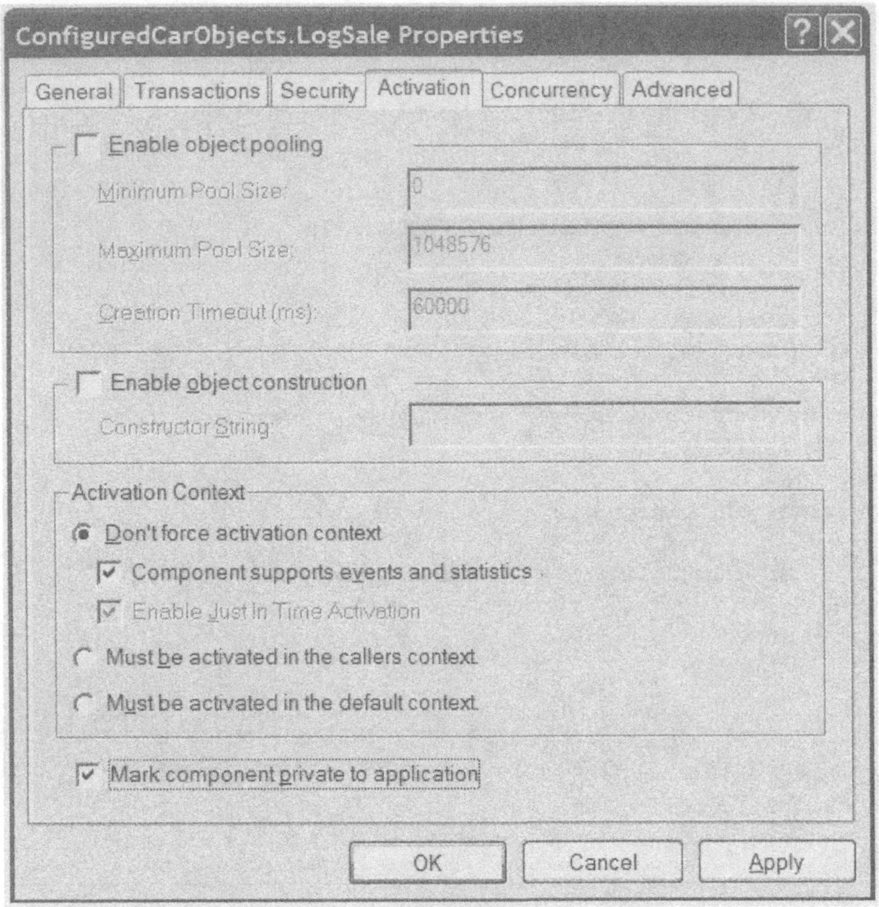

Figure 13-31. *Configuring a private component*

As you would guess, this can be controlled in code using the PrivateComponent attribute:

```
[PrivateComponent()]
public class LogSale : ServicedComponent
{...}
```

Building an ASP.NET Web Service Client

Of course, it is completely possible to build an ASP, ASP.NET Web application, or ASP.NET Web Service consumer for the configured car types. The process is identical to the Windows Forms client. By way of a quick illustration, assume you have created a new ASP.NET Web application project workspace. Using the necessary

Web Form controls, assemble a GUI that mimics the previous Windows Forms client. If you ensure that the names of your GUI widgets are identical between the two base clients, you can literally copy and paste the custom presentation logic between *.cs files (with an additional call to DataBind() to attach the DataSet to the Web Form DataGrid). Figure 13-32 shows the UI.

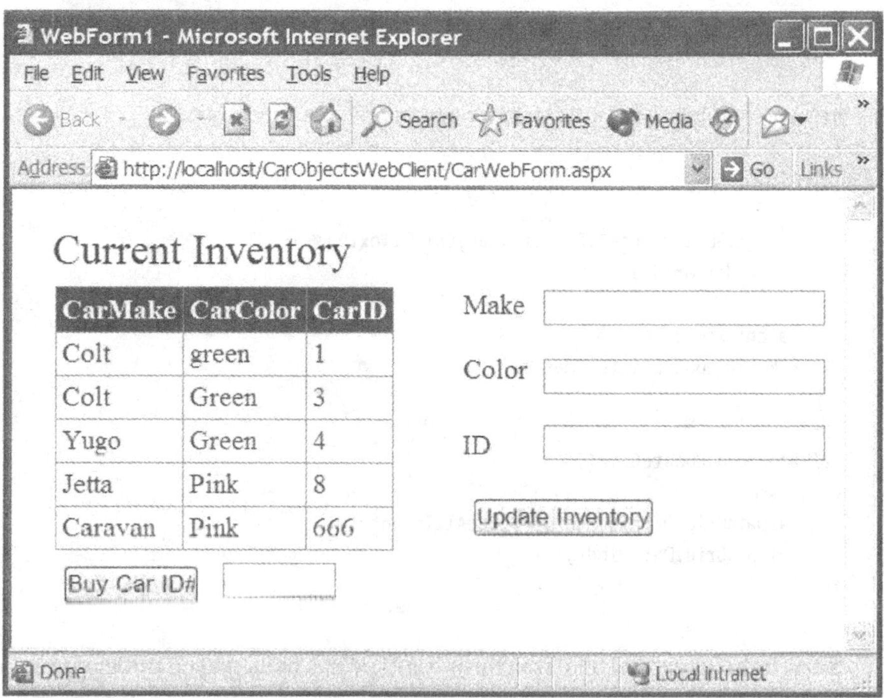

Figure 13-32. A Web-based base client

The code is (again) self-explanatory:

```
// Set a reference to the ConfiguredCarObjects.dll and
// System.EnterpriseServics.dll assemblies.
public class CarWebForm : System.Web.UI.Page
{
    ...
    CarInventory ci = new CarInventory();

    private void Page_Load(object sender, System.EventArgs e)
    {
        // Put user code to initialize the page here
        if(!IsPostBack)
            UpdateGrid();
    }
```

```
    private void btnUpdate_Click(object sender, System.EventArgs e)
    {
        try
        {
            ci.AddCar(txtMake.Text, txtColor.Text, Int32.Parse(txtID.Text));
            UpdateGrid();
        }
        catch(Exception ex)
        { MessageBox.Show(ex.Message); }
    }
    private void btnBuyCar_Click(object sender, System.EventArgs e)
    {
        try
        {
            ci.BuyCar(Int32.Parse(txtBuyCarID.Text));
            UpdateGrid();
        }
        catch(Exception ex)
        { MessageBox.Show(ex.Message); }
    }

    private void UpdateGrid()
    {
        carDataGrid.DataSource = ci.GetAllInventory();
        carDataGrid.DataBind();
    }
}
```

Slick, huh? Given that all of the business logic has been placed under component services, your choice of front end is more or less left to personal preference.

CODE *The *.aspx and *.aspx.cs files for this ASP.NET Web application are located under the Chapter 13 directory.*

Final Thoughts Regarding System.EnterpriseServices

Over the course of this chapter, you have been exposed to the core facets of the COM+ runtime and how to leverage these atoms from managed code. Depending on your current COM+ awareness, you are quite likely mindful that there are additional services I have not addressed. For example, using types within the System.EnterpriseServices namespace, you are able to programmatically establish role-based security settings, interact with the LCE model, as well as other more exotic techniques such as establishing compensating resource managers (CRMs). Although I will not address these topics in this text, you should now be in a position to check out the reaming types of System.EnterpriseServices at your leisure. If you wish to check out some addition COM+ services, look up the topic "Writing Serviced Components" using VS .NET online help.

Another point to be made aware of is that when you are designing configured components using a managed language, you need to spend some time considering the possible base client(s). For example, if you are creating a component that is designed *exclusively* for use by .NET base clients, you can make use of any construct supported by your language of choice. However, if you intend to allow COM-based and .NET-based clients to access the same object (which is certainly likely), keep in mind the design considerations shown in Table 13-11.

Table 13-11. Select Design Considerations

COM/.NET Base Client Design Consideration	Meaning in Life
Make use of the GuidAttribute type.	Regsvcs.exe will auto-generate GUIDs for each interface, class, and enumeration defined in your managed code. Thus, when you register and unregister assemblies, you may end up with COM clients that reference out-of-date GUIDs.
Don't make use of static (Shared) members.	As you have already learned, COM clients cannot access static members.
Avoid parameterized constructors.	COM clients are unable to view or interact with .NET class constructors. Recall, however, that .NET classes that derive from ServicedComponent should always support a default constructor.

Given that we made use of C# for all of the base clients using C# components, I have not bothered to adhere to each and every design recommendation. However, be mindful of these design tips if you wish to service COM and .NET base clients.

Summary

The COM+ runtime is a set of well-defined services designed to host objects in the middle tier. Although COM+ was originally designed to host classic COM types, .NET programmers are able to build configured components using the types defined within the System.EnterpriseServices.dll assembly. As you have seen, when you wish to build a COM+-aware .NET type, you are required to derive from the ServicedComponent type. This base class defines a number of COM+-specific virtual members that allow you to interact with JITA, control object pooling behaviors, and receive an object construction string.

Beyond deriving from ServicedComponent, most configured components built using managed code will tend to be decorated with a number of attributes that control how regsvcs.exe will initially configure the COM+ application. As you have seen over the course of this chapter, System.EnterpriseServices.dll defines attributes to control the very same attributes you may set using the Component Services Explorer. ContextUtil is a core type of the System.EnterpriseServices namespace. Using its numerous static members, you are able to interact with your contextual settings (including the happy and done bits) in a manner similar to using the classic COM+ IObjectContext interface.

Well, that's about it for this book. Over the course of these 13 chapters, you have become quite intimate with the COM(+) and .NET type systems. Hopefully you agree with me that understanding the details of COM and .NET is critical when engaging interoperability issues, and given this, you found the preliminary information of both architectures insightful. While the bulk of this book was spent examining how these extremely unique systems can coexist in harmony, as an extra bonus, this chapter pounded out the details of what one might consider "COM+ interop."

So then, thanks for reading. To those who have read my previous three books, I *promise* that my next Apress title will not make use of cars, DVD players, UFOs, or other startable objects (however, bicycles are still fair game).

Index

B

D

E

F

G

H

I

J

K

L

M

N

S

T

U

V

W

Apress Titles

ISBN	PRICE	AUTHOR	TITLE
1-893115-73-9	$34.95	Abbott	Voice Enabling Web Applications: VoiceXML and Beyond
1-893115-01-1	$39.95	Appleman	Dan Appleman's Win32 API Puzzle Book and Tutorial for Visual Basic Programmers
1-893115-23-2	$29.95	Appleman	How Computer Programming Works
1-893115-97-6	$39.95	Appleman	Moving to VB. NET: Strategies, Concepts, and Code
1-59059-023-6	$39.95	Baker	Adobe Acrobat 5: The Professional User's Guide
1-893115-09-7	$29.95	Baum	Dave Baum's Definitive Guide to LEGO MINDSTORMS
1-893115-84-4	$29.95	Baum, Gasperi, Hempel, and Villa	Extreme MINDSTORMS: An Advanced Guide to LEGO MINDSTORMS
1-893115-82-8	$59.95	Ben-Gan/Moreau	Advanced Transact-SQL for SQL Server 2000
1-893115-91-7	$39.95	Birmingham/Perry	Software Development on a Leash
1-893115-48-8	$29.95	Bischof	The .NET Languages: A Quick Translation Guide
1-893115-67-4	$49.95	Borge	Managing Enterprise Systems with the Windows Script Host
1-893115-28-3	$44.95	Challa/Laksberg	Essential Guide to Managed Extensions for C++
1-893115-39-9	$44.95	Chand	A Programmer's Guide to ADO.NET in C#
1-893115-44-5	$29.95	Cook	Robot Building for Beginners
1-893115-99-2	$39.95	Cornell/Morrison	Programming VB .NET: A Guide for Experienced Programmers
1-893115-72-0	$39.95	Curtin	Developing Trust: Online Privacy and Security
1-59059-008-2	$29.95	Duncan	The Career Programmer: Guerilla Tactics for an Imperfect World
1-893115-71-2	$39.95	Ferguson	Mobile .NET
1-893115-90-9	$49.95	Finsel	The Handbook for Reluctant Database Administrators
1-59059-024-4	$49.95	Fraser	Real World ASP.NET: Building a Content Management System
1-893115-42-9	$44.95	Foo/Lee	XML Programming Using the Microsoft XML Parser
1-893115-55-0	$34.95	Frenz	Visual Basic and Visual Basic .NET for Scientists and Engineers
1-893115-85-2	$34.95	Gilmore	A Programmer's Introduction to PHP 4.0
1-893115-36-4	$34.95	Goodwill	Apache Jakarta-Tomcat
1-893115-17-8	$59.95	Gross	A Programmer's Introduction to Windows DNA
1-893115-62-3	$39.95	Gunnerson	A Programmer's Introduction to C#, Second Edition
1-59059-009-0	$49.95	Harris/Macdonald	Moving to ASP.NET: Web Development with VB .NET
1-893115-30-5	$49.95	Harkins/Reid	SQL: Access to SQL Server
1-893115-10-0	$34.95	Holub	Taming Java Threads
1-893115-04-6	$34.95	Hyman/Vaddadi	Mike and Phani's Essential C++ Techniques
1-893115-96-8	$59.95	Jorelid	J2EE FrontEnd Technologies: A Programmer's Guide to Servlets, JavaServer Pages, and Enterprise JavaBeans
1-893115-49-6	$39.95	Kilburn	Palm Programming in Basic
1-893115-50-X	$34.95	Knudsen	Wireless Java: Developing with Java 2, Micro Edition
1-893115-79-8	$49.95	Kofler	Definitive Guide to Excel VBA
1-893115-57-7	$39.95	Kofler	MySQL
1-893115-87-9	$39.95	Kurata	Doing Web Development: Client-Side Techniques
1-893115-75-5	$44.95	Kurniawan	Internet Programming with VB

ISBN	PRICE	AUTHOR	TITLE
1-893115-38-0	$24.95	Lafler	Power AOL: A Survival Guide
1-893115-46-1	$36.95	Lathrop	Linux in Small Business: A Practical User's Guide
1-893115-19-4	$49.95	Macdonald	Serious ADO: Universal Data Access with Visual Basic
1-893115-06-2	$39.95	Marquis/Smith	A Visual Basic 6.0 Programmer's Toolkit
1-893115-22-4	$27.95	McCarter	David McCarter's VB Tips and Techniques
1-59059-021-X	$34.95	Moore	Karl Moore's Visual Basic .NET: The Tutorials
1-893115-76-3	$49.95	Morrison	C++ For VB Programmers
1-893115-80-1	$39.95	Newmarch	A Programmer's Guide to Jini Technology
1-893115-58-5	$49.95	Oellermann	Architecting Web Services
1-59059-020-1	$44.95	Patzer	JSP Examples and Best Practices
1-893115-81-X	$39.95	Pike	SQL Server: Common Problems, Tested Solutions
1-59059-017-1	$34.95	Rainwater	Herding Cats: A Primer for Programmers Who Lead Programmers
1-59059-025-2	$49.95	Rammer	Advanced .NET Remoting
1-893115-20-8	$34.95	Rischpater	Wireless Web Development
1-893115-93-3	$34.95	Rischpater	Wireless Web Development with PHP and WAP
1-893115-89-5	$59.95	Shemitz	Kylix: The Professional Developer's Guide and Reference
1-893115-40-2	$39.95	Sill	The qmail Handbook
1-893115-24-0	$49.95	Sinclair	From Access to SQL Server
1-893115-94-1	$29.95	Spolsky	User Interface Design for Programmers
1-893115-53-4	$44.95	Sweeney	Visual Basic for Testers
1-59059-002-3	$44.95	Symmonds	Internationalization and Localization Using Microsoft .NET
1-59059-010-4	$54.95	Thomsen	Database Programming with C#
1-893115-29-1	$44.95	Thomsen	Database Programming with Visual Basic .NET
1-893115-65-8	$39.95	Tiffany	Pocket PC Database Development with eMbedded Visual Basic
1-893115-59-3	$59.95	Troelsen	C# and the .NET Platform
1-59059-011-2	$59.95	Troelsen	COM and .NET Interoperability
1-893115-26-7	$59.95	Troelsen	Visual Basic .NET and the .NET Platform
1-893115-54-2	$49.95	Trueblood/Lovett	Data Mining and Statistical Analysis Using SQL
1-893115-68-2	$54.95	Vaughn	ADO.NET and ADO Examples and Best Practices for VB Programmers, Second Edition
1-59059-012-0	$49.95	Vaughn/Blackburn	ADO.NET Examples and Best Practices for C# Programmers
1-893115-83-6	$44.95	Wells	Code Centric: T-SQL Programming with Stored Procedures and Triggers
1-893115-95-X	$49.95	Welschenbach	Cryptography in C and C++
1-893115-05-4	$39.95	Williamson	Writing Cross-Browser Dynamic HTML
1-893115-78-X	$49.95	Zukowski	Definitive Guide to Swing for Java 2, Second Edition
1-893115-92-5	$49.95	Zukowski	Java Collections
1-893115-98-4	$54.95	Zukowski	Learn Java with JBuilder 6

books for professionals by professionals™

About Apress

Apress, located in Berkeley, CA, is a fast-growing, innovative publishing company devoted to meeting the needs of existing and potential programming professionals. Simply put, the "A" in Apress stands for *"The Author's Press™"* and its books have *"The Expert's Voice™"*. Apress' unique approach to publishing grew out of conversations between its founders Gary Cornell and Dan Appleman, authors of numerous best-selling, highly regarded books for programming professionals. In 1998 they set out to create a publishing company that emphasized quality above all else. Gary and Dan's vision has resulted in the publication of over 50 titles by leading software professionals, all of which have *The Expert's Voice™*.

Do You Have What It Takes to Write for Apress?

Apress is rapidly expanding its publishing program. If you can write and refuse to compromise on the quality of your work, if you believe in doing more than rehashing existing documentation, and if you're looking for opportunities and rewards that go far beyond those offered by traditional publishing houses, we want to hear from you!

Consider these innovations that we offer all of our authors:

- **Top royalties with *no* hidden switch statements**
  Authors typically only receive half of their normal royalty rate on foreign sales. In contrast, Apress' royalty rate remains the same for both foreign and domestic sales.

- **A mechanism for authors to obtain equity in Apress**
  Unlike the software industry, where stock options are essential to motivate and retain software professionals, the publishing industry has adhered to an outdated compensation model based on royalties alone. In the spirit of most software companies, Apress reserves a significant portion of its equity for authors.

- **Serious treatment of the technical review process**
  Each Apress book has a technical reviewing team whose remuneration depends in part on the success of the book since they too receive royalties.

Moreover, through a partnership with Springer-Verlag, New York, Inc., one of the world's major publishing houses, Apress has significant venture capital behind it. Thus, we have the resources to produce the highest quality books *and* market them aggressively.

If you fit the model of the Apress author who can write a book that gives the "professional what he or she needs to know™," then please contact one of our Editorial Directors, Gary Cornell (gary_cornell@apress.com), Dan Appleman (dan_appleman@apress.com), Peter Blackburn (peter_blackburn@apress.com), Jason Gilmore (jason_gilmore@apress.com), Karen Watterson (karen_watterson@apress.com), or John Zukowski (john_zukowski@apress.com) for more information.

Printed in the United States
By Bookmasters